THE OLYMPIC RECORD BOOK

GARLAND REFERENCE LIBRARY
OF SOCIAL SCIENCE
(Vol. 437)

THE OLYMPIC RECORD BOOK

Bill Mallon

GARLAND PUBLISHING, INC. · NEW YORK & LONDON
1988

Library of Congress Cataloging-in-Publication Data

Mallon, Bill.
The Olympic Record Book/Bill Mallon.
p. cm.
ISBN 0–8240–2948–8
1. Olympics—Records.   I. Title.

GV721.8.M34   1988   796.4′8—dc19   87-22511   CIP

Cover design by John M-Röblin

Printed on acid-free, 250-year-life paper
Manufactured in the United States of America

To Erich Kamper

CONTENTS

INTRODUCTION

Over the years, many sports have produced record books detailing the best, most, least, and worst in their own sport. Since their resurrection in 1896, the Olympic Games have been the most watched sporting events in the world, yet no record book of the Olympic Games has previously been produced. Several Olympic books have been produced using the term "Record Book" in their title, yet almost invariably these have been nothing more than lists of the medalists. This is the first true record book of the world's greatest sporting event, the Olympic Games.

Enclosed herein are myriad lists detailing the best records produced in the various phases of the Olympic Games. The book starts with the overall records, but the records are then subsetted into records for the summer Games (Games of the Olympiads, properly), and records for the Olympic Winter Games. Then, each sport is examined, giving the Olympic bests for all current sports, and also briefly touching on the discontinued and demonstration sports. The next section then gives Olympic records for each country which is now, or has ever been, a member of the International Olympic Committee or a participant in the Olympic Games. Finally the records of the previous Olympic Games are given.

Within each section, the lists detail most medals, most gold medals, most appearances, oldest and youngest to compete, to medal, and to win, as well as many lesser categories. The lists are of various lengths, starting out at least ten deep for the overall categories, and becoming shorter for the more esoteric records. In measurable sports, a progression of Olympic records is given in current events. In addition, in team sports, all-time records of all countries are given, as well as lists of the high point scorers in games, by individuals, nations, and both nations in one game.

In many sections, small portions are devoted to interesting bits of trivia relating to that category or sport, i.e., lists of torch bearers, lists of professional boxing champions who competed in the Olympics, lists of Olympic swimmers who swam the English Channel, lists of Olympic cyclists in the Tour de France, etc.

Thousands of books on the Olympics have been produced but none similar to this. Ideally this record book should be able to serve as a spectator or journalist's primary source for Olympic information, and hence heighten his enjoyment of the event or his work on the event.

The entire book has been produced by referring to multiple sources and books, as well as correspondance with many of the world's experts on the Olympics or the various Olympic sports. Through this research effort, all the information has been placed

ix

in a large computer database which enabled the various lists to be produced. Still there are certainly errors in such a large compendium of statistics and I would appreciate being informed of any error, great or small.

The book is dedicated to Erich Kamper, the doyen of Olympic statisticians. His three great books, Encyclopaedia of the Olympic Winter Games, Encyclopaedia of the Olympic Games, and Lexikon der 14,000 Olympioniken, were primary sources. In addition, his correspondence and friendship have been invaluable in the production of this record book. He was not the first to attempt to chronicle the records of the Olympics, that honor going to Dr. Fritz Wasner, and Dr. Ferenc Mező. However, Kamper has upgraded their works and produced by far the best records we have to date of the Olympics. Many times sources will conflict and it is difficult to tell which is correct. Often I have extensively researched some problem only to find time and again that Kamper was correct. This has led me to what I feel is the primary dictum of the Olympic researcher: "When in doubt, trust Kamper."

Several other people have been extremely helpful in the production of this book and I would like to acknowledge their help as follows: Ian Buchanan (HKG), Monique Berlioux (FRA), Peter Diamond (USA), John Grasso (USA), Pim Huurman (HOL), Richard Hymans (GBR), Magne Teigen (NOR), David Wallechinsky (GBR), and Ture Widlund (SWE). Special contributions by the above were as follows: Olympic boxing records (Grasso), speed skating Olympic record progressions (Teigen), track & field athletics Olympic record progressions (Hymans), and weightlifting Olympic record progressions (Widlund).

And of course, I thank Karen and our two dogs, Scruffy and Albert, for their patience during the many hours the work entailed.

Bill Mallon, M.D.
Durham, NC
November 1987

ABBREVIATIONS, NOTES, AND SOURCES

Age Records

All age records are listed as years-days (e.g. 17-303
means 17 years, 303 days old). All records are taken from the
athlete's date of birth to the day his or her event ended, even
though in a few cases the athlete may have been eliminated on an
earlier date. Age records which are given in italics indicate
that only the year of birth was known for that athlete. In those
cases a worst case estimate has been made. For youngest records,
the athlete is considered to have been born on 01 January of that
year, while for oldest records he is considered to have been born
on 31 December of that year. Thus for italicized dates, it would
be wise to remember the athlete could really be as much as a year
younger or older. All age records have been computed by a
specially designed computer program and checked twice,
eliminating, hopefully, virtually all errors in age records.

The 1906 Intercalated Olympic Games

In 1906, interim Olympics were held at the request of
Baron Pierre de Coubertin and the International Olympic Committee.
They were held in Athens and were designed to resuscitate the
Olympic Movement after the debacles of 1900 and 1904. Oddly,
despite having once given their imprimatur, the IOC no longer
recognizes these Olympic Games. However, the three modern
chroniclers of Olympic Results - Kamper, Greenberg, Wallechinsky -
all include these Games in their statistics and I have also. This
is because the Games were considered official in 1906 and because
of their importance in reviving the Olympic Movement. Still,
because a few purists will object, any records for numbers of
medals which includes medals won in the 1906 Games will be
qualified as follows: The number of medals won overall will be
listed first, followed by a slash, followed by the number of
medals won if the 1906 Olympics are not considered. For example:

9/4   Martin Sheridan

Sheridan won nine medals overall, but five of those medals came in
1906, so not including those years, he won only four medals.

Names

I have tried to be as accurate as possible with the spelling of names. In most cases, I was able to use special national lists of Olympic athletes which I have been able to obtain from various national Olympic Committees - mostly European. For certain countries, I used books specifically from those countries. For the names of Soviet athletes, the Soviet Olympic Encyclopaedia was used (see below). Transliteration was by the system given in A Transliterated Dictionary of the Russian Language, Eugene Garfield, editor. Finally for the athletes for whom I had no primary national source, I used either Kamper or Kluge's books (listed below).

Other Notes

After World War II, Germany was represented by a common team consisting of athletes from the FRG (West Germany) in 1952, and combined from both the FRG and the GDR (East Germany) from 1956 through 1964. From 1968 they have competed separately. I have chosen to correctly identify the German athletes who competed in 1956, 1960, and 1964 as being either from the FRG or the GDR. Medal lists by nation also reflect these correct nationalities.

In the sports section, best performance by country is listed at the end of each sport. This is determined by counting the medals won by countries at each Olympics and totalling points on a 5-3-1 basis for gold-silver-bronze medals, respectively.

There are many medal counts listed herein, reflecting the number of medals won by countries in various categories. Many similar lists exist in other books but none of these lists were merely copied from earlier works. A large computer spreadsheet of all Olympic medals won was created and these lists were generated from the spreadsheet. Thus the lists should be consistent throughout. In addition, all categories are separated into lists for men's medals and women's medals, where applicable. The only argument with these lists would be in early Games where controversy exists about the finish of certain events. In the sports section, all these controversies, as well as all events which did not award the standard set of medals, are mentioned.

Primary Sources

Gluszek, Zygmunt. *Polscy Olimpijczycy.* Warsaw: Sport i
    Turystyka, 1980.
Grasso, John. *The Olympic Boxing Record Book.* Guilford, NY:
    International Boxing Research Organization, 1984.
Greenberg, Stan. *The Guinness Book of Olympics Facts and Feats.*
    London: Guinness, 1983.

IAAF/ATFS. *I.A.A.F./A.T.F.S. Track & Field Statistics Handbook for the 1984 Los Angeles Olympic Games.* London: IAAF, 1984.
Kamper, Erich. *The Encyclopaedia of the Olympic Games.* New York: McGraw-Hill, 1972.
Kamper, Erich. *Lexikon der Olympischen Winterspiele.* Stuttgart: Union Verlag, 1964.
Kamper, Erich. *Lexikon der 14,000 Olympioniken.* Graz: Leykam-Verlag, 1983.
Kluge, Volker. *Die Olympischen Spiele von 1896 bis 1980.* Berlin: Sportverlag, 1981.
Mallon, Bill, Buchanan Ian, and Tishman, Jeffrey. *Quest for Gold: The Encyclopaedia of American Olympians.* Champaign, IL: Human Kinetics, 1984.
Parlov, S. P. *Olimpiyskaya Entsiklopediya.* Moscow: Izdatelstvo "Sovetskaya Entsiklopediya," 1980. (transliterated title)
Teigen, Magne. *Encyclopedia of Olympic Games 1924-80.* Veggli, Norway: World Speed Skating Statisticians Association, 1984.
Wallechinsky, David. *The Complete Book of the Olympics.* New York: Penguin Books, 1984.

Abbreviations

d.	defeated	ré1	repechage one
est.	estimate(d)	s1	semi-final one
f	final	sf1	semi-final one
f(2)	race two of final	sq. mi.	square mile(s)
h1	heat one	vs.	versus
h1r1	heat one, round one	WR	World Record
OR	Olympic Record		

Three-Letter Sport Abbreviations

ARC	Archery	NSK	Nordic Skiing
ASK	Alpine Skiing	POL	Polo
BAS	Basketball	ROW	Rowing & Sculling
BIA	Biathlon	RUG	Rugby Football
BOB	Bobsledding	SHO	Shooting
BOX	Boxing	SKE	Skeleton
CAN	Canoe & Kayaking	SOC	Soccer (Assoc. Football)
CYC	Cycling	SSK	Speed Skating
DIV	Diving	SWI	Swimming
EQU	Equestrian Events	TAF	Track & Field Athletics
FEN	Fencing	TEN	Tennis (Lawn Tennis)
FIH	Field Hockey	TOW	Tug-of-War
FSK	Figure Skating	VOL	Volleyball
GYM	Gymnastics	WAP	Water Polo
ICH	Ice Hockey	WLT	Weightlifting
JUD	Judo	WRE	Wrestling
LUG	Luge	YAC	Yachting
MOP	Modern Pentathlon		

Three-Letter National Abbreviations

AFG	Afghanistan	EST	Estonia
AHO	Neth. Antilles	ETH	Ethiopia
ALB	Albania	FIJ	Fiji
ALG	Algeria	FIN	Finland
AND	Andorra	FRA	France
ANG	Angola	FRG	Fed. Rep. Germany
ANT	Antigua	GAB	Gabon
ARG	Argentina	GAM	The Gambia
ARU	Aruba	GBR	Great Britain
AUS	Australia	GDR	German Demo. Republic
AUT	Austria	GEQ	Equatorial Guinea
BAH	The Bahamas	GER	Germany
BAN	Bangladesh	GHA	Ghana
BAR	Barbados	GRE	Greece
BEL	Belgium	GRN	Grenada
BEN	Benin	GUA	Guatemala
BER	Bermuda	GUI	Guinea
BHU	Bhutan	GUM	Guam
BIR	Burma	GUY	Guyana
BIZ	Belize	HAI	Haiti
BOL	Bolivia	HKG	Hong Kong
BOT	Botswana	HOL	The Netherlands
BRA	Brazil	HON	Honduras
BRN	Bahrain	HUN	Hungary
BRU	Brunei	INA	Indonesia
BUL	Bulgaria	IND	India
BUR	Burkina-Faso	IRL	Ireland
CAM	Kampuchea	IRN	Iran
CAN	Canada	IRQ	Iraq
CAY	Cayman Islands	ISL	Iceland
CEY	Ceylon	ISR	Israel
CGO	Congo	ISV	U.S. Virgin Islands
CHA	Chad	ITA	Italy
CHI	Chile	IVB	British Virgin Islands
CHN	China	JAM	Jamaica
CIV	Ivory Coast	JOR	Jordan
CMR	Cameroon	JPN	Japan
COL	Colombia	KEN	Kenya
CRC	Costa Rica	KOR	Korea (South)
CUB	Cuba	KUW	Kuwait
CYP	Cyprus	LAO	Laos
DEN	Denmark	LAT	Latvia
DJI	Djibouti	LBR	Liberia
DOM	Dominican Republic	LBA	Libya
ECU	Ecuador	LES	Lesotho
EGY	Egypt	LIB	Lebanon
ESA	El Salvador	LIE	Liechtenstein
ESP	Spain	LIT	Lithuania

Three-Letter National Abbreviations (cont'd)

LUX	Luxembourg	SUR	Suriname
MAD	Madagascar	SWE	Sweden
MAL	Malaysia	SWZ	Swaziland
MAR	Morocco	SYR	Syria
MAW	Malawi	TAN	Tanzania
MDV	Maldives	TCH	Czechoslovakia
MEX	Mexico	TGA	Tonga
MGL	Mongolia	THA	Thailand
MLI	Mali	TOG	Togo
MLT	Malta	TPE	Chinese Taipei
MON	Monaco	TRI	Trinidad & Tobago
MOZ	Mozambique	TUN	Tunisia
MRI	Mauritius	TUR	Turkey
MTN	Mauritania	UAE	United Arab Emirates
NCA	Nicaragua	UGA	Uganda
NEP	Nepal	URS	Soviet Union
NGR	Nigeria	URU	Uruguay
NGU	Papua-New Guinea	USA	United States
NIG	Niger	VAN	Vanuatu
NOR	Norway	VEN	Venezuela
NZL	New Zealand	VIE	Vietnam
OMA	Oman	VIN	St. Vincent/Grenadines
PAK	Pakistan	VOL	Upper Volta
PAN	Panama	YAR	Yemen AR (North)
PAR	Paraguay	YMD	Yemen DR (South)
PER	Peru	YUG	Yugoslavia
PHI	The Philippines	ZAI	Zaire
POL	Poland	ZAM	Zambia
POR	Portugal	ZIM	Zimbabwe
PRK	DPR Korea (North)		
PUR	Puerto Rico		
QAT	Qatar		
RHO	Rhodesia		
ROM	Romania		
RWA	Rwanda		
SAF	South Africa		
SAM	Western Samoa		
SAO	American Samoa		
SAU	Saudi Arabia		
SEN	Senegal		
SEY	Seychelles		
SIN	Singapore		
SLE	Sierra Leone		
SMR	San Marino		
SOL	Solomon Islands		
SOM	Somalia		
SRI	Sri Lanka		
SUD	The Sudan		
SUI	Switzerland		

The Olympic Record Book

RECORDS OF THE OLYMPIC GAMES

(OVERALL OLYMPIC RECORDS)

Following are the best records achieved in the modern Olympic Games since their inception in 1896. Lists are ten-deep for the major records and five-deep in more restricted categories. Where a great number of athletes are tied with the same mark, they are not always listed but that fact is noted. In some cases, the athletes so categorized may be deduced with reference to records for the summer or winter Games or the various sports. Age records are ten deep for medalists and gold medalists, and one-to-three deep for more restricted categories. A list of medals won by country, with sections for medals won by men and women, follows at the end of this section.

Most Medals
18	Larisa Latynina (URS-GYM)
15	Nikolai Andrianov (URS-GYM)
13	Edoardo Mangiarotti (ITA-FEN)
13	Takashi Ono (JPN-GYM)
13	Boris Shakhlin (URS-GYM)
12	Sawao Kato (JPN-GYM)
12	Paavo Nurmi (FIN-TAF)
11	Vera Cáslavská (TCH-GYM)
11	Carl Osburn (USA-SHO)
11	Mark Spitz (USA-SWI)
11	Viktor Chukarin (URS-GYM)
10	Polina Astakhova (URS-GYM)
10	Alexandr Dityatin (URS-GYM)
10	Aládár Gerevich (HUN-FEN)
10	Agnes Keleti (HUN-GYM)
10	Akinori Nakayama (JPN-GYM)
10/8	Raymond Ewry (USA-TAF)

Most Gold Medals
10/8	Raymond Ewry (USA-TAF)
9	Larisa Latynina (URS-GYM)
9	Paavo Nurmi (FIN-TAF)
9	Mark Spitz (USA-SWI)
8	Sawao Kato (JPN-GYM)
7	Nikolai Andrianov (URS-GYM)
7	Vera Cáslavská (TCH-GYM)
7	Viktor Chukarin (URS-GYM)
7	Aládár Gerevich (HUN-FEN)
7	Boris Shakhlin (URS-GYM)

1

Most Silver Medals
    6   Shirley Babashoff (USA-SWI)
    6   Alexandr Dityatin (URS-GYM)
    6   Mikhail Voronin (URS-GYM)
    5   Nine athletes tied with five

Most Bronze Medals
    6   Heikki Savolainen (FIN-GYM)
    5   Philip Edwards (CAN-TAF)
    5   Adrianus Jong (HOL-FEN)
    5   Daniel Revenu (FRA-FEN)
    4   Eleven athletes tied with four

Most Years Winning Medals
    6   Aládár Gerevich (HUN-FEN)
    6   Hans-Günter Winkler (GER-EQU)
    5   Edoardo Mangiarotti (ITA-FEN)
    5   Heikki Savolainen (FIN-GYM)
    5   Philippe Cattiau (FRA-FEN)
    5   Pál Kovács (HUN-FEN)
    5   Ildikó Saginé-Ujlakiné-Rejtö (HUN-FEN)
    5   Fernand de Montigny (BEL-FEN/FIH)
    5   John Michael Plumb (USA-EQU)
    5   Jack Beresford (GBR-ROW)
    5   Gustav Fischer (SUI-EQU)
    5   Deszö Gyarmati (HUN-WAP)

Most Years Winning Gold Medals
    6   Aládár Gerevich (HUN-FEN)
    5   Pál Kovács (HUN-FEN)
    4   Edoardo Mangiarotti (ITA-FEN)
    4   Gert Fredriksson (SWE-CAN)
    4   Reiner Klimke (GER-EQU)
    4   Hans-Günter Winkler (GER-EQU)
    4   Rudolf Kárpáti (HUN-FEN)
    4   Viktor Sidyak (URS-FEN)
    4   Aleksandr Tikhonov (URS-BIA)
    4   Alfred Oerter (USA-TAF)
    4   Paul Elvström (DEN-YAC)
    4/3 Raymond Ewry (USA-TAF)

Most Years Between Medals
    28   Aládár Gerevich (HUN-FEN)
    28   Tore Holm (SWE-YAC)
    24   Edoardo Mangiarotti (ITA-FEN)
    24   Heikki Savolainen (FIN-GYM)
    24   Pál Kovács (HUN-FEN)
    24   Gustaf-Adolf Boltenstern, Jr. (SWE-EQU)
    24   Magnus Konow (NOR-YAC)
    24   Joseph Petersen (DEN-ART)
    24   Hans Fogh (DEN/CAN-YAC)

Most Years Between Gold Medals
     28   Aládár Gerevich (HUN-FEN)
     24   Pál Kovács (HUN-FEN)
     24   Edoardo Mangiarotti (ITA-FEN)
     20   Hubert van Innis (BEL-ARC)
     20   Reiner Klimke (GER-EQU)
     20   Manlio DiRosa (ITA-FEN)
     20   Lars Jörgen Madsen (DEN-SHO)

Most Appearances
      8   Raimondo d'Inzeo (ITA-EQU, 1948-76)
      7   Ivan Osiier (DEN-FEN; 1908-32, 48)
      7   Durwood Knowles (GBR/BAH-YAC; 1948-72)
      7   Piero d'Inzeo (ITA-EQU, 1952-76)
      7   François La Fortune, Jr. (BEL-SHO, 1952-76)
      7   Paul Elvström (DEN-YAC; 1948-60, 68-72, 84)
      6   Nineteen athletes tied with six.

Most Years Between Appearances
     40   Ivan Osiier (DEN-FEN, 1908-48)
     40   Magnus Konow (NOR-YAC, 1908-48)
     36   François La Fortune, Sr. (BEL-SHO, 1924-60)
     36   Kroum Lekarski (BUL-EQU, 1924-60)
     36   Paul Elvström (DEN-YAC, 1948-84)

Most Medals, Women
     18   Larisa Latynina (URS-GYM)
     11   Vera Cáslavská (TCH-GYM)
     10   Polina Astakhova (URS-GYM)
     10   Agnes Keleti (HUN-GYM)
      9   Nadia Comǎneci (ROM-GYM)
      8   Shirley Babashoff (USA-SWI)
      8   Kornelia Ender (GDR-SWI)
      8   Dawn Fraser (AUS-SWI)
      8   Sofiya Muratova (URS-GYM)
      8   Lyudmila Turishcheva (URS-GYM)

Most Gold Medals, Women
      9   Larisa Latynina (URS-GYM)
      7   Vera Cáslavská (TCH-GYM)
      5   Polina Astakhova (URS-GYM)
      5   Agnes Keleti (HUN-GYM)
      5   Nadia Comǎneci (ROM-GYM)
      5   Nelli Kim (URS-GYM)

Most Silver Medals, Women
```
6    Shirley Babashoff (USA-SWI)
5    Larisa Latynina (URS-GYM)
5    Mariya Gorokhovskaya (URS-GYM)
4    Vera Cáslavská (TCH-GYM)
4    Kornelia Ender (GDR-GYM)
4    Dawn Fraser (AUS-SWI)
4    Erika Zuchold (GDR-GYM)
```

Most Bronze Medals, Women
```
4    Larisa Latynina (URS-GYM)
4    Sofiya Muratova (URS-GYM)
3    Nine athletes tied with three
```

Most Years Winning Medals, Women
```
5    Ildikó Saginé-Ujlakiné-Rejtö (HUN-FEN)
4    Irena Szewińska-Kirszenstein (POL-TAF)
4    Elena Belova-Novikova (URS-FEN)
4    Galina Gorokhova (URS-FEN)
4    Tatyana Samusenko-Petrenko (URS-FEN)
4    Michele Maffei (ITA-FEN)
4    Inna Ryskal (URS-VOL)
4    Galina Kulakova (URS-NSK)
```

Most Years Winning Gold Medals, Women
```
3    Larisa Latynina (URS-GYM)
3    Polina Astakhova (URS-GYM)
3    Dawn Fraser (AUS-SWI)
3    Lyudmila Turishcheva (URS-GYM)
3    Irena Szewińska-Kirszenstein (POL-TAF)
3    Elena Belova-Novikova (URS-FEN)
3    Galina Gorokhova (URS-FEN)
3    Lyudmila Pinayeva-Khvedosyuk (URS-CAN)
3    Tatyana Samusenko-Petrenko (URS-FEN)
3    Aleksandra Zabelina (URS-FEN)
3    Sonja Henie (NOR-FSK)
3    Irina Rodnina (URS-FSK)
```

Most Years Between Medals, Women
```
16   Ildikó Saginé-Ujlakiné-Rejtö (HUN-FEN)
16   Liselott Linsenhoff (FRG-EQU)
16   Ilona Elek (HUN-FEN)
16   Ellen Müller-Preiss (AUT-FEN)
```

Most Years Between Gold Medals, Women
```
16   Ilona Elek (HUN-FEN)
12   Irena Szewińska-Kirszenstein (POL-TAF)
12   Elena Belova-Novikvoa (URS-FEN)
12   Galina Gorokhova (URS-FEN)
12   Tatyana Samusenko-Petrenko (URS-FEN)
12   Aleksandra Zabelina (URS-FEN)
```

Most Appearances, Women
```
6    Janice Lee York-Romary (USA-FEN, 1948-68)
6    Lia Manoliu (ROM-TAF, 1952-72)
6    Kerstin Palm (SWE-FEN, 1964-84)
5    Eight athletes tied with five.
```

Most Years Between Appearances, Women
```
24   Ellen Müller-Preiss (AUT-FEN, 1932-56)
20   Jenny Addams (BEL-FEN, 1928-48)
20   Karen Lachman (DEN-FEN, 1936-56)
20   Dorothy Odam-Tyler (GBR-TAF, 1936-56)
20   Janice Lee York-Romary (USA-FEN, 1948-68)
20   Lia Manoliu (ROM-TAF, 1952-72)
20   Kerstin Palm (SWE-FEN, 1964-84)
20   Christilot Hanson-Boylen (CAN-EQU, 1964-84)
```

Most Medals, Men
```
15   Nikolai Andrianov (URS-GYM)
13   Edoardo Mangiarotti (ITA-FEN)
13   Takashi Ono (JPN-GYM)
13   Boris Shakhlin (URS-GYM)
12   Sawao Kato (JPN-GYM)
12   Paavo Nurmi (FIN-TAF)
```

Most Gold Medals, Men
```
10/8 Raymond Ewry (USA-TAF)
9    Paavo Nurmi (FIN-TAF)
9    Mark Spitz (USA-SWI)
8    Sawao Kato (JPN-GYM)
7    Nikolai Andrianov (URS-GYM)
7    Boris Shakhlin (URS-GYM)
7    Viktor Chukarin (URS-GYM)
7    Aládár Gerevich (HUN-FEN)
```

Most Silver Medals, Men
```
6    Mikhail Voronin (URS-GYM)
6    Aleksandr Dityatin (URS-GYM)
5    Nikolai Andrianov (URS-GYM)
5    Edoardo Mangiarotti (ITA-FEN)
5    Zoltán Halmay (HUN-SWI)
5    Yuriy Titov (URS-GYM)
5    Philippe Cattiau (FRA-FEN)
5    Gustavo Marzi (ITA-FEN)
5    Viktor Lisitsky (URS-GYM)
```

Most Bronze Medals, Men
```
6    Heikki Savolainen (FIN-GYM)
5    Philip Edwards (CAN-TAF)
5    Adrianus Jong (HOL-FEN)
5    Daniel Revenu (FRA-FEN)
4    Eight athletes tied with four
```

Most Years Winning Medals, Men
6   Aládár Gerevich (HUN-FEN)
6   Hans-Günther Winkler (FRG/GER-EQU)
5   Edoardo Mangiarotti (ITA-FEN)
5   Heikki Savolainen (FIN-GYM)
5   Philippe Cattiau (FRA-FEN)
5   Pál Kovács (HUN-FEN)
5   Fernand de Montigny (BEL-FEN/FIH)
5   Michael Plumb (USA-EQU)
5   Jack Beresford (GBR-ROW)
5   Gustav Fischer (SUI-EQU)
5   Deszö Gyarmati (HUN-WAP)

Most Years Winning Gold Medals, Men
6   Aládár Gerevich (HUN-FEN)
5   Pál Kovács (HUN-FEN)
4   Edoardo Mangiarotti (ITA-FEN)
4   Gert Fredriksson (SWE-CAN)
4   Reiner Klimke (FRG-EQU)
4   Hans-Günther Winkler (FRG/GER-EQU)
4   Rudolf Kárpáti (HUN-FEN)
4   Viktor Sidyak (URS-FEN)
4   Paul Elvström (DEN-YAC)
4   Alfred Oerter (USA-TAF)
4   Aleksandr Tikhonov (URS-BIA)
4/3   Raymond Ewry (USA-TAF)

Most Years Between Medals, Men
28   Aládár Gerevich (HUN-FEN)
28   Tore Holm (SWE-YAC)
24   Edoardo Mangiarotti (ITA-FEN)
24   Heikki Savolainen (FIN-GYM)
24   Pál Kovács (HUN-FEN)
24   Gustaf Adolf Boltenstern, Jr. (SWE-EQU)
24   Hans Fogh (DEN/CAN-YAC)
24   Magnus Konow (NOR-YAC)
24   Joseph Petersen (DEN-ART)

Most Years Between Gold Medals, Men
28   Aládár Gerevich (HUN-FEN)
24   Edoardo Mangiarotti (ITA-FEN)
24   Pál Kovács (HUN-FEN)
20   Hubert van Innis (BEL-ARC)
20   Reiner Klimke (FRG/GER-EQU)
20   Manlio DiRosa (ITA-FEN)
20   Lars Jörgen Madsen (DEN-SHO)

Most Appearances, Men
   8   Raimondo d'Inzeo (ITA-EQU, 1948-76)
   7   Ivan Osiier (DEN-FEN; 1908-32, 48)
   7   Durward Knowles (GBR/BAH-YAC, 1948-72)
   7   Piero d'Inzeo (ITA-EQU, 1952-76)
   7   François La Fortune, Jr. (BEL-SHO, 1952-76)
   7   Paul Elvström (DEN-YAC; 1948-60, 68-72, 84)
   6   Sixteen athletes tied with six.

Most Years Between Appearances, Men
   40   Ivan Osiier (DEN-FEN, 1908-48)
   40   Magnus Konow (NOR-YAC, 1908-48)
   36   François La Fortune, Sr. (BEL-SHO, 1924-60)
   36   Kroum Lekarski (BUL-EQU, 1924-60)
   36   Paul Elvström (DEN-YAC, 1948-84)

Most Medals, Individual
   14   Larisa Latynina (URS-GYM)
   12   Nikolai Andrianov (URS-GYM)
   10   Takashi Ono (JPN-GYM)
   10/8 Raymond Ewry (USA-TAF)
   9   Boris Shakhlin (URS-GYM)
   9   Sawao Kato (JPN-GYM)
   9   Paavo Nurmi (FIN-TAF)
   9   Viktor Chukarin (URS-GYM)
   9/4 Martin Sheridan (USA-TAF)

Most Gold Medals, Individual
   10/8 Raymond Ewry (USA-TAF)
   7   Vera Cáslavská (TCH-GYM)
   6   Larisa Latynina (URS-GYM)
   6   Nikolai Andrianov (URS-GYM)
   6   Boris Shakhlin (URS-GYM)
   6   Paavo Nurmi (FIN-TAF)
   6   Lidiya Skoblikova (URS-SSK)

Most Silver Medals, Individual
   5   Larisa Latynina (URS-GYM)
   5   Aleksandr Dityatin (URS-GYM)
   5   Shirley Babashoff (USA-SWI)
   4   Mikhail Voronin (URS-GYM)
   4   Zoltán Halmay (HUN-SWI)
   4   Mariya Gorokhovskaya (URS-GYM)

Most Bronze Medals, Individual
   4   Takashi Ono (JPN-GYM)
   4   Sofiya Muratova (URS-GYM)
   4   William Merz (USA-GYM)
   4   Roald Larsen (NOR-SSK)

Most Medals, Individual, Women
    12   Larisa Latynina (URS-GYM)
     8   Vera Cáslavská (TCH-GYM)
     7   Nadia Comăneci (ROM-GYM)
     6   Polina Astakhova (URS-GYM)
     6   Lidiya Skoblikova (URS-SSK)
     6   Agnes Keleti (HUN-GYM)
     6   Sofiya Muratova (URS-GYM)
     6   Irena Szewińska-Kirszenstein (POL-TAF)

Most Gold Medals, Individual, Women
     7   Vera Cáslavská (TCH-GYM)
     6   Larisa Latynina (URS-GYM)
     6   Lidiya Skoblikova (URS-SSK)
     5   Nadia Comăneci (ROM-GYM)
     4   Agnes Keleti (HUN-GYM)
     4   Patricia McCormick (USA-DIV)

Most Medals, Individual, Men
    12   Nikolai Andrianov (URS-GYM)
    10   Takashi Ono (JPN-GYM)
  10/8   Raymond Ewry (USA-TAF)
     9   Five athletes tied with nine

Most Gold Medals, Individual, Men
  10/8   Raymond Ewry (USA-TAF)
     6   Nikolai Andrianov (URS-GYM)
     6   Boris Shakhlin (URS-GYM)
     6   Paavo Nurmi (FIN-TAF)
     5   Gert Fredriksson (SWE-CAN)
     5   Viktor Chukarin (URS-GYM)
     5   Sawao Kato (JPN-GYM)
     5   Eric Heiden (USA-SSK)
     5   Clas Thunberg (FIN-SSK)
   5/3   Martin Sheridan (USA-TAF)

Most Medals, Games
     8   Aleksandr Dityatin (URS-GYM-1980)
     7   Willis Lee (USA-SHO-1920)
     7   Lloyd Spooner (USA-SHO-1920)
     7   Mariya Gorokhovskaya (URS-GYM-1952)
     7   Boris Shakhlin (URS-GYM-1960)
     7   Mikhail Voronin (URS-GYM-1968)
     7   Mark Spitz (USA-SWI-1972)
     7   Nikolai Andrianov (URS-GYM-1976)
     6   Eighteen athletes tied with six

Most Gold Medals, Games
      7   Mark Spitz (USA-SWI-1972)
      5   Anton Heida (USA-GYM-1904)
      5   Willis Lee (USA-SHO-1920)
      5   Nedo Nadi (ITA-FEN-1920)
      5   Paavo Nurmi (FIN-TAF-1924)
      5   Eric Heiden (USA-SSK-1980)

Most Silver Medals, Games
      5   Mariya Gorokhovskaya (URS-GYM-1952)
      4   Eugen Mack (SUI-GYM-1936)
      4   Viktor Lisitsky (URS-GYM-1964)
      4   Mikhail Voronin (URS-GYM-1968)
      4   Shirley Babashoff (USA-SWI-1976)
      4   Aleksandr Dityatin (URS-GYM-1980)

Most Bronze Medals, Games
      4   William Merz (USA-GYM-1904)
      4   Fritz Kucher (SUI-SHO-1920)
      3   Sixteen athletes tied with three

Most Medals, Games, Women
      7   Mariya Gorokhovskaya (URS-GYM-1952)
      6   Agnes Keleti (HUN-GYM-1956)
      6   Larisa Latynina (URS-GYM-1956)
      6   Larisa Latynina (URS-GYM-1960)
      6   Larisa Latynina (URS-GYM-1964)
      6   Vera Cáslavská (TCH-GYM-1968)

Most Gold Medals, Games, Women
      4   Francina Blankers-Koen (HOL-TAF-1948)
      4   Agnes Keleti (HUN-GYM-1956)
      4   Larisa Latynina (URS-GYM-1956)
      4   Vera Cáslavská (TCH-GYM-1968)
      4   Kornelia Ender (GDR-SWI-1976)
      4   Ecaterina Szabo (ROM-GYM-1984)
      4   Lidiya Skoblikova (URS-SSK-1964)

Most Medals, Games, Men
      8   Aleksandr Dityatin (URS-GYM-1980)
      7   Lloyd Spooner (USA-SHO-1920)
      7   Willis Lee (USA-SHO-1920)
      7   Boris Shakhlin (URS-GYM-1960)
      7   Mikhail Voronin (URS-GYM-1968)
      7   Mark Spitz (USA-SWI-1972)
      7   Nikolai Andrianov (URS-GYM-1976)

Most Gold Medals, Games, Men
  7   Mark Spitz (USA-SWI-1972)
  5   Anton Heida (USA-GYM-1904)
  5   Nedo Nadi (ITA-FEN-1920)
  5   Willis Lee (USA-SHO-1920)
  5   Paavo Nurmi (FIN-TAF-1924)

Most Medals, Games, Individual
  7   Aleksandr Dityatin (URS-GYM-1980)
  6   Nikolai Andrianov (URS-GYM-1976)
  6   Boris Shakhlin (URS-GYM-1960)
  6   Mikhail Voronin (URS-GYM-1968)
  6   Burton Downing (USA-CYC-1904)
  6   George Eyser (USA-GYM-1904)

Most Gold Medals, Games, Individual
  5   Eric Heiden (USA-SSK-1980)
  4   Alvin Kraenzlein (USA-TAF-1900)
  4   Anton Heida (USA-GYM-1904)
  4   Marcus Hurley (USA-CYC-1904)
  4   Boris Shakhlin (URS-GYM-1960)
  4   Lidiya Skoblikova (URS-SSK-1964)
  4   Vera Cáslavská (TCH-GYM-1968)
  4   Mark Spitz (USA-SWI-1972)
  4   Nikolai Andrianov (URS-GYM-1976)

Most Medals, Games, Individual, Women
  5   Mariya Gorokhovskaya (URS-GYM-1952)
  5   Vera Cáslavská (TCH-GYM-1968)
  5   Larisa Latynina (URS-GYM-1960)
  5   Larisa Latynina (URS-GYM-1964)
  5   Shane Gould (AUS-SWI-1972)

Most Gold Medals, Games, Individual, Women
  4   Lidiya Skoblikova (URS-SSK-1964)
  4   Vera Cáslavská (TCH-GYM-1968)
  3   Francina Blankers-Koen (HOL-TAF-1948)
  3   Agnes Keleti (HUN-GYM-1956)
  3   Larisa Latynina (URS-GYM-1956)
  3   Vera Cáslavská (TCH-GYM-1964)
  3   Debbie Meyer (USA-SWI-1968)
  3   Shane Gould (AUS-SWI-1972)
  3   Nadia Comăneci (ROM-GYM-1976)
  3   Kornelia Ender (GDR-SWI-1976)
  3   Marja-Liisa Hämäläinen (FIN-NSK-1984)
  3   Ecaterina Szabo (ROM-GYM-1984)

Most Medals, Games, Individual, Men
    7   Aleksandr Dityatin (URS-GYM-1980)
    6   Nikolai Andrianov (URS-GYM-1976)
    6   Boris Shakhlin (URS-GYM-1960)
    6   Mikhail Voronin (URS-GYM-1968)
    6   Burton Downing (USA-CYC-1904)
    6   George Eyser (USA-GYM-1904)

Most Gold Medals, Games, Individual, Men
    5   Eric Heiden (USA-SSK-1980)
    4   Alvin Kraenzlein (USA-TAF-1900)
    4   Anton Heida (USA-GYM-1904)
    4   Marcus Hurley (USA-CYC-1904)
    4   Boris Shakhlin (URS-GYM-1960)
    4   Mark Spitz (USA-SWI-1972)
    4   Nikolai Andrianov (URS-GYM-1976)

Most Consecutive Victories, Same Event, Individual
    4   Alfred Oerter (USA-TAF-Discus Throw, 1956-68)
    4   Paul Elvström (DEN-YAC-Monotype, 1948-60)
    4/3   Raymond Ewry (USA-TAF-Standing High Jump, 1900-08)
    4/3   Raymond Ewry (USA-TAF-Standing Long Jump, 1900-08)
    3   Fourteen athletes tied with three

Most Consecutive Victories, Same Event, Women, Individual
    3   Larisa Latynina (URS-GYM-Floor Exercises, 1956-64)
    3   Dawn Fraser (AUS-SWI-100 freestyle, 1956-64)
    3   Sonja Henie (NOR-FSK-Women, 1928-36)
    2   Twenty athletes tied with two

Most Consecutive Victories, Same Event, Men, Individual
    4   Alfred Oerter (USA-TAF-Discus Throw, 1956-68)
    4   Paul Elvström (DEN-YAC-Monotype, 1948-60)
    4/3   Raymond Ewry (USA-TAF-Standing High Jump, 1900-08)
    4/3   Raymond Ewry (USA-TAF-Standing Long Jump, 1900-08)
    3   Eleven athletes tied with three

Most Consecutive Victories, Team, Same Event, Same Team
   2   USA (Rowing Double Sculls, 1920-24)
          (John Kelly, Paul Costello)
   2   France (Pairs Figure Skating - 1928-32)
          (Andrée Brunet-Joly, Pierre Brunet)
   2   Norway (Dragon Yachting, 1948-52)
          (Thor Thorvaldsen, Sigvie Lie, Haakon Barfod)
   2   *Sweden (Equestrian Dressage, 1952-56)
          (Henri St. Cyr, Gustaf Boltenstern, Jr, Gehnall Persson)
   2   USSR (Pairs Figure Skating - 1964-68)
          (Lyudmila Byelousouva, Oleg Protopopov)
   2   FRG (500 metre Kayak Pairs Canoeing, 1964-68)
          (Roswitha Esser, Annemarie Zimmermann)
   2   GDR (Rowing Coxswainless Fours, 1968-72)
          (Frk. Forberger, Die. Grahn, Frk. Rühle, Die. Schubert)
   2   USSR (Pairs Figure Skating - 1976-80)
          (Irina Rodnina, Aleksandr Zaitsev)
   2   GDR (Luge Doubles - 1976-80)
          (Hans Rinn, Norbert Hahn)
   2   GDR (Rowing Coxed Pairs, 1976-80)
          (Harald Jährling, Friedrich-Wilhelm Ulrich, Georg Spohr)
   2   Denmark (Soling Yachting, 1976-80)
          (Poul Jensen, Valdemar Bandolowski, Erik Hansen)
   2   GDR (Rowing Coxswainless Pairs, 1976-80)
          (Jörg Landvoigt, Bernd Landvoigt)

*The Swedish dressage team of St. Cyr, Boltenstern, Persson can
claim, in effect, to be the only team to win an Olympic event
three times consecutively. In 1948 they "won" the dressage team
event but were disqualified when it was discovered that Persson
was a non-commisioned officer in the service, which was, at that
time, against Olympic rules in the equestrian events.

Youngest Known Competitor, Overall
   <10   Unknown French boy in 1900 ROW

Youngest Medalist, Overall
   <10   Unknown French boy in 1900 ROW
   10-216 Dimitrios Loundras (GRE-GYM, 1896)
   12-024 Inge Sörensen (DEN-SWI, 1936)
   12-233 Noël Vandernotte (FRA-ROW, 1936)
   13-024 Dorothy Poynton (USA-DIV, 1928)
   13-266 Marjorie Gestring (USA-DIV, 1936)
   13-308 Kornelia Ender (GDR-SWI, 1972)
   13-341 Robin Corsiglia (CAN-SWI, 1976)
   14-011 Nils Skoglund (SWE-DIV, 1920)
   14-012 Giorgia Cesana (ITA-ROW, 1906)

Youngest Gold Medalist, Overall
   <10   Unknown French boy in 1900 ROW
   13-266   Marjorie Gestring (USA-DIV, 1936)
   14-012   Giorgio Cesana (ITA-ROW, 1906)
   14-095   Bernard Malivoire (FRA-ROW, 1952)
   14-097   Debra "Pokey" Watson (USA-SWI, 1964)
   14-120   Aileen Riggin (USA-DIV, 1920)
   14-163   Franciscus Fidelis Joseph Hin (HOL-YAC, 1920)
   14-173   Günther Tiersch (GDR-ROW, 1968)
   14-184   Sandra Morgan (AUS-SWI, 1956)
   14-222   Hans Bourquin (SUI-ROW, 1928)

Youngest Medalist, Individual
   12-024   Inge Sörensen (DEN-SWI, 1936)
   13-024   Dorothy Poynton (USA-DIV, 1928)
   13-266   Marjorie Gestring (USA-DIV, 1936)

Youngest Gold Medalist, Individual
   13-266   Marjorie Gestring (USA-DIV, 1936)
   14-120   Aileen Riggin (USA-DIV, 1920)
   14-250   Nadia Comăneci (ROM-GYM, 1976)

Youngest Known Competitor, Women
   11-078   Cecilia Colledge (GBR-FSK, 1932)

Youngest Medalist, Women
   12-024   Inge Sörensen (DEN-SWI, 1936)
   13-024   Dorothy Poynton (USA-DIV, 1928)
   13-266   Marjorie Gestring (USA-DIV, 1936)
   13-308   Kornelia Ender (GDR-SWI, 1972)
   13-341   Robin Corsiglia (CAN-SWI, 1976)
   14-052   Zirvard Emirzyan (URS-DIV, 1980)
   14-058   Katherine Rawls (USA-DIV, 1932)
   14-097   Deborah "Pokey" Watson (USA-SWI, 1964)
   14-115   Ingeborg Schmitz (GER-SWI, 1936)
   14-120   Aileen Riggin (USA-DIV, 1920)

Youngest Gold Medalist, Women
   13-266   Marjorie Gestring (USA-DIV, 1936)
   14-096   Debra "Pokey" Watson (USA-SWI, 1964)
   14-120   Aileen Riggin (USA-DIV, 1920)
   14-184   Sandra Morgan (AUS-SWI, 1956)
   14-250   Nadia Comăneci (ROM-GYM, 1976)
   14-260   Carolyn Wood (USA-SWI, 1960)
   14-317   Simona Pauca (ROM-GYM, 1984)
   15-000   Mariya Filatova (URS-GYM, 1976)
   15-002   Susan Pederson (USA-SWI, 1968)
   15-072   Andrea Pollack (GDR-SWI, 1976)

Youngest Medalist, Women, Individual
 12-024   Inge Sörensen (DEN-SWI, 1936)
 13-024   Dorothy Poynton (USA-DIV, 1928)
 13-266   Marjorie Gestring (USA-DIV, 1936)

Youngest Gold Medalist, Women, Individual
 13-266   Marjorie Gestring (USA-DIV, 1936)
 14-120   Aileen Riggin (USA-DIV, 1920)
 14-250   Nadia Comăneci (ROM-GYM, 1976)

Youngest Known Competitor, Men
 <10   Unknown French boy in 1900 ROW

Youngest Medalist, Men
 <10   Unknown French boy in 1900 ROW
 10-216   Dimitrios Loundras (GRE-GYM, 1896)
 12-233   Noël Vandernotte (FRA-ROW, 1936)
 14-011   Nils Skoglund (SWE-DIV, 1920)
 14-012   Giorgio Cesana (ITA-ROW, 1906)
 14-055   Marcel Frébourg (FRA-ROW, 1906)
 14-095   Bernard Malivoire (FRA-ROW, 1952)
 14-163   Franciscus Hin (HOL-YAC, 1920)
 14-173   Günther Tiersch (FRG-ROW, 1968)
 14-222 Hans Bourquin (SUI-ROW, 1928)

Youngest Gold Medalist, Men
 <10   Unknown French boy in 1900 ROW
 14-012   Giorgio Cesana (ITA-ROW, 1906)
 14-095   Bernard Malivoire (FRA-ROW, 1952)
 14-163   Franciscus Hin (HOL-YAC, 1920)
 14-173   Günther Tiersch (FRG-ROW, 1968)
 14-222 Hans Bourquin (SUI-ROW, 1928)
 14-283   Klaus Zerta (GER-ROW, 1960)
 14-309   Kusuo Kitamura (JPN-SWI, 1932)
 15-226   Per Bertilsson (SWE-GYM, 1908)
 15-298   Yasuji Miyazaki (JPN-SWI, 1932)

Youngest Medalist, Men, Individual
 14-011   Nils Skoglund (SWE-DIV, 1920)
 14-309   Kusuo Kitamura (JPN-SWI, 1932)
 14-363   Scott Ethan Allen (USA-FSK, 1964)

Oldest Known Competitor, Overall
 72-280   Oscar Swahn (SWE-SHO, 1920)
 70-005   Lorna Johnstone (GBR-EQU, 1972)
 68-229   Roberto Soundy (ESA-SHO, 1968)

Oldest Medalist, Overall
   72-280   Oscar Swahn (SWE-SHO, 1920)
   68-194   Samuel Duvall (USA-ARC, 1904)
   66-155   Louis Noverraz (SUI-YAC, 1968)
   64-258   Oscar Swahn (SWE-SHO, 1912)
   64-002   Galen Spencer (USA-ARC, 1904)
   63-241   Robert Williams (USA-ARC, 1904)
   61-245   John Butt (GBR-SHO, 1912)
   61-131   William Roycroft (AUS-EQU, 1976)
   60-265   Oscar Swahn (SWE-SHO, 1908)
   60-104   William Milne (GBR-SHO, 1912)

Oldest Gold Medalist, Overall
   64-258   Oscar Swahn (SWE-SHO, 1912)
   64-002   Galen Spencer (USA-ARC, 1904)
   63-241   Robert Williams (USA-ARC, 1904)
   60-265   Oscar Swahn (SWE-SHO, 1908)
   59-113   Everard Endt (USA-YAC, 1952)
   59-024   William Northman (AUS-YAC, 1964)
   58-078   Allan Whitty (GBR-SHO, 1924)
   57-045   Johan Anker (NOR-YAC, 1928)
   56-212   Paul Smart (USA-YAC, 1948)
   56-195   William Thompson (USA-ARC, 1904)

Oldest Medalist, Individual
   64-258   Oscar Swahn (SWE-SHO, 1912)
   60-265   Oscar Swahn (SWE-SHO, 1908)
   60-104   William Milne (GBR-SHO, 1912)
   60-094   Josef Neckermann (FRG-EQU, 1972)

Oldest Gold Medalist, Individual
   60-265   Oscar Swahn (SWE-SHO, 1908)
   56-097   Walter Winans (USA-SHO, 1908)
   54-094   Henri St. Cyr (SWE-EQU, 1956)

Oldest Known Competitor, Women
   70-005   Lorna Johnstone (GBR-EQU, 1972)
   66-051   Lorna Johnstone (GBR-EQU, 1968)

Oldest Medalist, Women
   52-143   Patricia Dench (AUS-SHO, 1984)
   46-274   Ulla Håkanson (SWE-EQU, 1984)
   46-258   Maud von Rosen (SWE-EQU, 1972)
   45-072   Ilona Elek (HUN-FEN, 1952)
   45-025   Lida Howell (USA-ARC, 1904)
   45-012   Liselott Linsenhoff (FRG-EQU, 1972)
   44-226   Irena Szydłowska (POL-ARC, 1972)
   43-339   Edith Master (USA-EQU, 1976)
   43-015   Winifred McNair (GBR-TEN, 1920)
   42-246   Doreen Wilber (USA-ARC, 1972)

Oldest Gold Medalist, Women
  45-025 Lida Howell (USA-ARC, 1904)
  45-012 Liselott Linsenhoff (FRG-EQU, 1972)
  43-015 Winifred McNair (GBR-TEN, 1920)
  42-246 Doreen Wilber (USA-ARC, 1972)
  41-078 Ilona Elek (HUN-FEN, 1948)
  41-060 Liselott Linsenhoff (FRG-EQU, 1968)
  40-212 Linda Thom (CAN-SHO, 1984)
  38-132 Edith Hannam (GBR-TEN, 1912)
  38-016 Virginie Heriot (FRA-YAC, 1928)
  37-259 Sylvi Saimo (FIN-CAN, 1952)

Oldest Medalist, Women, Individual
  52-143 Patricia Dench (AUS-SHO, 1984)
  45-072 Ilona Elek (HUN-FEN, 1952)
  45-025 Lida Howell (USA-ARC, 1904)

Oldest Gold Medalist, Women, Individual
  45-025 Lida Howell (USA-ARC, 1904)
  45-012 Liselott Linsenhoff (FRG-EQU, 1972)
  42-246 Doreen Wilber (USA-ARC, 1972)

Oldest Known Competitor, Men
  72-280 Oscar Swahn (SWE-SHO, 1920)
  68-229 Roberto Soundy (ESA-SHO, 1968)
  68-194 Samuel Duvall (USA-ARC, 1904)

Oldest Medalist, Men
  72-280 Oscar Swahn (SWE-SHO, 1920)
  68-194 Samuel Duvall (USA-ARC, 1904)
  66-155 Louis Noverraz (SUI-YAC, 1968)
  64-258 Oscar Swahn (SWE-SHO, 1912)
  64-002 Galen Spencer (USA-ARC, 1904)
  63-241 Robert Williams (USA-ARC, 1904)
  61-245 John Butt (GBR-SHO, 1912)
  61-131 William Roycroft (AUS-EQU, 1976)
  60-265 Oscar Swahn (SWE-SHO, 1908)
  60-104 William Milne (GBR-SHO, 1912)

Oldest Gold Medalist, Men
  64-258 Oscar Swahn (SWE-SHO, 1912)
  64-002 Galen Spencer (USA-ARC, 1904)
  63-241 Robert Williams (USA-ARC, 1904)
  60-265 Oscar Swahn (SWE-SHO, 1908)
  59-113 Everard Endt (USA-YAC, 1952)
  59-024 William Northman (AUS-YAC, 1964)
  58-078 Allan Whitty (GBR-SHO, 1924)
  57-045 Johan Anker (NOR-YAC, 1928)
  56-212 Paul Smart (USA-YAC, 1948)
  56-195 William Thompson (USA-ARC, 1904)

Oldest Medalist, Men, Individual
  64-258   Oscar Swahn (SWE-SHO, 1912)
  60-265   Oscar Swahn (SWE-SHO, 1908)
  60-104   William Milne (GBR-SHO, 1912)
  60-094   Josef Neckermann (FRG-EQU, 1972)

Oldest Gold Medalist, Men, Individual
  60-265   Oscar Gomer Swahn (SWE-SHO, 1908)
  56-097   Walter Winans (USA-SHO, 1908)
  54-094   Henri St. Cyr (SWE-EQU, 1956)

Winning Gold Medals Both Winter and Summer Games
    Edward Eagan (USA) - 1920 BOX, 1932 BOB

Winning Medals Both Winter and Summer Games
    Edward Eagan (USA)- 1920 BOX (1), 1932 BOB (1)
    Jacob Tullin Thams (NOR) - 1924 NSK (1), 1936 YAC (2)

Winning Medals in Two Sports
    Gösta Asbrink (SWE) (1908 GYM, 1912 MOP)
    Edward Barrett (GBR) (1908 TOW, 1908 WRE)
    Victor Boin (BEL) (1908-12 WAP, 1920 FEN)
    Gustaf Dyrssen (SWE) (1920-24 MOP, 1936 FEN)
    Conn Findlay (USA) (1956-60-64 ROW, 1976 YAC)
    Charles Gondouin (FRA) (1900 TOW, 1900 RUG)
    Erik Granfelt (SWE) (1906 TOW, 1908 GYM)
    Nils Hellsten (SWE) (1908 GYM, 1924 FEN)
    Otto Herschmann (AUT) (1896 SWI, 1912 FEN)
    Fritz Hofmann (GER) (1896 TAF, 1896 GYM)
    Oswald Holmberg (SWE) (1906 TOW, 1908-12 GYM)
    Viggo Jensen (DEN) (1896 WLT, 1896 SHO)
    Roswitha Krause (GDR) (1968 SWI, 1976-80 THA)
    Georg de Laval (SWE) (1912 SHO, 1912 MOP)
    Joseph Lydon (USA) (1904 SOC, 1904 BOX)
    Fernand de Montigny (BEL) (1906-08-12-24 FEN, 1920 FIH)
    Holger Nielsen (DEN) (1896 SHO, 1896 FEN)
    Veli Nieminen (FIN) (1908 GYM, 1920 SHO)
    Axel Norling (SWE) (1906 TOW, 1908-12 GYM)
    Daniel Norling (SWE) (1908-12 GYM, 1920 EQU)
    Heinrich Schneidereit (GER) (1906 TOW, 1906 WLT)
    Karl Schumann (GER) (1896 WRE, 1896 GYM)
    Sven Thofelt (SWE) (1928 MOP, 1936-48 FEN)

Bertil Uggla (SWE) (1912 TAF, 1924 MOP)
Sotirios Versis (GRE) (1896 TAF, 1896 WLT)
Magnus Wegelius (FIN) (1908 GYM, 1920 SHO)
In addition to the above, four women and one man have won medals in the slightly artificial division of swimming and diving, while fourteen men have won medals in both swimming and water polo. Georg Hoffmann (GER) won swimming and diving medals in 1904. The women are listed below. The SWI/WAP doublers are as follows: Gerard Blitz (BEL), Austin Clapp (USA), Joseph De Combe (BEL), John Henry Derbyshire (GBR), Pontus Hanson (SWE), Harald Julin (SWE), Peter Kemp (GBR), Louis Martin (GBR), Desire Merchez (FRA), Wallace O'Connor (USA), Paul Radmiliovic (GBR), Erich Rademacher (GER), Tim Shaw (USA), and Johnny Weissmuller (USA).
Finally, two men won medals in both the art competitions and a sport. They are: Alfred Hájos (HUN) (1896 SWI, 1924 ART), and Walter Winans (USA) (1908-12 SHO, 1912 ART)

Winning Gold Medals in Two Sports
Daniel Norling (SWE) (1908-12 GYM, 1920 EQU)
Karl Schumann (GER) (1896 WRE, 1896 GYM)
Also, John Derbyshire (GBR) (SWI/WAP), Paul Radmilovic (GBR) (SWI/WAP), and Walter Winans (USA) (SHO/ART) - see above.

Winning Medals in Two Sports, Women
Roswitha Krause (GDR) (1968 SWI, 1976-80 THA)
In addition, four women have won medals in both swimming and diving as follows: Katherine Rawls (USA) (1936 SWI, 1932-36 DIV), Aileen Riggin (USA) (1924 SWI, 1920-24 DIV), Hjördis Töpel (SWE) (1924 SWI, 1924 DIV), Helen Wainwright (USA) (1924 SWI, 1920 DIV).

Winning Medals in Three Sports
Frank Kungler (USA) - 1904 TOW, WRE, WLT

Winning Medals in Two Sports, Winter
Jennison Heaton (USA) (1928 Skeleton, 1928 BOB)
John Heaton (USA) (1928 Skeleton, 1932 BOB)
This division is considered artificial by some who consider the skeleton race a form of bobsledding. Others, however, list the skeleton either as a separate sport or a form of luge (tobogganing).

Winning Gold Medals in Two Sports, Winter
This has not yet occurred.

Winning Medals While Representing Two Different Countries
Daniel Carroll (RUG) (1908 AUS, 1920 USA)
Latifur Rehman (FIH) (1948 IND, 1956 PAK)
Robert Zimonyi (ROW) (1948 HUN, 1964 USA)
Angelo Parisi (JUD) (1972 GBR, 1980-84 FRA)
Hans Fogh (YAC) (1960 DEN, 1984 CAN)

Winning Gold Medals While Representing Two Different Countries
       Daniel Carroll (RUG) (1908 AUS, 1920 USA)

Torch Bearers at the Opening Ceremonies
       1936   Fritz Schilgen
       1948   John Mark
       1952   Paavo Nurmi/Hannes Kolehmainen
       1956   Ron Clarke
       1960   Giancarlo Peris
       1964   Yoshinori Sakai
       1968   Enriqueta Basilio de Sotelo
       1972   Günter Zahn
       1976   Stéphane Prefontaine/Sandra Henderson
       1980   Sergei Belov
       1984   Rafer Johnson

Torch Bearers at the Opening Ceremonies, Winter
       1952   Eigil Nansen
       1956   Guido Caroli
       1960   Kenneth Henry
       1964   Joseph Rieder
       1968   Alain Calmat
       1972   Hideki Takada
       1976   Christl Haas/Josef Feistmantl
       1980   Charles Morgan Kerr
       1984   Sandra Dubravcič

Torch Bearers at the Opening Ceremonies, Female
       1968   Summer   Enriqueta Basilio de Sotelo
       1976   Winter   Christl Haas
       1984   Winter   Sandra Dubravcič

Speakers of the Oath at the Opening Ceremonies
       1920   Victor Boin
       1924   Georges Andre
       1928   Harry Denis
       1932   George Calnan
       1936   Rudolf Ismayr
       1948   Donald Finlay
       1952   Heikki Savolainen
       1956   John Landy
       1960   Adolfo Consolini
       1964   Takashi Ono
       1968   Pablo Garrido
       1972   Heidi Schueller
       1976   Pierre St. Jean
       1980   Nikolai Andrianov
       1984   Edwin Moses

Speakers of the Oath at the Opening Ceremonies, Winter
```
1924   Camille Mandrillon
1928   Hans Eidenbenz
1932   William Fiske
1936   Wilhelm Bogner
1948   Richard Torriani
1952   Torbjorn Falkanger
1956   Guilliana Chenal-Minuzzo
1960   Carol Heiss
1964   Paul Aste
1968   Leo Lacroix
1972   Keichi Suzuki
1976   Werner Delle-Kerth
1980   Eric Heiden
1984   Bojan Križaj
```

Speakers of the Oath at the Opening Ceremonies, Female
```
1956   Winter    Guilliana Chenal-Minuzzo
1960   Winter    Carol Heiss
1972   Summer    Heidi Schuller
```

Medals Won by Countries, Overall
        In the following tables, places are given according to
total medals. Ties are broken first by number of gold medals,
then number of silver medals, and finally number of bronze
medals.

		Gold	Silver	Bronze	Total
1.	United States	757.500	581.500	493.500	1832.500
2.	USSR	408.000	340.000	301.000	1049.000
3.	Great Britain	172.500	215.500	208.000	596.000
4.	Sweden	161.500	163.000	190.000	514.500
5.	France	160.000	170.000	184.000	514.000
6.	GDR	156.000	144.000	136.000	436.000
7.	Italy	152.000	124.000	127.000	403.000
8.	Finland	125.000	116.000	139.000	380.000
9.	Hungary	113.000	108.000	135.000	356.000
10.	FRG	82.000	106.000	121.000	309.000
11.	Norway	93.000	88.000	86.000	267.000
12.	Germany	75.500	86.000	84.000	245.500
13.	Japan	84.000	76.000	76.000	236.000
14.	Switzerland	59.000	83.000	78.000	220.000
15.	Australia	67.750	61.000	82.000	210.750
16.	Canada	50.000	70.000	84.000	204.000
17.	Netherlands	51.000	60.000	69.000	180.000
18.	Poland	39.000	52.000	88.000	179.000
19.	Romania	48.000	53.000	77.000	178.000
20.	Austria	42.000	60.000	63.000	165.000
21.	Czechoslovakia	44.000	53.000	57.500	154.500
22.	Denmark	30.500	57.000	52.000	139.500
23.	Belgium	36.000	49.000	43.000	128.000
24.	Bulgaria	27.000	50.000	40.000	117.000

25. Greece	22.000	40.000	39.000	101.000
26. Yugoslavia	23.000	26.000	23.000	72.000
27. Cuba	21.500	19.000	12.000	52.500
28. South Africa	16.000	15.000	20.000	51.000
29. Turkey	23.000	12.000	9.000	44.000
30. Argentina	13.000	18.000	13.000	44.000
31. New Zealand	22.250	4.000	15.000	41.250
32. Mexico	9.000	12.000	16.000	37.000
33. Korea	7.000	11.000	18.000	36.000
34. China	15.000	9.000	7.000	31.000
35. Brazil	6.000	7.000	17.000	30.000
36. Iran	4.000	10.000	15.000	29.000
37. Kenya	6.000	7.000	9.000	22.000
38. Spain	4.000	11.000	7.000	22.000
39. Estonia	6.000	6.000	9.000	21.000
40. Jamaica	4.000	8.000	8.000	20.000
41. Egypt	6.000	6.000	7.000	19.000
42. India	8.000	3.000	3.000	14.000
43. Ireland	4.000	5.000	5.000	14.000
44. Korea DPR	2.000	6.000	5.000	13.000
45. Portugal	1.000	4.000	7.000	12.000
46. Ethiopia	5.000	1.000	4.000	10.000
47. Mongolia	--	5.000	5.000	10.000
48. Uruguay	2.000	1.000	6.000	9.000
49. Pakistan	3.000	3.000	2.000	8.000
50. Liechtenstein	2.000	2.000	4.000	8.000
51. Venezuela	1.000	2.000	5.000	8.000
52. Trinidad	1.000	2.000	4.000	7.000
53. Chile	--	5.000	2.000	7.000
54. Philippines	--	1.000	5.000	6.000
55. Uganda	1.000	3.000	1.000	5.000
56. Tunisia	1.000	2.000	2.000	5.000
T57. Colombia	--	2.000	2.000	4.000
Lebanon	--	2.000	2.000	4.000
T59. Nigeria	--	1.000	3.000	4.000
Puerto Rico	--	1.000	3.000	4.000
61. Morocco	2.000	1.000	--	3.000
62. Latvia	--	2.000	1.000	3.000
T63. Ghana	--	1.000	2.000	3.000
Chinese Taipei	--	1.000	2.000	3.000
T65. Luxembourg	1.000	1.000	--	2.000
Peru	1.000	1.000	--	2.000
67. Bahamas	1.000	--	1.000	2.000
68. Tanzania	--	2.000	--	2.000
T69. Iceland	--	1.000	1.000	2.000
Cameroun	--	1.000	1.000	2.000
Haiti	--	1.000	1.000	2.000
Thailand	--	1.000	1.000	2.000
T73. Algeria	--	--	2.000	2.000
Panama	--	--	2.000	2.000

		Gold	Silver	Bronze	Total
75.	Zimbabwe	1.000	--	--	1.000
T76.	Singapore	--	1.000	--	1.000
	Ivory Coast	--	1.000	--	1.000
	Sri Lanka	--	1.000	--	1.000
	Syria	--	1.000	--	1.000
T80.	Dom. Republic	--	--	1.000	1.000
	Niger	--	--	1.000	1.000
	Bermuda	--	--	1.000	1.000
	Iraq	--	--	1.000	1.000
	Zambia	--	--	1.000	1.000
	Guyana	--	--	1.000	1.000
	Totals	3279.000	3255.000	3348.000	9882.000

Medals Won by Countries, Men

		Gold	Silver	Bronze	Total
1.	United States	622.750	468.250	402.500	1493.500
2.	USSR	297.333	251.167	205.500	754.000
3.	Great Britain	152.000	172.250	169.667	493.917
4.	Sweden	152.500	152.500	174.300	479.300
5.	France	147.833	157.500	171.000	476.333
6.	Italy	145.000	114.500	118.000	377.500
7.	Finland	116.500	103.500	130.000	350.000
8.	Hungary	95.000	89.000	109.000	293.000
9.	Norway	87.000	84.167	78.000	249.167
10.	GDR	79.000	71.500	86.500	237.000
11.	FRG	61.833	74.833	93.917	230.583
12.	Japan	80.000	72.000	71.000	223.000
13.	Germany	67.000	76.000	73.000	216.000
14.	Switzerland	51.000	78.333	73.667	203.000
15.	Canada	39.500	51.000	62.500	153.000
16.	Poland	33.000	41.000	74.000	148.000
17.	Australia	43.750	42.000	61.000	146.750
18.	Belgium	35.500	49.000	41.000	125.500
19.	Austria	31.000	45.000	45.500	121.500
20.	Czechoslovakia	31.000	42.000	47.500	120.500
21.	Netherlands	30.000	37.000	51.500	118.500
22.	Denmark	25.500	49.000	43.000	117.500
23.	Romania	23.000	35.000	51.667	109.667
24.	Bulgaria	24.000	41.000	33.000	98.000
25.	Greece	21.000	38.500	37.500	97.000
26.	Yugoslavia	21.000	24.000	22.000	67.000
27.	Cuba	20.500	18.000	10.000	48.500
28.	Turkey	23.000	12.000	9.000	44.000

29.	South Africa	14.000	14.000	16.000	44.000
30.	Argentina	13.000	16.000	13.000	42.000
31.	New Zealand	21.250	4.000	13.000	38.250
32.	Mexico	9.000	11.000	15.000	35.000
33.	Korea	6.000	10.000	16.000	32.000
34.	Brazil	6.000	7.000	17.000	30.000
35.	Iran	4.000	10.000	15.000	29.000
36.	China	10.000	7.000	5.000	22.000
37.	Kenya	6.000	7.000	9.000	22.000
38.	Spain	4.000	11.000	7.000	22.000
39.	Estonia	6.000	6.000	9.000	21.000
40.	Egypt	6.000	6.000	7.000	19.000
41.	Jamaica	4.000	8.000	5.000	17.000
42.	India	8.000	3.000	3.000	14.000
43.	Ireland	4.000	5.000	5.000	14.000
44.	Korea DPR	2.000	5.000	4.000	11.000
45.	Portugal	1.000	4.000	6.000	11.000
46.	Ethiopia	5.000	1.000	4.000	10.000
47.	Mongolia	--	5.000	5.000	10.000
48.	Uruguay	2.000	1.000	6.000	9.000
49.	Pakistan	3.000	3.000	2.000	8.000
50.	Venezuela	1.000	2.000	5.000	8.000
51.	Trinidad	1.000	2.000	4.000	7.000
52.	Chile	--	4.000	2.000	6.000
53.	Philippines	--	1.000	5.000	6.000
54.	Uganda	1.000	3.000	1.000	5.000
55.	Tunisia	1.000	2.000	2.000	5.000
T56.	Colombia	--	2.000	2.000	4.000
	Lebanon	--	2.000	2.000	4.000
T58.	Nigeria	--	1.000	3.000	4.000
	Puerto Rico	--	1.000	3.000	4.000
60.	Latvia	--	2.000	1.000	3.000
T61.	Ghana	--	1.000	2.000	3.000
	Liechtenstein	--	1.000	2.000	3.000
T63.	Morocco	1.000	1.000	--	2.000
	Luxembourg	1.000	1.000	--	2.000
	Peru	1.000	1.000	--	2.000
66.	Bahamas	1.000	--	1.000	2.000
67.	Tanzania	--	2.000	--	2.000
T68.	Chinese Taipei	--	1.000	1.000	2.000
	Cameroun	--	1.000	1.000	2.000
	Iceland	--	1.000	1.000	2.000
	Haiti	--	1.000	1.000	2.000
	Thailand	--	1.000	1.000	2.000
T73.	Algeria	--	--	2.000	2.000
	Panama	--	--	2.000	2.000
T75.	Singapore	--	1.000	--	1.000
	Ivory Coast	--	1.000	--	1.000
	Sri Lanka	--	1.000	--	1.000
	Syria	--	1.000	--	1.000

T79.	Dom. Republic	--	--	1.000	1.000
	Niger	--	--	1.000	1.000
	Bermuda	--	--	1.000	1.000
	Iraq	--	--	1.000	1.000
	Zambia	--	--	1.000	1.000
	Guyana	--	--	1.000	1.000
	Totals	2698.749	2672.000	2777.218	8147.967

Medals Won by Countries, Women

		Gold	Silver	Bronze	Total
1.	United States	134.750	113.250	91.000	339.000
2.	USSR	110.667	88.833	95.500	295.000
3.	GDR	77.000	72.500	49.500	199.000
4.	Great Britain	20.500	43.250	38.333	102.083
5.	FRG	20.167	31.167	27.083	78.417
6.	Romania	25.000	18.000	25.333	68.333
7.	Australia	24.000	19.000	21.000	64.000
8.	Hungary	18.000	19.000	26.000	63.000
9.	Netherlands	21.000	23.000	17.500	61.500
10.	Canada	10.500	19.000	21.500	51.000
11.	Austria	11.000	15.000	17.500	43.500
12.	France	12.167	12.500	13.000	37.667
13.	Sweden	9.000	10.500	15.700	35.200
14.	Czechoslovakia	13.000	11.000	10.000	34.000
15.	Poland	6.000	11.000	14.000	31.000
16.	Finland	8.500	12.500	9.000	30.000
17.	Germany	8.500	10.000	11.000	29.500
18.	Italy	7.000	9.500	9.000	25.500
19.	Denmark	5.000	8.000	9.000	22.000
20.	Bulgaria	3.000	9.000	7.000	19.000
21.	Norway	6.000	3.833	8.000	17.833
22.	Switzerland	8.000	4.667	4.333	17.000
23.	Japan	4.000	4.000	5.000	13.000
24.	China	5.000	2.000	2.000	9.000
25.	South Africa	2.000	1.000	4.000	7.000
26.	Yugoslavia	2.000	2.000	1.000	5.000
27.	Liechtenstein	2.000	1.000	2.000	5.000
28.	Greece	1.000	1.500	1.500	4.000

T29.	Cuba	1.000	1.000	2.000	4.000
	Korea	1.000	1.000	2.000	4.000
31.	New Zealand	1.000	--	2.000	3.000
32.	Jamaica	--	--	3.000	3.000
33.	Belgium	0.500	--	2.000	2.500
34.	Argentina	--	2.000	--	2.000
T35.	Mexico	--	1.000	1.000	2.000
	Korea DPR	--	1.000	1.000	2.000
T37.	Morocco	1.000	--	--	1.000
	Zimbabwe	1.000	--	--	1.000
39.	Chile	--	1.000	--	1.000
T40.	Portugal	--	--	1.000	1.000
	Chinese Taipei	--	--	1.000	1.000
	Totals	580.251	583.000	570.782	1734.033

Discrepancies in the number of total medals are due to various events in which a single medal of each type was not awarded. The specific events in which this occurred and the format of medals awarded is discussed under each sport.

Following are the best records achieved in the Games of
the Olympiads (Summer Olympics) since their inception in 1896.
Lists are ten-deep for the major records and five-deep in more
restricted categories. Where a great number of athletes are tied
with the same mark, they are not always listed but that fact is
noted. Age records are ten deep for medalists and gold medalists,
and one-to-three deep for more restricted categories. A list of
medals won by country in the summer Olympics, with sections for
medals won by men and women, follows at the end of this section.

Most Medals, Summer
```
 18     Larisa Latynina (URS-GYM)
 15     Nikolai Andrianov (URS-GYM)
 13     Edoardo Mangiarotti (ITA-FEN)
 13     Takashi Ono (JPN-GYM)
 13     Boris Shakhlin (URS-GYM)
 12     Sawao Kato (JPN-GYM)
 12     Paavo Nurmi (FIN-TAF)
 11     Vera Cáslavská (TCH-GYM)
 11     Carl Osburn (USA-SHO)
 11     Mark Spitz (USA-SWI)
 11     Viktor Chukarin (URS-GYM)
 10     Polina Astakhova (URS-GYM)
 10     Aleksandr Dityatin (URS-GYM)
 10     Aládár Gerevich (HUN-FEN)
 10     Agnes Keleti (HUN-GYM)
 10     Akinori Nakayama (JPN-GYM)
 10/8   Raymond Ewry (USA-TAF)
```

Most Gold Medals, Summer
```
 10/8   Raymond Ewry (USA-TAF)
  9     Larisa Latynina (URS-GYM)
  9     Paavo Nurmi (FIN-TAF)
  9     Mark Spitz (USA-SWI)
  8     Sawao Kato (JPN-GYM)
  7     Nikolai Andrianov (URS-GYM)
  7     Vera Cáslavská (TCH-GYM)
  7     Viktor Chukarin (URS-GYM)
  7     Aládár Gerevich (HUN-FEN)
  7     Boris Shakhlin (URS-GYM)
```

Most Silver Medals, Summer
    6   Shirley Babashoff (USA-SWI)
    6   Aleksandr Dityatin (URS-GYM)
    6   Mikhail Voronin (URS-GYM)
    5   Nine athletes tied with five

Most Bronze Medals, Summer
    6   Heikki Savolainen (FIN-GYM)
    5   Philip Edwards (CAN-TAF)
    5   Adrianus Jong (HOL-FEN)
    5   Daniel Revenu (FRA-FEN)
    4   Eleven athletes tied with four

Most Years Winning Medals, Summer
    6   Aládár Gerevich (HUN-FEN)
    6   Hans-Günter Winkler (FRG-EQU)
    5   Edoardo Mangiarotti (ITA-FEN)
    5   Heikki Savolainen (FIN-GYM)
    5   Philippe Cattiau (FRA-FEN)
    5   Pál Kovács (HUN-FEN)
    5   Ildikó Saginé-Ujlakiné-Rejtö (HUN-FEN)
    5   Fernand de Montigny (BEL-FEN/FIH)
    5   Michael Plumb (USA-EQU)
    5   Jack Beresford (GBR-ROW)
    5   Gustav Fischer (SUI-EQU)
    5   Deszö Gyarmati (HUN-WAP)

Most Years Winning Gold Medals, Summer
    6   Aládár Gerevich (HUN-FEN)
    5   Pál Kovács (HUN-FEN)
    4   Edoardo Mangiarotti (ITA-FEN)
    4/3 Raymond Ewry (USA-TAF)
    4   Gert Fredriksson (SWE-CAN)
    4   Reiner Klimke (GER-EQU)
    4   Hans-Günter Winkler (FRG-EQU)
    4   Rudolf Kárpáti (HUN-FEN)
    4   Viktor Sidyak (URS-FEN)
    4   Alfred Oerter (USA-TAF)
    4   Paul Elvström (DEN-YAC)

Most Years Between Medals, Summer
    28   Aládár Gerevich (HUN-FEN)
    28   Tore Holm (SWE-YAC)
    24   Edoardo Mangiarotti (ITA-FEN)
    24   Heikki Savolainen (FIN-GYM)
    24   Pál Kovács (HUN-FEN)
    24   Gustaf-Adolf Boltenstern, Jr. (SWE-EQU)
    24   Magnus Konow (NOR-YAC)
    24   Joseph Petersen (DEN-ART)
    24   Hans Fogh (DEN/CAN-YAC)

Most Years Between Gold Medals, Summer
    28   Aládár Gerevich (HUN-FEN)
    24   Pál Kovács (HUN-FEN)
    24   Edoardo Mangiarotti (ITA-FEN)
    20   Hubert van Innis (BEL-ARC)
    20   Reiner Klimke (FRG-EQU)
    20   Manlio DiRosa (ITA-FEN)
    20   Lars Jörgen Madsen (DEN-SHO)

Most Appearances, Summer
    8   Raimondo d'Inzeo (ITA-EQU, 1948-76)
    7   Ivan Osiier (DEN-FEN; 1908-32, 48)
    7   Durwood Knowles (GBR/BAH-YAC; 1948-72)
    7   Paul Elvström (DEN-YAC; 1948-60, 68-72, 84)
    7   Piero d'Inzeo (ITA-EQU, 1952-76)
    7   François La Fortune, Jr. (BEL-SHO, 1952-76)
    6   Eighteen athletes tied with six.

Most Years Between Appearances, Summer
    40   Ivan Osiier (DEN-FEN, 1908-48)
    40   Magnus Konow (NOR-YAC, 1908-48)
    36   François La Fortune, Sr. (BEL-SHO, 1924-60)
    36   Paul Elvström (DEN-YAC, 1948-84)

Most Medals, Summer, Women
    18   Larisa Latynina (URS-GYM)
    11   Vera Cáslavská (TCH-GYM)
    10   Polina Astakhova (URS-GYM)
    10   Agnes Keleti (HUN-GYM)
    9   Nadia Comăneci (ROM-GYM)
    8   Shirley Babashoff (USA-SWI)
    8   Kornelia Ender (GDR-SWI)
    8   Dawn Fraser (AUS-SWI)
    8   Sofiya Muratova (URS-GYM)
    8   Lyudmila Turishcheva (URS-GYM)

Most Gold Medals, Summer, Women
    9   Larisa Latynina (URS-GYM)
    7   Vera Cáslavská (TCH-GYM)
    5   Polina Astakhova (URS-GYM)
    5   Agnes Keleti (HUN-GYM)
    5   Nadia Comăneci (ROM-GYM)
    5   Nelli Kim (URS-GYM)

Most Silver Medals, Summer, Women
    6   Shirley Babashoff (USA-SWI)
    5   Larisa Latynina (URS-GYM)
    5   Mariya Gorokhovskaya (URS-GYM)
    4   Vera Cáslavská (TCH-GYM)
    4   Kornelia Ender (GDR-GYM)
    4   Dawn Fraser (AUS-SWI)
    4   Erika Zuchold (GDR-GYM)

Most Bronze Medals, Summer, Women
    4   Larisa Latynina (URS-GYM)
    4   Sofiya Muratova (URS-GYM)
    3   Nine athletes tied with three

Most Years Winning Medals, Summer, Women
    5   Ildikó Saginé-Ujlakiné-Rejtö (HUN-FEN)
    4   Irena Szewińska-Kirszenstein (POL-TAF)
    4   Elena Belova-Novikova (URS-FEN)
    4   Galina Gorokhova (URS-FEN)
    4   Tatyana Samusenko-Petrenko (URS-FEN)
    4   Michele Maffei (ITA-FEN)
    4   Inna Ryskal (URS-VOL)

Most Years Winning Gold Medals, Summer, Women
    3   Larisa Latynina (URS-GYM)
    3   Polina Astakhova (URS-GYM)
    3   Dawn Fraser (AUS-SWI)
    3   Lyudmila Turishcheva (URS-GYM)
    3   Irena Szewińska-Kirszenstein (POL-TAF)
    3   Elena Belova-Novikova (URS-FEN)
    3   Galina Gorokhova (URS-FEN)
    3   Lyudmila Pinayeva-Khvedosyuk (URS-CAN)
    3   Tatyana Samusenko-Petrenko (URS-FEN)
    3   Aleksandra Zabelina (URS-FEN)

Most Years Between Medals, Summer, Women
    16   Ildikó Saginé-Ujlakiné-Rejtö (HUN-FEN)
    16   Liselott Linsenhoff (FRG-EQU)
    16   Ilona Elek (HUN-FEN)
    16   Ellen Müller-Preiss (AUT-FEN)

Most Years Between Gold Medals, Summer, Women
    16   Ilona Elek (HUN-FEN)
    12   Irena Szewińska-Kirszenstein (POL-TAF)
    12   Elena Belova-Novikova (URS-FEN)
    12   Galina Gorokhova (URS-FEN)
    12   Tatyana Samusenko-Petrenko (URS-FEN)
    12   Aleksandra Zabelina (URS-FEN)

Most Appearances, Summer, Women
    6   Janice Lee York-Romary (USA-FEN, 1948-68)
    6   Lia Manoliu (ROM-TAF, 1952-72)
    6   Kerstin Palm (SWE-FEN, 1964-84)
    5   Eight athletes tied with five.

Most Years Between Appearances, Summer, Women
    24   Ellen Müller-Preiss (AUT-FEN, 1932-56)
    20   Jenny Addams (BEL-FEN, 1928-48)
    20   Karen Lachman (DEN-FEN, 1936-56)
    20   Dorothy Odam-Tyler (GBR-TAF, 1936-56)
    20   Janice Lee York-Romary (USA-FEN, 1948-68)
    20   Lia Manoliu (ROM-TAF, 1952-72)
    20   Kerstin Palm (SWE-FEN, 1964-84)
    20   Christilot Hanson-Boylen (CAN-EQU, 1964-84)

Most Medals, Summer, Men
15	Nikolai Andrianov (URS-GYM)
13	Edoardo Mangiarotti (ITA-FEN)
13	Takashi Ono (JPN-GYM)
13	Boris Shakhlin (URS-GYM)
12	Sawao Kato (JPN-GYM)
12	Paavo Nurmi (FIN-TAF)

Most Gold Medals, Summer, Men
10/8	Raymond Ewry (USA-TAF)
9	Paavo Nurmi (FIN-TAF)
9	Mark Spitz (USA-SWI)
8	Sawao Kato (JPN-GYM)
7	Nikolai Andrianov (URS-GYM)
7	Boris Shakhlin (URS-GYM)
7	Viktor Chukarin (URS-GYM)
7	Aládár Gerevich (HUN-FEN)

Most Silver Medals, Summer, Men
6	Mikhail Voronin (URS-GYM)
6	Aleksandr Dityatin (URS-GYM)
5	Nikolai Andrianov (URS-GYM)
5	Edoardo Mangiarotti (ITA-FEN)
5	Zoltán Halmay (HUN-SWI)
5	Yuriy Titov (URS-GYM)
5	Philippe Cattiau (FRA-FEN)
5	Gustavo Marzi (ITA-FEN)
5	Viktor Lisitsky (URS-GYM)

Most Bronze Medals, Summer, Men
6	Heikki Savolainen (FIN-GYM)
5	Philip Edwards (CAN-TAF)
5	Adrianus Jong (HOL-FEN)
5	Daniel Revenu (FRA-FEN)
4	Eight athletes tied with four

Most Years Winning Medals, Summer, Men
6	Aládár Gerevich (HUN-FEN)
6	Hans-Günther Winkler (FRG-EQU)
5	Edoardo Mangiarotti (ITA-FEN)
5	Heikki Savolainen (FIN-GYM)
5	Philippe Cattiau (FRA-FEN)
5	Pál Kovács (HUN-FEN)
5	Fernand de Montigny (BEL-FEN/FIH)
5	Michael Plumb (USA-EQU)
5	Jack Beresford (GBR-ROW)
5	Gustav Fischer (SUI-EQU)
5	Desző Gyarmati (HUN-WAP)

Most Years Winning Gold Medals, Summer, Men
6   Aládár Gerevich (HUN-FEN)
5   Pál Kovács (HUN-FEN)
4   Edoardo Mangiarotti (ITA-FEN)
4   Gert Fredriksson (SWE-CAN)
4   Reiner Klimke (FRG-EQU)
4   Hans-Günther Winkler (FRG-EQU)
4   Rudolf Kárpáti (HUN-FEN)
4   Viktor Sidyak (URS-FEN)
4   Paul Elvström (DEN-YAC)
4   Alfred Oerter (USA-TAF)
4/3   Raymond Ewry (USA-TAF)

Most Years Between Medals, Summer, Men
28   Aládár Gerevich (HUN-FEN)
28   Tore Holm (SWE-YAC)
24   Edoardo Mangiarotti (ITA-FEN)
24   Heikki Savolainen (FIN-GYM)
24   Pál Kovács (HUN-FEN)
24   Gustaf-Adolf Boltenstern, Jr. (SWE-EQU)
24   Hans Fogh (DEN/CAN-YAC)
24   Magnus Konow (NOR-YAC)
24   Joseph Petersen (DEN-ART)

Most Years Between Gold Medals, Summer, Men
28   Aládár Gerevich (HUN-FEN)
24   Edoardo Mangiarotti (ITA-FEN)
24   Pál Kovács (HUN-FEN)
20   Hubert van Innis (BEL-ARC)
20   Reiner Klimke (FRG/GER-EQU)
20   Manlio DiRosa (ITA-FEN)
20   Lars Jörgen Madsen (DEN-SHO)

Most Appearances, Summer, Men
8   Raimondo d'Inzeo (ITA-EQU, 1948-76)
7   Ivan Osiier (DEN-FEN; 1908-32, 48)
7   Durwood Knowles (GBR/BAH-YAC; 1948-72)
7   Paul Elvström (DEN-YAC; 1948-60, 68-72, 84)
7   Piero d'Inzeo (ITA-EQU, 1952-76)
7   François La Fortune, Jr. (BEL-SHO, 1952-76)
6   Fifteen athletes tied with six.

Most Years Between Appearances, Summer, Men
40   Ivan Osiier (DEN-FEN, 1908-48)
40   Magnus Konow (NOR-YAC, 1908-48)
36   François La Fortune, Sr. (BEL-SHO, 1924-60)
36   Paul Elvström (DEN-YAC, 1948-84)

Most Medals, Summer, Individual
```
14    Larisa Latynina (URS-GYM)
12    Nikolai Andrianov (URS-GYM)
10    Takashi Ono (JPN-GYM)
10/8  Raymond Ewry (USA-TAF)
9     Boris Shakhlin (URS-GYM)
9     Sawao Kato (JPN-GYM)
9     Paavo Nurmi (FIN-TAF)
9     Viktor Chukarin (URS-GYM)
9/4   Martin Sheridan (USA-TAF)
```

Most Gold Medals, Summer, Individual
```
10/8  Raymond Ewry (USA-TAF)
7     Vera Cáslavská (TCH-GYM)
6     Larisa Latynina (URS-GYM)
6     Nikolai Andrianov (URS-GYM)
6     Boris Shakhlin (URS-GYM)
6     Paavo Nurmi (FIN-TAF)
```

Most Medals, Summer, Individual, Women
```
12    Larisa Latynina (URS-GYM)
8     Vera Cáslavská (TCH-GYM)
7     Nadia Comãneci (ROM-GYM)
6     Polina Astakhova (URS-GYM)
6     Agnes Keleti (HUN-GYM)
6     Sofiya Muratova (URS-GYM)
6     Irena Szewińska-Kirszenstein (POL-TAF)
```

Most Gold Medals, Summer, Individual, Women
```
7     Vera Cáslavská (TCH-GYM)
6     Larisa Latynina (URS-GYM)
5     Nadia Comãneci (ROM-GYM)
4     Agnes Keleti (HUN-GYM)
4     Patricia McCormick (USA-DIV)
```

Most Medals, Summer, Individual, Men
```
12    Nikolai Andrianov (URS-GYM)
10    Takashi Ono (JPN-GYM)
10/8  Raymond Ewry (USA-TAF)
9     Five athletes tied with nine
```

Most Gold Medals, Summer, Individual, Men
```
10/8  Raymond Ewry (USA-TAF)
6     Nikolai Andrianov (URS-GYM)
6     Boris Shakhlin (URS-GYM)
6     Paavo Nurmi (FIN-TAF)
5     Gert Fredriksson (SWE-CAN)
5     Viktor Chukarin (URS-GYM)
5     Sawao Kato (JPN-GYM)
5/3   Martin Sheridan (USA-TAF)
```

Most Medals, Summer, Games
    8   Aleksandr Dityatin (URS-GYM-1980)
    7   Nikolai Andrianov (URS-GYM-1976)
    7   Mariya Gorokhovskaya (URS-GYM-1952)
    7   Willis Lee (USA-SHO-1920)
    7   Boris Shakhlin (URS-GYM-1960)
    7   Mark Spitz (USA-SWI-1972)
    7   Lloyd Spooner (USA-SHO-1920)
    7   Mikhail Voronin (URS-GYM-1968)

Most Gold Medals, Summer, Games
    7   Mark Spitz (USA-SWI-1972)
    5   Anton Heida (USA-GYM-1904)
    5   Willis Lee (USA-SHO-1920)
    5   Nedo Nadi (ITA-FEN-1920)
    5   Paavo Nurmi (FIN-TAF-1924)
    5   Eric Heiden (USA-SSK-1980)

Most Silver Medals, Summer, Games
    5   Mariya Gorokhovskaya (URS-GYM-1952)
    4   Eugen Mack (SUI-GYM-1936)
    4   Viktor Lisitsky (URS-GYM-1964)
    4   Mikhail Voronin (URS-GYM-1968)
    4   Shirley Babashoff (USA-SWI-1976)
    4   Aleksandr Dityatin (URS-GYM-1980)

Most Bronze Medals, Summer, Games
    4   William Merz (USA-GYM-1904)
    4   Fritz Kucher (SUI-SHO-1920)
    3   Sixteen athletes tied with three

Most Medals, Summer, Games, Women
    7   Mariya Gorokhovskaya (URS-GYM-1952)
    6   Agnes Keleti (HUN-GYM-1956)
    6   Larisa Latynina (URS-GYM-1956)
    6   Larisa Latynina (URS-GYM-1960)
    6   Larisa Latynina (URS-GYM-1964)
    6   Vera Cáslavská (TCH-GYM-1968)

Most Gold Medals, Summer, Games, Women
    4   Francina Blankers-Koen (HOL-TAF-1948)
    4   Agnes Keleti (HUN-GYM-1956)
    4   Larisa Latynina (URS-GYM-1956)
    4   Vera Cáslavská (TCH-GYM-1968)
    4   Kornelia Ender (GDR-SWI-1976)
    4   Ecaterina Szabo (ROM-GYM-1984)

Most Medals, Summer, Games, Men
    8   Aleksandr Dityatin (URS-GYM-1980)
    7   Lloyd Spooner (USA-SHO-1920)
    7   Willis Lee (USA-SHO-1920)
    7   Boris Shakhlin (URS-GYM-1960)
    7   Mikhail Voronin (URS-GYM-1968)
    7   Mark Spitz (USA-SWI-1972)
    7   Nikolai Andrianov (URS-GYM-1976)

Most Gold Medals, Summer, Games, Men
    7   Mark Spitz (USA-SWI-1972)
    5   Anton Heida (USA-GYM-1904)
    5   Nedo Nadi (ITA-FEN-1920)
    5   Willis Lee (USA-SHO-1920)
    5   Paavo Nurmi (FIN-TAF-1924)

Most Medals, Summer, Games, Individual
    7   Aleksandr Dityatin (URS-GYM-1980)
    6   Burton Downing (USA-CYC-1904)
    6   George Eyser (USA-GYM-1904)
    6   Boris Shakhlin (URS-GYM-1960)
    6   Mikhail Voronin (URS-GYM-1968)
    6   Nikolai Andrianov (URS-GYM-1976)

Most Gold Medals, Summer, Games, Individual
    4   Alvin Kraenzlein (USA-TAF-1900)
    4   Anton Heida (USA-GYM-1904)
    4   Marcus Hurley (USA-CYC-1904)
    4   Boris Shakhlin (URS-GYM-1960)
    4   Vera Cáslavská (TCH-GYM-1968)
    4   Mark Spitz (USA-SWI-1972)
    4   Nikolai Andrianov (URS-GYM-1976)

Most Medals, Summer, Games, Individual, Women
    5   Mariya Gorokhovskaya (URS-GYM-1952)
    5   Vera Cáslavská (TCH-GYM-1968)
    5   Larisa Latynina (URS-GYM-1960)
    5   Larisa Latynina (URS-GYM-1964)
    5   Shane Gould (AUS-SWI-1972)

Most Gold Medals, Summer, Games, Individual, Women
    4   Vera Cáslavská (TCH-GYM-1968)
    3   Francina Blankers-Koen (HOL-TAF-1948)
    3   Agnes Keleti (HUN-GYM-1956)
    3   Larisa Latynina (URS-GYM-1956)
    3   Vera Cáslavská (TCH-GYM-1964)
    3   Debbie Meyer (USA-SWI-1972)
    3   Shane Gould (AUS-SWI-1972)
    3   Nadia Comăneci (ROM-GYM-1976)
    3   Kornelia Ender (GDR-SWI-1976)
    3   Ecaterina Szabo (ROM-GYM-1984)

Most Medals, Summer, Games, Individual, Men
    7   Aleksandr Dityatin (URS-GYM-1980)
    6   Nikolai Andrianov (URS-GYM-1976)
    6   Boris Shakhlin (URS-GYM-1960)
    6   Mikhail Voronin (URS-GYM-1968)
    6   Burton Downing (USA-CYC-1904)
    6   George Eyser (USA-GYM-1904)

Most Gold Medals, Summer, Games, Individual, Men
   4   Alvin Kraenzlein (USA-TAF-1900)
   4   Anton Heida (USA-GYM-1904)
   4   Marcus Hurley (USA-CYC-1904)
   4   Boris Shakhlin (URS-GYM-1960)
   4   Mark Spitz (USA-SWI-1972)
   4   Nikolai Andrianov (URS-GYM-1976)

Most Consecutive Victories, Same Event, Summer, Individual
   4   Alfred Oerter (USA-TAF-Discus Throw, 1956-68)
   4   Paul Elvström (DEN-YAC-Monotype, 1948-60)
   4/3   Raymond Ewry (USA-TAF-Standing High Jump, 1900-06)
   4/3   Raymond Ewry (USA-TAF-Standing Long Jump, 1900-06)
   3   Eleven athletes tied with three.

Most Consecutive Victories, Same Event, Summer, Individual, Women
   3   Larisa Latynina (URS-GYM-Floor Exercises, 1956-64)
   3   Dawn Fraser (AUS-SWI-100 freestyle, 1956-64)
   2   Eighteen athletes tied with two

Most Consecutive Victories, Same Event, Summer, Individual, Men
   4   Alfred Oerter (USA-TAF-Discus Throw, 1956-68)
   4   Paul Elvström (DEN-YAC-Monotype, 1948-60)
   4/3   Raymond Ewry (USA-TAF-Standing High Jump, 1900-06)
   4/3   Raymond Ewry (USA-TAF-Standing Long Jump, 1900-06)
   3   Eleven athletes tied with three.

Most Consecutive Victories, Team, Same Event, Same Team, Summer
   2   USA (Rowing Double Sculls, 1920-24)
          (John Kelly, Paul Costello)
   2   Norway (Dragon Yachting, 1948-52)
          (Thor Thorvaldsen, Sigvie Lie, Haakon Barfod)
   2   *Sweden (Equestrian Dressage, 1952-56)
          (Henri St. Cyr, Gustaf Boltenstern, Jr, Gehnall Persson)
   2   FRG (500 metre Kayak Pairs Canoeing, 1964-68)
          (Roswitha Esser, Annemarie Zimmermann)
   2   GDR (Rowing Coxswainless Fours, 1968-72)
          (Frk. Forberger, Die. Grahn, Frk. Rühle, Die. Schubert)
   2   GDR (Rowing Coxswainless Pairs, 1976-80)
          (Jörg Landvoigt, Bernd Landvoigt)
   2   GDR (Rowing Coxed Pairs, 1976-80)
          (Harald Jährling, Friedrich-Wilhelm Ulrich, Georg Spohr)
   2   Denmark (Soling Yachting, 1976-80)
          (Poul Jensen, Valdemar Bandolowski, Erik Hansen)

*The Swedish dressage team of St. Cyr, Boltenstern, Persson can
claim, in effect, to be the only team to win an Olympic event
three times consecutively. In 1948 they "won" the dressage team
event but were disqualified when it was discovered that Persson
was a non-commisioned officer in the service, which was, at that
time, against Olympic rules in the equestrian events.

Youngest Known Competitor, Summer
   <10   Unknown French boy in 1900 ᴩOW

Youngest Medalist, Summer
   <10   Unknown French boy in 1900 ROW
   10-216   Dimitrios Loundras (GRE-GYM, 1896)
   12-024   Inge Sörensen (DEN-SWI, 1936)
   12-233   Noël Vandernotte (FRA-ROW, 1936)
   13-024   Dorothy Poynton (USA-DIV, 1928)
   13-266   Marjorie Gestring (USA-DIV, 1936)
   13-308   Kornelia Ender (GDR-SWI, 1972)
   13-341   Robin Corsiglia (CAN-SWI, 1976)
   14-011   Nils Skoglund (SWE-DIV, 1920)
   14-012   Giorgia Cesana (ITA-ROW, 1906)

Youngest Gold Medalist, Summer
   <10   Unknown French boy in 1900 ROW
   13-266   Marjorie Gestring (USA-DIV, 1936)
   14-012   Giorgio Cesana (ITA-ROW, 1906)
   14-095   Bernard Malivoire (FRA-ROW, 1952)
   14-097   Debra "Pokey" Watson (USA-SWI, 1964)
   14-120   Aileen Riggin (USA-DIV, 1920)
   14-163   Franciscus Fidelis Joseph Hin (HOL-YAC, 1920)
   14-173   Günther Tiersch (GDR-ROW, 1968)
   14-184   Sandra Morgan (AUS-SWI, 1956)
   14-222 Hans Bourquin (SUI-ROW, 1928)

Youngest Medalist, Individual, Summer
   12-024   Inge Sörensen (DEN-SWI, 1936)
   13-024   Dorothy Poynton (USA-DIV, 1928)
   13-266   Marjorie Gestring (USA-DIV, 1936)

Youngest Gold Medalist, Individual, Summer
   13-266   Marjorie Gestring (USA-DIV, 1936)
   14-120   Aileen Riggin (USA-DIV, 1920)
   14-250   Nadia Comăneci (ROM-GYM, 1976)

Youngest Known Competitor, Women, Summer
   11-078   Cecilia Colledge (GBR-FSK, 1932)

Youngest Medalist, Women, Summer
   12-024   Inge Sörensen (DEN-SWI, 1936)
   13-024   Dorothy Poynton (USA-DIV, 1928)
   13-266   Marjorie Gestring (USA-DIV, 1936)
   13-308   Kornelia Ender (GDR-SWI, 1972)
   13-341   Robin Corsiglia (CAN-SWI, 1976)
   14-052   Zirvard Emirzyan (URS-DIV, 1980)
   14-058   Katherine Rawls (USA-DIV, 1932)
   14-097   Deborah "Pokey" Watson (USA-SWI, 1964)
   14-115   Ingeborg Schmitz (GER-SWI, 1936)
   14-120   Aileen Riggin (USA-DIV, 1920)

Youngest Gold Medalist, Women, Summer
```
13-266   Marjorie Gestring (USA-DIV, 1936)
14-096   Debra "Pokey" Watson (USA-SWI, 1964)
14-120   Aileen Riggin (USA-DIV, 1920)
14-184   Sandra Morgan (AUS-SWI, 1956)
14-250   Nadia Comăneci (ROM-GYM, 1976)
14-260   Carolyn Wood (USA-SWI, 1960)
14-317   Simona Pauca (ROM-GYM, 1984)
15-000   Mariya Filatova (URS-GYM, 1976)
15-002   Susan Pederson (USA-SWI, 1968)
15-072   Andrea Pollack (GDR-SWI, 1976)
```

Youngest Medalist, Individual, Women, Summer
```
12-024   Inge Sörensen (DEN-SWI, 1936)
13-024   Dorothy Poynton (USA-DIV, 1928)
13-266   Marjorie Gestring (USA-DIV, 1936)
```

Youngest Gold Medalist, Individual, Women, Summer
```
13-266   Marjorie Gestring (USA-DIV, 1936)
14-120   Aileen Riggin (USA-DIV, 1920)
14-250   Nadia Comăneci (ROM-GYM, 1976)
```

Youngest Known Competitor, Men, Summer
```
<10      Unknown French boy in 1900 ROW
```

Youngest Medalist, Men, Summer
```
<10      Unknown French boy in 1900 ROW
10-216   Dimitrios Loundras (GRE-GYM, 1896)
12-233   Noël Vandernotte (FRA-ROW, 1936)
14-011   Nils Skoglund (SWE-DIV, 1920)
14-012   Giorgio Cesana (ITA-ROW, 1906)
14-055   Marcel Frébourg (FRA-ROW, 1906)
14-095   Bernard Malivoire (FRA-ROW, 1952)
14-163   Franciscus Hin (HOL-YAC, 1920)
14-173   Günther Tiersch (FRG-ROW, 1968)
14-222   Hans Bourquin (SUI-ROW, 1928)
```

Youngest Gold Medalist, Men, Summer
```
<10      Unknown French boy in 1900 ROW
14-012   Giorgio Cesana (ITA-ROW, 1906)
14-095   Bernard Malivoire (FRA-ROW, 1952)
14-163   Franciscus Hin (HOL-YAC, 1920)
14-173   Günther Tiersch (FRG-ROW, 1968)
14-222   Hans Bourquin (SUI-ROW, 1928)
14-283   Klaus Zerta (GER-ROW, 1960)
14-309   Kusuo Kitamura (JPN-SWI, 1932)
15-226   Per Bertilsson (SWE-GYM, 1908)
15-298   Yasuji Miyazaki (JPN-SWI, 1932)
```

Youngest Medalist, Individual, Men, Summer
```
14-011   Nils Skoglund (SWE-DIV, 1920)
14-309   Kusuo Kitamura (JPN-SWI, 1932)
14-363   Scott Ethan Allen (USA-FSK, 1964)
```

Oldest Known Competitor, Summer
  72-280 Oscar Swahn (SWE-SHO, 1920)
  70-005 Lorna Johnstone (GBR-EQU, 1972)
  68-229 Roberto Soundy (ESA-SHO, 1968)

Oldest Medalist, Summer
  72-280 Oscar Swahn (SWE-SHO, 1920)
  68-194 Samuel Duvall (USA-ARC, 1904)
  66-155 Louis Noverraz (SUI-YAC, 1968)
  64-258 Oscar Swahn (SWE-SHO, 1912)
  64-002 Galen Spencer (USA-ARC, 1904)
  63-241 Robert Williams (USA-ARC, 1904)
  61-245 John Butt (GBR-SHO, 1912)
  61-131 William Roycroft (AUS-EQU, 1976)
  60-265 Oscar Swahn (SWE-SHO, 1908)
  60-104 William Milne (GBR-SHO, 1912)

Oldest Gold Medalist, Summer
  64-258 Oscar Swahn (SWE-SHO, 1912)
  64-002 Galen Spencer (USA-ARC, 1904)
  63-241 Robert Williams (USA-ARC, 1904)
  60-265 Oscar Swahn (SWE-SHO, 1908)
  59-113 Everard Endt (USA-YAC, 1952)
  59-024 William Northman (AUS-YAC, 1964)
  58-078 Allan Whitty (GBR-SHO, 1924)
  57-045 Johan Anker (NOR-YAC, 1928)
  56-212 Paul Smart (USA-YAC, 1948)
  56-195 William Thompson (USA-ARC, 1904)

Oldest Medalist, Individual, Summer
  64-258 Oscar Swahn (SWE-SHO, 1912)
  60-265 Oscar Swahn (SWE-SHO, 1908)
  60-104 William Milne (GBR-SHO, 1912)
  60-094 Josef Neckermann (FRG-EQU, 1972)

Oldest Gold Medalist, Individual, Summer
  60-265 Oscar Swahn (SWE-SHO, 1908)
  56-097 Walter Winans (USA-SHO, 1908)
  54-094 Henri St. Cyr (SWE-EQU, 1956)

Oldest Known Competitor, Women, Summer
  70-005 Lorna Johnstone (GBR-EQU, 1972)
  66-051 Lorna Johnstone (GBR-EQU, 1968)

Oldest Medalist, Women, Summer
    52-143   Patricia Dench (AUS-SHO, 1984)
    46-274   Ulla Håkanson (SWE-EQU, 1984)
    46-258   Maud von Rosen (SWE-EQU, 1972)
    45-072   Ilona Elek (HUN-FEN, 1952)
    45-025   Lida Howell (USA-ARC, 1904)
    45-012   Liselott Linsenhoff (FRG-EQU, 1972)
    44-226   Irena Szydłowska (POL-ARC, 1972)
    43-339   Edith Master (USA-EQU, 1976)
    43-015   Winifred McNair (GBR-TEN, 1920)
    42-246   Doreen Wilber (USA-ARC, 1972)

Oldest Gold Medalist, Women, Summer
    45-025   Lida Howell (USA-ARC, 1904)
    45-012   Liselott Linsenhoff (FRG-EQU, 1972)
    43-015   Winifred McNair (GBR-TEN, 1920)
    42-246   Doreen Wilber (USA-ARC, 1972)
    41-078   Ilona Elek (HUN-FEN, 1948)
    41-060   Liselott Linsenhoff (FRG-EQU, 1968)
    40-212   Linda Thom (CAN-SHO, 1984)
    38-132   Edith Hannam (GBR-TEN, 1912)
    38-016   Virginie Heriot (FRA-YAC, 1928)
    37-259   Sylvi Saimo (FIN-CAN, 1952)

Oldest Medalist, Individual, Women, Summer
    52-143   Patricia Dench (AUS-SHO, 1984)
    45-072   Ilona Elek (HUN-FEN, 1952)
    45-025   Lida Howell (USA-ARC, 1904)

Oldest Gold Medalist, Individual, Women, Summer
    45-025   Lida Howell (USA-ARC, 1904)
    45-012   Liselott Linsenhoff (FRG-EQU, 1972)
    42-246   Doreen Wilber (USA-ARC, 1972)

Oldest Known Competitor, Men, Summer
    72-280   Oscar Swahn (SWE-SHO, 1920)
    68-229   Roberto Soundy (ESA-SHO, 1968)
    68-194   Samuel Duvall (USA-ARC, 1904)

Oldest Medalist, Men, Summer
    72-280   Oscar Swahn (SWE-SHO, 1920)
    68-194   Samuel Duvall (USA-ARC, 1904)
    66-155   Louis Noverraz (SUI-YAC, 1968)
    64-258   Oscar Swahn (SWE-SHO, 1912)
    64-002   Galen Spencer (USA-ARC, 1904)
    63-241   Robert Williams (USA-ARC, 1904)
    61-245   John Butt (GBR-SHO, 1912)
    61-131   William Roycroft (AUS-EQU, 1976)
    60-265   Oscar Swahn (SWE-SHO, 1908)
    60-104   William Milne (GBR-SHO, 1912)

Oldest Gold Medalist, Men, Summer
  64-258 Oscar Swahn (SWE-SHO, 1912)
  64-002 Galen Spencer (USA-ARC, 1904)
  63-241 Robert Williams (USA-ARC, 1904)
  60-265 Oscar Swahn (SWE-SHO, 1908)
  59-113 Everard Endt (USA-YAC, 1952)
  59-024 William Northman (AUS-YAC, 1964)
  58-078 Allan Whitty (GBR-SHO, 1924)
  57-045 Johan Anker (NOR-YAC, 1928)
  56-212 Paul Smart (USA-YAC, 1948)
  56-195 William Thompson (USA-ARC, 1904)

Oldest Medalist, Individual, Men, Summer
  64-258 Oscar Swahn (SWE-SHO, 1912)
  60-265 Oscar Swahn (SWE-SHO, 1908)
  60-104 William Milne (GBR-SHO, 1912)
  60-094 Josef Neckermann (FRG-EQU, 1972)

Oldest Gold Medalist, Individual, Men, Summer
  60-265 Oscar Gomer Swahn (SWE-SHO, 1908)
  56-097 Walter Winans (USA-SHO, 1908)
  54-094 Henri St. Cyr (SWE-EQU, 1956)

Medals Won by Countries, Summer
        In the following tables, places are given according to total medals. Ties are broken first by number of gold medals, then number of silver medals, and finally number of bronze medals.

		Gold	Silver	Bronze	Totals
1.	United States	717.500	536.500	461.500	1715.500
2.	USSR	340.000	292.000	252.000	884.000
3.	Great Britain	165.500	211.500	198.000	575.000
4.	France	148.000	160.000	169.000	477.000
5.	Sweden	129.500	138.000	161.000	428.500
6.	Italy	140.000	115.000	120.000	375.000
7.	Hungary	113.000	106.000	131.000	350.000
8.	GDR	122.000	115.000	106.000	343.000
9.	Finland	96.000	74.000	107.000	277.000
10.	FRG	66.000	91.000	104.000	261.000
11.	Germany	71.500	82.000	81.000	234.500
12.	Japan	83.000	72.000	75.000	230.000
13.	Australia	67.750	61.000	82.000	210.750
14.	Romania	48.000	53.000	76.000	177.000
15.	Poland	38.000	51.000	86.000	175.000
16.	Canada	36.000	60.000	69.000	165.000
17.	Switzerland	41.000	63.000	58.000	162.000
18.	Netherlands	41.000	45.000	59.000	145.000
19.	Denmark	30.500	57.000	52.000	139.500
20.	Czechoslovakia	42.000	46.000	46.500	134.500
21.	Belgium	35.000	48.000	41.000	124.000
22.	Bulgaria	27.000	50.000	39.000	116.000
23.	Norway	39.000	31.000	34.000	104.000
24.	Greece	22.000	40.000	39.000	101.000

25. Austria	17.000	27.000	33.000	77.000
26. Yugoslavia	23.000	25.000	23.000	71.000
27. Cuba	21.500	19.000	12.000	52.500
28. South Africa	16.000	15.000	20.000	51.000
29. Turkey	23.000	12.000	9.000	44.000
30. Argentina	13.000	18.000	13.000	44.000
31. New Zealand	22.250	4.000	15.000	41.250
32. Mexico	9.000	12.000	16.000	37.000
33. Korea	7.000	11.000	18.000	36.000
34. China	15.000	9.000	7.000	31.000
35. Brazil	6.000	7.000	17.000	30.000
36. Iran	4.000	10.000	15.000	29.000
37. Kenya	6.000	7.000	9.000	22.000
38. Estonia	6.000	6.000	9.000	21.000
39. Spain	3.000	11.000	7.000	21.000
40. Jamaica	4.000	8.000	8.000	20.000
41. Egypt	6.000	6.000	7.000	19.000
42. India	8.000	3.000	3.000	14.000
43. Ireland	4.000	5.000	5.000	14.000
44. Korea DPR	2.000	5.000	5.000	12.000
45. Portugal	1.000	4.000	7.000	12.000
46. Ethiopia	5.000	1.000	4.000	10.000
47. Mongolia	--	5.000	5.000	10.000
48. Uruguay	2.000	1.000	6.000	9.000
49. Pakistan	3.000	3.000	2.000	8.000
50. Venezuela	1.000	2.000	5.000	8.000
51. Trinidad	1.000	2.000	4.000	7.000
52. Chile	--	5.000	2.000	7.000
53. Philippines	--	1.000	5.000	6.000
54. Uganda	1.000	3.000	1.000	5.000
55. Tunisia	1.000	2.000	2.000	5.000
T56. Lebanon	--	2.000	2.000	4.000
Colombia	--	2.000	2.000	4.000
T58. Puerto Rico	--	1.000	3.000	4.000
Nigeria	--	1.000	3.000	4.000
60. Morocco	2.000	1.000	--	3.000
61. Latvia	--	2.000	1.000	3.000
T62. Chinese Taipei	--	1.000	2.000	3.000
Ghana	--	1.000	2.000	3.000
T64. Luxembourg	1.000	1.000	--	2.000
Peru	1.000	1.000	--	2.000
66. Bahamas	1.000	--	1.000	2.000
67. Tanzania	--	2.000	--	2.000
T68. Cameroun	--	1.000	1.000	2.000
Iceland	--	1.000	1.000	2.000
Haiti	--	1.000	1.000	2.000
Thailand	--	1.000	1.000	2.000
T72. Panama	--	--	2.000	2.000
Algeria	--	--	2.000	2.000

		Gold	Silver	Bronze	Totals
74.	Zimbabwe	1.000	--	--	1.000
T75.	Singapore	--	1.000	--	1.000
	Ivory Coast	--	1.000	--	1.000
	Syria	--	1.000	--	1.000
	Sri Lanka	--	1.000	--	1.000
T79.	Dom. Republic	--	--	1.000	1.000
	Guyana	--	--	1.000	1.000
	Zambia	--	--	1.000	1.000
	Niger	--	--	1.000	1.000
	Bermuda	--	--	1.000	1.000
	Iraq	--	--	1.000	1.000
	Totals	2896.000	2870.000	2971.000	8737.000

Medals Won by Countries, Summer, Men

		Gold	Silver	Bronze	Totals
1.	United States	594.750	442.750	386.000	1423.500
2.	USSR	257.333	223.667	178.000	659.000
3.	Great Britain	147.500	169.750	163.667	480.917
4.	France	139.833	153.500	162.500	455.833
5.	Sweden	124.250	130.000	148.500	402.750
6.	Italy	135.000	106.500	113.000	354.500
7.	Hungary	95.000	88.000	107.000	290.000
8.	Finland	95.000	72.000	106.000	273.000
9.	Japan	79.000	68.000	70.000	217.000
10.	Germany	65.000	74.000	70.000	209.000
11.	FRG	51.333	66.333	83.417	201.083
12.	GDR	59.000	56.000	65.000	180.000
13.	Switzerland	40.000	61.333	56.667	158.000
14.	Australia	43.750	42.000	61.000	146.750
15.	Poland	32.000	41.000	73.000	146.000
16.	Canada	30.000	45.000	50.000	125.000
17.	Belgium	35.000	48.000	39.000	122.000
18.	Denmark	25.500	49.000	43.000	117.500
19.	Romania	23.000	35.000	50.667	108.667
20.	Czechoslovakia	29.000	36.000	41.500	106.500
21.	Norway	38.191	29.667	33.000	100.858
22.	Netherlands	25.000	28.000	45.500	98.500
23.	Bulgaria	24.000	41.000	32.000	97.000
24.	Greece	21.000	38.500	37.500	97.000
25.	Yugoslavia	21.000	23.000	22.000	66.000
26.	Austria	14.000	25.000	26.000	65.000
27.	Cuba	20.500	18.000	10.000	48.500
28.	Turkey	23.000	12.000	9.000	44.000
29.	South Africa	14.000	14.000	16.000	44.000
30.	Argentina	13.000	16.000	13.000	42.000
31.	New Zealand	21.250	4.000	13.000	38.250
32.	Mexico	9.000	11.000	15.000	35.000
33.	Korea	6.000	10.000	16.000	32.000
34.	Brazil	6.000	7.000	17.000	30.000
35.	Iran	4.000	10.000	15.000	29.000
36.	China	10.000	7.000	5.000	22.000
37.	Kenya	6.000	7.000	9.000	22.000
38.	Estonia	6.000	6.000	9.000	21.000

39. Spain	3.000	11.000	7.000	21.000
40. Egypt	6.000	6.000	7.000	19.000
41. Jamaica	4.000	8.000	5.000	17.000
42. India	8.000	3.000	3.000	14.000
43. Ireland	4.000	5.000	5.000	14.000
44. Korea DPR	2.000	5.000	4.000	11.000
45. Portugal	1.000	4.000	6.000	11.000
46. Ethiopia	5.000	1.000	4.000	10.000
47. Mongolia	--	5.000	5.000	10.000
48. Uruguay	2.000	1.000	6.000	9.000
49. Pakistan	3.000	3.000	2.000	8.000
50. Venezuela	1.000	2.000	5.000	8.000
51. Trinidad	1.000	2.000	4.000	7.000
52. Chile	--	4.000	2.000	6.000
53. Philippines	--	1.000	5.000	6.000
54. Uganda	1.000	3.000	1.000	5.000
55. Tunisia	1.000	2.000	2.000	5.000
T56. Lebanon	--	2.000	2.000	4.000
Colombia	--	2.000	2.000	4.000
T58. Puerto Rico	--	1.000	3.000	4.000
Nigeria	--	1.000	3.000	4.000
60. Latvia	--	2.000	1.000	3.000
61. Ghana	--	1.000	2.000	3.000
T62. Morocco	1.000	1.000	--	2.000
Luxembourg	1.000	1.000	--	2.000
Peru	1.000	1.000	--	2.000
65. Bahamas	1.000	--	1.000	2.000
66. Tanzania	--	2.000	--	2.000
T67. Chinese Taipei	--	1.000	1.000	2.000
Thailand	--	1.000	1.000	2.000
Cameroun	--	1.000	1.000	2.000
Iceland	--	1.000	1.000	2.000
Haiti	--	1.000	1.000	2.000
T72. Panama	--	--	2.000	2.000
Algeria	--	--	2.000	2.000
T74. Singapore	--	1.000	--	1.000
Ivory Coast	--	1.000	--	1.000
Syria	--	1.000	--	1.000
Sri Lanka	--	1.000	--	1.000
T78. Dom. Republic	--	--	1.000	1.000
Guyana	--	--	1.000	1.000
Zambia	--	--	1.000	1.000
Niger	--	--	1.000	1.000
Bermuda	--	--	1.000	1.000
Iraq	--	--	1.000	1.000
Totals	2429.190	2404.000	2512.918	7346.108

Medals Won by Countries, Summer, Women

		Gold	Silver	Bronze	Totals
1.	United States	122.750	93.750	75.500	292.000
2.	USSR	82.667	68.333	74.000	225.000
3.	GDR	63.000	59.000	41.000	163.000
4.	Great Britain	18.000	41.750	34.333	94.083
5.	Romania	25.000	18.000	25.333	68.333
6.	Australia	24.000	19.000	21.000	64.000
7.	Hungary	18.000	18.000	24.000	60.000
8.	FRG	14.667	24.667	20.583	59.917
9.	Netherlands	16.000	17.000	13.500	46.500
10.	Canada	6.000	15.000	19.000	40.000
11.	Poland	6.000	10.000	13.000	29.000
12.	Czechoslovakia	13.000	10.000	5.000	28.000
13.	Sweden	5.250	8.000	12.500	25.750
14.	Germany	6.500	8.000	11.000	25.500
15.	Denmark	5.000	8.000	9.000	22.000
16.	France	8.167	6.500	6.500	21.167
17.	Italy	5.000	8.500	7.000	20.500
18.	Bulgaria	3.000	9.000	7.000	19.000
19.	Japan	4.000	4.000	5.000	13.000
20.	Austria	3.000	2.000	7.000	12.000
21.	China	5.000	2.000	2.000	9.000
22.	South Africa	2.000	1.000	4.000	7.000
23.	Yugoslavia	2.000	2.000	1.000	5.000
24.	Finland	1.000	2.000	1.000	4.000
25.	Switzerland	1.000	1.667	1.333	4.000
26.	Greece	1.000	1.500	1.500	4.000
T27.	Cuba	1.000	1.000	2.000	4.000
	Korea	1.000	1.000	2.000	4.000
29.	Norway	0.809	1.333	1.000	3.142
30.	New Zealand	1.000	--	2.000	3.000
31.	Jamaica	--	--	3.000	3.000
32.	Argentina	--	2.000	--	2.000
33.	Mexico	--	1.000	1.000	2.000
34.	Belgium	--	--	2.000	2.000
T35.	Morocco	1.000	--	--	1.000
	Zimbabwe	1.000	--	--	1.000
37.	Chile	--	1.000	--	1.000
T38.	Korea DPR	--	--	1.000	1.000
	Portugal	--	--	1.000	1.000
	Chinese Taipei	--	--	1.000	1.000
	Totals	466.810	466.000	458.082	1390.892

Discrepancies in the number of total medals are due to various events in which a single medal of each type was not awarded. The specific events in which this occurred and the format of medals awarded is discussed under each sport.

RECORDS OF THE OLYMPIC WINTER GAMES

(WINTER OLYMPIC RECORDS)

Following are the best records achieved in the Olympic Winter Games since their inception in 1924. In addition, the records include any marks by athletes competing in the figure skating events at the 1908 and 1920 Olympics or in the ice hockey event at the 1920 Olympics. Lists are ten-deep for the major records and five-deep in more restricted categories. Where a great number of athletes are tied with the same mark, they are not always listed but that fact is noted. Age records are ten deep for medalists and gold medalists, and one-to-three deep for more restricted categories. A list of medals won by country in the Olympic Winter Games, with sections for medals won by men and women, follows at the end of this section.

Most Medals, Winter
```
9     Sixten Jernberg (SWE-NSK)
8     Galina Kulakova (URS-NSK)
7     Ivar Ballangrud (NOR-SSK)
7     Veikko Hakulinen (FIN-NSK)
7     Eero Mäntyranta (FIN-NSK)
7     Raisa Smetanina (URS-NSK)
7     Clas Thunberg (FIN-SSK)
```

Most Gold Medals, Winter
```
6     Lidiya Skoblikova (URS-SSK)
5     Eric Heiden (USA-SSK)
5     Clas Thunberg (FIN-SSK)
4     Sixten Jernberg (SWE-NSK)
4     Galina Kulakova (URS-NSK)
4     Ivar Ballangrud (NOR-SSK)
4     Evgeniy Grishin (URS-SSK)
4     Nikolai Zimyatov (URS-NSK)
4     Aleksandr Tikhonov (URS-BIA)
```

Most Silver Medals, Winter
```
4     Raisa Smetanina (URS-NSK)
3     Twelve athletes tied with three
```

Most Bronze Medals, Winter
```
4     Roald Larsen (NOR-SSK)
3     Alevtina Kolchina (URS-NSK)
3     Pavel Kolchin (URS-NSK)
3     Nataliya Petruseva (URS-SSK)
3     Hans van Helden (HOL-SSK)
3     Harri Kirvesniemi (FIN-NSK)
```

47

Most Years Winning Medals, Winter
   4   Galina Kulakova (URS-NSK)
   4   Aleksandr Tikhonov (URS-BIA)
   4   Gillis Grafström (SWE-FSK)
   4   Jiŕi Holik (TCH-ICH)
   4   Vladislav Tretiak (URS-ICH)

Most Years Winning Gold Medals, Winter
   4   Aleksandr Tikhonov (URS-BIA)
   3   Sixten Jernberg (SWE-NSK)
   3   Veikko Hakulinen (FIN-NSK)
   3   Gillis Grafström (SWE-FSK)
   3   Vladislav Tretiak (URS-ICH)
   3   Vitali Davidov (URS-ICH)
   3   Sonja Henie (NOR-FSK)
   3   Viktor Kuskin (URS-ICH)
   3   Aleksandr Ragulin (URS-ICH)
   3   Irina Rodnina (URS-FSK)

Most Years Between Medals, Winter
  20   Richard "Bibi" Torriani (SUI-ICH)
  20   John Heaton (USA-LUG/SKE)
  16   Fritz Feierabend (SUI-BOB)
  16   Birger Ruud (NOR-NSK)
  12   Ten athletes tied with twelve

Most Years Between Gold Medals, Winter
  12   Aleksandr Tikhonov (URS-BIA)
  12   Vladislav Tretiak (URS-ICH)
  12   Paul Hildgartner (ITA-LUG)
   8   Nine athletes tied with eight

Most Appearances, Winter
   6   Carl-Erik Eriksson (SWE-BOB; 1964-1984)
   5   Örjan Sandler (SWE-SSK; 1964-1980)
   5   Colin Coates (AUS-SSK; 1968-1984)
   4   Fifty-two athletes tied with four

Most Years Between Appearances, Winter
  20   Max Houben (BEL-BOB, 1928-48)
  20   John Heaton (USA-LUG/SKE, 1928-48)
  20   Richard "Bibi" Torriani (SUI-ICH, 1928-48)
  20   Stanisław Marusarz (POL-NSK, 1932-52)
  20   Frank Stack (CAN-SSK, 1932-52)
  20   James Bickford (USA-BOB, 1936-56)
  20   Sepp Bradl (AUT-NSK, 1936-56)
  20   Carl-Erik Eriksson (SWE-BOB, 1964-84)

Most Medals, Winter, Women
  8   Galina Kulakova (URS-NSK)
  7   Raisa Smetanina (URS-NSK)
  6   Lidiya Skoblikova (URS-SSK)
  5   Alevtina Kolchina (URS-NSK)
  5   Helena Kivioja-Takalo (FIN-NSK)
  5   Karin Enke (GDR-SSK)

Most Gold Medals, Winter, Women
  6   Lidiya Skoblikova (URS-SSK)
  4   Galina Kulakova (URS-NSK)
  3   Sonja Henie (NOR-FSK)
  3   Irina Rodnina (URS-FSK)
  3   Marja-Liisa Hämäläinen (FIN-NSK)
  3   Klaudiya Boyarskikh (URS-NSK)
  3   Raisa Smetanina (URS-NSK)
  3   Karin Enke (GDR-SSK)

Most Silver Medals, Winter, Women
  4   Raisa Smetanina (URS-NSK)
  3   Helena Takalo (FIN-NSK)
  3   Lyubov Baranova-Kozyreva (URS-NSK)
  3   Radya Eroshina (URS-NSK)
  3   Marjatta Kajosmaa (FIN-NSK)
  3   Leah Poulos-Mueller (USA-SSK)
  3   Andrea Mitscherlich-Schöne (GDR-SSK)

Most Bronze Medals, Winter, Women
  3   Alevtina Kolchina (URS-NSK)
  3   Nataliya Petruseva (URS-SSK)

Most Years Winning Medals, Winter, Women
  4   Galina Kulakova (URS-NSK)
  3   Andrée Brunet-Joly (FRA-FSK)
  3   Sonja Henie (NOR-FSK)
  3   Beatrix Loughran (USA-FSK)
  3   Irina Rodnina (URS-FSK)
  3   Raisa Smetanina (URS-NSK)
  3   Alevtina Kolchina (URS-NSK)
  3   Helena Kivioja-Takalo (FIN-NSK)
  3   Siiri Rantanen (FIN-NSK)
  3   Britt Strandberg (SWE-NSK)

Most Years Winning Gold Medals, Winter, Women
  3   Sonja Henie (NOR-FSK)
  3   Irina Rodnina (URS-FSK)
  2   Marielle Goitschel (FRA-ASK)
  2   Trude Jochum-Beiser (AUT-ASK)
  2   Andrée Brunet-Joly (FRA-FSK)
  2   Lyudmila Belousova (URS-FSK)
  2   Galina Kulakova (URS-NSK)
  2   Raisa Smetanina (URS-NSK)
  2   Lidiya Skoblikova (URS-SSK)
  2   Karin Enke (GDR-SSK)
  2   Lyudmila Titova (URS-SSK)

Most Years Between Medals, Winter, Women
```
12    Alevtina Kolchina (URS-NSK, 1956-68)
12    Galina Kulakova (URS-NSK, 1968-80)
 8    Andrée Brunet-Joly (FRA-FSK, 1924-32)
 8    Beatrix Loughran (USA-FSK, 1924-32)
 8    Sonja Henie (NOR-FSK, 1928-36)
 8    Siiri Rantanen (FIN-NSK, 1952-60)
 8    Britt Strandberg (SWE-NSK, 1960-68)
 8    Irina Rodnina (URS-FSK, 1972-80)
 8    Helena Kivioja-Takalo (FIN-NSK, 1972-80)
 8    Raisa Smetanina (URS-NSK, 1976-84)
```

Most Years Between Gold Medals, Winter, Women
```
 8    Sonja Henie (NOR-FSK, 1928-36)
 8    Irina Rodnina (URS-FSK, 1972-80)
 4    Andrée Brunet-Joly (FRA-FSK, 1928-32)
 4    Trude Jochum-Beiser (AUT-ASK, 1948-52)
 4    Lidiya Skoblikova (URS-SSK, 1960-64)
 4    Marielle Goitschel (FRA-ASK, 1964-68)
 4    Lyudmila Belousova (URS-FSK, 1964-68)
 4    Galina Kulakova (URS-NSK, 1972-76)
 4    Raisa Smetanina (URS-NSK, 1976-80)
 4    Karin Enke (GDR-SSK, 1980-84)
```

Most Appearances, Winter, Women
```
 4    Sonja Henie (NOR-FSK, 1924-36)
 4    Alevtina Kolchina (URS-NSK, 1956-68)
 4    Barbro Martinsson (SWE-NSK, 1956-68)
 4    Helena Kivioja-Takalo (FIN-NSK, 1968-80)
 4    Galina Kulakova (URS-NSK, 1968-80)
 4    Lisbeth Korsmo-Berg (NOR-SSK, 1968-80)
 4    Sharon Firth (CAN-NSK, 1972-84)
 4    Shirley Firth (CAN-NSK, 1972-84)
 4    Monika Holzner-Pflug (FRG-SSK, 1972-84)
```

Most Years Between Appearances, Winter, Women
```
12    Sonja Henie (NOR-FSK, 1924-36)
12    Alevtina Kolchina (URS-NSK, 1956-68)
12    Barbro Martinsson (SWE-NSK, 1956-68)
12    Helena Kivioja-Takalo (FIN-NSK, 1968-80)
12    Galina Kulakova (URS-NSK, 1968-80)
12    Lisbeth Korsmo-Berg (NOR-SSK, 1968-80)
12    Sharon Firth (CAN-NSK, 1972-84)
12    Shirley Firth (CAN-NSK, 1972-84)
12    Monika Holzner-Pflug (FRG-SSK, 1972-84)
```

Most Medals, Winter, Men
```
 9    Sixten Jernberg (SWE-NSK)
 7    Ivar Ballangrud (NOR-SSK)
 7    Veikko Hakulinen (FIN-NSK)
 7    Eero Mäntyranta (FIN-NSK)
 7    Clas Thunberg (FIN-SSK)
```

Most Gold Medals, Winter, Men
5	Eric Heiden (USA-SSK)
5	Clas Thunberg (FIN-SSK)
4	Sixten Jernberg (SWE-NSK)
4	Ivar Ballangrud (NOR-SSK)
4	Evgeniy Grishin (URS-SSK)
4	Nikolai Zimyatov (URS-NSK)
4	Aleksandr Tikhonov (URS-BIA)

Most Silver Medals, Winter, Men
3	Sixten Jernberg (SWE-NSK)
3	Veikko Hakulinen (FIN-NSK)
3	Fritz Feierabend (SUI-BOB)
3	Pål Tyldum (NOR-NSK)
3	Cornelis "Kees" Verkerk (HOL-SSK)
3	Heikki Ikola (FIN-BIA)

Most Bronze Medals, Winter, Men
4	Roald Larsen (NOR-SSK)
3	Pavel Kolchin (URS-NSK)
3	Hans van Helden (HOL-SSK)
3	Harri Kirvesniemi (FIN-NSK)

Most Years Winning Medals, Winter, Men
4	Aleksandr Tikhonov (URS-BIA)
4	Gillis Grafström (SWE-FSK)
4	Jiří Holik (TCH-ICH)
4	Vladislav Tretiak (URS-ICH)

Most Years Winning Gold Medals, Winter, Men
4	Aleksandr Tikhonov (URS-BIA)
3	Sixten Jernberg (SWE-NSK)
3	Veikko Hakulinen (FIN-NSK)
3	Gillis Grafström (SWE-FSK)
3	Vladislav Tretiak (URS-ICH)
3	Vitali Davidov (URS-ICH)
3	Viktor Kuskin (URS-ICH)
3	Aleksandr Ragulin (URS-ICH)

Most Years Between Medals, Winter, Men
20	Richard "Bibi" Torriani (SUI-ICH, 1928-48)
20	John Heaton (USA-LUG/SKE, 1928-48)
16	Fritz Feierabend (SUI-BOB, 1936-52)
16	Birger Ruud (NOR-NSK, 1932-48)
12	Eight athletes tied with twelve

Most Years Between Gold Medals, Winter, Men
12	Aleksandr Tikhonov (URS-BIA, 1972-84)
12	Vladislav Tretiak (URS-ICH, 1972-84)
12	Paul Hildgartner (ITA-LUG, 1972-84)
8	Nine athletes tied with eight

Most Appearances, Winter, Men
6   Carl-Erik Eriksson (SWE-BOB; 1964-1984)
5   Örjan Sandler (SWE-SSK; 1964-1980)
5   Colin Coates (AUS-SSK; 1968-1984)
4   Forty-three athletes tied with four

Most Years Between Appearances, Winter, Men
20   Max Houben (BEL-BOB, 1928-48)
20   John Heaton (USA-LUG/SKE, 1928-48)
20   Richard "Bibi" Torriani (SUI-ICH, 1928-48)
20   Stanisław Marusarz (POL-NSK, 1932-52)
20   Frank Stack (CAN-SSK, 1932-52)
20   James Bickford (USA-BOB, 1936-56)
20   Sepp Bradl (AUT-NSK, 1936-56)
20   Carl-Erik Eriksson (SWE-BOB, 1964-84)

Most Medals, Winter, Individual
7   Sixten Jernberg (SWE-NSK)
7   Ivar Ballangrud (NOR-SSK)
7   Clas Thunberg (FIN-SSK)
6   Johan Gröttumsbråten (NOR-NSK)
6   Roald Larsen (NOR-SSK)
6   Lidiya Skoblikova (URS-SSK)

Most Gold Medals, Winter, Individual
6   Lidiya Skoblikova (URS-SSK)
5   Eric Heiden (USA-SSK)
5   Clas Thunberg (FIN-SSK)
4   Ivar Ballangrud (NOR-SSK)
4   Evgeniy Grishin (URS-SSK)

Most Medals, Winter, Individual, Women
6   Lidiya Skoblikova (URS-SSK)
5   Karin Enke (GDR-SSK)
5   Raisa Smetanina (URS-NSK)
4   Galina Kulakova (URS-NSK)
4   Tatyana Averina (URS-SSK)
4   Atje Keulen-Deelstra (HOL-SSK)
4   Dianne Holum (USA-SSK)
4   Kaija Mustonen (FIN-SSK)
4   Nataliya Petruseva (URS-SSK)

Most Gold Medals, Winter, Individual, Women
6   Lidiya Skoblikova (URS-SSK)
3   Karin Enke (GDR-SSK)
3   Marja Liisa Hämäläinen (FIN-NSK)
3   Sonja Henie (NOR-FSK)

Most Medals, Winter, Individual, Men
7   Ivar Ballangrud (NOR-SSK)
7   Sixten Jernberg (SWE-NSK)
7   Clas Thunberg (FIN-SSK)
6   Johan Gröttumsbråten (NOR-NSK)
6   Roald Larsen (NOR-SSK)

Most Gold Medals, Winter, Individual, Men
5   Clas Thunberg (FIN-SSK)
5   Eric Heiden (USA-SSK)
4   Evgeniy Grishin (URS-SSK)
4   Ivar Ballangrud (NOR-SSK)
3   Eight athletes tied with three

Most Medals, Winter, Games
5   Roald Larsen (NOR-SSK, 1924)
5   Clas Thunberg (FIN-SSK, 1924)
5   Eric Heiden (USA-SSK, 1980)
4   Thorleif Haug (NOR-NSK, 1924)
4   Ivar Ballangrud (NOR-SSK, 1936)
4   Sixten Jernberg (SWE-NSK, 1956)
4   Lidiya Skoblikova (URS-SSK, 1964)
4   Tatyana Averina (URS-SSK, 1976)
4   Gunde Anders Swan (SWE-NSK, 1984)
4   Karin Enke (GDR-SSK, 1984)
4   Marja-Liisa Hämäläinen (FIN-NSK, 1984)

Most Gold Medals, Winter, Games
5   Eric Heiden (USA-SSK, 1980)
4   Lidiya Skoblikova (URS-SSK, 1964)
3   Ten athletes tied with three

Most Medals, Winter, Games, Women
4   Lidiya Skoblikova (URS-SSK, 1964)
4   Tatyana Averina (URS-SSK, 1976)
4   Marja-Liisa Hämäläinen (FIN-NSK, 1984)
4   Karin Enke (GDR-SSK, 1984)
3   Twelve athletes tied with three

Most Gold Medals, Winter, Games, Women
4   Lidiya Skoblikova (URS-SSK, 1964)
3   Klaudiya Boyarskikh (URS-NSK, 1964)
3   Galina Kulakova (URS-NSK, 1972)
3   Marja-Liisa Hämäläinen (FIN-NSK, 1984)
2   Rosi Mittermaier (FRG-ASK, 1976)
2   Raisa Smetanina (URS-NSK, 1976)
2   Tatyana Averina (URS-SSK, 1976)
2   Hanni Wenzel (LIE-ASK, 1980)
2   Karin Enke (GDR-SSK, 1984)

Most Medals, Winter, Games, Men
5   Roald Larsen (NOR-SSK, 1924)
5   Clas Thunberg (FIN-SSK, 1924)
5   Eric Heiden (USA-SSK, 1980)
4   Thorleif Haug (NOR-NSK, 1924)
4   Ivar Ballangrud (NOR-SSK, 1936)
4   Sixten Jernberg (SWE-NSK, 1956)
4   Gunde Anders Swan (SWE-NSK, 1984)

Most Gold Medals, Winter, Games, Men
```
5      Eric Heiden (USA-SSK, 1980)
3      Clas Thunberg (FIN-SSK, 1924)
3      Thorleif Haug (NOR-NSK, 1924)
3      Ivar Ballangrud (FIN-SSK, 1936)
3      Hjalmar Andersen (NOR-SSK, 1952)
3      Anton "Toni" Sailer (AUT-ASK, 1956)
3      Jean-Claude Killy (FRA-ASK, 1968)
3      Adrianus "Ard" Schenck (HOL-SSK, 1972)
```

Most Medals, Winter, Games, Individual
```
5      Roald Larsen (NOR-SSK, 1924)
5      Clas Thunberg (FIN-SSK, 1924)
5      Eric Heiden (USA-SSK, 1980)
4      Thorleif Haug (NOR-NSK, 1924)
4      Ivar Ballangrud (NOR-SSK, 1936)
4      Lidiya Skoblikova (URS-SSK, 1964)
4      Tatyana Averina (URS-SSK, 1976)
4      Karin Enke (GDR-SSK, 1984)
```

Most Gold Medals, Winter, Games, Individual
```
5      Eric Heiden (USA-SSK, 1980)
4      Lidiya Skoblikova (URS-SSK, 1964)
3      Clas Thunberg (FIN-SSK, 1924)
3      Thorleif Haug (NOR-NSK, 1924)
3      Ivar Ballangrud (NOR-SSK, 1936)
3      Hjalmar Andersen (NOR-SSK, 1952)
3      Anton "Toni" Sailer (AUT-ASK, 1956)
3      Jean-Claude Killy (FRA-ASK, 1968)
3      Adrianus "Ard" Schenk (HOL-SSK, 1972)
3      Marja-Liisa Hämäläinen (FIN-NSK, 1984)
```

Most Medals, Winter, Games, Individual, Women
```
4      Lidiya Skoblikova (URS-SSK, 1964)
4      Tatyana Averina (URS-SSK, 1976)
4      Karin Enke (GDR-SSK, 1984)
3      Marja-Liisa Hämäläinen (FIN-NSK, 1984)
3      Annemarie "Mirl" Buchner (FRG-ASK, 1952)
3      Rosi Mittermaier (FRG-ASK, 1976)
3      Hanni Wenzel (LIE-ASK, 1980)
3      Atje Keulen-Deelstra (HOL-SSK, 1972)
3      Sheila Young (USA-SSK, 1976)
3      Andrea Mitscherlich-Schöne (GDR-SSK, 1984)
```

Most Gold Medals, Winter, Games, Individual, Women
```
4      Lidiya Skoblikova (URS-SSK, 1964)
3      Marja-Liisa Hämäläinen (FIN-NSK, 1984)
2      Klaudiya Boyarskikh (URS-NSK, 1964)
2      Galina Kulakova (URS-NSK, 1972)
2      Hanni Wenzel (LIE-ASK, 1980)
2      Rosi Mittermaier (FRG-ASK, 1976)
2      Tatyana Averina (URS-SSK, 1976)
2      Karin Enke (GDR-SSK, 1984)
```

Most Medals, Winter, Games, Individual, Men
 5   Eric Heiden (USA-SSK, 1980)
 5   Roald Larsen (NOR-SSK, 1924)
 5   Clas Thunberg (FIN-SSK, 1924)
 4   Ivar Ballangrud (NOR-SSK, 1936)
 3   Nine athletes tied with three

Most Gold Medals, Winter, Games, Individual, Men
 5   Eric Heiden (USA-SSK, 1980)
 3   Clas Thunberg (FIN-SSK, 1924)
 3   Thorleif Haug (NOR-NSK, 1924)
 3   Ivar Ballangrud (FIN-SSK, 1936)
 3   Hjalmar Andersen (NOR-SSK, 1952)
 3   Anton "Toni" Sailer (AUT-ASK, 1956)
 3   Jean-Claude Killy (FRA-ASK, 1968)
 3   Adrianus "Ard" Schenck (HOL-SSK, 1972)

Most Consecutive Victories, Same Event, Winter, Individual
 3   Gillis Grafström (SWE-FSK-Men, 1920-28)
 3   Sonja Henie (NOR-FSK-Women, 1928-36)
 3   Ulrich Wehling (GDR-NSK-Nordic Combined, 1972-80)
 2   Twelve athletes tied with two

Most Consecutive Victories, Same Event, Winter, Individual, Women
 3   Sonja Henie (NOR-FSK-Women, 1928-36)
 2   Lidiya Skoblikova (URS-SSK-1500, 1960-64)
 2   Lidiya Skoblikova (URS-SSK-3000, 1960-64)

Most Consecutive Victories, Same Event, Winter, Individual, Men
 3   Gillis Grafström (SWE-FSK-Men, 1920-28)
 3   Ulrich Wehling (GDR-NSK-Nordic Combined, 1972-80)
 2   Karl Schäfer (AUT-FSK-Men, 1932-36)
 2   Richard Button (USA-FSK-Men, 1948-52)
 2   Hallgeir Brenden (NOR-NSK-18/15 km, 1952-56)
 2   Birger Ruud (NOR-NSK-Jump, 1932-36)
 2   Johan Gröttumsbråten (NOR-NSK-Nordic Combined, 1928-32)
 2   Magnar Solberg (NOR-BIA-20K, 1968-72)
 2   Evgeniy Grishin (URS-SSK-500, 1956-60)
 2   Evgeniy Grishin (URS-SSK-500, 1956-60)
 2   Erhard Keller (FRG-SSK-500, 1968-72)
 2   Clas Thunberg (FIN-SSK-1500, 1924-28)

Most Consecutive Victories, Team, Same Event, Same Team, Winter
 2   France (Pairs Figure Skating - 1928-32)
            (Andrée Brunet-Joly, Pierre Brunet)
 2   USSR (Pairs Figure Skating - 1964-68)
            (Lyudmila Belousova, Oleg Protopopov)
 2   USSR (Pairs Figure Skating - 1976-80)
            (Irina Rodnina, Aleksandr Zaitsev)
 2   GDR (Luge Doubles - 1976-80)
            (Hans Rinn, Norbert Hahn)

Youngest Known Competitor, Winter
    11-074   Cecilia Colledge (GBR-FSK, 1932)
    11-108   Megan Taylor (GBR-FSK, 1932)
    11-162   Beatrice Hustiu (ROM-FSK, 1968)
    11-295   Sonja Henie (NOR-FSK, 1924)
    11-310   Marcelle Mathews (SAF-FSK, 1960)

Youngest Medalist, Winter
    14-363   Scott Ethan Allen (USA-FSK, 1964)
    15-008   Manuela Groß (GDR-FSK, 1972)
    15-076   Cecilia Colledge (GBR-FSK, 1936)
    15-091   Marina Cherkasova (URS-FSK, 1980)
    15-127   Maxi Herber (GER-FSK, 1936)
    15-129   Thomas Doe (USA-BOB, 1928)
    15-260   Ingrid Wendl (AUT-FSK, 1956)
    15-300   Erik Pausin (AUT-FSK, 1936)
    15-315   Sonja Henie (NOR-FSK, 1928)
    16-013   Carol Heiss (USA-FSK, 1956)

Youngest Gold Medalist, Winter
    15-127   Maxi Herber (GER-FSK, 1936)
    15-315   Sonja Henie (NOR-FSK, 1928)
    16-157   Anne Henning (USA-SSK, 1972)
    16-260   Billy Fiske (USA-BOB, 1928)
    17-306   Manfred Stengl (AUT-LUG, 1964)
    17-315   Michela Figini (SUI-ASK, 1984)
    17-337   Marie-Theres Nadig (SUI-ASK, 1972)
    17-347   Monika Pflug (FRG-SSK, 1972)
    18-054   John McKenzie (CAN-ICH, 1956)
    18-077   Katarina Witt (GDR-FSK, 1984)

Youngest Medalist, Winter, Individual
    14-363   Scott Ethan Allen (USA-FSK, 1964)
    15-076   Cecilia Colledge (GBR-FSK, 1936)
    15-260   Ingrid Wendl (AUT-FSK, 1956)
    15-315   Sonja Henie (NOR-FSK, 1928)
    16-013   Carol Heiss (USA-FSK, 1956)

Youngest Gold Medalist, Winter, Individual
    15-315   Sonja Henie (NOR-FSK, 1928)
    16-157   Anne Henning (USA-SSK, 1972)
    17-315   Michela Figini (SUI-ASK, 1984)
    17-337   Marie-Theres Nadig (SUI-ASK, 1972)
    17-347   Monika Pflug (FRG-SSK, 1972)

Youngest Known Competitor, Winter, Women
    11-074   Cecilia Colledge (GBR-FSK, 1932)
    11-108   Megan Taylor (GBR-FSK, 1932)
    11-162   Beatrice Hustiu (ROM-FSK, 1968)
    11-295   Sonja Henie (NOR-FSK, 1924)
    11-310   Marcelle Mathews (SAF-FSK, 1960)

Youngest Medalist, Winter, Women
```
15-008   Manuela Groß (GDR-FSK, 1972)
15-076   Cecilia Colledge (GBR-FSK, 1936)
15-091   Marina Cherkasova (URS-FSK, 1980)
15-127   Maxi Herber (GER-FSK, 1936)
15-260   Ingrid Wendl (AUT-FSK, 1956)
15-315   Sonja Henie (NOR-FSK, 1928)
16-013   Carol Heiss (USA-FSK, 1956)
16-145   Traudl Hecher (AUT-ASK, 1960)
16-157   Anne Henning (USA-SSK, 1972)
16-217   Tenley Albright (USA-FSK, 1952)
```

Youngest Gold Medalist, Winter, Women
```
15-127   Maxi Herber (GER-FSK, 1936)
15-315   Sonja Henie (NOR-FSK, 1928)
16-157   Anne Henning (USA-SSK, 1972)
17-315   Michela Figini (SUI-ASK, 1984)
17-337   Marie-Theres Nadig (SUI-ASK, 1972)
17-347   Monika Pflug (FRG-SSK, 1972)
18-077   Katarina Witt (GDR-FSK, 1984)
18-128   Marielle Goitschel (FRA-ASK, 1964)
18-240   Karin Enke (GDR-SSK, 1980)
19-003   Heidi Biebl (FRG-ASK, 1960)
```

Youngest Medalist, Winter, Individual, Women
```
15-076   Cecilia Colledge (GBR-FSK, 1936)
15-260   Ingrid Wendl (AUT-FSK, 1956)
15-315   Sonja Henie (NOR-FSK, 1928)
16-013   Carol Heiss (USA-FSK, 1956)
16-145   Traudl Hecher (AUT-ASK, 1960)
```

Youngest Gold Medalist, Winter, Individual, Women
```
15-315   Sonja Henie (NOR-FSK, 1928)
16-157   Anne Henning (USA-SSK, 1972)
17-315   Michela Figini (SUI-ASK, 1984)
17-337   Marie-Theres Nadig (SUI-ASK, 1972)
17-347   Monika Pflug (FRG-SSK, 1972)
```

Youngest Known Competitor, Winter, Men
```
12-113   Jan Hoffmann (GDR-FSK, 1968)
12-161   Alain Giletti (FRA-FSK, 1952)
```

Youngest Medalist, Winter, Men
```
14-363   Scott Ethan Allen (USA-FSK, 1964)
15-129   Thomas Doe (USA-BOB, 1928)
15-300   Erik Pausin (AUT-FSK, 1936)
16-141   Richard "Bibi" Torriani (SUI-ICH, 1928)
16-260   Billy Fiske (USA-BOB, 1928)
16-261   Mark Howe (USA-ICH, 1972)
17-306   Manfred Stengl (AUT-LUG, 1964)
17-320   Anton Innauer (AUT-NSK, 1976)
18-020   Frank Ullrich (GDR-BIA, 1976)
18-054   John McKenzie (CAN-ICH, 1956)
```

Youngest Gold Medalist, Winter, Men
    16-260 Billy Fiske (USA-BOB, 1928)
    17-306 Manfred Stengl (AUT-LUG, 1964)
    18-054 John McKenzie (CAN-ICH, 1956)
    18-202 Richard Button (USA-FSK, 1948)
    18-279 Heinrich Schläppi (SUI-BOB, 1924)
    19-009 Igor Malkov (URS-SSK, 1984)
    19-032 Reginald Smith (CAN-ICH, 1924)
    19-082 Mike Ramsey (USA-ICH, 1980)
    19-188 Wojciech Fortuna (POL-NSK, 1972)
    19-206 Jens Weißflog, (GDR-NSK, 1984)

Youngest Medalist, Winter, Individual, Men
    14-363 Scott Ethan Allen (USA-FSK, 1964)
    17-320 Anton Innauer (AUT-NSK, 1976)
    18-129 Ronald Robertson (USA-1956)
    18-137 Alv Gjestvang (NOR-1956)
    18-202 Richard Button (USA-FSK, 1948)

Youngest Gold Medalist, Winter, Individual, Men
    18-202 Richard Button (USA-FSK, 1948)
    19-009 Igor Malkov (URS-SSK, 1984)
    19-188 Wojciech Fortuna (POL-NSK, 1948)
    19-206 Jens Weißflog (GDR-1984)
    19-211 Ulrich Wehling (GDR-1972)

Oldest Known Competitor, Winter
    53-328 James Coats (GBR-SKE/LUG, 1948)
    53-280 Carl-Erik Eriksson (SWE-BOB, 1984)
    52-144 Joseph Savage (USA-FSK, 1932)
    51-031 Albert Tebbitt (GBR-SSK, 1924)

Oldest Medalist, Winter
    49-038 Max Houben (BEL-BOB, 1948)
    48-358 Jay O'Brien (USA-BOB, 1932)
    47-218 Giacomo Conti (ITA-BOB, 1956)
    46-341 Albert Madörin (SUI-BOB, 1952)
    45-035 John Crammond (GBR-LUG/SKE, 1948)
    44-362 Jay O'Brien (USA-BOB, 1932)
    44-078 Martin Stixrud (NOR-FSK, 1920)
    43-302 Edgar Syers (GBR-FSK, 1908)
    43-237 Fritz Feierabend (SUI-BOB, 1952)
    43-057 Francis Tyler (USA-BOB, 1948)

Oldest Gold Medalist, Winter
    48-358 Jay O'Brien (USA-BOB, 1932)
    47-217 Giacomo Conti (ITA-BOB, 1956)
    43-057 Francis Tyler (USA-BOB, 1948)
    42-182 Nion Tucker (USA-BOB, 1928)
    41-340 Hubert Stevens (USA-BOB, 1932)
    41-103 Franz Kemser (GER-BOB, 1952)
    40-172 Heinrich Angst (SUI-BOB, 1956)
    40-023 Eugenio Monti (ITA-BOB, 1968)
    40-017 Clifford Gray (USA-BOB, 1932)
    39-042 Meinhard Nehmer (GDR-BOB, 1980)

Oldest Medalist, Winter, Individual
    44-078 Martin Stixrud (NOR-FSK, 1920)
    38-247 Gillis Grafström (SWE-FSK, 1932)
    38-246 Julius Skutnabb (FIN-SSK, 1928)
    38-005 Alevtina Kolchina (URS-NSK, 1968)
    36-168 Birger Ruud (NOR-NSK, 1948)

Oldest Gold Medalist, Winter, Individual
    35-052 Veikko Hakulinen (FIN-NSK, 1960)
    35-005 Magnar Solberg (NOR-BIA, 1972)
    35-002 Sixten Jernberg (SWE-NSK, 1964)
    34-315 Clas Thunberg (FIN-SSK, 1928)
    34-255 Gillis Grafström (SWE-FSK, 1928)

Oldest Known Competitor, Winter, Women
    43-209 Ludowika Jakobsson (FIN-FSK, 1928)
    39-190 Ludowika Jakobsson (FIN-FSK, 1924)

Oldest Medalist, Winter, Women
    39-189 Ludowika Jakobsson (FIN-FSK, 1924)
    38-009 Marjatta Kajosmaa (FIN-NSK, 1976)
    38-005 Alevtina Kolchina (URS-NSK, 1968)
    37-298 Galina Kulakova (URS-NSK, 1980)
    37-184 Eevi Huttunen (FIN-SSK, 1960)
    35-275 Ludowika Jakobsson (FIN-FSK, 1920)
    35-116 Phyllis Johnson (GBR-FSK, 1920)
    35-073 Siiri Rantanen (FIN-NSK, 1960)
    34-009 Marjatta Kajosmaa (FIN-NSK, 1972)
    33-361 Alevtina Kolchina (URS-NSK, 1964)

Oldest Gold Medalist, Winter, Women
    35-275 Ludowika Jakobsson (FIN-FSK, 1920)
    33-362 Alevtina Kolchina (URS-NSK, 1964)
    33-289 Galina Kulakova (URS-NSK, 1976)
    33-268 Christina Baas-Kaiser (HOL-SSK, 1972)
    32-321 Evdokiya Mekshilo (URS-NSK, 1964)
    32-084 Lyudmila Belousova (URS-FSK, 1968)
    31-281 Lydia Wideman (FIN-NSK, 1952)
    31-048 Siiri Rantanen (FIN-NSK, 1956)
    30-158 Irina Rodnina (URS-FSK, 1980)
    30-149 Andrée Brunet-Joly (FRA-FSK, 1932)

Oldest Medalist, Winter, Individual, Women
  38-005   Alevtina Kolchina (URS-NSK, 1968)
  37-184   Eevi Huttunen (FIN-SSK, 1960)
  34-008   Marjatta Kajosmaa (FIN-NSK, 1972)
  33-268   Christina Baas-Kaiser (HOL-SSK, 1972)
  33-043   Atje Keulen-Deelstra (HOL-SSK, 1972)

Oldest Gold Medalist, Winter, Individual, Women
  33-268   Christina Baas-Kaiser (HOL-SSK, 1972)
  31-281   Lydia Wideman (FIN-NSK, 1952)
  30-033   Ossi Reichart (GER-ASK, 1956)
  28-359   Gretchen Fraser (USA-ASK, 1948)
  28-120   Annie Borckink (HOL-SSK, 1980)

Oldest Known Competitor, Winter, Men
  53-328   James Coats (GBR-SKE/LUG, 1948)
  53-280   Carl-Erik Eriksson (SWE-BOB, 1984)
  52-144   Joseph Savage (USA-FSK, 1932)
  51-031   Albert Tebbitt (GBR-SSK, 1924)

Oldest Medalist, Winter, Men
  49-038   Max Houben (BEL-BOB, 1948)
  48-358   Jay O'Brien (USA-BOB, 1932)
  47-217   Giacomo Conti (ITA-BOB, 1956)
  46-341   Albert Madörin (SUI-BOB, 1952)
  45-035   John Crammond (GBR-LUG/SKE, 1948)
  44-362   Jay O'Brien (USA-BOB, 1932)
  44-078   Martin Stixrud (NOR-FSK, 1920)
  43-302   Edgar Syers (GBR-FSK, 1908)
  43-237   Fritz Feierabend (SUI-BOB, 1952)
  43-057   Francis Tyler (USA-BOB, 1948)

Oldest Gold Medalist, Winter, Men
  48-358   Jay O'Brien (USA-BOB, 1932)
  47-217   Giacomo Conti (ITA-BOB, 1956)
  43-057   Francis Tyler (USA-BOB, 1948)
  42-182   Nion Tucker (USA-BOB, 1928)
  41-340   Hubert Stevens (USA-BOB, 1932)
  41-103   Franz Kemser (GER-BOB, 1952)
  40-172   Heinrich Angst (SUI-BOB, 1956)
  40-023   Eugenio Monti (ITA-BOB, 1968)
  40-017   Clifford Gray (USA-BOB, 1932)
  39-042   Meinhard Nehmer (GDR-BOB, 1980)

Oldest Medalist, Winter, Individual, Men
  44-078   Martin Stixrud (NOR-FSK, 1920)
  38-247   Gillis Grafström (SWE-FSK, 1932)
  38-246   Julius Skutnabb (FIN-SSK, 1928)
  36-168   Birger Ruud (NOR-NSK, 1948)
  35-052   Veikko Hakulinen (FIN-NSK, 1960)

Oldest Gold Medalist, Winter, Individual, Men
35-052 Veikko Hakulinen (FIN-NSK, 1960)
35-005 Magnar Solberg (NOR-BIA, 1972)
35-002 Sixten Jernberg (SWE-NSK, 1964)
34-315 Clas Thunberg (FIN-SSK, 1928)
34-255 Gillis Grafström (SWE-FSK, 1928)

Medals Won by Countries, Overall
          In the following tables, places are given according to
total medals. Ties are broken first by number of gold medals,
then number of silver medals, and finally number of bronze
medals.

		G	S	B	Tot
1.	USSR	68	48	49	165
2.	Norway	54	57	52	163
3.	Finland	29	42	32	103
4.	United States	40	45	32	117
5.	GDR	34	29	30	93
6.	Austria	25	33	30	88
7.	Sweden	32	25	29	86
8.	Switzerland	18	20	20	58
9.	FRG	16	15	17	48
10.	Canada	14	10	15	39
11.	France	12	10	15	37
12.	Netherlands	10	15	10	35
13.	Italy	12	9	7	28
14.	Great Britain	7	4	10	21
15.	Czechoslovakia	2	7	11	20
16.	Germany	4	4	3	11
17.	Liechtenstein	2	2	4	8
18.	Japan	1	4	1	6
19.	Hungary	–	2	4	6
T20.	Belgium	1	1	2	4
	Poland	1	1	2	4
22.	Spain	1	–	–	1
T23.	Yugoslavia	–	1	–	1
	Korea DPR	–	1	–	1
T25.	Romania	–	–	1	1
	Bulgaria	–	–	1	1
	Totals	383	385	377	1145

Medals Won by Countries, Men

		G	S	B	Tot
1.	Norway	48	54½	45	147½
2.	USSR	40	27½	27½	95
3.	Finland	21½	31½	24	77
4.	Sweden	28	22	26	76
5.	United States	28	25½	16½	70
6.	GDR	20	15½	21½	57
7.	Austria	17	20	19½	56½
8.	Switzerland	11	17	17	45
9.	FRG	10½	8½	10½	29½
10.	Canada	9½	6	12½	28
11.	Italy	10	8	5	23
12.	France	8	4	8½	20½
13.	Netherlands	5	9	6	20
14.	Czechoslovakia	2	6	6	14
15.	Great Britain	4½	2½	6	13
16.	Germany	2	2	3	7
17.	Japan	1	4	1	6
18.	Belgium	0½	1	2	3½
T19.	Liechtenstein	–	1	2	3
	Hungary	–	1	2	3
20.	Poland	1	–	1	2
21.	Spain	1	–	–	1
22.	Yugoslavia	–	1	–	1
T23.	Romania	–	–	1	1
	Bulgaria	–	–	1	1
	Totals	268½	267½	264½	800½

Medals Won by Countries, Women

		G	S	B	Tot
1.	USSR	28	20½	21½	70
2.	United States	12	19½	15½	47
3.	GDR	14	13½	8½	36
4.	Austria	8	13	10½	31½
5.	Finland	7½	10½	8	26
6.	FRG	5½	6½	6½	18½
7.	France	4	6	6½	16½
8.	Norway	6	2½	7	15½
9.	Netherlands	5	6	4	15
10.	Switzerland	7	3	3	13
11.	Canada	4½	4	2½	11
12.	Sweden	4	3	3	10
13.	Great Britain	2½	1½	4	8
14.	Czechoslovakia	–	1	5	6
T15.	Italy	2	1	2	5
	Liechtenstein	2	1	2	5
17.	Germany	2	2	–	4
18.	Hungary	–	1	2	3
19.	Poland	–	1	1	2
20.	Korea DPR	–	1	–	1
21.	Belgium	0½	–	–	0½
	Totals	114½	117½	112½	344½

Discrepancies in the number of total medals are due to various
events in which a single medal of each type was not awarded. The
specific events in which this occurred and the format of medals
awarded is discussed under each sport.

OLYMPIC RECORDS BY SPORT

     Following are the best records achieved in the various
sports of the Olympic Games. All sports ever contested at the
Olympics are included, although discontinued and demonstration
sports follow the current sports in special lists at the end.
Lists for medal records are five-deep, except in a few sports with
a relatively short Olympic history. Age records are five-deep in
most sports, three-deep in sports with a short Olympic history,
and ten-deep where it is appropriate, i.e., usually sports with a
great number of competitors at either extreme of age. Also listed
are the Olympic record progressions in the sports where the events
are comparable. Only the events on the current program are
included in these progressions. At the end of each section, are
lists of special interest individualized by sport. Also included
for each sport are lists of medals won by countries, lists of the
best performance by countries at each Olympics, and, in team
sports, a list of the won-lost records of all countries to have
competed at the Olympics.

THE GAMES OF THE OLYMPIADS

ARCHERY

International Federation: Fédération Internationale de Tir á
     l'Arc (FITA)
Countries Affiliated: 70 (1987)
Year of Formation: 1931
First Year of Olympic Appearance: 1900

Archery was first held as a sport in the 1900 Paris Olympics and
     again in 1904, 1908, and 1920. In those years it was possible
     for an athlete to compete in multiple events and win several
     medals. When the sport was revived in 1972, there was only one
     event for men and one for women, consequently all records for
     medals won are now inviable. Consequently, a list of modern
     (since 1972) records is also listed.

Overall Records

Most Medals, Men
     9   Hubert van Innis (BEL)
     5   Julien Brulé (FRA)
     4   Eugène Grisot (FRA)
     4   Louis Van de Perck (BEL)
     4   Leonce Gaston Quentin (FRA)

65

Most Gold Medals, Men
```
6       Hubert van Innis (BEL)
3       Emile Cloetens (BEL)
3       Edmond van Moer (BEL)
```

Most Silver Medals, Men
```
3       Hubert van Innis (BEL)
3       Julien Brulé (FRA)
3       Léonce Quentin (FRA)
```

Most Bronze Medals, Men
```
2       William Thompson (USA)
2       Henry Richardson (USA)
2       Charles-Frédéric Petit (FRA)
```

Most Medals, Games, Men
```
6       Hubert van Innis (BEL-1920)
5       Julien Brulé (FRA-1920)
4       Louis van de Perck (BEL-1920)
```

Most Gold Medals, Games, Men
```
4       Hubert van Innis (BEL-1920)
3       Emile Cloetens (BEL-1920)
3       Edmond van Moer (BEL-1920)
```

Most Medals, Individual, Men
```
6       Hubert van Innis (BEL-1920)
```

Most Gold Medals, Individual, Men
```
4       Hubert van Innis (BEL-1920)
```

Most Medals, Individual, Games, Men
```
3       Hubert van Innis (BEL-1900)
3       Hubert van Innis (BEL-1920)
```

Most Gold Medals, Individual, Games, Men
```
2       Hubert van Innis (BEL-1900)
2       Phillip Bryant (USA-1904)
2       Hubert van Innis (BEL-1920)
```

Most Medals, Women
```
3       Lida Howell (USA)
3       Emma Cooke (USA)
3       Jessie Pollock (USA)
```

Most Gold Medals, Women
```
3       Lida Howell (USA)
```

Most Silver Medals, Women
```
2       Emma Cooke (USA)
```

Most Bronze Medals, Women
```
2       Jessie Pollock (USA)
```

Modern Records (since 1972)

Most Medals
    2   Darrell Pace (USA)
    2   Giancarlo Ferrari (ITA)

Most Gold Medals
    2   Darrell Pace (USA)

Most Bronze Medals
    2   Giancarlo Ferrari (ITA)

Youngest Medalist, Men
    15-126   Henry Richardson (USA-1904)
    18-219   Tomi Poikolainen (FIN-1980)
    18-364   John Williams (USA-1972)
    19-060   Henry Richardson (USA-1908)
    19-280   Darrell Pace (USA-1976)

Youngest Gold Medalist, Men
    18-219   Tomi Poikolainen (FIN-1980)
    18-364   John Williams (USA-1972)
    19-280   Darrell Pace (USA-1976)
    24-148 Henri Herouin (FRA-1900)
    25-319   Adrianus van Merrienboer (HOL-1920)

Oldest Medalist, Men
    68-194   Samuel Duvall (USA-1904)
    64-002   Galen Spencer (USA-1904)
    63-241   Robert Williams (USA-1904)
    56-195   William Thompson (USA-1904)
    56-024   Eugène Richez (FRA-1920)

Oldest Gold Medalist, Men
    64-002   Galen Spencer (USA-1904)
    63-241   Robert Williams (USA-1904)
    56-195   William Thompson (USA-1904)
    54-187   Hubert van Innis (BEL-1920)
    53-265 Lewis Maxson (USA-1904)

Youngest Medalist, Women
    17-035   Hyang-Soon Seo (KOR-1984)
    18-124   Lingjuan Li (CHN-1984)
    21-183   Sebinisso Rustamova (URS-1976)
    23-199   Luann Ryon (USA-1976)
    26-153   Valentina Kovpan (URS-1976)

Youngest Gold Medalist, Women
    17-035   Hyang-Soon Seo (KOR-1984)
    23-199   Luann Ryon (USA-1976)
    31-002   Ketevan Lossaberidge (URS-1980)

Oldest Medalist, Women
```
45-025   Lida Howell (USA-1904)
44-226   Irena Szydłowska (POL-1972)
42-246   Doreen Wilber (USA-1972)
36-300   Charlotte Dod (GBR-1908)
34-199   Emma Gaptschenko (URS-1972)
```

Oldest Gold Medalist, Women
```
45-025   Lida Howell (USA-1904)
42-246   Doreen Wilber (USA-1972)
31-002   Ketevan Lossaberidge (URS-1980)
```

Olympic Record Progression

Men - FITA Round
```
1268   John Williams (USA) (Rd 1)    Munich        09SEP1972
1307   Darrell Pace (USA) (Rd 2)     Montreal      30JUL1976
1317   Darrell Pace (USA) (Rd 2)     Los Angeles   11AUG1984
```

Women - FITA Round
```
1224   Irena Szydłowska (POL) (Rd 1) Munich        09SEP1972
1226   Doreen Wilber (USA) (Rd 2)    Munich        10SEP1972
1282   Luann Ryon (USA) (Rd 2)       Montreal      30JUL1976
1293   Hyang-Soon Seo (KOR) (Rd 2)   Los Angeles   11AUG1984
```

Men - Double FITA Round
```
2528   John Williams (USA)           Munich        10SEP1972
2571   Darrell Pace (USA)            Montreal      30JUL1976
2616   Darrell Pace (USA)            Los Angeles   11AUG1984
```

Women - Double FITA Round
```
2424   Doreen Wilber (USA)           Munich        10SEP1972
2499   Luann Ryon (USA)              Montreal      30JUL1976
2568   Hyang-Soon Seo (KOR)          Los Angeles   11AUG1984
```

Top Olympic Performances at Each Distance - Single Round

Men

```
30m    352   Darrell Pace (USA)         Los Angeles   1984
50m    334   Darrell Pace (USA)         Los Angeles   1984
70m    331   Darrell Pace (USA)         Los Angeles   1984
       331   Armin Garnreiter (FRG)     Los Angeles   1984
90m    310   Darrell Pace (USA)         Los Angeles   1984
```

Women

```
30m    310   Yanan Wu (CHN)             Los Angeles   1984
50m    331   Jin-Ho Kim (KOR)           Los Angeles   1984
60m    320   Hyang-Soon Seo (KOR)       Los Angeles   1984
       320   Jin-Ho Kim (KOR)           Los Angeles   1984
70m    350   Jin-Ho Kim (KOR)           Los Angeles   1984
```

Top Olympic Performances at Each Distance - Double Round

Men

30m	702	Darrell Pace (USA)	Los Angeles	1984
50m	660	Darrell Pace (USA)	Los Angeles	1984
70m	653	Darrell Pace (USA)	Los Angeles	1984
90m	601	Darrell Pace (USA)	Los Angeles	1984

Women

30m	694	Lingjuan Li (CHN)	Los Angeles	1984
50m	631	Hyang-Soon Seo (KOR)	Los Angeles	1984
60m	648	Jin-Ho Kim (KOR)	Los Angeles	1984
70m	611	Hyang-Soon Seo (KOR)	Los Angeles	1984

Medals Won By Countries

	G	S	B	T
United States	11	7	6	24
France	6	9	6	21
Belgium	10	7	2	19
USSR	1	3	2	6
Great Britain	2	2	1	5
Finland	1	-	2	3
Korea	1	-	1	2
Japan	-	1	1	2
Italy	-	-	2	2
Netherlands	1	-	-	1
Sweden	-	1	-	1
Poland	-	1	-	1
China	-	1	-	1
Totals	33	32	23	88

Medals Won by Countries, Men

	G	S	B	T
United States	6	4	4	14
France	6	9	6	21
Belgium	10	7	2	19
Great Britain	1	1	-	2
Finland	1	-	1	2
Japan	-	1	1	2
Italy	-	-	2	2
Netherlands	1	-	-	1
Sweden	-	1	-	1
USSR	-	1	-	1
Totals	25	24	16	65

*Two seconds/no third in 1900 sur la perche à la herse; no third
  in 1900 sur la perche à la pyramide; no second/third in 1920
  fixed bird target, small birds, team; no second/third in 1920
  fixed bird target, large birds, team; no third in 1920 moving
  bird target, 28 metres, individual; no third in 1920 moving bird
  target, 33 metres, individual; no third in 1920 moving bird
  target, 50 metres, individual; no third in 1920 moving bird
  target, 33 metres, team; no third in 1920 moving bird target, 50
  metres, team.

Medals Won by Countries, Women

	G	S	B	T
United States	5	3	2	10
USSR	1	2	2	5
Great Britain	1	1	1	3
Korea	1	-	1	2
Poland	-	1	-	1
China	-	1	-	1
Finland	-	-	1	1
Totals	8	8	7	23

*No third place in 1904 women's team match.

Best Performance at Each Olympics

    1900 - France
    1904 - United States
    1908 - Great Britain
    1920 - Belgium
    1972 - United States
    1976 - United States
    1980 - USSR
    1984 - United States

ATHLETICS (TRACK & FIELD)

International Federation: International Amateur Athletic
     Federation (IAAF)
Countries Affiliated: 179 (1987)
Year of Formation: 1912
First Year of Olympic Appearance: 1896

Most Medals
   12   Paavo Nurmi (FIN)
   10/8   Ray Ewry (USA)
    9/4   Martin Sheridan (USA)
    8   Ville Ritola (FIN)
    7   Shirley Strickland de la Hunty (AUS)
    7   Irena Szewińska-Kirszenstein (POL)
    7/3   Erik Lemming (SWE)
    6   Robert Garrett (USA)
    6   Ralph Rose (USA)
    6   Renate Stecher (GDR)
    6/4   James Lightbody (USA)

Most Gold Medals
   10/8   Ray Ewry (USA)
    9   Paavo Nurmi (FIN)
    5   Ville Ritola (FIN)
    5/3   Martin Sheridan (USA)
    4   Fourteen athletes tied with four.

Most Silver Medals
    4   Edvin Wide (SWE)
    3   Paavo Nurmi (FIN)
    3   Ville Ritola (FIN)
    3   Irving Baxter (USA)
    3   Herb McKenley (JAM)
    3   Alain Mimoun (FRA)
    3   Raelene Boyle (AUS)
    3   Ernest Webb (GBR)
    3/0   Martin Sheridan (USA)

Most Bronze Medals
    5   Philip Edwards (CAN)
    3   Shirley Strickland de la Hunty (AUS)
    3   Erik Backman (SWE)
    3   Stanley Rowley (AUS/GBR)
    3   Alex Wilson (CAN)
    3   Kathryn Smallwood-Cook (GBR)
    3   Merlene Ottey-Page (JAM)
    3/0   Erik Lemming (SWE)

Most Years Winning Medals
4	Irena Szewińska-Kirszenstein (POL)
4	Vladimir Golubnichiy (URS)
4	Al Oerter (USA)
4	Viktor Saneev (URS)
4/3	Ray Ewry (USA)

Most Years Winning Gold Medals
4	Al Oerter (USA)
4/3	Ray Ewry (USA)
3	Irena Szewińska-Kirszenstein (POL)
3	Viktor Saneev (URS)
3	Paavo Nurmi (FIN)
3	John Flanagan (USA)
3	Ralph Rose (USA)
3/2	Meyer Prinstein (USA)
3/2	Erik Lemming (SWE)
3/2	Martin Sheridan (USA)

Most Years Between Medals
16	Matt McGrath (USA)
12	Irena Szewińska-Kirszenstein (POL)
12	Vladimir Golubnichy (URS)
12	Al Oerter (USA)
12	Viktor Saneev (URS)
12	John Ljunggren (SWE)
12	Lyudmila Maslakova-Scharkova (URS)
12	Albin Stenroos (FIN)

Most Years Between Gold Medals
12	Al Oerter (USA)
12	Irena Szewińska-Kirszenstein (POL)
8	Paavo Nurmi (FIN)
8	Ray Ewry (USA)
8	Ralph Rose (USA)
8	Hannes Kolehmainen (FIN)
8	John Flanagan (USA)
8	Vladimir Golubnichy (URS)
8	Viktor Saneev (URS)
8	Pat McDonald (USA)
8	Nina Ponomaryeva-Romaschkova (URS)
8	Elizabeth Robinson (USA)
8	Frank Wykoff (USA)

Most Appearances
6	Lia Manoliu (ROM, 1952-72)
5	Eleven athletes tied with five

Longest Span of Olympic Competition (in years)
24	František Janda-Suk (BOH/TCH, 1900-24)
20	Dorothy Odam-Tyler (GBR, 1936-56)
20	Toyoko Yoshino-Nakamura (JPN, 1936-56)
20	Lia Manoliu (ROM, 1952-72)
20	Alexander Oakley (CAN, 1956-76)
20	Ed Burke (USA, 1964-84)

Most Medals, Women
7	Shirley Strickland de la Hunty (AUS)
7	Irena Szewińska-Kirszenstein (POL)
6	Renate Stecher (GDR)
4	Eight athletes tied with four.

Most Gold Medals, Women
4	Francina Blankers-Koen (HOL)
4	Betty Cuthbert (AUS)
4	Barbel Wöckel-Eckert (GDR)
3	Eight athletes tied with four.

Most Silver Medals, Women
3	Raelene Boyle (AUS)
2	Many athletes tied with two.

Most Bronze Medals, Women
3	Shirley Strickland de la Hunty (AUS)
3	Kathryn Smallwood-Cook (GBR)
3	Merlene Ottey-Page (JAM)
2	Many athletes tied with two.

Most Years Winning Medals, Women
4	Irena Szewińska-Kirszenstein (POL)
3	Shirley Strickland de la Hunty (AUS)
3	Lia Manoliu (ROM)
3	Lyudmila Maslakova-Scharkova (URS)
3	Nina Ponomareva-Romashkova (URS)
3	Galina Zybina (URS)
3	Nadezhda Chizhova (URS)
3	Sara Simeoni (ITA)

Most Years Winning Gold Medals, Women
3	Irena Szewińska-Kirszenstein (POL)
2	Many athletes tied with two.

Most Years Between Medals, Women
12	Irena Szewińska-Kirszenstein (POL)
8	Betty Cuthbert (AUS)
8	Lia Manoliu (ROM)
8	Nina Ponomareva-Romashkova (URS)
8	Elizabeth Robinson (USA)
8	Galina Zybina (URS)
8	Nadyezhda Chizhova (URS)
8	Sara Simeoni (ITA)

Most Years Between Gold Medals, Women
12	Irena Szewińska-Kirszenstein (POL)
8	Betty Cuthbert (AUS)
8	Nina Ponomaryeva-Romaschkova (URS)
8	Elizabeth Robinson (USA)

Most Appearances, Women
      6   Lia Manoliu (ROM, 1952-72)
      5   Olga Fikotová-Connolly (TCH/USA, 1956-72)
      5   Willye White (USA, 1956-72)
      5   Irena Szewińska-Kirszenstein (POL, 1964-80)

Longest Span of Olympic Competition, Women (in years)
     20   Dorothy Odam-Tyler (GBR, 1936-56)
     20   Toyoko Yoshino-Nakamura (JPN, 1936-56)
     20   Lia Manoliu (ROM, 1952-72)
     16   Jadwiga Wajsówna (POL, 1932-48)
     16   Herma Bauma (AUT, 1936-52)
     16   Francina Blankers-Koen (HOL, 1936-52)
     16   Olga Fikotová-Connolly (TCH/USA, 1956-72)
     16   Willye White (USA, 1956-72)
     16   Irena Szewińska-Kirszenstein (POL, 1964-80)

Most Medals, Men
     12   Paavo Nurmi (FIN)
   10/8   Ray Ewry (USA)
    9/4   Martin Sheridan (USA)
      8   Ville Ritola (FIN)
    7/3   Erik Lemming (SWE)
      6   Robert Garrett (USA)
      6   Ralph Rose (USA)
    6/4   James Lightbody (USA)

Most Gold Medals, Men
   10/8   Ray Ewry (USA)
      9   Paavo Nurmi (FIN)
      5   Ville Ritola (FIN)
    5/3   Martin Sheridan (USA)
      4   Hannes Kolehmainen (FIN)
      4   Mel Sheppard (USA)
      4   Emil Zátopek (TCH)
      4   Harrison Dillard (USA)
      4   Alvin Kraenzlein (USA)
      4   Al Oerter (USA)
      4   Jesse Owens (USA)
      4   Lasse Virén (FIN)
    4/3   Erik Lemming (SWE)
    4/3   Archie Hahn (USA)
    4/3   Meyer Prinstein (USA)

Most Silver Medals, Men
      4   Edvin Wide (SWE)
      3   Paavo Nurmi (FIN)
      3   Ville Ritola (FIN)
      3   Irving Baxter (USA)
      3   Herb McKenley (JAM)
      3   Alain Mimoun (FRA)
      3   Ernest Webb (GBR)
    3/0   Martin Sheridan (USA)

Most Bronze Medals, Men
5	Phil Edwards (CAN)
3	Erik Backman (SWE)
3	Stanley Rowley (AUS/GBR)
3	Alex Wilson (CAN)
3/0	Erik Lemming (SWE)

Most Years Winning Medals, Men
4	Vladimir Golubnichiy (URS)
4	Al Oerter (USA)
4	Viktor Saneev (URS)
4/3	Ray Ewry (USA)

Most Years Winning Gold Medals, Men
4	Al Oerter (USA)
4/3	Ray Ewry (USA)
3	Viktor Saneev (URS)
3	Paavo Nurmi (FIN)
3	John Flanagan (USA)
3	Ralph Rose (USA)
3/2	Meyer Prinstein (USA)
3/2	Erik Lemming (SWE)
3/2	Martin Sheridan (USA)

Most Years Between Medals, Men
16	Matt McGrath (USA)
12	Vladimir Golubnichiy (URS)
12	Al Oerter (USA)
12	Viktor Saneev (URS)
12	John Ljunggren (SWE)
12	Albin Stenroos (FIN)

Most Years Between Gold Medals, Men
12	Al Oerter (USA)
8	Paavo Nurmi (FIN)
8	Ray Ewry (USA)
8	Ralph Rose (USA)
8	Hannes Kolehmainen (FIN)
8	John Flanagan (USA)
8	Vladimir Golubnichiy (URS)
8	Viktor Saneev (URS)
8	Pat McDonald (USA)
8	Frank Wykoff (USA)

Most Appearances, Men
5	Paul Martin (SUI, 1920-36)
5	John Ljunggren (SWE, 1948-64)
5	Janusz Sidlo (POL, 1952-68)
5	Abdon Pamich (ITA, 1956-72)
5	Igor Ter-Ovanesyan (URS, 1956-72)
5	Alex Oakley (CAN, 1956-76)
5	Vladimir Golubnichiy (URS, 1960-76)
5	Urs von Wartburg (SUI, 1960-76)

Longest Span of Olympic Competition, Men (in years)
24   František Janda-Suk (BOH/TCH, 1900-24)
20   Alexander Oakley (CAN, 1956-76)
20   Ed Burke (USA, 1964-84)
16   Twenty-one athletes tied with 16.

Most Medals, Individual
10/8   Ray Ewry (USA)
9   Paavo Nurmi (FIN)
9/4   Martin Sheridan (USA)
6   Ville Ritola (FIN)
6   Irena Szewińska-Kirszenstein (POL)
6   Robert Garrett (USA)
6   Ralph Rose (USA)
6/3   Erik Lemming (SWE)

Most Gold Medals, Individual
10/8   Ray Ewry (USA)
6   Paavo Nurmi (FIN)
5/3   Martin Sheridan (USA)
4   Hannes Kolehmainen (FIN)
4   Emil Zátopek (TCH)
4   Alvin Kraenzlein (USA)
4   Al Oerter (USA)
4   Lasse Virén (FIN)
4/3   Archie Hahn (USA)
4/3   Meyer Prinstein (USA)
4/3   James Lightbody (USA)
4/3   Erik Lemming (SWE)

Most Silver Medals, Individual
3   Paavo Nurmi (FIN)
3   Ville Ritola (FIN)
3   Irving Baxter (USA)
3   Herb McKenley (JAM)
3   Raelene Boyle (AUS)
3   Alain Mimoun (FRA)
3   Ernest Webb (GBR)
3/0   Martin Sheridan (USA)

Most Bronze Medals, Individual
3   Phil Edwards (CAN)
3   Edvin Wide (SWE)
3   Stanley Rowley (AUS/GBR)
3   Merlene Ottey-Page (JAM)

Most Medals, Individual, Women
6   Irena Szewińska-Kirszenstein (POL)
4   Renate Stecher (GDR)
4   Tamara Press (URS)

Most Gold Medals, Individual, Women
```
3        Francina Blankers-Koen (HOL)
3        Betty Cuthbert (AUS)
3        Tamara Press (URS)
```

Most Silver Medals, Individual, Women
```
3        Raelene Boyle (AUS)
2        Many athletes tied with two.
```

Most Bronze Medals, Individual, Women
```
3        Merlene Ottey-Page (JAM)
2        Many athletes tied with two.
```

Most Medals, Individual, Men
```
10/8     Ray Ewry (USA)
9        Paavo Nurmi (FIN)
9/4      Martin Sheridan (USA)
6        Ville Ritola (FIN)
6        Robert Garrett (USA)
6        Ralph Rose (USA)
6/3      Erik Lemming (SWE)
```

Most Gold Medals, Individual, Men
```
10/8     Ray Ewry (USA)
6        Paavo Nurmi (FIN)
5/3      Martin Sheridan (USA)
4        Hannes Kolehmainen (FIN)
4        Emil Zátopek (TCH)
4        Alvin Kraenzlein (USA)
4        Al Oerter (USA)
4        Lasse Virén (FIN)
4/3      Archie Hahn (USA)
4/3      Meyer Prinstein (USA)
4/3      James Lightbody (USA)
4/3      Erik Lemming (SWE)
```

Most Silver Medals, Individual, Men
```
3        Paavo Nurmi (FIN)
3        Ville Ritola (FIN)
3        Irving Baxter (USA)
3        Herb McKenley (JAM)
3        Alain Mimoun (FRA)
3        Ernest Webb (GBR)
3/0      Martin Sheridan (USA)
```

Most Bronze Medals, Individual, Men
```
3        Phil Edwards (CAN)
3        Edvin Wide (SWE)
3        Stanley Rowley (AUS/GBR)
```

Most Medals, Games
```
6        Ville Ritola (FIN-1924)
5        Irving Baxter (USA-1900)
5        Paavo Nurmi (FIN-1924)
5        Walter Tewksbury (USA-1900)
5        Martin Sheridan (USA-1906)
```

Most Gold Medals, Games
```
5          Paavo Nurmi (FIN-1924)
4          Alvin Kraenzlein (USA-1900)
4          Ville Ritola (FIN-1924)
4          Jesse Owens (USA-1936)
4          Francina Blankers-Koen (HOL-1948)
4          Carl Lewis (USA-1984)
```

Most Silver Medals, Games
```
3          Irving Baxter (USA-1900)
3          Martin Sheridan (USA-1906)
```

Most Bronze Medals, Games
```
3          Stanley Rowley (AUS/GBR-1900)
3          Erik Lemming (SWE-1906)
3          Erik Backman (SWE-1920)
3          Phil Edwards (CAN-1932)
```

Most Medals, Games, Women
```
4          Francina Blankers-Koen (HOL-1948)
3          Fifteen athletes tied with three.
```

Most Gold Medals, Games, Women
```
4          Francina Blankers-Koen (HOL-1948)
3          Betty Cuthbert (AUS-1956)
3          Wilma Rudolph (USA-1960)
3          Valerie Brisco-Hooks (USA-1984)
```

Most Medals, Games, Men
```
6          Ville Ritola (FIN-1924)
5          Irving Baxter (USA-1900)
5          Walter Tewksbury (USA-1900)
5          Martin Sheridan (USA-1906)
5          Paavo Nurmi (FIN-1924)
```

Most Gold Medals, Games, Men
```
5          Paavo Nurmi (FIN-1924)
4          Ville Ritola (FIN-1924)
4          Alvin Kraenzlein (USA-1900)
4          Jesse Owens (USA-1936)
4          Carl Lewis (USA-1984)
```

Most Medals, Games, Individual
```
5          Irving Baxter (USA-1900)
5          Walter Tewksbury (USA-1900)
5          Martin Sheridan (USA-1906)
4          Robert Garrett (USA-1896)
4          Alvin Kraenzlein (USA-1900)
4          Ville Ritola (FIN-1924)
```

Most Gold Medals, Games, Individual
```
4        Alvin Kraenzlein (USA-1900)
3        James Lightbody (USA-1904)
3        Ray Ewry (USA-1900)
3        Ray Ewry (USA-1904)
3        Archie Hahn (USA-1904)
3        Harry Hillman (USA-1904)
3        Hannes Kolehmainen (FIN-1912)
3        Jesse Owens (USA-1936)
3        Francina Blankers-Koen (HOL-1948)
3        Emil Zátopek (TCH-1952)
3        Carl Lewis (USA-1984)
```

Most Medals, Games, Women, Individual
```
3        Babe Didrikson (USA-1932)
3        Francina Blankers-Koen (HOL-1948)
3        Micheline Ostermeyer (FRA-1948)
3        Aleksandra Chudina (URS-1952)
```

Most Gold Medals, Games, Women, Individual
```
3        Francina Blankers-Koen (HOL-1948)
2        Betty Cuthbert (AUS-1956)
2        Wilma Rudolph (USA-1960)
2        Tamara Press (URS-1964)
2        Renate Stecher (GDR-1972)
2        Tatyana Kazankina (URS-1976)
```

Most Medals, Games, Men, Individual
```
5        Irving Baxter (USA-1900)
5        Walter Tewksbury (USA-1900)
5        Martin Sheridan (USA-1906)
4        Robert Garrett (USA-1896)
4        Alvin Kraenzlein (USA-1900)
4        Ville Ritola (FIN-1924)
```

Most Gold Medals, Games, Men, Individual
```
4        Alvin Kraenzlein (USA-1900)
3        Ray Ewry (USA-1900)
3        Ray Ewry (USA-1904)
3        Archie Hahn (USA-1904)
3        Harry Hillman (USA-1904)
3        James Lightbody (USA-1904)
3        Hannes Kolehmainen (FIN-1912)
3        Jesse Owens (USA-1936)
3        Francina Blankers-Koen (HOL-1948)
3        Emil Zátopek (TCH-1952)
3        Carl Lewis (USA-1984)
```

Youngest Known Competitor, Women
   14-104   Heather Gooding (BAR-1972, 800)
   15-057   Deborah Wells (AUS-1976, 100)
   15-065   Esther Stroy (USA-1968, 400)
   15-082   Meredith Ellis (USA-1956, 200)
   15-097   Cindy Gilbert (USA-1972, HJ)
   15-124   Pearl Jones (USA-1952, 4x100R)
   15-144   Pordis Gisladottir (ISL-1976, HJ)
   15-202   Marjorie Larney (USA-1952, JT)
   15-216   Stephanie Berto (CAN-1968, 100)
   15-240   Wassana Panyapuek (THA-1984, 4x100)

Youngest Medalist, Women
   15-124   Pearl Jones (USA-1952, 4x100R)
   16-123   Ulrike Meyfarth (FRG-1972, HJ)
   16-146   Dorothy Odam (GBR-1936, HJ)
   16-161   Wilma Rudolph (USA-1956, 4x100R)
   16-169   Linsey MacDonald (GBR-1980, 4x100R)
   16-332   Willye White (USA-1956, LJ)
   16-343   Elizabeth Robinson (USA-1928, 100)
   17-020   Maureen Caird (AUS-1968, 80H)
   17-087   Mihaela Penes (ROM-1964, JT)
   17-116   Raelene Boyle (AUS-1968, 200)

Youngest Gold Medalist, Women
   15-124   Pearl Jones (USA-1952, 4x100R)
   16-123   Ulrike Meyfarth (FRG-1972, HJ)
   16-343   Elizabeth Robinson (USA-1928, 100)
   17-020   Maureen Caird (AUS-1968, 80H)
   17-087   Mihaela Penes (ROM-1964, JT)
   17-271   Margaret Bailes (USA-1968, 4x100R)
   18-021   Eva Kłobukowska (POL-1964, 4x100R)
   18-036   Babe Didrikson (USA-1932, JT)
   18-088   Miloslava Rezková (TCH-1968, HJ)

Oldest Known Competitor, Women
   46-284   Joyce Smith (GBR-1984, Mar)
   42-087   Binta Jambane (MOZ-1984, 200)
   40-137   Lia Manoliu (ROM-1972, DT)
   39-300   Olga Connolly (USA-1972, DT)
   39-256   Priscilla Welch (GBR-1984, Mar)
   39-256   Antonina Ivanova (URS-1972, SP)
   39-139   Gabriella Andersen-Schiess (SUI-1984, Mar)
   38-292   Ileana Silai (ROM-1980, 1500)
   38-232   Nelly Wright (BOL-1984, Mar)
   37-348   Dana Zátopková (TCH-1960, JT)

Oldest Medalist, Women
```
37-348  Dana Zátopková (TCH-1960, JT)
36-176  Lia Manoliu (ROM-1968, DT)
34-254  Ivanka Khristova (BUL-1976, SP)
34-096  Karin Balzer (GDR-1972, 80H)
34-014  Maricica Puica (ROM-1984, 1500)
34-013  Maricica Puica (ROM-1984, 3000)
33-272  Galina Zybina (URS-1964, SP)
33-241  Kaisa Parviainen (FIN-1948, JT)
33-205  Fita Lovin (ROM-1984, 800)
33-190  Herma Bauma (AUT-1948, JT)
33-060  Mary Peters (GBR-1972, Pent)
```

Oldest Gold Medalist, Women
```
36-176  Lia Manoliu (ROM-1968, DT)
34-254  Ivanka Khristova (BUL-1976, SP)
34-013  Maricica Puica (ROM-1984, 3000)
33-190  Herma Bauma (AUT-1948, JT)
33-060  Mary Peters (GBR-1972, Pent)
32-244  Ria Stalman (HOL-1984, DT)
31-308  Nadezhda Tkachenko (URS-1980, Pent)
31-137  Shirley Strickland de la Hunty (AUS-1956, 4x100R)
31-134  Shirley Strickland de la Hunty (AUS-1956, 80H
31-132  Nina Ponomareva (URS-1960, DT)
```

Youngest Known Competitor, Men
```
13-196  Jakab Kauser (HUN-1900, PV)
16-061  Farhad Navab (IRN-1972, 100)
16-110  Willem Kaan (HOL-1928, 110H)
16-248  Herbert Gidney (USA-1908, HJ)
16-278  Douglas Melin (SWE-1912, SLJ)
16-306  Manikavasagam Jegathesan (MAL-1960, 400)
16-318  Fermin Donazar (URU-1956, LJ)
16-329  Renato Dionisi (ITA-1964, PV)
16-351  Carlos Abhuzamann (NCA-1976, HJ)
16-363  Carlo Speroni (ITA-1912, Mar)
```

Youngest Medalist, Men
```
17-169  Frank Castleman (USA-1904, 200LH)
17-206  Pál Simon (HUN-1908, 1600MR)
17-229  Ture Persson (SWE-1912, 4x100R)
17-263  Bob Mathias (USA-1948, Deca)
17-287  Dwayne Evans (USA-1976, 200)
17-360  Lee Barnes (USA-1924, PV)
18-011  Michail Dorizas (GRE-1906, Stone Throw)
18-119  Johnny Jones (USA-1976, 4x100R)
18-141  Valeriy Brumel (URS-1960, HJ)
18-234  Donald Lippincott (USA-1912, 100)
```

Youngest Gold Medalist, Men
    17-263   Bob Mathias (USA-1948, Deca)
    17-360   Lee Barnes (USA-1924, PV)
    18-119   Johnny Jones (USA-1976, 4x100R)
    18-281   Frank Wykoff (USA-1928, 4x100R)
    18-337   Ugo Frigerio (ITA-1920, 10K Wk)
    19-018   Randy Williams (USA-1972, LJ)
    19-101   Edgar Ablowich (USA-1932, 4x100R)
    19-126   Harvey Glance (USA-1976, 4x100R)
    19-129   Reggie Walker (SAF-1908, 100)
    19-168   Ralph Rose (USA-1904, SP)

Oldest Known Competitor, Men
    52-199   Percival Wyer (CAN-1936, Mar)
    49-075   John Deni (USA-1952, 50W)
    48-218   Harold Whitlock (GBR-1952, 50W)
    48-195   Bohumil Honzatko (TCH-1924, Mar)
    48-115   Tebbs Lloyd Johnson (GBR-1948, 50W)
    48-088   Alexander Oakley (CAN-1976, 20W)
    47-127   Guillermo Weller (ARG-1960, 50W)
    46-352   Edgar Bruun (NOR-1952, 50W)
    46-111   František Janda-Suk (TCH-1924, DT)
    45-205   Matt McGrath (USA, 1924 HT)

Oldest Medalist, Men
    48-115   Tebbs Lloyd-Johnson (GBR-1948, 50K Wk)
    45-205   Matt McGrath (USA-1924, HT)
    42-035   Evgeniy Ivchenko (URS-1980, 50K Wk)
    42-024   Pat McDonald (USA-1920, 56Wt)
    40-364   John Ljunggren (SWE-1960, 50K Wk)
    40-215   James Mitchel (USA-1904, 56Wt)
    40-090   Mamo Wolde (ETH-1972, Mar)
    39-335   Arthur Schwab (SUI-1936, 50K Wk)
    39-195   Ernest Webb (GBR-1912, 3500 Wk)
    39-039   Ossian Skiöld (SWE-1928, HT)

Oldest Gold Medalist, Men
    42-024   Pat McDonald (USA-1920, 56Wt)
    38-234   John Mikaelsson (SWE-1952, 10K Wk)
    38-127   Thomas Green (GBR-1932, 50K Wk)
    37-176   Carlos Lopes (POR-1984, Mar)
    36-130   Mamo Wolde (ETH-1968, Mar)
    36-078   Miruts Yifter (ETH-1980, 5000)
    36-058   Verner Järvinen (FIN-1906, DTg)
    35-335   Alain Mimoun (FRA-1956, Mar)
    35-240   Ludvik Danek (TCH-1972, DT)
    35-187   John Flanagan (USA-1908, HT)

Medals Won By Countries

	G	S	B	T
United States	262	197	155	614
USSR	54	49	64	167
Great Britain	45	70	51	166
Finland	46	34	27	107
GDR	33	36	28	97
Sweden	16	25	44	85
FRG	15	23	24	62
Australia	16	16	22	54
France	10	20	19	49
Canada	11	14	19	44
Poland	15	15	11	41
Hungary	9	14	18	41
Italy	14	8	18	40
Germany	6	13	19	38
Greece	3	8	12	23
Czechoslovakia	8	9	5	22
Romania	8	7	7	22
Jamaica	4	8	7	19
New Zealand	8	1	8	17
Kenya	6	6	5	17
South Africa	5	5	5	15
Japan	4	5	6	15
Netherlands	5	3	6	14
Cuba	3	6	3	12
Norway	2	3	7	12
Ethiopia	5	1	4	10
Belgium	2	6	2	10
Bulgaria	1	5	4	10
Brazil	3	1	4	8
Switzerland	-	6	1	7
Ireland	4	1	-	5
Mexico	3	2	-	5
Argentina	2	3	-	5
Austria	1	1	3	5
Tunisia	1	2	1	4
Trinidad	1	1	2	4
Portugal	1	1	2	4
Morocco	2	1	-	3
Denmark	-	1	2	3
Tanzania	-	2	-	2
Yugoslavia	-	2	-	2
Chile	-	2	-	2

India	–	2	–	2
Spain	–	1	1	2
Latvia	–	1	1	2
Estonia	–	1	1	2
Chinese Taipei	–	1	1	2
Panama	–	–	2	2
Philippines	–	–	2	2
Uganda	1	–	–	1
Luxembourg	1	–	–	1
Sri Lanka	–	1	–	1
Haiti	–	1	–	1
Iceland	–	1	–	1
Ivory Coast	–	1	–	1
Venezuela	–	–	1	1
China	–	–	1	1
Turkey	–	–	1	1
Nigeria	–	–	1	1
Totals	636	643	627	1906

Medals Won by Countries, Men

	G	S	B	T
United States	236	178	145	559
Great Britain	40	51	39	130
Finland	46	32	27	105
USSR	29	31	36	96
Sweden	16	25	41	82
France	7	19	17	43
GDR	11	16	11	38
FRG	7	13	18	38
Hungary	6	13	16	35
Italy	11	4	16	31
Canada	9	9	13	31
Germany	3	10	14	27
Australia	6	9	11	26
Greece	3	8	12	23
Poland	9	7	4	20
Kenya	6	6	5	17
Jamaica	4	8	4	16
New Zealand	7	1	7	15
Czechoslovakia	5	7	3	15
Japan	4	4	6	14

South Africa	4	4	4	12
Norway	2	2	7	11
Ethiopia	5	1	4	10
Belgium	2	6	2	10
Brazil	3	1	4	8
Cuba	2	5	1	8
Switzerland	-	6	1	7
Netherlands	-	1	5	6
Ireland	4	1	-	5
Mexico	3	2	-	5
Argentina	2	2	-	4
Tunisia	1	2	1	4
Trinidad	1	1	2	4
Portugal	1	1	1	3
Morocco	1	1	-	2
Tanzania	-	2	-	2
Yugoslavia	-	2	-	2
India	-	2	-	2
Denmark	-	1	1	2
Spain	-	1	1	2
Latvia	-	1	1	2
Estonia	-	1	1	2
Panama	-	-	2	2
Philippines	-	-	2	2
Uganda	1	-	-	1
Luxembourg	1	-	-	1
Chile	-	1	-	1
Chinese Taipei	-	1	-	1
Sri Lanka	-	1	-	1
Haiti	-	1	-	1
Iceland	-	1	-	1
Ivory Coast	-	1	-	1
Bulgaria	-	-	1	1
Venezuela	-	-	1	1
China	-	-	1	1
Romania	-	-	1	1
Turkey	-	-	1	1
Nigeria	-	-	1	1
Totals	498	503	491	1492

*Two seconds/no third in 1896 high jump; no third in 1896 110 metre high hurdles; no third in 1900 team race; no third in 1904 team race; two thirds in 1906 high jump; three seconds/no third in 1906 standing high jump; no second/third in 1908 400 metres; three seconds/no third in 1908 high jump; two firsts and three thirds in 1908 pole vault; two seconds/no third in 1908 standing high jump; two seconds/no third in 1912 pole vault; no third in 1912 400 metre relay; two thirds in 1956 400 metres; two seconds/no thirds in 1980 pole vault; and two thirds in 1984 pole vault.

**Decathlon/pentathlon results in 1912 are recorded as they actually occurred, i.e. Decathlon - 1) Thorpe (USA), 2) Wieslander (SWE), 3) Lomberg (SWE); and Pentathlon - 1) Thorpe (USA), 2) Bie (NOR), 3) Donahue (USA).

Medals Won by Countries, Women

	G	S	B	T
USSR	25	18	28	71
GDR	22	20	17	59
United States	26	19	10	55
Great Britain	5	19	12	36
Australia	10	7	11	28
FRG	8	10	6	24
Romania	8	7	6	21
Poland	6	8	7	21
Canada	2	5	6	13
Germany	3	3	5	11
Italy	3	4	2	9
Bulgaria	1	5	3	9
Netherlands	5	2	1	8
Czechoslovakia	3	2	2	7
France	3	1	2	6
Hungary	3	1	2	6
Austria	1	1	3	5
Cuba	1	1	2	4
South Africa	1	1	1	3
Sweden	–	–	3	3
Jamaica	–	–	3	3
New Zealand	1	–	1	2
Finland	–	2	–	2
Morocco	1	–	–	1
Chile	–	1	–	1
Japan	–	1	–	1
Norway	–	1	–	1
Argentina	–	1	–	1
Portugal	–	–	1	1
Denmark	–	–	1	1
Chinese Taipei	–	–	1	1
Totals	138	140	136	414

*Two seconds/no third in 1956 high jump; two seconds/no third in 1960 high jump.

Best Performance at Each Olympics

	Men	Women	Overall
1896 –	United States	-----	-----
1900 –	United States	-----	-----
1904 –	United States	-----	-----
1906 –	United States	-----	-----
1908 –	United States	-----	-----
1912 –	United States	-----	-----
1920 –	United States	-----	-----
1924 –	United States	-----	-----
1928 –	United States	Canada	United States
1932 –	United States	United States	United States
1936 –	United States	Germany	United States
1948 –	United States	The Netherlands	United States
1952 –	United States	USSR	United States
1956 –	United States	Australia	United States
1960 –	United States	USSR	United States
1964 –	United States	USSR	United States
1968 –	United States	United States	United States
1972 –	United States	GDR	USSR
1976 –	United States	GDR	GDR
1980 –	USSR	USSR	USSR
1984 –	United States	United States	United States

Track & Field Athletics - Olympic Record Progressions - Men

     Following are the Olympic record progressions for the events on the current program. The marks must have been set under conditions which would currently qualify it for record consideration, the only exception to this being the early tracks which were often slightly oversized (from 500 metres up to 1/3 mile). Marks set in other circumstances are listed separately or so noted.

     Altitude assisted marks are noted in the affected events. In addition, a progression is provided which disregards the altitude-assisted marks, so that the reader can tell what the best "sea-level" performances have been. Automatic timing was present as early as 1932, but did not become official until 1972. Consequently, we have given the progression according to hand times through 1968, although we note the automatic time, where known, and, in addition, give a separate automatic record progression.

100 metres

12.2	h1		Francis Lane (USA)	1896
12.2	h2		Thomas Curtis (USA)	1896
11.8	h3		Thomas Burke (USA)	1896
11.4	h1		Arthur Duffey (USA)	1900
11.4	h2		Walter Tewksbury (USA)	1900
10.8	h3	=WR	Frank Jarvis (USA)	1900
10.8	s2	=WR	Walter Tewksbury (USA)	1900
10.8	h15		James Rector (USA)	1908
*10.8	s1		Reginald Walker (SAF)	1908
[10.8]	s3		James Rector (USA)	1908
[10.8]	1		Reginald Walker (SAF)	1908
[10.8]	h10		David Jacobs (GBR)	1912
10.6	h16	WR	Donald Lippincott (USA)	1912
10.6	q4		Harold Abrahams (GBR)	1924
10.6	s2		Harold Abrahams (GBR)	1924
10.6	1		Harold Abrahams (GBR)	1924
10.6	q4		Percy Williams (CAN)	1928
10.6	s1		Robert McAllister (USA)	1928
10.6	s1		Percy Williams (CAN)	1928
10.6	s2		Jack London (GBR)	1928

10.6	10.67	h3	Arthur Jonath (GER)	1932
10.4	10.53	q1	Eddie Tolan (USA)	1932
10.3	10.38	1	=WR Eddie Tolan (USA)	1932
10.3	10.38	2	=WR Ralph Metcalfe (USA)	1932
10.3		h1	Jesse Owens (USA)	1936
[10.2w]		q2	Jesse Owens (USA)	1936
10.3		1	Harrison Dillard (USA)	1948
10.3	10.56	q1	Bobby Joe Morrow (USA)	1956
10.3	10.56	q2	Ira Murchison (USA)	1956
10.3	10.52	s2	Bobby Joe Morrow (USA)	1956
10.2	10.32	q2	Armin Hary (FRG)	1960
10.2	10.32	1	Armin Hary (FRG)	1960
10.2	10.35	2	Dave Sime (USA)	1960
[9.9w]	{9.91w}	s1	Bob Hayes (USA)	1964
10.0	10.05	1	=WR Bob Hayes (USA)	1964
[10.0A]	{10.10A}	q2	Hermes Ramirez (CUB)	1968
[10.0A]	{10.02A}	q4	Charlie Greene (USA)	1968
[10.0A]	{10.08A}	s1	Jim Hines (USA)	1968
[9.9A]	{9.95A}	1	=WR Jim Hines (USA)	1968
9.99	9.99	1	Carl Lewis (USA)	1984

*Actual time was 10.7, rounded up to the nearest fifth, in accordance with rules in force at that time.

Automatic Record Progression

10.67	h3	Arthur Jonath (GER)	1932
10.53	q1	Eddie Tolan (USA)	1932
10.38	1	WRa Eddie Tolan (USA)	1932
10.38	2	Ralph Metcalfe (USA)	1932
10.32	q2	Armin Hary (FRG)	1960
10.32	1	Armin Hary (FRG)	1960
10.05	1	WRa Bob Hayes (USA)	1964
[9.95A]	1	WRa Jim Hines (USA)	1968
9.99	1	Carl Lewis (USA)	1984

200 metres

24.0*		h1		William Holland (USA)	1900
22.2*		1		Walter Tewksbury (USA)	1900
22.2+		h1		Archie Hahn (USA)	1904
21.6+		1		Archie Hahn (USA)	1904
21.6*		1		Jackson Scholz (USA)	1924
21.6		q6		Helmut Körnig(GER)	1928
21.5		q1		Ralph Metcalfe (USA)	1932
21.5	21.56	q2		Eddie Tolan (USA)	1932
21.5	21.46	q3		Carlos Bianchi Luti (ARG)	1932
21.4		q4		Arthur Jonath (GER)	1932
21.2	21.12	1		Eddie Tolan (USA)	1932
21.1		h3		Jesse Owens (USA)	1936
[21.1w]		q3		Jesse Owens (USA)	1936
20.7		1		Jesse Owens (USA)	1936
20.7	20.81	1		Andy Stanfield (USA)	1952
20.6	20.75	1		Bobby Joe Morrow (USA)	1956
20.5	20.65	s2	=WR	Livio Berruti (ITA)	1960
20.5	20.62	1	=WR	Livio Berruti (ITA)	1960
20.5	20.58	s1		Paul Drayton (USA)	1964
20.3	20.36	1		Henry Carr (USA)	1964
[20.3A]		h2		Tommie Smith (USA)	1968
[20.2A]	{20.23A}	h6		Peter Norman (AUS)	1968
[20.2A]	{20.29A}	q3		Tommie Smith (USA)	1968
[20.1A]	{20.12A}	s1		John Carlos (USA)	1968
[20.1A]	{20.13A}	s2		Tommie Smith (USA)	1968
[19.8A]	{19.83A}	1	WR	Tommie Smith (USA)	1968
20.30		q1		Valeriy Borzov (URS)	1972
20.28		q4		Larry Black (USA)	1972
20.00		1		Valeriy Borzov (URS)	1972
19.80		1		Carl Lewis (USA)	1984

*Track 500 metres in circumference.
+Straight course.

Automatic Record Progression

21.83	h2		William Walters (SAF)	1932
21.59	q1		Ralph Metcalfe (USA)	1932
21.56	q2		Eddie Tolan (USA)	1932
21.46	q3		Carlos Bianchi Luti (ARG)	1932
21.12	1	WRa	Eddie Tolan (USA)	1932
20.81	1	WRa	Andy Stanfield (USA)	1952
20.75	1	WRa	Bobby Joe Morrow (USA)	1956
20.65	s2	WRa	Livio Berruti (ITA)	1960
20.62	1	WRa	Livio Berruti (ITA)	1960
20.58	s1	WRa	Paul Drayton (USA)	1964
20.36	1	WRa	Henry Carr (USA)	1964
[20.23A]	h6	WRa	Peter Norman (AUS)	1968
[20.12A]	s1	WRa	John Carlos (USA)	1968
[19.83A]	1	WRa	Tommie Smith (USA)	1968
20.30	q1		Valeriy Borzov (URS)	1972
20.00	1		Valeriy Borzov (URS)	1972
19.80	1		Carl Lewis (USA)	1968

400 metres

56.8		h1		Herbert Jamison (USA)	1896
54.2		1		Tom Burke (USA)	1896
50.4*		h1		Maxie Long (USA)	1900
49.4*		1		Maxie Long (USA)	1900
49.2+		1		Harry Hillman (USA)	1904
48.4+		q2		Wyndham Halswelle (GBR)	1908
48.2		1		Charles Reidpath (USA)	1912
48.0*		q6		Joseph Imbach (SUI)	1924
47.8*		s1		Horacio Fitch (USA)	1924
47.6*		1		Eric Liddell (GBR)	1924
47.2	47.25	s1		William Carr (USA)	1932
46.2	46.28	1	WR	William Carr (USA)	1932
46.2		1		Arthur Wint (JAM)	1948
45.9	46.09	1		George Rhoden (JAM)	1952
45.9	46.20	2		Herb McKenley (JAM)	1952
45.9	46.02	q4		Otis Davis (USA)	1960
45.5	45.62	s1		Otis Davis (USA)	1960
44.9	45.07	1	WR	Otis Davis (USA)	1960
44.9	45.08	2	=WR	Carl Kauffman (USA)	1960
[44.8A]	{44.82A}	s2		Lee Evans (USA)	1968
[43.8A]	{43.86A}	1	WR	Lee Evans (USA)	1968
44.66		1		Vince Matthews (USA)	1972
44.26		1		Alberto Juantorena (CUB)	1976

*Track 500 metres in circumference.
+Track 536.45 metres (1/3 mile) in circumference.

Automatic Record Progression

49.02	h2		Ben Eastman (USA)	1932
48.70	h4		William Carr (USA)	1932
48.31	q1		Ben Eastman (USA)	1932
47.25	s1		William Carr (USA)	1932
46.28	1		William Carr (USA)	1932
46.09	1		George Rhoden (JAM)	1952
46.02	q4		Otis Davis (USA)	1960
45.62	s1		Otis Davis (USA)	1960
45.07	1	WRa	Otis Davis (USA)	1960
[44.82A]	s2		Lee Evans (USA)	1968
[43.86A]	1	WRa	Lee Evans (USA)	1968
44.92	s1		Vince Matthews (USA)	1972
44.66	1		Vince Matthews (USA)	1972
44.26	1		Alberto Juantorena (CUB)	1976

800 metres

2:10.0		h1		Edwin Flack (AUS)	1896
1:59.0#		h1		David Hall (USA)	1900
1:56.0*		1		James Lightbody (USA)	1904
1:52.8*		1	WR	Mel Sheppard (USA)	1908
1:51.9		1	WR	Ted Meredith (USA)	1912
1:51.8		1		Douglas Lowe (GBR)	1928
1:49.8+	1:49.70	1	WR	Thomas Hampson (GBR)	1932
1:49.2		1		Mal Whitfield (USA)	1948
1:49.2	1:49.34	1		Mal Whitfield (USA)	1952
1:47.7	1:47.75	1		Tom Courtney (USA)	1956
1:47.1	1:47.26	s1		George Kerr (JAM)	1960
1:46.3	1:46.48	1		Peter Snell (NZL)	1960
1:46.1		s2 <1>		George Kerr (JAM)	1964
1:46.1		s2 <2>		Wilson Kiprugut (KEN)	1964
1:45.1		1		Peter Snell (NZL)	1964
1:44.3	1:44.40	1	WR	Ralph Doubell (AUS)	1968
1:43.50		1	WR	Alberto Juantorena (CUB)	1976
1:43.00		1		Joaquim Cruz (BRA)	1984

#Track 500 metres in circumference.
*Track 536.45 metres (1/3 mile) in circumference.
+Hand time was 1:49.7, rounded up to the nearest fifth, in
  accordance with rules in force at that time.

1,500 metres

4:33.2		1		Edwin Flack (AUS)	1896
4:06.2#		1	WR	Charles Bennett (GBR)	1900
4:05.4*		1	WR	James Lightbody (USA)	1904
4:05.0*		h2		Mel Sheppard (USA)	1908
4:03.4*		h3		Norman Hallows (GBR)	1908
4:03.4*		1		Mel Sheppard (GBR)	1908
3:56.8		1		Arnold Jackson (GBR)	1912
3:53.6		1		Paavo Nurmi (FIN)	1924
3:53.2		1		Harry Larva (FIN)	1928
3:51.2	3:51.20	1		Luigi Beccali (ITA)	1932
3:47.8		1	WR	Jack Lovelock (NZL)	1936
3:45.2+	3:45.28	1		Joseph Barthel (LUX)	1952
3:45.2	[3:45.39]	2		Bob McMillen (USA)	1952
3:41.2	3:41.49	1		Ron Delany (IRL)	1956
3:35.6		1	WR	Herb Elliott (AUS)	1960
3:34.9	3:34.91	1		Kipchoge Keino (KEN)	1968
3:32.53		1		Sebastian Coe (GBR)	1984

#Track 500 metres in circumference.
*Track 536.45 metres (1/3 mile) in circumference.
+Hand time 3:45.1, rounded up to the nearest fifth, in accordance
  with rules in force at that time.

5,000 metres

15:20.0*+		1	Charles Bennett (GBR)	1900
15:05.0		h5	Jean Bouin (FRA)	1912
14:36.6		1 WR	Hannes Kolehmainen (FIN)	1912
14:31.2+		1	Paavo Nurmi (FIN)	1924
14:30.0		1	Lauri Lehtinen (FIN)	1932
14:30.0		2	Ralph Hill (USA)	1932
14:22.2		1	Gunnar Höckert (FIN)	1936
14:17.6		1	Gaston Reiff (BEL)	1948
14:15.4		h2	Herbert Schade (FRG)	1952
14:06.6	14:06.72	1	Emil Zátopek (TCH)	1952
13:39.6	13:39.86	1	Vladimir Kuts (URS)	1956
13:31.8	13:31.65	h2	Emile Puttemans (BEL)	1972
13:26.4	13:36.42	1	Lasse Virén (FIN)	1972
13:20.34		h3	Brendan Foster (GBR)	1976
13:05.59		1	Said Aouita (MAR)	1984

*Winning time in team race.
+Track 500 metres in circumference.

10,000 metres

33:49.0		h1	Hannes Kolehmainen (FIN)	1912
32:30.8		h2	Len Richardson (SAF)	1912
31:20.8		1	Hannes Kolehmainen (FIN)	1912
30:23.2*		1 WR	Ville Ritola (FIN)	1924
30:18.8		1	Paavo Nurmi (FIN)	1928
30:11.4		1	Janusz Kusociński (POL)	1932
29:59.6		1	Emil Zátopek (TCH)	1948
29:17.0		1	Emil Zátopek (TCH)	1952
28:45.6	28:45.60	1	Vladimir Kuts (URS)	1956
28:32.2	28:32.18	1	Petr Bolotnikov (URS)	1960
28:24.4		1	Billy Mills (USA)	1964
27:53.4	27:53.28	h1	Emile Puttemans (BEL)	1972
27:38.4	27:38.34	1 WR	Lasse Virén (FIN)	1972

*Track 500 metres in circumference.

Marathon (42,385 metres)

[2-58:50]*	1		Spiridon Loues (GRE)	1896
<2-51:23.6>^	1		William Sherring (CAN)	1906
2-55:18.4+	1		John Hayes (USA)	1908
[2-36:54.8]&	1		Kenneth McArthur (SAF)	1912
2-32:35.8#	1	WR	Hannes Kolehmainen (FIN)	1920
2-31:36.0	1		Juan Carlos Zabala (ARG)	1932
2-29:19.2	1		Kee-Chung Sohn (KOR)@	1936
2-23:03.2	1		Emil Zátopek (TCH)	1952
2-15:16.2	1		Abebe Bikila (ETH)	1960
2-12:11.2	1	WR	Abebe Bikila (ETH)	1964
2-09:55.0	1		Waldemar Cierpinski (GDR)	1976
2-09:21.0	1		Carlos Lopes (POR)	1984

*Distance 40.0 km.
^Distance 41.86 km.
+Dorando Pietri (ITA) finished first in 2-54:46.4 but was
 disqualified for having been assisted near the finish line.
&Distance 40.2 km.
#Distance 42.75 km.
@This is the correct name and affiliation. He is usually listed
 as Kitei Son (JPN), as Korea was annexed to Japan at the time.

3,000 metre steeplechase

10:56.2*		h1	Arthur Russell (GBR)	1908
10:47.8*		1	Arthur Russell (GBR)	1908
10:23.0		h1	Michael Devaney (USA)	1920
10:17.4		h3	Percy Hodge (GBR)	1920
10:00.4		1	Percy Hodge (GBR)	1920
9:43.8+		h1	Elias Katz (FIN)	1924
9:33.6+		1	Ville Ritola (FIN)	1924
9:21.8		1	Toivo Loukola (FIN)	1928
9:18.8		h1	Tom Evenson (GBR)	1932
9:14.6#		h2	Volmari Iso-Hollo (FIN)	1932
9:03.8		1	Volmari Iso-Hollo (FIN)	1936
8:58.0	8:58.17	h1	Vladimir Kazantsev (URS)	1952
8:51.0	8:51.18	h3	Horace Ashenfelter (USA)	1952
8:45.4	8:45.68	1 WR	Horace Ashenfelter (USA)	1952
8:41.2	8:41.35	1	Chris Brasher (GBR)	1956
8:34.2	8:34.31	1	Zdzisław Krzyszkowiak (POL)	1960
8:33.0		h2	Maurice Herriott (GBR)	1964
8:31.8		h3	Adolfas Alekseyunas (URS)	1964
8:30.8		1	Gaston Roelants (BEL)	1964
8:24.8	8:24.78	h1	Tapio Kantanen (FIN)	1972
8:23.8	8:23.73	h4	Amos Biwott (KEN)	1972
8:23.6	8:23.64	1	Kipchoge Keino (KEN)	1972
8:18.6	8:18.56	h1	Bronisław Malinowski (POL)	1976
8:08.0	8:08.02	1 WR	Anders Gärderud (SWE)	1976

*3,200 metres. Equivalent times are 10:16.0 (heat) and 10:08.0
 (final)
+Track 500 metres in circumference.
#Final was one lap too long. 3,000 metre equivalent for the final
 was 9:10.0

110 metre high hurdles

18.4		h1		Grantley Goulding (GBR)	1896
18.0		h2		Thomas Curtis (USA)	1896
17.6		1		Thomas Curtis (USA)	1896
15.6		h1		Alvin Kraenzlein (USA)	1900
15.4		1		Alvin Kraenzlein (USA)	1900
15.4		s2		Forrest Smithson (USA)	1908
15.0		1	WR	Forrest Smithson (USA)	1908
15.0		s1		Harold Barron (USA)	1920
15.0		s2		Earl Thomson (CAN)	1920
14.8		1	WR	Earl Thomson (CAN)	1920
14.8		h3		George Weightman-Smith (SAF)	1928
14.8		s1		Leighton Dye (USA)	1928
14.8		s2		Steve Anderson (USA)	1928
14.6		s3	WR	George Weightman-Smith (SAF)	1928
14.5		s1		Jack Keller (USA)	1932
14.4		s2	=WR	George Saling (USA)	1932
14.1		s1	=WR	Forrest Towns (USA)	1936
14.1		s2		William Porter (USA)	1948
13.9		1		William Porter (USA)	1948
13.9	14.01	h1		Harrison Dillard (USA)	1952
13.7	13.91	1		Harrison Dillard (USA)	1952
13.7	[14.00]	2		Jack Davis (USA)	1952
13.5	13.70	1		Lee Calhoun (USA)	1956
13.5	[13.73]	2		Jack Davis (USA)	1956
[13.5A]	{13.61A}	h3		Eddy Ottoz (ITA)	1968
[13.3A]	{13.38A}	s1		Erv Hall (USA)	1968
[13.3A]	{13.33A}	1		Willie Davenport (USA)	1968
13.47		s1		Tom Hill (USA)	1972
13.44		s2		Rod Milburn (USA)	1972
13.24		1	WR	Rod Milburn (USA)	1972
13.24		h4		Greg Foster (USA)	1984
13.24		s1		Roger Kingdom (USA)	1984
13.24		s2		Greg Foster (USA)	1984
13.20		1		Roger Kingdom (USA)	1984

Automatic Record Progression

14.80	h1		Percy Beard (USA)	1932
14.63	s1		Jack Keller (USA)	1932
14.55	s2	WRa	George Saling (USA)	1932
14.01	h1		Harrison Dillard (USA)	1952
13.91	1		Harrison Dillard (USA)	1952
13.70	1	WRa	Lee Calhoun (USA)	1956
13.67	1	WRa	Hayes Jones (USA)	1964
[13.65A]	h2		Willie Davenport (USA)	1968
[13.61A]	h3		Eddy Ottoz (ITA)	1968
[13.38A]	s1	WRa	Erv Hall (USA)	1968
[13.33A]	1	WRa	Willie Davenport (USA)	1968
13.47	s1		Tom Hill (USA)	1972
13.44	s2		Rod Milburn (USA)	1972
13.24	1	WRa	Rod Milburn (USA)	1972
13.24	h4		Greg Foster (USA)	1984
13.24	s1		Roger Kingdom (USA)	1984
13.24	s2		Greg Foster (USA)	1984
13.20	1		Roger Kingdom (USA)	1984

400 metre intermediate hurdles

61.2		h1		Walter Tewksbury (USA)	1900
60.2		h2		George Orton (CAN)	1900
60.2		h2<2>		Henri Tauzin (FRA)	1900
57.6		1		Walter Tewksbury (USA)	1900
57.0*		h3	WR	Charles Bacon (USA)	1908
56.4		s1	WR	Harry Hillman (USA)	1908
55.0		1	WR	Charles Bacon (USA)	1908
54.0		1	WR	Frank Loomis (USA)	1920
52.6+#		1		Morgan Taylor (USA)	1924
[53.8]#		2		Erik Wilén (FIN)	1924
[53.4]		s1		Morgan Taylor (USA)	1928
[53.4]		1		Lord Burghley (GBR)	1928
[52.8]		s1		Glenn Hardin (USA)	1932
[52.8]		s2		Robert Tisdall (IRL)	1932
51.8+@	51.67	1		Robert Tisdall (IRL)	1932
[52.0]	[51.85]	2	WR	Glenn Hardin (USA)	1932
[51.9]		s1		Rune Larsson (SWE)	1948
[51.9]		s2		Roy Cochran (USA)	1948
51.1		1		Roy Cochran (USA)	1948

50.8	50.98	q1		Charles Moore (USA)	1952
50.8	[51.06]	1		Charles Moore (USA)	1952
50.1	50.26	s1		Eddie Southern (USA)	1956
50.1	[50.29]	1		Glenn Davis (USA)	1956
49.3	49.51	1		Glenn Davis (USA)	1960
[49.0A]	{49.05A}	h3		Ron Whitney (USA)	1968
[48.1A]	{48.12A}	1	WR	David Hemery (GBR)	1968
49.25		s1		John Akii-Bua (UGA)	1972
47.82		1	WR	John Akii-Bua (UGA)	1972
47.63|		1	WR	Edwin Moses (USA)	1976

*In 1904, Harry Hillman (USA) ran 53.0 but the hurdles were only
2' 6" high.
+Neither Taylor's nor Tisdall's record could be accepted as they
knocked over a hurdle, which was against the rules in force at
that time. The records following their marks are those given
official credit if one does not allow the Taylor/Tisdall marks.
#Track 500 metres in circumference.
@Hand time was 51.7, rounded up to the nearest fifth, in
accordance with rules in force at that time.
|Officially 47.64 but photo re-read by ATFS President, Bob Sparks.

Automatic Record Progression

55.65		h1		F. Morgan Taylor (USA)	1932
54.63		h2		Robert Tisdall (IRL)	1932
54.06		h3		Joseph Healey (USA)	1932
52.79		s1		Glenn Hardin (USA)	1932
52.60		s2		Robert Tisdall (IRL)	1932
51.67*		1		Robert Tisdall (IRL)	1932
[51.85]		2	WRa	Glenn Hardin (USA)	1932
50.98		q1	WRa	Charles Moore (USA)	1952
50.26		s1		Eddie Southern (USA)	1956
49.51		1	WRa	Glenn Davis (USA)	1960
[49.05A]		h3		Ron Whitney (USA)	1968
[48.12A]		1	WRa	David Hemery (GBR)	1968
49.25		s1		John Akii-Bua (UGA)	1972
47.82		1	WRa	John Akii-Bua (UGA)	1972
47.63|		1	WRa	Edwin Moses (USA)	1976

*Tisdall's record could not be accepted as he knocked over a
hurdle, which was against the rules in force at that time.
Hardin's mark is the mark given official credit if one does not
allow Tisdall's mark.
|Officially 47.64 but photo re-read by ATFS President, Bob Sparks.

20 kilometre walk

1-31:28		1		Leonid Spirin (URS)	1956
1-29:34		1		Ken Matthews (GBR)	1964
1-26:43	1-26:42.4	1		Peter Frenkel (GDR)	1972
1-24:41	1-24:40.6	1	WR	Daniel Bautista (MEX)	1976
1-23:36	1-23:35.5	1		Maurizio Damilano (ITA)	1980
1-23:13		1		Ernesto Canto (MEX)	1984

```
50 kilometre walk
    4-50:10              1      Thomas Green (GBR)          1932
    4-30:42   4-30:41.1  1      Harold Whitlock (GBR)       1936
    4-28:08   4-28:07.8  1      Giuseppe Dordoni (ITA)      1952
    4-25:30              1      Donald Thompson (GBR)       1960
    4-11:13   4-11:12.4  1      Abdon Pamich (ITA)          1964
    3-56:12   3-56:11.57 1      Bernd Kannenberg (FRG)      1972
    3-49:24   3-49:23.40 1      Hartwig Gauder (GDR)        1980
    3-47:26              1      Raul Gonzalez (MEX)         1984


4 x 100 metre relay
    46.2                 h1        Canada                        1912
                                   (McConnell, Lukeman, Beasley, Howard)
    43.7                 h2  WR    United States                 1912
                                   (Courtney, Belote, Wilson, Cooke)
    43.6                 h3  WR    Sweden                        1912
                                   (Möller, Luther, Persson, Lindberg)
    43.6                 h5  =WR   Germany                       1912
                                   (Röhr, Herrmann, Kern, Rau)
    43.0                 s1  WR    Great Britain/North. Ireland  1912
                                   (Applegarth, Jacobs, MacIntosh, D'Arcy)
    42.5                 s2  WR    Sweden                        1912
                                   (Möller, Luther, Persson, Lindberg)
    42.3                 s3  WR    Germany                       1912
                                   (Röhr, Herrmann, Kern, Rau)
    42.2                 1   WR    United States                 1920
                                   (Paddock, Scholz, Murchison, Kirksey)
    42.0*                h1  WR    Great Britain/North. Ireland  1924
                                   (Abrahams, Rangeley, Royle, Nichol)
    42.0*                h2  =WR   The Netherlands               1924
                                   (Boot, Broos, de Vries, van den Berghe)
    41.2*                h6  WR    United States                 1924
                                   (Hussey, Clarke, Murchison, LeConey)
    41.0*                s1  WR    United States                 1924
                                   (Hussey, Clarke, Murchison, LeConey)
    41.0*                1   =WR   United States                 1924
                                   (Hussey, Clarke, Murchison, LeConey)
    41.0                 1   =WR   United States                 1928
                                   (Wykoff, Quinn, Borah, Russell)
    40.6                 h2  WR    United States                 1932
                                   (Kiesel, Toppino, Dyer, Wykoff)
    40.0                 1   WR    United States                 1932
                                   (Kiesel, Toppino, Dyer, Wykoff)
    40.0                 h1  =WR   United States                 1936
                                   (Owens, Metcalfe, Draper, Wykoff)
    39.8                 1   WR    United States                 1936
                                   (Owens, Metcalfe, Draper, Wykoff)
    39.5     39.59       1   WR    United States                 1956
                                   (Murchison, King, Baker, Morrow)
    39.5     [39.61]     h3  =WR   German Federal Republic       1960
                                   (Cullman, Hary, Mahlendorf, Lauer)
```

```
39.5+    [39.66]    1   =WR German Federal Republic     1960
                         (Cullman, Hary, Mahlendorf, Lauer)
39.5      39.50     s1       United States              1964
                         (Drayton, Ashworth, Stebbins, Hayes)
39.0      39.06     1    WR  United States              1964
                         (Drayton, Ashworth, Stebbins, Hayes)
[38.7A]  {38.76A}   h1       Cuba                       1968
                         (Ramirez, Morales, Montes, Figuerola)
[38.6A]  {38.65A}   h2  =WR Jamaica                     1968
                         (Stewart, Fray, Forbes, Miller)
[38.3A]  {38.39A}   s1  WR  Jamaica                     1968
                         (Stewart, Fray, Forbes, Miller)
[39.2A]  {38.24A}   1   WR  United States              1968
                         (Greene, Pender, Smith, Hines)
38.19               1   WR  United States              1972
                         (Black, Taylor, Tinker, Hart)
37.83               1   WR  United States              1984
                         (Graddy, Brown, Smith, Lewis)
```

*Track 500 metres in circumference.

Automatic Record Progression
```
41.22               h1       Germany                    1932
                         (Köring, Jonath, Hendrix, Borchmeyer)
40.61               h2       United States              1932
                         (Toppino, Kiesel, Dyer, Wykoff)
40.10               1   WRa United States              1932
                         (Toppino, Kiesel, Dyer, Wykoff)
39.59               1   WRa United States              1956
                         (Murchison, King, Baker, Morrow)
39.50               s1       United States              1964
                         (Drayton, Ashworth, Stebbins, Hayes)
39.06               1   WRa United States              1964
                         (Drayton, Ashworth, Stebbins, Hayes)
[38.76A]            h1       Cuba                       1968
                         (Ramirez, Morales, Montes, Figuerola)
[38.65A]            h2  WRa Jamaica                     1968
                         (Stewart, Fray, Forbes, Miller)
[38.39A]            s1  WRa Jamaica                     1968
                         (Stewart, Fray, Forbes, Miller)
[38.24A]            1   WRa United States              1968
                         (Greene, Pender, Smith, Hines)
38.54               s1       United States              1972
                         (Black, Taylor, Tinker, Hart)
38.19               1   WRa United States              1972
                         (Black, Taylor, Tinker, Hart)
37.83               1   WRa United States              1984
                         (Graddy, Brown, Smith, Lewis)
```

4 x 400 metre relay

3:19.0		h1		Great Britain/North. Ireland	1912
				(Seedhouse, Soutter, Henley, Nicol)	
3:16.6		1	WR	United States	1912
				(Sheppard, Lindberg, Meredith, Reidpath)	
3:16.0*		1	WR	United States	1924
				(Cochran, Stevenson, MacDonald, Helffrich)	
3:14.2		1	WR	United States	1928
				(Baird, Spencer, Alderman, Barbuti)	
3:11.8		s1	WR	United States	1932
				(Fuqua, Ablowich, Warner, Carr)	
3:08.2		1	WR	United States	1932
				(Fuqua, Ablowich, Warner, Carr)	
3:03.9	3:04.04	1		Jamaica	1952
				(Wint, Laing, McKenley, Rhoden)	
3:02.2	3:02.37	1	WR	United States	1960
				(Yerman, Young, Davis, Davis)	
3:00.7		1	WR	United States	1964
				(Cassell, Larrabee, Williams, Carr)	
[3:00.7A]	{3:00.71A}	h1	=WR	United States	1968
				(Matthews, Freeman, James, Evans)	
[2:56.1A]	{2:56.16A}	1	WR	United States	1968
				(Matthews, Freeman, James, Evans)	
2:59.83		1		Keny	1972
				(Asati, Nyamau, Ouko, Sang)	
2:59.52		s1		United States	1976
				(Frazier, Brown, Newhouse, Parks)	
2:58.66		1		United States	1976
				(Frazier, Brown, Newhouse, Parks)	
2:57.91		1		United States	1984
				(Nix, Armstead, Babers, McKay)	

*Track 500 metres in circumference.

Automatic Record Progression

3:04.04	1		Jamaica	1952
			(Wint, Laing, McKenley, Rhoden)	
3:02.37	1	WRa	United States	1960
			(Yerman, Young, Davis, Davis)	
[3:00.71A]	h1	WRa	United States	1968
			(Matthews, Freeman, James, Evans)	
[2:56.16A]	1	WRa	United States	1968
			(Matthews, Freeman, James, Evans)	
2:59.83	1		Kenya	1972
			(Asati, Nyamau, Ouko, Sang)	
2:59.52	s1		United States	1976
			(Frazier, Brown, Newhouse, Parks)	
2:58.66	1		United States	1976
			(Frazier, Brown, Newhouse, Parks)	
2:57.91	1		United States	1984
			(Nix, Armstead, Babers, McKay)	

High Jump

1.81	[5-11 1/4]	1	Ellery Clark (USA)	1896
1.85	[6-0 3/4]	-	Irving Baxter (USA)	1900
1.90	[6-2 3/4]	1	Irving Baxter (USA)	1900
1.905	[6-3]	1	Harry Porter (USA)	1908
1.91	[6-3 1/4]	2	Hans Liesche (GER)	1912
1.91	[6-3 1/4]	-	Alma Richards (USA)	1912
1.93	[6-4]	1	Alma Richards (USA)	1912
1.94	[6-4 1/4]	1	Richmond Landon (USA)	1920
1.95	[6-4 3/4]	-	Harold Osborn (USA)	1924
1.95	[6-4 3/4]	2	Leroy Brown (USA)	1924
1.98	[6-6]	1	Harold Osborn (USA)	1924
2.00	[6-6 3/4]	-	Cornelius Johnson (USA)	1936
2.00	[6-6 3/4]	3	Delos Thurber (USA)	1936
2.00	[6-6 3/4]	2	Dave Albritton (USA)	1936
2.00	[6-6 3/4]	4	Kalevi Kotkas (FIN)	1936
2.03	[6-8]	1	Cornelius Johnson (USA)	1936
2.04	[6-8 1/4]	1	Walter Davis (USA)	1952
2.06	[6-9]	-	Charles Dumas (USA)	1956
2.06	[6-9]	-	Charles Porter (AUS)	1956
2.06	[6-9]	-	Igor Kashkarov (URS)	1956
2.06	[6-9]	4	Stig Pettersson (SWE)	1956
2.08	[6-9 3/4]	-	Charles Dumas (USA)	1956
2.08	[6-9 3/4]	-	Charles Porter (AUS)	1956
2.08	[6-9 3/4]	3	Igor Kashkarov (URS)	1956
2.10	[6-10 1/4]	-	Charles Dumas (USA)	1956
2.10	[6-10 1/4]	2	Charles Porter (AUS)	1956
2.12	[6-11 1/2]	1	Charles Dumas (USA)	1956
2.12	[6-11 1/2]	-	Valeriy Brumel (URS)	1960
2.12	[6-11 1/2]	-	Viktor Bolshov (URS)	1960
2.12	[6-11 1/2]	-	Robert Shavlakadze (URS)	1960
2.14	[7-0 1/4]	-	Valeriy Brumel (URS)	1960
2.14	[7-0 1/4]	4	Viktor Bolshov (URS)	1960
2.14	[7-0 1/4]	-	Robert Shavlakadze (URS)	1960
2.14	[7-0 1/4]	3	John Thomas (USA)	1960
2.16	[7-1]	1	Robert Shavlakadze (URS)	1960
2.16	[7-1]	2	Valeriy Brumel (URS)	1960
2.16	[7-1]	-	Valeriy Brumel (URS)	1964
2.16	[7-1]	-	John Thomas (USA)	1964
2.16	[7-1]	3	John Rambo (USA)	1964
2.18	[7-1 3/4]	1	Valeriy Brumel (URS)	1964
2.18	[7-1 3/4]	2	John Thomas (USA)	1964

2.18	[7-1 3/4]	–		Dick Fosbury (USA)	1968
2.18	[7-1 3/4]	–		Ed Caruthers (USA)	1968
2.20	[7-2 1/2]	–		Dick Fosbury (USA)	1968
2.20	[7-2 1/2]	3		Valentin Gavrilov (URS)	1968
2.20	[7-2 1/2]	–		Ed Caruthers (USA)	1968
2.22	[7-3 1/4]	–		Dick Fosbury (USA)	1968
2.22	[7-3 1/4]	2		Ed Caruthers (USA)	1968
2.24	[7-4 1/4]	1		Dick Fosbury (USA)	1968
2.25	[7-4 1/2]	1		Jacek Wszoła (POL)	1976
2.27	[7-5 1/4]	–		Gerd Wessig (GDR)	1980
2.27	[7-5 1/4]	–		Jacek Wszoła (POL)	1980
2.27	[7-5 1/4]	–		Henry Lauterbach (GDR)	1980
2.27	[7-5 1/4]	–		Jörg Freimuth (GDR)	1980
2.29	[7-6]	–		Jörg Freimuth (GDR)	1980
2.29	[7-6]	–		Jacek Wszoła (POL)	1980
2.29	[7-6]	4		Henry Lauterbach (GDR)	1980
2.29	[7-6]	–		Gerd Wessig (GDR)	1980
2.31	[7-7]	–		Gerd Wessig (GDR)	1980
2.31	[7-7]	3		Jörg Freimuth (GDR)	1980
2.31	[7-7]	2		Jacek Wszoła (POL)	1980
2.33	[7-7 3/4]	–	WR	Gerd Wessig (GDR)	1980
2.36	[7-8 3/4]	1		Gerd Wessig (GDR)	1980

Pole Vault

3.30	[10-10]	1	William Hoyt (USA)	1896
3.30	[10-10]	1	Irving Baxter (USA)	1900
[3.35]	10-11 3/4	5	Claude Allen (USA)	1904
[3.35]	10-11 3/4	4	Ward McLanahan (USA)	1904
[3.35]	10-11 3/4	–	Louis Wilkins (USA)	1904
[3.35]	10-11 3/4	–	LeRoy Samse (USA)	1904
[3.35]	10-11 3/4	–	Charles Dvorak (USA)	1904
[3.43]	11-3	3	Louis Wilkins (USA)	1904
[3.43]	11-3	2	Charles Dvorak (USA)	1904
[3.43]	11-3	–	Charles Dvorak (USA)	1904
[3.50]	11-5 3/4	1	Charles Dvorak (USA)	1904
3.50	[11-5 3/4]	1	Fernand Gonder (FRA)	1906
3.50	[11-5 3/4]	6=	Samuel Bellah (USA)	1908
3.50	[11-5 3/4]	6=	Giorgios Banikas (GRE)	1908
3.50	[11-5 3/4]	–	Bruno Söderström (SWE)	1908
3.50	[11-5 3/4]	–	Charles Jacobs (USA)	1908
3.50	[11-5 3/4]	–	Ed Archibald (CAN)	1908
3.50	[11-5 3/4]	–	Alfred Gilbert (USA)	1908
3.50	[11-5 3/4]	–	Edward Cooke (USA)	1908
3.58	[11-9]	3=	Bruno Söderström (SWE)	1908

3.58	[11-9]	3=		Charles Jacobs (USA)	1908
3.58	[11-9]	3=		Ed Archibald (CAN)	1908
3.58	[11-9]	-		Alfred Gilbert (USA)	1908
3.58	[11-9]	-		Edward Cooke (USA)	1908
3.66	[12-0]	-		Alfred Gilbert (USA)	1908
3.66	[12-0]	-		Edward Cooke (USA)	1908
3.71	[12-2]	1=		Alfred Gilbert (USA)	1908
3.71	[12-2]	1=		Edward Cooke (USA)	1908
3.75	[12-3 1/2]	-		Frank Nelson (USA)	1912
3.75	[12-3 1/2]	-		Bertil Uggla (SWE)	1912
3.75	[12-3 1/2]	-		Harry Babcock (USA)	1912
3.75	[12-3 1/2]	-		Marc Wright (USA)	1912
3.75	[12-3 1/2]	-		William Happenny (CAN)	1912
3.75	[12-3 1/2]	-		Frank Murphy (USA)	1912
3.75	[12-3 1/2]	7		Samuel Bellah (USA)	1912
3.80	[12-5 1/2]	-		Frank Nelson (USA)	1912
3.80	[12-5 1/2]	-		Harry Babcock (USA)	1912
3.80	[12-5 1/2]	-		Marc Wright (USA)	1912
3.80	[12-5 1/2]	4=		Bertil Uggla (SWE)	1912
3.80	[12-5 1/2]	4=		William Happenny (CAN)	1912
3.80	[12-5 1/2]	4=		Frank Murphy (USA)	1912
3.85	[12-7 1/2]	-		Harry Babcock (USA)	1912
3.85	[12-7 1/2]	2=		Frank Nelson (USA)	1912
3.85	[12-7 1/2]	2=		Marc Wright (USA)	1912
3.90	[12-9 1/2]	-		Harry Babcock (USA)	1912
3.95	[12-11 1/2]	1		Harry Babcock (USA)	1912
4.00	[13-1 1/2]	-		Frank Foss (USA)	1920
4.09	[13-5]	1	WR	Frank Foss (USA)	1920
4.10	[13-5 1/4]	-		Sabin Carr (USA)	1928
4.10	[13-5 1/4]	2		William Droegemuller (USA)	1928
4.20	[13-9 1/4]	1		Sabin Carr (USA)	1928
4.20	[13-9 1/4]	-		Bill Miller (USA)	1932
4.20	[13-9 1/4]	3		George Jefferson (USA)	1932
4.20	[13-9 1/4]	-		Shuhei Nishida (JPN)	1932
4.25	[13-11 1/4]	-		Bill Miller (USA)	1932
4.25	[13-11 1/4]	-		Shuhei Nishida (JPN)	1932
4.30	[14-1 1/4]	-		Bill Miller (USA)	1932
4.30	[14-1 1/4]	2		Shuhei Nishida (JPN)	1932
4.315	[14-1 3/4]	1		Bill Miller (USA)	1932
4.35	[14-3 1/4]	1		Earle Meadows (USA)	1936
4.40	[14-5 1/4]	3		Ragnar Lundberg (SWE)	1952
4.40	[14-5 1/4]	-		Don Laz (USA)	1952

4.40	[14-5 1/4]	4	Pyotr Denisenko (URS)	1952
4.40	[14-5 1/4]	–	Bob Richards (USA)	1952
4.50	[14-9]	2	Don Laz (USA)	1952
4.50	[14-9]	–	Bob Richards (USA)	1952
4.55	[14-11]	1	Bob Richards (USA)	1952
4.56	[14-11 1/2]	1	Bob Richards (USA)	1956
4.60	[15-1]	–	Don Bragg (USA)	1960
4.60	[15-1]	2	Ron Morris (USA)	1960
4.70	[15-5]	1	Don Bragg (USA)	1960
4.70	[15-5]	–	Gennadiy Bliznetsov (URS)	1964
4.70	[15-5]	–	Fred Hansen (USA)	1964
4.70	[15-5]	–	Pentti Nikula (FIN)	1964
4.70	[15-5]	–	Billy Pemelton (USA)	1964
4.70	[15-5]	–	Klaus Lehnertz (FRG)	1964
4.70	[15-5]	10	Guerrino Moro (CAN)	1964
4.70	[15-5]	–	Rudolf Tomášek (TCH)	1964
4.70	[15-5]	11	John Pennel (USA)	1964
4.70	[15-5]	12	Risto Ankio (FIN)	1964
4.70	[15-5]	13	Roman Lesek (YUG)	1964
4.70	[15-5]	–	Igor Feld (URS)	1964
4.80	[15-9]	–	Fred Hansen (USA)	1964
4.80	[15-9]	8	Billy Pemelton (USA)	1964
4.80	[15-9]	–	Manfred Preußger (GDR)	1964
4.80	[15-9]	–	Klaus Lehnertz (FRG)	1964
4.80	[15-9]	–	Wolfgang Reinhardt (FRG)	1964
4.80	[15-9]	–	Rudolf Tomášek (TCH)	1964
4.80	[15-9]	9	Igor Feld (URS)	1964
4.80	[15-9]	–	Pentti Nikula (FIN)	1964
4.85	[15-11]	–	Gennadiy Bliznetsov (URS)	1964
4.85	[15-11]	–	Fred Hansen (USA)	1964
4.85	[15-11]	–	Klaus Lehnertz (FRG)	1964
4.85	[15-11]	–	Pentti Nikula (FIN)	1964
4.90	[16-0 3/4]	7	Pentti Nikula (FIN)	1964
4.90	[16-0 3/4]	–	Manfred Preußger (GDR)	1964
4.90	[16-0 3/4]	–	Klaus Lehnertz (FRG)	1964
4.90	[16-0 3/4]	6	Rudolf Tomášek (TCH)	1964
4.90	[16-0 3/4]	–	Wolfgang Reinhardt (FRG)	1964
4.95	[16-2 3/4]	5	Gennadiy Bliznetsov (URS)	1964
4.95	[16-2 3/4]	–	Klaus Lehnertz (FRG)	1964
5.00	[16-4 3/4]	–	Fred Hansen (USA)	1964
5.00	[16-4 3/4]	–	Wolfgang Reinhardt (FRG)	1964
5.00	[16-4 3/4]	4	Manfred Preußger (GDR)	1964

5.00	[16-4 3/4]	3	Klaus Lehnertz (FRG)	1964
5.00	[16-4 3/4]	2	Wolfgang Reinhardt (FRG)	1964
5.05	[16-6 3/4]	1	Fred Hansen (USA)	1964
5.10	[16-8 3/4]	–	Gennadiy Bliznetsov (URS)	1968
5.10	[16-8 3/4]	–	Kiyoshi Niwa (JPN)	1968
5.10	[16-8 3/4]	–	Claus Schiprowski (FRG)	1968
5.10	[16-8 3/4]	–	Ignacio Sola (ESP)	1968
5.10	[16-8 3/4]	–	Heinfried Engel (FRG)	1968
5.15	[16-10 3/4]	–	Ignacio Sola (ESP)	1968
5.15	[16-10 3/4]	–	Christos Papanikolau (GRE)	1968
5.15	[16-10 3/4]	10	Kjell Isaksson (SWE)	1968
5.15	[16-10 3/4]	11	Kiyoshi Niwa (JPN)	1968
5.15	[16-10 3/4]	–	Herve D'Encausse (FRA)	1968
5.20	[17-0 3/4]	–	Gennadiy Bliznetsov (URS)	1968
5.20	[17-0 3/4]	–	Wolfgang Nordwig (GDR)	1968
5.20	[17-0 3/4]	8	Heinfried Engel (FRG)	1968
5.20	[17-0 3/4]	–	Claus Schiprowski (FRG)	1968
5.20	[17-0 3/4]	–	Bob Seagren (USA)	1968
5.20	[17-0 3/4]	–	John Pennel (USA)	1968
5.20	[17-0 3/4]	9	Ignacio Sola (ESP)	1968
5.25	[17-2 3/4]	7	Herve D'Encausse (FRA)	1968
5.25	[17-2 3/4]	–	Christos Papanikolau (GRE)	1968
5.25	[17-2 3/4]	–	Claus Schiprowski (FRG)	1968
5.30	[17-4 1/2]	–	Wolfgang Nordwig (GDR)	1968
5.30	[17-4 1/2]	–	Bob Seagren (USA)	1968
5.30	[17-4 1/2]	–	Claus Schiprowski (FRG)	1968
5.30	[17-4 1/2]	–	Christos Papanikolau (GRE)	1968
5.30	[17-4 1/2]	6	Gennadiy Bliznetsov (URS)	1968
5.30	[17-4 1/2]	–	John Pennel (USA)	1968
5.35	[17-6 1/2]	4	Christos Papanikolau (GRE)	1968
5.35	[17-6 1/2]	–	Wolfgang Nordwig (GDR)	1968
5.35	[17-6 1/2]	–	Claus Schiprowski (FRG)	1968
5.35*	[17-6 1/2]	5	John Pennel (USA)	1968
5.40	[17-8 1/2]	1	Bob Seagren (USA)	1968
5.40	[17-8 1/2]	2	Claus Schiprowski (FRG)	1968
5.40	[17-8 1/2]	3	Wolfgang Nordwig (GDR)	1968
5.40	[17-8 1/2]	–	Wolfgang Nordwig (GDR)	1972
5.40	[17-8 1/2]	2	Bob Seagren (USA)	1972
5.45	[17-10 1/2]	–	Wolfgang Nordwig (GDR)	1972
5.50	[18-0 1/2]	1	Wolfgang Nordwig (GDR)	1972
5.50	[18-0 1/2]	2	Antti Kalliomäki (FIN)	1976
5.50	[18-0 1/2]	1	Tadeusz Slusarski (POL)	1976

5.50	[18-0 1/2]	3		Dave Roberts (USA)	1976
5.50	[18-0 1/2]	-		Jean-Michel Bellot (FRA)	1980
5.50	[18-0 1/2]	-		WładysIaw Kozakiewicz (POL)	1980
5.55	[18-2 1/2]	6		Mariusz Klimczyk (POL)	1980
5.55	[18-2 1/2]	-		Konstantin Volkov (URS)	1980
5.55	[18-2 1/2]	-		Philippe Houvion (FRA)	1980
5.55	[18-2 1/2]	-		Tadeusz Slusarski (POL)	1980
5.60	[18-4 1/2]	5		Jean-Michel Bellot (FRA)	1980
5.60	[18-4 1/2]	-		WładysIaw Kozakiewicz (POL)	1980
5.65	[18-6 1/2]	-		WładysIaw Kozakiewicz (POL)	1980
5.65	[18-6 1/2]	2=		Konstantin Volkov (URS)	1980
5.65	[18-6 1/2]	4		Philippe Houvion (FRA)	1980
5.65	[18-6 1/2]	2=		Tadeusz Slusarski (POL)	1980
5.70	[18-8 1/4]	-		WładysIaw Kozakiewicz (POL)	1980
5.75	[18-10 1/4]	-		WładysIaw Kozakiewicz (POL)	1980
5.78	[18-11 1/2]	1	WR	WładysIaw Kozakiewicz (POL)	1980

*Pennel cleared 5.40 immediately after Seagren, but jump
disallowed as pole passed under bar contrary to rules then in
force.

Long Jump

6.35	[20-10]	1		Ellery Clark (USA)	1896
7.175	[23-6 1/2]	Q		Meyer Prinstein (USA)	1900
7.185	[23-7]	1		Alvin Kraenzlein (USA)	1900
[7.34]	24-1	1		Meyer Prinstein (USA)	1904
7.44	[24-5]	-		Frank Irons (USA)	1908
7.48	[24-6 1/2]	1		Frank Irons (USA)	1908
7.60	[24-11 1/4]	1-r1		Albert Gutterson (USA)	1912
7.76	[25-5 1/2]	P*	WR	Robert LeGendre (USA)	1924
[7.87w]	{25-10}	r2		Jesse Owens (USA)	1936
[7.87w]	{25-10}	2-r5		Luz Long (GER)	1936
7.94	[26-0 3/4]	r5		Jesse Owens (USA)	1936
[8.06w]	{26-5 1/2}	1-r6		Jesse Owens (USA)	1936
8.03	[26-4 1/4]	r2		Bo Roberson (USA)	1960
8.12	[26-7 3/4]	1-r3		Ralph Boston (USA)	1960
[8.27A]	{27-1¾}	Q		Ralph Boston (USA)	1960
[8.90A]	{29-2 1/2}	1-r1	WR	Bob Beamon (USA)	1968
8.34	[27-4 1/2]	Q		Randy Williams (USA)	1972
8.35	[27-4 3/4]	1-r1		Arni Robinson (USA)	1976
8.54	[28-0 1/4]	1-r5		Lutz Dombrowski (GDR)	1980
8.54	[28-0 1/4]	1-r1		Carl Lewis (USA)	1984

*Mark made in pentathlon competition.

Triple Jump

13.71	[44-11 3/4]	1		James Connolly (USA)	1896
14.47	[47-5 3/4]	1		Meyer Prinstein (USA)	1900
14.73	[48-4]	r2		Tim Ahearne (GBR)	1908
14.76	[48-5 1/4]	2-r6		Garfield MacDonald (GBR)	1908
14.92	[48-11 1/2]	1-r6		Tim Ahearne (GBR)	1908
15.425	[50-7 1/4]	2-r1		Luis Brunetto (ARG)	1924
15.525	[50-11 1/4]	1-r6	WR	Anthony Winter (AUS)	1924
15.72	[51-7]	1-r5	WR	Chuhei Nambu (JPN)	1932
15.76	[51-8 1/2]	r1		Naoto Tajima (JPN)	1936
16.00	[52-6]	1-r4	WR	Naoto Tajima (JPN)	1936
16.12	[52-10 3/4]	r2		Adhemar da Silva (BRA)	1952
16.22	[53-2 3/4]	1-r5	WR	Adhemar da Silva (BRA)	1952
16.25	[53-3 3/4]	2-r2		Vilhjalmur Einarsson (ISL)	1956
16.35	[53-7 3/4]	1-r4		Adhemar da Silva (BRA)	1956
16.44	[53-11 1/4]	Q		Józef Szmidt (POL)	1960
16.78	[55-0 3/4]	r1		Józef Szmidt (POL)	1960
16.81	[55-2]	1-r3		Józef Szmidt (POL)	1960
16.85	[55-3 1/2]	1-r6		Józef Szmidt (POL)	1964
[17.10A]	{56-1 1/4}	Q	WR	Giuseppe Gentile (ITA)	1968
[17.22A]	{56-6}	3-r1	WR	Giuseppe Gentile (ITA)	1968
[17.23A]	{56-6 1/2}	r3	WR	Viktor Saneev (URS)	1968
[17.27A]	{56-8}	2-r5	WR	Nelson Prudencio (BRA)	1968
[17.39A]	{57-0 3/4}	1-r6	WR	Viktor Saneev (URS)	1968
[16.85w]	{55-3 1/2}	Q		Viktor Saneev (URS)	1972
16.87	[55-4 1/4]	3-r1		Nelson Prudencio (BRA)	1972
[17.35w]	{56-11 /14}	1-r1		Viktor Saneev (URS)	1972
17.02	[55-10 1/4]	r2		Jörg Drehmel (GDR)	1972
17.19	[56-4 3/4]	r3		Viktor Saneev (URS)	1972
17.31	[56-9 1/2]	2-r5		Jörg Drehmel (GDR)	1972
17.35	[56-11 1/4]	r3		Jaak Uudmäe (URS)	1980
17.36	[56-11 1/2]	Q		Mike Conley (USA)	1984

Shot Put

11.22	[36-9 3/4]	1		Robert Garrett (USA)	1896
13.80	[45-3 1/2]	Q		Richard Sheldon (USA)	1900
14.10	[46-3 1/4]	1		Richard Sheldon (USA)	1900
[14.35]	47-1	r1		Ralph Rose (USA)	1904
[14.40]	47-3	2-r1		Wesley Coe (USA)	1904
[14.81]	48-7 1/4	1	WR	Ralph Rose (USA)	1904
14.98	[49-1 3/4]	r1		Ralph Rose (USA)	1912
15.25	[50-0 1/2]	2-r3		Ralph Rose (USA)	1912
15.34	[50-4]	1-r4		Pat McDonald (USA)	1912
15.75	[51-8 1/4]	Q		Herman Brix (USA)	1928
15.87	[52-0 3/4]	1	WR	John Kuck (USA)	1928
15.94	[52-3 3/4]	r4		Leo Sexton (USA)	1932
16.005	[52-6 1/4]	1-r6		Leo Sexton (USA)	1932
16.03	[52-7 1/4]	r2		Sulo Bärlund (FIN)	1936
16.20	[53-1 3/4]	1-r5		Hans Woellke (GER)	1936
16.32	[53-6 1/2]	r1		James Fuchs (USA)	1948
16.47	[54-0 1/2]	r1		Wilbur Thompson (USA)	1948
16.68	[54-8 3/4]	2-r2		James Delaney (USA)	1948
17.12	[56-2]	1-r2		Wilbur Thompson (USA)	1948
17.41	[57-1 1/2]	1-r1		Parry O'Brien (USA)	1952
17.92	[58-9 1/2]	r1		Parry O'Brien (USA)	1956
18.47	[60-7 1/4]	r2		Parry O'Brien (USA)	1956
18.57	[60-11 1/4]	1-r5		Parry O'Brien (USA)	1956
18.77	[61-7]	r1		Parry O'Brien (USA)	1960
19.11	[62-8 1/2]	2-r2		Parry O'Brien (USA)	1960
19.68	[64-6 3/4]	1-r5		Bill Nieder (USA)	1960
19.88	[65-2 3/4]	r3		Randy Matson (USA)	1964
20.20	[66-3 1/4]	2-r4		Randy Matson (USA)	1964
20.33	[66-8 1/2]	1-r4		Dallas Long (USA)	1964
20.68	[67-10 1/4]	Q		Randy Matson (USA)	1968
20.97	[68-9 3/4]	r1		Hartmut Briesenick (GDR)	1972
21.14	[69-4 1/4]	4-r1		Hans-Peter Gies (GDR)	1972
21.18	[69-6]	1-r1		Władysław Komar (POL)	1972
21.32	[69-11 1/2]	Q		Aleksandr Baryshnikov (URS)	1976
21.35	[70-0 1/2]	1-r6		Vladimir Kiselyov (URS)	1980

Discus Throw

29.15	[95-7 1/2]	1	Robert Garrett (USA)	1896
36.04	[118-3]	Q	Rudolf Bauer (HUN)	1900
[39.28]	128-10	2	Ralph Rose (USA)	1904
[39.28]	128-10	1-r5	Martin Sheridan (USA)	1904
<41.02>	{134-7}	-	Martin Sheridan (USA)	1906
<41.46>	{136-0}	1	Martin Sheridan (USA)	1906
40.70	[133-6]	2-r1	Merritt Giffin (USA)	1908
40.89	[134-1 1/2]	1	Martin Sheridan (USA)	1908
43.91	[144-0 1/2]	r2	Armas Taipale (FIN)	1912
44.34	[145-6]	r4	Armas Taipale (FIN)	1912
45.21	[148-3 1/2]	1-r6	Armas Taipale (FIN)	1912
46.155	[151-4 3/4]	1-r3	Clarence Houser (USA)	1924
47.00	[154-2]	3	James Corson (USA)	1928
47.32	[155-3]	1-r6	Clarence Houser (USA)	1928
47.87	[157-0 1/2]	r1	John Anderson (USA)	1932
48.23	[158-2 1/2]	r1	Henri Laborder (USA)	1932
48.86	[160-4]	r2	John Anderson (USA)	1932
49.39	[162-0 1/2]	r3	John Anderson (USA)	1932
49.49	[162-4 1/2]	1-r5	John Anderson (USA)	1932
50.48	[165-7]	1-r5	Kenneth Carpenter (USA)	1936
51.08	[167-7]	Q	Adolfo Consolini (ITA)	1948
51.78	[169-10]	2-r1	Giuseppe Tosi (ITA)	1948
52.78	[173-2]	1-r2	Adolfo Consolini (ITA)	1948
53.46	[175-5]	r1	Sim Iness (USA)	1952
54.60	[179-1]	r2	Sim Iness (USA)	1952
55.03	[180-6 1/2]	1-r3	Sim Iness (USA)	1952
56.36	[184-11]	1-r1	Al Oerter (USA)	1956
58.43	[191-8 1/2]	Q	Al Oerter (USA)	1960
59.18	[194-2]	1-r5	Al Oerter (USA)	1960
60.54	[198-7]	Q	Al Oerter (USA)	1964
61.00	[200-1]	1-r5	Al Oerter (USA)	1964
63.34	[207-10]	Q	Jay Silvester (USA)	1968
64.78	[212-6]	1-r3	Al Oerter (USA)	1968
68.28	[224-0]	Q	Mac Wilkins (USA)	1976

Hammer Throw

49.73	[163-1 1/2]	1	John Flanagan (USA)	1900
[50.27]	164-11	2	John Dewitt (USA)	1904
[51.23]	168-0 1/2	1	John Flanagan (USA)	1904
51.92	[170-4]	1-r6	John Flanagan (USA)	1908
54.13	[177-7]	r1	Matt McGrath (USA)	1912
54.74	[179-7]	1	Matt McGrath (USA)	1912
55.04	[180-7]	2-r2	Erwin Blask (GER)	1936
56.49	[185-4]	1-r6	Karl Hein (GER)	1936
57.20	[184-4]	Q	József Csermák (HUN)	1952
58.45	[191-9]	r1	József Csermák (HUN)	1952
60.34	[197-11]	1-r3 WR	József Csermák (HUN)	1952
62.10	[203-9]	r1	Anatoliy Samotsvetov (URS)	1956
63.00	[206-8]	r2	Mikhail Krivonosov (URS)	1956
63.03	[206-9 1/2]	2-r3	Mikhail Krivonosov (URS)	1956
63.19	[210-7]	1-r5	Hal Connolly (USA)	1956
64.80	[212-7]	Q	Gyula Zsivótsky (HUN)	1960
67.03	[219-10 1/2]	Q	Vasiliy Rudenkov (URS)	1960
67.10	[220-2]	1-r3	Vasiliy Rudenkov (URS)	1960
67.10	[220-2]	Q	Romuald Klim (URS)	1964
67.40	[221-1]	Q	Hal Connolly (USA)	1964
67.99	[223-0 1/2]	Q	Gyula Zsivótsky (HUN)	1964
69.09	[226-8]	2-r1	Gyula Zsivótsky (HUN)	1964
69.74	[228-10]	1-r4	Romuald Klim (URS)	1964
72.60	[238-2]	Q	Gyula Zsivótsky (HUN)	1968
72.82	[238-11]	r3	Romuald Klim (URS)	1968
73.28	[240-5]	2-r4	Romuald Klim (URS)	1968
73.36	[240-8]	1-r5	Gyula Zsivótsky (HUN)	1968
75.50	[247-8]	1-r1	Anatoliy Bondarchuk (URS)	1972
75.64	[248-2]	r1	Yuriy Sedykh (URS)	1976
75.74	[248-6]	r1	Aleksei Spiridonov (URS)	1976
77.52	[254-4]	1-r2	Yuriy Sedykh (URS)	1976
78.22	[256-7]	Q	Yuriy Sedykh (URS)	1980
81.80	[268-4]	1-r1	Yuriy Sedykh (URS)	1980

Javelin Throw

[49.66]	{162-11}	-		Eric Lemming (SWE)	1906
[53.90]	{176-10}	1		Eric Lemming (SWE)	1906
[46.04]*	<151-0>	6		Armas Pesonen (FIN)	1908
[49.72]*	<163-1>	3		Arne Halse (NOR)	1908
[54.44]*	<178-7>	1		Eric Lemming (SWE)	1908
47.09	[154-5 1/2]	Q		Otto Nilsson (SWE)	1908
53.68	[176-1]	Q		Eric Lemming (SWE)	1908
54.83	[179-10 1/2]	1	WR	Eric Lemming (SWE)	1908
55.37	[181-7 1/2]	Q		Julius Saaristo (FIN)	1912
57.42	[188-5]	Q		Eric Lemming (SWE)	1912
60.64	[198-11]	1-r4	WR	Eric Lemming (SWE)	1912
61.00+	[200-1]	Q	WR	Julius Saaristo (FIN)	1912
63.60	[208-8]	Q		Urho Peltonen (FIN)	1920
65.78	[215-10]	1-r1		Jonni Myyrä (FIN)	1920
66.60	[218-6]	1		Erik Lundkvist (SWE)	1928
71.25	[233-9]	r1		Matti Järvinen (FIN)	1932
72.71	[238-6 1/2]	1-r3		Matti Järvinen (FIN)	1932
73.78	[242-1]	1-r2		Cy Young (USA)	1952
74.76	[245-3]	Q		Cy Young (USA)	1956
74.96	[245-11]	r1		Viktor Tsybulenko (URS)	1956
75.84	[248-10]	r2		Viktor Tsybulenko (URS)	1956
79.98	[262-5]	2-r3		Janusz Sidło (POL)	1956
85.71	[281-2 1/2]	1-r4	WR	Egil Danielsen (NOR)	1956
86.30	[283-2]	r1		Jorma Kinnunen (FIN)	1968
86.34	[283-3]	r2		Yanis Lusis (URS)	1968
87.06	[285-7]	3-r4		Gergely Kulcsar (HUN)	1968
88.58	[290-7]	2-r6		Jorma Kinnunen (FIN)	1968
90.10	[295-7]	1-r6		Yanis Lusis (URS)	1968
90.48	[296-10]	1-r5		Klaus Wolfermann (FRG)	1972
94.58	[310-4]	1-r1	WR	Miklos Nemeth (HUN)	1976

*Made in the conventional manner, but in the freestyle competition held prior to the regular competition.
+Saaristo's mark was made in the both arms combined competition.

Decathlon

6565	8412.955	[1912A] 1	WR	Jim Thorpe (USA)	1912

{11.2 679 1289 187 52.2 15.6 3698 325 4570 4:40.1}

[6161]* {7724.495} [1912A] 2   Hugo Wieslander (SWE)   1912
{11.8 642 1214 175 53.6 17.2 3629 310 5040 4:45.0}

[6476]* {7710.775} [1920] 1 WR+ Harold Osborn (USA)   1924
{11.2 692 11435 197 53.2 16.0 3451 350 4669 4:50.0}

6587   8053.29 [1920] 1 WR Paavo Yrjölä (FIN)   1928
{11.8 672 1411 187 53.2 16.6 4209 330 5570 4:44.0}

6879   8292.48 [1920] 2   Akilles Järvinen (FIN)   1932
{11.1 700 1311 175 50.6 15.7 3680 360 6100 4:47.0}

6835   8462.23 [1920] 1 WR James Bausch (USA)   1932
{11.7 695 1532 170 54.2 16.2 4458 400 6191 5:17.0}

7254   7900 [1934] 1 WR Glenn Morris (USA)   1936
{11.1 697 1410 185 49.4 14.9 4302 350 5452 4:33.2}

7580   7887 [1950] 1 WR Bob Mathias (USA)   1952
{10.9 698 1530 190 50.2 14.7 4689 400 5921 4:50.8}

7565   7937 [1950] 1   Milt Campbell (USA)   1956
{10.8 733 1476 189 48.8 14.0 4498 340 5708 4:50.6}

7820   8334 [1950] 2   C. K. Yang (TAI)   1960
{10.7 746 1333 190 48.1 14.6 3983 430 6822 4:48.5}

7901   8392 [1950] 1   Rafer Johnson (USA)   1960
{10.9 735 1582 185 48.3 15.3 4849 410 6976 4:49.7}

8064   8193 [1962] 1   Bill Toomey (USA)   1968
{10.4 787 1375 195 45.6 14.9 4368 420 6280 4:57.1}

8458   8454 [1971] 1 WR Nikolai Avilov (URS)   1972
{11.00 768 1436 212 48.5 14.31 4698 455 6164 4:22.8}

8634   8618 [1971] 1 WR Bruce Jenner (USA)   1976
{10.94 722 1535 203 47.51 14.84 5004 480 6852 4:12.6}

8696   8673 [1977] 2   Jürgen Hingsen (FRG)   1984
{10.91 780 1587 212 47.69 14.29 5082 450 6044 4:22.60}

8847   8797 [1977] 1 WR@ Daley Thompson (GBR)   1984
{10.44 801 1572 203 46.97 14.33 4656 500 6524 4:35.00}

*Wieslander's and Osborn's marks were inferior to Thorpe's record on all scoring tables.
+Although credited as a world record, Osborn's mark was inferior to Thorpe's world record which had been stricken from the record books.
@Thompson's mark was not a world record on the 1977 tables but when the 1985 tables came into use, it became equal to Hingsen's world record and he was given credit for a world record.

Track & Field Athletics - Olympic Record Progressions - Women

100 metres

13.0		h1		Anni Holdmann (GER)	1928
12.8		h2		Erna Steinberg (GER)	1928
12.8		h3		Kinue Hitomi (JPN)	1928
12.8		h4		Leni Junker (GER)	1928
12.8		h6		Leni Schmidt (GER)	1928
12.6		h7		Fanny Rosenfeld (CAN)	1928
12.6		h9		Ethel Smith (CAN)	1928
12.4		s1		Fanny Rosenfeld (CAN)	1928
12.4		s2		Elizabeth Robinson (USA)	1928
12.2		1	WR	Elizabeth Robinson (USA)	1928
12.2		h1		Marie Dollinger (GER)	1932
11.9		h2	WR	Stanisława Walasiewiczowna (POL)	1932
11.9		s2	=WR	Stanisława Walasiewiczowna (POL)	1932
11.9		1	=WR	Stanisława Walasiewiczowna (POL)	1932
11.9		2		Hilda Strike (CAN)	1932
[11.4w]		h2		Helen Stephens (USA)	1936
[11.5w]		s1		Helen Stephens (USA)	1936
[11.5w]		1		Helen Stephens (USA)	1936
11.9		1		Francina Blankers-Koen (HOL)	1948
11.9	12.18	h7		Catherine Hardy (USA)	1952
11.6	11.86	h8		Marjorie Jackson (AUS)	1952
11.6	11.84	q4		Marjorie Jackson (AUS)	1952
11.5	11.72	s1	=WR	Marjorie Jackson (AUS)	1952
11.5	11.65	1		Marjorie Jackson (AUS)	1952
11.4		h3		Betty Cuthbert (AUS)	1956
11.3	11.41	s1	=WR	Wilma Rudolph (USA)	1960
[11.0w]	[11.18w]	1		Wilma Rudolph (USA)	1960
11.2	11.23	q1	=WR	Wyomia Tyus (USA)	1964
[11.2A]	[11.21A]	h1		Wyomia Tyus (USA)	1968
[11.2A]	[11.29A]	h2		Margaret Bailes (USA)	1968
[11.2A]	[11.28A]	h6		Barbara Ferrell (USA)	1968
[11.1A]	[11.12A]	q1	=WR	Barbara Ferrell (USA)	1968
[11.0Aw]	[11.08Aw]	q2		Wyomia Tyus (USA)	1968
[11.1A]	[11.19A]	q4	=WR	Irena Szewińska (POL)	1968
[11.0A]	[11.07A]	1	WR	Wyomia Tyus (USA)	1968
11.18		h1		Silvia Chivas (CUB)	1972
11.18		s1		Renate Stecher (GDR)	1972
11.07		1	=WR	Renate Stecher (GDR)	1972
11.05		q1		Annegret Richter (FRG)	1976
11.01		s1	WR	Annegret Richter (FRG)	1976
10.97		1		Evelyn Ashford (USA)	1984

Automatic Record Progression

12.18	h1	Winsome Cripps (AUS)	1952
12.18	h7	Catherine Hardy (USA)	1952
11.86	h8	Marjorie Jackson (AUS)	1952
11.84	q4	Marjorie Jackson (AUS)	1952
11.72	s1	Marjorie Jackson (AUS)	1952

11.65		1		Marjorie Jackson (AUS)	1952
11.65		h6		Wilma Rudolph (USA)	1960
11.41		s1	WRa	Wilma Rudolph (USA)	1960
[11.18w]		1		Wilma Rudolph (USA)	1960
11.23		q1	WRa	Wyomia Tyus (USA)	1964
[11.21A]		h1	WRa	Wyomia Tyus (USA)	1968
[11.12A]		q1	WRa	Barbara Ferrell (USA)	1968
[11.08Aw]		q2		Wyomia Tyus (USA)	1968
[11.07A]		1	WRa	Wyomia Tyus (USA)	1968
11.18		h1		Silvia Chivas (CUB)	1972
11.18		s1		Renate Stecher (GDR)	1972
11.07		1	=WRa	Renate Stecher (GDR)	1972
11.05		q1		Annegret Richter (FRG)	1976
11.01		s1	WRa	Annegret Richter (FRG)	1976
10.97		1		Evelyn Ashford (USA)	1984

200 metres

25.7		h1		Francina Blankers-Koen (HOL)	1948
25.6		h2		Cynthia Thompson (JAM)	1948
25.3		h4		Daphne Robb (SAF)	1948
24.3		s1		Francina Blankers-Koen (HOL)	1948
24.3	24.48	h2		Nadezhda Chnykina (URS)	1952
23.6	23.74	h3	=WR	Marjorie Jackson (AUS)	1952
23.4	23.59	s1	WR	Marjorie Jackson (AUS)	1952
23.4	23.55	1		Betty Cuthbert (AUS)	1956
23.2	23.30	h6		Wilma Rudolph (USA)	1960
23.0	23.05	1		Edith McGuire (USA)	1964
[23.0A]	[23.09A]	h2		Raelene Boyle (AUS)	1968
[22.9A]	[22.94A]	h3		Barbara Ferrell (USA)	1968
[22.9A]	[22.95A]	s1		Raelene Boyle (AUS)	1968
[22.8A]	[22.87A]	s2 <1>		Barbara Ferrell (USA)	1968
[22.8A]		s2 <2>		Jennifer Lamy (AUS)	1968
[22.5A]	[22.58A]	1	WR	Irena Szewińska (POL)	1968
22.96		h2		Renate Stecher (GDR)	1972
22.79		q1		Irena Szewińska (POL)	1972
22.40		1	WR	Renate Stecher (GDR)	1972
22.37		1		Bärbel Eckert (GDR)	1976
22.26		q3		Natalya Bochina (URS)	1980
22.03		1		Bärbel Wöckel-Eckert (GDR)	1980
21.81		1		Valerie Brisco-Hooks (USA)	1984

Automatic Record Progression

24.48		h2	Nadezhda Chnykina (URS)	1952
23.74		h3	WRa Marjorie Jackson (AUS)	1952
23.59		s1	WRa Marjorie Jackson (AUS)	1952
23.55		1	WRa Betty Cuthbert (AUS)	1956
23.30		h6	WRa Wilma Rudolph (USA)	1960
23.05		1	WRa Edith McGuire (USA)	1964
[22.94A]		h3	WRa Barbara Ferrell (USA)	1968
[22.87A]		s2	WRa Barbara Ferrell (USA)	1968
[22.58A]		1	WRa Irena Szewińska (POL)	1968
22.96		h2	Renate Stecher (GDR)	1972
22.79		q1	Irena Szewińska (POL)	1972
22.40		1	WRa Renate Stecher (GDR)	1972
22.37		1	Bärbel Eckert (GDR)	1976
22.26		q3	Natalya Bochina (URS)	1980
22.03		1	Bärbel Wöckel-Eckert (GDR)	1980
21.81		1	Valerie Brisco-Hooks (USA)	1984

400 metres

54.4	54.42	h1	Antónia Munkácsi (HUN)	1964
53.1	53.18	h3	Ann Packer (GBR)	1964
52.7	52.77	s1	Ann Packer (GBR)	1964
52.0	52.01	1	Betty Cuthbert (AUS)	1964
[52.0]	[52.03A]	1	Colette Besson (FRA)	1968
51.94		h1	Charlene Rendina (AUS)	1972
51.71		q3	Györgyi Balogh (HUN)	1972
51.68		s1	Helga Seidler (GDR)	1972
51.47		s2	Monika Zehrt (GDR)	1972
51.08		1	Monika Zehrt (GDR)	1972
50.48		s1	Irena Szewińska (POL)	1976
49.28*		1 WR	Irena Szewińska (POL)	1976
48.88		1	Marita Koch (GDR)	1980
48.83		1	Valerie Brisco-Hooks (USA)	1984

*Officially 49.29 - photo re-read by ATFS President Bob Sparks.

800 metres

2:22.4		h1	Marie Dollinger (GER)	1928
2:16.8		1 WR	Lina Radke (GER)	1960
2:10.9	2:11.07	h1	Antje Gleichfeld (FRG)	1960
2:07.8	2:07.91	h2	Ursula Donath (GDR)	1960
2:05.9	2:06.03	h4	Dixie Willis (AUS)	1960
2:04.3	2:04.50	1 =WR	Lyudmila Shevtsova (URS)	1960
2:04.1		s1	Maryvonne Dupureur (FRA)	1964
2:01.1		1 WR	Ann Packer (GBR)	1964
2:00.9	2:00.92	1	Madeline Manning (USA)	1968
1:58.9	1:58.93	h2	Svetla Zlateva (BUL)	1972
1:58.6	1:58.55	1	Hildegard Falck (FRG)	1972
1:56.5	1:56.53	s1	Anita Weiß (GDR)	1976
1:54.9	1:54.94	1 WR	Tatyana Kazankina (URS)	1976
1:53.5	1:53.43	1 WR	Nadyezhda Olizaryenko (URS)	1980

1,500 metres
```
4:06.5   4:04.47  h1  WR   Lyudmila Bragina (URS)         1972
4:05.1   4:05.07  s2  WR   Lyudmila Bragina (URS)         1972
4:01.4   4:01.38  1   WR   Lyudmila Bragina (URS)         1972
3:59.2   3:59.12  h1       Tatyana Kazankina (URS)        1980
3:56.6   3:56.56  1        Tatyana Kazankina (URS)        1980
```

3,000 metres
```
8:44.38           h1       Mary Decker-Slaney (USA)       1984
8:43.32           h3       Maricica Puica (ROM)           1984
8:35.96           1        Maricica Puica (ROM)           1984
```

Marathon (42,385 metres)
```
2-24:52           1        Joan Benoit (USA)              1984
```

100 metre high hurdles
```
13.3     13.34    P*       Heidemarie Rosendahl (FRG)     1972
13.3     13.25    P*       Christine Bodner (GDR)         1972
12.7     12.70    h1       Annelie Ehrhardt (GDR)         1972
12.6     12.59    1   WR   Annelie Ehrhardt (GDR)         1972
12.56             1        Vera Komisova (URS)            1980
```

*Mark made in pentathlon competition.

400 metre intermediate hurdles
```
55.97             h1       Judi Brown (USA)               1984
55.75             h4       Ann Louise Skoglund (SWE)      1984
55.17             s1       Ann Louise Skoglund (SWE)      1984
54.61             1        Nawal El Moutawakel (MAR)      1984
```

4 x 100 metre relay
```
49.3            h1  WR    Canada                          1928
                          (Smith, Rosenfeld, Bell, Cook)
48.4            1   WR    Canada                          1928
                          (Smith, Rosenfeld, Bell, Cook)
47.0            1   WR    United States                   1932
                          (Carew, Furtsch, Rogers, von Bremen)
47.0            2   =WR   Canada                          1932
                          (Frizzell, Palmer, Frizzell, Strike)
46.4            h2  WR    Germany                         1936
                          (Albus, Krause, Dollinger, Dörffeldt)
46.1     46.23  h1  WR    Australia                       1952
                          (Strickland, Johnson, Cripps, Jackson)
45.9     46.14  1   WR    United States                   1952
                          (Faggs, Jones, Moreau, Hardy)
45.9    [46.18] 2   =WR   German Federal Republic         1952
                          (Knab, Sander, Klein, Petersen)
44.9            h1  WR    Australia                       1956
                          (de la Hunty, Croker, Mellor, Cuthbert)
```

```
44.9              h1  WR   FRG/GDR                       1956
                       (Sander [FRG], Stubnick, Köhler, Mayer)
44.5     44.65    1   WR   Australia                     1956
                       (de la Hunty, Croker, Mellor, Cuthbert)
44.4     44.51    h2  WR   United States                 1960
                       (Hudson, Williams, Jones, Rudolph)
43.6     43.69    1   WR   Poland                        1964
                       (Ciepɫy, Kirszenstein, Górecka, Klobukowska)
[43.4A]  [43.50A] h1  WR   United States                 1968
                       (Ferrell, Bailes, Netter, Tyus)
[43.4A]  [43.49A] h2  =WR  The Netherlands               1968
                       (Hennipman, van den Berg, Sterk, Bakker)
[42.8A]  [42.88A] 1   WR   United States                 1968
                       (Ferrell, Bailes, Netter, Tyus)
42.81             1   WR   German Federal Republic       1972
                       (Krause, Mickler, Richter, Rosendahl)
42.61             h1        German Federal Republic      1976
                       (Poßekel, Helten, Richter, Kroniger)
42.55             1         German Democratic Republic   1976
                       (Oelsner, Stecher, Bodendorf, Eckert)
41.60             1   WR   German Democracti Republic    1980
                       (Müller, Wöckel, Auerswald, Göhr)

Automatic Record Progression
46.23             h1  WRa  Australia                     1952
                       (Strickland, Johnson, Cripps, Jackson)
46.14             1   WRa  United States                 1952
                       (Faggs, Jones, Moreau, Hardy)
44.65             1   WRa  Australia                     1956
                       (de la Hunty, Croker, Mellor, Cuthbert)
44.51             h2  WRa  United States                 1960
                       (Hudson, Williams, Jones, Rudolph)
43.69             1   WRa  Poland                        1964
                       (Ciepɫy, Kirszenstein, Górecka, Klobukowska)
[43.50A]          h1  WRa  United States                 1968
                       (Ferrell, Bailes, Netter, Tyus)
[43.49A]          h2  WRa  The Netherlands               1968
                       (van den Berg, Sterk, Hennipman, Bakker)
[42.88A]          1   WRa  United States                 1968
                       (Ferrell, Bailes, Netter, Tyus)
43.67             h1        Cuba                         1972
                       (Elejarde, Valdes, Romay, Chivas)
42.88             h2  =WRa German Democratic Republic    1972
                       (Kaufer, Heinich, Struppert, Stecher)
42.81             1   WRa  German Federal Republic       1972
                       (Krause, Mickler, Richter, Rosendahl)
42.61             h1        German Federal Republic      1976
                       (Poßekel, Helten, Richter, Kroniger)
42.55             1         German Democratic Republic   1976
                       (Oelsner, Stecher, Bodendorf, Eckert)
41.60             1   WRa  German Democracti Republic    1980
                       (Müller, Wöckel, Auerswald, Göhr)
```

4 x 400 metre relay

3:29.3	3:29.32	s1		German Federal Republic	1972
				(Rückes, Bödding, Falck, Wilden)	
3:28.5	3:28.48	s2	WR	German Democratic Republic	1972
				(Käsling, Kühne, Seidler, Zehrt)	
3:23.0	3:22.95	1	WR	German Democratic Republic	1972
				(Käsling, Kühne, Seidler, Zehrt)	
3:19.2	3:19.23	1	WR	German Democratic Republic	1976
				(Maletzki, Rohde, Streidt, Brehmer)	
	3:18.29	1		United States	1984
				(Leatherwood, Howard, Brisco-Hooks, Cheeseborough)	

High Jump

1.54	[5-0 1/2]	–		Ethel Catherwood (CAN)	1928
1.54	[5-0 1/2]	–		Carolina Gisolf (HOL)	1928
1.54	[5-0 1/2]	–		Mildred Wiley (USA)	1928
1.56	[5-1 1/4]	–		Ethel Catherwood (CAN)	1928
1.56	[5-1 1/4]	2		Carolina Gisolf (HOL)	1928
1.56	[5-1 1/4]	3		Mildred Wiley (USA)	1928
1.59	[5-2 1/2]	1	WR	Ethel Catherwood (CAN)	1928
1.60	[5-3]	–		Jean Shiley (USA)	1932
1.60	[5-3]	–		Babe Didrikson (USA)	1932
1.60	[5-3]	3		Eva Dawes (CAN)	1932
1.625	[5-4]	–		Jean Shiley (USA)	1932
1.625	[5-4]	–		Babe Didrikson (USA)	1932
1.65	[5-5]	1	WR	Jean Shiley (USA)	1932
1.65	[5-5]	2	=WR	Babe Didrikson (USA)	1932
1.67	[5-5¾]	jo*	WR	Jean Shiley (USA)	1932
1.68	[5-6]	–		Alice Coachman (USA)	1948
1.68	[5-6]	–		Dorothy Tyler (GBR)	1948
1.70	[5-7]	1		Alice Coachman (USA)	1948
1.70	[5-7]	2		Dorothy Tyler (GBR)	1948
1.70	[5-7]	–		Mildred McDaniel (USA)	1956
1.76	[5-9 1/4]	1		Mildred McDaniel (USA)	1956
1.77	[5-9 3/4]	–		Iolanda Balas (ROM)	1960
1.81	[5-11 1/4]	–		Iolanda Balas (ROM)	1960
1.85	[6-0 3/4]	1		Iolanda Balas (ROM)	1960
1.86	[6-1 1/4]	–		Iolanda Balas (ROM)	1964
1.90	[6-2 3/4]	1		Iolanda Balas (ROM)	1964
1.92	[6-3 1/2]	1	=WR	Ulrike Meyfarth (FRG)	1972
1.93	[6-4]	1		Rosemarie Ackermann (GDR)	1976
1.94	[6-4 1/4]	2		Urszula Kielan (POL)	1980
1.94	[6-4 1/4]	–		Sara Simeoni (ITA)	1980
1.94	[6-4 1/4]	3		Jutta Kirst (GDR)	1980
1.97	[6-5 1/2]	1		Sara Simeoni (ITA)	1980
1.97	[6-5 1/2]	–		Sara Simeoni (ITA)	1984
1.97	[6-5 1/2]	–		Ulrike Meyfarth (FRG)	1984
1.97	[6-5 1/2]	3		Joni Huntley (USA)	1984
2.00	[6-6 3/4]	2		Sara Simeoni (ITA)	1984
2.00	[6-6 3/4]	–		Ulrike Meyfarth (FRG)	1984
2.02	[6-7 1/2]	1		Ulrike Meyfarth (FRG)	1984

*Shiley's 1.67 was done in a jump-off for first place. Didrikson
cleared the same height but her jump was disallowed for diving
over the bar.

Long Jump

5.64	[18-6]	Q		Yvonne Curtet-Chabot (FRA)	1948
5.695	[18-8 1/4]	1		Olga Gyarmati (HUN)	1948
5.73	[18-9 3/4]	Q		Shirley Cawley (GBR)	1952
5.77	[18-11 1/4]	Q		Aleksandra Chudina (URS)	1952
5.77	[18-11 1/4]	Q		Nina Tyurkina (URS)	1952
5.88	[19-3 1/2]	Q		Mabel Landry (USA)	1952
6.16	[20-2 1/2]	Q		Yvette Williams (NZL)	1952
6.24	[20-5 3/4]	1-r4		Yvette Williams (NZL)	1952
6.35	[20-10]	1-r2	WR	Elzbieta Krzesińska (POL)	1956
6.37	[20-10 3/4]	1-r4		Vera Krepkina (URS)	1960
[6.44w]	{21-1 1/2}	Q		Helga Hoffmann (FRG)	1964
6.37	[20-10 3/4]	Q		Ingrid Becker (FRG)	1964
6.52	[21-4 3/4]	Q		Mary Rand (GBR)	1964
6.59	[21-7 1/2]	r1		Mary Rand (GBR)	1964
6.63	[21-9]	r4		Mary Rand (GBR)	1964
6.76	[22-2 1/4]	1-r5	WR	Mary Rand (GBR)	1964
[6.82A]	{22-4 1/2}	1-r1	WR	Viorica Viscopoleanu (ROM)	1968
6.78	[22-3]	1-r1		Heidemarie Rosendahl (FRG)	1972
[6.83w]	{22-5}	P*		Heidemarie Rosendahl (FRG)	1972
6.79	[22-3 1/2]	P*		Olga Rukavishnikova (URS)	1980
6.96	[22-10]	r1		Tatyana Skachko (URS)	1980
7.01	[23-0]	3-r3		Tatyana Skachko (URS)	1980
7.06	[23-2]	1-r6		Tatyana Kolpakova (URS)	1980

*Mark made in the pentathlon competition.

Shot Put

13.14	[43-1 1/2]	Q		Micheline Ostermeyer (FRA)	1948
13.75	[45-1 1/2]	1		Micheline Ostermeyer (FRA)	1948
13.88	[45-2 1/2]	Q		Klaudiya Tochenova (URS)	1952
13.89	[45-3]	r1		Marianne Werner (FRG)	1952
14.42	[47-3 3/4]	r1		Klaudiya Tochenova (URS)	1952
14.42	[47-3 3/4]	4-r1		Tamara Tyshkevich (URS)	1952
15.00	[49-2 1/2]	r1		Galina Zybina (URS)	1952
15.28	[50-1 3/4]	1-r4	WR	Galina Zybina (URS)	1952
15.61	[51-2 3/4]	3-r1		Marianne Werner (FRG)	1956
16.35	[53-7 3/4]	r1		Galina Zybina (URS)	1956
16.48	[54-1]	r5		Galina Zybina (URS)	1956
16.53	[54-2 3/4]	2-r6		Galina Zybina (URS)	1956
16.59	[54-5 1/4]	1-r6		Tamara Tyshkevich (URS)	1956
16.59	[54-5 1/4]	r2		Johanna Lüttge (GDR)	1960
17.32	[56-10]	1-r2		Tamara Press (URS)	1960
17.51	[57-5 1/2]	r1		Tamara Press (URS)	1964
17.72	[58-1 3/4]	r2		Tamara Press (URS)	1964
18.14	[59-6 1/4]	1-r6		Tamara Press (URS)	1964
18.53	[60-9 1/2]	r1		Margitta Gummel (GDR)	1968
18.78	[61-7 1/2]	2-r1		Marita Lange (GDR)	1968
19.07	[62-6 3/4]	r3		Margitta Gummel (GDR)	1968
19.61	[64-4]	1-r5	WR	Margitta Gummel (GDR)	1968
21.03	[69-0]	1-r1	WR	Nadezhda Chizhova (URS)	1972
21.16	[69-5 1/4]	1-r5		Ivanka Khristova (BUL)	1976
21.20	[69-6 3/4]	3-r1		Margitta Pufe (GDR)	1980
22.41	[73-6 1/4]	1-r1		Ilona Slupianek (GDR)	1980

Discus Throw

35.56	[119-11]	5		Grete Heublein (GER)	1928
36.33	[119-2 1/2]	–		Lillian Copeland (USA)	1928
39.17	[128-6]	–		Halina Konopacka (POL)	1928
39.62	[130-0]	1	WR	Halina Konopacka (POL)	1928
40.13	[131-7 1/2]	2-r6		Ruth Osborn (USA)	1932
40.59	[133-2]	1-r6		Lillian Copeland (USA)	1932
44.69	[146-7 1/2]	r1		Jadwiga Wajsówna (POL)	1936
47.63	[156-3]	1-r1		Gisela Mauermayer (GER)	1936
50.84	[166-9]	r2		Nina Ponomareva (URS)	1952
51.42	[168-8]	1-r3		Nina Ponomareva (URS)	1952
51.74	[169-9]	r1		Irina Beglyakova (URS)	1956
52.04	[170-9]	r3		Olga Fikotová (TCH)	1956
52.54	[172-4]	2-r3		Irina Beglyakova (URS)	1956
52.54	[172-4]	r4		Irina Beglyakova (URS)	1956
53.69	[176-1 1/2]	1-r5		Olga Fikotová (TCH)	1956
55.10	[180-9]	1-r5		Nina Ponomareva (URS)	1960
55.17	[181-0]	5-r1		Yevgeniya Kuznetsova (URS)	1964
55.90	[183-5]	r1		Lia Manoliu (ROM)	1964
57.21	[187-8 1/2]	2-r1		Ingrid Lotz (GDR)	1964
57.27	[187-10 1/2]	1-r5		Tamara Press (URS)	1964
58.28	[191-2]	1-r1		Lia Manoliu (ROM)	1968
61.58	[202-0]	Q		Argentina Menis (ROM)	1972
62.64	[205-6]	r1		Tamara Danilova (URS)	1972
64.28	[210-11]	r1		Argentina Menis (ROM)	1972
65.06	[213-5]	2-r4		Argentina Menis (ROM)	1972
66.62	[218-7]	1-r4		Faina Melnik (URS)	1972
66.68	[218-9]	r1		Gabriele Hinzmann (GDR)	1976
69.00	[226-4]	1-r1		Evelin Schlaak (GDR)	1976
69.76	[228-10]	r2		Evelin Jahl-Schlaak (GDR)	1980
69.96	[229-6]	1-r3		Evelin Jahl-Schlaak (GDR)	1980

Javelin Throw

43.69	[143-4]	1		Babe Didrikson (USA)	1932
44.69	[146-7 1/2]	r2		Tilly Fleischer (GER)	1936
45.18	[148-3]	1-r5		Tilly Fleischer (GER)	1936
45.57	[149-6]	1		Herma Bauma (AUT)	1948
46.17	[151-5 1/2]	Q		Aleksandra Chudina (URS)	1952
46.23	[151-8]	5-r1		Lily Kelsby-Carlstedt (DEN)	1952
46.71	[153-2 1/2]	2-r1		Aleksandra Chudina (URS)	1952
50.47	[165-7]	1-r1		Dana Zátopková (TCH)	1952
51.63	[169-4 1/2]	r1		Inese Yaunzeme (URS)	1956
53.40	[175-2]	r4		Inese Yaunzeme (URS)	1956
53.86	[176-8]	1-r6		Inese Yaunzeme (URS)	1956
55.98	[183-8]	1-r1		Elvira Ozolina (URS)	1960
62.40	[204-9]	Q	WR	Elena Gorchakova (URS)	1964
63.88	[209-7]	1-r5		Ruth Fuchs (GDR)	1972
65.14	[213-8]	Q		Marion Becker (FRG)	1976
65.94	[216-4]	1-r1		Ruth Fuchs (GDR)	1976
66.66	[218-8]	Q		Ute Richter (GDR)	1980
68.40	[224-5]	1-r1		Maria Colon (CUB)	1980
69.56	[228-2]	1-r1		Tessa Sanderson (GBR)	1984

Heptathlon

5798	5904	[1971]	15	Jill Ross Giffin (CAN)	1984

{13.72 168 1171 25.22 600 3938 2:11.97}

6085	6147	[1971]	8	Tineke Hidding (HOL)	1984

{13.70 174 1348 24.12 635 3394 2:12.84}

6388	6363	[1971]	3	Sabine Everts (FRG)	1984

{13.54 189 1249 24.05 671 3262 2:09.05}

6387	6390	[1971]	1	Glynis Nunn (AUS)	1984

{13.02 180 1282 24.06 666 3558 2:10.57}

BASKETBALL

International Federation: Fédération Internationale de Basketball Amateur (FIBA)
Year of Formation: 1932
Countries Affiliated: 165 (1987)
First Year of Olympic Appearance: 1936 (exhibition in 1904)

Most Medals, Men

4	Sergei Belov (URS)
4	Gennadiy Volnov (URS)
3	Krešimir Cošić (YUG)
3	Yanis Kruminsh (URS)
3	Valdis Muiznieks (URS)
3	Maigonis Valdmanis (URS)
3	Dražen Dalipagić (YUG)
3	Andro Knego (YUG)

Most Gold Medals, Men

2	Burdette Haldorson (USA)
2	Bill Hougland (USA)
2	Bob Kurland (USA)

Most Silver Medals, Men

3	Yanis Kruminsh (URS)
3	Valdis Muiznieks (URS)
3	Maigonis Valdmanis (URS)

Most Bronze Medals, Men

3	Sergei Belov (URS)

Most Years Between Medals, Men
    12   Sergei Belov (URS)
    12   Gennadiy Volnov (URS)
    12   Krešimir Cošić (YUG)

Most Years Between Gold Medals, Men
    4   Burdette Haldorson (USA)
    4   Bill Hougland (USA)
    4   Bob Kurland (USA)

Most Medals, Women
    2   Angele Rupshene (URS)
    2   Tatyana Nadyrova-Sakharova (URS)
    2   Olga Korostelyova-Barysheva (URS)
    2   Tatyana Ovechkina (URS)
    2   Nadezhda Olkhova-Shuvaeva (URS)
    2   Iuliyana Semenova (URS)
    2   Nelli Feryabnikova (URS)
    2   Olga Sukharnova (URS)
    2   Nadka Golcheva (BUL)
    2   Penka Metodiyeva (BUL)
    2   Petkana Makaveyeva (BUL)
    2   Sneschana Michailova (BUL)
    2   Krassimira Bogdanova (BUL)
    2   Diyana Brainova-Dilova (BUL)
    2   Penka Stoyanova (BUL)

Most Gold Medals, Women
    2   Angele Rupshene (URS)
    2   Tatyana Nadyrova-Sakharova (URS)
    2   Olga Korostelyova-Barysheva (URS)
    2   Tatyana Ovechkina (URS)
    2   Nadezhda Olkhova-Shuvaeva (URS)
    2   Iuliyana Semenova (URS)
    2   Nelli Feryabnikova (URS)
    2   Olga Sukharnova (URS)

Most Silver Medals, Women
    1   Many athletes tied with one.

Most Bronze Medals, Women
    1   Many athletes tied with one.

Most Years Between Medals, Women
    4   Angele Rupshene (URS)
    4   Tatyana Nadyrova-Sakharova (URS)
    4   Olga Korostelyova-Barysheva (URS)
    4   Tatyana Ovechkina (URS)
    4   Nadezhda Olkhova-Shuvaeva (URS)
    4   Iuliyana Semenova (URS)
    4   Nelli Feryabnikova (URS)
    4   Olga Sukharnova (URS)
    4   Nadka Golcheva (BUL)
    4   Penka Metodiyeva (BUL)
    4   Petkana Makaveyeva (BUL)
    4   Sneschana Michailova (BUL)
    4   Krassimira Bogdanova (BUL)
    4   Diyana Brainova-Dilova (BUL)
    4   Penka Stoyanova (BUL)

Most Years Between Gold Medals, Women
    4   Angele Rupshene (URS)
    4   Tatyana Nadyrova-Sakharova (URS)
    4   Olga Korostelyova-Barysheva (URS)
    4   Tatyana Ovechkina (URS)
    4   Nadezhda Olkhova-Shuvaeva (URS)
    4   Iuliyana Semenova (URS)
    4   Nelli Feryabnikova (URS)
    4   Olga Sukharnova (URS)

Most Appearances
    5   Teofilo Cruz Downs (PUR, 1960-76)
    4   Zenny de Azevedo (BRA, 1948-60)
    4   Sergei Belov (URS, 1968-80)
    4   Krešimir Cošić (YUG, 1968-80)
    4   Carlos Domingos Massoni (BRA, 1960-72)
    4   Ruperto Herrera Tabio (CUB, 1968-80)
    4   Vladimir Marques (BRA, 1956-68)
    4   Pier-Luigi Marzorati (ITA, 1972-84)
    4   Dino Meneghin (ITA, 1972-84)
    4   Gennadiy Volnov (URS, 1960-72)

Youngest Medalist, Men
    19-187   Spencer Haywood (USA-1968)
    19-222   Viktor Subkov (URS-1956)
    19-226   Phil Hubbard (USA-1976)
    19-242   Sergio De Toledo Machado (BRA-1964)
    19-260   Steve Alford (USA-1984)

Youngest Gold Medalist, Men
    19-187   Spencer Haywood (USA-1968)
    19-226   Phil Hubbard (USA-1976)
    19-260   Steve Alford (USA-1984)
    19-314   Charlie Scott (USA-1968)
    20-012   Chris Mullin (USA-1984)

Oldest Medalist, Men
   36-189   Sergei Belov (URS-1980)
   35-194   Zenny De Azevedo (BRA-1960)
   34-267   Yanis Kruminsh (URS-1964)
   33-303   Armenak Alachachyan (URS-1964)
   32-287   Gennadiy Volnov (URS-1972)

Oldest Gold Medalist, Men
   32-287   Gennadiy Volnov (URS-1972)
   31-246   Krešimir Cošić (YUG-1980)
   30-319   Jesse Renick (USA-1948)
   30-278   Zoran Slavnić (YUG-1980)
   29-052   R. C. Pitts (USA-1948)

Youngest Medalist, Women
   18-027   Nancy Lieberman (USA-1976)
   18-035   Kostadinka Radkova (BUL-1980)
   18-156   Yevladia Slavcheva (BUL-1980)
   18-164   Kyung-Hee Choi (KOR-1984)
   18-226   Jung-A Sung (KOR-1984)

Youngest Gold Medalist, Women
   20-019   Teresa Edwards (USA-1984)
   20-217   Cheryl Miller (USA-1984)
   21-065   Lyudmile Rogoshina (URS-1980)
   21-164   Olga Sukharnova (URS-1976)
   21-250   Pamela McGee (USA-1984)

Oldest Medalist, Women
   31-169   Nadezhda Sakharova (URS-1976)
   31-078   Nelli Feryabnikova (URS-1980)
   31-056   Krassimira Bogdanova (BUL-1980)
   30-336   Vera Djurašković (YUG-1980)
   30-347   Raisa Kurvyakova (URS-1976)

Oldest Gold Medalist, Women
   31-169   Nadezhda Sakharova (URS-1976)
   31-078   Nelli Feryabnikova (URS-1980)
   30-347   Raissa Kurvyakova (URS-1976)
   30-134   Tatyana Ovechkina (URS-1980)
   29-183   Tatyana Nadyrova-Sakharova (URS-1980)

Most Points, Game, Men, Individual
   48   Edward Palubinskas (AUS-1976, v. MEX)
   44   Ricardo Duarte (PER-1964, v. KOR)
   41   Arturo Guerrero (MEX-1976, v. JPN)
   40   Arturo Guerrero (MEX-1976, v. AUS)
   39   Masatomo Taniguchi (JPN-1972, v. ESP)
   39   Horacio Lopez (URU-1984, v. ITA)
   38   Radivoje Korać (YUG-1960, v. URU)
   38   · Shigeaki Abe (JPN-1976, v. PUR)
   37   Dražen Dalipagić (YUG-1984, v. CAN)
   36   Ian Davies (AUS-1980, v. TCH)
   36   Ian Davies (AUS-1980, v. IND)

Most Rebounds, Game, Men, Individual (not recorded prior to 1972)

22	Marcos Leite Abdalla (BRA-1972, v. PUR)
20	Milun Marović (YUG-1972, v. PHI)
19	Clifford Luyk (ESP-1972, v. JPN)
17	Ruben Rodriquez (PUR-1972, v. PHI)
17	Ruben Rodriquez (PUR-1972, v. SEN)
17	Marcos Leite Abdalla (BRA-1972, v. CUB)
17	Clifford Luyk (ESP-1972, v. GER)
17	Rafael Paloma (MEX-1976, v. JPN)

Most Assists, Game, Men, Individual (not recorded prior to 1972)

20	Manuel Saenz (MEX-1976, v. JPN)
14	Pier-Luigi Marzorati (ITA-1976, v. PUR)
14	Fengwu Sun (CHN-1984, v. FRA)
14	Amir Abdelmeguid (EGY-1984, v. FRA)
13	Zoran Slavnić (YUG-1976, v. USA)
13	Jacques Monclar (FRA-1984, v. EGY)

Most Points, Game, Men, Team

137	Brazil (1980 v. India)
133	Czechoslovakia (1980 v. India)
129	USSR (1976 v. Japan)
129	Yugoslavia (1980 v. Poland)
125	China (1948 v. Iraq)
125	USA (1960 v. Japan)
123	USSR (1968 v. Morocco)
121	USA (1956 v. The Philippines)
121	USSR (1980 v. India)
121	Canada (1984 v. China)

Most Points, Game, Men, Both Teams

237	Australia d. Mexico, 120-117 - 1976
221	USSR d. Spain, 119-102 - 1980
220	Yugoslavia d. Poland, 129-91 - 1980
213	Uruguay d. Italy, 111-102 - 1984
205	USA d. Yugoslavia, 112-93 - 1976
202	Puerto Rico d. Japan, 111-91 - 1976
201	Brazil d. India, 137-64 - 1980
201	Canada d. China, 121-80 - 1984
200	Cuba d. Australia, 111-89 - 1976
199	USSR d. Cuba, 109-90 - 1980

Most Points, Game, Women, Individual

38	Miyako Otsuka (JPN-1976, v. CAN)
35	Keiko Namai (JPN-1976, v. USA)
32	Iuliyana Semenova (URS-1976, v. USA)
30	Olga Sukharnova (URS-1980, v. HUN)
29	Sofija Pekić (YUG-1980, v. HUN)
28	Petkana Makaveeva (BUL-1976, v. CAN)
28	Sofija Pekić (YUG-1980, v. HUN)
27	Iuliyana Semenova (URS-1970, v. BUL)
27	Xiaobo Song (CHN-1984, v. YUG)

Most Rebounds, Game, Women, Individual
    21   Iuliyana Semenova (URS-1980, v. BUL)
    20   Caridad Despaigne (CUB-1980, v. BUL)
    19   Iuliyana Semenova (URS-1976, v. USA)
    18   Iuliyana Semenova (URS-1976, v. JPN)
    16   Nelli Feryabnikova (URS-1976, v. JPN)

Most Assists, Game, Women, Individual
    14   Joanne Sargent (CAN-1976, v. TCH)
    11   Nadezhda Sakharova (URS-1976, v. USA)
    10   Ann Meyers (USA-1976, v. CAN)
    10   Keiko Namai (JPN-1976, v. CAN)
     9   Ann Meyers (USA-1976, v. BUL)
     9   Ivana Korinková (TCH-1976, v. BUL)
     9   Ivana Korinková (TCH-1976, v. JPN)

Most Points, Game, Women, Team
    122   USSR (1980 v. Bulgaria)
    121   Japan (1976 v. Canada)
    120   USSR (1980 v. Hungary)
    119   USSR (1980 v. Italy)
    115   USSR (1976 v. Canada)
    112   USSR (1976 v. USA)
    104   USSR (1980 v. Bulgaria)
    102   Bulgaria (1980 v. Italy)
     98   USSR (1976 v. Japan)
     97   USSR (1980 v. Yugoslavia)

Most Points, Game, Women, Both Teams
    210   Japan d. Canada, 121-89 - 1976
    205   USSR d. Bulgaria, 122-83 - 1980
    189   USSR d. USA, 112-77 - 1976
    182   USSR d. Hungary, 120-62 - 1980
    177   USSR d. Bulgaria, 104-73 - 1980
    173   USSR d. Japan, 98-75 - 1976
    172   USSR d. Italy, 119-53 - 1980

Triple Champions (Olympic, NCAA, and NBA)
    Clyde Lovelette (USA-1952, U. Kansas, Minneapolis Lakers/Boston
        Celtics)
    Bill Russell (USA-1956, U. San Francisco, Boston Celtics)
    K. C. Jones (USA-1956, U. San Francisco, Boston Celtics)
    Jerry Lucas (USA-1960, Ohio State U., New York Knicks)
    Quinn Buckner (USA-1976, Indiana U., Boston Celtics)

Medals Won by Countries

	G	S	B	T
United States	10	2	–	12
USSR	3	4	3	10
Yugoslavia	1	2	2	5
Brazil	–	–	3	3
Bulgaria	–	1	1	2
Canada	–	1	1	2
Uruguay	–	–	2	2
France	–	1	–	1
Italy	–	1	–	1
Spain	–	1	–	1
Korea	–	1	–	1
Mexico	–	–	1	1
Cuba	–	–	1	1
Totals	14	14	14	42

Medals Won by Countries, Men

	G	S	B	T
United States	9	1	–	10
USSR	1	4	3	8
Yugoslavia	1	2	1	4
Brazil	–	–	3	3
Uruguay	–	–	2	2
France	–	1	–	1
Italy	–	1	–	1
Canada	–	1	–	1
Spain	–	1	–	1
Mexico	–	–	1	1
Cuba	–	–	1	1
Totals	11	11	11	33

Medals Won by Countries, Women

	G	S	B	T
USSR	2	–	–	2
United States	1	1	–	2
Bulgaria	–	1	1	2
Korea	–	1	–	1
Yugoslavia	–	–	1	1
Canada	–	–	1	1
Totals	3	3	3	9

Overall Records by Countries, Men

	W	L	%%%%
United States	78	1	.987
USSR	55	12	.821
Yugoslavia	44	13	.772
Argentina	8	5	.615
Italy	39	27	.591
Brazil	45	32	.584
Mexico	23	19	.548
Uruguay	29	25	.537
Czechoslovakia	24	23	.511
Spain	19	19	.500
Bulgaria	13	13	.500
Puerto Rico	17	18	.486
Chile	12	13	.480
Australia	19	22	.463
Poland	22	26	.458
France	16	19	.457
Canada	18	22	.450
Cuba	17	21	.447
Belgium	3	4	.429
The Philippines	16	23	.410
China	6	10	.375
Peru	6	10	.375
Sweden	3	5	.375
Latvia	1	2	.333
Estonia	1	2	.333
Taiwan	1	2	.333
Hungary	6	14	.300
Finland	3	7	.300
Germany/FRG	6	15	.286
Panama	2	5	.286
Japan	9	23	.281
Switzerland	2	6	.250
Iran	1	3	.250
Korea	4	21	.160
Egypt	3	32	.086
Senegal	2	22	.083
Turkey	0	2	.000
Singapore	0	3	.000
Thailand	0	3	.000
Ireland	0	4	.000
Great Britain	0	5	.000
Iraq	0	5	.000
Morocco	0	7	.000
India	0	8	.000
Totals	573	573	.500

Overall Records by Countries, Women

	W	L	%%%%
USSR	11	0	1.000
United States	9	2	.818
Korea	4	2	.667
Bulgaria	7	4	.636
China	3	3	.500
Yugoslavia	5	6	.454
Czechoslovakia	2	3	.400
Japan	2	3	.400
Hungary	2	4	.333
Cuba	1	4	.200
Australia	1	4	.200
Canada	2	9	.182
Italy	0	5	.000
Totals	49	49	.500

BOXING

International Federation: Association Internationale de Boxe
    Amateur (AIBA)
Countries Affiliated: 137 (1987)
Year of Formation: 1946
First Year of Olympic Appearance: 1904

Most Medals
    3   László Papp (HUN)
    3   Téofilo Stevenson (CUB)
    3   Zbigniew Pietrzykowski (POL)
    3   Boris Lagutin (URS)

Most Gold Medals
    3   László Papp (HUN)
    3   Téofilo Stevenson (CUB)
    2   Angel Herrera (CUB)
    2   Harry Mallin (GBR)
    2   Jerzy Kulej (POL)
    2   Boris Lagutin (URS)
    2   Oliver Kirk (USA)

Most Silver Medals
    2   Sören Petersen (DEN)
    2   Artur Olech (POL)
    2   Aleksei Kiselev (URS)

Most Bronze Medals
  2   Zbigniew Pietrzykowski (POL)
  2   Zvonimir Vujin (YUG)
  2   Leszek Blazynski (POL)
  2   Janusz Gortat (POL)
  2   Kazimierz Szczerba (POL)
  2   Viktor Rybakov (URS)

Most Medals, Games
  2   George Finnegan (USA-1904)
  2   Oliver Kirk (USA-1904)
  2   Harry Spanger (USA-1904)
  2   Charles Mayer (USA-1904)

Most Gold Medals, Games
  2   Oliver Kirk (USA-1904)

Most Appearances
  4   György Gedó (HUN, 1968-80)
  3   Fifty-five athletes tied with three.

Most Years Winning Medals
  3   László Papp (HUN)
  3   Téofilo Stevenson (CUB)
  3   Zbigniew Pietrzykowski (POL)
  3   Boris Lagutin (URS)

Most Years Winning Gold Medals
  3   László Papp (HUN)
  3   Téofilo Stevenson (CUB)

Most Years Between Appearances
  12   György Gedó (HUN, 1968-80)
  12   Frederick Grace (GBR, 1908-20)
  12   Peter Hussing (GER, 1972-84)

Most Years Between Medals
  8   László Papp (HUN)
  8   Téofilo Stevenson (CUB)
  8   Zbigniew Pietrzykowski (POL)
  8   Boris Lagutin (URS)
  8   Rolando Garbey (CUB)

Most Years Between Gold Medals
  8   Téofilo Stevenson (CUB)
  8   László Papp (HUN)
  4   Angel Herrera (CUB)
  4   Harry Mallin (GBR)
  4   Jerzy Kulej (POL)
  4   Boris Lagutin (URS)

Youngest Medalist
  16-162 Jackie Fields (USA-1924)
  16-270 Louis Lauria (USA-1936)
  17-045 William Meyers (SAF-1960)
  17-072 Orlando Maldonado (PUR-1976)
  17-211 Floyd Patterson (USA-1952)

Youngest Gold Medalist
  16-162 Jackie Fields (USA-1924)
  17-211 Floyd Patterson (USA-1952)
  17-297 Meldrick Taylor (USA-1984)
  18-111 Carlo Orlandi (ITA-1928)
  18-155 Leo Randolph (USA-1976)

Oldest Medalist
  37-301 Richard Gunn (GBR-1908)
  32-295 Jan Szczepański (POL-1972)
  32-255 János Kajdi (HUN-1972)
  32-049 Harry Mallin (GBR-1924)
  30-296 Hans Huber (FRG-1964)

Oldest Gold Medalist
  37-301 Richard Gunn (GBR-1908)
  32-295 Jan Szczepański (POL-1972)
  32-049 Harry Mallin (GBR-1924)
  30-252 László Papp (HUN-1956)
  30-125 Boris Lagutin (URS-1968)

Professional Champions Who Boxed in the Olympics
    (Olympic experience mentioned first, followed by professional
championships. Olympic medals mentioned after year and division.
Updated through July 1987.)

  ARG - Pascual Perez (1948 FL <1>, 1954 FL), Victor Galindez
      (1968 LM, 1974 LH), Miguel Cuello (1972 LH, 1977 LH)
  AUS - Jimmy Carruthers (1948 BA, 1952 BA), Jeffrey Fenech (1984
      FL, 1985 BA)
  BRA - Eder Jofre (1956 BA; 1961 BA, 1973 FE)
  CAN - Jimmy Callura (1932 FL, 1943 FE)
  COL - Prudencio Cardona (1972 LF, 1982 FL)
  DEN - Waldemar Holberg (1908 LI, 1914 WE)
  DOM - Eleoncio Mercedes (1976 LF, 1982 FL)
  ESP - José Duran (1968 WE, 1976 JM), Miguel Velasquez (1964 LW,
      1976 JW)
  GBR - Alan Minter (1972 LM <3>, 1980 MI), Maurice Hope (1972 WE,
      1979 JM), Matt Wells (1908 LI, 1914 WE), John Stracey (1968
      LI, 1975 WE), Charlie Magri (1976 FL, 1983 FL)
  IRL - Johnny Caldwell (1956 FL <3>, 1961 BA), Barry McGuigan
      (1980 FE, 1985 FE)
  ITA - Giovanni "Nino" Benvenuti (1960 WE <1>; 1965 JM, 1967 MI),
      Carmello Bossi (1960 LM <2>, 1970 JM), Sandro Lopopolo (1960
      LI <2>, 1966 JW), Bruno Arcari (1964 LI, 1970 JW),
      Salvatore Burruni (1956 FL, 1965 FL). Franco Udella (1968 LF,
      1972 FL; 1975 JFl), Francesco Damiani (1984 HE <2>, 1986
      JrHE), Patrizio Oliva (1980 LW <1>, 1986 JW)

JAM - Mike McCallum (1976 WE, 1984 JM), Trevor Berbick (1976 HE,
   1986 HE)
JPN - Kazuo "Royal" Kobayashi (1972 FE, 1976 JFe)
KOR - Ki-Soo Kim (1960 WE, 1966 JM), Chan-Hee Park (1976 LF,
   1979 FL)
MEX - Vicente Saldivar (1960 FE, 1964 FE), Raul Macias (1952 BA,
   1955 BA), Alfonso Zamora (1972 BA <2>, 1975 BA),
   Daniel Zaragoza (1980 BA, 1985 BA)
PAN - Alfonso Frazer (1964 FE, 1972 JW)
PUR - Wilfredo Gomez (1972 FL; 1977 JFe, 1984 FE, 1985 JL),
   Carlos Santos (1976 WE, 1984 JM),
SAF - Willie Smith (1924 BA <1>, 1927 BA), Vic Toweel (1948 BA,
   1950 BA)
SWE - Ingemar Johansson (1952 HE <2>, 1959 HE)
THA - Payao Pooltarat (1976 LF <3>, 1984 JB)
UGA - Cornelius Bbosa [Boza-Edwards] (1976 FE, 1981 JL)
USA - Floyd Patterson (1952 MI <1>, 1956 HE), Cassius Clay
   [Muhammed Ali] (1960 LH <1>, 1964 HE), Joe Frazier (1964 HE
   <1>, 1968 HE), George Foreman (1968 HE <1>, 1973 HE),
   Leon Spinks (1976 LH <1>, 1978 HE), John Tate (1976 HE <3>,
   1979 HE), Michael Spinks (1976 MI <1>; 1981 LH, 1985 HE),
   Evander Holyfield (1984 MH <3>, 1986 CR), José Torres (1956 LH
   <2>, 1965 LH), Marvin Johnson (1976 MI <3>; 1981 LH, 1986 CR),
   Mark Breland (1984 WE <1>, 1986 WE), Sugar Ray Leonard (1976
   LW <1>; 1979 WE, 1981 JM, 1987 MI), Jackie Fields (1924 FE
   <1>, 1929 WE), Wallace "Bud" Smith (1948 LI, 1955 LI),
   Davey Moore (1952 BA, 1959 FE), Leo Randolph (1976 FL <1>,
   1980 JFe), Lou Salica (1932 FL <3>, 1935 BA), Fidel LaBarba
   (1924 FL <1>, 1925 FL), Frankie Genaro [Frank DiGennara](1920
   FL <1>, 1928 FL), 1986 CR). {Also the following who were
   unable to compete in 1980: Donald Curry (1980 WE, 1983 WE),
   Johnny Bumphus (1980 LW, 1984 JW), Richard Sandoval (1980 FL,
   1984 BA), Lee Roy Murphy (1980 LH, 1984 CR), Joe Louis Manley
   (1980 LI, 1986 JW)}
VEN - Bernardo Pinango (1980 BA <2>, 1986 BA), Antonio
   Esparragoza (1980 FE, 1987 FE)
YUG - Mate Parlov (1968 MI, 1972 LH <1>; 1978 LH), Slobodan
   Katar (1980 LH, 1985 MI)

Val Barker Award Winners
         The Val Barker Award is given at each Olympic Games to
the boxer who is judged to be the best overall technical boxer.
It is named in honor of Val Barker of Great Britain, a former
president of the AIBA.

1936	-	Louis Laurie (USA)	Bronze	Flyweight
1948	-	George Hunter (SAF)	Gold	Light-heavyweight
1952	-	Norvel Lee (USA)	Gold	Light-heavyweight
1956	-	Dick McTaggart (GBR)	Gold	Lightweight
1960	-	Giovanni Benvenuti (ITA)	Gold	Welterweight
1964	-	Valeriy Popenchenko (URS)	Gold	Middleweight
1968	-	Philip Waruinge (KEN)	Bronze	Featherweight
1972	-	Téofilo Stevenson (CUB)	Gold	Heavyweight
1976	-	Howard Davis (USA)	Gold	Lightweight
1980	-	Patrizio Oliva (ITA)	Gold	Light-welterweight
1984	-	Paul Gonzalez (USA)	Gold	Light-flyweight

Medals Won by Countries

	G	S	B	T
United States	42	17	26	85
USSR	13	18	16	47
Great Britain	12	10	19	41
Italy	13	12	13	38
Poland	8	9	21	38
Cuba	12	8	5	25
Argentina	7	7	9	23
South Africa	6	4	9	19
Romania	1	7	10	18
Hungary	9	2	3	14
GDR	4	1	8	13
Finland	2	1	10	13
France	3	3	6	12
Canada	2	4	5	11
Denmark	1	5	5	11
Yugoslavia	3	2	5	10
Mexico	2	3	5	10
FRG	1	4	5	10
Germany	2	6	1	9
Bulgaria	2	1	6	9
Korea	1	4	4	9
Sweden	-	4	5	9
Ireland	-	2	5	7
Czechoslovakia	3	1	2	6
Venezuela	1	2	2	5
Norway	1	2	2	5
Kenya	-	1	4	5
PR Korea	1	2	1	4
Belgium	1	1	2	4
Uganda	-	3	1	4
Australia	-	1	3	4
Puerto Rico	-	1	3	4
Japan	1	-	2	3
Netherlands	1	-	2	3
Nigeria	-	1	2	3
Ghana	-	1	2	3
Chile	-	1	2	3
New Zealand	1	1	-	2
Philippines	-	1	1	2
Thailand	-	1	1	2
Cameroun	-	1	1	2
Turkey	-	-	2	2
Algeria	-	-	2	2
Colombia	-	-	2	2
Estonia	-	1	-	1
Tunisia	-	-	1	1
Bermuda	-	-	1	1
Dominican Rep	-	-	1	1

Uruguay	– –	1	1
Egypt/UAR	– –	1	1
Guyana	– –	1	1
Zambia	– –	1	1
Spain	– –	1	1
Brazil	– –	1	1
Niger	– –	1	1
Totals	156 156	250	562

*A single bronze was awarded in all classes through 1948, except in the exceptions given below. Since 1952, two bronzes have been awarded in all classes.

**No third in 1904 flyweight, bantamweight, and middleweight classes. Two thirds in 1904 welterweight class.

Best Record by Country at Each Olympics

1904	–	United States
1908	–	Great Britain
1920	–	United States/Great Britain
1924	–	United States
1928	–	Argentina/Italy
1932	–	United States
1936	–	Germany
1948	–	South Africa
1952	–	United States
1956	–	USSR
1960	–	Italy
1964	–	USSR
1968	–	USSR
1972	–	Cuba
1976	–	United States
1980	–	Cuba
1984	–	United States

CANOEING

International Federation: Fédération Internationale de Canoe (FIC)
Countries Affiliated: 40 (1987)
Year of Formation: 1924
First Year of Olympic Appearance: 1936 (exhibition in 1924)

Most Medals

8	Gert Fredriksson (SWE)
6	Rüdiger Helm (GDR)
5	Ivan Patzaichin (ROM)
4	Vasile Diba (ROM)
4	Bernd Olbricht (GDR)
4	Lyudmila Pinaeeva-Khvedosyuk (URS)
4	Matija Ljubek (YUG)

Most Gold Medals
6	Gert Fredriksson (SWE)
3	Rüdiger Helm (GDR)
3	Ivan Patzaichin (ROM)
3	Lyudmila Pinaeeva-Khvedosyuk (URS)
3	Vladimir Morozov (URS)
3	Vladimir Parvenovitch (URS)
3	Sergei Chukhrai (URS)
3	Ian Ferguson (NZL)

Most Silver Medals
3	Therese Zenz (FRG)
3	Lars-Erik Moberg (SWE)

Most Bronze Medals
3	Rüdiger Helm (GDR)
3	Georges Dransart (FRA)

Most Years Winning Medals
4	Gert Fredriksson (SWE)
3	Ivan Patzaichin (ROM)
3	Lyudmila Pinaeeva-Khvedosyuk (URS)
3	Jan Brzák-Felix (TCH)
3	Vladimir Morozov (URS)
3	János Parti (HUN)
3	Anna Pfeffer (HUN)
3	Tamás Wichmann (HUN)

Most Years Winning Gold Medals
4	Gert Fredriksson (SWE)
3	Ivan Patzaichin (ROM)
3	Lyudmila Pinaeeva-Khvedosyuk (URS)
3	Vladimir Morozov (URS)

Most Years Between Medals
16	Jan Brzák-Felix (TCH)
12	Gert Fredriksson (SWE)
12	Ivan Patzaichin (ROM)

Most Years Between Gold Medals
12	Jan Brzák-Felix (TCH)
12	Gert Fredriksson (SWE)
12	Ivan Patzaichin (ROM)
8	Lyudmila Pinaeeva-Khvedosyuk (URS)
8	Matija Ljubek (YUG)
8	Vladimir Morozov (URS)

Most Medals, Women
4	Lyudmila Pinaeeva-Khvedosyuk (URS)
3	Anna Pfeffer (HUN)
3	Antonina Seredina (URS)
3	Therese Zenz (FRG)
3	Agneta Andersson (SWE)

Most Gold Medals, Women
3	Lyudmila Pinaeeva-Khvedosyuk (URS)
2	Antonina Seredina (URS)
2	Agneta Andersson (SWE)
2	Roswitha Esser (GDR)
2	Annemarie Zimmermann (GDR)

Most Years Winning Medals, Women
3	Lyudmila Pinaeeva-Khvedosyuk (URS)
3	Anna Pfeffer (HUN)

Most Years Winning Gold Medals, Women
3	Lyudmila Pinaeeva-Khvedosyuk (URS)
2	Roswitha Esser (GDR)
2	Annemarie Zimmermann (GDR)

Most Years Between Medals, Women
8	Lyudmila Pinaeeva-Khvedosyuk (URS)
8	Anna Pfeffer (HUN)

Most Years Between Gold Medals, Women
8	Lyudmila Pinaeeva-Khvedosyuk (URS)
4	Roswitha Esser (GDR)
4	Annemarie Zimmermann (GDR)

Most Medals, Men
8	Gert Fredriksson (SWE)
6	Rüdiger Helm (GDR)
5	Ivan Patzaichin (ROM)
4	Vasile Diba (ROM)
4	Bernd Olbricht (GDR)
4	Matija Ljubek (YUG)

Most Gold Medals, Men
6	Gert Fredriksson (SWE)
3	Rüdiger Helm (GDR)
3	Ivan Patzaichin (ROM)
3	Vladimir Morozov (URS)
3	Vladimir Parvenovitch (URS)
3	Sergei Chukrai (URS)
3	Ian Ferguson (NZL)

Most Years Winning Medals, Men
4	Gert Fredriksson (SWE)
3	Ivan Patzaichin (ROM)
3	Vladimir Morozov (URS)

Most Years Winning Gold Medals, Men
4	Gert Fredriksson (SWE)
3	Ivan Patzaichin (ROM)
3	Vladimir Morozov (URS)

Most Years Between Medals, Men
  16   Jan Brzák-Felix (TCH)
  16   Ivan Patzaichin (ROM)
  12   Gert Fredriksson (SWE)

Most Years Between Gold Medals, Men
  12   Jan Brzák-Felix (TCH)
  12   Gert Fredriksson (SWE)
  12   Ivan Patzaichin (ROM)
   8   Matija Ljubek (YUG)
   8   Vladimir Morozov (URS)

Most Medals, Games
   3   Rüdiger Helm (GDR-1976)
   3   Rüdiger Helm (GDR-1980)
   3   Vladimir Parvenovitch (URS-1980)
   3   Ian Ferguson (NZL-1984)
   3   Lars-Erik Moberg (SWE-1984)
   3   Agneta Andersson (SWE-1984)

Most Gold Medals, Games
   3   Vladimir Parvenovitch (URS-1980)
   3   Ian Ferguson (NZL-1984)

Most Medals, Games, Men
   3   Rüdiger Helm (GDR-1976)
   3   Rüdiger Helm (GDR-1980)
   3   Vladimir Parvenovitch (URS-1980)
   3   Ian Ferguson (NZL-1984)
   3   Lars-Erik Moberg (SWE-1984)

Most Gold Medals, Games, Men
   3   Vladimir Parvenovitch (URS-1980)
   3   Ian Ferguson (NZL-1984)

Most Medals, Games, Women
   3   Agneta Andersson (SWE-1984)

Most Gold Medals, Games, Women
   2   Antonina Seredina (URS-1960)
   2   Agneta Andersson (SWE-1984)

Most Appearances
   5   Ivan Patzaichin (ROM, 1968-84)
   5   Adrian Powell (AUS, 1960-76)
   4   Thirteen athletes tied with four.

Youngest Medalist, Women
  15-221 Francine Anne Fox (USA-1964)
  17-192 Gisela Grothaus (FRG-1972)
  18-158 Birgit Fischer (GDR-1980)
  19-066 Bärbel Köster (GDR-1976)
  19-081 Eva Rakusz (HUN-1980)

Youngest Gold Medalist, Women
  18-158 Birgit Fischer (GDR-1980)
  20-149 Anna Olsson (SWE-1984)
  20-151 Angelika Bahmann (GDR-1972)
  20-245 Carsta Genäuß (GDR-1980)
  21-319 Carola Zirzov (GDR-1976)

Oldest Medalist, Women
  37-307 Antonina Seredina (URS-1968)
  37-259 Sylvia Saimo (FIN-1952)
  36-303 Nina Savina (URS-1952)
  36-239 Lyudmila Pinaeeva-Khvedosyuk (URS-1972)
  35-216 Glorianne Perrier (USA-1964)

Oldest Gold Medalist, Women
  37-259 Sylvi Saimo (FIN-1952)
  36-239 Lyudmila Pinaeeva-Khvedosyuk (URS-1972)
  32-285 Lyudmila Pinaeeva-Khvedosyuk (URS-1968)
  30-177 Maria Stefan (ROM-1984)
  30-160 Nastasia Ionescu (ROM-1984)

Youngest Medalist, Men
  17-348 Gábor Novák (HUN-1952)
  18-059 Bent Peder Rasch (DEN-1952)
  18-132 Erik Bladström (SWE-1936)
  18-191 Olaf Heukrodt (GDR-1980)
  18-334 Ivan Patzaichin (ROM-1968)

Youngest Gold Medalist, Men
  18-059 Bent Peder Rasch (DEN-1952)
  18-132 Eric Bladström (SWE-1936)
  18-334 Ivan Patzaichin (ROM-1968)
  19-041 Vladimir Romanovskiy (URS-1976)
  19-235 Sergei Nagorny (URS-1976)

Oldest Medalist, Men
  40-282 Gert Fredriksson (SWE-1960)
  40-113 Jan Brzák-Felix (TCH-1952)
  40-041 Wilfried Soltau (FRG-1952)
  37-011 Gert Fredriksson (SWE-1956)
  36-178 Bernhard Jensen (DEN-1948)

Oldest Gold Medalist, Men
  40-282 Gert Fredriksson (SWE-1960)
  37-011 Gert Fredriksson (SWE-1956)
  36-128 Jan Brzák-Felix (TCH-1948)
  34-259 Ivan Patzaichin (ROM-1984)
  33-361 Stephen Lysak (USA-1948)

Medals Won by Countries

	G	S	B	T
USSR	26	10	9	45
Hungary	5	18	15	38
Romania	9	9	11	29
Sweden	13	8	2	23
FRG	4	11	8	23
GDR	12	3	7	22
France	1	5	9	15
Austria	3	5	5	13
Canada	3	6	4	13
Denmark	3	3	5	11
Czechoslovakia	6	3	1	10
Finland	4	2	3	9
United States	2	3	4	9
Germany	3	3	2	8
Netherlands	–	3	4	7
Bulgaria	1	2	3	6
Yugoslavia	2	2	1	5
New Zealand	4	–	–	4
Norway	1	1	2	4
Poland	–	1	3	4
Spain	–	2	2	4
Australia	–	1	2	3
Italy	–	1	–	1
Totals	102	102	102	306

Medals Won by Countries, Men

	G	S	B	T
USSR	18	8	6	32
Hungary	5	16	11	32
Romania	8	8	8	24
Sweden	11	7	2	20
GDR	8	2	6	16
France	1	5	9	15
FRG	2	5	6	13
Canada	3	5	3	11
Austria	3	4	4	11
Czechoslovakia	6	3	1	10
Denmark	2	3	4	9
Finland	3	2	3	8
Germany	3	3	2	8
United States	2	2	3	7
Yugoslavia	2	2	1	5
Bulgaria	1	1	3	5
New Zealand	4	–	–	4
Norway	1	1	2	4
Spain	–	2	2	4
Netherlands	–	1	3	4
Poland	–	1	2	3
Australia	–	1	2	3
Italy	–	1	–	1
Totals	83	83	83	249

Medals Won by Countries, Women

	G	S	B	T
USSR	8	2	3	13
FRG	2	6	2	10
GDR	4	1	1	6
Hungary	–	2	4	6
Romania	1	1	3	5
Sweden	2	1	–	3
Netherlands	–	2	1	3
Denmark	1	–	1	2
Austria	–	1	1	2
Canada	–	1	1	2
United States	–	1	1	2
Finland	1	–	–	1
Bulgaria	–	1	–	1
Poland	–	–	1	1
Totals	19	19	19	57

Best Performance by Country at Each Olympics

		Men	Women	Overall
1936	–	Austria	-----	-----
1948	–	Sweden	one event only	-----
1952	–	Finland	one event only	-----
1956	–	USSR	one event only	-----
1960	–	Hungary	USSR	USSR
1964	–	USSR	USSR/Germany	USSR
1968	–	Hungary	FRG	Hungary
1972	–	USSR	USSR	USSR
1976	–	USSR	USSR	USSR
1980	–	USSR	GDR	USSR
1984	–	New Zealand	Sweden	Sweden

CYCLING

International Federation: Fédération Internationale Amateur de
     Cyclisme (FIAC)
Countries Affiliated: 122 (1987)
Year of Formation: 1900
First Year of Olympic Appearance: 1896

Most Medals
   6   Burton Downing (USA)
   5   Marcus Hurley (USA)
   5   Daniel Morelon (FRA)
   4   Teddy Billington (USA)
   4   Pierre Trentin (FRA)

Most Gold Medals
   4   Marcus Hurley (USA)
   3   Daniel Morelon (FRA)
   3   Robert Charpentier (FRA)
   3   Paul Masson (FRA)
   3/0   Francesco Verri (FRA)

Most Silver Medals
   3   Burton Downing (USA)
   3   Cyril Alden (GBR)
   3   H. Thomas Johnson (GBR)

Most Bronze Medals
   3   Teddy Billington (USA)

Most Years Winning Medals
   4   Daniel Morelon (FRA)
   3   Niels Fredborg (DEN)
   3   Ragnar Malm (SWE)

Most Years Winning Gold Medals
   2   Daniel Morelon (FRA)
   2   Sergio Bianchetto (ITA)
   2   Günther Schumacher (FRG)

Most Years Between Medals
   12   Daniel Morelon (FRA)
   12   H. Thomas Johnson (GBR)
   12   Ragnar Malm (SWE)

Most Years Between Gold Medals
   4   Daniel Morelon (FRA)
   4   Sergio Bianchetto (ITA)
   4   Günther Schumacher (FRG)

Most Medals, Games
```
6        Burton Downing (USA-1904)
5        Marcus Hurley (USA-1904)
4        Teddy Billington (USA-1904)
3        Ten athletes tied with three.
```

Most Gold Medals, Games
```
4        Marcus Hurley (USA-1904)
3        Robert Charpentier (FRA-1936)
3        Paul Masson (FRA-1896)
3/0      Francesco Verri (ITA-1906)
```

Most Medals, Individual
```
6        Burton Downing (USA)
5        Marcus Hurley (USA)
4        Daniel Morelon (FRA)
4        Teddy Billington (USA)
```

Most Gold Medals, Individual
```
4        Marcus Hurley (USA)
3        Paul Masson (FRA)
3        Francesco Verri (ITA)
2        Daniel Morelon (FRA)
2        Burton Downing (USA)
```

Most Medals, Games, Individual
```
6        Burton Downing (USA)
5        Marcus Hurley (USA)
4        Teddy Billington (USA)
```

Most Gold Medals, Games, Individual
```
4        Marcus Hurley (USA-1904)
3        Paul Masson (FRA-1896)
3        Francesco Verri (ITA-1906)
```

Most Appearances
```
4        Gerardus van Drakestein (HOL, 1908-20, 28)
4        Niels Fredborg (DEN, 1964-76)
4        Harry Hannus (FIN, 1972-84)
4        Joseph Kono (CMR, 1972-84)
4        Daniel Morelon (FRA, 1964-76)
4        Pierre Trentin (FRA, 1964-76)
```

Youngest Medalist, Women
```
17-217  Sandra Schumacher (FRG-1984)
```

Oldest Medalist, Women
```
27-160  Connie Carpenter-Phinney (USA-1984)
```

Youngest Medalist, Men
```
17-304  Franco Giorgetti (ITA-1920)
18-043  Dean Woods (AUS-1984)
18-115  Villy Falck Hansen (DEN-1924)
18-146  Benedykt Kocot (POL-1972)
18-155  Louis Chaillot (FRA-1932)
```

Youngest Gold Medalist, Men
  17-304   Franco Giorgetti (ITA-1920)
  18-043   Dean Woods (AUS-1984)
  18-155   Louis Chaillot (FRA-1932)
  18-235   Evart Dolman (HOL-1964)
  18-329   Leon Delathouwer (BEL-1948)

Oldest Medalist, Men
  42-084   Maurice Peeters (HOL-1924)
  39-208   Cyril Alden (GBR-1924)
  38-100   Maurice Peeters (HOL-1920)
  36-225   W. G. "Jock" Stewart (GBR-1920)
  35-224   Cyril Alden (GBR-1920)

Oldest Gold Medalist, Men
  38-100   Maurice Peeters (HOL-1920)
  30-006   Leonard Meredith (GBR-1908)
  28-245   Igor Tselovalnikov (URS-1972)
  28-134   Primo Magnani (ITA-1920)
  28-036   Daniel Morelon (FRA-1972)

Olympic Cyclists and the Tour de France
  Among the greatest professional cyclists who have starred in the
    Tour de France, only a few have had Olympic experience.
    Three-time winner Philippe Thys (BEL-1913/14/20) never
    competed in the Olympics, nor did Fausto Coppi (ITA-1949/52)
    Louison Bobet (FRA-1953/54/55), nor Bernard Hinault (FRA-
    1978/79/81/82/85)
  Eddy Merckx (BEL-1969/70/71/72/74), arguably the greatest
    cyclist ever, competed in the 1964 Olympics in the individual
    road race, finishing 12th.
  Jacques Anquetil (FRA-1957/61/62/63/64), whose record of five
    wins has been tied by Merckx and Hinault, competed in the 1952
    Olympic individual road race, oddly also finishing 12th. But
    Anquetil did win an Olympic medal, having been a member of the
    French team in the road race, which finished third in the
    overall team event.
  The only Olympic gold medalist to also have won the Tour de
    France is Gerardes Jozef "Joop" Zoetemelk (HOL). Zoetemelk
    won his gold medal in the 1968 104 kilometre team time trial
    as a member of the Dutch team. At 34 years of age, he won his
    Tour de France in 1980 and, amazingly, in 1985, aged 39 years,
    he won the world professional road race championship.
  The feat of winning the Olympic road race and the world
    professional road race, has also been achieved. Hennie Kuiper
    (HOL) won his Olympic gold in 1972 and took the world
    professional title in 1975.
  Greg LeMond (USA-1986), first American to win the Tour de
    France, qualified for the United States Olympic team in 1980,
    but as a member of that ill-fated team, did not compete in the
    Olympics.

Cycling - Olympic Record Progressions

1,000 metre time trial

1:16.0	4		Octave Dayen (FRA)	1928
1:15.2	2		Gerard van Drakestein (HOL)	1928
1:14.4	1		Willy Falck-Hansen (DEN)	1928
1:13.0	1		Edgar Gray (AUS)	1932
1:12.0	1		Arie van Vliet (HOL)	1936
1:11.1	1		Russell Mockridge (AUS)	1952
1:09.8	1		Leandro Faggin (ITA)	1956
1:09.20	4		Pieter van der Touw (HOL)	1960
1:08.75	2		Dieter Gieseler (FRG)	1960
1:07.27	1	WR	Sante Gaiardoni (ITA)	1960
[1:04.65A]	4		Gianni Sartori (ITA)	1968
[1:04.61A]	2	=WR	Niels Fredborg (DEN)	1968
[1:03.91A]	1	WR	Pierre Trentin (FRA)	1968
1:07.02	3		Jürgen Schütze (GDR)	1972
1:06.87	2		Daniel Clark (AUS)	1972
1:06.44	1		Niels Fredborg (DEN)	1972
1:05.93	1		Klaus-Jürgen Grunke (GDR)	1976
1:05.478	4		Guido Bontempi (ITA)	1980
1:04.845	2		Aleksandr Panfilov (URS)	1980
1:02.955	1	WR	Lothar Thoms (GDR)	1980

Match Sprint (time measured only for last 200 metres)

15.4	h1	Hildebrand (FRA)	1900
14.2	h2	Cayron (FRA)	1900
14.0	h6	John Lake (USA)	1900
13.6	h9	Restelli (ITA)	1900
13.2	q1	John Lake (USA)	1900
13.0	q4	Restelli (ITA)	1900
12.6	q5	Georges Taillandier (FRA)	1900
12.6	h6	H. Thomas Johnson (GBR)	1920
12.6	h12	Gerald Halpin (AUS)	1920
12.6	q2	Gerald Halpin (AUS)	1920
11.8	q5	H. Thomas Johnson (GBR)	1920
11.8	f(1)	Toni Merkens (GER)	1936
11.8	f(2)	Toni Merkens (GER)	1936
11.7	h6	Cyril Peacock (GBR)	1952
11.7	ré1	Werner Potzernheim (FRG)	1952
11.7	ré3	J. Millman (CAN)	1952
11.7	q2	Cyril Peacock (GBR)	1952
11.6	q4	Werner Potzernheim (FRG)	1952
11.6	s2	Lionel Cox (AUS)	1952

11.6	ré2r2	Werner Potzernheim (FRG)	1952
11.6	h2	Michel Rousseau (FRA)	1956
11.4	q1(2)	Michel Rousseau (FRA)	1956
11.4	q4(1)	Warren Johnston (NZL)	1956
11.4	f(1)	Michel Rousseau (FRA)	1956
11.4	f(2)	Michel Rousseau (FRA)	1956
11.4	3p(2)	Richard Ploog (AUS)	1956
11.4	h3r1	Leo Sterckx (BEL)	1960
11.4	h4r2	Anesio Argenton (BRA)	1960
11.3	h5r2	Leo Sterckx (BEL)	1960
11.3	q4(2)	Sante Gaiardoni (ITA)	1960
11.1	s1(1)	Valentino Gasparella (ITA)	1960
11.1	f(1)	Sante Gaiardoni (ITA)	1960
[11.10]	h8r1	Johannes Janssen (HOL)	1968
[10.87]	h9r1	Dino Verzini (ITA)	1968
[10.70]	h5r2	Roger Gibbon (TRI)	1968
[10.66]	h2r3	Leijn Loevesijn (HOL)	1968
10.78	f(2)	Anton Tkáč (TCH)	1976
10.70	h3r1	Yavé Cahard (FRA)	1980
10.55	h4r2	Sergei Kopylov (URS)	1980
10.47	3p(2)	Sergei Kopylov (URS)	1980

4,000 metre team pursuit

6:20.1	q1	Italy	1920
		(Giorgetti, Ferrario, Carli, Magnani)	
6:13.4	q2	Belgium	1920
		(Janssens, de Buinne, van Doorselaer, Deschryver)	
5:23.8	q3	Great Britain	1920
		(White, Johnson, Stewart, Alden)	
5:21.0	q4	South Africa	1920
		(Smith, Walker, Goosen, Kaltenbrun)	
5:14.0	s1	Great Britain	1920
		(White, Johnson, Stewart, Alden)	
5:10.8	s2	Italy	1920
		(Giorgetti, Ferrario, Carli, Magnani)	
5:01.6	q1	Great Britain	1928
		(Wyld, Wyld, Wyld, Southall)	
4:52.9	h1	Italy	1932
		(Cimatti, Pedretti, Ghilardi, Borsari)	
4:49.6	h1	Italy	1936
		(Bianchi, Gentili, Latini, Rigoni)	
4:49.4	h3	Denmark	1936
		(Magnussen, Friis, Jacobsen, Nielsen)	

4:48.6	h6	Germany	1936
		(Arndt, Hassleberg, Hoffmann, Klöchner)	
4:41.8	h7	France	1936
		(Charpentier, Goujan, Lapébie, Le Nizerhy)	
4:40.4	s2	South Africa	1952
		(Shardelow, Swift, Fowler, Estman)	
4:38.4	s1	Italy	1956
		(Faggin, Gasparella, Gandini, Domenicali)	
4:37.4	1	Italy	1956
		(Faggin, Gasparella, Gandini, Domenicali)	
4:29.98	q1	Italy	1960
		(Arienti, Testa, Vallotto, Vigna)	
4:29.32	q3	German Democratic Republic	1960
		(Gröning, Klieme, Köhler, Barleben)	
4:28.88	s2	Italy	1960
		(Arienti, Testa, Vallotto, Vigna)	
[4:26.14A]	Q	Belgium	1968
		(Bens, van Marcke, de Bosscher, Crapez)	
[4:23.58A]	Q	Denmark	1968
		(Asmussen, Lyngemark, Olsen, Frey-Jensen)	
[4:21.88A]	Q	Czechoslovakia	1968
		(Daler, Kondr, Puzrla, Rezac)	
[4:19.90A]	Q WR	German Federal Republic	1968
		(Hempel, Link, Henrichs, Kissner)	
[4:19.29A]	Q WR	USSR	1968
		(Moskvin, Koliushev, Latsis, Kusnetsov)	
[4:16.10A]	Q WR	Italy	1968
		(Bosisio, Morbiato, Roncaglia, Chemello)	
[4:15.76A]	s1 WR	German Federal Republic	1968
		(Hempel, Link, Henrichs, Kissner)	
4:27.30	Q	The Netherlands	1972
		(Dekkers, Kamper, Ponsteen, Schuiten)	
4:26.53	Q	Soviet Union	1972
		(Bykov, Kuznetsov, Stepanenko, Yudin)	
4:23.54	Q	German Federal Republic	1972
		(Colombo, Haritz, Hempel, Schumacher)	
4:23.26	q3	German Democratic Republic	1972
		(Huschke, Richter, Richter, Unterwalder)	
4:23.14	s2	German Democratic Republic	1972
		(Huschke, Richter, Richter, Unterwalder)	
4:22.14	1	German Federal Republic	1972
		(Colombo, Haritz, Hempel, Schumacher)	
4:20.10	q2	German Federal Republic	1976
		(Braun, Lutz, Schumacher, Vonhof)	
4:16.62	Q	Soviet Union	1980
		(Manakov, Movchan, Osokin, Petrakov)	
4:14.64	q4 WR	Soviet Union	1980
		(Manakov, Movchan, Osokin, Petrakov)	

4,000 metre individual pursuit

4:57.48	Q		Tiemen Groen (HOL)	1964
4:56.64	s1		Giorgio Ursi (ITA)	1964
[4:40.41A]	Q	WR	Xaver Kurmann (SUI)	1968
[4:39.87A]	q3	WR	Daniel Rebillard (FRA)	1968
[4:37.54A]	q4	WR	Mogens Frey Jensen (DEN)	1968
4:56.10	Q		Roy Schuiten (HOL)	1972
4:54.50	Q		Xaver Kurmann (SUI)	1972
4:50.06	Q		John Bylsma (AUS)	1972
4:49.06	Q		Knut Knudsen (NOR)	1972
4:47.43	q4		Knut Knudsen (NOR)	1972
4:47.04	s1		Knut Knudsen (NOR)	1972
4:45.74	1		Knut Knudsen (NOR)	1972
4:45.10	q2		Vladimir Osokin (URS)	1976
4:39.96	Q		Harald Wolf (GDR)	1980
4:34.92	q1		Robert Dill-Bundi (SUI)	1980
4:32.29	s2	WR	Robert Dill-Bundi (SUI)	1980

Medals Won by Countries, Men and Women

	G	S	B	T
France	27	15	20	62
Italy	26	14	6	46
Great Britain	8	21	14	43
United States	11	9	13	33
Netherlands	8	10	4	22
Belgium	6	6	9	21
Denmark	5	6	7	18
USSR	7	3	7	17
FRG	5	5	5	15
GDR	3	7	3	13
Sweden	3	2	7	12
Australia	5	4	2	11
Germany	2	3	5	10
South Africa	1	4	3	8
Poland	-	4	3	7
Czechoslovakia	2	2	2	6
Switzerland	1	3	2	6
Greece	1	3	1	5
Austria	1	-	2	3
Canada	-	2	1	3
Norway	1	-	1	2
Jamaica	-	-	1	1
Japan	-	-	1	1
Mexico	-	-	1	1
Totals	123	123	120	366

*No third in 1896 100 kilometre race. Third-place in 1972 individual road race and 100 kilometre team time trial were both declared void because of a disqualification for drug use. In 1908, the match sprint finals were declared void because the contestants exceeded the time limit. No medals were awarded.

Medals Won by Countries, Women

	G	S	B	T
United States	1	-	1	2
FRG	-	1	-	1
Totals	1	1	1	3

Best Performance by Country at Each Olympics

1896	-	France
1900	-	France
1904	-	United States
1906	-	Great Britain
1908	-	Great Britain
1912	-	Great Britain
1920	-	Great Britain
1924	-	France
1928	-	Denmark
1932	-	Italy
1936	-	France
1948	-	France
1952	-	Italy
1956	-	Italy
1960	-	Italy
1964	-	Italy
1968	-	France
1972	-	USSR
1976	-	FRG
1980	-	USSR
1984	-	United States

DIVING

International Federation: Fédération Internationale de Natation
     Amateur (FINA)
Countries Affiliated: 125 (1987)
First Year of Olympic Appearance: 1896
Year of Formation: 1908

Most Medals

| 5 | Klaus Dibiasi (ITA) |
| 4 | Nine athletes tied with four. |

Most Gold Medals

4	Pat McCormick (USA)
3	Klaus Dibiasi (ITA)
3	Ingrid Engel-Krämer (GDR)
2	Ten athletes tied with two.

Most Silver Medals

| 3 | Paula Jean Myers-Pope (USA) |
| 2 | Nine athletes tied with two. |

Most Bronze Medals
   2   Clarence Pinkston (USA)
   2   Joaquin Capilla Peréz (MEX)
   2   Franco Cagnotto (ITA)
   2   John Jansson (SWE)

Most Years Winning Medals
   4   Klaus Dibiasi (ITA)
   3   Franco Cagnotto (ITA)
   3   Joaquin Capilla Peréz (MEX)
   3   Dorothy Poynton-Hill (USA)
   3   Paula Jean Myers-Pope (USA)
   3   John Jansson (SWE)

Most Years Winning Gold Medals
   3   Klaus Dibiasi (ITA)
   2   Samuel Lee (USA)
   2   Robert Webster (USA)
   2   Pat McCormick (USA)
   2   Ingrid Engel-Krämer (GDR)
   2   Elizabeth Becker-Pinkston (USA)
   2   Dorothy Poynton-Hill (USA)

Most Years Between Medals
   12   Klaus Dibiasi (ITA)
   8   Franco Cagnotto (ITA)
   8   Joaquin Capilla Peréz (MEX)
   8   Dorothy Poynton-Hill (USA)
   8   Paula Jean Myers-Pope (USA)
   8   Gregory Louganis (USA)

Most Years Between Gold Medals
   8   Klaus Dibiasi (ITA)
   4   Six athletes tied with four.

Most Medals, Women
   4   Pat McCormick (USA)
   4   Georgia Coleman (USA)
   4   Ingrid Engel-Krämer (GDR)
   4   Dorothy Poynton-Hill (USA)
   4   Paula Jean Myers-Pope (USA)

Most Gold Medals, Women
   4   Pat McCormick (USA)
   3   Ingrid Engel-Krämer (GDR)
   2   Dorothy Hill-Poynton (USA)
   2   Elizabeth Becker-Pinkston (USA)

Most Silver Medals, Women
   3   Paula Jean Myers-Pope (USA)
   2   Katherine Rawls (USA)
   2   Ulrika Knape (SWE)
   2   Georgia Coleman (USA)

Most Bronze Medals, Women
   1   Many athletes tied with one.

Most Years Winning Medals, Women
   3   Dorothy Poynton-Hill (USA)
   3   Paula Jean Myers-Pope (USA)

Most Years Winning Gold Medals, Women
   2   Pat McCormick (USA)
   2   Ingrid Engel-Krämer (GDR)
   2   Elizabeth Becker-Pinkston (USA)
   2   Dorothy Poynton-Hill (USA)

Most Years Between Medals, Women
   8   Dorothy Poynton-Hill (USA)
   8   Paula Jean Myers-Pope (USA)

Most Years Between Gold Medals, Women
   4   Pat McCormick (USA)
   4   Ingrid Engel-Krämer (GDR)
   4   Elizabeth Becker (USA)
   4   Dorothy Poynton-Hill (USA)

Most Medals, Men
   5   Klaus Dibiasi (ITA)
   4   Franco Cagnotto (ITA)
   4   Joaquin Capilla Peréz (MEX)
   4   Michael Galitzen (USA)
   4   Clarence Pinkston (USA)

Most Gold Medals, Men
   3   Klaus Dibiasi (ITA)
   2   Gregory Louganis (USA)
   2   Albert White (USA)
   2   Peter Desjardins (USA)
   2   Samuel Lee (USA)
   2   Robert Webster (USA)
   2   Erik Adlerz (SWE)

Most Silver Medals, Men
   2   Michael Galitzen (USA)
   2   Miller Anderson (USA)
   2   Franco Cagnotto (ITA)
   2   Georg Hoffmann (GER)
   2   Gary Tobian (USA)

Most Bronze Medals, Men
   2   Clarence Pinkston (USA)
   2   Joaquin Capilla Peréz (MEX)
   2   Franco Cagnotto (ITA)
   2   John Jansson (SWE)

Most Years Winning Medals, Men
   4   Klaus Dibiasi (ITA)
   3   Franco Cagnotto (ITA)
   3   Joaquin Capilla Peréz (MEX)
   3   John Jansson (SWE)

Most Years Winning Gold Medals, Men
   3   Klaus Dibiasi (ITA)
   2   Samuel Lee (USA)
   2   Robert Webster (USA)

Most Years Between Medals, Men
  12   Klaus Dibiasi (ITA)
   8   Franco Cagnotto (ITA)
   8   Joaquin Capilla Peréz (MEX)
   8   Gregory Louganis (USA)

Most Years Between Gold Medals, Men
   8   Klaus Dibiasi (ITA)
   4   Samuel Lee (USA)
   4   Robert Webster (USA)

Most Appearances
   5   Franco Cagnotto (ITA, 1964-80)
   4   Erik Adlerz (SWE, 1908-24)
   4   Klaus Dibiasi (ITA, 1964-76)
   4   Carlos Giron (MEX, 1972-84)
   4   Nicolle Pellissard-Darrigrand (FRA, 1968-80)
   4   Juno Stover-Irwin (USA, 1948-60)

Most Appearances, Men
   5   Franco Cagnotto (ITA, 1964-80)
   4   Erik Adlerz (SWE, 1908-24)
   4   Klaus Dibiasi (ITA, 1964-76)
   4   Carlos Giron (MEX, 1972-84)

Most Appearances, Women
   4   Nicolle Pellissard-Darrigrand (FRA, 1968-80)
   4   Juno Stover-Irwin (USA, 1948-60)

Winning Platform and Springboard, Same Year
   1924   Albert White (USA)
   1928   Peter Desjardins (USA)
   1948   Victoria Draves (USA)
   1952   Pat McCormick (USA)
   1956   Pat McCormick (USA)
   1960   Ingrid Krämer (GDR)
   1984   Gregory Louganis (USA)

Winning Platform and Springboard, Different Years
   Elizabeth Becker-Pinkston (USA) (1924 Springboard, 1928
      Platform)

Youngest Medalist, Women
    13-024   Dorothy Poynton (USA-1928)
    13-268   Marjorie Gestring (USA-1936)
    14-052   Sirvard Emirzian (URS-1980)
    14-058   Katherine Rawls (USA-1932)
    14-120   Aileen Riggin (USA-1920)
    14-168   Helen Wainwright (USA-1920)
    16-181   Milena Duchková (TCH-1968)
    16-199   Georgia Coleman (USA-1928)
    16-228   Eva Ollivier (SWE-1920)
    17-027   Dorothy Poynton (USA-1932)

Youngest Gold Medalist, Women
    13-268   Marjorie Gestring (USA-1936)
    14-120   Aileen Riggin (USA-1920)
    16-181   Milena Duchková (TCH-1968)
    17-027   Dorothy Poynton (USA-1932)
    17-029   Lesley Bush (USA-1964)
    17-030   Ingrid Krämer (GDR-1960)
    17-038   Jennifer Chandler (USA-1976)
    17-130   Ulrika Knape (SWE-1972)
    17-186   Greta Johansson (SWE-1912)
    18-000   Caroline Smith (USA-1924)

Oldest Medalist, Women
    33-293   Ninel Krutova (URS-1960)
    28-033   Micki King (USA-1972)
    27-206   Christina Seufert (USA-1984)
    26-210   Pat McCormick (USA-1956)
    25-328   Cynthia McIngvale (USA-1976)

Oldest Gold Medalist, Women
    28-033   Micki King (USA-1972)
    26-210   Pat McCormick (USA-1956)
    25-159   Elizabeth Becker-Pinkston (USA-1928)
    23-237   Helen Meany (USA-1928)
    23-218   Victoria Draves (USA-1948)

Youngest Medalist, Men
    14-011   Nils Skoglund (SWE-1920)
    16-134   Brian Phelps (GBR-1960)
    16-180   Gregory Louganis (USA-1976)
    16-319   Vladimir Aleinik (URS-1976)
    17-013   Klaus Dibiasi (ITA-1964)

Youngest Gold Medalist, Men
    18-170   Albert Zürner (GER-1908)
    18-310   Aleksandr Portnov (URS-1980)
    19-148   Louis Kuehn (USA-1920)
    19-204   Arvid Wallman (SWE-1920)
    19-244   Kenneth Sitzberger (USA-1964)

Oldest Medalist, Men
  38-173 Hjalmar Johansson (SWE-1912)
  35-196 Harold Clarke (GBR-1924)
  34-186 Hjalmar Johansson (SWE-1908)
  33-052 Franco Cagnotto (ITA-1980)
  32-210 Karl Malmström (SWE-1908)

Oldest Gold Medalist, Men
  34-186 Hjalmar Johansson (SWE-1908)
  32-000 Samuel Lee (USA-1952)
  30-114 George Sheldon (USA-1904)
  29-072 Albert White (USA-1924)
  28-323 Paul Günther (GER-1912)

Medals Won by Countries

	G	S	B	T
United States	43	38	36	117
Sweden	6	8	7	21
USSR	4	4	6	14
Germany	3	5	5	13
GDR	5	3	3	11
Italy	3	4	2	9
Mexico	1	3	3	7
Great Britain	-	1	4	5
China	1	1	1	3
Czechoslovakia	1	1	-	2
Canada	1	-	1	2
Denmark	1	-	1	2
Egypt	-	1	1	2
Australia	1	-	-	1
France	-	1	-	1
FRG	-	-	1	1
Austria	-	-	1	1
Totals	70	70	72	212

Medals Won by Countries, Men

	G	S	B	T
United States	24	19	19	62
Sweden	4	5	4	13
Germany	3	5	4	12
Italy	3	4	2	9
Mexico	1	3	3	7
USSR	2	1	3	6
China	-	1	1	2
Egypt	-	1	1	2
Great Britain	-	-	2	2
GDR	1	-	-	1
Australia	1	-	-	1
FRG	-	-	1	1
Austria	-	-	1	1
Totals	39	39	41	119

*Two thirds in 1904 platform; two thirds in 1908 springboard.

Medals Won by Countries, Women

	G	S	B	T
United States	19	19	17	55
GDR	4	3	3	10
Sweden	2	3	3	8
USSR	2	3	3	8
Great Britain	-	1	2	3
Czechoslovakia	1	1	-	2
Canada	1	-	1	2
Denmark	1	-	1	2
China	1	-	-	1
France	-	1	-	1
Germany	-	-	1	1
Totals	31	31	31	93

Best Performance by Country at Each Olympics

Year	Men	Women	Overall
1904 -	United States	-----	-----
1906 -	Germany	-----	-----
1908 -	Sweden/Germany	-----	-----
1912 -	Germany	one event only	-----
1920 -	United States	United States	United States
1924 -	United States	United States	United States
1928 -	United States	United States	United States
1932 -	United States	United States	United States
1936 -	United States	United States	United States
1948 -	United States	United States	United States
1952 -	United States	United States	United States
1956 -	United States	United States	United States
1960 -	United States	GDR	United States
1964 -	United States	United States	United States
1968 -	Italy	United States	United States
1972 -	Italy	Sweden	USA/Italy
1976 -	USA/Italy	United States	United States
1980 -	USSR	USSR/GDR	USSR
1984 -	United States	United States	United States

EQUESTRIAN EVENTS

International Federation: Fédération Equestre Internationale
     (FEI)
Countries Affiliated: 80 (1987)
First Year of Olympic Appearance: 1900
Year of Formation: 1921

Most Medals
   7   Reiner Klimke (FRG)
   7   Hans-Günter Winkler (FRG)
   6   Piero D'Inzeo (ITA)
   6   Raimondo D'Inzeo (ITA)
   6   Josef Neckermann (FRG)
   6   Michael Plumb (USA)
   5   Henri Chammartin (SUI)
   5   Gustav Fischer (SUI)
   5   André Jousseaume (FRA)
   5   Liselott Linsenhoff (FRG)
   5   Earl Thomson (USA)

Most Gold Medals
   5   Reiner Klimke (FRG)
   5   Hans-Günter Winkler (FRG)
   4   Henri St. Cyr (SWE)
   3   Xavier Lesage (FRA)
   3   Richard Meade (GBR)
   3   Adolph van der Voort van Zijp (HOL)

Most Silver Medals
   4   Michael Plumb (USA)
   3   Gustav Fischer (SUI)
   3   Earl Thomson (USA)

Most Bronze Medals
   4   Piero D'Inzeo (ITA)
   3   Raimondo D'Inzeo (ITA)
   3   Fritz Ligges (FRG)

Most Years Winning Medals
   6   Hans-Günter Winkler (FRG)
   5   Michael Plumb (USA)
   5   Gustav Fischer (SUI)
   4   Reiner Klimke (FRG)
   4   Piero D'Inzeo (ITA)
   4   Raimondo D'Inzeo (ITA)
   4   Josef Neckermann (FRG)
   4   Henri Chammartin (SUI)
   4   André Jousseaume (FRA)
   4   Gustaf-Adolf Boltenstern, Jr. (SWE)
   4   William Steinkraus (USA)

Most Years Winning Gold Medals
    4   Reiner Klimke (FRG)
    4   Hans-Günter Winkler (FRG)

Most Years Between Medals
    24   Gustaf-Adolf Boltenstern, Jr. (SWE)
    20   Reiner Klimke (FRG)
    20   Hans-Günter Winkler (FRG)
    20   Michael Plumb (USA)
    20   André Jousseaume (FRA)
    20   William Steinkraus (USA)
    20   José Navaro Morenes (ESP)

Most Years Between Gold Medals
    20   Reiner Klimke (FRG)
    16   Hans-Günter Winkler (FRG)
    16   André Jousseaume (FRA)
    16   Earl Thomson (USA)
    16   Alwin Schockemöhle (FRG)
    12   Harry Boldt (FRG)

Most Medals, Women
    5   Liselott Linsenhoff (FRG)
    3   Yelena Petushkova (URS)
    3   Christine Stückelberger (SUI)

Most Gold Medals, Women
    2   Liselott Linsenhoff (FRG)
    1   Twelve athletes tied with one.

Most Appearances
    8   Raimondo d'Inzeo (ITA, 1948-76)
    7   Piero d'Inzeo (ITA, 1952-76)
    6   Frank Chapot (USA, 1956-76)
    6   James Elder (CAN, 1956-60, 68, 76, 84)
    6   Michael Plumb (USA, 1960-76, 84)
    6   Hans-Günter Winkler (FRG/GER, 1956-76)

Most Appearances, Men
    8   Raimondo d'Inzeo (ITA, 1948-76)
    7   Piero d'Inzeo (ITA, 1952-76)
    6   Frank Chapot (USA, 1956-76)
    6   James Elder (CAN, 1956-60, 68, 76, 84)
    6   Michael Plumb (USA, 1960-76, 84)
    6   Hans-Günter Winkler (FRG/GER, 1956-76)

Most Appearances, Women
    5   Christilot Hanson-Boylen (CAN, 1964-76, 84)

Youngest Medalist, Women
    20-235 Mary Anne Tauskey (USA-1976)
    21-162 Marianne Gossweiler (SUI-1964)
    21-257 Marina Sciocchetti (ITA-1980)
    21-270 Bettina Overesch (FRG-1984)
    22-015 Ann Moore (GBR-1972)

Youngest Gold Medalist, Women
    20-235   Mary Anne Tauskey (USA-1976)
    23-315   Elisabeth "Sissy" Theurer (AUT-1980)
    23-345   Gabriella Grillo (FRG-1976)

Oldest Medalist, Women
    46-274   Ulla Håkanson (SWE-1984)
    46-258   Maud von Rosen (SWE-1972)
    45-012   Liselott Linsenhoff (FRG-1972)
    43-339   Edith Master (USA-1976)
    41-060   Liselott Linsenhoff (FRG-1968)

Oldest Gold Medalist, Women
    45-012   Liselott Linsenhoff (FRG-1972)
    41-060   Liselott Linsenhoff (FRG-1968)
    35-005   Torrance Fleischmann (USA-1984)
    33-274   Karen Stives (USA-1984)
    33-240   Bridget Parker (GBR-1972)

Youngest Medalist, Men
    18-094   Antonio Borges de Almeida (POR-1924)
    19-070   Stanny van Paeschen (BEL-1976)
    21-078   Edmund "Tad" Coffin (USA-1976)
    21-114   John Wofford (USA-1952)
    21-233   Mauro Checcoli (ITA-1964)

Youngest Gold Medalist, Men
    21-078   Edmund "Tad" Coffin (USA-1976)
    21-233   Mauro Checcoli (ITA-1964)
    22-113   Jim Day (GBR-1968)
    23-343   Hans van Rosen (SWE-1912)
    23-344   Mark Phillips (GBR-1972)

Oldest Medalist, Men
    61-131   William Roycroft (AUS-1976)
    60-094   Josef Neckermann (FRG-1972)
    58-003   André Jousseaume (FRA-1952)
    57-283   Petre Rosca (ROM-1980)
    56-142   Josef Neckermann (FRG-1968)
    56-105   Carl Bonde (SWE-1928)
    56-091   Ernst Linder (SWE-1924)
    54-286   Derek Allhusen (GBR-1968)
    54-094   Henri St. Cyr (SWE-1956)
    54-014   André Jousseaume (FRA-1948)

Oldest Gold Medalist, Men
```
56-142   Josef Neckermann (FRG-1968)
56-091   Ernst Linder (SWE-1924)
54-286   Derek Allhusen (GBR-1968)
54-094   Henri St. Cyr (SWE-1956)
54-014   André Jousseaume (FRA-1948)
52-140   Josef Neckermann (FRG-1964)
52-032   Gustav Boltenstern, Jr. (SWE-1956)
52-020   Friedrich Gerhard (GER-1936)
50-137   Henri St. Cyr (SWE-1952)
48-208   Reiner Klimke (FRG-1984)
```

Medals Won by Countries, Men and Women

	G	S	B	T
Sweden	17	8	14	39
FRG	12	11	14	37
United States	8	13	9	30
France	10	11	8	29
Italy	7	9	7	23
Great Britain	5	5	8	18
Switzerland	4	7	6	17
Germany	8	4	3	15
USSR	6	5	4	15
Belgium	4	2	5	11
Netherlands	5	3	1	9
Mexico	2	1	4	7
Poland	1	3	2	6
Australia	2	1	2	5
Denmark	-	4	1	5
Canada	1	1	1	3
Portugal	-	-	3	3
Spain	1	1	-	2
Austria	1	-	1	2
Chile	-	2	-	2
Romania	-	1	1	2
Czechoslovakia	1	-	-	1
Japan	1	-	-	1
New Zealand	1	-	-	1
Norway	-	1	-	1
Bulgaria	-	1	-	1
Argentina	-	1	-	1
Hungary	-	-	1	1
Totals	97	95	95	287

*Two firsts/no second in 1900 high jump event; no third in 1932 3-day event, team. Grand prix jumping event, team, in 1932 declared void as no nation had three riders complete the course.

Medals Won by Countries, Women

	G	S	B	Total
FRG	1.667	1.667	1.583	4.917
Great Britain	0.500	2.750	1.333	4.583
Switzerland	1.000	1.667	1.333	4.000
United States	1.250	1.250	1.000	3.500
Denmark	-	3.000	-	3.000
Sweden	-	-	2.000	2.000
Austria	1.000	-	-	1.000
USSR	0.667	0.333	-	1.000
Italy	-	0.500	-	0.500
Romania	-	-	0.333	0.333

Best Performance by Country at Each Olympics
```
1900 -  Belgium
1912 -  Sweden
1920 -  Sweden
1924 -  Sweden
1928 -  The Netherlands
1932 -  Unietd States
1936 -  Germany
1948 -  France/Mexico
1952 -  Sweden
1956 -  FRG
1960 -  Australia
1964 -  FRG
1968 -  Great Britain
1972 -  FRG
1976 -  FRG
1980 -  USSR
1984 -  United States
```

FENCING

International Federation: Fédération Internationale d'Escrime
    (FIE)
Countries Affiliated: 73 (1987)
First Year of Olympic Appearance: 1896
Year of Formation: 1913

Most Medals
```
13      Edoardo Mangiarotti (ITA)
10      Aládár Gerevich (HUN)
 9      Giulio Gaudini (ITA)
 8      Philippe Cattiau (FRA)
 8      Roger Ducret (FRA)
 7      Pál Kovács (HUN)
 7      Gustavo Marzi (ITA)
 7      Ildikó Saginé-Ujlakiné-Rejtö (HUN)
 6      Eleven athletes tied with six.
```

Most Gold Medals
7   Aládár Gerevich (HUN)
6   Edoardo Mangiarotti (ITA)
6   Pál Kovács (HUN)
6   Rudolf Kárpáti (HUN)
6   Nedo Nadi (ITA)
4   Eleven athletes tied with four.

Most Silver Medals
5   Edoardo Mangiarotti (ITA)
5   Philippe Cattiau (FRA)
5   Gustavo Marzi (ITA)
4   Giulio Gaudini (ITA)
4   Roger Ducret (FRA)
4   Renzo Nostini (ITA)
4   Vicenzo Pinton (ITA)

Most Bronze Medals
5   Daniel Revenu (FRA)
5   Adrianus Jong (HOL)
4   Christian Noel (FRA)
4   Jetze Doorman (HOL)

Most Years Winning Medals
6   Aládár Gerevich (HUN)
5   Edoardo Mangiarotti (ITA)
5   Philippe Cattiau (FRA)
5   Pál Kovács (HUN)
5   Ildikó Saginé-Ujlakiné-Rejtö (HUN)

Most Years Winning Gold Medals
6   Aládár Gerevich (HUN)
5   Pál Kovács (HUN)
4   Viktor Sidyak (URS)
4   Rudolf Kárpáti (HUN)
4   Edoardo Mangiarotti (ITA)

Most Years Between Medals
28   Aládár Gerevich (HUN)
24   Edoardo Mangiarotti (ITA)
24   Pál Kovács (HUN)
20   Manlio DiRosa (ITA)
20   Carlo Agostini (ITA)
20   Marcello Bertinetti (ITA)

Most Years Between Gold Medals
28   Aládár Gerevich (HUN)
24   Edoardo Mangiarotti (ITA)
24   Pál Kovács (HUN)
20   Manlio DiRosa (ITA)
16   Tibor Berczelly (HUN)
16   Alexandre Lippmann (FRA)
16   René Bougnol (FRA)
16   László Rajcsányi (HUN)

Most Medals, Women
7	Ildikó Saginé-Ujlakiné-Rejtö (HUN)
6	Elena Belova-Novikova (URS)
5	Galina Gorochova (URS)
4	Ildikó Bóbis (HUN)
4	Michele Maffei (ITA)
4	Tatyana Samusenko-Petrenko (URS)
4	Ildikó Tordasi-Schwarczenberger (HUN)

Most Gold Medals, Women
4	Elena Belova-Novikova (URS)
3	Galina Gorochova (URS)
3	Tatyana Samusenko-Petrenko (URS)
3	Aleksandra Zabelina (URS)
2	Ildikó Saginé-Ujlakiné-Rejtö (HUN)
2	Ilona Elek (HUN)
2	Pascale Trinquet-Hachin (FRA)
2	Svetlana Chirkova (URS)

Most Silver Medals, Women
3	Ildikó Saginé-Ujlakiné-Rejtö (HUN)
3	Ildikó Bóbis (HUN)
2	Valentina Rastvorova (URS)
2	Lidia Sákovitsné-Dömölky (HUN)

Most Bronze Medals, Women
2	Ildikó Saginé-Ujlakiné-Rejtö (HUN)
2	Ildikó Tordasi-Schwarczenberger (HUN)
2	Antonella Lonzi-Ragno (ITA)
2	Magda Maros (HUN)
2	Edit Kovács (HUN)
2	Ellen Müller-Preiss (AUT)
2	Ecaterina Iencic-Stahl (ROM)
2	Ileana Drimba (ROM)
2	Olga Szabo (ROM)
2	Ana Pascu-Ene-Dersidan (ROM)

Most Years Winning Medals, Women
5	Ildikó Saginé-Ujlakiné-Rejtö (HUN)
4	Elena Belova-Novikova (URS)
4	Galina Gorochova (URS)
4	Tatyana Samusenko-Petrenko (URS)

Most Years Winning Gold Medals, Women
3	Elena Belova-Novikova (URS)
3	Galina Gorochova (URS)
3	Tatyana Samusenko-Petrenko (URS)
3	Aleksandra Zabelina (URS)

Most Years Between Medals, Women
16	Ildikó Saginé-Ujlakiné-Rejtö (HUN)
16	Ilona Elek (HUN)
12	Elena Belova-Novikova (URS)
12	Galina Gorochova (URS)
12	Tatyana Samuesenko-Petrenko (URS)
12	Aleksandra Zabelina (URS)

Most Years Between Gold Medals, Women
12	Galina Gorochova (URS)
12	Tatyana Samusenko-Petrenko (URS)
12	Ilona Elek (HUN)
12	Aleksandra Zabelina (URS)
8	Elena Belova-Novikova (URS)
8	Brigitte Gaudin-Latrille (FRA)

Most Medals, Men
13	Edoardo Mangiarotti (ITA)
10	Aládár Gerevich (HUN)
9	Giulio Gaudini (ITA)
8	Philippe Cattiau (FRA)
8	Roger Ducret (FRA)
7	Pál Kovács (HUN)
7	Gustavo Marzi (ITA)
6	Ten athletes tied with six.

Most Gold Medals, Men
7	Aládár Gerevich (HUN)
6	Edoardo Mangiarotti (ITA)
6	Pál Kovács (HUN)
6	Rudolf Kárpáti (HUN)
6	Nedo Nadi (ITA)
4	Ten athletes tied with four.

Most Silver Medals, Men
5	Edoardo Mangiarotti (ITA)
5	Philippe Cattiau (FRA)
5	Gustavo Marzi (ITA)
4	Giulio Gaudini (ITA)
4	Roger Ducret (FRA)
4	Renzo Nostini (ITA)
4	Vicenzo Pinton (ITA)

Most Bronze Medals, Men
5	Daniel Revenu (FRA)
5	Adrianus Jong (HOL)
4	Christian Noel (FRA)
4	Jetze Doorman (HOL)

Most Years Winning Medals, Men
6	Aládár Gerevich (HUN)
5	Edoardo Mangiarotti (ITA)
5	Philippe Cattiau (FRA)
5	Pál Kovács (HUN)

Most Years Winning Gold Medals, Men
```
6        Aládár Gerevich (HUN)
5        Pál Kovács (HUN)
4        Viktor Sidyak (URS)
4        Rudolf Kárpáti (HUN)
4        Edoardo Mangiarotti (ITA)
```

Most Years Between Medals, Men
```
28       Aládár Gerevich (HUN)
24       Edoardo Mangiarotti (ITA)
24       Pál Kovács (HUN)
20       Manlio DiRosa (ITA)
20       Carlo Agostini (ITA)
20       Marcello Bertinetti (ITA)
```

Most Years Between Gold Medals, Men
```
28       Aládár Gerevich (HUN)
24       Edoardo Mangiarotti (ITA)
24       Pál Kovács (HUN)
20       Manlio DiRosa (ITA)
16       Tibor Berczelly (HUN)
16       Alexandre Lippmann (FRA)
16       René Bougnol (FRA)
16       László Rajcsányi (HUN)
```

Most Medals, Games
```
5        Roger Ducret (FRA-1924)
5        Nedo Nadi (ITA-1920)
5        Albertson van zo Post (USA-1904)
4        Gustav Casmir (GER-1906)
4        Edoardo Mangiarotti (ITA-1932)
4        Aldo Nadi (ITA-1920)
4        Giulio Gaudini (ITA-1936)
```

Most Gold Medals, Games
```
5        Nedo Nadi (ITA-1920)
3        Roger Ducret (FRA-1924)
3        Aldo Nadi (ITA-1920)
3        Ramón Fonst (CUB-1904)
```

Most Medals, Individual
```
4        Edoardo Mangiarotti (ITA)
4        Giulio Gaudini (ITA)
4        Roger Ducret (FRA)
4        Ramón Fonst (CUB)
4        Albertson van zo Post (USA)
4        Jeno Fuchs (HUN)
```

Most Gold Medals, Individual
3	Nedo Nadi (ITA)
3	Ramón Fonst (CUB)
2	Lucien Gaudin (FRA)
2	Rudolf Kárpáti (HUN)
2	Christian d'Oriola (FRA)
2	Jeno Fuchs (HUN)
2	Viktor Krovopuskov (URS)
2	Ilona Elek (HUN)
2/1	Georges de la Falaise (FRA)

Most Medals, Games, Individual
4	Albertson van zo Post (USA-1904)
3	Roger Ducret (FRA-1924)
3	Gustav Casmir (GER-1906)

Most Gold Medals, Games, Individual
2	Nedo Nadi (ITA-1920)
2	Ramón Fonst (CUB-1904)

Most Appearances
7	Ivan Osiier (DEN, 1908-32, 48)
6	Norman Armitage (né Cohn) (USA, 1928-56)
6	Aládár Gerevich (HUN, 1932-60)
6	William Hoskyns (GBR, 1956-76)
6	Adrianus de Jong (HOL, 1906-28)
6	Kerstin Palm (SWE, 1964-84)
6	Jerzy Pawłowski (POL, 1952-72)
6	Janice-Lee Romary-York (USA, 1948-68)

Most Appearances, Men
7	Ivan Osiier (DEN, 1908-32, 48)
6	Norman Armitage (né Cohn) (USA, 1928-56)
6	Aládár Gerevich (HUN, 1932-60)
6	William Hoskyns (GBR, 1956-76)
6	Adrianus de Jong (HOL, 1906-28)
6	Jerzy Pawłowski (POL, 1952-72)

Most Appearances, Women
6	Kerstin Palm (SWE, 1964-84)
6	Janice-Lee Romary-York (USA, 1948-68)
5	Ecaterina Iencic-Stahl (ROM, 1964-80)
5	Olga Orban-Szabo (ROM, 1956-72)
5	Ellen Müller-Preiss (AUT, 1932-56)
5	Ildikó Saginé-Ujlakiné-Rejtö (HUN, 1960-76)

Winning Gold Medals, Foil/Epée/Sabre
  Nedo Nadi (ITA)
  Aldo Nadi (ITA)

Winning Gold Medals, Foil/Epée Individual
  Ramón Fonst (CUB)
  Lucien Gaudin (FRA)

Winning Gold Medals, Foil/Sabre, Individual
  Nedo Nadi (ITA)

Winning Gold Medals, Epée/Sabre, Individual
  Georges de la Falaise (FRA) (includes 1906)

Winning Gold Medals, Foil/Epée
  Philippe Cattiau (FRA)
  Georges Dillon-Kavanagh (FRA) (both 1906)
  Lucien Gaudin (FRA)
  Roger Ducret (FRA)
  André Labatut (FRA)
  Edoardo Mangiarotti (ITA)

Winning Gold Medals, Foil/Sabre
  Abelardo Olivier (ITA)
  Oreste Puliti (IT)

Winning Gold Medals, Epée/Sabre
  Marcello Bertinetti (ITA)
  George de la Falaise (FRA) (includes 1906)

Winning Medals, Foil/Epée/Sabre, Individual
  Roger Ducret (FRA)
  Albertson van zo Post (USA)

Winning Medals, Foil/Epée, Individual
  Georges Dillon-Kavanagh (FRA) (all 1906)
  Ramón Fonst (CUB)
  Lucien Gaudin (FRA)
  Edoardo Mangiarotti (ITA)
  Charles Tatham (USA)

Winning Medals, Foil/Sabre, Individual
  Gustav Casmir (GER) (all 1906)
  Giulio Gaudini (ITA)
  Gustavo Marzi (ITA)
  Nedo Nadi (ITA)

Winning Medals, Epée/Sabre, Individual
  Georges de la Falaise (FRA) (includes 1906)

Youngest Medalist, Women
  17-225   Helene Mayer (GER-1928)
  18-038   Zita Funkhauser (FRG-1984)
  18-052   Olga Orban (ROM-1956)
  18-105   Brigitte Latrille (FRA-1976)
  18-109   Zsuzsa Szöcz (HUN-1980)

Youngest Gold Medalist, Women
  17-225   Helene Mayer (GER-1928)
  18-038   Zita Funkhauser (FRG-1984)
  20-020   Isabelle Boeri-Bégard (FRA-1980)
  20-089   Ellen Müller-Preiss (AUT-1932)
  20-094   Lyudmila Shishova (URS-1960)

Oldest Medalist, Women
45-072 Ilona Elek (HUN-1952)
41-078 Ilona Elek (HUN-1948)
41-073 Olga Oelkers (GER-1928)
40-201 Velleda Cesari (ITA-1960)
39-079 Ildikó Saginé-Ujlakiné-Rejtö (HUN-1976)

Oldest Gold Medalist, Women
41-078 Ilona Elek (HUN-1948)
35-182 Aleksandra Zabelina (URS-1972)
34-219 Tatyana Samusenko-Petrenko (URS-1972)
34-009 Galina Gorokhova (URS-1972)
33-326 Ellen Osiier (AUT-1924)

Youngest Medalist, Men
16-288 Ramón Fonst (CUB-1900)
17-124 Edoardo Mangiarotti (ITA-1936)
17-304 Jacques Brodin (FRA-1964)
18-030 Nedo Nadi (ITA-1912)
18-340 Michel Poffet (SUI-1976)

Youngest Gold Medalist, Men
16-288 Ramón Fonst (CUB-1900)
17-124 Edoardo Mangiarotti (ITA-1936)
18-030 Nedo Nadi (ITA-1912)
19-005 Fabio Dal Zotto (ITA-1976)
19-136 Carlo Agostini (ITA-1928)

Oldest Medalist, Men
52-196 Charles Newton-Robinson (GBR-1906)
50-252 Charles Tatham (USA-1904)
50-180 Lord William Henry Grenfell Desborough (GBR-1906)
50-179 Aládár Gerevich (HUN-1960)
49-268 Guido Balzarini (ITA-1924)
48-294 Lajos Maszlay (HUN-1952)
48-192 Sydney Martineau (GBR-1912)
48-055 Pál Kovács (HUN-1960)
46-263 Aládár Gerevich (HUN-1956)
46-180 Fiorenzo Marini (ITA-1960)

Oldest Gold Medalist, Men
50-179 Aládár Gerevich (HUN-1960)
49-268 Guido Balzarini (ITA-1924)
48-055 Pál Kovács (HUN-1960)
46-263 Aládár Gerevich (HUN-1956)
46-180 Fiorenzo Marini (ITA-1960)
44-182 Henri Jobier (FRA-1924)
44-139 Pál Kovács (HUN-1956)
43-328 Pietro Speciale (ITA-1920)
43-190 Alexander Lippmann (FRA-1924)
43-102 Marcello Bertinetti (ITA-1928)

Medals Won by Countries

	G	S	B	T
France	32	31	26	89
Italy	31	32	20	83
Hungary	30	17	22	69
USSR	17	14	13	44
United States	1½	6	11	18½
Poland	4	5	7	16
Belgium	5	3	5	13
FRG	5	6	2	13
Germany	3	4	3	10
Great Britain	1	9	–	10
Greece	3	3	2	8
Romania	1	2	5	8
Netherlands	–	1	7	8
Sweden	2	3	2	7
Austria	1	1	5	7
Cuba	4½	1	–	5½
Denmark	1	2	3	6
Switzerland	–	2	3	5
Czechoslovakia	–	–	2	2
China	1	–	–	1
Argentina	–	–	1	1
Portugal	–	–	1	1
Mexico	–	1	–	1
Totals	143	143	140	426

Medals Won by Countries, Men

	G	S	B	T
France	30	30	24	84
Italy	29	31	17	77
Hungary	25	11	18	54
USSR	12	11	11	34
United States	1½	6	11	18½
Poland	4	5	6	15
Belgium	5	3	5	13
FRG	3	4	1	8
Greece	3	3	2	8
Netherlands	–	1	7	8
Germany	2	3	2	7
Sweden	2	3	2	7
Great Britain	–	6	–	6
Cuba	4½	1	–	5½
Switzerland	–	2	3	5
Austria	–	1	3	4
Romania	1	–	2	3
Denmark	–	1	1	2
Czechoslovakia	–	–	2	2
Argentina	–	–	1	1
Portugal	–	–	1	1
Totals	122	122	119	363

*No third in 1896 foil masters event; no third in 1904 team foil;
no third in 1906 sabre masters event.

Medals Won by Countries, Women

	G	S	B	T
Hungary	5	6	4	15
USSR	5	3	2	10
Italy	2	1	3	6
FRG	2	2	1	5
France	2	1	2	5
Romania	–	2	3	5
Great Britain	1	3	–	4
Denmark	1	1	2	4
Germany	1	1	1	3
Austria	1	–	2	3
China	1	–	–	1
Mexico	–	1	–	1
Poland	–	–	1	1
Totals	21	21	21	63

Best Performance by Country at Each Olympics

	Men	Women	Overall
1896 –	Greece	-----	-----
1900 –	France	-----	-----
1904 –	United States	-----	-----
1906 –	France	-----	-----
1908 –	France	-----	-----
1912 –	Hungary	-----	-----
1920 –	Italy	-----	-----
1924 –	France	one event only	-----
1928 –	France	one event only	-----
1932 –	Italy	one event only	-----
1936 –	Italy	one event only	-----
1948 –	France/Italy	one event only	-----
1952 –	Italy	one event only	-----
1956 –	Italy	one event only	-----
1960 –	USSR/Italy	USSR	USSR
1964 –	USSR	Hungary	USSR/Hungary
1968 –	USSR	USSR	USSR
1972 –	Hungary	USSR/Hungary	Hungary
1976 –	USSR	USSR/Hungary	USSR
1980 –	USSR	France	USSR
1984 –	Italy	FRG	Italy

FOOTBALL (ASSOCIATION FOOTBALL - SOCCER)

International Federation: Fédération Internationale de Football
    Association (FIFA)
Countries Affiliated: 151 (1987)
First Year of Olympic Appearance: 1900
Year of Formation: 1904

Most Medals
3   Dezsö Novák (HUN)
3/2   Charles Buchwald (DEN)
3/2   Oscar Nielsen-Nörlund (DEN)

Most Gold Medals
2   Dezsö Novák (HUN)
2   José Nasazzi (URU)
2   José Andrade (URU)
2   Hector Scarone (URU)
2   Andrés Mazali (URU)
2   Pedro Arispe (URU)
2   Santos Urdinaran (URU)
2   Pedro Petrone (URU)
2   Pedro Céa (URU)
2   Arthur Berry (GBR)
2   Vivian Woodward (GBR)

Most Silver Medals
2   Charles Buchwald (DEN)
2   Oscar Nielsen-Nörlund (DEN)
2   Harald Hansen (DEN)
2   Nils Middleboe (DEN)
2   Sophus Nielsen (DEN)
2   Vilhelm Wolfhagen (DEN)
2   Branislav Stanković (YUG)
2   Zlatko Cajkovski (YUG)
2   Rajko Mitić (YUG)
2   Bernard Vukas (YUG)
2   Stjepan Bobek (YUG)

Most Bronze Medals
2   Oleg Blochin (URS)
2   Viktor Kolotov (URS)
2   Johannes Marius de Korver (HOL)

Most Appearances
4/3   Nils Middleboe (DEN)
3   Seventeen athletes tied with three

Most Years Between Medals
8   Dezsö Novák (HUN)
6/4   Charles Buchwald (DEN)
6/4   Oscar Nielsen-Nörlund (DEN)

Most Years Between Gold Medals
    4   Dezsö Novák (HUN)
    4   José Nasazzi (URU)
    4   José Andrade (URU)
    4   Hector Scarone (URU)
    4   Andrés Mazali (URU)
    4   Pedro Arispe (URU)
    4   Santos Urdinaran (URU)
    4   Pedro Petrone (URU)
    4   Pedro Céa (URU)
    4   Arthur Berry (GBR)
    4   Vivian Woodward (GBR)

Youngest Medalist
    16-026   Louis Menges (USA-1904)
    16-298   Charles January (USA-1904)
    16-329   Alexander Cudmore (USA-1904)
    17-329   Peter Ratican (USA-1904)
    18-068   Johannes Boutmy (HOL-1912)

Youngest Gold Medalist
    18-364   Pedro Petrone (URU-1924)
    19-005   László Nagy (HUN-1968)
    19-141   Eduard Streltsov (URS-1956)
    19-296   Zoltán Varga (HUN-1964)
    19-306   Silvester Takać (YUG-1960)

Oldest Medalist
    35-361   Erik Nilsson (SWE-1952)
    35-217   Shigeo Yaegashi (JPN-1968)
    35-157   Johannes Gandil (DEN-1908)
    34-102   Henry From (DEN-1960)
    33-173   Werner Unger (GDR-1964)

Oldest Gold Medalist
    33-033   Vivian Woodward (GBR-1912)
    32-333   Hans-Ulrich Grapenthin (GDR-1976)
    32-289   Anatoliy Bashashkin (URS-1956)
    32-007   Erik Nilsson (SWE-1948)
    31-310   Bernd Bransch (GDR-1976)

Athletes Who Played on Both an Olympic and a World Cup Champion
    Hector Castro (URU) (1924, 1928 Olympic, 1930 World)
    Pedro Cea (URU) (1928 Olympic, 1930 World)
    José Nasazzi (URU) (1924, 1928 Olympic, 1930 World)
    José Andrade (URU) (1924, 1928 Olympic, 1930 World)
    Lorenzo Fernandez (URU) (1928 Olympic, 1930 World)
    Alvaro Gestido (URU) (1928 Olympic, 1930 World)
    Hector Scarone (URU) (1924, 1928 Olympic, 1930 World)
    Alfredo Foni (ITA) (1936 Olympic, 1938 World)
    Pietro Rava (ITA) (1936 Olympic, 1938 World)
    Ugo Locatelli (ITA) (1936 Olympic, 1938 World)

Most Goals, Individual
```
10       Sophus Nielsen (DEN) (1908 v. France)
10       Gottfried Fuchs (GER) (1912 v. Russia)
 6       Ferenc Bene (HUN) (1964 v. Morocco)
 6       Ibrahim Riad (UAE) (1964 v. Korea)
 5       Ernest Pohl (POL) (1960 v. Tunisia)
 4       Nine athletes tied - most recent:
            Bernd Nickel (FRG) (1972 v. USA)
```

Most Goals, Team
```
17       Denmark (1908 v. France)
16       Germany (1912 v. Russia)
12       Great Britain (1908 v. Sweden)
12       Sweden (1948 v. Korea)
11       Argentina (1928 v. USA)
11       Italy (1928 v. Egypt)
10       Yugoslavia (1952 v. India)
10       United Arab Emirates (1964 v. Korea)
```

Most Goals, Both Teams (Both Teams Scoring)
```
18       Denmark d. France, 17-1 (1908)
14       Italy d. Egypt, 11-3 (1928)
13       Great Britain d. Sweden, 12-1 (1908)
13       Argentina d. USA, 11-2 (1928)
11       Hungary d. Yugoslavia, 6-5 (1964)
10       Peru d. Finland, 7-3, (1936)
10       Yugoslavia tied USSR, 5-5 (1952)
10       Yugoslavia d. USA, 9-1 (1956)
 9       Holland d. Sweden, 5-4 (1920)
 9       Sweden d. Belgium, 8-1 (1924)
 9       Argentina d. Belgium, 6-3 (1928)
 9       Poland d. Great Britain, 5-4 (1936)
```

Medals Won by Countries

	G	S	B	T
Hungary	3	1	1	5
Denmark	1	3	1	5
Yugoslavia	1	3	1	5
USSR	1	-	3	4
Great Britain	3	-	-	3
GDR	1	1	1	3
Sweden	1	-	2	3
The Netherlands	-	-	3	3
Uruguay	2	-	-	2
Czechoslovakia	1	1	-	2
Poland	1	1	-	2
France	1	1	-	2

Belgium	1	–	1	2
Italy	1	–	1	2
Bulgaria	–	1	1	2
Greece	–	1	1	2
United States	–	1	1	2
Canada	1	–	–	1
Argentina	–	1	–	1
Austria	–	1	–	1
Spain	–	1	–	1
Switzerland	–	1	–	1
Brazil	–	1	–	1
Germany	–	–	1	1
Japan	–	–	1	1
Norway	–	–	1	1
Total	19	19	20	58

*Two thirds in 1972.

Overall Records by Countries

	W	L	T	%%%%
Uruguay	9	0	1	.950
Hungary	27	5	2	.824
USSR	20	4	2	.808
Czechoslovakia	14	4	4	.727
Denmark	18	8	1	.685
Poland	14	6	2	.682
GDR	11	5	2	.667
Switzerland	4	2	1	.643
Great Britain	12	7	1	.625
Yugoslavia	21	12	4	.622
Bulgaria	7	4	3	.607
Italy	19	12	3	.603
Argentina	5	3	2	.600
Belgium	4	3	0	.571
Brazil	12	9	5	.558
France	14	11	4	.552
Sweden	11	9	1	.548
Austria	6	5	0	.545
Germany/FRG	14	12	2	.536
Spain	7	6	5	.528
Smyrna	1	1	0	.500
Australia	1	1	0	.500
Athens	1	1	0	.500
Portugal	1	1	0	.500
Kuwait	1	1	2	.500
Israel	2	2	4	.500
Peru	2	2	0	.500
Japan	5	5	2	.500
The Netherlands	9	9	1	.500
Canada	3	4	1	.438
Guatemala	2	3	2	.429
Norway	5	7	1	.423
Romania	2	3	1	.417
Cuba	2	3	1	.417

Egypt	6	9	1	.406
Finland	3	5	1	.389
Colombia	3	5	1	.389
Algeria	1	2	1	.375
Iraq	1	3	3	.357
Mexico	5	11	4	.350
Malaysia	1	2	0	.333
Venezuela	1	2	0	.333
Ireland	1	2	0	.333
Burma	1	2	0	.333
Cameroun	1	2	0	.333
PR Korea	1	2	0	.333
UAR	2	5	2	.333
Chile	1	4	2	.286
Ghana	1	5	3	.278
Iran	2	6	1	.278
Indonesia	0	1	1	.250
Luxembourg	2	6	0	.250
Turkey	2	7	1	.250
Morocco	2	8	1	.227
Korea	1	4	0	.200
United States	2	11	2	.200
India	1	6	1	.188
El Salvador	0	2	1	.167
Syria	0	2	1	.167
Qatar	0	2	1	.167
Nigeria	0	4	2	.167
Costa Rica	1	5	0	.167
Estonia	0	1	0	.000
Lithuania	0	1	0	.000
Latvia	0	1	0	.000
Neth. Antilles	0	1	0	.000
Afghanistan	0	1	0	.000
Russia	0	2	0	.000
Greece	0	2	0	.000
Thessalonika	0	2	0	.000
Taiwan	0	3	0	.000
Sudan	0	3	0	.000
Tunisia	0	3	0	.000
Guinea	0	3	0	.000
Zambia	0	3	0	.000
Saudi Arabia	0	3	0	.000
Thailand	0	4	0	.000
Totals	328	328	90	.500

GYMNASTICS

International Federation: Fédération Internationale de
     Gymnastique (FIG)
Countries Affiliated: 88 (1987)
Year of Formation: 1881
First Year of Olympic Appearance: 1896

Most Medals
18	Larisa Latynina (URS)
15	Nikolai Andrianov (URS)
13	Takashi Ono (JPN)
13	Boris Shakhlin (URS)
12	Sawao Kato (JPN)
11	Vera Cáslavská (TCH)
11	Viktor Chukarin (URS)
10	Polina Astakhova (URS)
10	Aleksandr Dityatin (URS)
10	Agnes Keleti (HUN)
10	Akinori Nakayama (JPN)

Most Gold Medals
9	Larisa Latynina (URS)
8	Sawao Kato (JPN)
7	Nikolai Andrianov (URS)
7	Boris Shakhlin (URS)
7	Vera Cáslavská (TCH)
7	Viktor Chukarin (URS)
6	Akinori Nakayama (JPN)

Most Silver Medals
6	Aleksandr Dityatin (URS)
6	Akinori Nakayama (JPN)
6	Mikhail Voronin (URS)
5	Larisa Latynina (URS)
5	Nikolai Andrianov (URS)
5	Yuriy Titov (URS)
5	Mariya Gorokhovskaya (URS)
5	Viktor Lisitskiy (URS)

Most Bronze Medals
6	Heikki Savolainen (FIN)
4	Larisa Latynina (URS)
4	Takashi Ono (JPN)
4	Sofiya Muratova (URS)
4	William Merz (USA)

Most Years Winning Medals
5	Heikki Savolainen (FIN)
4	Takashi Ono (JPN)
4	Georges Miez (SUI)
4	Peter Hol (NOR)

Most Years Winning Gold Medals
     3   Eleven athletes tied with three.

Most Years Between Medals
    24   Heikki Savolainen (FIN)
    16   Alfred Schwarzmann (SUI)
    16   Einari Teräsvirta (FIN)
    14/12   Peter Hol (NOR)
    12   Trygve Bøysen (NOR)
    12   Luigi Maiocca (ITA)
    12   Takashi Ono (JPN)
    12   Leon Stukelj (YUG)
    12   Michael Reusch (SUI)
    12   Giorgio Zampori (ITA)

Most Years Between Gold Medals
    12   Giorgio Zampori (ITA)
    12   Luigi Maiocca (ITA)

Most Medals, Women
    18   Larisa Latynina (URS)
    11   Vera Cáslavská (TCH)
    10   Polina Astakhova (URS)
    10   Agnes Keleti (HUN)
     9   Nadia Comăneci (ROM)
     8   Sofiya Muratova (URS)
     8   Lyudmila Turishcheva (URS)

Most Gold Medals, Women
     9   Larisa Latynina (URS)
     7   Vera Cáslavská (TCH)
     5   Polina Astakhova (URS)
     5   Agnes Keleti (HUN)
     5   Nadia Comăneci (ROM)
     5   Nelli Kim (URS)
     4   Lyudmila Turishcheva (URS)
     4   Olga Korbut (URS)

Most Silver Medals, Women
     5   Larisa Latynina (URS)
     5   Mariya Gorokhovskaya (URS)
     4   Vera Cáslavská (TCH)
     4   Erika Zuchold (GDR)

Most Bronze Medals, Women
     4   Larisa Latynina (URS)
     4   Sofiya Muratova (URS)
     3   Polina Astakhova (URS)
     3   Margit Korondi (HUN)
     3   Steffi Kräker (GDR)
     3   Elena Leusteanu (ROM)

Most Years Winning Medals, Women
    3   Larisa Latynina (URS)
    3   Vera Cáslavská (TCH)
    3   Polina Astakhova (URS)
    3   Lyudmila Turishcheva (URS)
    3   Erzsébet Gulyás (HUN)
    3   Olga Tass (HUN)
    3   Eva Bosáková-Vechtová (TCH)

Most Years Winning Gold Medals, Women
    3   Larisa Latynina (URS)
    3   Polina Astakhova (URS)
    3   Lyudmila Turishcheva (URS)

Most Years Between Medals, Women
    8   Many athletes tied with eight.

Most Years Between Gold Medals, Women
    8   Larisa Latynina (URS)
    8   Polina Astakhova (URS)
    8   Lyudmila Turishcheva (URS)

Most Medals, Men
   15   Nikolai Andrianov (URS)
   13   Takashi Ono (JPN)
   13   Boris Shakhlin (URS)
   12   Sawao Kato (JPN)
   11   Viktor Chukarin (URS)
   10   Aleksandr Dityatin (URS)
   10   Akinori Nakayama (JPN)

Most Gold Medals, Men
    8   Sawao Kato (JPN)
    7   Nikolai Andrianov (URS)
    7   Boris Shakhlin (URS)
    7   Viktor Chukarin (URS)
    6   Akinori Nakayama (JPN)

Most Silver Medals, Men
    6   Aleksandr Dityatin (URS)
    6   Akinori Nakayama (JPN)
    6   Mikhail Voronin (URS)
    5   Nikolai Andrianov (URS)
    5   Yuriy Titov (URS)
    5   Viktor Lisitskiy (URS)

Most Bronze Medals, Men
    6   Heikki Savolainen (FIN)
    4   Takashi Ono (JPN)
    4   William Merz (USA)
    3   Ten athletes tied with three.

Most Years Winning Medals, Men
    5   Heikki Savolainen (FIN)
    4   Takashi Ono (JPN)
    4   Georges Miez (SUI)
    4   Peter Hol (NOR)

Most Years Winning Gold Medals, Men
    3   Eight athletes tied with three.

Most Years Between Medals, Men
    24   Heikki Savolainen (FIN)
    16   Alfred Schwarzmann (SUI)
    16   Einari Teräsvirta (FIN)
    14/12   Peter Hol (NOR)

Most Years Between Gold Medals, Men
    12   Giorgio Zampori (ITA)
    12   Luigi Maiocca (ITA)

Most Medals, Individual
    14   Larisa Latynina (URS)
    12   Nikolai Andrianov (URS)
    10   Takashi Ono (JPN)
    9   Boris Shakhlin (URS)
    9   Sawao Kato (JPN)
    9   Viktor Chukarin (URS)

Most Gold Medals, Individual
    7   Vera Cáslavská (TCH)
    6   Larisa Latynina (URS)
    6   Boris Shakhlin (URS)
    6   Nikolai Andrianov (URS)

Most Medals, Individual, Women
    14   Larisa Latynina (URS)
    8   Vera Cáslavská (TCH)
    7   Nadia Comăneci (ROM)
    6   Agnes Keleti (HUN)
    6   Polina Astakhova (URS)
    6   Sofiya Muratova (URS)

Most Gold Medals, Individual, Women
    7   Vera Cáslavská (TCH)
    6   Larisa Latynina (URS)
    5   Nadia Comăneci (ROM)
    4   Agnes Keleti (HUN)
    3   Nelli Kim (URS)

Most Medals, Individual, Men
    12   Nikolai Andrianov (URS)
    10   Takashi Ono (JPN)
    9   Boris Shakhlin (URS)
    9   Sawao Kato (JPN)
    9   Viktor Chukarin (URS)
    8   Aleksandr Dityatin (URS)
    8   Akinori Nakayama (JPN)

Most Gold Medals, Individual, Men
    6   Boris Shakhlin (URS)
    6   Nikolai Andrianov (URS)
    5   Sawao Kato (JPN)
    5   Viktor Chukarin (URS)

Most Medals, Games
    8   Aleksandr Dityatin (URS-1980)
    7   Mariya Gorokhovskaya (URS-1952)
    7   Boris Shakhlin (URS-1960)
    7   Mikhail Voronin (URS-1968)
    7   Nikolai Andrianov (URS-1976)

Most Gold Medals, Games
    5   Anton Heida (USA-1904)
    4   Viktor Chukarin (URS-1952)
    4   Agnes Keleti (HUN-1956)
    4   Larisa Latynina (URS-1956)
    4   Boris Shakhlin (URS-1960)
    4   Vera Cáslavská (TCH-1968)
    4   Akinori Nakayama (JPN-1968)
    4   Nikolai Andrianov (URS-1976)
    4   Ecaterina Szabo (ROM-1984)

Most Medals, Games, Women
    7   Mariya Gorokhovskaya (URS-1952)
    6   Agnes Keleti (HUN-1956)
    6   Larisa Latynina (URS-1956)
    6   Larisa Latynina (URS-1960)
    6   Larisa Latynina (URS-1964)
    6   Vera Cáslavská (TCH-1968)

Most Gold Medals, Games, Women
    4   Agnes Keleti (HUN-1956)
    4   Larisa Latynina (URS-1956)
    4   Vera Cáslavská (TCH-1968)
    4   Ecaterina Szabo (ROM-1984)

Most Medals, Games, Men
    8   Aleksandr Dityatin (URS-1980)
    7   Boris Shakhlin (URS-1960)
    7   Mikhail Voronin (URS-1968)
    7   Nikolai Andrianov (URS-1976)

Most Gold Medals, Games, Men
    5   Anton Heida (USA-1904)
    4   Viktor Chukarin (URS-1952)
    4   Boris Shakhlin (URS-1960)
    4   Akinori Nakayama (JPN-1968)
    4   Nikolai Andrianov (URS-1976)

Most Medals, Games, Individual
  7   Aleksandr Dityatin (URS-1980)
  6   Nikolai Andrianov (URS-1976)
  6   Boris Shakhlin (URS-1960)
  6   Mikhail Voronin (URS-1968)
  6   George Eyser (USA-1904)

Most Gold Medals, Games, Individual
  4   Nikolai Andrianov (URS-1976)
  4   Boris Shakhlin (URS-1960)
  4   Vera Cáslavská (TCH-1968)
  4   Anton Heida (USA-1904)

Most Medals, Games, Individual, Women
  5   Mariya Gorokhovskaya (URS-1952)
  5   Vera Cáslavská (TCH-1968)
  5   Larisa Latynina (URS-1960)
  5   Larisa Latynina (URS-1964)

Most Gold Medals, Games, Individual, Women
  4   Vera Cáslavská (TCH-1968)
  3   Vera Cáslavská (TCH-1964)
  3   Agnes Keleti (HUN-1956)
  3   Larisa Latynina (URS-1956)
  3   Nadia Comăneci (ROM-1976)
  3   Ecaterina Szabo (ROM-1984)

Most Medals, Games, Individual, Men
  7   Aleksandr Dityatin (URS-1980)
  6   Nikolai Andrianov (URS-1976)
  6   Boris Shakhlin (URS-1960)
  6   Mikhail Voronin (URS-1968)
  6   George Eyser (USA-1904)

Most Gold Medals, Games, Individual, Men
  4   Nikolai Andrianov (URS-1976)
  4   Boris Shakhlin (URS-1960)
  4   Anton Heida (USA-1904)
  3   George Eyser (USA-1904)
  3   Akinori Nakayama (JPN-1968)
  3   Ning Li (CHN-1984)
  3   Viktor Chukarin (URS-1952)

Most Appearances
  5   Joseph Stoffel (LUX, 1948-64)
  5   Heikki Savolainen (FIN, 1928-52)
  4   Petter Hol (NOR, 1906-20)
  4   Alfred Jochim (USA, 1924-36)
  4   Michel Mathiot (FRA, 1948-60)
  4   Georges Miez (SUI, 1924-36)
  4   Ole Olsen (DEN, 1906-20)
  4   Takashi Ono (JPN, 1952-64)
  4   Hans Sauter (AUT, 1948-60)
  4   Olga Tass (HUN, 1948-60)
  4   William Thoresson (SWE, 1952-64)

Most Appearances, Women
    4   Olga Tass (HUN, 1948-60)

Youngest Medalist, Women
    14-137   Krisztina Medveczky (HUN-1972)
    14-163   Christina Elena Grigoras (ROM-1980)
    14-191   Georgeta Gabor (ROM-1976)
    14-250   Nadia Comăneci (ROM-1976)
    14-317   Simona Pauca (ROM-1984)
    15-000   Maria Filatova (URS-1976)
    15-069   Rodica Dunca (ROM-1980)
    15-137   Qun Huang (CHN-1984)
    15-196   Lyubov Burda (URS-1968)
    15-218   Michelle Dusserre (USA-1984)

Youngest Gold Medalist, Women
    14-250   Nadia Comăneci (ROM-1976)
    14-317   Simona Pauca (ROM-1984)
    15-000   Maria Filatova (URS-1976)
    15-196   Lyubov Burda (URS-1968)
    15-288   Maxi Gnauck (GDR-1980)
    15-322   Laura Cutina (ROM-1984)
    16-016   Lyudmila Turishcheva (URS-1968)
    16-190   Mary Lou Retton (USA-1984)
    17-012   Stella Sakharova (URS-1980)
    17-017   Mihaela Stanulet (ROM-1984)

Oldest Medalist, Women
    35-182   Agnes Keleti (HUN-1956)
    35-049   Zdenka Veřmiřovská (TCH-1948)
    34-350   Helena Rakoczy (POL-1956)
    34-293   Galina Urbanovich (URS-1952)
    34-082   Pelageya Danilova (URS-1952)

Oldest Gold Medalist, Women
    35-182   Agnes Keleti (HUN-1956)
    35-049   Zdenka Veřmiřovská (TCH-1948)
    34-293   Galina Urbanovich (URS-1952)
    34-082   Pelageya Danilova (URS-1952)
    32-034   Erzsébet Gulyás (HUN-1956)

Youngest Medalist, Men
    10-216   Dimitrios Loundras (GRE-1896)
    15-226   Per Daniel Bertilsson (SWE-1908)
    17-237   Einari Teräsvirta (FIN-1932)
    17-292   Harald Eriksen (NOR-1906)
    17-305   Sverre Gröner (NOR-1908)

Youngest Gold Medalist, Men
    15-226   Per Daniel Bertilsson (SWE-1908)
    17-292   Harald Eriksen (NOR-1906)
    18-075   Albert Andersen (SWE-1920)
    18-099   Nicolaos Andriakopoulos (GRE-1896)
    18-108   Guido Boni (ITA-1912)

Oldest Medalist, Men
    45-267   Lucien Démanet (FRA-1920)
    44-297   Heikki Savolainen (FIN-1952)
    41-117   Manlio Pastorini (ITA-1920)
    40-344   Maseo Takemoto (JPN-1960)
    40-320   Heikki Savolainen (FIN-1948)

Oldest Gold Medalist, Men
    41-117   Manlio Pastorini (ITA-1920)
    40-344   Maseo Takemoto (JPN-1960)
    40-320   Heikki Savolainen (FIN-1948)
    36-230   Giorgio Zampori (ITA-1924)
    35-323   Oskar Bye (NOR-1906)

First Man to Score a 10.0 (Modern Scoring - since 1948)
    Aleksandr Dityatin (URS-1980-Horse Vault)

First Women to Score a 10.0 (Modern Scoring - since 1948)
    Nadia Comăneci (ROM-1976-Balance Beam)

Medals Won by Countries

	G	S	B	T
USSR	61	62	39	162
Japan	27	27	27	81
United States	23	19	23	65
Switzerland	15	19	13	47
Hungary	11	10	15	36
Czechoslovakia	12	13	10	35
Italy	12	8	9	29
GDR	5	11	13	29
Germany	11	5	11	27
Romania	10	7	10	27
Finland	8	5	12	25
France	4	7	9	20
Yugoslavia	5	2	4	11
China	5	4	2	11
Greece	3	2	4	9
Sweden	5	2	1	8
Norway	2	2	1	5
Denmark	1	3	1	5
FRG	1	1	2	4
Bulgaria	1	-	2	3
Great Britain	-	1	2	3
Austria	1	1	-	2
Poland	-	1	1	2
Belgium	-	1	1	2
Netherlands	1	-	-	1
Canada	1	-	-	1
Totals	225	213	212	650

Medals Won by Countries, Men

	G	S	B	T
USSR	31	35	16	82
Japan	27	27	26	80
United States	21	16	19	56
Switzerland	15	19	13	47
Italy	12	7	9	28
Germany	10	5	11	26
Finland	8	5	12	25
France	4	7	9	20
Czechoslovakia	3	7	9	19
Hungary	5	5	5	15
Yugoslavia	5	2	4	11
GDR	2	1	7	10
China	4	4	1	9
Greece	3	2	4	9
Sweden	4	1	-	5
Norway	2	2	1	5
Denmark	1	3	1	5
FRG	1	1	1	3
Bulgaria	1	-	2	3
Austria	1	1	-	2
Great Britain	-	1	1	2
Belgium	-	1	1	2
Poland	-	1	-	1
Romania	-	-	1	1
Totals	160	153	153	466

*No second/third in 1896 horizontal bar, team; two firsts/no
 second in 1904 parallel bars; two firsts/no second in 1904
 horizontal bar; no third in 1920 team freestyle; two seconds/no
 third in 1924 side horse vault; two thirds in 1924 rope climb;
 two thirds in 1936 floor exercises; three firsts in 1948
 pommelled horse (but with a second and a third awarded); three
 thirds in 1948 horse vault; two thirds in 1948 parallel bar; two
 seconds/no third in 1952 floor exercises; two seconds/no third
 in 1952 pommelled horse; two thirds in 1952 horse vault; two
 seconds/no third in 1952 horizontal bar; two thirds in 1952
 still rings; three seconds/no third in 1956 floor exercises; two
 thirds in 1956 still rings; two firsts/no second in 1956 horse
 vault; two thirds in 1956 parallel bars; two firsts/no second in
 1960 pommelled horse; two firsts/no second in 1960 horse vault;
 two thirds in 1960 still rings; three seconds/no third in 1964
 all-around, individual; two seconds/no third in 1964 floor
 exercises; two firsts/no second in 1968 horizontal bar; two
 thirds in 1976 pommelled horse; two thirds in 1976 horizontal
 bar; two thirds in 1984 floor exercises; two firsts/no second in
 1984 pommelled horse; two firsts/no second in 1984 still rings;
 and four seconds/no third in 1984 horse vault.

Medals Won by Countries, Women

	G	S	B	T
USSR	30	27	23	80
Romania	10	7	9	26
Hungary	6	5	10	21
GDR	3	10	6	19
Czechoslovakia	9	6	1	16
United States	2	3	4	9
Sweden	1	1	1	3
China	1	–	1	2
Germany	1	–	–	1
Netherlands	1	–	–	1
Canada	1	–	–	1
Italy	–	1	–	1
FRG	–	–	1	1
Great Britain	–	–	1	1
Japan	–	–	1	1
Poland	–	–	1	1
Totals	65	60	59	184

*Two firsts/no second in 1956 floor exercises; two seconds/no
third in 1956 balance beam; two thirds in 1956 horse vault; two
seconds/no third in 1964 horse vault; two firsts/no second in
1968 floor exercises; two seconds/no third in 1972 uneven
parallel bars; two seconds/no third in 1976 horse vault; two
seconds/no third in 1980 all-around, individual; three thirds in
1980 uneven parallel bars; two firsts/no second/two thirds in
1980 floor exercises; two firsts/no second in 1984 uneven
parallel bars; and two firsts/no second in 1984 balance beam.

Best Performance by Country at Each Olympics

	Men	Women	Overall
1896 –	Germany	-----	-----
1900 –	France	-----	-----
1904 –	United States	-----	-----
1906 –	France	-----	-----
1908 –	Sweden/Italy	-----	-----
1912 –	Italy	-----	-----
1920 –	Italy	-----	-----
1924 –	Czechoslovakia	-----	-----
1928 –	Switzerland	one event only	-----
1932 –	United States	one event only	-----
1936 –	Germany	one event only	-----
1948 –	Finland	one event only	-----
1952 –	USSR	USSR	USSR
1956 –	USSR	USSR	USSR
1960 –	USSR	USSR	USSR
1964 –	Japan	USSR	USSR
1968 –	Japan	Czechoslovakia	USSR
1972 –	Japan	USSR	USSR
1976 –	USSR	USSR	USSR
1980 –	USSR	USSR	USSR
1984 –	China	Romania	United States

HANDBALL (TEAM HANDBALL)

International Federation: Fédération Internationale de Handball
    (IHF)
Countries Affiliated: 94 (1987)
Year of Formation: 1946
First Year of Olympic Appearance: 1936 (as an outdoor game), 1972
    (as indoor team handball)

Most Medals
   3   Stefan Birtalan (ROM)
   3   Adrian Cosma (ROM)
   3   Radu Voina (ROM)
   3   Nicolae Munteanu (ROM)
   2   Forty-seven athletes tied with two.

Most Gold Medals
   1   Many athletes tied with one.

Most Silver Medals
   1   Many athletes tied with one.

Most Bronze Medals
   2   Stefan Birtalan (ROM)
   2   Adrian Cosma (ROM)
   2   Radu Voina (ROM)
   2   Nicolae Munteanu (ROM)

Most Medals, Women
   2   Twenty-one athletes tied with two.

Most Gold Medals, Women
   2   Nataliya Timoshkina-Sherstyuk (URS)
   2   Larisa Karlova (URS)
   2   Sinaida Turchina (URS)
   2   Tatyana Kochergina-Makarets (URS)
   2   Lyudmila Poradnik-Bobruss (URS)
   2   Aldona Neneniene-Chesaityte (URS)
   2   Lyubov Odinokova-Bereshnaya (URS)

Most Silver Medals, Women
   1   Many athletes tied with one.

Most Bronze Medals, Women
   1   Many athletes tied with one.

Most Medals, Men
```
3        Stefan Birtalan (ROM)
3        Adrian Cosma (ROM)
3        Radu Voina (ROM)
3        Nicolae Munteanu (ROM)
2        Twenty-six athletes tied with two.
```

Most Gold Medals, Men
```
1        Many athletes tied with one.
```

Most Silver Medals, Men
```
1        Many athletes tied with one.
```

Most Bronze Medals, Men
```
2        Stefan Birtalan (ROM)
2        Adrian Cosma (ROM)
2        Radu Voina (ROM)
2        Nicolae Munteanu (ROM)
```

Youngest Medalist, Women
```
17-356   Larisa Karlova (URS-1976)
19-009   Nina Lobova (URS-1976)
19-042   Rada Savić (YUG-1980)
19-095   Svetlana Anastasovski (YUG-1980)
19-141   Mirjana Djurica (YUG-1980)
```

Youngest Gold Medalist, Women
```
17-356   Larisa Karlova (URS-1976)
19-009   Nina Lobova (URS-1976)
19-269   Svetlana Mugosa (YUG-1984)
20-016   Tatyana Glushenko (URS-1976)
20-124   Tatyana Kochergina-Makarets (URS-1976)
```

Oldest Medalist, Women
```
34-200   Lyudmila Poradnik-Bobrus (URS-1980)
34-074   Sinaida Turchina (URS-1980)
33-279   Kristina Richter (GDR-1980)
33-267   Hannelore Zober (GDR-1980)
33-057   Agota Bujdosó (HUN-1976)
```

Oldest Gold Medalist, Women
```
34-200   Lyudmila Poradnik-Bobrus (URS-1980)
34-074   Sinaida Turchina (URS-1980)
32-271   Rafiga Schabanova (URS-1976)
30-327   Mirjana Ognjenović (YUG-1984)
30-304   Biserka Visnjič (YUG-1984)
```

Youngest Medalist, Men
```
17-310   Willy Hufschmid (SUI-1936)
18-199   Rudolf Wirz (SUI-1936)
18-218   Willy Gysi (SUI-1936)
19-257   Günther Ortmann (GER-1936)
19-300   Rolf Faes (SUI-1936)
```

Youngest Gold Medalist, Men
```
19-257  Günther Ortmann (GER-1936)
20-135  Sergei Kushniryuk (URS-1976)
21-040  Heinz Körvers (GER-1936)
21-151  Yuriy Kidyayev (URS-1976)
22-001  Zdravko Miljak (YUG-1972)
```

Oldest Medalist, Men
```
34-290  Vladimir Maksimov (URS-1980)
33-159  Evgeniy Chernyshov (URS-1980)
33-134  Ernst Gerlach (GDR-1980)
33-013  Fritz Wurmböck (GER-1936)
32-248  Nicolae Munteanu (ROM-1984)
```

Oldest Gold Medalist, Men
```
33-134  Ernst Gerlach (GDR-1980)
31-340  Zdravko Radjenović (YUG-1984)
30-288  Vladimir Maksimov (URS-1976)
30-209  Petar Fajfrić (YUG-1972)
29-301  Siegfried Voigt (GDR-1980)
```

Most Goals, Game, Individual, Men
```
13  Istvan Varga (HUN-1972, v. USA)
12  Zdravko Miljak (YUG-1976, v. JPN)
11  Jerzy Klempel (POL-1980, v. CUB)
11  Aleksandr Anpilogov (URS-1980, v. KUW)
11  Ernst Zuellig (SUI-1980, v. ALG)
11  Musa'ed Al-Randi (KUW-1980, v. CUB)
11  Vasile Stinga (ROM-1984, v. JPN)
10  Ten athletes tied with ten goals
```

Most Goals, Game, Team, Men
```
44  Yugoslavia (1980 v. Kuwait)
38  USSR (1980 v. Kuwait)
37  FRG (1984 v. Korea)
36  Hungary (1976 v. USA)
36  Sweden (1984 v. Korea)
34  Poland (1980 v. Cuba)
33  USSR (1980 v. Algeria)
32  Romania (1976 v. USA)
32  Romania (1980 v. Kuwait)
32  Switzerland (1980 v. Kuwait)
32  Cuba (1980 v. Kuwait)
32  Yugoslavia (1984 v. Japan)
```

Most Goals, Game, Both Teams, Men
```
62      FRG d. Korea, 37-25 (1984)
59      Sweden d. Korea, 36-23 (1984)
59      Denmark d. Korea, 31-28 (1984)
57      Hungary d. USA, 36-21 (1976)
56      Cuba d. Kuwait, 32-24 (1980)
56      Spain d. Korea, 31-25 (1984)
54      Yugoslavia d. Kuwait, 44-10 (1980)
53      Poland d. Cuba, 34-19 (1980)
51      Sweden d. Spain, 26-25 (1984)
50      Romania d. USA, 32-19 (1976)
50      Denmark d. Tunisia, 29-21 (1972)
50      Sweden d. Iceland, 26-24 (1984)
```

Most Goals, Game, Individual, Women
```
17      Jasna Kolar-Merdan (YUG-1984, v. USA)
16      Byung-Soon Yoon (KOR-1984, v. FRG)
14      Svetlana Kitić (YUG-1980, v. CON)
13      Marianna Nagy (HUN-1980, v. CON)
11      Cynthia Stinger (USA-1984, v. YUG)
10      Kristina Richter (GDR-1976, v. CAN)
10      Biserka Visnjić (YUG-1980, v. GDR)
10      Cynthia Stinger (USA-1984, v. AUT)
 9      Seven athletes tied with nine goals
```

Most Goals, Game, Team, Women
```
39      Hungary (1980 v. The Congo)
39      Yugoslavia (1980 v. The Congo)
33      Yugoslavia (1984 v. USA)
31      USSR (1976 v. Japan)
31      Yugoslavia (1984 v. China)
30      USSR (1980 v. The Congo)
30      Yugoslavia (1984 v. Austria)
29      GDR (1976 v. Canada)
29      Korea (1984 v. USA)
29      Yugoslavia (1984 v. Korea)
```

Most Goals, Game, Both Teams, Women
```
56      Korea d. USA, 29-27 (1984)
56      Yugoslavia d. China, 31-25 (1984)
53      Yugoslavia d. USA, 33-20 (1984)
52      Yugoslavia d. Korea, 29-23 (1984)
49      Hungary d. Congo, 39-10 (1980)
48      Yugoslavia d. Congo, 39-9 (1980)
48      China tied Korea, 24-24 (1984)
47      USA d. China, 25-22 (1984)
46      USA d. Austria, 25-21 (1984)
45      Korea d. Austria, 23-22 (1984)
45      Yugoslavia d. Austria, 30-15 (1984)
```

Medals Won by Countries

	G	S	B	T
USSR	3	1	–	4
Yugoslavia	3	1	–	4
Romania	–	1	3	4
GDR	1	1	1	3
Germany	1	–	–	1
FRG	–	1	–	1
Austria	–	1	–	1
Czechoslovakia	–	1	–	1
China	–	1	–	1
United States	–	–	1	1
Hungary	–	–	1	1
Poland	–	–	1	1
Switzerland	–	–	1	1
Totals	8	8	8	24

Medals Won by Countries, Men

	G	S	B	T
Romania	–	1	3	4
USSR	1	1	–	2
Yugoslavia	2	–	–	2
GDR	1	–	–	1
Germany	1	–	–	1
FRG	–	1	–	1
Austria	–	1	–	1
Czechoslovakia	–	1	–	1
Poland	–	–	1	1
Switzerland	–	–	1	1
Totals	5	5	5	15

Medals Won by Countries, Women

	G	S	B	T
USSR	2	–	–	2
Yugoslavia	1	1	–	2
GDR	–	1	1	2
China	–	1	–	1
United States	–	–	1	1
Hungary	–	–	1	1
Totals	3	3	3	9

Overall Record by Countries, Men

	W	L	T	%%%%
Yugoslavia	21	3	1	.860
GDR	10	2	1	.808
Austria	4	1	0	.800
Romania	20	6	1	.759
USSR	12	4	3	.711
Norway	3	1	1	.700
Germany/FRG	16	7	1	.688
Poland	9	5	2	.625
Sweden	6	4	3	.577
Czechoslovakia	5	5	2	.500
Denmark	10	12	1	.457
Switzerland	5	6	0	.455
Iceland	4	5	2	.455
Hungary	8	13	2	.391
Spain	6	10	1	.382
Japan	7	16	0	.304
Korea	1	4	1	.250
Cuba	1	4	1	.250
United States	2	16	1	.132
Algeria	1	11	0	.083
Canada	0	5	0	.000
Kuwait	0	6	0	.000
Tunisia	0	5	0	.000
Totals	151	151	24	.500

Overall Records by Country, Women

	W	L	T	%%%%
USSR	10	0	0	1.000
Yugoslavia	8	1	1	.850
GDR	6	2	2	.700
Korea	3	1	1	.700
Hungary	4	4	2	.500
China	2	2	1	.500
FRG	2	3	0	.400
United States	2	3	0	.400
Romania	2	3	0	.400
Czechoslovakia	1	3	1	.300
Japan	1	4	0	.200
Congo	0	5	0	.000
Canada	0	5	0	.000
Austria	0	5	0	.000
Totals	41	41	8	.500

HOCKEY (FIELD HOCKEY)

International Federation: Fédération Internationale de Hockey
     (FIH)
Countries Affiliated: 102 (1987)
Year of Formation: 1924
First Year of Olympic Appearance: 1908

Most Medals
     4   Leslie Claudius (IND)
     4   Abdul Rashid (IND)
     4   Udham Singh (IND)
     3   Fifteen athletes tied with three.

Most Gold Medals
     3   Leslie Claudius (IND)
     3   Udham Singh (IND)
     3   Dhyan Chand (IND)
     3   Ranganandhan Francis (IND)
     3   Balbir Singh (IND)
     3   Randhir Singh Gentle (IND)

Most Silver Medals
     2   Abdul Hamid (PAK)
     2   Munir Ahmad Dar (PAK)
     2   Manzur Hussain Atif (PAK)
     2   Saeed Anwar (PAK)
     2   Anwar Ahmad Khan (PAK)
     2   Mohammed Asad Malik (PAK)
     2   Mutih Ullah (PAK)
     2   Robert Haigh (AUS)
     2   Ronald Riley (AUS)

Most Bronze Medals
     2   Ajitpal Singh (IND)
     2   Krishnamurty Perumal (IND)
     2   Harbinder Singh (IND)
     2   Harmik Singh (IND)

Most Years Between Medals
     16   Abdul Rashid (IND)
     12   Leslie Claudius (IND)
     12   Udham Singh (IND)

Most Years Between Gold Medals
     16   Abdul Rashid (IND)
     12   Udham Singh (IND)

Most Medals, Women
1   Many athletes tied with one.

Most Appearances, Men
4   Eighteen athletes tied with four.

Youngest Medalist, Women
16-304   Iveta Sranková (TCH-1980)
19-264   Tatyana Shvyganova (URS-1980)
19-290   Marta Urbanová (TCH-1980)
19-315   Viera Podhányiová (TCH-1980)
20-060   Martine Ohr (HOL-1984)

Youngest Gold Medalist, Women
20-060   Martine Ohr (HOL-1984)
20-299   Anneloes Nieuwenhuizen (HOL-1984)
22-141   Laurien Willemse (HOL-1984)
22-195   Brenda Joan Philips (ZIM-1980)
23-056   Marjolein Eysvogel (HOL-1984)

Oldest Medalist, Women
36-081   Jarmila Králíčková (TCH-1980)
35-256   Jirina Cermaková (TCH-1980)
35-253   Anthea Doreen Stewart (ZIM-1980)
35-043   Elisabeth Sevene (HOL-1984)
34-115   Berta Hrubá (TCH-1980)

Oldest Gold Medalist, Women
35-253   Anthea Doreen Stewart (ZIM-1980)
35-043   Elisabeth Sevene (HOL-1984)
33-060   Sonia Robertson (ZIM-1980)
33-060   Sandra Chick (ZIM-1980)
30-097   Elizabeth Chase (ZIM-1980)

Youngest Medalist, Men
17-025   Haneef Khan (PAK-1976)
17-123   Agathan de Roos (HOL-1936)
17-256   Rene Sparenberg (HOL-1936)
17-275   Manzoor Hussain (PAK-1976)
18-240   Rasool Akhtar (PAK-1972)

Youngest Gold Medalist, Men
19-228   Shahid Ali Khan (PAK-1984)
19-272   Chinadorai Deshmutu (IND-1952)
19-286   Ayaz Mehmood (PAK-1984)
19-334   Fernandes Peter (IND-1936)
20-103   Shahid Mohamed (IND-1980)

Oldest Medalist, Men
45-278   Dharam Singh (IND-1964)
42-260   Michael Walford (GBR-1948)
40-335   Hans Hansen (DEN-1920)
39-033   Hans Herlak (DEN-1920)
38-249   Stanley Shoveller (GBR-1920)

Oldest Gold Medalist, Men
      45-278   Dharam Singh (IND-1964)
      38-249   Stanley Shoveller (GBR-1920)
      38-101   Abdul Rashid (PAK-1960)
      37-211   Harry Haslam (GBR-1920)
      37-112   Shankar Laxman (IND-1964)

Most Goals, Game, Individual, Men
      12   Roop Singh (IND) (1932 v. USA)
       8   Juan Amat (ESP) (1980 v. Cuba)
       7   Dhyan Chand (IND) (1932 v. USA)
       7   Udham Singh (IND) (1956 v. USA)
       6   Dhyan Chand (IND) (1936 v. Germany)
       5   Surinder Singh (IND) (1980 v. Tanzania)
       5   Juan Luis Coghen (ESP) (1980 v. Tanzania)
       5   Vyacheslav Lampeev (URS) (1980 v. Tanzania)

Most Goals, Game, Team, Men
      24   India (1932 v. USA)
      18   India (1980 v. Tanzania)
      16   India (1956 v. USA)
      14   India (1956 v. Afghanistan)
      13   India (1980 v. Cuba)
      12   Great Britain (1920 v. Belgium)
      12   Spain (1980 v. Tanzania)
      11   India (1932 v. Japan)
      11   Great Britain (1948 v. USA)
      11   USSR (1980 v. Cuba)
      11   USSR (1980 v. Tanzania)
      11   Spain (1980 v. Cuba)

Most Goals, Game, Both Teams, Men (Both Teams Scoring)
      25   India d. USA, 24-1 (1932)
      13   Great Britain d. Belgium, 12-1 (1920)
      13   USSR d. Tanzania, 11-2 (1980)
      13   USSR d. Cuba, 11-2 (1980)
      12   India d. Japan, 11-1 (1932)
      11   Great Britain d. France, 10-1 (1908)
      11   Japan d. USA, 9-2 (1932)
      10   Denmark d. France, 9-1 (1920)
      10   India d. Argentina, 9-1 (1948)
      10   FRG d. Spain, 9-1 (1976)

Most Goals, Game, Individual, Women
       4   Natalia Krasnikova (URS) (1980 v. Poland)
       3   Jirina Cermáková (TCH) (1980 v. Austria)
       3   Beth Anders (USA) (1984 v. Canada)

Most Goals, Game, Team, Women
    6   USSR (1980 v. Poland)
    6   Holland (1984 v. FRG)
    5   Czechoslovakia (1980 v. Austria)
    4   Zimbabwe (1980 v. Poland)
    4   India (1980 v. Poland)
    4   Zimbabwe (1980 v. Austria)
    4   USA (1984 v. Canada)
    4   Canada (1984 v. New Zealand)

Most Goals, Game, Both Teams, Women (Both Teams Scoring)
    8   Holland d. FRG, 6-2 (1984)
    6   USSR d. Poland, 6-0 (1980)
    5   Czechoslovakia d. Austria, 5-0 (1980)
    5   Zimbabwe d. Austria, 4-1 (1980)
    5   Italy d. Czechoslovakia, 3-2 (1980)
    5   USA d. Canada, 4-1 (1984)

Medals Won by Countries

	G	S	B	T
India	8	1	2	11
Great Britain**	2	2	4	8
Pakistan	3	3	1	7
The Netherlands	1	2	2	5
FRG	1	2	1	4
Australia	-	2	1	3
Spain	-	1	1	2
Germany	-	1	1	2
USSR	-	-	2	2
United States	-	-	2	2
Zimbabwe	1	-	-	1
New Zealand	1	-	-	1
Czechoslovakia	-	1	-	1
Denmark	-	1	-	1
Japan	-	1	-	1
Belgium	-	-	1	1
Totals	17	17	18	52

Medals Won by Countries, Men

	G	S	B	T
India	8	1	2	11
Great Britain	2	2	4	8
Pakistan	3	3	1	7
The Netherlands	-	2	2	4
FRG	1	1	1	3
Australia	-	2	1	3
Spain	-	1	1	2
Germany	-	1	1	2
New Zealand	1	-	-	1
Denmark	-	1	-	1
Japan	-	1	-	1
Belgium	-	-	1	1
USSR	-	-	1	1
United States	-	-	1	1
Totals	15	15	16	46

*Two thirds in 1908.
**In 1908, England, Ireland, Scotland, and Wales competed as separate teams. All of these medals are credited to Great Britain.

Medals Won by Countries, Women

	G	S	B	T
Zimbabwe	1	-	-	1
The Netherlands	1	-	-	1
Czechoslovakia	-	1	-	1
FRG	-	1	-	1
USSR	-	-	1	1
United States	-	-	1	1
Totals	2	2	2	6

Overall Records by Country, Men

	W	L	T	%%%%
England	3	0	0	1.000
India	63	8	7	.853
Pakistan	44	9	7	.792
Germany/FRG	36	15	11	.669
Singapore	2	1	0	.667
USSR	4	2	0	.667
The Netherlands	36	20	7	.627
Australia	30	18	5	.613
Great Britain	25	18	8	.569
Spain	21	20	16	.509
Scotland	1	1	0	.500
Ireland	1	1	0	.500
Hungary	2	2	0	.500
Afghanistan	4	4	2	.500
New Zealand	16	17	12	.489
Kenya	14	18	7	.449
GDR	2	3	2	.429
Belgium	18	26	8	.423
Poland	5	9	4	.389
Japan	8	14	1	.370

Malaysia	10	20	6	.361
Malaya	0	1	2	.333
Switzerland	4	9	2	.333
France	8	23	4	.286
Denmark	4	12	2	.278
Rhodesia	1	4	1	.250
Argentina	3	15	5	.239
Austria	1	6	2	.222
Uganda	0	4	3	.214
Canada	3	16	1	.175
Cuba	1	5	0	.167
Tanzania	1	5	0	.167
Hong Kong	0	6	1	.071
Wales	0	1	0	.000
Finland	0	1	0	.000
Italy	0	4	0	.000
Mexico	0	14	0	.000
United States	0	19	0	.000
Totals	371	371	126	.500

**In 1908, England, Ireland, Scotland, and Wales competed as separate teams. All of these medals are credited to Great Britain in the medal lists, but above they are listed separately.

Overall Records by Country, Women

	W	L	T	%%%%
Netherlands	4	0	1	.900
Zimbabwe	3	0	2	.800
Czechoslovakia	3	1	1	.700
USSR	3	2	0	.600
FRG	2	1	2	.600
Canada	2	2	1	.500
United States	2	2	1	.500
Australia	2	2	1	.500
India	2	2	1	.500
Austria	2	3	0	.400
New Zealand	0	5	0	.000
Poland	0	5	0	.000
Totals	25	25	10	.500

JUDO

International Federation: International Judo Federation (IJF)
Countries Affiliated: 123 (1987)
Year of Formation: 1951
First Year of Olympic Appearance: 1964

Most Medals
    4   Angelo Parisi (GBR/FRA)
    2   Dietmar Lorenz (GDR)
    2   Shota Chochoshvili (URS)
    2   Ezio Gamba (ITA)
    2   Neil Adams (GBR)
    2   Wilhelm Ruska (HOL)
    2   David Starbrook (GBR)
    2   Jürg Röthlisberger (SUI)
    2   Felice Mariani (ITA)

Most Gold Medals
    2   Wilhelm Ruska (HOL)

Most Silver Medals
    2   Neil Adams (GBR)
    2   Angelo Parisi (GBR/FRA)

Most Bronze Medals
    2   Felice Mariani (ITA)

Most Appearances
    4   Antonio Roquete Andrade (POR, 1972-84)

Youngest Medalist
    19-080   Jae-Yup Kim (KOR-1984)
    19-250   Angelo Parisi (GBR-1972)
    20-171   Tibor Kincses (HUN-1980)
    20-182   Dimitr Sapryanov (BUL-1980)
    20-355   Günther Neureuther (FRG-1976)

Youngest Gold Medalist
    20-275   Isao Okano (JPN-1964)
    21-062   Thierry Rey (FRA-1980)
    21-216   Shota Chabareli (URS-1980)
    21-241   Ezio Gamba (ITA-1980)
    22-054   Shota Chochishvili (URS-1972)

Oldest Medalist
    35-329   Arthur Schnabel (FRG-1984)
    32-011   Wilhelm Ruska (HOL-1972)
    31-221   Angelo Parisi (FRA-1984)
    31-206   Vitaliy Kuznetsov (URS-1972)
    30-363   Seiki Nose (JPN-1984)

Oldest Gold Medalist
    32-011   Wilhelm Ruska (HOL-1972)
    30-201   Antonius Geesink (HOL-1964)
    29-314   Dietmar Lorenz (GDR-1980)
    29-267   Isamu Sonoda (JPN-1976)
    29-242   Kazuhiro Ninomiya (JPN-1976)

Medals Won by Countries

	G	S	B	T
Japan	13	2	3	18
USSR	5	4	9	18
France	2	2	7	11
Korea	2	4	4	10
Great Britain	-	4	6	10
FRG	1	3	4	8
GDR	1	-	5	6
Netherlands	3	-	1	4
Cuba	1	3	-	4
Italy	1	1	2	4
Brazil	-	1	3	4
Switzerland	1	1	1	3
Poland	-	1	2	3
United States	-	1	2	3
Hungary	-	-	3	3
Austria	1	-	1	2
Bulgaria	-	1	1	2
Mongolia	-	1	1	2
Canada	-	1	1	2
Yugoslavia	-	-	2	2
Romania	-	-	2	2
Belgium	1	-	-	1
Egypt	-	1	-	1
DPR Korea	-	-	1	1
Czechoslovakia	-	-	1	1
Australia	-	-	1	1
Iceland	-	-	1	1
Totals	32	31	64	127

*No second in 1972 63 kilogram class. Place declared void due to drug disqualification. Two thirds have been awarded in all classes at all Olympics.

Best Performance by Country at Each Olympics
    1964 - Japan
    1972 - Japan
    1976 - Japan
    1980 - USSR
    1984 - Japan

MODERN PENTATHLON

International Federation: Union Internationale de Pentathlon
    Moderne et Biathlon (UIPMB)
Countries Affiliated: 87 (1987)
Year of Formation: 1948
First Year of Olympic Appearance: 1912

Most Medals
7	Pavel Lednev (URS)
5	András Balczó (HUN)
4	Igor Novikov (URS)
3	Lars Hall (SWE)
3	Bo Lindman (SWE)
3	Olavi Mannonen (FIN)
3	Imre Nagy (HUN)
3	Ferenc Török (HUN)

Most Gold Medals
3	András Balczó (HUN)
2	Pavel Lednev (URS)
2	Igor Novikov (URS)
2	Lars Hall (SWE)
2	Ferenc Török (HUN)
2	Daniele Masala (ITA)

Most Silver Medals
2	Pavel Lednev (URS)
2	András Balczó (HUN)
2	Igor Novikov (URS)
2	Bo Lindman (SWE)
2	Tamás Szombathelyi (HUN)

Most Bronze Medals
3	Pavel Lednev (URS)
2	Olavi Mannonen (FIN)
2	Wäinö Korhonen (FIN)
2	Robert Beck (USA)

Most Years Winning Medals
3	Pavel Lednev (URS)
3	András Balczó (HUN)
3	Igor Novikov (URS)
3	Bo Lindman (SWE)

Most Years Winning Gold Medals
3	András Balczó (HUN)
2	Pavel Lednev (URS)
2	Igor Novikov (URS)
2	Lars Hall (SWE)
2	Ferenc Török (HUN)

Most Years Between Medals
    12   András Balczó (HUN)
    12   Pavel Lednev (URS)
     8   Igor Novikov (URS)
     8   Bo Lindman (SWE)

Most Years Between Gold Medals
    12   András Balczó (HUN)
     8   Pavel Lednev (URS)
     8   Igor Novikov (URS)

Most Appearances
     5   Peter Macken (AUS, 1960-76)
     4   Jeremy Fox (GBR, 1964-76)
     4   Pavel Lednev (URS, 1968-80)
     4   Igor Novikov (URS, 1952-64)

Youngest Medalist
    19-226 Aládár Kovácsi (HUN-1952)
    20-132 George Horvath (SWE-1980)
    20-188 Anatoli Starostin (URS-1980)
    21-120 Raoul Gueguen (FRA-1968)
    21-188 Jan Bártu (TCH-1976)

Youngest Gold Medalist
    19-226 Aládár Kovácsi (HUN-1952)
    20-188 Anatoli Starostin (URS-1980)
    22-015 András Balczó (HUN-1960)
    22-063 Robert Nightingale (GBR-1976)
    22-147 Yevgeni Lipeyev (URS-1980)

Oldest Medalist
    37-122 Pavel Lednev (URS-1980)
    36-178 Claes Egnell (SWE-1952)
    34-174 Gregory Losey (USA-1984)
    34-015 András Balczó (HUN-1972)
    33-076 Ferenc Török (HUN-1968)

Oldest Gold Medalist
    37-122 Pavel Lednev (URS-1980)
    34-015 András Balczó (HUN-1972)
    33-076 Ferenc Török (HUN-1968)
    33-322 William Grut (SWE-1948)
    33-362 Igor Novikov (URS-1964)

Medals Won by Countries

	G	S	B	T
Sweden	9	7	5	21
Hungary	6	6	3	15
USSR	5	5	4	14
United States	–	5	3	8
Finland	–	1	4	5
Italy	2	–	2	4
Germany	1	–	1	2
Czechoslovakia	–	1	1	2
France	–	–	2	2
Great Britain	1	–	–	1
Poland	1	–	–	1
Totals	25	25	25	75

Highest Scores in Measurable Events
SHOOTING –	200	[1132]	Charles Leonard (USA-1936)
	200	[1132]	Daniel Massala (ITA-1976)
	200	[1132]	George Horvath (SWE-1980)
SWIMMING –	3:10.856	[1348]	Ivan Sisniega (MEX-1980)

Best Performance by Country at Each Olympics
```
1912 -  one event only
1920 -  one event only
1924 -  one event only
1928 -  one event only
1932 -  one event only
1936 -  one event only
1948 -  one event only
1952 -  Hungary
1956 -  USSR/Sweden/Finland
1960 -  Hungary
1964 -  USSR
1968 -  Hungary
1972 -  USSR
1976 -  Poland/Great Britain
1980 -  USSR
1984 -  Italy
```

ROWING & SCULLING

International Federation: Fédération Internationale des Sociétés d'Aviron (FISA)
Countries Affiliated: 62 (1987)
Year of Formation: 1892
First Year of Olympic Appearance: 1900

Most Medals
5	Jack Beresford (GBR)
3	Seventeen athletes tied with three.

Most Gold Medals
    3   Jack Beresford (GBR)
    3   Siegfried Brietzke (GDR)
    3   Paul Costello (USA)
    3   John Kelly, Sr. (USA)
    3   Pertti Karppinen (FIN)
    3   Vyacheslav Ivanov (URS)
    3/0   Emilio Fontanella (ITA)
    3/0   Enrico Bruna (ITA)
    3/0   Giorgio Cesana (ITA)

Most Silver Medals
    2   Many athletes tied with two.

Most Bronze Medals
    2   Many athletes tied with two.

Most Years Winning Medals
    5   Jack Beresford (GBR)
    3   Eleven athletes tied with three.

Most Years Winning Gold Medals
    3   Jack Beresford (GBR)
    3   Siegfried Brietzke (GDR)
    3   Paul Costello (USA)
    3   Pertti Karppinen (FIN)
    3   Vyacheslav Ivanov (URS)

Most Years Between Medals
    16   Jack Beresford (GBR)
    16   Robert Zimonyi (HUN/USA)
    16   Simon Dickie (NZL)
    12   Hermann Wilker (GER)
    12   Kenneth Myers (USA)

Most Years Between Gold Medals
    12   Jack Beresford (GBR)
    12   Simon Dickie (NZL)
    8   Siegfried Brietzke (GDR)
    8   Paul Costello (USA)
    8   Conn Findlay (USA)
    8   Pertti Karppinen (FIN)
    8   Vyacheslav Ivanov (URS)

Most Medals, Women
    2   Seventeen women tied with two.

Most Gold Medals, Women
2   Jutta Lau (GDR)
2   Roswietha Zobelt (GDR)
2   Liane Buhr (GDR)
2   Gabriele Kühn-Lohs (GDR)
2   Christiane Köpke-Knetsch (GDR)
2   Ilona Richter (GDR)
2   Karin Metze (GDR)
2   Marina Wilke (GDR)

Most Silver Medals, Women
2   Joan Lind (USA)
2   Ginka Gyurova (BUL)

Most Bronze Medals, Women
1   Many athletes tied with one.

Most Appearances, Men
5   Jack Beresford (GBR, 1920-36)
5   Yuri Lorentsson (URS, 1960-76)
4   Yves Fraisse (FRA, 1964-76)
4   Kauko Hänninen (FIN, 1956-68)
4   John Kelly, Jr. (USA, 1948-60)
4   Toimi Pitkänen (FIN, 1952-64)
4   Jiři Ptak (TCH, 1968-80)
4   Igor Rudakov (URS, 1960-72)
4   Romano Sgheiz (ITA, 1956-68)
4   Alfons Slusarski (POL, 1964-76)

Youngest Medalist, Women
17-297   Sabine Heß (GDR-1976)
18-059   Susan Lee (AUS-1984)
18-083   Rodica Puscatu (ROM-1980)
18-147   Marina Wilke (GDR-1976)
18-298   Andrea Kurth (GDR-1976)

Youngest Gold Medalist, Women
17-297   Sabine Heß (GDR-1976)
18-147   Marina Wilke (GDR-1976)
18-298   Andrea Kurth (GDR-1976)
19-136   Gabriele Lohs (GDR-1976)
19-150   Kirsten Wenzel (GDR-1980)

Oldest Medalist, Women
31-312   Joan Lind (USA-1984)
31-039   Carie Graves (USA-1984)
30-190   Elena Giurca (ROM-1976)
30-133   Ecaterina Oancia (ROM-1984)
30-112   Martha Laurijsen (HOL-1984)

Oldest Gold Medalist, Women
31-039   Carie Graves (USA-1984)
30-133   Ecaterina Oancia (ROM-1984)
28-056   Carol Bower (USA-1984)
27-279   Angelika Noack (GDR-1980)
27-274   Kathryn Keeler (USA-1984)

Youngest Medalist, Men
```
 <10      unknown French boy
12-233   Noël Vandernotte (FRA-1936)
14-012   Giorgia Cesana (ITA-1906)
14-053   Marcel Frébourg (FRA-1906)
14-095   Bernard Malivoire (FRA-1952)
14-173   Günther Tiersch (FRG-1968)
14-222   Hans Bourquin (SUI-1928)
14-283   Klaus Zerta (GER-1960)
14-307   Marcel Lepan (FRA-1924)
14-362   Josip Reić (YUG-1980)
```

Youngest Gold Medalist, Men
```
 <10      unknown French boy
14-012   Giorgia Cesana (ITA-1906)
14-095   Bernard Malivoire (FRA-1952)
14-173   Günther Tiersch (FRG-1968)
14-222   Hans Bourquin (SUI-1928)
15-135   Carl Goßler (GER-1900)
15-299   Bruno Cipolla (ITA-1968)
15-342   Guido De Filip (ITA-1920)
16-073   Michael Obst (FRG-1960)
16-238   Louis Abell (USA-1900)
```

Oldest Medalist, Men
```
46-180   Robert Zimonyi (USA-1964)
45-304   Sigurd Monssen (NOR-1948)
45-235   Yuriy Lorentsson (URS-1976)
44-020   Julius Beresford (GBR-1912)
42-170   Guy Nickalls (GBR-1908)
```

Oldest Gold Medalist, Men
```
46-180   Robert Zimonyi (USA-1964)
42-170   Guy Nickalls (GBR-1908)
40-003   Harry Blackstaffe (GBR-1908)
37-302   Alfred Felber (SUI-1924)
37-226   Jack Beresford (GBR-1936)
```

Medals Won by Countries

	G	S	B	T
United States	29	21	16	66
GDR	25	8	7	40
USSR	12	18	10	40
Great Britain	15	15	5	35
Italy	10	10	8	28
France	4	13	9	26
Canada	3	8	11	22
FRG	7	6	6	19
Switzerland	4	6	9	19
Germany	9	3	5	17

Netherlands	3	5	6	14
Romania	7	2	4	13
Denmark	3	3	7	13
Australia	3	4	5	12
Czechoslovakia	2	1	7	10
Norway	1	2	6	9
Poland	–	2	7	9
New Zealand	3	2	3	8
Belgium	–	6	2	8
Bulgaria	2	2	3	7
Finland	3	–	3	6
Greece	1	2	1	4
Argentina	1	1	2	4
Yugoslavia	1	1	2	4
Austria	–	2	2	4
Uruguay	–	1	3	4
Hungary	–	1	2	3
Sweden	–	2	–	2
Spain	–	1	–	1
Totals	148	148	151	447

Medals Won by Countries, Men

	G	S	B	T
United States	28	18	15	61
Great Britain	15	15	5	35
USSR	11	13	6	30
GDR	17	5	6	28
Italy	10	10	8	28
France	4	13	9	26
Canada	3	6	10	19
Switzerland	4	6	9	19
Germany	9	3	5	17
FRG	7	6	4	17
Netherlands	3	4	5	12
Denmark	3	3	6	12
Australia	3	4	4	11
Czechoslovakia	2	1	7	10
Norway	1	2	6	9
Poland	–	1	7	8
New Zealand	3	2	3	8
Belgium	–	6	1	7
Finland	3	–	3	6

Greece	1	2	1	4
Argentina	1	1	2	4
Yugoslavia	1	1	2	4
Austria	–	2	2	4
Uruguay	–	1	3	4
Romania	1	1	1	3
Hungary	–	1	2	3
Sweden	–	2	–	2
Spain	–	1	–	1
Bulgaria	–	–	1	1
Totals	130	130	133	393

*No third in 1904 eights; no third in 1906 single sculls; two thirds in 1908 single sculls; two thirds in 1908 pairs with coxswain; two thirds in 1908 fours with coxswain; two thirds in 1908 eights; two thirds in 1912 single sculls; two thirds in 1912 fours with coxswain; and no third in 1924 pairs without coxswain.

+Included in the above is the 1906 "single sculls" event. Recent evidence indicates that this may have actually been a canoeing event.

Medals Won by Countries, Women

	G	S	B	T
GDR	8	3	1	12
Romania	6	1	3	10
USSR	1	5	4	10
Bulgaria	2	2	2	6
United States	1	3	1	5
Canada	–	2	1	3
Netherlands	–	1	1	2
FRG	–	–	2	2
Poland	–	1	–	1
Denmark	–	–	1	1
Australia	–	–	1	1
Belgium	–	–	1	1
Totals	18	18	18	54

Best Performance by Country at Each Olympics

	Men	Women	Overall
1900 -	France	-----	-----
1904 -	United States	-----	-----
1906 -	Italy	-----	-----
1908 -	Great Britain	-----	-----
1912 -	Great Britain	-----	-----
1920 -	United States	-----	-----
1924 -	United States	-----	-----
1928 -	United States	-----	-----
1932 -	United States	-----	-----
1936 -	Germany	-----	-----
1948 -	Great Britain	-----	-----
1952 -	USSR/United States	-----	-----
1956 -	United States	-----	-----
1960 -	USSR	-----	-----
1964 -	United States	-----	-----
1968 -	GDR	-----	-----
1972 -	GDR	-----	-----
1976 -	GDR	GDR	GDR
1980 -	GDR	GDR	GDR
1984 -	United States	Romania	Romania

SHOOTING

International Federation: Union Internationale de Tir
Countries Affiliated: 118 (1987)
Year of Formation: 1907
First Year of Olympic Appearance: 1896

Most Medals
11	Carl Osburn (USA)
9/4	Konrad Stäheli (SUI)
8	Otto Olsen (NOR)
8/7	Vilhelm Carlberg (SWE)
8/6	Albert Helgerud (NOR)
8/3	Léon Moreaux (FRA)
8/2	Louis Richardet (SUI)
7	Willis Lee (USA)
7	Einar Liberg (NOR)
7	Lloyd Spooner (USA)
7/3	Gudbrand Skatteboe (NOR)

Most Gold Medals
6	Alfred Lane (USA)
5	Carl Osburn (USA)
5	Willis Lee (USA)
5	Ole Andreas Lilloe-Olsen (NOR)
5	Morris Fisher (USA)
5/3	Konrad Stäheli (SUI)
5/2	Louis Richardet (SUI)

Most Silver Medals
```
4        Carl Osburn (USA)
4/4      Vilhelm Carlberg (SWE)
4/3      Albert Helgerud (NOR)
3        Eleven athletes tied with three.
```

Most Bronze Medals
```
4        Fritz Kuchen (SUI)
4/2      Maurice Lecoq (FRA)
3        Nine athletes tied with three.
```

Most Years Winning Medals
```
4        Einar Liberg (NOR)
4/3      Vilhelm Carlberg (SWE)
4/3      Albert Helgerud (NOR)
4/3      Gudbrand Skatteboe (NOR)
```

Most Years Winning Gold Medals
```
3        Einar Liberg (NOR)
2        Many athletes tied with two.
```

Most Years Between Medals
```
20       Lars Jörgen Madsen (DEN)
20       Anders Peter Nielsen (DEN)
18/16    Vilhelm Carlberg (SWE)
16       Einar Liberg (NOR)
16       Albert Courquin (FRA)
16       George Beattie (CAN)
16       Paul Colas (FRA)
```

Most Years Between Gold Medals
```
20       Lars Jörgen Madsen (DEN)
16       Einar Liberg (NOR)
12       Torsten Ullman (SWE)
10/0     Georgios Orphanidas (GRE)
```

Most Medals, Individual
```
6/2      Konrad Stäheli (SUI)
5/1      Leon Moreaux (FRA)
5/0      Louis Richardet (SUI)
4        Carl Osburn (USA)
4/0      Jean Reich (SUI)
3        Fourteen athletes tied with three.
```

Most Gold Medals, Individual
```
3/0      Gudbrand Skatteboe (NOR)
3        Alfred Lane (USA)
2        Many athletes tied with two.
```

Most Medals, Games
    7   Willis Lee (USA-1920)
    7   Lloyd Spooner (USA-1920)
    6   Carl Osburn (USA-1920)
    6   Louis Richardet (SUI-1906)
    5   Vilhelm Carlberg (SWE-1912)
    5   Léon Moreaux (FRA-1906)
    5   Lawrence Nuesslein (USA-1829)
    5   Otto Olsen (NOR-1920)
    5   Jean Reich (SUI-1906)
    5   Konrad Stäheli (SUI-1906)

Most Gold Medals, Games
    5   Willis Lee (USA-1920)
    4   Lloyd Spooner (USA-1920)
    4   Carl Osburn (USA-1920)
    3   Twelve athletes tied with three.

Most Medals, Games, Individual
    5   Louis Richardet (SUI-1906)
    4   Léon Moreaux (FRA-1920)
    4   Jean Reich (SUI-1906)
    4   Konrad Stäheli (SUI-1906)
    3   Ole Östmo (NOR-1900)
    3   Gudbrand Skatteboe (NOR-1906)
    3   Anders Peter Nielsen (DEN-1900)

Most Gold Medals, Games, Individual
    3   Gudbrand Skatteboe (NOR-1906)
    2   Léon Moreaux (FRA-1906)
    2   Louis Richardet (SUI-1906)
    2   Alfred Lane (USA-1912)
    2   Otto Olsen (NOR-1920)

Most Appearances, Men
    7   François La Fortune, Jr. (BEL, 1952-76)
    6   Paul van Asbroeck (BEL; 1906-08, 20-28, 36)
    6   Bill McMillan (USA; 1952, 60-76)
    6   Adam Smelczyński (POL, 1956-76)
    5   Eighteen athletes tied with five.

Youngest Medalist, Women
    16-301   Ulrike Holmer (FRG-1984)
    18-356   Pat Spurgin (USA-1984)

Youngest Gold Medalist, Women
    18-356   Pat Spurgin (USA-1984)

Oldest Medalist, Women
    52-143   Patricia Dench (AUS-1984)
    40-212   Linda Thom (CAN-1984)
    38-353   Ruby Fox (USA-1984)

Oldest Gold Medalist, Women
  40-212 Linda Thom (CAN-1984)

Youngest Medalist, Men
  16-301 Marcus Dinwiddie (USA-1924)
  17-128 Szilárd Kun (HUN-1952)
  17-148 George Genereux (CAN-1952)
  18-196 René Guyot (FRA-1900)
  18-337 Peter Kohnke (GER-1960)

Youngest Gold Medalist, Men
  17-148 George Genereux (CAN-1952)
  18-337 Peter Kohnke (GER-1960)
  19-012 Yuwei Li (CHN-1984)
  19-099 Pantelis Karasevdas (GRE-1896)
  20-137 Arthur Cook (USA-1948)

Oldest Medalist, Men
  72-280 Oscar Swahn (SWE-1920)
  64-258 Oscar Swahn (SWE-1912)
  61-245 John Butt (GBR-1912)
  60-265 Oscar Swahn (SWE-1908)
  60-104 William Milne (GBR-1912)
  60-090 Walter Winans (USA-1912)
  57-255 John Butt (GBR-1908)
  57-009 William Libbey (USA-1912)
  56-097 Walter Winans (USA-1908)
  56-078 Allen Whitty (GBR-1924)

Oldest Gold Medalist, Men
  64-258 Oscar Swahn (SWE-1912)
  60-265 Oscar Swahn (SWE-1908)
  56-097 Walter Winans (USA-1908)
  56-078 Allen Whitty (GBR-1924)
  53-066 Anders Nielsen (DEN-1920)
  52-031 Maurice Lecoq (FRA-1906)
  52-023 Harald Natvig (NOR-1924)
  50-261 Einar Liberg (NOR-1924)
  50-176 Henry Sears (USA-1912)
  49-253 Cornelius van Oyen (GER-1936)

Shooting - Olympic Record Progressions

Many of the rules for Olympic shooting have changed over the years. The following Olympic record progressions pertain only to those years which in the events have been contested in the manner currently in use.

Rapid-Fire Pistol

580	1	Károly Tákacs (HUN)	1948
587	1	Stefan Petrescu (ROM)	1956
587	1	William McMillan (USA)	1960
587	2	Pentti Linnosvuo (FIN)	1960
587	3	Aleksandr Zabelin (URS)	1960
592	1	Pentti Linnosvuo (FIN)	1964
593	1	Józef Zapedzki (POL)	1968
595	1	Józef Zapedzki (POL)	1972
597	1	Norbert Klaar (GDR)	1976

Free Pistol

559	1	Torsten Ullman (SWE)	1936
560	1	Aleksei Gushchin (URS)	1960
560	1	Väinö Markkanen (FIN)	1964
562	1	Grigoriy Kosykh (URS)	1968
562	2	Heinz Mertel (FRG)	1968
567	1	Ragnar Skanåker (SWE)	1972
573	1	Uwe Potteck (GDR)	1976
581	1	Aleksandr Melentev (URS)	1980

Small-Bore Rifle, Prone (English Match)

590	1	Peter Kohnke (FRG)	1960
597	1	László Hammerl (HUN)	1964
597	2	Lones Wigger (USA)	1964
598	1	Jan Kurka (TCH)	1968
598	2	László Hammerl (HUN)	1968
599	1	Ho-Jun Li (PRK)	1972
599	1	Karlheinz Smieszek (FRG)	1976
599	1	Károly Varga (HUN)	1980
599	2	Hellfried Heilfort (GDR)	1980
599	1	Edward Etzel (USA)	1984

Small-Bore Rifle, Three Positions

1149	1	Viktor Shamburkin (URS)	1960
1164	1	Lones Wigger (USA)	1964
1166	1	John Writer (USA)	1972
1173	1	Viktor Vlasov (URS)	1980
1173	1	Malcolm Cooper (GBR)	1984

Trap Shooting

192	1	George Généréux (CAN)	1952
195	1	Galliano Rossini (ITA)	1956
198	1	Ennio Mattarelli (ITA)	1964
198	1	John Braithwaite (GBR)	1968
199	1	Angelo Scalzone (ITA)	1972

Skeet Shooting

198	1	Evgeniy Petrov (URS)	1968
198	2	Romano Garagnani (ITA)	1968
198	3	Konrad Wirnhier (FRG)	1968
198	1	Josef Panáček (TCH)	1976
198	2	Eric Swinkels (HOL)	1976
198	1	Matthew Dryke (USA)	1984

Moving Target Event

569	1	Yakov Zheleznyak (URS)	1972
579	1	Aleksandr Gazov (URS)	1976
589	1	Igor Sokolov (URS)	1980

Air Rifle

589	1	Philippe Heberle (FRA)	1984

Sport Pistol, Women

585	1	Linda Thom (CAN)	1984
585	2	Ruby Fox (USA)	1984

Air Rifle, Women

393	1	Pat Spurgin (USA)	1984

Small-Bore Rifle, Three Positions; Women

581*	1	Xiaoxuan Wu (CHN)	1984

*In 1976, Margaret Murdock (USA), competing in the men's small-bore rifle, three position event, scored 1162 and tied for first place, losing the gold medal on examination of the targets. The event is conducted slightly differently and it is not possible to exactly compare scores, although 1162 is exactly twice 581, so her performance is at least comparable, and probably superior to the listed Olympic record.

Medals Won by Countries, Men and Women

	G	S	B	Tot
United States	43	23	19	85
Sweden	13	22	18	53
Great Britain	12	13	19	44
USSR	13	15	12	40
France	12	14	12	38
Norway	15	8	11	34
Switzerland	11	11	12	34
Greece	5	7	6	18
Finland	3	5	9	17
Denmark	3	8	6	17

Italy	6	4	6	16
GDR	2	7	5	14
Hungary	6	3	4	13
Romania	4	4	3	11
FRG	4	3	3	10
Canada	4	3	2	9
Belgium	2	3	2	7
China	3	-	3	6
Poland	2	1	3	6
Germany	1	4	1	6
Czechoslovakia	2	2	1	5
Austria	1	1	3	5
Brazil	1	1	1	3
Japan	1	-	2	3
Bulgaria	-	1	2	3
Peru	1	1	-	2
Colombia	-	2	-	2
Netherlands	-	1	1	2
Australia	-	-	2	2
DPR Korea	1	-	-	1
Portugal	-	1	-	1
South Africa	-	1	-	1
Mexico	-	1	-	1
Spain	-	1	-	1
Argentina	-	1	-	1
Haiti	-	-	1	1
New Zealand	-	-	1	1
Cuba	-	-	1	1
Venezuela	-	-	1	1
Totals	171	172	172	515

*Two seconds/no third in 1900 free rifle, kneeling; two thirds in 1900 free rifle, three positions; two thirds in 1900 pigeon shooting; no third in 1908 running deer, team; and two thirds in 1908 trap shooting.

Medals Won by Countries, Women

	G	S	B	T
United States	1	2	1	4
China	1	-	1	2
Canada	1	-	-	1
Italy	-	1	-	1
FRG	-	1	-	1
Australia	-	-	1	1
Totals	3	4	3	10

*The extra silver medal is credited to Margaret Murdock, who won a silver medal in 1976 small-bore rifle, three positions, while competing against men.

Best Performance by Country at Each Olympics
     1896 - Greece
     1900 - France
     1906 - Switzerland
     1908 - Great Britain
     1912 - Sweden
     1920 - United States
     1924 - United States
     1932 - Italy
     1936 - Germany
     1948 - Switzerland/United States
     1952 - USSR/Norway
     1956 - USSR
     1960 - USSR
     1964 - United States
     1968 - USSR
     1972 - United States
     1976 - GDR
     1980 - USSR
     1984 - United States

SWIMMING
(see also Diving and Water Polo)

International Federation: Fédération Internationale de Natation
     Amateur (FINA)
Countries Affiliated: 125 (1987)
Year of Formation: 1908
First Year of Olympic Appearance: 1896

Most Medals
     11   Mark Spitz (USA)
      9/7   Zoltán Halmay (HUN)
      8   Shirley Babashoff (USA)
      8   Kornelia Ender (GDR)
      8   Dawn Fraser (AUS)
      8/7   Charles Daniels (USA)
      8/5   Henry Taylor (GBR)
      7   Roland Matthes (GDR)

Most Gold Medals
      9   Mark Spitz (USA)
      5/4   Charles Daniels (USA)
      5   Don Schollander (USA)
      5   Johnny Weissmuller (USA)
      4   Kornelia Ender (GDR)
      4   Dawn Fraser (AUS)
      4   Roland Matthes (GDR)
      4   Murray Rose (AUS)
      4   John Naber (USA)
      4/3   Henry Taylor (GBR)

Most Silver Medals
    6   Shirley Babashoff (USA)
    5/4   Zoltán Halmay (HUN)
    4   Kornelia Ender (GDR)
    4   Dawn Fraser (AUS)
    4   Frank Wiegand (GDR)
    4   Tsuyoshi Yamanaka (JPN)

Most Bronze Medals
    3   Frank Beaurepaire (AUS)
    3   George Breen (USA)
    3   Vladimir Bure (URS)
    3   Margaret Cooper (GBR)
    3   Peter Evans (AUS)
    3   Heidemarie Reineck (FRG)
    3   Per Johansson (SWE)
    3/2   Henry Taylor (GBR)

Most Years Winning Medals
    4/3   Zoltán Halmay (HUN)
    4/3   Henry Taylor (GBR)
    3   Dawn Fraser (AUS)
    3   Roland Matthes (GDR)
    3   Frank Beaurepaire (AUS)
    3   Duke Kahanamoku (USA)
    3   David Dickson (AUS)
    3   Gary Hall (USA)
    3/2   Charles Daniels (USA)

Most Years Winning Gold Medals
    3   Dawn Fraser (AUS)
    3/2   Charles Daniels (USA)
    2   Many athletes tied with two.

Most Years Between Medals
    16   Frank Beaurepaire (AUS)
    14/12   Henry Taylor (GBR)
    12   Duke Kahanamoku (USA)

Most Years Between Gold Medals
    8   Duke Kahanamoku (USA)
    8   Dawn Fraser (AUS)

Most Medals, Women
    8   Shirley Babashoff (USA)
    8   Kornelia Ender (GDR)
    8   Dawn Fraser (AUS)
    6   Andrea Pollack (GDR)
    5   Ines Diers (GDR)
    5   Shane Gould (AUS)

Most Gold Medals, Women
```
  4        Kornelia Ender (GDR)
  4        Dawn Fraser (AUS)
  3        Sixteen athletes tied with three.
```

Most Silver Medals, Women
```
  6        Shirley Babashoff (USA)
  4        Kornelia Ender (GDR)
  4        Dawn Fraser (AUS)
  3        Andrea Pollack (GDR)
```

Most Bronze Medals, Women
```
  3        Margaret Cooper (GBR)
  3        Heidemarie Reineck (GDR)
  2        Many athletes tied with two.
```

Most Years Winning Medals, Women
```
  3        Dawn Fraser (AUS)
  2        Many athletes tied with two.
```

Most Years Winning Gold Medals, Women
```
  3        Dawn Fraser (AUS)
  2        Many athletes tied with two.
```

Most Medals, Men
```
 11        Mark Spitz (USA)
  9/7      Zoltán Halmay (HUN)
  8/7      Charles Daniels (USA)
  8/5      Henry Taylor (GBR)
  7        Roland Matthes (GDR)
  6        Don Schollander (USA)
  6        Johnny Weissmuller (USA)
  6        Murray Rose (AUS)
  6        Frank Beaurepaire (AUS)
```

Most Gold Medals, Men
```
  9        Mark Spitz (USA)
  5        Don Schollander (USA)
  5        Johnny Weissmuller (USA)
  5/4      Charles Daniels (USA)
  4        Roland Matthes (GDR)
  4        Murray Rose (AUS)
  4        John Naber (USA)
  4/3      Henry Taylor (GBR)
```

Most Silver Medals, Men
```
  5/4      Zoltán Halmay (HUN)
  4        Frank Wiegand (GDR)
  4        Tsuyoshi Yamanaka (JPN)
```

Most Bronze Medals, Men
```
  3       Frank Beaurepaire (AUS)
  3       George Breen (USA)
  3       Vladimir Bure (URS)
  3       Peter Evans (AUS)
  3       Per Johansson (SWE)
 3/2      Henry Taylor (GBR)
```

Most Years Winning Medals, Men
```
 4/3      Zoltán Halmay (HUN)
 4/3      Henry Taylor (GBR)
  3       Roland Matthes (GDR)
  3       Frank Beaurepaire (AUS)
  3       Duke Kahanamoku (USA)
  3       David Dickson (AUS)
  3       Gary Hall (USA)
 3/2      Charles Daniels (USA)
```

Most Years Winning Gold Medals, Men
```
 3/2      Charles Daniels (USA)
  2       Many athletes tied with two.
```

Most Years Between Medals, Men
```
 16       Frank Beaurepaire (AUS)
14/12     Henry Taylor (GBR)
 12       Duke Kahanamoku (USA)
```

Most Years Between Gold Medals, Men
```
  8       Duke Kahanamoku (USA)
  4       Many athletes tied with four.
```

Most Medals, Games
```
  7       Mark Spitz (USA-1972)
  5       Charles Daniels (USA-1904)
  5       Shane Gould (AUS-1972)
  5       John Naber (USA-1976)
  5       Shirley Babashoff (USA-1976)
  5       Kornelia Ender (GDR-1976)
  5       Ines Diers (GDR-1980)
```

Most Gold Medals, Games
```
  7       Mark Spitz (USA-1972)
  4       Don Schollander (USA-1964)
  4       Kornelia Ender (GDR-1976)
  4       John Naber (USA-1976)
  3       Twenty-six athletes tied with three.
```

Most Silver Medals, Games
```
  4       Shirley Babashoff (USA-1976)
  3       Francis Gailey (USA-1904)
  3       Hans-Joachim Klein (FRG-1964)
  3       Frank Wiegand (GDR-1964)
```

Most Bronze Medals, Games
    3   Louis Martin (FRA-1900)
    2   Many athletes tied with two.

Most Medals, Women, Games
    5   Shirley Babashoff (USA-1976)
    5   Ines Diers (GDR-1980)
    5   Kornelia Ender (GDR-1976)
    5   Shane Gould (AUS-1972)
    4   Nine athletes tied with four.

Most Gold Medals, Women, Games
    4   Kornelia Ender (GDR-1976)
    3   Ethelda Bleibtrey (USA-1920)
    3   Helene Madison (USA-1932)
    3   Hendrika Mastenbroek (HOL-1936)
    3   Chris Von Saltza (USA-1960)
    3   Sharon Stouder (USA-1964)
    3   Debbie Meyer (USA-1968)
    3   Sandra Neilson (USA-1972)
    3   Shane Gould (AUS-1972)
    3   Melissa Belote (USA-1972)
    3   Ulrike Richter (GDR-1976)
    3   Barbara Krause (GDR-1980)
    3   Caren Metschuck (GDR-1980)
    3   Rica Reinisch (GDR-1980)
    3   Nancy Hogshead (USA-1984)
    3   Tracy Caulkins (USA-1984)
    3   Mary T. Meagher (USA-1984)

Most Silver Medals, Women, Games
    4   Shirley Babashoff (USA-1976)
    3   Kornelia Ender (GDR-1972)
    2   Many athletes tied with two.

Most Bronze Medals, Women, Games
    2   Many athletes tied with two.

Most Medals, Men, Games
    7   Mark Spitz (USA-1972)
    5   Charles Daniels (USA-1904)
    5   Shane Gould (AUS-1972)
    5   John Naber (USA-1976)
    4   Ten athletes tied with four.

Most Gold Medals, Men, Games
    7   Mark Spitz (USA-1972)
    4   John Naber (USA-1976)
    4   Don Schollander (USA-1964)
    3   Ten athletes tied with three.

Most Silver Medals, Men, Games
    3   Francis Gailey (USA-1904)
    3   Hans-Joachim Klein (FRG-1964)
    3   Frank Wiegand (GDR-1964)

Most Bronze Medals, Men, Games
```
3        Louis Martin (FRA-1900)
2        Many athletes tied with two.
```

Most Medals, Individual
```
7/6      Zoltán Halmay (HUN)
6        Mark Spitz (USA)
6/5      Charles Daniels (USA)
5        Shirley Babashoff (USA)
5        Roland Matthes (GDR)
5        Shane Gould (AUS)
```

Most Gold Medals, Individual
```
4        Mark Spitz (USA)
4/3      Charles Daniels (USA)
4        Roland Matthes (GDR)
3        Kornelia Ender (GDR)
3        Dawn Fraser (AUS)
3        Murray Rose (AUS)
3        John Weissmuller (USA)
3        Shane Gould (AUS)
3        Debbie Meyer (USA)
3        Michael Burton (USA)
3/2      Henry Taylor (GBR)
```

Most Silver Medals, Individual
```
5        Shirley Babashoff (USA)
4/3      Zoltán Halmay (HUN)
3        Francis Gailey (USA)
3        Tsuyoshi Yamanaka (JPN)
3        Tor Henning (SWE)
3        Georg Hoffmann (GER)
3        Tim McKee (USA)
```

Most Bronze Medals, Individual
```
3        Frank Beaurepaire (AUS)
3        George Breen (USA)
```

Most Medals, Women, Individual
```
5        Shirley Babashoff (USA)
5        Shane Gould (AUS)
4        Kornelia Ender (GDR)
4        Dawn Fraser (AUS)
4        Ines Diers (GDR)
```

Most Gold Medals, Women, Individual
```
3        Kornelia Ender (GDR)
3        Dawn Fraser (AUS)
3        Shane Gould (AUS)
3        Debbie Meyer (USA)
```

Most Silver Medals, Women, Individual
   5   Shirley Babashoff (USA)
   2   Many athletes tied with two.

Most Bronze Medals, Women, Individual
   2   Many athletes tied with two.

Most Medals, Men, Individual
   7/6   Zoltán Halmay (HUN)
   6   Mark Spitz (USA)
   6/5   Charles Daniels (USA)
   5   Roland Matthes (GDR)

Most Gold Medals, Men, Individual
   4   Mark Spitz (USA)
   4   Roland Matthes (GDR)
   4/3   Charles Daniels (USA)
   3   Murray Rose (AUS)
   3   John Weissmuller (USA)
   3   Michael Burton (USA)
   3/2   Henry Taylor (GBR)

Most Silver Medals, Men, Individual
   4/3   Zoltán Halmay (HUN)
   3   Francis Gailey (USA)
   3   Tsuyoshi Yamanaka (JPN)
   3   Tor Henning (SWE)
   3   Georg Hoffmann (GER)
   3   Tim McKee (USA)

Most Bronze Medals, Men, Individual
   3   Frank Beaurepaire (AUS)
   3   George Breen (USA)

Most Medals, Games, Individual
   5   Shane Gould (AUS-1972)
   4   Mark Spitz (USA-1972)
   4   Charles Daniels (USA-1904)
   4   Ines Diers (GDR-1980)
   4   Francis Gailey (USA-1904)

Most Gold Medals, Games, Individual
   4   Mark Spitz (USA-1972)
   3   Kornelia Ender (GDR-1976)
   3   Shane Gould (AUS-1972)
   3   Debbie Meyer (USA-1968)

Most Medals, Women, Games, Individual
   5   Shane Gould (AUS-1972)
   4   Ines Diers (GDR-1980)
   3   Shirley Babashoff (USA-1976)
   3   Kornelia Ender (GDR-1976)
   3   Jan Henne (USA-1968)
   3   Hendrika Mastenbroek (HOL-1936)
   3   Novella Calligaris (ITA-1972)
   3   Debbie Meyer (USA-1968)

Most Gold Medals, Women, Games, Individual
   3   Kornelia Ender (GDR-1976)
   3   Shane Gould (AUS-1972)
   3   Debbie Meyer (USA-1968)

Most Medals, Men, Games, Individual
   4   Mark Spitz (USA-1972)
   4   Charles Daniels (USA-1904)
   4   Francis Gailey (USA-1904)
   3   John Naber (USA-1976)
   3   Charles Hickcox (USA-1968)
   3   Michael Groß (FRG-1984)
   3   Efstathios Choraphas (GRE-1896)
   3   Zoltán Halmay (HUN-1900)
   3   Georg Hoffmann (GER-1904)
   3   Emil Rausch (GER-1904)

Most Gold Medals, Men, Games, Individual
   4   Mark Spitz (USA-1972)
   2   Many athletes tied with two.

Most Appearances
   4/3   Zoltán Halmay (HUN, 1900-08)
   4/3   John Derbyshire (GBR; 1900, 06-12)
   4/3   Henry Taylor (GBR, 1906-20)
   4/3   Robert Andersson (SWE, 1906-20)
   4   John Hatfield (GBR, 1912-28)
   4   Phyllis Harding (GBR, 1924-36)
   4   Gudmundur Gislasson (ISL, 1960-72)

Most Appearances, Men
   4/3   Zoltán Halmay (HUN, 1900-08)
   4/3   John Derbyshire (GBR; 1900, 06-12)
   4/3   Henry Taylor (GBR, 1906-20)
   4/3   Robert Andersson (SWE, 1906-20)
   4   John Hatfield (GBR, 1912-28)
   4   Gudmundur Gislasson (ISL, 1960-72)

Most Appearances, Women
   4   Phyllis Harding (GBR, 1924-36)

Youngest Medalist, Women
  12-024 Inge Sörensen (DEN-1936)
  13-308 Kornelia Ender (GDR-1972)
  13-341 Robin Corsiglia (CAN-1976)
  14-097 Debra "Pokey" Watson (USA-1964)
  14-115 Inge Schmitz (GER-1936)
  14-156 Sylvia Ruuska (USA-1956)
  14-184 Sandra Morgan (AUS-1956)
  14-220 Willemijntje den Ouden (HOL-1932)
  14-260 Carolyn Wood (USA-1960)
  14-288 Karen Moras (AUS-1968)

Youngest Gold Medalist, Women
```
14-097   Debra "Pokey" Watson (USA-1964)
14-184   Sandra Morgan (AUS-1956)
14-260   Carolyn Wood (USA-1960)
15-002   Susan Pederson (USA-1968)
15-072   Andrea Pollack (GDR-1976)
15-106   Rica Reinisch (GDR-1980)
15-115   Deena Deardurff (USA-1972)
15-172   Faith Leech (AUS-1956)
15-173   Petra Thümer (GDR-1976)
15-188   Keena Rothhammer (USA-1972)
```

Oldest Medalist, Women
```
30-042   Ursula Happe (GER-1956)
28-253   Eva Riise (DEN-1948)
27-159   Irma Heijting-Schuhmacher (HOL-1952)
27-141   Frances Schroth (USA-1920)
27-078   Ilona Novák (HUN-1952)
```

Oldest Gold Medalist, Women
```
30-042   Ursula Happe (GER-1956)
27-141   Frances Schroth (USA-1920)
27-078   Ilona Novák (HUN-1952)
27-040   Dawn Fraser (AUS-1964)
26-146   Lucy Morton (GBR-1924)
```

Youngest Medalist, Men
```
14-309   Kusuo Kitamura (JPN-1932)
15-298   Yasuji Miyazaki (JPN-1932)
16-061   John Kinsella (USA-1968)
16-101   Ioannis Malokinis (GRE-1896)
16-131   John Nelson (USA-1964)
16-134   Otto Scheff (AUT-1906)
16-173   Warren Kealoha (USA-1920)
16-338   Andrew Charlton (AUS-1924)
17-008   Sándor Wladár (HUN-1980)
17-019   Dick Roth (USA-1964)
```

Youngest Gold Medalist, Men
```
14-309   Kusuo Kitamura (JPN-1932)
15-298   Yasuji Miyazaki (JPN-1932)
16-061   John Kinsella (USA-1968)
16-101   Ioannis Malokinis (GRE-1896)
16-134   Otto Scheff (AUT-1906)
16-173   Warren Kealoha (USA-1920)
16-338   Andrew Charlton (AUS-1924)
17-008   Sándor Wladár (HUN-1980)
17-019   Dick Roth (USA-1964)
17-110   Brian Goodell (USA-1976)
```

Oldest Medalist, Men
```
46-302  William Henry (GBR-1906)
37-200  William Robinson (GBR-1908)
35-166  Henry Taylor (GBR-1920)
34-061  John Jarvis (GBR-1906)
33-331  Duke Kahanamoku (USA-1924)
```

Oldest Gold Medalist, Men
```
30-230  Cecil Healy (AUS-1912)
30-206  Louis Handley (USA-1904)
30-006  Duke Kahanamoku (USA-1920)
29-238  John Derbyshire (GBR-1908)
28-286  Yoshiyuki Tsuruta (JPN-1932)
```

Medals Won by Countries

	G	S	B	T
United States	148	104	80	332
Australia	35¾	29	35	99¾
GDR	27	25	15	67
Great Britain	13	20	23	56
USSR	10	19	21	50
Japan	13	18	14	45
Hungary	11	14	13	38
Netherlands	9	12	12	33
Canada	6	13	14	33
Germany	10	13	8	31
Sweden	7	8	11	26
FRG	3	5	16	24
France	2	6	7	15
Austria	2	3	6	11
Denmark	2	4	4	10
Greece	1	4	3	8
South Africa	1	–	3	4
Brazil	–	1	3	4
Belgium	–	1	2	3
Italy	–	1	2	3
Yugoslavia	1	1	–	2
Argentina	1	1	–	2
Mexico	1	–	1	2
Philippines	–	–	2	2
Finland	–	–	2	2
New Zealand	¼	–	1	1¼
Spain	–	–	1	1
Switzerland	–	–	1	1
Poland	–	–	1	1
Venezuela	–	–	1	1
Romania	–	–	1	1
Totals	304	302	303	909

Medals Won by Countries, Men

	G	S	B	T
United States	86	64	47	197
Australia	21¾	17	27	65¾
Japan	11	17	11	39
USSR	7	13	13	33
Great Britain	9	11	11	31
Hungary	7	10	10	27
Germany	9	10	4	23
Sweden	7	6	9	22
Canada	5	6	5	16
FRG	2	3	9	14
GDR	5	5	3	13
France	2	5	6	13
Austria	2	3	5	10
Greece	1	4	3	8
Brazil	-	1	3	4
Belgium	-	1	1	2
Denmark	-	1	1	2
Philippines	-	-	2	2
Netherlands	-	-	2	2
Finland	-	-	2	2
Mexico	1	-	-	1
Argentina	1	-	-	1
Spain	-	-	1	1
Switzerland	-	-	1	1
Venezuela	-	-	1	1
New Zealand	¼	-	-	¼
Totals	177	177	177	531

*The 1912 800 metre freestyle relay team represented Australasia and was composed of three Australians and one New Zealander.

Medals Won by Countries, Women

	G	S	B	T
United States	62	40	33	135
GDR	22	20	12	54
Australia	14	12	8	34
Netherlands	9	12	10	31
Great Britain	4	9	12	25
USSR	3	6	8	17
Canada	1	7	9	17
Hungary	4	4	3	11
FRG	1	2	7	10
Denmark	2	3	3	8

Germany	1	3	4	8
Japan	2	1	3	6
South Africa	1	-	3	4
Sweden	-	2	2	4
Italy	-	1	2	3
Yugoslavia	1	1	-	2
France	-	1	1	2
Argentina	-	1	-	1
New Zealand	-	-	1	1
Austria	-	-	1	1
Belgium	-	-	1	1
Mexico	-	-	1	1
Poland	-	-	1	1
Romania	-	-	1	1
Totals	127	125	126	378

Two firsts/no second in 1984 100 metre freestyle.

Olympic Swimmers and The English Channel

Gertrude Ederle (USA) was the first Olympic swimmer to successfully swim the English Channel. She won three medals at the 1924 Olympics (4x100 freestyle relay <1>, 100 freestyle <3>, 400 freestyle <3>) and in 1926 swam from France to England in 14:39 (hours:minutes). She was the first woman to cross the channel, the third person to swim from France-to-England, and the sixth person overall to make a successful crossing.

Greta Andersen (DEN/USA) five times swam the English channel. As a Danish citizen she won two medals in the 1948 Olympics (100 freestyle <1>, 4x100 freestyle relay <2>). Still a Dane, in 1957 she swam from France-to-England in 13:55. She repeated this route in 1958 in 11:01 (then a record for women), and again in 1959 in 15:25, having by 1958 become a U.S. citizen. In 1964, she reversed directions, swimming England-to-France in 13:40, making her the third woman to swim in that direction. Finally in 1965 she swam England-to-France in 13:49, her fifth crossing, at the time a record for women.

John Kinsella (USA) swam from England-to-France in 9:10 in 1979. As an Olympian he won two medals (1968 1500 freestyle <2>, 1972 4x200 freestyle relay <1>).

Edward H. "Ted" Temme (GBR) was a water poloist at the 1928 Olympics and in 1934 swam from England-to-France in 15:34, becoming the first male Olympian to achieve a successful crossing.

Linda McGill (AUS) competed in four events at the 1964 Olympics, her best finish being fifth in the 400 metre individual medley. She made the following Channel crossings: 1965 - France-to-England, 11:12; 1967 - France-to-England (twice), 13:02, and 9:59 (a new female record at the time).

Best Performance by Country at Each Olympics

	Men	Women	Overall
1896 -	Greece	-----	-----
1900 -	France	-----	-----
1904 -	United States	-----	-----
1906 -	Great Britain	-----	-----
1908 -	Great Britain	-----	-----
1912 -	Germany	Australia	Germany
1920 -	United States	United States	United States
1924 -	United States	United States	United States
1928 -	United States	United States	United States
1932 -	Japan	United States	Japan
1936 -	Japan	The Netherlands	Japan
1948 -	United States	USA/Denmark	United States
1952 -	United States	Hungary	United States
1956 -	Australia	Australia	Australia
1960 -	Australia	United States	United States
1964 -	United States	United States	United States
1968 -	United States	United States	United States
1972 -	United States	United States	United States
1976 -	United States	GDR	United States
1980 -	USSR	GDR	GDR
1984 -	United States	United States	United States

Swimming - Olympic Record Progressions - Men

100 metre freestyle

1:22.2	1		Alfred Hájos (HUN)	1896
1:13.4	1		Charles Daniels (USA)	1906
1:08.2	h1		Zoltán Halmay (HUN)	1908
1:05.8	h5		Charles Daniels (USA)	1908
1:05.6	1	WR	Charles Daniels (USA)	1908
1:04.8	h4		Perry McGillivray (USA)	1912
1:02.6	h5		Duke Kahanamoku (USA)	1912
1:02.4	s3	=WR	Duke Kahanamoku (USA)	1912
1:01.8	h1		Duke Kahanamoku (USA)	1920
1:01.4	s1		Duke Kahanamoku (USA)	1920
[1:00.4*]	1	WR	Duke Kahanamoku (USA)	1920
1:00.8	s1		Johnny Weissmuller (USA)	1924
59.0	1		Johnny Weissmuller (USA)	1924
58.6	s3		Johnny Weissmuller (USA)	1928
58.6	1		Johnny Weissmuller (USA)	1928
58.0	s1		Yasuji Miyazaki (JPN)	1932
57.6	h1		Peter Fick (USA)	1936
57.5	h5		Masaharu Taguchi (JPN)	1936

57.5	s2		Masanori Yusa (JPN)	1936
57.5	s2		Walter Ris (USA)	1948
57.3	1		Walter Ris (USA)	1948
57.1	s1		Clarke Scholes (USA)	1952
56.8	h4		L. Reid Patterson (USA)	1956
55.7	s1		Jon Henricks (AUS)	1956
55.4	1		Jon Henricks (AUS)	1956
55.2+	1		John Devitt (AUS)	1960
55.1+	2		Lance Larson (USA)	1960
54.0	h1		Gary Ilman (USA)	1964
53.9	s1		Gary Ilman (USA)	1964
53.4	1		Donald Schollander (USA)	1964
52.9	R	WR	Stephen Clark (USA)	1964
52.9	s3		Michael Wenden (AUS)	1968
52.2	1	WR	Michael Wenden (AUS)	1968
52.26	R		Vladimir Bure (URS)	1972
51.22	1	WR	Mark Spitz (USA)	1972
50.39	s1	WR	James Montgomery (USA)	1976
49.99	1	WR	James Montgomery (USA)	1976
49.80	1		Ambrose "Rowdy" Gaines (USA)	1984

*Kahanamoku's time was done in the first final, which was ordered re-swum. In the re-swim, he recorded 1:01.4.
+Devitt was declared the winner over Larson in the most controversial finish in Olympic swimming history. The times taken for this race were 55.0, 55.1, and 55.1 for Larson; and 55.2, 55.2, and 55.2 for Devitt. Larson's official time was given as 55.2.
R-Time was recorded as the first leg of the 4x100 metre freestyle relay.

200 metre freestyle

[2:35.6]*	h1	Otto Wahle (AUT)	1900
[2:22.0]*	h5	Karl Ruberl (AUT)	1900
2:14.1	R-f	Yasaji Myazaki (JPN)	1932
2:13.4	R-f	Masanori Yusa (JPN)	1936
2:11.4	R-h2	Wallace Wolf (USA)	1952
2:10.1	R-h3	Yoshihiro Hamaguchi (JPN)	1952
2:07.0	R-f	Hiroshi Suzuki (JPN)	1952
2:06.8	R-f	Kevin O'Halloran (AUS)	1956
2:01.8	R-h1	Tsuyoshi Yamanaka (JPN)	1960
2:00.0	R-f	Stephen Clark (USA)	1964
1:58.6	R-f	John Nelson (USA)	1968

1:55.2	1		Michael Wenden (AUS)	1968
1:52.78	1	WR	Mark Spitz (USA)	1972
1:52.71	h2		Andrei Bogdanov (URS)	1976
1:51.41	h3		Klaus Steinbach (FRG)	1976
1:50.93	h8		Bruce Furniss (USA)	1976
1:50.29	1	WR	Bruce Furniss (USA)	1976
1:49.81	1		Sergei Koplyakov (URS)	1980
1:48.03	h7		Michael Groß (FRG)	1984
1:47.44	1	WR	Michael Groß(FRG)	1984

*The 1900 swimming events were held in the River Seine and the 200
metre freestyle was noted to be swum downstream.
R-Time recorded as the first leg of the 4x200 metre freestyle
relay.

400 metre freestyle

6:23.8	1		Otto Scheff (AUT)	1906
5:48.8	h1		T. Sydney Battersby (GBR)	1908
5:42.2	h6		Henry Taylor (GBR)	1908
5:40.6	s2		Henry Taylor (GBR)	1908
5:36.8	1		Henry Taylor (GBR)	1908
5:36.0	h1		Harold Hardwick (AUS)	1912
5:34.0	h5		Cecil Healy (AUS)	1912
5:25.4	s1		George Hodgson (CAN)	1912
5:24.4	1		George Hodgson (CAN)	1912
5:22.4	h1		Ralph Breyer (USA)	1924
5:22.2	h3		Johnny Weissmuller (USA)	1924
5:13.6	s1		Johnny Weissmuller (USA)	1924
5:04.2	1		Johnny Weissmuller (USA)	1924
5:01.6	1		Alberto Zorilla (ARG)	1928
4:53.2	h1		Takashi Yokoyama (JPN)	1932
4:51.4	s1		Takashi Yokoyama (JPN)	1932
4:48.4	1		Clarence "Buster" Crabbe (USA)	1932
4:45.5	h5		Shumpei Uto (JPN)	1936
4:44.5	1		Jack Medica (USA)	1936
4:42.2	h1		James McLane (USA)	1948
4:41.0	1		William Smith (USA)	1948
4:38.6	h6		Per-Olof Astrand (SWE)	1952
4:33.1	s1		Jean Boiteaux (FRA)	1952
4:30.7	1		Jean Boiteaux (FRA)	1952
4:27.3	1		Murray Rose (AUS)	1956
4:21.0	h1		Tsuyoshi Yamanaka (JPN)	1960
4:19.2	h6		Alan Somers (USA)	1960
4:18.3	1		Murray Rose (AUS)	1960
4:17.2	h6		Frank Wiegand (FRG)	1964
4:15.8	h7		Donald Schollander (USA)	1964
4:12.2	1	WR	Donald Schollander (USA)	1964
4:09.0	1		Michael Burton (USA)	1968
4:06.59	h2		Bengt Gingsjö (SWE)	1972
4:05.89	h3		Steve Genter (USA)	1972
4:04.59	h4		Brad Cooper (AUS)	1972

[4:00.26]*	dq	Rick DeMont (USA)	1972
4:00.27	1	Brad Cooper (AUS)	1972
3:59.62	h2	Djan Madruga (BRA)	1976
3:57.56	h3	Vladimir Raskatov (URS)	1976
3:56.40	h6	Tim Shaw (USA)	1976
3:55.24	h7	Brian Goodell (USA)	1976
3:51.93	1 WR	Brian Goodell (USA)	1976
3:51.31	1	Vladimir Salnikov (URS)	1980
3:51.23	1	George DiCarlo (USA)	1984
3:50.91+	9	Thomas Fahrner (FRG)	1984

*DeMont was disqualified for having used an illegal asthma drug.
+Fahrner did not qualify for the final. He set this mark in the
consolation final.

1,500 metre freestyle

25:02.4	h1	Paul Radmilovic (GBR)	1908
23:45.8	h2	Frank Beaurepaire (AUS)	1908
23:42.8	h4	T. Sydney Battersby (GBR)	1908
23:24.4	h6	Henry Taylor (GBR)	1908
22:54.0	s1	Henry Taylor (GBR)	1908
22:48.4	1	Henry Taylor (GBR)	1908
22:23.0	h3 WR	George Hodgson (CAN)	1912
22:00.0	1 WR	George Hodgson (CAN)	1912
21:20.4	h3	Andrew "Boy" Charlton (AUS)	1924
21:11.4	h4 WR	Arne Borg (SWE)	1924
20:06.6	1 WR	Andrew "Boy" Charlton (AUS)	1924
19:51.8	1	Arne Borg (SWE)	1928
19:51.6	s1	Kusuo Kitamura (JPN)	1932
19:38.7	s2	Shozo Makino (JPN)	1932
19:12.4	1	Kusuo Kitamura (JPN)	1932
18:34.0	h1	Shiro Hashizume (JPN)	1952
18:30.3	1	Ford Konno (USA)	1952
18:04.0	h1	Murray Rose (AUS)	1956
17:52.9	h3 WR	George Breen (USA)	1956
17:46.5	h1	Tsuyoshi Yamanaka (JPN)	1960
17:32.8	h5	Murray Rose (AUS)	1960
17:19.6	1	Jon Konrads (AUS)	1960
17:15.9	h1	Robert Windle (AUS)	1964
17:01.7	1	Robert Windle (AUS)	1964
16:38.9	1	Michael Burton (USA)	1968
16:34.63	h1	Hans-Joachim Faßnacht (FRG)	1972
15:59.63	h2	Graham Windeatt (AUS)	1972
15:52.58	1 WR	Michael Burton (USA)	1972
15:37.61	h1	Zoltán Wladár (HUN)	1976
15:20.74	h2	Paul Hartloff (USA)	1976
15:02.40	1 WR	Brian Goodell (USA)	1976
14:58.27	1 WR	Vladimir Salnikov (URS)	1980

100 metre backstroke

1:25.6	h1		Arno Bieberstein (GER)	1908
1:25.6	s1		Arno Bieberstein (GER)	1908
1:24.6	1	WR	Arno Bieberstein (GER)	1908
1:21.0	h1		Harry Hebner (USA)	1912
1:20.8	s1		Harry Hebner (USA)	1912
1:17.8	h1		Ray Kegeris (USA)	1920
1:14.8	h2	WR	Warren Kealoha (USA)	1920
1:13.4	h1		Warren Kealoha (USA)	1924
1:13.2	1		Warren Kealoha (USA)	1924
1:09.2	h1		George Kojac (USA)	1928
1:08.2	1	WR	George Kojac (USA)	1928
1:06.9	h1		Adolf Kiefer (USA)	1936
1:06.8	s1		Adolf Kiefer (USA)	1936
1:05.9	1		Adolf Kiefer (USA)	1936
1:05.7	s1		Yoshinobu Oyakawa (JPN)	1952
1:05.4	1		Yoshinobu Oyakawa (JPN)	1952
1:04.2	h1		Robert Christophe (FRA)	1956
1:03.4	h4		John Monckton (AUS)	1956
1:02.2	1		David Thiele (AUS)	1956
1:02.0	h2		Robert Bennett (USA)	1960
1:01.9	1		David Thiele (AUS)	1960
1:01.1	R-h1		Richard McGeagh (USA)	1964
59.6	R-f	WR	Thompson Mann (USA)	1964
58.7	1		Roland Matthes (GDR)	1968
58.0	R-f	WR	Roland Matthes (GDR)	1968
57.99	s2		Mitchell Ivey (USA)	1972
56.58	1		Roland Matthes (GDR)	1972
56.30	R-f	=WR	Roland Matthes (GDR)	1972
56.19	h2	WR	John Naber (USA)	1976
55.49	1	WR	John Naber (USA)	1976
55.41	R-f		Richard Carey (USA)	1984

R-Time was recorded in the first leg of the 4x100 metre medley relay.

200 metre backstroke

2:54.2	h1		Ernst Hoppenberg (GER)	1900
2:47.0	1		Ernst Hoppenberg (GER)	1900
2:16.1*	h1		Robert Bennett (USA)	1964
2:14.7	h2		Shigeo Fukushima (JPN)	1964
2:14.5	h3		Jed Graef (USA)	1964
2:14.2	h5		Gary Dilley (USA)	1964
2:13.8	s1		Gary Dilley (USA)	1964
2:13.7	s2		Jed Graef (USA)	1964
2:10.3	1	WR	Jed Graef (USA)	1964
2:09.6	1		Roland Matthes (GDR)	1968
2:07.51	h2		Mike Stamm (USA)	1972
2:06.62	h5		Roland Matthes (GDR)	1972
2:02.82	1	=WR	Roland Matthes (GDR)	1972
2:02.25	h2		Dan Harrigan (USA)	1976
2:02.01	h5		John Naber (USA)	1976
1:59.19	1	WR	John Naber (USA)	1976
1:58.99	h5		Richard Carey (USA)	1984

*This event was not held from 1904-1960.

100 metre breaststroke

1:08.9	h1		Nikolai Pankin (URS)	1968
1:08.1	h5		Donald McKenzie (USA)	1968
1:08.1	s2		Nikolai Pankin (URS)	1968
1:07.9	s3		Vladimir Kosinskiy (URS)	1968
1:07.7	1		Donald McKenzie (USA)	1968
1:05.89	h1		Mark Chatfield (USA)	1972
1:05.68	s1	WR	John Hencken (USA)	1972
1:05.13	s2	WR	Nobutaka Taguchi (JPN)	1972
1:04.94	1	WR	Nobutaka Taguchi (JPN)	1972
1:04.92	h1		Duncan Goodhew (GBR)	1976
1:04.78	h2		Arvidas Yuozaitis (URS)	1976
1:03.88	h5	=WR	John Hencken (USA)	1976
1:03.62	s2	WR	John Hencken (USA)	1976
1:03.11	1	WR	John Hencken (USA)	1976
1:02.87	h2		Peter Evans (AUS)	1984
1:02.16	h7		John Moffet (USA)	1984
1:01.65	1		Steve Lundquist (USA)	1984

200 metre breaststroke

3:10.6	h1		Frederick Holman (GBR)	1908
3:10.0	s1		Frederick Holman (GBR)	1908
3:09.2	1		Frederick Holman (GBR)	1908
3:07.4	h1		WIlhelm Lützow (GER)	1912
3:03.4	h4		Walter Bathe (GER)	1912
3:02.2	s2		Walter Bathe (GER)	1912
3:01.8	1		Walter Bathe (GER)	1912
2:56.0	h1		Robert Skelton (USA)	1924
2:52.0	h3		Erich Rademacher (GER)	1928
2:50.0	h4		Yoshiyuki Tsuruta (JPN)	1928

2:49.2	s1		Yoshiyuki Tsuruta (JPN)	1928
2:48.8	1		Yoshiyuki Tsuruta (JPN)	1928
2:46.2	h1		Yoshiyuki Tsuruta (JPN)	1932
2:46.2	h2		Reizo Koike (JPN)	1932
2:44.9	s1		Reizo Koike (JPN)	1932
2:42.5	h1		Tetsuo Hamuro (JPN)	1936
2:42.5	1		Tetsuo Hamuro (JPN)	1936
[2:40.0]*	h2		Joseph Verdeur (USA)	1948
[2:39.3]*	1		Joseph Verdeur (USA)	1948
[2:38.9]*	h3		Ludevit Komadel (TCH)	1952
[2:36.8]*	h5		Gerald Holan (USA)	1952
[2:36.8]*	s1		John Davies (AUS)	1952
[2:34.4]*	1		John Davies (AUS)	1952
[2:36.1]+	h1		Masaru Furukawa (JPN)	1956
[2:34.7]+	1		Masaru Furukawa (JPN)	1956
2:38.0	h1		William Mulliken (USA)	1960
2:37.2	s1		William Mulliken (USA)	1960
2:31.4	h1		Ian O'Brien (AUS)	1964
2:30.1	h2		Egon Henninger (GDR)	1964
2:28.7	s2		Ian O'Brien (AUS)	1964
2:27.8	1	WR	Ian O'Brien (AUS)	1964
2:26.32	h1		Klaus Katzur (GDR)	1972
2:23.45	h2		Nobutaka Taguchi (JPN)	1972
2:21.55	1	WR	John Hencken (USA)	1972
2:21.08	h2		Rick Colella (USA)	1976
2:18.29	h4		David Wilkie (GBR)	1976
2:15.11	1	WR	David Wilkie (GBR)	1976
2:13.34	1	WR	Victor Davis (CAN)	1984

*These marks were all set in the 200 metre breaststroke event, but using the butterfly stroke, which was then permissible.
+Furukawa's marks were set using the now disallowed underwater technique of swimming the breaststroke.

100 metre butterfly

57.3	h1		Douglas Russell (USA)	1968
55.9	s3		Douglas Russell (USA)	1968
55.9	1		Douglas Russell (USA)	1968
54.27	1	WR	Mark Spitz (USA)	1972
54.02	h6		Michael Groß (FRG)	1984
53.78	h7		Pedro Pablo Morales (USA)	1984
53.08	1	WR	Michael Groß (FRG)	1984

200 metre butterfly

[2:44.9]*	h1		Robert Sohl (USA)	1948
[2:40.7]*	h2		Joseph Verdeur (USA)	1948
[2:39.3]*	1		Joseph Verdeur (USA)	1948
[2:38.9]*	h3		Ludevit Komadel (TCH)	1952
[2:36.8]*	h5		Gerald Holan (USA)	1952
[2:36.8]*	s1		John Davies (AUS)	1952
[2:34.4]*	1		John Davies (AUS)	1952
2:18.6	h1		William Yorzyk (USA)	1956
2:15.5	h1		Michael Troy (USA)	1960
2:12.8	1	WR	Michael Troy (USA)	1960
2:10.0	h1		Carl Robie (USA)	1964
2:09.3	s1		Carl Robie (USA)	1964
2:06.6	1	WR	Kevin Berry (AUS)	1964
2:03.70	h1		Gary Hall (USA)	1972
2:03.11	h2		Robin Backhaus (USA)	1972
2:02.11	h4		Mark Spitz (USA)	1972
2:00.70	1	WR	Mark Spitz (USA)	1972
2:00.24	h3		Steve Gregg (USA)	1976
1:59.23	1	WR	Michael Bruner (USA)	1976
1:59.19	h4		Pedro Pablo Morales (USA)	1984
1:58.72	h5		Michael Groß (FRG)	1984
1:57.04	1	WR	Jon Sieben (AUS)	1984

*All of these marks were set in the 200 metre breaststroke by swimmers using the butterfly stroke, which was then permissible.

200 metre individual medley

2:16.1	h1		Charles Hickcox (USA)	1968
2:14.6	h3		John Ferris (USA)	1968
2:12.0	1		Charles Hickcox (USA)	1968
2:10.88	h2		András Hargitay (HUN)	1972
2:09.70	h3		Gunnar Larsson (SWE)	1972
2:07.17	1	WR	Gunnar Larsson (SWE)	1972
2:05.39	h1		Neil Cochran (GBR)	1984
2:04.13	h3		Robin Brew (GBR)	1984
2:03.60	h5		Alex Baumann (CAN)	1984
2:01.42	1	WR	Alex Baumann (CAN)	1984

400 metre individual medley

4:52.0	h1		Carl Robie (USA)	1964
4:45.4	1	WR	Dick Roth (USA)	1964
4:37.51	h1		András Hargitay (HUN)	1972
4:34.99	h2		Gunnar Larsson (SWE)	1972
4:31.98*	1		Gunnar Larsson (SWE)	1972
4:31.98*	2		Tim McKee (USA)	1972
4:27.76	h1		Steve Furniss (USA)	1976
4:27.15	h3		Rod Strachan (USA)	1976
4:23.68	1	WR	Rod Strachan (USA)	1976
4:22.89	1		Aleksandr Sidorenko (URS)	1980
4:22.46	h3		Alex Baumann (CAN)	1984
4:17.41	1	WR	Alex Baumann (CAN)	1984

*The automatic timer broke the tie and awarded first place to Larsson by the margin of 2/1000th of a second - 4:31.981 to 4:31.983.

4 x 100 metre freestyle relay

3:40.6	h1		Australia	1964
			(Doak, Dickson, Ryan, Windle)	
3:38.8	h2		United States	1964
			(Clark, Schulhof, Austin, Ilman)	
3:33.2	1	WR	United States	1964
			(Clark, Austin, Ilman, Schollander)	
3:31.7	1	WR	United States	1968
			(Zorn, Rerych, Spitz, Walsh)	
3:28.84	h2	=WR	United States	1972
			(Fairbank, Conelly, Edgar, Heidenreich)	
3:26.42	1	WR	United States	1972
			(Edgar, Murphy, Heidenreich, Spitz)	
3:24.69	h1		German Federal Republic	1984
			(Korthals, Schowtka, Klapkarek, Schmidt)	
3:23.86	h2		Sweden	1984
			(Milton, Soderlund, Orn, Johansson)	
3:19.94	h3		Australia	1984
			(Brooks, Fasala, Delaney, Stockwell)	
3:19.03	1	WR	United States	1984
			(Cavanaugh, Heath, Biondi, Gaines)	

4 x 100 metre medley relay

4:14.8	h1		Australia	1960

(Carroll, Burton, Berry, Shipton)

| 4:08.2 | h3 | WR | United States | 1960 |

(Bennett, Hait, Gillanders, Clark)

| 4:05.4 | 1 | WR | United States | 1960 |

(McKinney, Hait, Larson, Farrell)

| 4:05.1 | h2 | | United States | 1964 |

(McGeagh, Luken, Richardson, Bennett)

| 3:58.4 | 1 | WR | United States | 1964 |

(Mann, Craig, Schmidt, Clark)

| 3:54.9 | 1 | WR | United States | 1968 |

(Hickcox, McKenzie, Russell, Walsh)

| 3:51.98 | h3 | | United States | 1972 |

(Ivey, Hencken, Hall, Fairbank)

| 3:48.16 | 1 | WR | United States | 1972 |

(Stamm, Bruce, Spitz, Heidenreich)

| 3:47.28 | h2 | WR | United States | 1976 |

(Rocca, Woo, Bottom, Babashoff)

| 3:42.22 | 1 | WR | United States | 1976 |

(Naber, Hencken, Vogel, Montgomery)

| 3:39.30 | 1 | WR | United States | 1984 |

(Carey, Lundquist, Morales, Gaines)

4 x 200 metre freestyle relay

11:35.0	h1	Australasia	1908

(Beaurepaire, Springfield, Baker, Tartakover)

| 10:53.4 | h2 | Great Britain | 1908 |

(Foster, Radmilovic, Derbyshire, Taylor)

| 10:26.4 | h1 | United States | 1912 |

(Huszagh, Kahanamoku, Hebner, McGillivray)

| 10:14.0 | h2 | Australasia | 1912 |

(Hardwick, Champion, Boardman, Healy)

| 10:11.6 | 1 | Australia/New Zealand | 1912 |

(Hardwick, Champion, Boardman, Healy)

| 10:04.4 | 1 | United States | 1920 |

(McGillivray, Kealoha, Ross, Kahanamoku)

| 9:59.4 | s2 | United States | 1924 |

(Breyer, Glancy, Howell, O'Connor)

| 9:53.4 | 1 | United States | 1924 |

(O'Connor, Glancy, Breyer, Weissmuller)

| 9:38.8 | h1 | United States | 1928 |

(Samson, Clapp, Young, Weissmuller)

| 9:36.2 | 1 | United States | 1928 |

(Clapp, Laufer, Kojac, Weissmuller)

8:58.4	1	WR	Japan	1932
			(Miyazaki, Yusa, Yokoyama, Toyoda)	
8:56.1	h3		Japan	1936
			(Arai, Sugiura, Taguchi, Yusa)	
8:51.5	1	WR	Japan	1936
			(Arai, Sugiura, Taguchi, Yusa)	
8:46.0	1	WR	United States	1948
			(Ris, McLane, Wolf, Smith)	
8:42.1	h3		Japan	1952
			(Hamaguchi, Suzuki, Goto, Tanikawa)	
8:31.1	1		United States	1952
			(Moore, Woolsey, Konno, McLane)	
8:23.6	1	WR	Australia	1956
			(O'Halloran, Devitt, Rose, Henricks)	
8:17.1	h1		Japan	1960
			(Yamanaka, Fukui, Ishii, Fujimoto)	
8:10.2	1	WR	United States	1960
			(Harrison, Blick, Troy, Farrell)	
8:09.7	h1		Germany	1964
			(Gregor, Hetz, Wiegand, Klein)	
8:09.0	h2		United States	1964
			(Mettler, Lyons, Wall, Townsend)	
7:52.1	1	WR	United States	1964
			(Clark, Saari, Ilman, Schollander)	
7:49.03	h1		Australia	1972
			(Cooper, Featherstone, White, Wenden)	
7:46.42	h2		United States	1972
			(Connelly, McBreen, Burton, Kinsella)	
7:35.78	1	WR	United States	1972
			(Kinsella, Tyler, Genter, Spitz)	
7:33.21	h2		Soviet Union	1976
			(Smirnov, Minheev, Raskatov, Koplyakov)	
7:30.33	h3	WR	United States	1976
			(Northway, Shaw, Bruner, Furniss)	
7:23.22	1	WR	United States	1976
			(Bruner, Furniss, Naber, Montgomery)	
7:18.87	h1		United States	1984
			(Gaberino, Larson, Hayes, Saeger)	
7:15.69	1	WR	United States	1984
			(Heath, Larson, Float, Hayes)	

Swimming - Olympic Record Progressions - Women

100 metre freestyle

1:29.8	h1		Bella Moore (GBR)	1912
1:23.6	h2		Daisy Curwen (GBR)	1912
1:19.8	h4	WR	Fanny Durack (AUS)	1912
1:18.0	h1		Frances Schroth (USA)	1920
1:14.4	h3	WR	Ethelda Bleibtrey (USA)	1920
1:13.6	1	WR	Ethelda Bleibtrey (USA)	1920
1:12.2	h1	WR	Mariechen Wehselau (USA)	1924
1:12.2	h4		Albina Osipowich (USA)	1928
1:11.4	s2		Eleanor Garatti (USA)	1928
1:11.0	1		Albina Osipowich (USA)	1928
1:09.0	h2		Joyce Cooper (GBR)	1932
1:08.9	h3		Helene Madison (USA)	1932
1:08.5	h4		Eleanor Garatti-Saville (USA)	1932
1:07.6	s1		Willemijntje den Ouden (HOL)	1932
1:06.8	1		Helene Madison (USA)	1932
1:06.4	h1		Hendrika Mastenbroek (HOL)	1936
1:06.4	s1		Hendrika Mastenbroek (HOL)	1936
1:05.9	1		Hendrika Mastenbroek (HOL)	1936
1:05.9	s1		Greta Andersen (DEN)	1948
1:05.5	h5		Judit Temes (HUN)	1952
1:03.4	h1		Lorraine Crapp (AUS)	1956
1:02.4	h5		Dawn Fraser (AUS)	1956
1:02.0	1	WR	Dawn Fraser (AUS)	1956
1:01.9	h4		Chris von Saltza (USA)	1960
1:01.4	h2		Dawn Fraser (AUS)	1960
1:01.2	1		Dawn Fraser (AUS)	1960
1:00.6	h5		Dawn Fraser (AUS)	1964
59.9	s1		Dawn Fraser (AUS)	1964
59.5	1		Dawn Fraser (AUS)	1964
59.47	h3		Magdolna Patoh (HUN)	1972
59.44	h6		Shane Gould (AUS)	1972
59.05	s1		Shirley Babashoff (USA)	1972
58.59	1		Sandra Neilson (USA)	1972
56.95	h1		Petra Priemer (GDR)	1976
56.61	h6		Enith Brigitha (HOL)	1976
55.81	h7		Kornelia Ender (GDR)	1976
55.65	1	WR	Kornelia Ender (GDR)	1976
54.98	h3	WR	Barbara Krause (GDR)	1980
54.79	1	WR	Barbara Krause (GDR)	1980

200 metre freestyle

2:13.1	h1		Debbie Meyer (USA)	1968
2:10.5	1		Debbie Meyer (USA)	1968
2:08.12	h1		Ann Marshall (USA)	1972
2:07.48	h3		Keena Rothhammer (USA)	1972
2:07.05	h5		Andrea Eife (GDR)	1972
2:03.56	1	WR	Shane Gould (AUS)	1972
2:03.36	h1		Claudia Hempel (GDR)	1976
2:01.54	h4		Enith Brigitha (HOL)	1976
1:59.26	1	WR	Kornelia Ender (GDR)	1976
1:58.33	1		Barbara Krause (GDR)	1980

400 metre freestyle

6:12.2	h1		Gertrude Ederle (USA)	1924
6:02.2	1		Martha Norelius (USA)	1924
5:45.4	h1	WR	Martha Norelius (USA)	1928
5:42.8	1	WR	Martha Norelius (USA)	1928
5:40.9	h3		Lenore Kight (USA)	1932
5:28.5	1	WR	Lenore Kight (USA)	1932
5:28.0	h1		Ragnhild Hveger (DEN)	1936
5:26.4	1		Hendrika Mastenbroek (HOL)	1936
5:25.7	s1		Karen-Margrethe Harup (DEN)	1948
5:17.8	1		Ann Curtis (USA)	1948
5:16.6	h4		Evelyn Kawamoto (USA)	1952
5:16.6	h4<2>		Daphne Wilkinson (GBR)	1952
5:12.1	1		Valéria Gyenge (HUN)	1952
5:07.6	h2		Marley Shriver (USA)	1956
5:02.5	h3		Dawn Fraser (AUS)	1956
5:00.2	h4		Lorraine Crapp (AUS)	1956
4:54.6	1		Lorraine Crapp (AUS)	1956
4:53.6	h1		Chris von Saltza (USA)	1960
4:50.6	1		Chris von Saltza (USA)	1960
4:48.6	h1		Virginia Duenkel (USA)	1964
4:47.7	h4		Marilyn Ramenofsky (USA)	1964
4:43.3	1		Virginia Duenkel (USA)	1964
4:35.0	h2		Debbie Meyer (USA)	1968
4:31.8	1		Debbie Meyer (USA)	1968
4:27.53	h1		Jenny Wylie (USA)	1972
4:24.14	h4		Novella Calligaris (ITA)	1972
4:19.04	1	WR	Shane Gould (AUS)	1972
4:15.71	h1		Rebecca Perrott (NZL)	1976
4:09.89	1	WR	Petra Thümer (GDR)	1976
4:08.76	1		Ines Diers (GDR)	1980
4:07.10	1		Tiffany Cohen (USA)	1984

800 metre freestyle

9:42.8	h1		Debbie Meyer (USA)	1968
9:38.3	h2		Karen Moras (AUS)	1968
9:24.0	1		Debbie Meyer (USA)	1968
9:02.96	h1		Novella Calligaris (ITA)	1972
8:59.69	h2		Keena Rothhammer (USA)	1972
8:53.68	1	WR	Keena Rothhammer (USA)	1972
8:46.81	h1		Nicole Kramer (USA)	1976
8:46.58	h2		Petra Thümer (GDR)	1976
8:37.14	1	WR	Petra Thümer (GDR)	1976
8:36.09	h1		Heike Dähne (GDR)	1980
8:28.90	1		Michelle Ford (AUS)	1980
8:24.95	1		Tiffany Cohen (USA)	1984

100 metre backstroke

1:24.0	h1		Sybil Bauer (USA)	1924
1:23.2	1		Sybil Bauer (USA)	1924
1:22.0	h1	=WR	Ellen King (GBR)	1928
1:21.6	h2	WR	Marie Braun (HOL)	1928
1:18.3	h1		Eleanor Holm (USA)	1932
1:16.6	h1		Dina Senff (HOL)	1936
1:15.6	h2		Karen-Margrethe Harup (DEN)	1948
1:15.5	s1		Karen-Margrethe Harup (DEN)	1948
1:14.4	1		Karen-Margrethe Harup (DEN)	1948
1:13.8	h1		Geertje Wielema (HOL)	1952
1:13.1	h1		Judith Grinham (GBR)	1956
1:13.0	h3		Margaret Edwards (GBR)	1956
1:12.9	1		Judith Grinham (GBR)	1956
1:12.9	2		Carin Cone (USA)	1956
1:10.3	R-h1		Lynn Burke (USA)	1960
1:09.4	h2		Lynn Burke (USA)	1960
1:09.0	R-f	WR	Lynn Burke (USA)	1960
1:08.9	h2		Virginia Duenkel (USA)	1964
1:08.8	h3		Cathy Ferguson (USA)	1964
1:08.5	h4		Christine Caron (FRA)	1964
1:07.7	1	WR	Cathy Ferguson (USA)	1964
1:07.6	R-h3		Elaine Tanner (CAN)	1968
1:07.6	h3		Elaine Tanner (CAN)	1968
1:07.4	s2		Elaine Tanner (CAN)	1968
1:06.2	1	WR	Kaye Hall (USA)	1968
1:06.08	s1		Melissa Belote (USA)	1972
1:05.78	1		Melissa Belote (USA)	1972
1:04.57	R-h1		Linda Jezek (USA)	1976
1:03.90	R-h3		Birgit Treiber (GDR)	1976
1:02.23	R-f		Ulrike Richter (GDR)	1976
1:01.83	1		Ulrike Richter (GDR)	1976
1:01.51	R-f		Rica Reinisch (GDR)	1980
1:01.50	h4	WR	Rica Reinisch (GDR)	1980
1:00.86	1	WR	Rica Reinisch (GDR)	1980

R-Time was recorded as the first leg of the 4x100 metre medley relay.

200 metre backstroke

2:31.1	h1		Kaye Hall (USA)	1968
2:30.9	h4		Elaine Tanner (CAN)	1968
2:29.2	h5		Debra "Pokey" Watson (USA)	1968
2:24.8	1		Debra "Pokey" Watson (USA)	1968
2:22.13	h2		Susan Atwood (USA)	1972
2:20.58	h5	WR	Melissa Belote (USA)	1972
2:19.19	1	WR	Melissa Belote (USA)	1972
2:16.49	h1		Nancy Garapick (CAN)	1976
2:13.43	1		Ulrike Richter (GDR)	1976
2:11.77	1	WR	Rica Reinisch (GDR)	1980

100 metre breaststroke

1:18.8	h1		Catie Ball (USA)	1968
1:17.7	h2		Djurdjica Bjedov (YUG)	1968
1:17.4	h5		Ana Maria Norbis (URU)	1968
1:16.8	s1		Sharon Wichman (USA)	1968
1:16.7	s2		Ana Maria Norbis (URU)	1968
1:15.8	1		Djurdjica Bjedov (YUG)	1968
1:15.00	s2		Catherine Carr (USA)	1972
1:13.58	1	WR	Catherine Carr (USA)	1972
1:11.11	h5	WR	Hannelore Anke (GDR)	1976
1:10.86	s2	WR	Hannelore Anke (GDR)	1976
1:10.11	h4	WR	Ute Geweniger (GDR)	1980
1:09.88	1		Petra Van Staveren (HOL)	1984

200 metre breaststroke

3:27.6	h1		Agnes Geraghty (USA)	1924
3:11.6	h1		Hilde Schrader (GER)	1928
3:11.2	s2	=WR	Hilde Schrader (GER)	1928
3:08.2	h1		Claire Dennis (AUS)	1932
3:06.3	1		Claire Dennis (AUS)	1932
3:03.0	h2		Martha Genenger (GER)	1936
3:01.9	h3		Hideko Machata (JPN)	1936
[3:01.2]*	h2		Eva Székely (HUN)	1948
2:57.4	h3		Petronella van Vliet (HOL)	1948
2:57.0	s2		Petronella van Vliet (HOL)	1948
2:54.0	h1		Eva Novák (HUN)	1952
[2:54.0]*	s2		Eva Székely (HUN)	1952
[2:51.7]*	1		Eva Székely (HUN)	1952
[2:53.1]+	1		Ursula Happe (GER)	1956
2:53.3	h2		Anita Lonsbrough (GBR)	1960
2:52.0	h3		Wiltrud Urselmann (FRG)	1960
2:49.5	1	WR	Anita Lonsbrough (GBR)	1960
2:48.6	h2		Bärbel Grimmer (GDR)	1964
2:48.3	h3		Svetlana Babanina (URS)	1964
2:46.4	1		Galina Prozumenshchikova (URS)	1964
2:44.4	1		Sharon Wichman (USA)	1968
2:43.13	h3		Agnes Kaczander (HUN)	1972
2:41.71	1		Beverley Whitfield (AUS)	1972
2:35.14	h1		Marina Koshevaya (URS)	1976
2:33.35	1	WR	Marina Koshevaya (URS)	1976
2:29.77	h3		Svetlana Varganova (URS)	1980
2:29.54	1		Lina Kachushite (URS)	1980

*These marks were all set in the 200 metre breaststroke event, but using the butterfly stroke, which was then permissible.
+Happe's mark was set using the now disallowed underwater technique of swimming the breaststroke.

100 metre butterfly
1:11.2	h1		Shelley Mann (USA)	1956
1:11.0	1		Shelley Mann (USA)	1956
1:09.8	h1		Carolyn Schuler (USA)	1960
1:09.5	1		Carolyn Schuler (USA)	1960
1:07.8	h1		Kathleen Ellis (USA)	1964
1:07.5	h2		Donna De Varona (USA)	1964
1:07.0	h4		Sharon Stouder (USA)	1964
1:05.6	h4		Sharon Stouder (USA)	1964
1:04.7	1	WR	Sharon Stouder (USA)	1964
1:04.01	h2	WR	Andrea Gyarmati (HUN)	1972
1:04.00	h4	WR	Mayumi Aoki (JPN)	1972
1:03.80	s1		Andrea Gyarmati (HUN)	1972
1:03.34	1		Mayumi Aoki (JPN)	1972
1:02.67	h1		Helene Boivin (CAN)	1976
1:01.82	h2		Wendy Boglioli (USA)	1976
1:01.43	h6		Andrea Pollack (GDR)	1976
1:01.03	s2		Kornelia Ender (GDR)	1976
1:00.13	1	=WR	Kornelia Ender (GDR)	1976
59.05	h4		Mary T. Meagher (USA)	1984

200 metre butterfly
[3:01.2]*	h2		Eva Székely (HUN)	1948
[2:55.1]*	h4		Eva Székely (HUN)	1952
[2:54.0]*	s2		Eva Székely (HUN)	1952
[2:51.7]*	1		Eva Székely (HUN)	1952
2:33.0	h1		Diane Giebel (USA)	1968
2:29.4	h2		Ellie Daniel (USA)	1968
2:29.1	h3		Toni Hewitt (USA)	1968
2:26.3	h4		Ada Kok (HOL)	1968
2:24.7	1		Ada Kok (HOL)	1968
2:18.32	h1		Rosemarie Kother (GDR)	1972
2:17.18	h2		Ellie Daniel (USA)	1972
2:15.57	1	WR	Karen Moe (USA)	1972
2:14.53	h1		Karen Moe-Thornton (USA)	1976
2:14.39	h2		Tamara Shelofastova (URS)	1976
2:11.56	h3		Andrea Pollack (GDR)	1976
2:11.41	1		Andrea Pollack (GDR)	1976
2:10.44	1		Ines Geißler (GDR)	1980
2:06.90	1		Mary T. Meagher (USA)	1984

*All of these marks were set in the 200 metre breaststroke by
swimmers using the butterfly stroke, which was then permissible.

200 metre individual medley
2:33.2	h1		Sabine Steinbach (GDR)	1968
2:31.5	h3		Yoshimi Nishigawa (JPN)	1968
2:28.8	h4		Claudia Kolb (USA)	1968
2:24.7	1		Claudia Kolb (USA)	1968
2:23.07	1	WR	Shane Gould (AUS)	1972
2:19.17	h1		Christiane Pielke (FRG)	1984
2:16.29	h3		Nancy Hogshead (USA)	1984
2:14.47	h4		Tracy Caulkins (USA)	1984
2:12.64	1		Tracy Caulkins (USA)	1984

400 metre individual medley

5:30.6	h1		Anita Lonsbrough (GBR)	1964
5:27.8	h2		Martha Randall (USA)	1964
5:26.8	h3		Veronika Holletz (GDR)	1964
5:24.2	h4		Donna De Varona (USA)	1964
5:18.7	1		Donna De Varona (USA)	1964
5:17.2	h5		Claudia Kolb (USA)	1968
5:08.5	1		Claudia Kolb (USA)	1968
5:06.96	h4		Evelyn Stolze (GDR)	1972
5:02.97	1	WR	Gail Neall (AUS)	1972
4:52.90	h1		Becky Smith (CAN)	1976
4:51.24	h3		Ulrike Tauber (GDR)	1976
4:42.77	1	WR	Ulrike Tauber (GDR)	1976
4:36.29	1	WR	Petra Schneider (GDR)	1980

4 x 100 metre freestyle relay

5:52.8	1	WR	Great Britain	1912
			(Moore, Fletcher, Spiers, Steer)	
5:11.6	1	WR	United States	1920
			(Woodbridge, Schroth, Guest, Bleibtrey)	
4:58.8	1	WR	United States	1924
			(Ederle, Donnelly, Lackie, Wehselau)	
4:55.6	h1	WR	United States	1928
			(Lambert, McKim, Laird, Osipowich)	
4:47.6	1	WR	United States	1928
			(Lambert, Garatti, Osipowich, Norelius)	
4:38.0	1	WR	United States	1932
			(McKim, Johns, Garatti-Saville, Madison)	
4:36.0	1		The Netherlands	1936
			(Selbach, Wagner, den Ouden, Mastenbroek)	
4:33.5	h1		Denmark	1948
			(Riise, Harup, Carstensen, Andersen)	
4:31.3	h2		The Netherlands	1948
			(Schuhmacher, Marsman, Vaessen, Termeulen)	
4:29.2	1		United States	1948
			(Corridon, Kalama, Helser, Curtis)	
4:28.1	h2		United States	1952
			(Kawamoto, Lavine, Stepan, Alderson)	
4:24.4	1	WR	Hungary	1952
			(Novák, Temes, Novák, Szöke)	
4:17.1	1	WR	Australia	1956
			(Fraser, Leech, Morgan, Crapp)	
4:08.9	1	WR	United States	1960
			(Spillane, Stobs, Wood, von Saltza)	
4:03.8	1	WR	United States	1964
			(Stouder, De Varona, Watson, Ellis)	
4:02.5	1		United States	1968
			(Barkman, Gustavson, Pederson, Henne)	
3:58.11	h1	=WR	German Democratic Republic	1972
			(Eife, Eichner, Sehmisch, Ender)	

```
3:55.19    1    WR   United States                    1972
                     (Neilson, Kemp, Barkman, Babashoff)
3:50.27    h1        United States                    1976
                     (Sterkel, Boglioli, Hooker, Peyton)
3:48.95    h2        German Democratic Republic       1976
                     (Ender, Priemer, Pollock, Hempel)
3:44.82    1    WR   United States                    1976
                     (Peyton, Boglioli, Sterkel, Babashoff)
3:42.71    1    WR   German Democratic Republic       1980
                     (Krause, Metschuck, Diers, Hülsenbeck)
```

4 x 100 metre medley relay

```
4:49.0     h1        Great Britain                    1960
                     (Lewis, Lonsbrough, Oldroyd, Steward)
4:47.7     h2        The Netherlands                  1960
                     (van Velsen, den Haan, Lagerberg, Terpstra)
4:41.1     1    WR   United States                    1960
                     (Burke, Kempner, Schuler, von Saltza)
4:39.1     h1        Soviet Union                     1964
                     (Saveleva, Babanina, Devyatova, Bystrova)
4:33.9     1    WR   United States                    1964
                     (Ferguson, Goyette, Stouder, Ellis)
4:28.3     1         United States                    1968
                     (Hall, Ball, Daniel, Pederson)
4:27.57    h2        United States                    1972
                     (Atwood, Melick, Schrader, Babashoff)
4:20.75    1    WR   United States                    1972
                     (Belote, Carr, Deardurff, Neilson)
4:20.10    h2        Canada                           1976
                     (Hogg, Corsiglia, Sloan, Clarke)
4:13.98    h3        German Democratic Republic       1976
                     (Treiber, Nitschke, Gabriel, Pollock)
4:07.95    1    WR   German Democratic Republic       1976
                     (Richter, Anke, Pollack, Ender)
4:06.67    1    WR   German Democratic Republic       1980
                     (Reinisch, Geweniger, Pollack, Metschuck)
```

TENNIS (LAWN TENNIS)

International Federation: International Tennis Federation (ITF)
Countries Affiliated: 125 (1987)
Year of Formation: 1913
First Year of Olympic Appearance: 1896

Tennis, then called lawn tennis, was contested at every Olympic
 Games from 1896 through 1924 as a regular medal sport. It was
 then discontinued although it was on the schedule as a
 demonstration sport in 1968 and 1984. It returns as a regular
 medal sport in 1988.

Most Medals
  6   Max Decugis (FRA)
  5   Kathleen "Kitty" McKane (GBR)
  4   Charles Dixon (GBR)
  4   Reginald Doherty (GBR)
  4   Gunnar Setterwall (SWE)

Most Gold Medals
  4   Max Decugis (FRA)
  3   Reginald Doherty (GBR)
  3   Suzanne Lenglen (FRA)
  3   Vincent Richards (USA)

Most Medals, Women
  5   Kathleen "Kitty" McKane (GBR)
  3   Suzanne Lenglen (FRA)

Most Gold Medals, Women
  3   Suzanne Lenglen (FRA-1920)
  2   Charlotte Cooper (GBR-1900)
  2   Ethel Hannam (GBR-1912)
  2   Hazel Wightman (USA-1924)

Most Medals, Men
  6   Max Decugis (FRA)
  4   Charles Dixon (GBR)
  4   Reginald Doherty (GBR)
  4   Gunnar Setterwall (SWE)

Most Gold Medals, Men
  4   Max Decugis (FRA)
  3   Reginald Doherty (GBR)
  3   Vincent Richards (USA)

Most Medals, Games
```
3        Max Decugis (FRA-1906)
3        Charles Dixon (GBR-1912)
3        Hugh Doherty (GBR-1900)
3        Reginald Doherty (GBR-1900)
3        Suzanne Lenglen (FRA-1920)
3        Harold Mahony (GBR-1900)
3        Vincent Richards (USA-1924)
3        Major Josiah Ritchie (GBR-1908)
3        Gunnar Setterwall (SWE-1912)
```

Most Gold Medals, Games
```
3        Max Decugis (FRA-1906)
3        Suzanne Lenglen (FRA-1920)
3        Vincent Richards (USA-1924)
```

Most Medals, Games, Women
```
3        Suzanne Lenglen (FRA-1920)
3        Kathleen "Kitty" McKane (GBR-1920)
2        Charlotte Cooper (GBR-1900)
2        Hélène Prévost (FRA-1900)
2        Hedwiga Rosenbaumová (TCH/BOH-1900)
2        Marion Jones (USA-1900)
2        Sophia Marinou (GRE-1906)
2        Dora Köring (GER-1912)
2        Marguerite Broquedis (FRA-1912)
2        Ethel Hannam (GBR-1912)
2        Kathleen "Kitty" McKane (GBR-1924)
2        Hazel Wightman (USA-1924)
```

Most Gold Medals, Games, Women
```
3        Suzanne Lenglen (FRA-1920)
2        Charlotte Cooper (GBR-1900)
2        Ethel Hannam (GBR-1912)
2        Hazel Wightman (USA-1924)
```

Most Medals, Games, Men
```
3        Max Decugis (FRA-1906)
3        Charles Dixon (GBR-1912)
3        Hugh Doherty (GBR-1900)
3        Reginald Doherty (GBR-1900)
3        Harold Mahony (GBR-1900)
3        Vincent Richards (USA-1924)
3        Major Josiah Ritchie (GBR-1908)
3        Gunnar Setterwall (SWE-1912)
```

Most Gold Medals, Games, Men
```
3        Max Decugis (FRA-1906)
3        Vincent Richards (USA-1924)
```

Youngest Medalist, Women
```
18-287   Helen Wills (USA-1924)
19-079   Marguerite Broquedis (FRA-1912)
20-241   Kornelia Bouman (HOL-1924)
20-250   Marion Jones (USA-1900)
21-115   Aspasia Matsa (GRE-1906)
```

Youngest Gold Medalist, Women
    18-287   Helen Wills (USA-1924)
    19-079   Marguerite Broquedis (FRA-1912)
    21-261   Marie Decugis (FRA-1906)
    22-115   Esmée Simiriotou (GRE-1906)
    24-274   Gwendoline Eastlake-Smith (GBR-1908)

Oldest Medalist, Women
    43-015   Winifred Margaret McNair (GBR-1920)
    39-332   Märtha Adlerstråhle (SWE-1908)
    38-132   Edith Hannam (GBR-1912)
    37-214   Hazel Wightman (USA-1924)
    29-316   Dorothea Chambers (GBR-1908)

Oldest Gold Medalist, Women
    43-015   Winifred Margaret McNair (GBR-1920)
    38-132   Edith Hannam (GBR-1912)
    37-214   Hazel Wightman (USA-1924)
    29-316   Dorothea Chambers (GBR-1908)
    29-291   Charlotte Cooper (GBR-1900)

Youngest Medalist, Men
    17-289   Max Decugis (FRA-1900)
    18-170   Ladislav "Rázný" Zemda (TCH/BOH-1906)
    19-209   Robert LeRoy (USA-1904)
    20-013   Friedrich "Fritz" Traun (GER-1896)
    20-019   René Lacoste (FRA-1924)

Youngest Gold Medalist, Men
    20-013   Friedrich "Fritz" Traun (GER-1896)
    21-123   Vincent Richards (USA-1924)
    21-241   André Gobert (FRA-1912)
    23-077   Edgar Leonard (USA-1904)
    23-157   Maurice Germot (FRA-1906)

Oldest Medalist, Men
    44-160   George Hillyard (GBR-1908)
    40-218   Wilberforce Eaves (GBR-1908)
    40-133   Arthur Gore (GBR-1908)
    39-095   Charles Dixon (GBR-1912)
    39-084   George Caridia (GBR-1908)

Oldest Gold Medalist, Men
    44-160   George Hillyard (GBR-1908)
    40-133   Arthur Gore (GBR-1908)
    39-095   Charles Dixon (GBR-1912)
    38-018   Harold Kitson (SAF-1912)
    37-334   Max Decugis (FRA-1920)

Medals Won by Countries

	G	S	B	T
Great Britain	15½	12½	14	42
France	8	6	6	20
United States	7	3½	5½	16
Greece	1	5	2	8
Sweden	–	2	3	5
Germany	1½	2	1	4½
Czechoslovakia	–	–	4½	4½
South Africa	3	1	–	4
Japan	–	2	–	2
Austria	–	1	–	1
Denmark	–	1	–	1
New Zealand	–	–	1	1
Italy	–	–	1	1
Norway	–	–	1	1
Netherlands	–	–	1	1
Totals	36	36	40	112

*Two thirds awarded in 1900 men's singles, men's doubles, women's singles and mixed doubles. In other years, a single bronze only was awarded in all events. Mixed doubles medals are equally divided between men and women in the following tables. In 1896, Germany and Great Britain shared in the men's doubles first place. In 1900 France and Great Britain shared the mixed doubles second place. In 1900 Great Britain and Bohemia (Czechoslovakia) shared one of the third place awards in mixed doubles, and the United States and Great Britain shared the other mixed doubles third place.

Medals Won by Countries, Men

	G	S	B	T
Great Britain	9½	6½	9	25
France	5	3½	4½	13
United States	4½	3	4	11½
South Africa	3	1	–	4
Greece	–	3½	½	4
Germany	1	1	1	3
Sweden	–	1½	1½	3
Czechoslovakia	–	–	2½	2½
Japan	–	2	–	2
Austria	–	1	–	1
New Zealand	–	–	1	1
Italy	–	–	1	1
Netherlands	–	–	½	½
Totals	23	23	25½	71½

Medals Won by Countries, Women

	G	S	B	T
Great Britain	6	6	5	17
France	3	2½	1½	7
United States	2½	½	1½	4½
Greece	1	1½	1½	4
Sweden	-	½	1½	2
Czechoslovakia	-	-	2	2
Germany	½	1	-	1½
Denmark	-	1	-	1
Norway	-	-	1	1
Netherlands	-	-	½	½
Totals	13	13	14½	40½

Best Performance by Country at Each Olympics (Overall Only)
```
1896 -  Great Britain
1900 -  Great Britain
1904 -  United States
1906 -  France
1908 -  Great Britain
1912 -  Great Britain
1920 -  Great Britain
1924 -  United States
```

VOLLEYBALL

International Federation: Fédération Internationale de Volleyball (FIVB)
Countries Affiliated: 161 (1987)
Year of Formation: 1947
First Year of Olympic Appearance: 1964

Most Medals
```
4        Inna Ryskal (URS)
3        Lyudmila Buldakova (URS)
3        Vladimir Kondra (URS)
3        Masayuki Minami (JPN)
3        Katsutoshi Nekoda (JPN)
3        Yuriy Poyarkov (URS)
3        Nina Smoleeva (URS)
```

Most Gold Medals
    2   Inna Ryskal (URS)
    2   Lyudmila Buldakova (URS)
    2   Nina Smoleeva (URS)
    2   Vera Duyunova-Galuschka (URS)
    2   Tatyana Tretyakova-Ponyaeva (URS)
    2   Rosa Salichova (URS)
    2   Galina Leontyeva (URS)
    2   Tatyana Sarycheva (URS)
    2   Yuri Poyarkov (URS)
    2   Ivan Bugayenkov (URS)
    2   Georgiy Mondzolevskiy (URS)
    2   Eduard Sibiryakov (URS)

Most Silver Medals
    2   Inna Ryskal (URS)
    2   Sumie Oinuma (JPN)
    2   Toyoko Iwahara (JPN)

Most Bronze Medals
    2   Krystyna Czajkowska-Rawska (POL)
    2   Józefa Ledwigowa (POL)
    2   Zofia Szczesniewska-Bryszewska (POL)
    2   Krystyna Jakubowska (POL)
    2   Krystyna Krupowa (POL)

Most Medals, Women
    4   Inna Ryskal (URS)
    3   Lyudmila Buldakova (URS)
    3   Nina Smoleeva (URS)

Most Gold Medals, Women
    2   Inna Ryskal (URS)
    2   Lyudmila Buldakova (URS)
    2   Nina Smoleeva (URS)
    2   Vera Duyunova-Galuschka (URS)
    2   Tatyana Tretyakova-Ponyayeva (URS)
    2   Rosa Salichova (URS)
    2   Galina Leontyeva (URS)
    2   Tatyana Sarycheva (URS)

Most Silver Medals, Women
    2   Inna Ryskal (URS)
    2   Sumie Oinuma (JPN)
    2   Toyoko Iwahara (JPN)

Most Bronze Medals, Women
    2   Krystyna Czajkowska-Rawska (POL)
    2   Józefa Ledwigowa (POL)
    2   Zofia Szczesniewska-Bryszewska (POL)
    2   Krystyna Jakubowska (POL)
    2   Krystyna Krupowa (POL)

Most Medals, Men
  3   Vladimir Kondra (URS)
  3   Masayuki Minami (JPN)
  3   Katsutoshi Nekoda (JPN)
  3   Yuri Poyarkov (URS)

Most Gold Medals, Men
  2   Yuri Poyarkov (URS)
  2   Ivan Bugayenkov (URS)
  2   Georgiy Mondzolevskiy (URS)
  2   Eduard Sibiryakov (URS)

Most Silver Medals, Men
  1   Many athletes tied with one.

Most Bronze Medals, Men
  1   Many athletes tied with one.

Most Appearances
  4   Katsutoshi Nekoda (JPN, 1964-76)
  4   Inna Ryskal (URS, 1964-76)
  4   Antonio Moreno (BRA, 1968-80)

Most Appearances, Men
  4   Katsutoshi Nekoda (JPN, 1964-76)
  4   Antonio Moreno (BRA, 1968-80)

Most Appearances, Women
  4   Inna Ryskal (URS, 1964-76)

Youngest Medalist, Women
  18-123   Heike Lehmann (GDR-1980)
  18-196   Myong-Suk Paek (DPK-1972)
  18-215   Ute Kostrzewa (GDR-1980)
  18-249   Lyudmila Borozna (URS-1972)
  18-298   Elena Achaiminova (URS-1972)

Youngest Gold Medalist, Women
  18-249   Lyudmila Borozna (URS-1972)
  18-298   Elena Achaiminova (URS-1980)
  19-262   Tatyana Sarycheva (URS-1968)
  19-268   Yoko Shinozaki (JPN-1964)
  19-276   Svetlana Badulina (URS-1980)

Oldest Medalist, Women
  34-106   Lyudmila Buldakova (URS-1972)
  32-184   Krystyna Czajkowski-Rawska (POL-1968)
  32-056   Maria Golimowska (POL-1964)
  30-339   Lyudmila Michailovskaya (URS-1968)
  30-306   Galina Leonteeva (URS-1972)

Oldest Gold Medalist, Women
    34-106   Lyudmila Buldakova (URS-1972)
    30-339   Lyudmila Michailovskaya (URS-1968)
    30-306   Galina Leonteeva (URS-1972)
    30-178   Takako Iida (JPN-1976)
    30-155   Lyudmila Buldakova (URS-1972)

Youngest Medalist, Men
    19-030   Aleksandr Savin (URS-1976)
    19-088   Wolfgang Löwe (GDR-1972)
    19-171   Kenji Shimaoka (JPN-1968)
    19-224   Victoriano Sarmientos (CUB-1976)
    19-229   Tetsuo Sato (JPN-1968)

Youngest Gold Medalist, Men
    20-058   Lech Lasko (POL-1976)
    20-356   Oleg Antropov (URS-1968)
    21-178   Yuri Panchenko (URS-1980)
    21-268   Tetsuo Nishimoto (JPN-1972)
    22-264   Viktor Michalchuk (URS-1968)

Oldest Medalist, Men
    37-216   Bohumil Golián (TCH-1968)
    36-115   Josef Musil (TCH-1968)
    35-212   Yuri Poyarkov (URS-1972)
    35-140   Wolfgang Webner (GDR-1972)
    34-274   Georgiy Mondsolevskiy (URS-1968)

Oldest Gold Medalist, Men
    34-274   Georgiy Mondsolevskiy (URS-1968)
    33-048   Edward Skorek (POL-1976)
    32-318   Chris Marlowe (USA-1984)
    32-135   Paul Sunderland (USA-1984)
    31-275   Yuriy Chesnokov (URS-1964)

Medals Won by Countries

	G	S	B	T
USSR	6	3	1	10
Japan	3	3	2	8
Poland	1	–	2	3
United States	1	1	–	2
GDR	–	2	–	2
Bulgaria	–	1	1	2
Czechoslovakia	–	1	1	2
China	1	–	–	1
Brazil	–	1	–	1
Romania	–	–	1	1
Cuba	–	–	1	1
Italy	–	–	1	1
Korea	–	–	1	1
DPR Korea	–	–	1	1
Totals	12	12	12	36

Medals Won by Countries, Men

	G	S	B	T
USSR	3	2	-	5
Japan	2	2	1	5
Poland	-	-	2	2
China	1	-	-	1
United States	-	1	-	1
GDR	-	1	-	1
Bulgaria	-	-	1	1
Korea	-	-	1	1
DPR Korea	-	-	1	1
Totals	6	6	6	18

Medals Won by Countries, Women

	G	S	B	T
USSR	3	1	1	5
Japan	1	1	1	3
Czechoslovakia	-	1	1	2
Poland	1	-	-	1
United States	1	-	-	1
Bulgaria	-	1	-	1
GDR	-	1	-	1
Brazil	-	1	-	1
Romania	-	-	1	1
Cuba	-	-	1	1
Italy	-	-	1	1
Totals	6	6	6	18

Overall Records by Country, Men

	W	L	%%%%
USSR	32	4	.888
Japan	27	9	.750
GDR	11	5	.687
Czechoslovakia	24	13	.648
Romania	14	8	.636
Poland	17	10	.629
Bulgaria	17	14	.548
Yugoslavia	3	3	.500
United States	11	13	.458
Cuba	8	10	.444
Hungary	4	5	.444
Brazil	16	26	.380
Italy	6	10	.375
Korea	10	18	.357
Argentina	2	4	.333
Canada	3	7	.300
Belgium	2	7	.222
The Netherlands	2	7	.222
FRG	1	5	.166
China	1	5	.166
Tunisia	1	10	.090
Libya	0	5	.000
Egypt	0	5	.000
Mexico	0	9	.000
Totals	212	212	.500

Overall Records by Country, Women

	W	L	%%%%
USSR	25	2	.925
Japan	24	3	.888
China	4	1	.800
Poland	8	4	.666
PR Korea	3	2	.600
Bulgaria	3	2	.600
Cuba	8	7	.533
Hungary	7	8	.466
Korea	11	16	.407
Romania	4	6	.400
GDR	4	6	.400
Peru	8	14	.363
Czechoslovakia	4	8	.333
United States	5	12	.294
FRG	2	8	.200
Brazil	2	8	.200
Mexico	1	6	.142
Canada	0	10	.000
Totals	123	123	.500

WATER POLO

International Federation: Fédération Internationale de Natation
    Amateur (FINA)
Countries Affiliated: 125 (1987)
Year of Formation: 1908
First Year of Olympic Appearance: 1896

Most Medals
    5   Deszö Gyarmati (HUN)
    4   András Bodnár (HUN)
    4   László Jeney (HUN)
    4   György Kárpáti (HUN)
    4   Mihály Mayer (HUN)
    4   Endre Molnár (HUN)
    4   Joseph Pletincx (BEL)
    4   István Szivós (HUN)

Most Gold Medals
    3   Deszö Gyarmati (HUN)
    3   György Kárpáti (HUN)
    3   Charles Smith (GBR)
    3   George Wilkinson (GBR)

Most Silver Medals
    3   Joseph Pletincx (BEL)
    2   Many athletes tied with two.

Most Bronze Medals
   3   Pontus Hansen (SWE)
   2   Many athletes tied with two.

Most Years Between Medals
  16   Deszö Gyarmati (HUN)
  16   Joseph Pletincx (BEL)
  12   Fourteen athletes tied with twelve.

Most Years Between Gold Medals
  12   Deszö Gyarmati (HUN)
  12   György Kárpáti (HUN)
  12   Charles Smith (GBR)
  12   George Wilkinson (GBR)

Most Appearances
   5   Paul Radmilovic (GBR, 1908-28)
   5   Dezsö Gyarmati (HUN, 1948-64)
   5   Gianni De Magistris (ITA, 1968-84)
   4   Nineteen athletes tied with four.

Youngest Medalist
  15-306   Paul Vasseur (FRA-1900)
  16-223 Albert Vandeplancke (FRA-1928)
  17-041   György Kárpáti (HUN-1952)
  17-264   Perica Bukić (YUG-1984)
  18-117   Harald Julin (SWE-1908)

Youngest Gold Medalist
  17-041   György Kárpáti (HUN-1952)
  17-264   Perica Bukić (YUG-1984)
  18-236   Igor Milanović (YUG-1984)
  19-173   Franco Lavoratori (ITA-1960)
  19-323   Fritz Gunst (GER-1928)

Oldest Medalist
  41-215   Charles Smith (GBR-1920)
  38-073   Mario Maioni (ITA-1948)
  36-362   István Barta (HUN-1932)
  36-361   Dezsö Gyarmati (HUN-1964)
  35-109   István Szivós (HUN-1956)

Oldest Gold Medalist
  41-215   Charles Smith (GBR-1920)
  38-073   Mario Maioni (ITA-1948)
  36-362   István Barta (HUN-1932)
  36-361   Dezsö Gyarmati (HUN-1964)
  35-109   István Szivós (HUN-1956)

Most Goals, Game, Individual
```
9        Zoran Janković (YUG) (1968 v. Japan)
9        Manuel Estiarte (ESP) (1984 v. Brazil)
8        Velt Hermans (GDR) (1968 v. UAR)
7        László Felkai (HUN) (1968 v. Italy)
7        Aleksei Barkalov (URS) (1968 v. Yugoslavia)
6        Nine athletes tied with six.
```

Most Points, Game, Team
```
19       GDR (1968 v. UAE)
19       Spain (1984 v. Brazil)
17       Hungary (1932 v. Japan)
17       Yugoslavia (1968 v. Japan)
16       France (1928 v. Malta)
16       Italy (1952 v. India)
16       Romania (1972 v. Canada)
16       USSR (1976 v. Iran)
16       Italy (1984 v. Canada)
```

Most Points, Game, Both Teams
```
31       Spain d. Brazil, 19-12 (1984)
25       Italy d. Canada, 16-9 (1984)
23       FRG d. Japan, 15-8 (1984)
22       Yugoslavia d. Spain, 14-8 (1984)
21       Spain d. Greece, 12-9 (1984)
21       Greece d. Japan, 14-7 (1984)
20       Italy d. Japan, 15-5 (1984)
20       Canada tied Brazil, 10-10 (1984)
20       China d. Brazil, 11-9 (1984)
20       Australia tied Spain, 10-10 (1984)
```

Medals Won by Countries

	G	S	B	T
Hungary	6	3	3	12
United States	1	2	4	7
Yugoslavia	2	4	–	6
USSR	2	2	2	6
Belgium	–	4	2	6
Great Britain	4	–	–	4
Italy	2	1	1	4
Germany	1	2	–	3
France	1	–	2	3
Sweden	–	1	2	3
Netherlands	–	–	2	2
FRG	–	–	1	1
Total	19	19	19	57

Overall Records by Country

	W	L	T	%%%%
Hungary	66	10	17	.801
USSR	41	12	13	.720
Yugoslavia	50	14	21	.712
Italy	46	20	18	.655
GDR	6	2	7	.633
Great Britain	16	11	4	.581
United States	39	30	11	.556
Romania	19	15	8	.548
Belgium	27	23	5	.536
Germany/FRG	32	27	12	.535
France	18	16	2	.528
Netherlands	40	35	19	.527
China	4	4	0	.500
Cuba	13	13	10	.500
Sweden	20	20	3	.500
South Africa	3	4	1	.438
Egypt	3	5	3	.409
Austria	6	10	1	.382
Spain	16	30	4	.360
Canada	6	12	3	.357
Czechoslovakia	3	7	0	.300
Greece	7	21	5	.288
Australia	8	30	6	.250
Mexico	3	15	5	.239
India	1	4	0	.200
Malta	1	4	0	.200
Argentina	1	8	2	.182
Japan	4	25	4	.182
Brazil	2	22	5	.155
Switzerland	1	7	0	.125
Bulgaria	1	13	2	.125
Uruguay	0	4	1	.100
UAR	0	10	2	.083
Luxembourg	0	1	0	.000
Chile	0	2	0	.000
Singapore	0	2	0	.000
Ireland	0	2	0	.000
Portugal	0	2	0	.000
Iceland	0	3	0	.000
Iran	0	8	0	.000
Totals	503	503	194	.500

WEIGHTLIFTING

International Federation: International Weightlifting Federation
   (IWF)
Countries Affiliated: 83 (1987)
Year of Formation: 1907
First Year of Olympic Appearance: 1896

Most Medals
4	Norbert Schemansky (USA)
3	Isaac Berger (USA)
3	Imre Foldi (HUN)
3	Carlo Galimberti (ITA)
3	Peter George (USA)
3	Louis Hostin (FRA)
3	Thomas Kono (USA)
3	Yoshinobu Miyake (JPN)
3	Mohammed Nassiri-Seresht (IRN)
3	Arkadi Vorobiev (URS)
3	Marion Zieliński (POL)

Most Gold Medals
2	Charles Vinci (USA)
2	Norair Nurikian (BUL)
2	Yoshinobu Miyake (JPN)
2	Tommy Kono (USA)
2	Waldemar Baszanowski (POL)
2	Louis Hostin (FRA)
2	Arkadiy Vorobiev (URS)
2	John Davis (USA)
2	Leonid Zhabotinskiy (URS)
2	Vasiliy Alexeev (URS)

Most Silver Medals
2	Imre Földi (HUN)
2	Isaac Berger (USA)
2	Dito Shanidze (URS)
2	Carlo Galimberti (ITA)
2	Peter George (USA)
2	Fritz Hünenberger (SUI)
2	Václav Pšenička (TCH)
2	James Bradord (USA)

Most Bronze Medals
3	Marian Zieliński (POL)
2	Sung-Jip Kim (KOR)
2	Gyözö Veres (HUN)
2	Frank Kungler (USA)
2	Heinrich Schneidereit (GER)
2	Norbert Schemansky (USA)
2	Tadeusz Rutkowski (POL)

Most Years Between Medals
   16   Norbert Schemansky (USA)
   12   Marian Zieliński (POL)
    8   Many athletes tied with eight.

Most Years Between Gold Medals
    4   Charles Vinci (USA)
    4   Norair Nurikian (BUL)
    4   Yoshinobu Miyake (JPN)
    4   Tommy Kono (USA)
    4   Waldemar Baszanowski (POL)
    4   Louis Hostin (FRA)
    4   Arkadiy Vorobiev (URS)
    4   John Davis (USA)
    4   Leonid Zhabotinskiy (URS)
    4   Vasiliy Alexeev (URS)

Most Appearances
    5   Imre Földi (HUN, 1960-76)
    4   Fifteen athletes tied with four

Most Years Between Appearances
   20   Walter Legel (AUT, 1960-80)
   16   Imre Földi (HUN, 1960-76)
   16   Norbert Schemansky (USA, 1948-64)

Youngest Medalist
   18-044   Andrei Socaci (ROM-1984)
   18-259   Mincho Pashov (BUL-1980)
   18-342   Yuriy Sarkisian (URS-1980)
   19-043   Peter George (USA-1948)
   19-134   Guoqiang Zeng (CHN-1984)

Youngest Gold Medalist
   19-134   Guoqiang Zeng (CHN-1984)
   20-007   Isaac Berger (USA-1956)
   20-060   Pierino Gabetti (ITA-1924)
   20-062   Asen Zlatev (BUL-1980)
   20-110   Jordan Mitkov (BUL-1976)

Oldest Medalist
   40-141   Norbert Schemansky (USA-1964)
   38-296   Marian Zieliński (POL-1968)
   37-364   Carlo Galimberti (ITA-1932)
   37-345   Josef Straßberger (GER-1932)
   37-328   *Mahmoud Namdjou (IRN-1956)*

Oldest Gold Medalist
   36-040   Rudolf Pflukfelter (URS-1964)
   35-336   Arkadiy Vorobiev (URS-1960)
   34-202   Vasiliy Alekseev (URS-1976)
   34-113   Imre Földi (HUN-1972)
   34-063   Joseph DePietro (USA-1948)

Medals Won by Countries

	G	S	B	T
USSR	33	19	2	54
United States	15	16	10	41
Poland	4	2	15	21
Bulgaria	7	10	3	20
France	9	2	4	15
Italy	5	5	5	15
Hungary	2	5	8	15
Germany	4	3	7	14
Japan	2	2	8	12
Austria	4	5	2	11
Egypt	5	2	2	9
Iran	1	3	5	9
Czechoslovakia	3	2	3	8
Romania	2	5	1	8
GDR	-	3	5	8
Estonia	1	3	3	7
Great Britain	1	3	3	7
China	4	2	-	6
FRG	2	1	1	4
Greece	2	-	2	4
Belgium	1	2	1	4
Switzerland	-	2	2	4
Sweden	-	-	4	4
Denmark	1	2	-	3
Australia	1	1	1	3
Finland	1	-	2	3
Trinidad	-	1	2	3
Korea	-	-	3	3
Holland	-	-	3	3
Cuba	1	-	1	2
Canada	-	2	-	2
Argentina	-	1	1	2
DPR Korea	-	1	1	2
Norway	1	-	-	1
Luxembourg	-	1	-	1
Lebanon	-	1	-	1
Singapore	-	1	-	1
Chinese Taipei	-	-	1	1
Iraq	-	-	1	1
Totals	112	108	112	332

*Three thirds in 1906 two-hand event; two firsts in 1928
lightweight class; and two firsts in 1936 lightweight class.

Best Performance by Country at Each Olympics
```
1896 -  Great Britain/Denmark
1900 -  not held
1904 -  United States
1906 -  Austria
1908 -  not held
1912 -  not held
1920 -  France
1924 -  Italy
1928 -  Germany
1932 -  France
1936 -  Egypt
1948 -  United States
1952 -  United States
1956 -  United States/USSR
1960 -  USSR
1964 -  USSR
1968 -  USSR
1972 -  Bulgaria
1976 -  USSR
1980 -  USSR
1984 -  China/Romania
```

Weightlifting - Olympic Record Progressions

From 1932 until 1976, the overall classifications were decided based on three lifts: press, snatch, and clean & jerk. Starting in 1976, the press was eliminated. In the lists below the overall records for the triathlon (press, snatch, and clean & jerk) are listed through 1972, and the records from 1976 on are for the biathlon (snatch and clean & jerk). However, the best performance prior to 1976 for the biathlon is listed as a "starting" record.

The first time the three triathlon lifts were held was in 1924 as part of a five-event pentathlon. The best triathlon marks have been extrapolated from those performances. Prior to 1932 the exact format differed a great deal.

The second column below reflects the finish by that lifter. It is not necessarily his Olympic record which earned him this finish. Because of the order of lifting, a lifter may have surpassed his record lift to earn his final placing without setting another Olympic record.

Flyweight Class (< 52 kg.)

287.5	11		Anil Kumar Mondal (IND)	1972
287.5	13		Chan Chun-Hon (CAN)	1972
302.5	8		Ioan Hortopan (ROM)	1972
315	-		Aung Gyi (BIR)	1972
320	5		Aung Gyi (BIR)	1972
322.5	4		Tetsuhide Sasaki (JPN)	1972
325	2		Lajos Szücs (HUN)	1972
327.5	3		Sándor Holczreiter (HUN)	1972
337.5	1		Zygmunt Smalcerz (POL)	1972
225	-		Aung Gyi (BIR)	1972
225	-		Zygmunt Smalcerz (POL)	1972
232.5	4		Masatomo Takeuchi (JPN)	1976
235	-		Aleksandr Voronin (URS)	1976
237.5	2		György Köszegi (HUN)	1976
240	-		Aleksandr Voronin (URS)	1976
242.5	1		Aleksandr Voronin (URS)	1976
245	2	=WR	Ho Bong-Choi (PRK)	1980
245	3		Han Gyong-Si (PRK)	1980
245	4		Béla Oláh (HUN)	1980
245	1		Kanybek Osmonaliev (URS)	1980

Bantamweight Class (< 56 kg.)

225	19		M. Salas-Maravilla (MEX)	1948
240	18		Pentti Kotvio (FIN)	1948
262.5	13		Abe Greenhalgh (GBR)	1948
262.5	9		Keith Caple (AUS)	1948
265	15		Maung Win Maung (BIR)	1948
270	6		Marcel Thevenet (FRA)	1948
300	-	=WR	Joseph DePietro (USA)	1948
305	-	WR	Joseph DePietro (USA)	1948
307.5	1	WR	Joseph DePietro (USA)	1948
310	-		Ivan Udodov (URS)	1952
315	1	=WR	Ivan Udodov (URS)	1952
337.5	2	WR	Vladimir Stogov (URS)	1956
337.5	-	WR	Charles Vinci (USA)	1956
342.5	1	WR	Charles Vinci (USA)	1956
345	1	=WR	Charles Vinci (USA)	1960
350	-		Imre Földi (HUN)	1964
352.5	-	=WR	Aleksei Vakhonin (URS)	1964
355	2	WR	Imre Földi (URS)	1964
357.5	1	WR	Aleksei Vakhonin (URS)	1964
362.5	-		Imre Földi (HUN)	1968
367.5	2	=WR	Imre Földi (HUN)	1968
367.5	1	=WR	Mohammad Nassiri-Seresht (IRN)	1968
372.5	-		Imre Földi (HUN)	1972
377.5	1	WR	Imre Földi (HUN)	1972
255	-	WR	Mohammad Nasiri-Seresht (IRN)	1968
257.5	-		Norair Nurikian (BUL)	1976
262.5	1	WR	Norair Nurikian (BUL)	1976
270	-		Daniel Nunez (CUB)	1980
275	1	WR	Daniel Nunez (CUB)	1980

Featherweight Class (< 60 kg.)

260	1		Pierino Gabetti (ITA)	1924
265	5		Arthur Reinmann (SUI)	1928
277.5	4		Giuseppe Conca (ITA)	1928
277.5	-		Pierino Gabetti (ITA)	1928
282.5	3		Hans Wölpert (GER)	1928
282.5	2		Pierino Gabetti (ITA)	1928
282.5	-		Franz Andrysek (AUT)	1928
287.5	1		Franz Andrysek (AUT)	1928
287.5	1		Raymond Suvigny (FRA)	1932
290	5		Georg Liebsch (GER)	1936
295	2		Saleh Mohamed Soliman (EGY)	1936
295	3		Ibrahim Hassanien Shams (EGY)	1936
297.5	4		Anton Richter (AUT)	1936
312.5	1		Anthony Terlazzo (USA)	1936
312.5	3		Jaffar Mohammad Salmassi (IRN)	1948
312.5	2		Rodney Wilkes (TRI)	1948
327.5	-	WR	Mahmoud Fayad (EGY)	1948
332.5	1	WR	Mahmoud Fayad (EGY)	1948
332.5	-	=WR	Rafael Chimishkyan (URS)	1952
337.5	1	WR	Rafael Chimishkyan (URS)	1952
342.5	2		Evgeniy Minaev (URS)	1956
347.5	-		Isaac Berger (URS)	1956
352.5	1	WR	Isaac Berger (USA)	1956
353.5	3		Sebastiano Mannironi (ITA)	1960
365	-		Evgeniy Minaev (URS)	1960
370	-		Evgeniy Minaev (URS)	1960
372.5	1	=WR	Evgeniy Minaev (URS)	1960
375	4		Hiroshi Fukuda (JPN)	1964
375	2		Isaac Berger (USA)	1964
390	-	WR	Yoshinobu Miyake (JPN)	1964
395	-	WR	Yoshinobu Miyake (JPN)	1964
397.5	1	WR	Yoshinobu Miyake (JPN)	1964
400	2		Dito Shanidze (URS)	1972
402.5	1	=WR	Nurair Nurikian (BUL)	1972
275	-		Yoshinobu Miyake (JPN)	1964
275	-		Nurair Murikian (BUL)	1972
275	3		Kazumasa Hirai (JPN)	1976
275	-		Georgi Todorov (BUL)	1976
280	-		Nikolai Kolesnikov (URS)	1976
280	2		Georgi Todorov (BUL)	1976
285	1		Nikolai Kolesnikov (URS)	1976
285	-		Viktor Mazin (URS)	1980
290	1		Viktor Mazin (URS)	1980

Lightweight Class (< 67.5 kg.)

277.5	1		Edmond Decottignies (FRA)	1924
277.5	8		Gastone Pierini (ITA)	1928
287.5	6		Jules Meese (FRA)	1928
292.5	-		Albert Äschmann (SUI)	1928
297.5	-		Fernand Arnout (FRA)	1928
297.5	4		Albert Äschmann (SUI)	1928
307.5	3		Fernand Arnout (FRA)	1928
312.5	-		Kurt Helbig (GER)	1928
317.5	-		Hans Haas (AUT)	1928
317.5	-		Kurt Helbig (GER)	1928
322.5	=1		Hans Haas (AUT)	1928
322.5	=1		Kurt Helbig (GER)	1928
325	1		René Duverger (FRA)	1932
335	-		Robert Fein (AUT)	1936
340	-		Robert Fein (AUT)	1936
342.5	=1		Robert Fein (AUT)	1936
342.5	=1		Mohamed Ahmed Mesbah (EGY)	1936
350	-		Attia Hamouda (EGY)	1948
352.5	-		Ibrahim Hassanien Shams (EGY)	1948
355	-		Attia Hamouda (EGY)	1948
360	2		Attia Hamouda (EGY)	1948
360	1		Ibrahim Hassanien Shams (EGY)	1948
362.5	1		Tommy Kono (USA)	1952
372.5	2		Ravel Khabutdinov (URS)	1956
372.5	-		Igor Rybak (URS)	1956
377.5	-		Igor Rybak (URS)	1956
380	1		Igor Rybak (URS)	1956
392.5	-	WR	Viktor Bushuev (URS)	1960
397.5	1	WR	Viktor Bushuev (URS)	1960
397.5	-		Zdenek Otahal (TCH)	1964
400	5		Zdenek Otahal (TCH)	1964
407.5	4		Anthony Garcy (USA)	1964
420	3		Marian Zieliński (POL)	1964
427.5	-		Vladimir Kaplunov (URS)	1964
427.5	-		Waldemar Baszanowski (POL)	1964
432.5	2	WR	Vladimir Kaplunov (URS)	1964
432.5	1	WR	Waldemar Baszanowski (POL)	1964
432.5	-		Waldemar Baszanowski (POL)	1968
437.5	1		Waldemar Baszanowski (POL)	1968
437.5	3		Zbigniew Kaczmarek (POL)	1972
450	-	=WR	Mukharbiy Kirzhinov (URS)	1972
450	2	=WR	Mladen Kuchev (BUL)	1972
455	-	WR	Mukharbiy Kirzhinov (URS)	1972
460	1	WR	Mukharbiy Kirzhinov (URS)	1972
312.5	-	WR	Mukharbiy Kirzhinov (URS)	1972
317.5	-		Daniel Senet (FRA)	1980
317.5	7		Raul Gonzalez (CUB)	1980
322.5	4		Daniel Senet (FRA)	1980
325	3		Mincho Pashov (BUL)	1980
330	-		Joachim Kunz (GDR)	1980
332.5	-		Janko Rusev (BUL)	1980
335	2		Joachim Kunz (GDR)	1980
337.5	-	=WR	Janko Rusev (BUL)	1980
342.5	1	WR	Janko Rusev (BUL)	1980

Middleweight Class (< 75 kg.)

320	1		Carlo Galimberti (ITA)	1924
330	-		Roger François (FRA)	1928
332.5	2		Carlo Galimberti (ITA)	1928
335	1		Roger François (FRA)	1928
335	2		Carlo Galimberti (ITA)	1932
345	1		Rudolf Ismayr (GER)	1932
345	2		Rudolf Ismayr (GER)	1936
345	3		Adolf Wagner (GER)	1936
377.5	-		Khadr Sayed El Touni (EGY)	1936
387.5	1		Khadr Sayed El Touni (EGY)	1936
387.5	-		Frank Spellman (USA)	1948
390	1		Frank Spellman (USA)	1948
392.5	-		Peter George (USA)	1952
400	1		Peter George (USA)	1952
407.5	-		Peter George (USA)	1956
412.5	-		Fedor Bogdanovskiy (URS)	1956
412.5	2		Peter George (USA)	1956
417.5	-	WR	Fedor Bogdanovskiy (URS)	1956
420	1	WR	Fedor Bogdanovskiy (URS)	1956
427.5	2		Tommy Kono (USA)	1960
430	-	=WR	Aleksandr Kurynov (URS)	1960
435	-	WR	Aleksandr Kurynov (URS)	1960
437.5	1	WR	Aleksandr Kurynov (URS)	1960
437.5	3		Masashi Ohuchi (JPN)	1964
440	-		Hans Zdražila (TCH)	1964
440	2		Viktor Kurentsov (URS)	1964
445	1	=WR	Hans Zdražila (TCH)	1964
450	2		Masashi Ohuchi (JPN)	1968
462.5	-		Viktor Kurentsov (URS)	1968
467.5	-		Viktor Kurentsov (URS)	1968
475	1		Viktor Kurentsov (URS)	1968
477.5	-		Jordan Bikov (BUL)	1972
485	1	WR	Jordan Bikov (BUL)	1972
325	-	=WR	Jordan Bikov (BUL)	1972
327.5	-		Jordan Mitkov (BUL)	1976
327.5	3		Peter Wentzel (GDR)	1976
330	2		Vartan Militosyan (URS)	1976
335	1		Jordan Mitkov (BUL)	1976
345	3		Nedelcho Kolev (BUL)	1980
347.5	-		Aleksandr Perviy (URS)	1980
350	-		Asen Zlatev (BUL)	1980
357.5	2	WR	Aleksandr Perviy (URS)	1980
360	1	WR	Asen Zlatev (BUL)	1980

Light-Heavyweight Class (< 82.5 kg.)

322.5	1		Charles Rigoulet (FRA)	1924
335	=4		Jakob Vogt (GER)	1928
335	=4		Václav Pšenička, Sr. (TCH)	1928
342.5	-		Louis Hostin (FRA)	1928
347.5	2		Louis Hostin (FRA)	1928
352.5	-		El Sayed Mohamed Nossseir (EGY)	1928
355	1		El Sayed Mohamed Nossseir (EGY)	1928
355	-		Louis Hostin (FRA)	1932
360	-		Louis Hostin (FRA)	1932
360	2		Svend Olsen (DEN)	1932
365	1		Louis Hostin (FRA)	1932
367.5	-		Louis Hostin (FRA)	1936
372.5	1		Louis Hostin (FRA)	1936
375	3		Gösta Magnusson (SWE)	1948
377.5	-		Harold Sakata (USA)	1948
380	2		Harold Sakata (USA)	1948
417.5	1		Stanley Stanczyk (USA)	1948
417.5	1		Trofim Lomakin (URS)	1952
432.5	-		Tommy Kono (USA)	1956
440	-	WR	Tommy Kono (USA)	1956
447.5	1	WR	Tommy Kono (USA)	1956
450	7		Kaarlo Kangasniemi (FIN)	1964
455	5		Gary Cleveland (USA)	1964
465	-		Rudolf Plyukfelder (URS)	1964
467.5	3		Gyözo Veres (HUN)	1964
472.5	-		Rudolf Plyukfelder (URS)	1964
475	1		Rudolf Plyukfelder (URS)	1964
480	-		Vladimir Beliaev (URS)	1968
485	2	=WR	Vladimir Beliaev (URS)	1968
485	1	=WR	Boris Selitskiy (URS)	1968
502.5	-		Leif Jenssen (NOR)	1972
507.5	1		Leif Jenssen (NOR)	1972
335	-		Leif Jenssen (NOR)	1972
335	-		György Horváth (HUN)	1972
335	4		Nikolaos Iliadis (GRE)	1976
345	3		Peter Baczakó (HUN)	1976
355	-		Valeriy Shariy (URS)	1976
355	-		Trendafil Stojchev (BUL)	1976
357.5	-	dq	Blagoj Blagoev (BUL)	1976
360	-		Valeriy Shariy (URS)	1976
360	2		Trendafil Stojchev (BUL)	1976
362.5	dq	dq	Blagoj Blagoev (BUL)	1976
365	1		Valeriy Shariy (URS)	1976
367.5	-		Blagoj Blagoev (BUL)	1980
372.5	2		Blagoj Blagoev (BUL)	1980
382.5	-		Yurik Vardanian (URS)	1980
392.5	-		Yurik Vardanian (URS)	1980
400	1		Yurik Vardanian (URS)	1980

*Blagoev was disqualified for failing the drug test.

Middle-Heavyweight Class (< 90 kg.)

325	16		Gheorghe Piticaru (ROM)	1952
350	10		Kai Outa (FIN)	1952
357.5	–		Börje Jeppsson (SWE)	1952
357.5	9		Luciano Zardi (ITA)	1952
357.5	12		Jorgé Soto (PUR)	1952
362.5	8		Theunis Jonck (SAF)	1952
362.5	11		Börje Jeppsson (SWE)	1952
365	7		Francisco Hector Rensonnet (ARG)	1952
410	2		Grigoriy Novak (URS)	1952
432.5	–	WR	Norbert Schemansky (USA)	1952
440	–	WR	Norbert Schemansky (USA)	1952
445	1	WR	Norbert Schemansky (USA)	1952
455	–		Arkadiy Vorobiev (URS)	1956
460	–	=WR	Arkadiy Vorobiev (URS)	1956
462.5	1	WR	Arkadiy Vorobiev (URS)	1956
467.5	–		Arkadiy Vorobiev (URS)	1960
472.5	1	WR	Arkadiy Vorobiev (URS)	1960
475	2		Louis Martin (GBR)	1964
487.5	1		Vladimir Golovanov (URS)	1964
490	3		Marek Gołab (POL)	1968
512.5	–		Kaarlo Kangasniemi (FIN)	1968
517.5	–		Kaarlo Kangasniemi (FIN)	1968
520	–		Andon Nikolov (BUL)	1972
525	1		Andon Nikolov (BUL)	1972
347.5	–		Yaan Talts (URS)	1968
355	–		Lee James (USA)	1976
362.5	2		Lee James (USA)	1976
372.5	–		David Rigert (URS)	1976
382.5	1		David Rigert (URS)	1976
387.5	–		Nicu Vlad (ROM)	1984
392.5	1		Nicu Vlad (ROM)	1984

Heavyweight I Class (< 100 kg.)

225	14	Addison Brian Dale (ZIM)	1980
312.5	13	Omar Yousfi (ALG)	1980
337.5	11	John Burns (GBR)	1980
352.5	–	Michael Persson (SWE)	1980
357.5	–	Michael Persson (SWE)	1980
360	9	Michael Persson (SWE)	1980
367.5	8	László Varga (HUN)	1980
385	–	Otakar Zaremba (TCH)	1980
390	–	Otakar Zaremba (TCH)	1980
392.5	2	Igor Nitikin (URS)	1980
395	1	Otakar Zaremba (TCH)	1980

Heavyweight II Class (< 110 kg.)

455	23		H. Phillips (PAN)	1972
457.5	21		Bent Harsmann (DEN)	1972
457.5	22		Morris Price (CAN)	1972
465	20		Pablo Juan Campos (PUR)	1972
470	19		Oskar Sigurpalsson (ISL)	1972
480	18		Kenneth Price (GBR)	1972
495	16		Edgar Kjerran (NOR)	1972
510	-		Alan Ball (USA)	1972
515	11		Alan Ball (USA)	1972
515	-		Rainer Dörrzapf (FRG)	1972
522.5	8		Rainer Dörrzapf (FRG)	1972
535	5		Roberto Vezzani (ITA)	1972
542.5	6		János Hanzlik (HUN)	1972
557.5	-		Aleksandr Krajchev (BUL)	1972
562.5	2		Aleksandr Krajchev (BUL)	1972
580	1		Yaan Talts (URS)	1972
370	-		Yaan Talts (URS)	1972
370	-		Stefan Grutzner (GDR)	1972
372.5	5		Jürgen Ciezki (GDR)	1976
377.5	3		Tadeusz Rutkowski (POL)	1976
380	-		Krastio Semerdzhiev (BUL)	1976
380	-		Yuriy Zaitsev (URS)	1976
385	2		Krastio Semerdzhiev (BUL)	1976
395	-	DQ	Valentin Khristov (BUL)	1976
385	1		Yuriy Zaitsev (URS)	1976
400	DQ	DQ	Valentin Khristov (BUL)	1976
385	-		György Szalai (HUN)	1980
390	3		György Szalai (HUN)	1980
402.5	-		Leonid Taranenko (URS)	1980
405	2		Valentin Khristov (BUL)	1980
417.5	-		Leonid Taranenko (URS)	1980
422.5	1	WR	Leonid Taranenko (URS)	1980

Super-Heavyweight Class (Unlimited Class) (> 110 kg. currently)

342.5	1	Giuseppe Tonani (ITA)	1924
342.5	-	Giuseppe Tonani (ITA)	1928
345	5	Josef Leppelt (AUT)	1928
350	7	Giuseppe Tonani (ITA)	1928
355	6	Rudolf Schilberg (AUT)	1928
367.5	-	Josef Straßberger (GER)	1928
372.5	1	Josef Straßberger (GER)	1928
372.5	-	Josef Straßberger (GER)	1932
377.5	3	Josef Straßberger (GER)	1932
377.5	2	Václav Pšenička (TCH)	1932
377.5	-	Jaroslav Skobla (TCH)	1932
380	1	Jaroslav Skobla (TCH)	1932
400	-	Josef Manger (GER)	1936
407.5	-	Josef Manger (GER)	1936
410	1	Josef Manger (GER)	1936
415	2	Norbert Schemansky (USA)	1948
440	-	John Davis (USA)	1948
452.5	1	John Davis (USA)	1948
460	1	John Davis (USA)	1952
490	-	Humberto Selvetti (ARG)	1956

500	2		Humberto Selvetti (ARG)	1956
500	1		Paul Anderson (USA)	1956
507.5	-		James Bradford (USA)	1960
512.5	2		James Bradford (USA)	1960
520	-	WR	Yuriy Vlasov (URS)	1960
530	-	WR	Yuriy Vlasov (URS)	1960
537.5	1	WR	Yuriy Vlasov (URS)	1960
537.5	3		Norbert Schemansky (USA)	1964
555	-		Leonid Zhabotinskiy (URS)	1964
565	-		Yuriy Vlasov (URS)	1964
570	2		Yuriy Vlasov (URS)	1964
572.5	1		Leonid Zhabotinskiy (URS)	1964
572.5	1		Leonid Zhabotinskiy (URS)	1968
572.5	4		Jouko Leppä (FIN)	1972
610	2		Rudolf Mang (FRG)	1972
635	-		Vasiliy Alekseev (URS)	1972
640	-		Vasiliy Alekseev (URS)	1972
405	1		Vasiliy Alekseev (URS)	1972
415	-		Vasiliy Alekseev (URS)	1976
440	1		Vasiliy Alekseev (URS)	1976
440	1		Sultanbyj Rakhmanov (URS)	1980

WRESTLING

International Federation: Fédération Internationale de Lutte
     Amateur (FILA)
Countries Affiliated: 103 (1987)
Year of Formation: 1912
First Year of Olympic Appearance: 1896

Most Medals
     5   Wilfred Dietrich (FRG)
     4   Sören Jensen (DEN)
     4   Eino Leino (FIN)
     4   Imré Polyák (HUN)
     4   Rudolf Svensson (SWE)

Most Gold Medals
     3   Ivar Johansson (SWE)
     3   Aleksandr Medved (URS)
     3   Carl Westergren (SWE)
     2   Twenty-one athletes tied with two.

Most Silver Medals
3	Imré Polyák (HUN)
3	Alexander Tomov (BUL)
2	Richard Sanders (USA)
2	Stantcho Ivanov (BUL)
2	Wolfgang Ehrl (GER)
2	Daniel Robin (FRA)
2	Rudolf Svensson (SWE)
2	Bertil Antonsson (SWE
2	József Balla (HUN)
2	Ignazio Fabra (ITA)
2	Arthur Lindfors (FIN)
2	Wilfrid Dietrich (FRG)
2	Anatoliy Roshchin (URS)

Most Bronze Medals
2	Wilfrid Dietrich (FRG)
2	Sören Jensen (DEN)
2	Eino Leino (FIN)
2	Karl-Erik Nilsson (SWE)
2	Einar Karlsson (SWE)
2	Stefan Anghelov (BUL)
2	Onni Pellinen (FIN)
2	Karl-Erik Nilsson (SWE)
2	Czesław Kwieciński (POL)
2	Károly Bajkó (HUN)
2	Nikolaus Hirschl (AUT)

Most Years Winning Medals
4	Wilfred Dietrich (FRG)
4	Eino Leino (FIN)
4	Imré Polyák (HUN)

Most Years Winning Gold Medals
3	Aleksandr Medved (URS)
3	Carl Westergren (SWE)

Most Years Between Medals
12	Wilfred Dietrich (FRG)
12	Eino Leino (FIN)
12	Imré Polyák (HUN)
12	Kustaa Pihlajamäki (FIN)

Most Years Between Gold Medals
12	Kustaa Pihlajamäki (FIN)
8	Aleksandr Medved (URS)
8	Carl Westergren (SWE)

Most Years Competing
5	George MacKenzie (GBR; 1908-28)
5	Mario Tovar Gonzalez (MEX, 1952-68)
5	Wilfrid Dietrich (GER/FRG, 1956-72)
5	Khorloogyn Baianmunkh (MON, 1964-80)
4	Twenty-six athletes tied with four

Most Appearances, Greco-Roman
   4   Carl Westergren (SWE, 1920-32)
   4   Aleardo Donati (ITA, 1924-36)
   4   Ercole Gallegati (ITA, 1932-52)
   4   Josef Lipién (POL, 1968-80)
   4   Harald Barlie (NOR, 1960-72)
   4   Ignazio Fabra (ITA, 1952-64)
   4   Maurice Mewis (BEL, 1952-64)
   4   Dumitru Pirvulescu (ROM, 1952-64)
   4   Imré Polyák (HUN, 1952-64)
   4   Lothar Metz (GER/GDR, 1960-72)
   4   Nicolae Martinescu (ROM, 1964-76)
   4   Vitezlav Macha (TCH, 1968-80)

Most Appearances, Freestyle
   5   Khorloogyn Baianmunkh (MON, 1964-80)
   4   George MacKenzie (GBR; 1908, 20-28)
   4   Eino Leino (FIN, 1920-32)
   4   Kustaa Pihlajamäki (FIN, 1924-36)
   4   Garibaldo Nizzola (ITA, 1948-60)
   4   Mario Tovar Gonzalez (MEX, 1952-64)
   4   Tauno Jaskari (FIN, 1952-64)
   4   Gholam-Reza Takhti (IRN, 1952-64)
   4   Stefanos Ioannidis (GRE, 1960-72)
   4   Wilfrid Dietrich (GER/FRG, 1960-72)
   4   Moises Lopez Ruiz (MEX, 1964-76)
   4   José Ramos Cardoso (CUB, 1968-80)

Most Tournaments
   7   Wilfrid Dietrich (FRG; 56[G], 60[FG], 64[FG], 68[F], 72[F])
   6   George MacKenzie (GBR; 08[FG], 12[G], 20[F], 24[F], 28[F])
   6   Mario Tovar Gonzalez (MEX;52[F], 56[F], 60[F], 64[FG], 68[G])
   5   Carl Westergren (SWE; 20[G], 24[FG], 28[G], 32[G])
   5   Ercole Gallegati (ITA; 32[G], 36[FG], 48[G], 52[G])
   5   Kenneth Richmond (GBR; 48[G], 52[FG], 56[F], 60[F])
   5   Taisto Kangasniemi (FIN; 48[F], 52[F], 56[FG], 64[G])
   5   Maurice Mewis (BEL; 52[FG], 56[G], 60[G], 64[G])
   5   Harald Barlie (NOR; 60[G], 64[FG], 68[G], 72[G])
   5   Moises Lopez Ruiz (MEX; 64[FG], 68[F], 72[F], 76[F])
   5   Khorloogyn Baianmunkh (MON;64[F], 68[F], 72[F], 76[F], 80[F])

Most Years Between Appearances
   20   George MacKenzie (GBR; 1908-12, 24-28)
   20   Ercole Gallegati (ITA, 1932-52)
   16   Taisto Kangasniemi (FIN; 1948-56, 64)
   16   Mario Tovar Gonzalez (MEX, 1952-68)
   16   Wilfrid Dietrich (GER/FRG, 1956-72)
   16   Khorloogyn Bainanmunkh (MON, 1964-80)

Winning Medals in Freestyle and Greco-Roman
    Per Gunnar Berlin (SWE)
    Wilfried Dietrich (GER)
    Wolfgang Ehrl (GER)
    Olle Anderberg (SWE)
    Kalle Anttila (FIN)
    Karoly Bajko (HUN)
    Nikolaus Hirschl (AUT)
    Ahmet Kireççi (TUR)
    August Neo (EST)
    Ivar Johansson (SWE)
    Hjalmar Nyström (FIN)
    Kristyan Palusalu (EST)
    Daniel Robin (FRA)
    Rudolf Svensson (SWE)

Winning Gold Medals in Freestyle and Greco-Roman
    Kalle Anttila (FIN)
    Ivar Johansson (SWE)
    Kristyan Palusalu (EST)

Winning Medals in Freestyle and Greco-Roman, Same Year
    Rudolf Svensson (SWE-1924)
    Ivar Johansson (SWE-1932)
    Nikolaus Hirschl (AUT-1932)
    August Neo (EST-1936)
    Kristyan Palusalu (EST-1936)
    Wilfried Dietrich (FRG-1960)
    Daniel Robin (FRA-1968)

Winning Gold Medals in Freestyle and Greco-Roman, Same Year
    Ivar Johansson (SWE-1932)
    Kristyan Palusalu (EST-1936)

Youngest Medalist
    16-254 Nasser Guivehtchi (IRN-1952)
    18-120 Ferenc Holuban (HUN-1906)
    18-262 John Hein (USA-1904)
    18-358 Albert Zirkel (USA-1904)
    19-094 Ignazio Fabra (ITA-1952)

Youngest Gold Medalist
    19-222 Saben Trstena (YUG-1984)
    20-051 Suren Nalbandyan (URS-1976)
    20-175 Sanasar Organesyan (URS-1980)
    20-202 George de Relwyskow (GBR-1908)
    21-155 Aleksandr Kolchinskiy (URS-1976)

Oldest Medalist
    40-184 Anatoli Roshin (URS-1972)
    40-102 Arsen Mekokishvili (URS-1952)
    39-219 Ferenc Tóth (HUN-1948)
    39-208 Shalva Chikhladze (URS-1952)
    39-192 Richard Garrard (AUS-1948)

Oldest Gold Medalist
   40-184   Anatoli Roshin (URS-1972)
   40-102   Arsen Mekokishvili (URS-1952)
   38-298   Gyula Bóbis (HUN-1948)
   37-175   Iokhannes Kotkas (URS-1952)
   36-315   Kalle Anttila (FIN-1924)

Medals Won by Countries, Overall

	G	S	B	T
USSR	54	30	20	104
United States	38	30	19	87
Finland	27	25	27	79
Sweden	27	25	24	76
Bulgaria	13	24	12	49
Hungary	15	12	18	45
Turkey	23	12	6	41
Japan	18	11	8	37
Romania	6	8	16	30
Iran	3	7	10	20
Italy	5	3	9	17
Germany	3	8	6	17
Great Britain	3	4	10	17
Yugoslavia	4	5	6	15
FRG	2	7	6	15
Switzerland	4	4	6	14
Czechoslovakia	1	7	6	14
Poland	1	5	7	13
France	3	3	5	11
Denmark	1	3	7	11
Estonia	5	1	4	10
Korea	3	2	5	10
GDR	2	4	2	8
Greece	1	3	4	8
Mongolia	–	4	4	8
Canada	–	3	5	8
Egypt/UAR	1	2	3	6
Austria	1	2	2	5
Belgium	–	3	1	4
Norway	–	2	1	3
DPR Korea	–	2	1	3
Australia	–	1	2	3
Lebanon	–	1	2	3
Latvia	–	1	–	1
Syria	–	1	–	1
Mexico	–	1	–	1
India	–	–	1	1
Pakistan	–	–	1	1
Totals	264	266	266	796

Medals Won by Countries, Freestyle

	G	S	B	T
United States	36	29	18	83
USSR	24	12	11	47
Turkey	15	9	4	28
Japan	14	8	6	28
Sweden	8	10	8	26
Finland	8	7	10	25
Bulgaria	6	13	6	25
Iran	3	6	9	18
Great Britain	3	4	10	17
Hungary	3	4	7	14
Switzerland	4	4	5	13
Korea	2	2	4	8
Mongolia	–	4	4	8
Canada	–	3	5	8
France	2	2	3	7
FRG	1	2	3	6
Poland	–	1	3	4
Romania	–	–	4	4
Estonia	2	1	–	3
Yugoslavia	1	–	2	3
DPR Korea	–	2	1	3
Germany	–	1	2	3
Czechoslovakia	–	1	2	3
Australia	–	1	2	3
Belgium	–	3	–	3
GDR	–	2	–	2
Italy	1	–	–	1
Norway	–	1	–	1
Syria	–	1	–	1
Greece	–	–	1	1
Egypt/UAR	–	–	1	1
Austria	–	–	1	1
India	–	–	1	1
Pakistan	–	–	1	1
Totals	133	133	134	400

*Two thirds in 1920 heavyweight class.

Medals Won by Countries, Greco-Roman

	G	S	B	T
USSR	30	18	9	57
Finland	19	18	17	54
Sweden	19	15	16	50
Hungary	12	8	11	31
Romania	6	8	12	26
Bulgaria	7	11	6	24
Italy	4	3	9	16
Germany	3	7	4	14
Turkey	8	3	2	13
Yugoslavia	3	5	4	12
Czechoslovakia	1	6	4	11
Denmark	1	3	7	11
Japan	4	3	2	9
FRG	1	5	3	9
Poland	1	4	4	9
Estonia	3	-	4	7
Greece	1	3	3	7
GDR	2	2	2	6
Egypt/UAR	1	2	2	5
United States	2	1	1	4
Austria	1	2	1	4
France	1	1	2	4
Lebanon	-	1	2	3
Korea	1	-	1	2
Iran	-	1	1	2
Norway	-	1	1	2
Latvia	-	1	-	1
Mexico	-	1	-	1
Switzerland	-	-	1	1
Belgium	-	-	1	1
Totals	131	133	132	396

*No firsts/two seconds in 1912 light-heavyweight class.

Best Performance by Country at Each Olympics (one style until 1920

	Freestyle	Greco-Roman	Overall
1896 –	- - - - -	Germany	- - - - -
1904 –	United States	- - - - - -	- - - - -
1906 –	- - - - -	Austria	- - - - -
1908 –	Great Britain	- - - - - -	- - - - -
1912 –	- - - - -	Finland	- - - - -
1920 –	USA/Finland	Finland	Finland
1924 –	United States	Finland	Finland
1928 –	Finland	Germany	Finland
1932 –	United States	Sweden	Sweden
1936 –	United States	Sweden	Sweden
1948 –	Turkey	Sweden	Turkey
1952 –	Sweden	USSR	USSR
1956 –	Iran	USSR	USSR
1960 –	Turkey	USSR	Turkey
1964 –	Bulgaria	USSR	USSR
1968 –	Japan	USSR	USSR
1972 –	USSR	USSR	USSR
1976 –	USSR	USSR	USSR
1980 –	USSR	USSR	USSR
1984 –	United States	Romania	United States

YACHTING

International Federation: International Yacht Racing Union (IYRU)
Countries Affiliated: 83 (1987)
Year of Formation: 1907
First Year of Olympic Appearance: 1900

Most Medals
4	Paul Elvström (DEN)
4	Tore Holm (SWE)
4	Valentin Mankin (URS)
3	Ole Berntsen (DEN)
3	Martin Hindorff (SWE)
3	Léon Huybrechts (BEL)
3	Magnus Konow (NOR)
3	Rodney Pattison (GBR)

Most Gold Medals
4	Paul Elvström (DEN)
3	Valentin Mankin (URS)
2	Thirteen athletes tied with two.

Most Silver Medals
2	Léon Huybrechts (BEL)
2	Hubert Raudaschl (AUT)
2	Vilhelm Vett (DEN)
2	Lauritz Schmidt (NOR)

Most Bronze Medals
    2   Tore Holm (SWE)
    2   Martin Hindorff (SWE)
    2   Adriaan Maas (HOL)
    2   Reinaldo Conrad (BRA)
    2   Torsten Lord (SWE)

Most Years Winning Medals
    4   Paul Elvström (DEN)
    4   Tore Holm (SWE)
    4   Valentin Mankin (URS)
    3   Ole Berntsen (DEN)
    3   Martin Hindorff (SWE)
    3   Louis Huybrechts (BEL)
    3   Magnus Konow (NOR)
    3   Rodney Pattison (GBR)

Most Years Winning Gold Medals
    4   Paul Elvström (DEN)
    3   Valentin Mankin (URS)
    2   Thirteen athletes tied with two.

Most Years Between Medals
   28   Tore Holm (SWE)
   24   Hans Fogh (DEN/CAN)
   24   Magnus Konow (NOR)
   16   Johan Anker (NOR)
   16   Lauritz Schmidt (NOR)
   16   Ole Berntsen (DEN)
   16   Martin Hindorff (SWE)
   16   Louis Huybrechts (BEL)

Most Years Between Gold Medals
   16   Johan Anker (NOR)
   12   Paul Elvström (DEN)
   12   Valentin Mankin (URS)
   12   Tore Holm (SWE)

Most Medals, Women
    1   Vibeke Lunde (NOR)
    1   Dagmar Salén (SWE)
    1   Frances Rivett-Carnac (GBR)
    1   Dorothy Wright (GBR)
    1   Virginie Hériot (FRA)

Most Gold Medals, Women
    1   Frances Rivett-Carnac (GBR)
    1   Dorothy Wright (GBR)
    1   Virginie Hériot (FRA)

Most Appearances
```
7        Paul Elvström (DEN; 1948-60, 68-72, 84)
7        Durward Knowles (GBR/BAH, 1948-72)
6        Magnus Konow (NOR; 1908-20, 28, 36-48)
6        Hubert Raudaschl (AUT, 1964-84)
5        Eleven athletes tied with five.
```

Youngest Medalist, Men
```
14-163   Franciscus Hin (HOL-1920)
15-041   Donald Douglas (USA-1932)
16-036   Carlos De Cárdenas Culmell, Jr. (CUB-1948)
18-091   Michael Mooney (USA-1948)
18-176   Karsten Konow (NOR-1936)
```

Youngest Gold Medalist, Men
```
14-163   Franciscus Hin (HOL-1920)
18-091   Michael Mooney (USA-1948)
18-211   Peder Lunde (NOR-1960)
19-085   Bernard Carp (HOL-1920)
19-164   Marcos Pinto Rizzo Soares (BRA-1980)
```

Oldest Medalist, Men
```
66-155   Louis Noverraz (SUI-1968)
60-025   Lars Thörn (SWE-1964)
59-132   Ernst Westerlund (FIN-1952)
59-113   Everard Endt (USA-1952)
59-024   William Northman (AUS-1964)
57-045   Johan Anker (NOR-1928)
57-035   John Sandblom (SWE-1928)
56-212   Paul Smart (USA-1948)
56-160   Julio Sieburger (ARG-1948)
55-168   Charles Rivett-Carnac (GBR-1908)
```

Oldest Gold Medalist, Men
```
59-113   Everard Endt (USA-1952)
59-024   William Northman (AUS-1964)
57-045   Johan Anker (NOR-1928)
56-212   Paul Smart (USA-1948)
55-168   Charles Rivett-Carnac (GBR-1908)
54-322   Blair Cochrane (GBR-1908)
53-224   Johan Friele (NOR-1920)
53-055   Herman de Pourtales (SUI-1900)
52-070   Lars Thörn (SWE-1956)
50-330   Emile Cornellie (FRA-1920)
```

The America's Cup and Olympic Yachtsmen
   This has only been achieved a few times, virtually always by
   United States' athletes. Dennis Conner (USA) won a bronze
   medal in the 1976 Tempest class, and in 1980 skippered **Freedom**
   to an America's Cup victory. Conner had skippered **Mariner** at
   the 1974 Cup trials but was not chosen to defend. In 1983,
   Conner was the first American skipper to lose the America's
   Cup but in 1987 he returned with the boat **Stars & Stripes** to
   regain the Cup.

One of his crewman in the 1974 Cup trials and the 1976 Olympics
was Conn Findlay, who first won three Olympic medals as an
oarsman, before his yachting successes. He won a gold medal
in 1956, a bronze in 1960, and another gold in 1964, all in
the pair-oars with coxswain event. In 1977, Findlay was a
member of the crew for Ted Turner's **Courageous** as they
defended the America's Cup.

John Bertrand (AUS) won a bronze medal in the 1976 Finn Monotype
class. In 1983, he made sailing history when he broke the
132-year-old American stranglehold on the America's Cup,
winning the event in seven races with his yacht, **Australia
III**.

Britton Chance (USA) won a gold medal in the 1952 5.5 metre
class. He has since become a designer of yachts, having
designed several American yachts which took part in the Cup
Defender Trials, including **Mariner**, and **Valiant**, both in 1974.
In 1987 he helped design the winning American yacht, **Stars &
Stripes**.

Colin Ratsey (GBR) won a silver medal in 1932 and twice was
involved with the America's Cup as a challenger. In 1934 he
was a member of the J-boat Endeavour, which challenged the
United States. In 1958 Ratsey was in the afterguard of the
12-metre yacht, Scepter, during her America's Cup challenge.

Medals Won by Countries

	G	S	B	T
United States	14	11	9	34
Great Britain	13	9	7	29
Sweden	9	10	9	28
Norway	15	10	1	26
France	8	6	9	23
Denmark	7	8	2	17
Netherlands	4	4	4	12
USSR	4	4	3	11
FRG	3	2	5	10
Australia	3	1	4	8
Italy	2	1	5	8
Finland	1	1	6	8
Belgium	2	3	2	7
GDR	1	3	2	6
Canada	-	2	4	6
New Zealand	4	-	1	5
Brazil	2	1	2	5
Germany	1	2	2	5
Spain	2	1	1	4
Switzerland	1	1	1	3
Greece	1	1	1	3
Austria	-	3	-	3
Portugal	-	2	1	3
Bahamas	1	-	1	2
Argentina	-	2	-	2
Ireland	-	1	-	1
Cuba	-	1	-	1
Estonia	-	-	1	1
Hungary	-	-	1	1
Totals	98	90	84	272

*Results of 1900 yachting events are listed variably. Those used
were the ones listed in Kamper's <u>Lexikon der 14,000
Olympioniken</u>. Two thirds in 1900 3-10 ton class; no
second/third in 1908 7 metre class; no third in 1908 12 metre
class; no third in 1920 12-foot dinghy class; no second/third in
1920 18-foot dinghy class+; no second/third in 1920 30 metres^2
class; no third in 1920 40 metres^2 class; no third in 1920 6
metre class; no third in 1920 6.5 metre class; no second/third
in 1920 7 metre class; no third in 1920 8 metre class, 1907
rating; no second/third in 1920 10 metre class, 1907 rating; no
second/third in 1920 10 metre class, 1919 rating; no
second/third in 1920 12 metre class, 1907 rating; and no
second/third in 1920 12 metre class, 1919 rating.
+It is probable that the 18-foot dinghy class in 1920 was not
actually held and that not only were second and third not
awarded, but first was also not awarded. This has only recently
been discovered and may be correct. However, I have given Great
Britain credit for this gold medal pending verification of these
facts.

Medals Won by Countries, Women

	G	S	B	T
Great Britain	0.500	--	--	0.500
Norway	--	0.333	--	0.333
Sweden	--	--	0.200	0.200
France	0.167	--	--	0.167

*Women's medals are based on the number of women on board the crew
compared to the number of total crew members.

Best Performance by Country at each Olympics
    1900 - France
    1908 - Great Britain
    1912 - Sweden
    1920 - Norway
    1924 - Norway
    1928 - Sweden
    1932 - United States
    1936 - Germany
    1948 - United States
    1952 - United States
    1956 - Sweden
    1960 - Denmark
    1964 - United States
    1968 - United States
    1972 - Australia
    1976 - FRG
    1980 - Brazil
    1984 - United States

THE OLYMPIC WINTER GAMES

ALPINE SKIING

International Federation: Fédération Internationale de Ski (FIS)
Countries Affiliated: 55 (1987)
Year of Formation: 1924
First Year of Olympic Appearance: 1936

Most Medals
    4   Hanni Wenzel (LIE)
    3   Thirteen athletes tied with three.

Most Gold Medals
    3   Jean-Claude Killy (FRA)
    3   Anton "Toni" Sailer (AUT)

Most Silver Medals
    2   Gustavo Thöni (ITA)
    2   Annemarie Moser-Pröll (AUT)
    2   Penelope "Penny" Pitou (USA)

Most Bronze Medals
    2   Annemarie "Mirl" Buchner (GER)
    2   Perrine Pelen (FRA)
    2   Giuliana Chenal-Minuzzo (ITA)
    2   Traudl Hecher (AUT)

Most Medals, Women
    4   Hanni Wenzel (LIE)
    3   Annemarie "Mirl" Buchner (GER)
    3   Marielle Goitschel (FRA)
    3   Trude Jochum-Beiser (AUT)
    3   Rosi Mittermaier (FRG)
    3   Marie-Theres Nadig (SUI)
    3   Annemarie Moser-Pröll (AUT)
    3   Perrine Pelen (FRA)

Most Gold Medals, Women
    2   Hanni Wenzel (LIE)
    2   Marielle Goitschel (FRA)
    2   Trude Jochum-Beiser (AUT)
    2   Rosi Mittermaier (FRG)
    2   Marie-Theres Nadig (SUI)
    2   Andrea Mead-Lawrence (USA)

Most Silver Medals, Women
    2   Annemarie Moser-Pröll (AUT)
    2   Penelope "Penny" Pitou (USA)

Most Bronze Medals, Women
     2   Annemarie "Mirl" Buchner (GER)
     2   Perrine Pelen (FRA)
     2   Giuliana Chenal-Minuzzo (ITA)
     2   Traudl Hecher (AUT)

Most Medals, Men
     3   Jean-Claude Killy (FRA)
     3   Anton "Toni" Sailer (AUT)
     3   Henri Oreiller (FRA)
     3   Ingemar Stenmark (SWE)
     3   Josef "Pepi" Stiegler (AUT)
     3   Gustavo Thöni (ITA)

Most Gold Medals, Men
     3   Jean-Claude Killy (FRA)
     3   Anton "Toni" Sailer (AUT)

Most Silver Medals, Men
     2   Gustavo Thöni (ITA)

Most Bronze Medals, Men
     1   Many athletes tied with one.

Most Medals, Games
     3   Henri Oreiller (FRA-1948)
     3   Annemarie "Mirl" Buchner (GER-1952)
     3   Anton "Toni" Sailer (AUT-1956)
     3   Jean-Claude Killy (FRA-1968)
     3   Rosi Mittermaier (FRG-1976)
     3   Hanni Wenzel (LIE-1980)

Most Gold Medals, Games
     3   Jean-Claude Killy (FRA-1968)
     3   Anton "Toni" Sailer (AUT-1956)

Most Medals, Games, Women
     3   Annemarie "Mirl" Buchner (GER-1952)
     3   Rosi Mittermaier (FRG-1976)
     3   Hanni Wenzel (LIE-1980)

Most Gold Medals, Games, Women
     2   Andrea-Mead Lawrence (USA-1952)
     2   Rosi Mittermaier (FRG-1976)
     2   Hanni Wenzel (LIE-1980)

Most Medals, Games, Men
     3   Henri Oreiller (FRA-1948)
     3   Anton "Toni" Sailer (AUT-1956)
     3   Jean-Claude Killy (FRA-1968)

Most Gold Medals, Games, Men
    3   Anton "Toni" Sailer (AUT-1956)
    3   Jean-Claude Killy (FRA-1968)

Most Appearances
    4   Ibrahim Geagea (LIB, 1948-60)
    4   Georges Schneider (SUI, 1948-60)
    4   Luis Arias Carraion (ESP, 1948-60)
    4   Muzaffer Demirhan (TUR, 1948, 56-64)
    4   Francisco Fernandez Ochoa (ESP, 1968-80)

Youngest Medalist, Women
    16-145 Traudl Hecher (AUT-1960)
    16-327 Laila Schou Nilsen (NOR-1936)
    17-205 Danielle Debernard (FRA-1972)
    17-315 Michela Figini (SUI-1984)
    17-337 Marie-Theres Nadig (SUI-1972)

Youngest Gold Medalist, Women
    17-315 Michela Figini (SUI-1984)
    17-337 Marie-Theres Nadig (SUI-1972)
    18-128 Marielle Goitschel (FRA-1964)
    19-003 Heidi Biebl (GER-1960)
    19-212 Kathy Kreiner (CAN-1976)

Oldest Medalist, Women
    30-201 Dorothea Hochleitner (AUT-1956)
    30-033 Ossi Reichart (GER-1956)
    28-359 Gretchen Fraser (USA-1948)
    28-089 Giuliana Chenal-Minuzzo (ITA-1960)
    28-004 Annemarie "Mirl" Buchner (GER-1952)

Oldest Gold Medalist, Women
    30-033 Ossi Reichart (GER-1956)
    28-359 Gretchen Fraser (USA-1948)
    26-327 Annemarie Moser-Pröll (AUT-1980)
    26-057 Ossi Reichart (GER-1952)
    25-190 Rosi Mittermaier (GER-1976)

Youngest Medalist, Men
    19-281 Alfred Matt (AUT-1968)
    19-363 Guy Perillat (FRA-1960)
    20-073 Anton "Toni" Sailer (AUT-1956)
    20-139 James Heuga (USA-1964)
    20-226 Jacques Lüthy (SUI-1980)

Youngest Gold Medalist, Men
    20-073 Anton "Toni" Sailer (AUT-1956)
    20-347 Gustav Thöni (ITA-1972)
    21-107 Piero Gros (ITA-1976)
    21-337 Leonhard Stock (AUT-1980)
    21-353 Francisco Fernandez Ochoa (ESP-1972)

Oldest Medalist, Men
    32-159   Heini Messner (AUT-1972)
    31-230   Zeno Colo (ITA-1952)
    29-220   Stig Sollander (SWE-1956)
    28-301   Edmund Bruggman (SUI-1972)
    28-164   Heini Messner (AUT-1968)

Oldest Gold Medalist, Men
    31-230   Zeno Colo (ITA-1952)
    27-361   Ernst Hinterseer (SUI-1960)
    27-079   Franz Pfnur (GER-1936)
    27-042   Edy Reinalter (SUI-1948)
    27-023   Heini Hemmi (SUI-1976)

Medals Won by Countries

	G	S	B	T
Austria	14	17	19	50
Switzerland	12	11	8	31
France	10	9	11	30
United States	7	8	5	20
FRG	4	6	4	14
Italy	4	3	4	11
Liechtenstein	2	2	4	8
Canada	3	1	2	6
Sweden	2	–	2	4
Norway	1	1	2	4
Germany	2	2	–	4
Spain	1	–	–	1
Japan	–	1	–	1
USSR	–	–	1	1
Yugoslavia	–	1	–	1
Czechoslovakia	–	–	1	1
Totals	62	62	63	187

Medals Won by Countries, Men

	G	S	B	T
Austria	9	9	11	29
Switzerland	5	8	5	18
France	7	3	6	16
Italy	3	2	2	7
United States	2	3	1	6
Sweden	2	–	2	4
Norway	1	1	1	3
Liechtenstein	–	1	2	3
Germany	1	1	–	2
FRG	–	1	1	2
Spain	1	–	–	1
Japan	–	1	–	1
Yugoslavia	–	1	–	1
Canada	–	–	1	1
Totals	31	31	32	94

*Two thirds in 1948 downhill event.

Medals Won by Countries, Women

	G	S	B	T
Austria	5	8	8	21
France	3	6	5	14
United States	5	5	4	14
Switzerland	7	3	3	13
FRG	4	5	3	12
Liechenstein	2	1	2	5
Canada	3	1	1	5
Italy	1	1	2	4
Germany	1	1	–	2
Norway	–	–	1	1
USSR	–	–	1	1
Czechoslovakia	–	–	1	1
Totals	31	31	31	93

Best Performance by Country at Each Olympics

		Men	Women	Overall
1936	–	one event only	one event only	Germany
1948	–	France	Austria	France
1952	–	Austria	United States	Liechtenstein
1956	–	Austria	Switzerland	Sweden
1960	–	Austria	United States	Germany
1964	–	Austria	France	France
1968	–	France	France	France
1972	–	Switzerland	Switzerland	Switzerland
1976	–	Switzerland	FRG	FRG
1980	–	Sweden	Liechtenstein	Liechtenstein
1984	–	United States	USA/Switzerland	United States

BIATHLON

International Federation: Union Internationale de Pentathlon
     Moderne et Biathlon (UIPMB)
Countries Affiliated: 87 (1987)
Year of Formation: 1948
First Year of Olympic Appearance: 1960

Most Medals

5	Aleksandr Tikhonov (URS)
4	Frank Ullrich (GDR)
4	Peter Angerer (FRG)
3	Anatoli Alyabiev (URS)
3	Heikki Ikola (FIN)
3	Magnar Solberg (NOR)
3	Eirik Kvallfoss (NOR)

Most Gold Medals
    4   Aleksandr Tikhonov (URS)
    2   Anatoli Alyabiev (URS)
    2   Magnar Solberg (NOR)
    2   Viktor Mamatov (URS)
    2   Ivan Byakov (URS)

Most Silver Medals
    3   Heikki Ikola (FIN)

Most Bronze Medals
    2   Peter Angerer (FRG)

Most Years Winning Medals
    4   Aleksandr Tikhonov (URS)

Most Years Winning Gold Medals
    4   Aleksandr Tikhonov (URS)
    2   Magnar Solberg (NOR)

Most Medals, Games
    3   Anatoli Alyabiev (URS-1980)
    3   Frank Ullrich (GDR-1980)
    3   Eirik Kvallfoss (NOR-1984)
    3   Peter Angerer (FRG-1984)

Most Gold Medals, Games
    2   Anatoli Aliabiev (URS-1980)

Most Appearances
    4   Aleksandr Tikhonov (URS, 1968-80)

Youngest Medalist
    18-020 Frank Ullrich (GDR-1976)
    19-297 Frank Peter Rötsch (GDR-1984)
    20-075 Yuri Kachkarov (URS-1984)
    20-222 Sergei Bouligin (URS-1984)
    20-223 Peter Angerer (FRG-1980)

Youngest Gold Medalist
    20-075 Yuri Kachkarov (URS-1984)
    20-222 Sergei Bouligin (URS-1984)
    21-044 Aleksandr Tikhonov (URS-1968)
    21-171 Dimitri Vassiliev (URS-1984)
    22-026 Frank Ullrich (GDR-1980)

Oldest Medalist
    37-244 Esko Saira (FIN-1976)
    35-005 Magnar Solberg (NOR-1972)
    34-205 Viktor Mamatov (URS-1972)
    33-242 Esko Saira (FIN-1972)
    33-051 Aleksandr Tikhonov (URS-1980)

Oldest Gold Medalist
     35-005   Magnar Solberg (NOR-1972)
     34-205   Viktor Mamatov (URS-1972)
     33-051   Aleksandr Tikhonov (URS-1980)
     31-165   Rinnat Safin (URS-1972)
     31-144   Ivan Byakov (URS-1976)

Medals Won by Countries

	G	S	B	T
USSR	8	3	4	15
GDR	1	4	4	9
Sweden	1	-	2	3
Norway	3	2	2	7
Finland	-	4	-	4
FRG	1	1	2	4
Totals	14	14	14	42

Best Performance by Country at Each Olympics
     1960   -   one event only
     1964   -   one event only
     1968   -   USSR
     1972   -   Norway/USSR
     1976   -   USSR
     1980   -   USSR
     1984   -   Norway/FRG

BOBSLEDDING

International Federation: Fédération Internationale de Bobsleigh
     et de Tobogganing (FIBT)
Countries Affiliated: 28 (1987)
Year of Formation: 1923
First Year of Olympic Appearance: 1924

Most Medals
     6   Eugenio Monti (ITA)
     5   Fritz Feierabend (SUI)
     4   Bernhard Germeshausen (GDR)
     4   Meinhard Nehmer (GDR)
     4   Erich Schärer (SUI)
     4   Wolfgang Zimmerer (FRG)
     4   Bogdan Musiol (GDR)

Most Gold Medals
     3   Bernhard Germeshausen (GDR)
     3   Meinhard Nehmer (GDR)

Most Silver Medals
    3   Fritz Feierabend (SUI)
    2   Fourteen athletes tied with two.

Most Bronze Medals
    2   Eugenio Monti (ITA)
    2   Fritz Feierabend (SUI)
    2   Peter Utzschneider (FRG)
    2   Jean Wicki (SUI)
    2   Stephan Waser (SUI)
    2   Sergio Siorpaes (ITA)
    2   Hanns Kilian (GER)
    2   Sebastian Huber (GER)
    2   Wolfgang Zimmerer (FRG)

Most Years Winning Medals
    3   Eugenio Monti (ITA)
    3   Fritz Feierabend (SUI)

Most Years Winning Gold Medals
    2   Bernhard Germeshausen (GDR)
    2   Meinhard Nehmer (GDR)
    2   Billy Fiske (USA)
    2   Clifford Gray (USA)

Most Years Between Medals
    16   Fritz Feierabend (SUI)
    12   Eugenio Monti (ITA)

Most Years Between Gold Medals
    4   Bernhard Germeshausen (GDR)
    4   Meinhard Nehmer (GDR)
    4   Billy Fiske (USA)
    4   Clifford Gray (USA)

Most Appearances
    6   Carl-Erik Eriksson (SWE, 1964-84)
    4   James Bickford (USA, 1936-56)
    4   Ion Panturu (ROM, 1964-76)
    4   Denys Malcolm Lloyd (GBR, 1972-84)

Youngest Medalist
    15-129   Thomas Doe (USA-1928)
    16-260   Billy Fiske (USA-1928)
    18-279   Heinrich Schläppi (SUI-1924)
    19-342   Reto Capadrutt (ITA-1932)
    20-215   Roland Wetzig (GDR-1980)

Youngest Gold Medalist
    16-260   Billy Fiske (USA-1928)
    18-279   Heinrich Schläppi (SUI-1924)
    20-256   Billy Fiske (USA-1932)
    22-172   Jochen Babock (GDR-1976)
    22-214   Bogdan Musiol (GDR-1980)

Oldest Medalist
   49-038 Max Houben (BEL-1948)
   48-358 Jay O'Brien (USA-1932)
   47-217 Giacomo Conti (ITA-1956)
   46-342 Albert Madörin (SUI-1952)
   44-362 Jay O'Brien (USA-1928)
   43-237 Fritz Feierabend (SUI-1952)
   43-057 Francis Tyler (USA-1948)
   42-182 Nion Tucker (USA-1928)
   42-122 Paul Stevens (USA-1932)
   42-034 René Mortiaux (BEL-1924)

Oldest Gold Medalist
   48-358 Jay O'Brien (USA-1932)
   47-217 Giacomo Conti (ITA-1956)
   43-057 Francis Tyler (USA-1948)
   42-182 Nion Tucker (USA-1928)
   41-340 Hubert Stevens (USA-1932)
   41-103 Franz Kemser (GER-1932)
   40-172 Heinrich Angst (SUI-1956)
   40-023 Eugenio Monti (ITA-1968)
   40-017 Clifford Gray (USA-1932)
   39-042 Meinhard Nehmer (GDR-1980)

Medals Won by Countries

	G	S	B	T
Switzerland	6	6	7	19
United States	5	4	5	14
GDR	5	3	2	10
Italy	3	4	2	9
FRG	3	3	2	8
Great Britain	1	1	1	3
Austria	-	2	-	2
Belgium	-	1	1	2
Germany	-	-	2	2
Canada	1	-	-	1
Romania	-	-	1	1
USSR	-	-	1	1
Totals	24	24	24	72

Best Performance by Country at Each Olympics
   1924   -   one event only
   1928   -   one event only
   1932   -   United States
   1936   -   Switzerland
   1948   -   Switzerland
   1952   -   Germany
   1956   -   Italy
   1960   -   not held
   1964   -   Great Britain/Canada/Italy
   1968   -   Italy
   1972   -   FRG
   1976   -   GDR
   1980   -   GDR
   1984   -   GDR

FIGURE SKATING

International Federation: Internationale Skating Union (ISU)
Countries Affiliated: 34 (1987)
Year of Formation: 1892
First Year of Olympic Appearance: 1908

Most Medals
    4   Gillis Grafström (SWE)
    3   Andrée Brunet-Joly (FRA)
    3   Pierre Brunet (FRA)
    3   Sonja Henie (NOR)
    3   Beatrix Loughran (USA)
    3   Irina Rodnina (URS)

Most Gold Medals
    3   Gillis Grafström (SWE)
    3   Sonja Henie (NOR)
    3   Irina Rodnina (URS)

Most Silver Medals
    2   Willy Böckl (AUT)
    2   Fritzi Burger (AUT)
    2   Beatrix Loughran (USA)

Most Bronze Medals
    2   Patrick Péra (FRA)
    2   Emilia Rotter (HUN)
    2   László Szollás (HUN)
    2   Marianna Nagy (HUN)
    2   László Nagy (HUN)
    2   Manuella Groß (GDR)
    2   Uwe Kagelmann (GDR)

Most Medals, Women
    3   Andrée Brunet-Joly (FRA)
    3   Sonja Henie (NOR)
    3   Beatrix Loughran (USA)
    3   Irina Rodnina (URS)

Most Gold Medals, Women
    3   Sonja Henie (NOR)
    3   Irina Rodnina (URS)

Most Silver Medals, Women
    2   Fritzi Burger (AUT)
    2   Beatrix Loughran (USA)

Most Bronze Medals, Women
   2   Emilia Rotter (HUN)
   2   Marianna Nagy (HUN)
   2   Manuella Groß (GDR)

Most Medals, Men
   4   Gillis Grafström (SWE)
   3   Pierre Brunet (FRA)

Most Gold Medals, Men
   3   Gillis Grafström (SWE)
   2   Karl Schäfer (AUT)
   2   Richard Button (USA)
   2   Pierre Brunet (FRA)
   2   Oleg Protopopov (URS)
   2   Aleksandr Zaitsev (URS)

Most Silver Medals, Men
   2   Willy Böckl (AUT)

Most Bronze Medals, Men
   2   Patrick Péra (FRA)
   2   László Szollás (HUN)
   2   László Nagy (HUN)
   2   Uwe Kagelmann (GDR)

Most Appearances
   4   Gillis Grafström (SWE, 1920-32)
   4   Sonja Henie (NOR, 1924-36)
   4   Jan Hoffmann (GDR, 1968-80)

Youngest Medalist, Women
   15-008 Manuela Groß (GDR-1972)
   15-076 Cecilia Colledge (GBR-1936)
   15-091 Marina Cherkasova (URS-1980)
   15-127 Maxi Herber (GER-1936)
   15-260 Ingrid Wendl (AUT-1956)

Youngest Gold Medalist, Women
   15-127 Maxi Herber (GER-1936)
   15-315 Sonja Henie (NOR-1928)
   18-077 Katarina Witt (GDR-1984)
   19-172 Annet Pötzsch (GDR-1980)
   19-198 Peggy Fleming (USA-1968)

Oldest Medalist, Women
   39-189 Ludowika Jakobsson (FIN-1924)
   35-275 Ludowika Jakobsson (FIN-1920)
   35-116 Phyllis Johnson (GBR-1920)
   32-084 Lyudmila Belousova (URS-1968)
   31-226 Beatrix Loughran (USA-1932)

Oldest Gold Medalist, Women
   35-275   Ludowika Jakobsson (FIN-1920)
   32-084   Lyudmila Belousova (URS-1968)
   30-158   Irina Rodnina (URS-1980)
   30-149   Andrée Brunet-Joly (FRA-1932)
   29-085   Ria Falk (GER-1952)

Youngest Medalist, Men
   14-363   Scott Allen (USA-1964)
   15-300   Erik Pausin (AUT-1936)
   18-022   Hans-Jürgen Bäumler (FRG-1960)
   18-037   Wallace Diestelmeyer (CAN-1948)
   18-129   Ronald Robertson (USA-1956)

Youngest Gold Medalist, Men
   18-202   Richard Button (USA-1948)
   20-155   Wolfgang Schwarz (AUT-1968)
   20-280   Manfred Schnelldorfer (FRG-1964)
   21-020   Ondrej Nepela (TCH-1972)
   22-199   Pierre Baugniet (FRA-1948)

Oldest Medalist, Men
   44-078   Martin Stixrud (NOR-1920)
   43-302   Edgar Syers (GBR-1908)
   41-359   Walter Jakobsson (FIN-1924)
   38-247   Gillis Grafström (SWE-1932)
   38-131   Yngvar Bryn (NOR-1920)

Oldest Gold Medalist, Men
   38-080   Walter Jakobsson (FIN-1920)
   35-222   Oleg Protopopov (URS-1968)
   34-255   Gillis Grafström (SWE-1928)
   31-196   Oleg Protopopov (URS-1964)
   30-237   Gillis Grafström (SWE-1924)

Medals Won by Countries

	G	S	B	T
United States	9	10	12	31
Austria	7	9	4	20
USSR	9	7	4	20
Great Britain	5	3	6	14
Sweden	5	3	2	10
Canada	2	4	5	11
GDR	2	3	4	9
France	2	1	4	7
Norway	3	2	1	6
Hungary	–	2	4	6
FRG	2	1	2	5
Germany	2	2	–	4
Czechoslovakia	1	1	2	4
Netherlands	1	2	–	3
Finland	1	1	–	2
Belgium	1	–	1	2
Switzerland	–	1	1	2
Totals	52	52	52	156

*Pairs and ice dancing medals are equally divided among men and women in the tables below.

Medals Won by Countries, Men

	G	S	B	T
United States	5	3½	5½	14
USSR	5	4½	1½	11
Austria	4	4	2½	10½
Sweden	4	2	1	7
Great Britain	2½	1½	2	6
Canada	½	2	3½	6
France	1	1	2½	4½
Czechoslovakia	1	1	1	3
Hungary	–	1	2	3
GDR	–	1½	1½	3
FRG	1½	½	½	2½
Norway	–	1½	1	2½
Germany	1	1	–	2
Switzerland	–	1	1	2
Belgium	½	–	1	1½
Finland	½	½		1
Totals	26½	26½	26½	79½

Medals Won by Countries, Women

	G	S	B	T
United States	4	6½	6½	17
Austria	3	5	1½	9½
USSR	4	2½	2½	9
Great Britain	2½	1½	4	8
GDR	2	1½	2½	6
Canada	1½	2	1½	5
Norway	3	½	–	3½
Netherlands	1	2	–	3
Sweden	1	1	1	3
Hungary	–	1	2	3
France	1	–	1½	2½
FRG	½	½	1½	2½
Germany	1	1	–	2
Czechoslovakia	–	–	1	1
Finland	½	½	–	1
Belgium	½	–	–	½
Totals	25½	25½	25½	76½

Best Performance by Country at Each Olympics

1908	–	Great Britain
1920	–	Sweden
1924	–	Austria
1928	–	Austria
1932	–	Austria
1936	–	Austria
1948	–	Canada
1952	–	United States
1956	–	United States
1960	–	United States
1964	–	Germany/The Netherlands/USSR
1968	–	United States/USSR
1972	–	USSR
1976	–	USSR
1980	–	USSR
1984	–	United States/USSR

ICE HOCKEY

International Federation: International Ice Hockey Federation
    (IIHF)
Countries Affiliated: 34 (1987)
Year of Formation: 1908
First Year of Olympic Appearance: 1920

Most Medals

4	Jiři Holik (TCH)
4	Vladislav Tretiak (URS)
3	Twelve athletes tied with three.

Most Gold Medals
    3   Vitali Davidov (URS)
    3   Viktor Kuskin (URS)
    3   Aleksandr Ragulin (URS)
    3   Vladislav Tretiak (URS)
    3   Anatoliy Firsov (URS)

Most Silver Medals
    2   Jiři Holik (TCH)
    2   Oldřich Machač (TCH)
    2   František Pospišil (TCH)
    2   Herb Drury (USA)
    2   Frank Synott (USA)
    2   Milan Chalupa (TCH)

Most Bronze Medals
    2   Richard "Bibi" Torriani (SUI)
    2   Mats Waltin (SWE)
    2   Jiři Holik (TCH)
    2   Josef Cerný (TCH)
    2   Vladimir Dzurilla (TCH)

Most Years Between Medals
    20   Richard "Bibi" Torriani (SUI)
    12   Jiři Holik (TCH)
    12   Vladislav Tretiak (URS)
    12   Boris Mikhailov (URS)

Most Years Between Gold Medals
    12   Vladislav Tretiak (URS)
    8   Vitali Davidov (URS)
    8   Viktor Kuzkin (URS)
    8   Boris Mikhailov (URS)
    8   Aleksandr Ragulin (URS)
    8   Anatoliy Firsov (URS)

Most Appearances
    4   Vlastimil Bubnik (TCH, 1952-64)
    4   Josef Cerný (TCH, 1960-72)
    4   Jiři Holik (TCH, 1964-76)
    4   Sven "Tumba" Johansson (SWE, 1952-64)
    4   Thor Martinsen (NOR; 1964-72, 80)
    4   Bert-Ola Nordlander (SWE, 1960-72)
    4   Esa Peltonen (FIN, 1968-80)
    4   Otto Schneitberger (GER/FRG, 1960-72)
    4   Vladislav Tretiak (URS, 1972-84)

Youngest Medalist
    16-141   Richard "Bibi" Torriani (SUI-1928)
    16-261   Mark Howe (USA-1972)
    18-054   John McKenzie (CAN-1956)
    18-328   Robert Breiter (SUI-1928)
    19-032   Reginald Smith (CAN-1924)

Youngest Gold Medalist
   18-054   John McKenzie (CAN-1956)
   19-032   Reginald Smith (CAN-1924)
   19-082   Mike Ramsey (USA-1980)
   19-293   Vladislav Tretiak (URS-1972)
   19-316   Tom Williams (USA-1960)

Oldest Medalist
   42-194   Irving Small (USA-1924)
   38-184   Harold Simpson (CAN-1932)
   37-256   Erich Römer (GER-1932)
   36-331   Allan Van (USA-1952)
   36-130   Richard "Bibi" Torriani (SUI-1948)

Oldest Gold Medalist
   38-184   Harold Simpson (CAN-1932)
   36-001   George Abel (CAN-1952)
   35-046   Carl Erhardt (GBR-1936)
   35-028   Evgeniy Babitsch (URS-1956)
   34-262   Francis Sullivan (CAN-1952)

Athletes Competing for Both an Olympic and a Stanley Cup Champion
   Ken Morrow (USA-1980/New York Islanders)
   Duncan Monro (CAN-1924/Montreal Maroons)
   Reginald Smith (CAN-1924/Ottawa Senators and Montreal Maroons)
   Albert McCaffrey (CAN-1924/Montreal Canadiens)
   David Trottier (CAN-1928/Montreal Maroons)

Most Goals, Game, Individual
   13   Harry Watson (CAN-1924 v. Czechoslovakia)
   7   Herb Drury (USA-1924 v. France)
   7   Herb Drury (USA-1924 v. Sweden)
   6   David Miller (CAN-1952 v. Germany)
   6   Václav Nedomanský (TCH-1972 v. Poland)
   5   Sándor Miklós (HUN-1936 v. Belgium)
   5   Paul Knox (CAN-1956 v. Austria)
   5   Vladimir Golikov (URS-1980 v. Japan)
   5   Marian Stastný (TCH-1980 v. Canada)

*Complete records not kept prior to 1932.

Most Goals, Game, Team
   33   Canada (1924 v. Switzerland)
   31   USA (1948 v. Italy)
   30   Canada (1924 v. Czechoslovakia)
   29   USA (1920 v. Switzerland)
   23   Sweden (1948 v. Italy)
   23   Canada (1956 v. Austria)
   22   Canada (1924 v. Sweden)
   22   USA (1924 v. France)
   21   Canada (1948 v. Italy)
   20   USA (1924 v. Sweden)

Most Goals, Game, Both Teams (Both Teams Scoring)
```
32      USA d. Italy, 31-1 (1948)
27      USA d. Poland, 23-4 (1948)
25      Czechoslovakia d. Italy, 22-3 (1948)
22      Great Britain d. Belgium, 19-3 (1924)
22      Canada d. Italy, 21-1 (1948)
21      Canada d. Great Britain, 19-2 (1924)
21      Great Britain d. Italy, 14-7 (1948)
21      Austria d. Italy, 16-5 (1948)
21      Finland d. Australia, 19-2 (1960)
21      USSR d. Holland, 17-4 (1980)
```

Medals Won by Countries

	G	S	B	T
Canada	6	2	2	10
United States	2	6	1	9
USSR	6	1	1	8
Czechoslovakia	-	4	3	7
Sweden	-	2	3	5
Great Britain	1	-	1	2
Switzerland	-	-	2	2
FRG	-	-	1	1
Germany	-	-	1	1
Totals	15	15	15	45

Overall Record by Countries

	W	L	T	%%%%
USSR	47	4	2	.906
Canada	68	15	3	.808
United States	59	27	7	.672
Czechoslovakia	54	28	2	.655
Sweden	44	34	8	.558
Great Britain	14	12	2	.536
Japan	15	16	4	.486
Yugoslavia	12	14	2	.464
Romania	10	12	2	.458
Finland	21	28	4	.434
Switzerland	17	31	3	.363
Germany/FRG	23	44	6	.356
Norway	11	23	2	.333
The Netherlands	1	3	1	.300
Austria	11	30	4	.289
Poland	16	42	2	.283
France	4	11	0	.267
Italy	7	21	2	.267
Belgium	2	8	0	.200
GDR	1	7	0	.125
Hungary	2	15	0	.118
Latvia	0	3	0	.000
Bulgaria	0	5	0	.000
Australia	0	6	0	.000
Totals	439	439	56	.500

LUGE & TOBOGGANING (includes Skeleton)

International Federation: Fédération Internationale de Luge de
     Course (FIL)
Countries Affiliated: 28 (1987)
Year of Formation: 1957
First Year of Olympic Appearance: 1964

Most Medals
    4   Klaus-Michael Bonsack (GDR)
    3   Thomas Khler (GDR)
    3   Hans Rinn (GDR)
    3   Paul Hildgartner (ITA)

Most Gold Medals
    2   Thomas Khler (GDR)
    2   Hans Rinn (GDR)
    2   Paul Hildgartner (ITA)
    2   Norbert Hahn (GDR)

Most Silver Medals
    2*   John Heaton (USA)
*Heaton competed in the Skeleton event at St. Moritz (1928 &
    1948), not exactly the same as the luge.

Most Bronze Medals
    2   Klaus-Michael Bonsack (GDR)
    2   Wolfram Fiedler (GDR)

Most Medals, Women
    2   Margit Schumann (GDR)
    2   Ute Rhrold (GDR)

Most Gold Medals, Women
    1   Six athletes tied with one.

Most Medals, Men
    4   Klaus-Michael Bonsack (GDR)
    3   Thomas Khler (GDR)
    3   Hans Rinn (GDR)
    3   Paul Hildgartner (ITA)

Most Gold Medals, Men
    2   Thomas Khler (GDR)
    2   Hans Rinn (GDR)
    2   Paul Hildgartner (ITA)
    2   Norbert Hahn (GDR)

Most Silver Medals, Men
   2*   John Heaton (USA)
*Heaton competed in the Skeleton event at St. Moritz (1928 &
   1948), not exactly the same as the luge.

Most Bronze Medals, Men
   2   Klaus-Michael Bonsack (GDR)
   2   Wolfram Fiedler (GDR)

Most Appearances
   4   Paul Hildgartner (ITA, 1972-84)
   4   Manfred Schmid (AUT, 1964-76)

Youngest Medalist, Men
   17-306   Manfred Stengl (AUT-1964)
   19-246   Paul Hildgartner (ITA-1972)
   20-076   Jochen Pietzsch (GDR-1984)

Youngest Gold Medalist, Men
   17-306   Manfred Stengl (AUT-1964)
   19-246   Paul Hildgartner (ITA-1972)
   20-109   Walter Plaikner (ITA-1972)

Youngest Medalist, Women
   17-060   Ute Rhrold (GDR-1972)
   19-145   Margit Schumann (GDR-1972)

Youngest Gold Medalist, Women
   20-065   Ortrun Enderlein (GDR-1964)
   20-263   Erika Lechner (ITA-1968)

Oldest Medalist, Men
   45-035   John Crammond [SKE] (GBR-1948)
   39-147   John Heaton [SKE] (USA-1948)
   38-186   Fritz Nachmann (FRG-1968)
   32-249   Paul Hildgartner (ITA-1984)
   30-036   Klaus-Michael Bonsack (GDR-1972)

Oldest Gold Medalist, Men
   32-248   Paul Hildgartner (ITA-1984)
   28-343   Wolfgang Scheidel (GDR-1972)
   27-237   Thomas Köhler (GDR-1968)

Oldest Medalist, Women
   25-176   Helen Thurner (AUT-1964)
   24-032   Vera Sosulya (URS-1980)

Oldest Gold Medalist, Women
   24-032   Vera Sosulya (URS-1980)
   23-145   Margit Schumann (GDR-1976)

Medals Won by Countries

	G	S	B	T
GDR	12	8	7	27
FRG	1	3	5	9
Austria	2	2	3	7
Italy	4	2	1	7
United States	1	2	–	3
USSR	1	2	2	5
Great Britain	–	–	2	2
Totals	21	19	20	60

Medals Won by Countries, Men

	G	S	B	T
GDR	8	3	5	16
Italy	3	2	1	6
Austria	2	2	2	6
FRG	1	2	3	6
United States	1	2	–	3
USSR	–	2	1	3
Great Britain	–	–	2	2
Totals	15	13	14	42

*Two firsts/no second in 1972 two-man luge event.
**The 1928 and 1948 skeleton contests are included in the above totals.

Medals Won by Countries, Women

	G	S	B	T
GDR	4	5	2	11
FRG	–	1	2	3
USSR	1	–	1	2
Austria	–	–	1	1
Italy	1	–	–	1
Totals	6	6	6	18

Best Performance by Country at Each Olympics (Luge Only)

		Men	Women	Overall
1964	–	Germany	Germany	Germany
1968	–	GDR	Italy	GDR
1972	–	GDR	GDR	GDR
1976	–	GDR	GDR	GDR
1980	–	GDR	USSR	GDR
1984	–	USSR	GDR	GDR

NORDIC SKIING

International Federation: Fédération Internationale de Ski (FIS)
Countries Affiliated: 55 (1987)
Year of Formation: 1924
First Year of Olympic Appearance: 1924

Most Medals
9	Sixten Jernberg (SWE)
8	Galina Kulakova (URS)
7	Veikko Hakulinen (FIN)
7	Eero Mäntyranta (FIN)
7	Raisa Smetanina (URS)
6	Johan Gröttumsbråten (NOR)

Most Gold Medals
4	Sixten Jernberg (SWE)
4	Galina Kulakova (URS)
4	Nikolai Zimyatov (URS)
3	Nine athletes tied with three.

Most Silver Medals
4	Raisa Smetanina (URS)
3	Sixten Jernberg (SWE)
3	Veikko Hakulinen (FIN)
3	Helena Kivioja-Takalo (FIN)
3	Pal Tyldum (NOR)
3	Lyubov Baranova-Kozyreva (URS)
3	Radya Eroshina (URS)
3	Marjatta Kajosmaa (FIN)

Most Bronze Medals
3	Alevtina Kolchina (URS)
3	Pavel Kolchin (URS)
3	Harri Kirvesniemi (FIN)

Most Years Winning Medals
4	Galina Kulakova (URS)
3	Fifteen athletes tied with three.

Most Years Winning Gold Medals
3	Sixten Jernberg (SWE)
3	Ulrich Wehling (GDR)
3	Veikko Hakulinen (FIN)

Most Years Between Medals
16	Birger Ruud (NOR)
12	Galina Kulakova (URS)
12	Alevtina Kolchina (URS)
8	Seventeen athletes tied with eight.

Most Years Between Gold Medals
8   Sixten Jernberg (SWE)
8   Ulrich Wehling (GDR)
8   Veikko Hakulinen (FIN)

Most Medals, Women
8   Galina Kulakova (URS)
7   Raisa Smetanina (URS)
5   Alevtina Kolchina (URS)
5   Helena Kivioja-Takalo (FIN)
4   Lyubov Baranova-Kozyreva (URS)
4   Toini Gustafsson (SWE)
4   Radya Eroshina (URS)
4   Marjatta Kajosmaa (FIN)
4   Marja-Liisa Hämäläinen (FIN)

Most Gold Medals, Women
4   Galina Kulakova (URS)
3   Marja-Liisa Hämäläinen (FIN)
3   Klaudiya Boyarskikh (URS)
3   Raisa Smetanina (URS)

Most Silver Medals, Women
4   Raisa Smetanina (URS)
3   Helena Kivioja-Takalo (FIN)
3   Lyubov Baranova-Kozyreva (URS)
3   Radya Eroshina (URS)
3   Marjatta Kajosmaa (FIN)

Most Bronze Medals, Women
3   Alevtina Kolchina (URS)

Most Years Winning Medals, Women
4   Galina Kulakova (URS)
3   Raisa Smetanina (URS)
3   Alevtina Kolchina (URS)
3   Helena Takalo (FIN)
3   Siiri Rantanen (FIN)
3   Britt Strandberg (SWE)

Most Years Winning Gold Medals, Women
2   Galina Kulakova (URS)
2   Raisa Smetanina (URS)

Most Years Between Medals, Women
12   Galina Kulakova (URS)
12   Alevtina Kolchina (URS)
8   Raisa Smetanina (URS)
8   Helena Takalo (FIN)

Most Years Between Gold Medals, Women
4   Galina Kulakova (URS)
4   Raisa Smetanina (URS)

Most Medals, Men
9	Sixten Jernberg (SWE)
7	Veikko Hakulinen (FIN)
7	Eero Mäntyranta (FIN)
6	Johan Gröttumsbråten (NOR)
5	Harald Grönningen (NOR)
5	Juha Mieto (FIN)
5	Nikolai Zimyatov (URS)
5	Pål Tyldum (FIN)

Most Gold Medals, Men
4	Sixten Jernberg (SWE)
3	Veikko Hakulinen (FIN)
3	Eero Mäntyranta (FIN)
3	Johan Gröttumsbråten (NOR)
3	Thorleif Haug (NOR)
3	Ulrich Wehling (GDR)
3	Thomas-Lars Wassberg (SWE)

Most Silver Medals, Men
3	Sixten Jernberg (SWE)
3	Veikko Hakulinen (FIN)
3	Pål Tyldum (NOR)

Most Bronze Medals, Men
3	Pavel Kolchin (URS)
3	Harri Kirvesniemi (FIN)

Most Years Winning Medals, Men
3	Sixten Jernberg (SWE)
3	Veikko Hakulinen (FIN)
3	Eero Mäntyranta (FIN)
3	Johan Gröttumsbråten NOR)
3	Harald Grönningen (NOR)
3	Juha Mieto (FIN)
3	Pål Tyldum (NOR)
3	Hallgeir Brenden (NOR)
3	Birger Ruud (NOR)
3	Ulrich Wehling (GDR)

Most Years Winning Gold Medals, Men
3	Sixten Jernberg (SWE)
3	Ulrich Wehling (GDR)
3	Veikko Hakulinen (FIN)

Most Years Between Medals, Men
16	Birger Ruud (NOR)
8	Eleven athletes tied with eight.

Most Years Between Gold Medals, Men
8	Sixten Jernberg (SWE)
8	Ulrich Wehling (GDR)
8	Veikko Hakulinen (FIN)

Most Medals, Games
4	Thorleif Haug (NOR-1924)
4	Sixten Jernberg (SWE-1956)
4	Marja-Liisa Hämäläinen (FIN-1984)
4	Gunde Anders Swan (SWE-1984)

Most Gold Medals, Games
3	Thorleif Haug (NOR-1924)
3	Klaudiya Boyarskikh (URS-1964)
3	Galina Kulakova (URS-1972)
3	Nikolai Zimyatov (URS-1980)
3	Marja-Liisa Hämäläinen (FIN-1984)

Most Medals, Games, Men
4	Thorleif Haug (NOR-1924)
4	Sixten Jernberg (SWE-1956)
4	Gunde Anders Swan (SWE-1984)

Most Gold Medals, Games, Men
3	Thorleif Haug (NOR-1924)
3	Nikolai Zimyatov (URS-1980)
2	Johan Gröttumsbråten (NOR-1928)
2	Martin Lundström (SWE-1948)
2	Sixten Jernberg (SWE-1964)
2	Eero Mäntyranta (FIN-1964)
2	Harald Grönningen (NOR-1968)
2	Ole Ellefsaeter (NOR-1968)
2	Vyacheslav Vedenin (URS-1972)
2	Gunde Anders Swan (SWE-1984)

Most Medals, Games, Women
4	Marja-Liisa Hämäläinen (FIN-1984)
3	Klaudiya Boyarskikh (URS-1964)
3	Toini Gustafsson (SWE-1968)
3	Marjatta Kajosmaa (FIN-1972)
3	Galina Kulakova (URS-1972)
3	Raisa Smetanina (URS-1976)
3	Helena Takalo (FIN-1976)

Most Gold Medals, Games, Women
3	Klaudiya Boyarskikh (FIN-1964)
3	Galina Kulakova (URS-1972)
3	Marja Liisa Hämälainen (FIN-1984)
2	Toini Gustafsson (SWE-1968)
2	Raisa Smetanina (URS-1976)
2	Barbara Petzold (GDR-1980)

Most Appearances
4	Sixteen athletes tied with four.

Most Appearances, Men
4   Victor Arbez (FRA, 1956-68)
4   Oddvar Brå (NOR, 1972-84)
4   Timothy Caldwell (USA, 1972-84)
4   Benoit Carrara (FRA, 1948-60)
4   Walter Demel (GER/FRG, 1964-76)
4   Yukio Kasaya (JPN, 1964-76)
4   Juha Mieto (FIN, 1972-84)
4   Eero Mäntyranta (FIN, 1960-72)
4   Arto Tiainen (FIN, 1956-68)
4   Koba Tsakadse (URS; 1956-64, 72)

Most Appearances, Women
4   Sharon Firth (CAN, 1972-84)
4   Shirley Firth (CAN, 1972-84)
4   Helena Kivioja-Takalo (FIN, 1968-80)
4   Alevtina Kolchina (URS, 1956-68)
4   Galina Kulakova (URS, 1968-80)
4   Barbro Martinsson (SWE, 1956-68)

Youngest Medalist, Men
17-320 Anton Innauer (AUT-1976)
18-323 Manfred Deckert (GDR-1980)
19-064 Niilo Halonen (FIN-1960)
19-146 Hubert Neuper (AUT-1980)
19-188 Wojciech Fortuna (POL-1972)

Youngest Gold Medalist, Men
19-188 Wojciech Fortuna (POL-1972)
19-206 Jens Weißflog (GDR-1984)
19-211 Ulrich Wehling (GDR-1972)
20-173 Birger Ruud (NOR-1932)
20-216 Matti Nykänen (FIN-1984)

Youngest Medalist, Women
18-311 Brit Pettersen (NOR-1980)
19-012 Marjo Matikainen (FIN-1984)
19-049 Hilkka Kuntola (FIN-1972)
19-053 Carola Anding (GDR-1980)
19-306 Marlies Rostock (GDR-1980)

Youngest Gold Medalist, Women
19-053 Carola Anding (GDR-1980)
19-306 Marlies Rostock (GDR-1980)
20-240 Anne Jahren (NOR-1984)
23-346 Raisa Smetanina (URS-1976)
24-082 Klaudiya Boyarskikh (URS-1964)

Oldest Medalist, Men
36-245 Olav Ökern (NOR-1948)
36-168 Birger Ruud (NOR-1948)
35-169 Enar Josefsson (SWE-1952)
35-052 Veikko Hakulinen (FIN-1960)
35-002 Sixten Jernberg (SWE-1964)

Oldest Gold Medalist, Men
35-052   Veikko Hakulinen (FIN-1960)
35-002   Sixten Jernberg (SWE-1964)
34-209   Simon Slåttvik (NOR-1952)
33-128   Harald Grönningen (NOR-1968)
32-364   Johan Gröttumsbråten (NOR-1932)

Oldest Medalist, Women
38-009   Marjatta Kajosmaa (FIN-1976)
38-005   Alevtina Kolchina (URS-1968)
37-298   Galina Kulakova (URS-1980)
35-073   Siiri Rantanen (FIN-1960)
34-009   Marjatta Kajosmaa (FIN-1972)

Oldest Gold Medalist, Women
33-362   Galina Kulakova (URS-1976)
32-231   Evdokiya Mekshilo (URS-1964)
31-281   Lydia Wideman (FIN-1952)
31-048   Siiri Rantanen (FIN-1956)
29-100   Sonja Ruthström-Edström (SWE-1960)

Medals Won by Countries

	G	S	B	Tot
Norway	28	28	24	80
Finland	21	29	23	73
USSR	21	18	19	58
Sweden	19	16	15	50
GDR	8	4	8	20
Austria	2	3	3	8
Czechoslovakia	1	2	5	8
FRG	2	1	1	4
Japan	1	2	1	4
Switzerland	-	2	2	4
Poland	1	-	1	2
United States	-	1	1	2
Italy	1	-	-	1
Bulgaria	-	-	1	1
Totals	105	106	104	315

Medals Won by Countries, Men

	G	S	B	Tot
Norway	26	26	19	71
Finland	15	21	17	53
Sweden	16	14	13	43
USSR	10	7	12	29
GDR	6	4	7	17
Austria	2	3	3	8
FRG	2	1	1	4
Japan	1	2	1	4
Czechoslovakia	1	1	2	4
Switzerland	–	2	2	4
Poland	1	–	1	2
United States	–	1	1	2
Italy	1	–	–	1
Bulgaria	–	–	1	1
Totals	81	82	80	243

*Two seconds/no third in 1980 70 metre ski jumping.
**Third in 1924 ski jumping credited to Anders Haugen (USA), not
Thorleif Haug (NOR) as originally given. An error in scoring
was discovered in 1974 and the medal was presented to Haugen by
Haug's daughter.

Medals Won by Countries, Women

	G	S	B	Tot
USSR	11	11	7	29
Finland	6	8	6	20
Norway	2	2	5	9
Sweden	3	2	2	7
Czechoslovakia	–	1	3	4
GDR	2	–	1	3
Totals	24	24	24	72

Best Performance by Country at Each Olympics

		Men	Women	Overall
1924	–	Norway	-----	-----
1928	–	Norway	-----	-----
1932	–	Norway	-----	-----
1936	–	Norway	-----	-----
1948	–	Sweden	-----	-----
1952	–	Norway	one event only	Finland
1956	–	Finland	USSR	Finland
1960	–	Finland	USSR	Finland
1964	–	Finland	USSR	Finland
1968	–	Norway	Sweden	Norway
1972	–	Norway	USSR	USSR
1976	–	GDR	USSR	USSR
1980	–	USSR	GDR	USSR
1984	–	Finland	Finland	Finland

SPEED SKATING

International Federation: Internationale Skating Union (ISU)
Countries Affiliated: 34 (1987)
Year of Formation: 1892
First Year of Olympic Appearance: 1924

Most Medals
7	Ivar Ballangrud (NOR)
7	Clas Thunberg (FIN)
6	Roald Larsen (NOR)
6	Lidiya Skoblikova (URS)
5	Evgeniy Grishin (URS)
5	Eric Heiden (USA)
5	Knut Johannesen (NOR)
5	Karin Enke (GDR)

Most Gold Medals
6	Lidiya Skoblikova (URS)
5	Clas Thunberg (FIN)
5	Eric Heiden (USA)
4	Ivar Ballangrud (NOR)
4	Evgeniy Grishin (URS)

Most Silver Medals
3	Cornelis "Kees" Verkerk (HOL)
3	Leah Poulos-Mueller (USA)
3	Andrea Mitscherlich-Schöne (GDR)

Most Bronze Medals
4	Roald Larsen (NOR)
3	Natalya Petruseva (URS)
3	Hans van Helden (HOL)

Most Years Winning Medals
3	Ivar Ballangrud (NOR)
3	Evgeniy Grishin (URS)
3	Knut Johannesen (NOR)
3	Cornelis "Kees" Verkerk (HOL)

Most Years Winning Gold Medals
2	Ivar Ballangrud (NOR)
2	Clas Thunberg (FIN)
2	Lidiya Skoblikova (URS)
2	Evgeniy Grishin (URS)
2	Knut Johannesen (NOR)
2	Karin Enke (GDR)
2	Lyudmila Titova (URS)

Most Years Between Medals
8	Ivar Ballangrud (NOR)
8	Evgeniy Grishin (URS)
8	Knut Johannesen (NOR)
8	Cornelis "Kees" Verkerk (HOL)
8	Alv Gjestvang (NOR)
8	Andrea Mitscherlich-Schöne (GDR)

Most Years Between Gold Medals
8	Ivar Ballangrud (NOR)
4	Clas Thunberg (FIN)
4	Lidiya Skoblikova (URS)
4	Evgeniy Grishin (URS)
4	Knut Johannesen (NOR)
4	Karin Enke (GDR)
4	Lyudmila Titova (URS)

Most Medals, Women
6	Lidiya Skoblikova (URS)
5	Karin Enke (GDR)
4	Tatyana Averina (URS)
4	Christina Baas-Kaiser (HOL)
4	Dianne Holum (USA)
4	Kaija Mustonen (FIN)
4	Natalya Petruseva (URS)

Most Gold Medals, Women
6	Lidiya Skoblikova (URS)
3	Karin Enke (GDR)
2	Tatyana Averina (URS)

Most Silver Medals, Women
3	Leah Poulos-Mueller (USA)
3	Andrea Mitscherlich-Schöne (GDR)
2	Karin Enke (GDR)
2	Dianne Holum (USA)
2	Kaija Mustonen (FIN)
2	Irina Egorova (URS)
2	Valentina Stenina (URS)

Most Bronze Medals, Women
3	Natalya Petruseva (URS)
2	Tatyana Averina (URS)
2	Christina Baas-Kaiser (HOL)
2	Atje Keulen-Deelstra (HOL)

Most Years Winning Medals, Women
   2   Lidiya Skoblikova (URS)
   2   Karin Enke (GDR)
   2   Christina Baas-Kaiser (HOL)
   2   Dianne Holum (USA)
   2   Kaija Mustonen (FIN)
   2   Natalya Petruseva (URS)
   2   Leah Poulos-Mueller (USA)
   2   Lyudmila Titova (URS)
   2   Andrea Mitscherlich-Schöne (GDR)
   2   Valentina Stenina (URS)

Most Years Winning Gold Medals, Women
   2   Lidiya Skoblikova (URS)
   2   Karin Enke (GDR)

Most Years Between Medals, Women
   8   Andrea Mitscherlich-Schöne (GDR)
   4   Lidiya Skoblikova (URS)
   4   Karin Enke (GDR)
   4   Christina Baas-Kaiser (HOL)
   4   Dianne Holum (USA)
   4   Kaija Mustonen (FIN)
   4   Natalya Petruseva (URS)
   4   Leah Poulos-Mueller (USA)
   4   Lyudmila Titova (URS)
   4   Valentina Stenina (URS)

Most Years Between Gold Medals, Women
   4   Lidiya Skoblikova (URS)
   4   Karin Enke (GDR)

Most Medals, Men
   7   Ivar Ballangrud (NOR)
   7   Clas Thunberg (FIN)
   6   Roald Larsen (NOR)
   5   Evgeniy Grishin (URS)
   5   Eric Heiden (USA)
   5   Knut Johannesen (NOR)

Most Gold Medals, Men
   5   Clas Thunberg (FIN)
   5   Eric Heiden (USA)
   4   Ivar Ballangrud (NOR)
   4   Evgeniy Grishin (URS)
   3   Adrianus "Ard" Schenk (HOL)
   3   Hjalmar Andersen (NOR)

Most Silver Medals, Men
   3   Cornelis "Kees" Verkerk (HOL)
   2   Twelve athletes tied with two.

Most Bronze Medals, Men
4	Roald Larsen (NOR)
3	Hans van Helden (HOL)
2	Six athletes tied with two.

Most Years Winning Medals, Men
3	Ivar Ballangrud (NOR)
3	Evgeniy Grishin (URS)
3	Knut Johannesen (NOR)
3	Cornelis "Kees" Verkerk (HOL)

Most Years Winning Gold Medals, Men
2	Ivar Ballangrud (NOR)
2	Clas Thunberg (FIN)
2	Evgeniy Grishin (URS)
2	Knut Johannesen (NOR)

Most Years Between Medals, Men
8	Ivar Ballangrud (NOR)
8	Evgeniy Grishin (URS)
8	Knut Johannesen (NOR)
8	Cornelis "Kees" Verkerk (HOL)
8	Alv Gjestvang (NOR)

Most Years Between Gold Medals, Men
8	Ivar Ballangrud (NOR)

Most Medals, Games
5	Roald Larsen (NOR-1924)
5	Clas Thunberg (FIN-1924)
5	Eric Heiden (USA-1980)
4	Ivar Ballangrud (NOR-1936)
4	Lidiya Skoblikova (URS-1964)
4	Tatiana Averina (URS-1976)
4	Karin Enke (GDR-1984)

Most Gold Medals, Games
5	Eric Heiden (USA-1980)
4	Lidiya Skoblikova (URS-1964)
3	Clas Thunberg (FIN-1924)
3	Ivar Ballangrud (NOR-1936)
3	Hjalmar Andersen (NOR-1952)
3	Adrianus "Ard" Schenk (HOL-1972)

Most Medals, Games, Women
4	Ivar Ballangrud (NOR-1936)
4	Tatyana Averina (URS-1976)
4	Karin Enke (GDR-1984)
3	Atje Keulen-Deelstra (HOL-1972)
3	Sheila Young (USA-1976)
3	Andrea Mitscherlich-Schöne (GDR-1984)

Most Gold Medals, Games, Women
4	Lidiya Skoblikova (URS-1964)
2	Lidiya Skoblikova (URS-1960)
2	Tatyana Averina (URS-1976)
2	Karin Enke (GDR-1984)

Most Medals, Games, Men
5	Eric Heiden (USA-1980)
5	Roald Larsen (NOR-1924)
5	Clas Thunberg (FIN-1924)
4	Ivar Ballangrud (NOR-1936)

Most Gold Medals, Games, Men
5	Eric Heiden (USA-1980)
3	Clas Thunberg (FIN-1924)
3	Ivar Ballangrud (NOR-1936)
3	Hjalmar Andersen (NOR-1952)
3	Adrianus "Ard" Schenk (HOL-1972)

Most Appearances
5	Colin Coates (AUS, 1968-84)
5	Örjan Sandler (SWE, 1964-80)
4	Cornelis "Kees" Broekman (HOL, 1948-60)
4	Ralph Olin (CAN, 1952-64)
4	Toivo Salonen (FIN, 1952-64)
4	Hroar Elvenes (NOR, 1952-64)
4	Evgeniy Grishin (URS, 1956-68)
4	Lisbeth Korsmo-Berg (NOR, 1968-80)
4	Monika Holzner-Pflug (FRG, 1972-84)

Most Appearances, Men
5	Colin Coates (AUS, 1968-84)
5	Örjan Sandler (SWE, 1964-80)
4	Cornelis "Kees" Broekman (HOL, 1948-60)
4	Hroar Elvenes (NOR, 1952-64)
4	Ralph Olin (CAN, 1952-64)
4	Toivo Salonen (FIN, 1952-64)
4	Evgeniy Grishin (URS, 1956-68)

Most Appearances, Women
4	Lisbeth Korsmo-Berg (NOR, 1968-80)
4	Monika Holzner-Pflug (FRG, 1972-84)

Youngest Medalist, Women
16-157	Anne Henning (USA-1972)
16-266	Dianne Holum (USA-1968)
17-112	Sylvia Albrecht (GDR-1980)
17-347	Monika Pflug (FRG-1972)
18-209	Ria Visser (HOL-1980)

Youngest Gold Medalist, Women
16-157	Anne Henning (USA-1972)
17-347	Monika Pflug (FRG-1972)
18-240	Karin Enke (GDR-1980)
20-005	Björg Eva Jensen (NOR-1980)
20-266	Dianne Holum (USA-1972)

Youngest Medalist, Men
   18-137 Alv Gjestvang (NOR-1956)
   19-009 Igor Malkov (URS-1984)
   19-063 Antero Ojala (FIN-1936)
   19-087 Per Ivar Moe (NOR-1964)
   19-131 Villy Haugen (NOR-1964)

Youngest Gold Medalist, Men
   19-009 Igor Malkov (URS-1984)
   20-363 Jonny Nilsson (SWE-1964)
   21-006 Sergei Fokichev (URS-1984)
   21-147 Jack Shea (USA-1932)
   21-291 Peter Mueller (USA-1976)

Oldest Medalist, Women
   37-184 Eevi Huttunen (FIN-1960)
   33-268 Christina Baas-Kaiser (HOL-1972)
   33-043 Atje Keulen-Deilstra (HOL-1972)
   29-268 Christina Baas-Kaiser (HOL-1968)
   29-035 Valentina Stenina (URS-1964)

Oldest Gold Medalist, Women
   33-268 Christina Baas-Kaiser (HOL-1972)
   28-120 Annie Borckink (HOL-1980)
   27-009 Galina Stepanskaya (URS-1976)
   26-190 Kaija Mustonen (FIN-1968)
   25-256 Helga Haase (GER-1960)

Oldest Medalist, Men
   38-246 Julius Skutnabb (FIN-1928)
   34-315 Clas Thunberg (FIN-1928)
   34-229 Julius Skutnabb (FIN-1924)
   31-343 Ivar Ballangrud (NOR-1936)
   31-337 Ruald Os (URS-1960)

Oldest Gold Medalist, Men
   34-315 Clas Thunberg (FIN-1928)
   34-229 Julius Skutnabb (FIN-1924)
   31-343 Ivar Ballangrud (NOR-1936)
   31-337 Ruald Os (URS-1960)
   30-201 Reidar Liaklev (NOR-1948)

Medals Won by Countries

	G	S	B	Tot
Norway	19	24	23	66
USSR	23	17	17	57
United States	16	14	8	38
The Netherlands	9	13	10	32
Finland	7	8	9	24
GDR	6	7	5	18
Sweden	5	4	5	14
Canada	2	3	6	11
FRG	3	-	-	3
Poland	-	1	1	2
North Korea	-	1	-	1
Japan	-	1	-	1
Austria	-	-	1	1
Totals	90	93	85	268

Medals Won by Countries, Men

	G	S	B	Tot
Norway	18	24	22	64
USSR	11	10	7	28
United States	13	6	3	22
The Netherlands	5	9	6	20
Finland	6	6	7	19
Sweden	5	4	5	14
Canada	2	2	6	10
FRG	2	-	-	2
GDR	-	-	2	2
Japan	-	1	-	1
Austria	-	-	1	1
Totals	62	62	59	183

*Two thirds in 1924 500 metres; two firsts/no second/three thirds in 1928 500 metres; three seconds/no third in 1948 500 metres; two thirds in 1952 500 metres; two firsts/no second in 1956 1500 metres; two firsts/no second in 1960 1500 metres; three seconds/no third in 1964 500 metres; two seconds/no third in 1968 500 metres; two seconds/no third in 1968 1500 metres; and two thirds in 1980 1000 metres.

Medals Won by Countries, Women

	G	S	B	Tot
USSR	12	7	10	29
United States	3	8	5	16
GDR	6	7	3	16
The Netherlands	4	4	4	12
Finland	1	2	2	5
Norway	1	-	1	2
Poland	-	1	1	2
FRG	1	-	-	1
Canada	-	1	-	1
North Korea	-	1	-	1
Totals	28	31	26	85

*Three seconds/no third in 1968 500 metres; and two seconds/no third in 1964 3000 metres.

Best Performance by Country at Each Olympics

		Men	Women	Overall
1924	-	Finland	---	---
1928	-	Norway	---	---
1932	-	United States	---	---
1936	-	Norway	---	---
1948	-	Norway	---	---
1952	-	Norway	---	---
1956	-	USSR	---	---
1960	-	USSR	USSR	USSR
1964	-	Norway	USSR	USSR
1968	-	Norway	Netherlands	Netherlands
1972	-	Netherlands	Netherlands	Netherlands
1976	-	USSR	USSR	USSR
1980	-	United States	GDR	United States
1984	-	USSR	GDR	GDR

Speed Skating - Olympic Record Progressions - Men

500 metres

45.6	=8	Joseph Moore (USA)	1924
45.0	5	Asser Wallenius (FIN)	1924
44.2	2	Oscar Olsen (NOR)	1924
44.0	1	Charles Jewtraw (USA)	1924
43.6	=3	John Farrell (USA)	1928
43.4	=1	Clas Thunberg (FIN)	1928
43.4	=1	Bernt Evensen (NOR)	1928
43.4	1	Jack Shea (USA)	1932
43.4	1	Ivar Ballangrud (NOR)	1936
43.2	=2	Robert Fitzgerald (USA)	1948
43.1	1	Finn Helgesen (NOR)	1948
40.2	1	Evgeniy Grishin (URS)	1956
40.2	1	Evgeniy Grishin (URS)	1960
40.1	1	Terry McDermott (USA)	1964
39.69	2	Hasse Börjes (SWE)	1972
39.44	1	Erhard Keller (FRG)	1972
39.17	1	Evgeniy Kulikov (URS)	1976
38.03	1	Eric Heiden (USA)	1980

1,000 metres

1:21.23	6	Gaetan Boucher (CAN)	1976
1:19.32	1	Peter Mueller (USA)	1976
1:15.18	1	Eric Heiden (USA)	1980

1,500 metres

2:54.4	16		André Gegout (FRA)	1924
2:20.8	1		Clas Thunberg (FIN)	1924
2:20.2	2		Ivar Ballangrud (NOR)	1936
2:19.2	1		Charles Mathiesen (NOR)	1936
2:17.6	1		Sverre Farstad (NOR)	1948
2:09.4	3		Toivo Salonen (FIN)	1956
2:08.6	=1	WR	Evgeniy Grishin (URS)	1956
2:08.6	=1	WR	Yuriy Mikhailov (URS)	1956
2:07.1	11		Aleksandr Kerchenko (URS)	1968
2:05.0	=2		Adrianus "Ard" Schenk (HOL)	1968
2:03.4	1		Cornelis "Kees" Verkerk (HOL)	1968
2:02.96	1		Adrianus "Ard" Schenk (HOL)	1972
2:00.87	3		Hans van Helden (HOL)	1976
1:59.38	1		Jan Egil Storholt (NOR)	1976
1:57.95	6		Jan Egil Storholt (NOR)	1980
1:55.44	1		Eric Heiden (USA)	1980

5,000 metres

9:08.6	9		Leonhard Quaglia (FRA)	1924
8:59.0	7		Frithjof Paulsen (NOR)	1924
8:54.6	5		Harald Strøm (NOR)	1924
8:48.4	2		Julius Skutnabb (FIN)	1924
8:39.0	1		Clas Thunberg (FIN)	1924
8:30.1	3		Antero Ojala (FIN)	1936
8:19.6	1		Ivar Ballangrud (NOR)	1936
8:10.6	1		Hjalmar Andersen (NOR)	1952
8:04.1	9		Helmut Kuhnert (GDR)	1956
8:00.2	=4		Willem de Graaff (HOL)	1956
7:48.7	1		Boris Shilkov (URS)	1956
7:48.3	5		Hermann Strutz (AUT)	1964
7:45.1	4		Viktor Kosichkin (URS)	1964
7:38.6	2		Per Ivar Moe (NOR)	1964
7:38.4	1		Knut Johannesen (NOR)	1964
7:35.9	9		Kimmo Koskinen (FIN)	1968
7:23.3	2	WR	Cornelis "Kees" Verkerk (HOL)	1968
7:22.4	1	WR	Fred Anton Maier (HOL)	1968
7:05.59	3		Tom Erik Oxholm (NOR)	1980
7:02.29	1		Eric Heiden (USA)	1980

10,000 metres

19:36.2	12		Joseph Moore (USA)	1924
18:18.6	5		Harald Strøm (NOR)	1924
18:12.2	3		Roald Larsen (NOR)	1924
18:04.8	1		Julius Skutnabb (FIN)	1924
[17:41.3]	*		Alexander Hurd (CAN)	1932
17:56.5	h1		Alexander Hurd (CAN)	1932
17:41.2	4		Charles Mathiesen (NOR)	1936
17:30.0	3		Max Stiepl (AUT)	1936
17:24.3	1		Ivar Ballangrud (NOR)	1936
16:45.8	1		Hjalmar Andersen (NOR)	1952
16:42.3	3		Oleg Goncharenko (URS)	1956
16:36.9	2		Knut Johannesen (NOR)	1956
16:35.9	1		Sigvard Ericsson (SWE)	1956
16:14.2	3	WR	Kjell Bäckman (SWE)	1960
15:46.6	1	WR	Knut Johannesen (NOR)	1960
15:23.9	2		Fred Anton Maier (NOR)	1968
15:23.6	1		Johnny Höglin (SWE)	1968
15:20.08	5		Valeri Lavrushkin (URS)	1972
15:07.08	3		Sten Stensen (NOR)	1972
15:04.70	2		Cornelis "Kees" Verkerk (HOL)	1972
15:01.35	1		Adrianus "Ard" Schenk (HOL)	1972
14:53.30	2		Sten Stensen (NOR)	1976
14:50.59	1		Piet Kleine (HOL)	1976
14:36.60	3		Tom Erik Oxholm (NOR)	1980
14:28.13	1	WR	Eric Heiden (USA)	1980

*Hurd's time was done in heats which were later annulled because of protests.

Speed Skating - Olympic Record Progressions - Women

500 metres

46.0	2	Natalya Donchenko (URS)	1960
45.9	1	Helga Haase (GDR)	1960
45.4	2	Irina Egorova (URS)	1964
45.0	1	Lidiya Skoblikova (URS)	1964
44.75	5	Monika Pflug (FRG)	1972
44.45	3	Lyudmila Titova (URS)	1972
43.73	*	Anne Henning (USA)	1972
43.33	1	Anne Henning (USA)	1972
43.12	2	Cathy Priestner (CAN)	1976
42.76	1	Sheila Young (USA)	1976
42.47	4	Ann-Sofie Järnström (SWE)	1980
41.78	1	Karin Enke (GDR)	1980
41.50	3	Natalya Chive (URS)	1984
41.02	1	Christa Rothenburger (GDR)	1984

*Henning was interfered with on this skate and was allowed to restart.

1,000 metres

1:34.1	1		Klara Guseva (URS)	1960
1:33.2	1		Lidiya Skoblikova (URS)	1964
1:32.9	2		Lyudmila Titova (URS)	1968
1:32.6	1		Carolina Geijssen (HOL)	1968
1:31.40	1		Monika Pflug (FRG)	1972
1:29.54	5		Monika Pflug-Holzner (FRG)	1976
1:28.57	2		Leah Poulos (USA)	1976
1:28.43	1		Tatyana Averina (URS)	1976
1:28.18	9		Sylvia Filipsson (SWE)	1980
1:24.10	1		Natalya Petruseva (URS)	1980
1:23.98	5		Christa Rothenberger (GDR)	1984
1:22.83	2		Andrea Schöne (GDR)	1984
1:21.61	1		Karin Enke (GDR)	1984

1,500 metres

2:28.7	4		Klara Guseva (URS)	1960
2:25.7	2		Elwira Seroczynska (POL)	1960
2:25.2	1		Lidiya Skoblikova (URS)	1960
2:22.6	1		Lidiya Skoblikova (URS)	1964
2:22.4	1		Kaija Mustonen (FIN)	1968
2:22.05	3		Atje Keulen-Deelstra (HOL)	1972
2:20.85	1		Dianne Holum (USA)	1972
2:18.99	4		Lisbeth Korsmo (NOR)	1976
2:17.96	3		Tatyana Averina (URS)	1976
2:16.58	1		Galina Stepanskaya (URS)	1976
2:13.10	7		Beth Heiden (USA)	1980
2:12.35	2		Ria Visser (HOL)	1980
2:10.95	1		Annie Borckink (HOL)	1980
2:05.29	2		Andrea Schöne (GDR)	1984
2:03.42	1	WR	Karin Enke (GDR)	1984

3,000 metres

5:48.3	17	Gisela Toews (GDR)	1960
5:32.2	11	Elsa Einarsson (SWE)	1960
5:30.0	9	Tamara Rylova (URS)	1960
5:26.2	6	Helena Pilejczykowa (POL)	1960
5:25.5	5	Christina Scherling (SWE)	1960
5:16.9	2	Valentina Stenina (URS)	1960
5:14.3	1	Lidiya Skoblikova (URS)	1960
5:05.1	5	Wilhelmina Burgmeijer (HOL)	1968
5:03.9	4	Kaija-Liisa Keskivitikka (FIN)	1968
4:56.2	1	Johanna Schut (HOL)	1968
4:52.14	1	Christina Baas-Kaiser (HOL)	1972
4:46.67	5	Ines Bautzmann (GDR)	1976
4:45.19	1	Tatyana Averina (URS)	1976
4:32.13	1	Björg Eva Jensen (NOR)	1980
4:24.79	1	Andrea Schöne (GDR)	1984

DISCONTINUED SPORTS

CRICKET

Years in the Olympics: 1900

CROQUET & ROGUE

Years in the Olympics: 1900, 1904. (In 1900, this event was
  contested as croquet, while in 1904 the slightly more difficult
  form of roque was used.)

GOLF

Years in the Olympics: 1900, 1904. (Women competed in 1900.)

JEU DE PAUME (COURT TENNIS or REAL TENNIS)

Years in the Olympics: 1908. (In addition it was contested as a
  demonstration sport in 1928.)

LACROSSE

Years in the Olympics: 1904, 1908. (In addition it was contested
  as a demonstration sport in 1928, 1932, and 1948.)

MOTORBOATING

Years in the Olympics: 1908

POLO

Years in the Olympics: 1900, 1908, 1920, 1924, 1936.

Most Medals
    2   Sir John Wodehouse (GBR)
    2   Frederick Barrett (GBR)
    2   Walter Buckmaster (GBR)
    2   Frederick Freake (GBR)

Most Gold Medals
    1   Many athletes tied with one.

Youngest Medalist
    19-243   Frederick Roe (USA-1924)
    21-239   Roberto Cavanagh (ARG-1936)
    24-087   Frederick Freake (GBR-1900)

Youngest Gold Medalist
    21-239   Roberto Cavanagh (ARG-1936)
    29-019   Juan Miles (ARG-1924)
    30-125   Luis Duggan (ARG-1936)

Oldest Medalist
    52-358   John Beresford (GBR-1900)
    52-169   Foxhall Keene (GBR/USA-1900)
    49-029   Frederick Guest (GBR-1924)

Oldest Gold Medalist
    52-169   Foxhall Keene (GBR/USA-1900)
    46-181   Manuel Andrada (ARG-1936)
    42-181   Teignmouth Melvill (GBR-1920)

RACKETS

Years in the Olympics: 1908

RUGBY UNION FOOTBALL

Years in the Olympics: 1900, 1908, 1920, 1924

Most Medals
    2   Daniel Carroll (AUS/USA)
    2   Charles Doe (USA)
    2   John O'Neil (USA)
    2   Jack Patrick (USA)
    2   Rudolph Scholz (USA)

Most Gold Medals
    2   Daniel Carroll (AUS/USA)
    2   Charles Doe (USA)
    2   John O'Neil (USA)
    2   Jack Patrick (USA)
    2   Rudolph Scholz (USA)

Youngest Medalist
    16-245 Daniel Carroll (AUS-1908)
    17-138 Eugen Sfetescu (ROM-1924)
    18-138 Soare Sterian (ROM-1924)

Youngest Gold Medalist
    16-245 Daniel Carroll (AUS-1908)
    20-231 Heaton Wrenn (USA-1920)
    21-289 John Hickey (AUS-1908)

Oldest Medalist
    32-302 Marcel Lubin-Lubrère (FRA-1924)
    31-138 Atanasie Tanasescu (ROM-1924)
    30-224 Alan Williams (USA-1924)

Oldest Gold Medalist
    30-224 Alan Williams (USA-1924)
    30-116 Norman Slater (USA-1924)
    29-227 Frantz Reichel (FRA-1900)

TENNIS (LAWN TENNIS)

Tennis was contested in every Olympics from 1896 through 1924. It
    was revised purely as a demonstration sport at the Olympic Games
    of 1968 and 1984. It is scheduled to return to the Olympic
    program as a full medal sport in 1988. The records for tennis
    in the Olympics may, therefore, be found in the section on
    current summer sports under "Tennis".

TUG-OF-WAR

Years in the Olympics: 1900, 1904, 1906, 1908, 1912, 1920. (Tug-
    of-war was always contested as a part of the track & field
    athletics program.)

Most Medals
    3   John Shepherd (GBR)
    3   Frederick Humphreys (GBR)
    3   Edwin Mills (GBR)
    2   Alexander Munro (GBR)
    2   Walter Chaffe (GBR)
    2   Joseph Dowler (GBR)
    2   John Sewell (GBR)

Most Gold Medals
    2   John Shepherd (GBR)
    2   Frederick Humphreys (GBR)
    2   Edwin Mills (GBR)

Youngest Medalist
    19-102   Karl Gustaf Staaf (SWE-1900)
    21-127   Heinrich Schneidereit (GER-1906)
    22-013   Axel Norling (SWE-1906)

Youngest Gold Medalist
    19-102   Karl Gustaf Staaf (SWE-1900)
    21-127   Heinrich Schneidereit (GER-1906)
    23-119   Karl Kaltenbach (GER-1906)

Oldest Medalist
    42-203   Frederick Humphreys (GBR-1920)
    42-098   Walter Chaffe (GBR-1912)
    42-094   Edwin Mills (GBR-1920)

Oldest Gold Medalist
    42-203   Frederick Humphreys (GBR-1920)
    42-094   Edwin Mills (GBR-1920)
    38-300   Harry Stiff (GBR-1920)

DEMONSTRATION SPORTS - SUMMER OLYMPIC GAMES

AMERICAN FOOTBALL

Years in the Olympics: 1932

AUSSIE RULES (AUSTRALIAN RULES FOOTBALL)

Years in the Olympics: 1956

BADMINTON

Years in the Olympics: 1972

BASEBALL (American and Finnish)

Years in the Olympics: 1912, 1936, 1956, 1964, 1984 (American).
    1952 (Finnish)

BASKETBALL

Years in the Olympics: 1904.   (Basketball became a regular Olympic
    sport in 1936.)

BUDO

Years in the Olympics: 1964   (Included exhibitions of Japanese
   archery, fencing, and wrestling.)

CANOEING

Years in the Olympics: 1924.   (Canoeing became a regular Olympic
   sport in 1936 and has not since left the Olympic program.   In
   addition, it has only recently been discovered that a single
   canoe race was held at the 1906 Intercalated Games which has
   been included in the rowing results.)

GLIDING

Years in the Olympics: 1936

JEU DE PAUME (COURT TENNIS or REAL TENNIS)

Years in the Olympics: 1928   (In addition, it was contested as a
   regular medal sport in 1908.)

LACROSSE

Years in the Olympics: 1928, 1932, 1948.   (In addition, lacrosse
   was contested as a regular medal sport in 1904 and 1908.)

PELOTA BASQUE

Years in the Olympics: 1924, 1968

TABLE TENNIS

Years in the Olympics: Scheduled to be a demonstration sport in
   1988 at Seoul.

TENNIS (LAWN TENNIS)

Tennis was a regular Olympic sport from 1896-1924, was
   discontinued and then appeared in 1968 and 1984 as a
   demonstration.   See "Tennis" under the section on current summer
   sports for the records of tennis in the Olympics.

WATER SKIING

Years in the Olympics: 1972

DEMONSTRATION SPORTS - OLYMPIC WINTER GAMES

BANDY

Years in the Olympics: 1952

CURLING

Years in the Olympics: 1924, 1932, 1936, 1964. It is also
  scheduled to be a demonstration sport in 1988 at Calgary.

DOGSLED RACING

Years in the Olympics: 1932

MILITARY PATROL

Years in the Olympics: 1924, 1928, 1936, 1948.

WINTER PENTATHLON

Years in the Olympics: 1948

ART COMPETITIONS

Years in the Olympics: 1912, 1920, 1924, 1928, 1932, 1936, 1948.

Most Medals
    3   Alex Walter Diggelmann (SUI)
    3   Joseph Petersen (DEN)
    2   Jean Jacoby (LUX)
    2   Werner March (GER)

Most Gold Medals
    2   Jean Jacoby (LUX)

Winners of Art and Sport Medals in the Olympics
    Walter Winans (USA) [1908 Shooting, 1912 Sculpture]
    Alfred Hájos (HUN) [1896 Swimming, 1924 Architecture]

Following are synopses of the Olympic records of every
country to have ever competed in the Olympic Games. After each
country can be found the proper name of the country, in English
and its native language, the name of its Olympic Committee, and
data about the country, including area, population, location,
government, religions and languages. That is followed by a short
history of the country's Olympic participation. For all countries
that have won three or more medals, a list is given with the
medals separated into categories for winter, summer, men and
women. Finally, for each country with three or more Olympic
medals, a list of Olympic records for that country is given,
including most medals, most gold medals, youngest, oldest, and
first medalist and gold medalist. All the records are separated
into categories for winter, summer, men and women. In this
section, records are two-deep for medals, and one-deep for age
records.

AFGHANISTAN (AFG)
De Afghanistan Democrateek Jamhuriat
Democratic Republic of Afghanistan
National Olympic Committee of Afghanistan - 1935

Area: 251,773 sq. mi. Population (1985 est.): 15,056,000
Located: Between Soviet Central Asia and the Indian subcontinent.
Language(s): Pashta, Dari Persian, Uzbek.
Religion(s): Sunni Muslim 80%, Shiite Muslim 20%
Government: People's Republic

Olympic History: Afghanistan first competed at the 1936 Olympics
  in Berlin. The country has since failed to compete at the
  Olympics of 1952, 1980, and 1984. They have yet to win a medal
  and have never competed at the Olympic Winter Games.

ALBANIA (ALB)
Republika Popullore Socialiste e Shqiperise
Socialist Republic of Albania
Comité Olympique de la République Populaire Socialiste d'Albanie -
  1959

Area: 11,100 sq. mi. Population (1985 est.): 3,046,000
Located: On the Southeast coast of the Adriatic sea, north of
  Greece.
Language(s): Albanian (Tosk is official dialect), Greek
Religion(s): officially atheist, historically mostly Muslims
Government: Communist

Olympic History: Albania has competed at only one Olympic Games, those of 1972 in Munich. They did not win any medals but did have one successful competitor, Ymez Pampuri, a weightlifter in the featherweight category who broke the Olympic record in the press and led the competition briefly. He eventually finished ninth.

ALGERIA (ALG)
al-Jumhuriya al-Jazairiya ad-Dimuqratiya ash-Shabiya
Democratic and Popular Republic of Algeria
Comité National Olympique Algérien - 1964

Area: 918,497 sq. mi. Population (1985 est.):   22,107,000
Located: Northwest Africa.
Language(s):   Arabic (official), Berber, French
Religion(s):   Sunni Muslim
Government: Republic

Olympic History: Algeria first competed at the 1964 Olympic Games. They have since competed at every summer Games with the exception of 1980. They have not yet competed at the Winter Olympics. They have, however, won two medals, both bronzes. These were won in 1984 boxing events by Mohammed Zaoui in the middleweight class, and by Mustapha Moussa in the light-heavyweight class. It can be argued that they have won a gold medal, however. In 1928, Mohammed Boughéra El-Ouafi won the marathon race representing France, although he was a native Algerian.

ANDORRA (AND)
Principat d'Andorra
Principality of Andorra
Comité Olympique Andorran - 1975

Area: 188 sq. mi. Population (1985 est.):   43,000
Located: In Pyrenees Mountains, between France and Spain.
Language(s):   Catalan (official), Spanish, French
Religion(s):   Roman Catholic
Government: Co-principality

Olympic History: Andorra first competed at the Olympic Winter Games in Innsbruck in 1976. They have competed at every Olympics, summer and winter, since.

ANGOLA (ANG)
Republica Popular de Angola
People's Republic of Angola
Comité Olímpico Angolano - 1979

Area: 481,353 sq. mi. Population (1985 est.): 7,948,000
Located: In Southwest Africa on the Atlantic coast.
Language(s): Portuguese (official), various Bantu languages
Religion(s): Roman Catholic 46%, Protestant 12%, animist 42%
Government: People's Republic, one party rule

Olympic History: Angola competed at the 1980 Olympics in Moscow,
  their only Olympic appearance.

ANTIGUA (ANT)
Antigua and Barbuda
Antigua Olympic and Commonwealth Games Association - 1976

Area: 171 sq. mi. Population (1985 est.): 80,000
Located: Islands in the Eastern Caribbean.
Language(s): English
Religion(s): Anglican
Government: Constitutional monarchy with a British-style
  parliament

Olympic History: Antigua has competed twice at the Olympics - at
  the celebrations of 1976 and 1984.

ANTILLES
  See Jamaica and Trinidad and Tobago.

ARGENTINA (ARG)
Republica Argentina
Argentine Republic
Comité Olímpico Argentino - 1927

Area: 1,065,189 sq. mi. Population (1985 est.): 30,708,000
Located: Southern South America, facing the east coast.
Language(s): Spanish (official), English, Italian, German, French
Religion(s): Roman Catholic 92%
Government: Republic

Olympic History: In 1908 Henri Torromé became Argentina's first
  Olympian when he competed at the "Summer" Games in figure
  skating. In 1920, Rodriquez, a boxer, competed in the
  lightweight class, losing his first match, but becoming
  Argentina's first true summer Olympian in the process. In 1924
  Argentina was finally represented at the Olympics in Paris with
  a full team. They have since competed at every summer Games
  with the exception of the 1980 Moscow Olympics. In the Olympic
  Winter Games, their first "true" appearance (after Torromé in
  1908) came in 1928 when they entered two five-man bobsled teams.
  They have since missed the Winter Games of 1932, 1936, and 1956.

Medal Count:

	Men				Women				Totals			
	GO	SI	BR	TOT	GO	SI	BR	TOT	GO	SI	BR	TOT
Summer	13	16	13	42	–	2	–	2	13	18	13	44
Winter	–	–	–	–	–	–	–	–	–	–	–	–
Totals	13	16	13	42	–	2	–	2	13	18	13	44

Most Medals, Men
2   Alberto Demiddi (ROW)
2   Humberto Selvetti (WLT)

Most Gold Medals, Men
1   Twenty-athletes tied with one

First Medalist, Men
12 JUL 1924 Luis Brunetto (TAF-TJ)
12 JUL 1924 Polo Team

First Gold Medalist, Men
12 JUL 1924 Polo Team

Youngest Medalist, Men
18-213 Guillermo Lovell (BOX-1936)

Youngest Gold Medalist, Men
20-112 Santiago Alberto Lovell (BOX-1932)

Oldest Medalist, Men
56-160 Julio Sieburger (YAC-1948)

Oldest Gold Medalist, Men
46-181 Manuel Andrada (POL-1936)

Most Medals, Women
1   Jeannette Campbell (SWI)
1   Noemi Simonetto de Portela (TAF)

First Medalist, Women
10 AUG 1936 Jeannette Campbell (SWI-100 free)

Youngest Medalist, Women
20-115 Jeannette Campbell (SWI-1936)

Oldest Medalist, Women
22-185 Noemi Simonetto de Portela (TAF-1948)

ARUBA (ARU)
Aruba Olympic Committee - 1986

Area: 75 sq. mi. Population (1985 est.): 244,000
Located: Islands in the Caribbean
Language(s): Dutch
Religion(s): Roman Catholic
Government: Autonomous member of The Netherlands, became
  independent 01 JAN 1986

Olympic History: Aruba has not yet competed in the Olympic Games.

AUSTRALIA (AUS)
Commonwealth of Australia
Australian Olympic Federation - 1895

Area: 2,966,200 sq. mi. Population (1985 est.): 15,345,000
Language(s): English, aboriginal languages
Religion(s): Anglican 36%, other Protestant 25%, Roman Catholic
  33%
Government: Democratic, federal state system

Olympic History: Australia has competed at every summer Olympic
  Games with the sole exception of the 1980 Moscow Olympics. They
  have also competed at the Olympic Winter Games - those of 1936
  and continuously since 1956. Australia has been successful in
  many sports, but particularly so in swimming and track & field.
  In swimming, several times they have been the top nation
  overall. They have yet to win a medal in the Winter Olympics.

Olympic Hosts:
        1956 - Melbourne - The Games of the XVIth Olympiad

Medal Count:

	Men				Women				Totals			
	GO	SI	BR	TOT	GO	SI	BR	TOT	GO	SI	BR	TOT
Summer	43+	42	61	146+	24	19	21	64	67+	61	82	210+
Winter	-	-	-	-	-	-	-	-	-	-	-	-
Totals	43+	42	61	146+	24	19	21	64	67+	61	82	210+

Most Medals, Men
    6   Frank Beaurepaire (SWI)
    6   Murray Rose (SWI)

Most Gold Medals, Men
    4   Murray Rose (SWI)
    2   John Devitt (SWI)
    2   Michael Wenden (SWI)
    2   David Thiele (SWI)
    2   Lawrence Morgan (EQU)
    2   Henry Pearce (ROW)
    2   Jon Henricks (SWI)
    2   Edwin Flack (TAF)
    2   John Anderson (YAC)

First Medalist/Gold Medalist, Men
  07 APR 1896 Edwin Flack (TAF-1500)

Youngest Medalist/Gold Medalist, Men
  16-245 Daniel Carroll (RUG-1908)

Oldest Medalist, Men
  61-131 William Roycroft (EQU-1976)

Oldest Gold Medalist, Men
  59-024 William Northman (YAC-1964)

Most Medals, Women
  8   Dawn Fraser (SWI)
  7   Shirley Strickland de la Hunty (TAF)

Most Gold Medals, Women
  4   Dawn Fraser (SWI)
  4   Betty Cuthbert (TAF)

First Medalist, Women
  02 JUL 1912 Fanny Durack (SWI-100 free)
  02 JUL 1912 Wilhelmina Wylie (SWI-100 free)

First Gold Medalist, Women
  02 JUL 1912 Fanny Durack (SWI-100 free)

Youngest Medalist/Gold Medalist, Women
  14-184 Sandra Anne Morgan (SWI-1956)

Oldest Medalist, Women
  52-143 Patricia Dench (SHO-1984)

Oldest Gold Medalist, Women
  31-137 Shirley Strickland de la Hunty (TAF-1956)

Most Medals, Men, Games
  4   Stanley Rowley (TAF-1900)
  4   Michael Wenden (SWI-1968)

Most Gold Medals, Men, Games
  3   Murray Rose (SWI-1956)
  2   Edwin Flack (TAF-1896)
  2   Jon Henricks (SWI-1956)
  2   Lawrence Morgan (EQU-1960)
  2   Michael Wenden (SWI-1968)

Most Medals, Women, Games
  5   Shane Gould (SWI-1972)
  3   Shirley Strickland (TAF-1948)
  3   Lorraine Crapp (SWI-1956)
  3   Betty Cuthbert (TAF-1956)
  3   Dawn Fraser (SWI-1956)
  3   Dawn Fraser (SWI-1960)

Most Gold Medals, Women, Games
    3   Betty Cuthbert (TAF-1956)
    3   Shane Gould (SWI-1972)

AUSTRALASIA
    See Australia and New Zealand.

AUSTRIA (AUT)
Republik Österreich
Republic of Austria
Österreichisches Olympisches Komitee - 1912

Area: 32,374 sq. mi. Population (1985 est.): 7,451,000
Located: South Central Europe, southeast of Germany.
Language(s): German 95%, Slovene
Religion(s): Roman Catholic 85%
Government: Parliamentary democracy

Olympic History: Austria competed at the first Olympics in 1896
    and has missed only one Games since - those of 1920 when they
    were not invited, having been an aggressor nation in World War
    I. Austria has also competed at every Olympic Winter Games,
    where it has often been the dominant nation in alpine skiing.
    It is one of only three countries (Norway, Liechtenstein) to
    have won more medals at the Winter Olympics than at the Summer
    Olympics.

Olympic Hosts:
        1964 - Innsbruck - The IXth Olympic Winter Games
        1976 - Innsbruck - The XIIth Olympic Winter Games

Medal Count:

| | Men | | | | Women | | | | Totals | | | |
	GO	SI	BR	TOT	GO	SI	BR	TOT	GO	SI	BR	TOT
Summer	14	25	26	65	3	2	7	12	17	27	33	77
Winter	17	20	19+	56+	8	13	10+	31+	25	33	30	88
Totals	31	45	45+	121+	11	15	17+	43+	42	60	63	165

Most Medals, Men
    3   Julius Lenhart (GYM)
    3   Anton "Toni" Sailer (ASK)
    3   Otto Scheff (SWI)
    3   Josef "Pepi" Stiegler (ASK)
    3   Otto Wahle (SWI)
    3   Adolf Schmal (CYC)

Most Gold Medals, Men
    3   Anton "Toni" Sailer (ASK)
    2   Julius Lenhart (GYM)

First Medalist, Men
   11 APR 1896   Paul Neumann (SWI-500 free)
   11 APR 1896   Otto Herschmann (SWI-100 free)
   11 APR 1896   Adolf Schmal (CYC-10K)

First Gold Medalist, Men
   11 APR 1896   Paul Neumann (SWI-500 free)

Youngest Medalist/Gold Medalist, Men
   16-134   Otto Scheff (SWI-1906)

Oldest Medalist, Men
   39-327   Gerhard Petritsch (SHO-1980)

Oldest Gold Medalist, Men
   34-361   Hubert Hammerer (SHO-1960)

Most Medals, Women
   3   Trude Jochum-Beiser (ASK)
   3   Annemarie Moser-Pröll (ASK)
   3   Ellen Müller-Preiss (FEN)

Most Gold Medals, Women
   2   Trude Jochum-Beiser (ASK)
   1   Ellen Müller-Preiss (ASK)
   1   Elisabeth "Sissy" Theurer (EQU)
   1   Herma Bauma (TAF)
   1   Christl Haas (ASK)
   1   Olga Pall (ASK)
   1   Annemarie Moser-Pröll (ASK)
   1   Herma Planck-Szabo (FSK)
   1   Beatrix Schuba (FSK)
   1   Helene Engelmann (FSK)
   1   Elisabeth Schwarz (FSK)

First Medalist, Women
   15 JUL 1912   Swimming Freestyle Relay Team

First Gold Medalist, Women, Summer
   03 AUG 1932   Ellen Preis (FEN-Foil)

Youngest Medalist, Women, Summer
   16-153   Margarete Adler (SWI-1912)

Youngest Gold Medalist, Women, Summer
   20-089   Ellen Müller-Preiss (FEN-1932)

Oldest Medalist, Women
   36-088   Ellen Müller-Preiss (FEN-1948)

Oldest Gold Medalist, Women
   33-190   Herma Bauma (TAF-1948)

Most Medals, Winter, Men
3   Anton "Toni" Sailer (ASK)
3   Josef "Pepi" Stiegler (ASK)

Most Gold Medals, Winter, Men
3   Anton "Toni" Sailer (ASK)
2   Karl Schäfer (FSK)

First Medalist/Gold Medalist, Winter, Men
31 JAN 1924 Alfred Berger (FSK-Pairs)

Youngest Medalist, Winter, Men
17-306 Manfred Stengl (LUG-1964)

Youngest Gold Medalist, Winter, Men
20-073 Anton "Toni" Sailer (ASK-1956)

Oldest Medalist, Winter, Men
32-159 Heinrich "Heini" Messner (ASK-1972)

Oldest Gold Medalist, Winter, Men
26-273 Karl Schäfer (FSK-1936)

Most Medals, Winter, Women
3   Trude Jochum-Beiser (ASK)
3   Annemarie Moser-Pröll (ASK)

Most Gold Medals, Winter, Women
2   Trude Jochum-Beiser (ASK)
1   Christl Haas (ASK)
1   Olga Pall (ASK)
1   Annemarie Moser-Pröll (ASK)
1   Herma Planck-Szabo (FSK)
1   Beatrix Schuba (FSK)
1   Helene Engelmann (FSK)
1   Elisabeth Schwarz (FSK)

First Medalist/Gold Medalist, Winter, Women
29 JAN 1924 Herma Planck-Szabo (FSK-Women)

Youngest Medalist, Winter, Women
15-260 Ingrid Wendl (FSK-1956)

Youngest Gold Medalist, Winter, Women
19-259 Elisabeth Schwarz (FSK-1956)

Oldest Medalist, Winter, Women
30-201 Dorothea Hochleitner (ASK-1956)

Oldest Gold Medalist, Winter, Women
26-327 Annemarie Moser-Pröll (ASK-1980)

Most Medals, Men, Games
    3   Adolf Schmal (CYC-1896)
    3   Julius Lenhart (GYM-1904)
    3   Anton "Toni" Sailer (ASK-1956)

Most Gold Medals, Men, Games
    3   Anton "Toni" Sailer (ASK-1956)
    2   Julius Lenhart (GYM-1904)

Most Medals, Women, Games
    2   Trude Beiser (ASK-1948)
    2   Erika Mahringer (ASK-1948)
    2   Annemarie Pröll (ASK-1972)

Most Gold Medals, Women, Games
    1   Herma Planck-Szabo (FSK-1924)
    1   Helene Engelmann (FSK-1924)
    1   Ellen Müller-Preiss (FEN-1932)
    1   Herma Bauma (TAF-1932)
    1   Trude Beiser (ASK-1948)
    1   Trude Jochum-Beiser (ASK-1952)
    1   Elisabeth Schwarz (FSK-1956)
    1   Christl Haas (ASK-1964)
    1   Olga Pall (ASK-1968)
    1   Beatrix Schuba (FSK-1972)
    1   Annemarie Moser-Pröll (ASK-1980)
    1   Elisabeth "Sissy" Theurer (EQU-1980)

Most Medals, Winter, Men, Games
    3   Anton "Toni" Sailer (ASK-1956)
    2   Manfred Schmid (LUG-1968)
    2   Karl Schnabl (NSK-1976)

Most Gold Medals, Winter, Men, Games
    3   Anton "Toni" Sailer (ASK-1956)
    1   Seventeen athletes tied with one

Most Medals, Winter, Women, Games
    2   Trude Beiser (ASK-1948)
    2   Erika Mahringer (ASK-1948)
    2   Annemarie Pröll (ASK-1972)

Most Gold Medals, Winter, Women, Games
    1   Herma Planck-Szabo (FSK-1924)
    1   Helene Engelmann (FSK-1924)
    1   Trude Beiser (ASK-1948)
    1   Trude Jochum-Beiser (ASK-1952)
    1   Elisabeth Schwarz (FSK-1956)
    1   Christl Haas (ASK-1964)
    1   Olga Pall (ASK-1968)
    1   Beatrix Schuba (FSK-1972)
    1   Annemarie Moser-Pröll (ASK-1980)

THE BAHAMAS (BAH)
The Commonwealth of the Bahamas
Bahamas Olympic Association - 1952

Area: 5,380 sq. mi. Population (1985 est.): 230,000
Located: A group of islands east of Florida in the Atlantic.
Language(s): English
Religion(s): Baptist 29%, Anglican 23%, Roman Catholic 22%
Government: Independent commonwealth

Olympic History: The Bahamas competed at every Olympics from 1952
through 1976 and again competed at Los Angeles in 1984. Their
top sport has been yachting in which they have won their only
two medals. These both came in the Star Class, a bronze in 1956
and a gold medal in 1964. A member of both of these crews was
Durwood Knowles, who competed seven times in the Olympics as a
yachtsman. In 1948, he competed for Great Britain, but then
through 1972 he represented The Bahamas.

BAHRAIN (BRN)
Dawlat al-Bahraya
State of Bahrain
Bahrain Olympic Committee - 1979

Area: 258 sq. mi. Population (1985 est.): 431,000
Located: Island in the Persian Gulf.
Language(s): Arabic (official), Persian
Religion(s): Sunni Muslim 40%, Shiite Muslim 60%
Government: Traditional emirate

Olympic History: Bahrain competed at its first Olympic Games at
Los Angeles in 1984 with a team of one track & field athlete,
four modern pentathletes, five shooters, and two swimmers. All
of these were men.

BANGLADESH (BAN)
Gama Prajatantri Bangladesh
People's Republic of Bangladesh
Bangladesh Olympic Association - 1980

Former Name: Pakistan (East Pakistan) (independence declared 26
MAR 1971)
Area: 55,598 sq. mi. Population (1985 est.): 101,408,000
Located: In Southern Asia, on north bend of Bay of Bengal.
Language(s): Bengali (official), English
Religion(s): Muslims 83%, Hindu 16%
Government: Martial law.

Olympic History: Finishing eighth and last in heat eight, round
one of the men's 100 metre dash at the 1984 Los Angeles Olympics
was Saidurrahman Dawn. He is, to date, the only Olympic
competitor from this relatively new country.

BARBADOS (BAR)
Barbados Olympic Association - 1955

Area: 166 sq. mi. Population (1985 est.): 252,000
Located: In Atlantic, farthest east of the West Indies.
Language(s): English
Religion(s): Anglican 70%, Methodist 9%, Roman Catholic 4%
Government: Independent sovereign state

Olympic History: As an independent country, Barbados competed at
the Olympics of 1968, 1972, 1976, and 1984. It has not won a
medal in those years. In 1960 Barbados competed with Jamaica
and Trinidad as part of The Antilles team, representing the West
Indies Federation. One of the Barbados runners, James
Wedderburn, ran with three Jamaicans as a member of the 4 x 400
metre relay team, and helped win a bronze medal.

BELGIUM (BEL)
Koninkrijk België (Dutch); Royaume de Belgique (French)
Kingdom of Belgium
Comité Olympique et Interfédéral Belge - 1906

Area: 11,779 sq. mi. Population (1985 est.): 9,858,000
Located: In Northwest Europe, on the North Sea.
Language(s): Flemish 57%, French 33%, legally bilingual 10%
Religion(s): Roman Catholic 96%
Government: Parliamentary democracy under a constitutional
monarch.

Olympic History: Belgium has competed at every Olympic Games,
with the exception of 1896 and 1904. Belgium began competing at
the Olympic Winter Games in 1924, and as well competed in figure
skating in 1920, but missed the 1960 and 1968 Olympic Winter
Games.

Olympic Hosts: 1920 - Antwerp - The Games of the VIIth Olympiad

Medal Count:

	Men				Women				Totals			
	GO	SI	BR	TOT	GO	SI	BR	TOT	GO	SI	BR	TOT
Summer	35	48	39	122	–	–	2	2	35	48	41	124
Winter	0+	1	2	3+	0+	–	–	0+	1	1	2	4
Totals	35+	49	41	125+	0+	–	2	2+	36	49	43	128

Most Medals, Men
9   Hubert van Innis (ARC)
6   Fernand de Montigny (FEN/FIH)

Most Gold Medals, Men
6   Hubert van Innis (ARC)
3   Emile Cloetens (ARC)
3   Edmond van Moer (ARC)

First Medalist/Gold Medalist, Men
   26 MAY 1900   Hubert van Innis (ARC-several)

First Medalist, Women
   04 AUG 1984   Ann Haesebrouck (ROW-SS)

Youngest Medalist/Gold Medalist, Men
   18-329   Leon Delathouwer (CYC-1948)

Oldest Medalist/Gold Medalist, Men
   54-187   Hubert van Innis (ARC-1920)

Most Medals, Winter, Men
   1   Eleven athletes tied with one

Most Gold Medals, Winter, Men
   1   Pierre Baugniet (FSK)

First Medalist, Winter, Men
   03 FEB 1924   Five-Man Bobsled Team

First Gold Medalist, Winter, Men
   07 FEB 1948   Pierre Baugniet (FSK-Pairs)

Youngest Medalist, Winter, Men
   20-033   Paul van den Broeck (BOB-1924)

Oldest Medalist, Winter, Men
   49-038   Max Houben (BOB-1948)

Most Medals/Gold Medals, Winter, Women
   1   Micheline Lannoy (FSK)

First Medalist/Gold Medalist, Winter, Women
   07 FEB 1948   Micheline Lannoy (FSK-Pairs)

Most Medals, Men, Games
   6   Hubert van Innis (ARC-1920)
   4   Louis van de Perck (ARC-1920)

Most Gold Medals, Men, Games
   4   Hubert van Innis (ARC-1920)
   3   Emile Cloetens (ARC-1920)
   3   Edmond van Moer (ARC-1920)

BELIZE (BIZ)
Belize Olympic and Commonwealth Games Association - 1967

Former Name: British Honduras (declared independence on
    21 SEP 1981).
Area: 8,867 sq. mi. Population (1985 est.): 166,400
Located: Eastern coast of Central America.
Language(s): English (official), Spanish, native Creole dialects
Religion(s): Roman Catholic 66%, Methodist 13%, Anglican 13%
Government: Parliamentary

Olympic History: As British Honduras, this country made three
    Olympics appearances, in 1968, 1972, and 1976. Belize made its
    first Olympic appearance at Los Angeles in 1984 with four
    athletes, and six cyclists.

BENIN (BEN)
République Populaire du Benin
People's Republic of Benin
Comité Olympique Béninois - 1962

Former Names: French West Africa (declared independence on 01 AUG
    1960). Renamed Dahomey in 1960, the name was changed to Benin
    in 1975.
Area: 43,483 sq. mi. Population (1984 est.): 4,005,000
Located: In West Africa on the Gulf of Guinea.
Language(s): French (official), local dialects
Religion(s): Mainly animist with Christian, Muslim minorities
Government: Marxist-Leninist

Olympic History: Benin has competed three times at the Olympic
    Games. In 1972 it competed as Dahomey, and in 1980 and 1984 it
    competed as Benin. It has yet to win a medal.

BERMUDA (BER)
Bermuda Olympic Association - 1936

Area: 21 sq. mi. Population (1984 est.): 56,652
Located: 360 islands (21 inhabited) in the western Atlantic
Language(s): English
Religion(s): Protestant, Roman Catholic
Government: British dependency

Olympic History: Bermuda has competed at the Olympics since 1936,
    failing to appear only in 1980. They have not competed at the
    Olympic Winter Games. They have won one medal, a bronze in 1976
    heavyweight boxing, won by Clarence Hill.

BHUTAN (BHU)
Druk-Yul
Kingdom of Bhutan
Bhutan Olympic Committee - 1983

Area: 18,147 sq. mi. Population (1985 est.): 1,417,000
Located: In the Eastern Himalayan Mountains
Language(s): Dzongkha (official), Nepali
Religion(s): Buddhist 70%, Hindu 25%, Muslim 5%
Government: Monarchy

Olympic History: Recognized in 1983, Bhutan sent three women and
three men to the 1984 Los Angeles Olympics, all archers. Their
best finishes were 43rd by Sonam Chuki (women) and 53rd by
Thinley Dorji (men).

BOHEMIA
See Czechoslovakia.

Olympic History: Prior to forming the bulk of Czechoslovakia,
Bohemia appeared at the Olympics of 1900, 1906, 1908, and 1912.

BOLIVIA (BOL)
Republica de Bolivia
Republic of Bolivia
Comité Olímpico Boliviano - 1936

Area: 424,165 sq. mi. Population (1985 est.): 6,195,000
Located: In Central Andes Mountains, in central South America.
Language(s): Spanish (official), Quechua, Aymara
Religion(s): Roman Catholic 95%
Government: Republic

Olympic History: Bolivia had a single swimmer at the 1936
Olympics in Berlin, but did not compete at the Olympics again
until 1964. They have competed since except at Moscow in 1980.
They have not yet won a medal. Oddly, Bolivia has also competed
three times at the Olympic Winter Games, sending alpine skiiers
in 1956, 1980, and 1984.

BOTSWANA (BOT)
Republic of Botswana
Botswana Olympic Committee - 1980

Former Name: Bechuanaland (declared independence on 30 SEP 1966).
Area: 231,804 sq. mi. Population (1985 est.): 1,068,000
Located: In southern Africa, just north of South Africa.
Language(s): English (official), Setswana (national)
Religion(s): Mostly indigenous beliefs, Christian 15%
Government: Republic, parliamentary democracy.

Olympic History: Botswana competed at both the 1980 and 1984
   Olympic Games.   The country never made an Olympic appearance as
   Bechuanaland.

BRAZIL (BRA)
Republica Federativa do Brasil
Federative Republic of Brazil
Comité Olímpico Brasileiro - 1935

Former Name: United States of Brazil.   Became independent of
   Portugal on 07 SEP 1822.
Area: 3,286,470 sq. mi.   Population (1985 est.):   135,000,000
Located: Eastern half of South America.
Language(s):   Portuguese (official), English
Religion(s):   Roman Catholic 89%
Government: Federal Republic

Olympic History: Brazil has competed at every Olympics since
   1920, with the sole exception of 1928.   It has never competed at
   the Olympic Winter Games.
      Brazil's successes have come in a variety of sports.   It has
   won medals in athletics, basketball, boxing, judo, shooting,
   soccer (football), swimming, and yachting.   It has always had
   one of the top basketball teams, and in 1984, its soccer team
   won the gold medal to finally fulfill the promise shown by its
   professional teams.

Medal Count:

| | Men | | | | Women | | | | Totals | | | |
	GO	SI	BR	TOT	GO	SI	BR	TOT	GO	SI	BR	TOT
Summer	6	7	17	30	-	-	-	-	6	7	17	30
Winter	-	-	-	-	-	-	-	-	-	-	-	-
Totals	6	7	17	30	-	-	-	-	6	7	17	30

Most Medals, Men
   2   Adhemar Ferreira da Silva (TAF)
   2   João de Oliveira (TAF)
   2   Afranio Da Costa (SHO)
   2   Guilherme Paraense (SHO)
   2   Zenny De Azevedo (BAS)
   2   Amaury Antônio Pasos (BAS)
   2   Wlamir Marques (BAS)
   2   Carlos Domingos Massoni (BAS)
   2   Carmo De Souza (BAS)
   2   Jatyr Eduardo Schall (BAS)
   2   Edson Bispo dos Santos (BAS)
   2   Antônio Salvador Sucar (BAS)
   2   Reinaldo Conrad (YAC)

Most Gold Medals, Men
   2   Adhemar Ferreira da Silva (TAF)
   1   Joaquim Cruz (TAF)
   1   Marcos Soares (YAC)
   1   Eduardo Penido (YAC)
   1   Alexandre Welter (YAC)
   1   Lars Bjorkstrom (YAC)
   1   Guilherme Paraense (SHO)

First Medalist, Men
   02 AUG 1920 Afranio Da Costa (SHO-Free Pistol)
   02 AUG 1920 Military Pistol Team

First Gold Medalist, Men
   03 AUG 1920 Guilherme Paraense (SHO-Rapid-Fire Pistol)

Youngest Medalist, Men
   18-112 Jorge Luiz Fernandes (SWI-1980)

Youngest Gold Medalist, Men
   19-164 Marcos Soares (YAC-1980)

Oldest Medalist/Gold Medalist, Men
   36-253 Lars Bjorkstrom (YAC-1980)

BRITISH HONDURAS
   See Belize.

BRUNEI (BRU)
Negara Brunei Darussalam
The Sultanate of Brunei - 1984

Area: 2,226 sq. mi. Population (1985 est.): 232,000
Located: On the north coast of the island of Borneo.
Language(s): Malay (official), English
Religion(s): Muslim 64%, Buddhist 14%, Christian 10%
Government: Independent sultanate; became independent of Great
   Britain in 1983.

Olympic History: Brunei has yet to compete at the Olympic Games.

BULGARIA (BUL)
Narodna Republika Bulgaria
People's Republic of Bulgaria
Comité Olympique Bulgare - 1923

Area: 44,365 sq. mi. Population (1985 est.): 8,974,000
Located: North of Greece bordering on the Black Sea
Language(s): Bulgarian, Turkish, Greek
Religion(s): Orthodox 85%, Muslim 13%
Government: Communist; became an independent kingdom in 1908.
   The monarchy was abolished on 08 SEP 1946.

Olympic History: Bulgaria had a single competitor at the first
Olympics in 1896, gymnast Charles Champov, a physical education
teacher with the "lounak" society. No Bulgarians then competed
until 1924, and they have since missed the Games of 1932, 1948,
and 1984. Their first appearance in the Winter Games was in
1936 and they have competed at all celebrations since.
   Bulgaria has had its greatest successes in strength sports,
mainly weightlifting and wrestling, and today they are the
premier nation in the world in weightlifting. Their only winter
medal to date came in 1980 when Ivan Lebanov finished third in
the 30 kilometre nordic skiing event.

Medal Count:

	Men				Women				Totals			
	GO	SI	BR	TOT	GO	SI	BR	TOT	GO	SI	BR	TOT
Summer	24	41	32	97	3	9	7	19	27	50	39	116
Winter	–	–	1	1	–	–	–	–	–	–	1	1
Totals	24	41	33	98	3	9	7	19	27	50	40	117

Most Medals, Men
   3   Aleksander Tomov (WRE)
   3   Enyu Dimov-Valtchev (WRE)

Most Gold Medals, Men
   2   Norair Nurikian (WLT)
   2   Petar Kirov (WRE)
   2   Boyan Radev (WRE)

First Medalist, Men
   02 AUG 1952 Boris Nikolov (BOX-Middleweight)

First Gold Medalist, Men
   01 DEC 1956 Nikolai Stanchev (WRE-Middleweight Freestyle)

Youngest Medalist, Men
   18-259 Mincho Pashov (WLT-1980)

Youngest Gold Medalist, Men
   19-233 Petar Lessov (BOX-1980)

Oldest Medalist, Men
   50-268 Petar Mandachiyev (EQU-1980)

Oldest Gold Medalist, Men
   29-359 Petar Kirov (WRE-1972)

Most Medals, Women
    2   Siika Barbulova-Kelbecheva (ROW)
    2   Stoyanka Kurbatova-Gruicheva (ROW)
    2   Ginka Gjurova (ROW)
    2   Marijka Modeva (ROW)
    2   Nadka Golcheva (BAS)
    2   Penka Metodijeva (BAS)
    2   Petkana Makavejeva (BAS)
    2   Sneschana Michailova (BAS)
    2   Krassimira Bogdanova (BAS)
    2   Dijana Dilova (BAS)
    2   Penka Stoyanova (BAS)
    2   Yordanko Blagoyeva (TAF)
    2   Ivanka Khristova (TAF)
    2   Marija Petkova-Vergova (TAF)

Most Gold Medals, Women
    1   Ivanka Khristova (TAF)
    1   Svetlana Otzetova (ROW)
    1   Sdravka Yordanova (ROW)
    1   Siika Kelbecheva (ROW)
    1   Stoyanka Gruicheva (ROW)

First Medalist, Women
    04 SEP 1972 Yordanka Blagoyeva (TAF-HJ)

First Gold Medalist, Women
    24 JUL 1976 Double Sculls Rowing
    24 JUL 1976 Pairs without Rowing

Youngest Medalist, Women
    18-035 Kostadinka Radkova (BAS-1980)

Youngest Gold Medalist, Women
    21-129 Stoyanka Gruicheva (ROW-1976)

Oldest Medalist/Gold Medalist, Women
    34-254 Ivanka Khristova (TAF-1976)

BURKINA FASO (BUR)
Republic of Burkina Faso
Conseil National Olympique et des Sports Voltaques - 1972

Former Name: Upper Volta (changed 04 AUG 1984)
Area: 105,869 sq. mi. Population (1985 est.): 6,907,000
Located: In Western Africa, south of the Sahara.
Language(s): French (official), More, Sudanic tribal languages
Religion(s): animist 50%, Muslims 16%, Roman Catholic 8%
Government: Republic

Olympic History: Burkina Faso sent a single competitor to the
    1972 Olympics, representing Upper Volta. They have not competed
    since although they did send an entourage to observe the 1984
    Olympics in Los Angeles.

BURMA (BIR)
Pyidaungsu Socialist Thammada Myanma Naingngandaw
Socialist Republic of the Union of Burma
Burma Olympic Committee - 1947

Area: 261,789 sq. mi. Population (1985 est.): 36,919,000
Located: Between south and southeast Asia, on the Bay of Bengal.
Language(s): Burmese (official)
Religion(s): Buddhist 85%, animists, Christian
Government: Socialist Republic; became independent of the
   Commonwealth on 04 JAN 1948.

Olympic History: Burma has competed at all Olympics since 1948,
   with the exception of the 1980 Olympics. They have never
   attended the Olympic Winter Games nor have they won a medal.

CAMBODIA (KAMPUCHEA) (CAM)
Cambodian People's Republic

Area: 69,898 sq. mi. Population (1985 est.): 6,249,000
Located: In the Indochina Peninsula.
Language(s): Khmer (official), French
Religion(s): Theravada Buddhism, animism
Government: Country not currently governed as a whole.
   Vietnamese-installed government controls Phnom Penh.

Olympic History: Cambodia made its first Olympic appearance at
   the Olympic Equestrian Games of 1956 in Stockholm. It again
   competed in 1964 and 1972 but has not competed since. It has
   yet to win a medal. Its current government does not have a
   recognized Olympic Committee.

CAMEROON (CMR)
United Republic of Cameroon
Comité Olympique Camerounais - 1963

Area: 185,568 sq. mi. Population (1985 est.): 9,737,000
Located: Between west and central Africa.
Language(s): English, French (both official), Bantu, Sudanic
Religion(s): Roman Catholic 35%, animist 25%, Muslim 22%,
   Protestant 18%.
Government: Formerly under the control of France and Britain as
   French and British Cameroon. Became independent on 01 JAN 1960,
   with part of British Cameroon joining Nigeria, and the rest
   joining French Cameroon to form Cameroon.

Olympic History: Cameroon made its Olympic début in 1964 at Tokyo
   and has appeared at all Games since. It has not yet attended
   the Olympic Winter Games, however. In 1968, Joseph Bessala won
   a silver medal in welterweight boxing to garner the country's
   first medal. Martin Ndongo Ebanga added a second medal by
   winning the bronze in the lightweight class in the 1984 boxing
   tournament.

CANADA (CAN)
Canadian Olympic Association - 1907

Area: 3,851,790 sq. mi. Population (1985 est.): 25,399,000
Language(s): French, English (both official)
Religion(s): Roman Catholic 46%, Protestant 41%
Government: Constitutional monarchy with a parliamentary
   democracy.

Olympic History: Canada first appeared officially at the 1904
   Olympic Games in St. Louis. However, in 1900, two Canadian
   citizens competed, both under U.S. colors. George Orton is well
   known, for as a student representing the University of
   Pennsylvania, he won the 2,500 metre steeplechase. In the
   marathon, however, it has been recently discovered that Ronald
   MacDonald, a Nova Scotia native who later returned there to
   practise medicine, ran and finished, while representing Boston
   College.
      Since 1900, Canada has failed to be represented only at the
   1980 Moscow Olympic Games. They have appeared at every Olympic
   Winter Games since their inception in 1924, and, in addition,
   their ice hockey team competed in the 1920 hockey tournament,
   winning decisively. This began a trend which continued until
   the Soviet Union entered the Olympic ice hockey tournaments,
   starting in 1956.

Olympic Hosts:
   1976 - Montréal - Games of the XXIst Olympiad
   1988 - Calgary - The XVth Olympic Winter Games

Medal Count:

	Men				Women				Totals			
	GO	SI	BR	TOT	GO	SI	BR	TOT	GO	SI	BR	TOT
Summer	30	45	50	125	6	15	19	40	36	60	69	165
Winter	9+	6	12+	28	4+	4	2+	11	14	10	15	39
Totals	39+	51	62+	153	10+	19	21+	51	50	70	84	204

Most Medals, Men
   5   Phil Edwards (TAF)
   4   Alex Wilson (TAF)
   4   Gaeten Boucher (SSK)

Most Gold Medals, Men
   2   George Hodgson (SWI)
   2   Percy Williams (TAF)
   2   Gaeten Boucher (SSK)
   2   Alex Baumann (SWI)

First Medalist, Men
   15 JUL 1900 George Orton (CAN/USA-TAF-2,500 steeple/400 IH)
   07 JUL 1904 Lacrosse Team

First Gold Medalist, Men
   15 JUL 1900   George Orton (CAN/USA-TAF-2,500 steeple/400 IH)
   07 JUL 1904   Lacrosse Team

Youngest Medalist/Gold Medalist, Men
   17-148   George Genereux (SHO-1952)

Oldest Medalist/Gold Medalist, Men
   46-029   George Lyon (GOL-1904)

Most Medals, Women
   3   Elaine Tanner (SWI)
   3   Anne Ottenbrite (SWI)

Most Gold Medals, Women
   1   Fanny Rosenfeld (TAF)
   1   Florence Bell (TAF)
   1   Ethel Smith (TAF)
   1   Myrtle Cook (TAF)
   1   Ethel Catherwood (TAF)
   1   Anne Ottenbrite (SWI)
   1   Barbara Ann Scott (FSK)
   1   Anne Heggtveit (ASK)
   1   Barbara Wagner (FSK)
   1   Nancy Greene (ASK)
   1   Kathy Kreiner (ASK)

First Medalist, Women
   31 JUL 1928   Fanny Rosenfeld (TAF-100)
   31 JUL 1928   Ethel Smith (TAF-100)

First Gold Medalist, Women
   05 AUG 1928   Ethel Catherwood (TAF-HJ)
   05 AUG 1928   Sprint Relay Team (TAF-400R)

Youngest Medalist, Women
   13-341   Robin Corsiglia (SWI-1976)

Youngest Gold Medalist, Women
   18-096   Ethel Catherwood (SWI-1928)

Oldest Medalist/Gold Medalist, Women
   40-211   Linda Thom (SHO-1984)

Most Medals, Winter, Men
   4   Gaeten Boucher (SSK)
   2   Alexander Hurd (SSK)
   2   William Logan (SSK)

Most Gold Medals, Winter, Men
   2   Gaeten Boucher (SSK)
   1   Many tied with one.

First Medalist, Winter, Men
<u>30 APR 1920 Ice Hockey Team</u>
08 FEB 1924 Ice Hockey Team

First Gold Medalist, Winter, Men
<u>30 APR 1920 Ice Hockey Team</u>
08 FEB 1924 Ice Hockey Team

Youngest Medalist, Winter, Men
18-037 Wallace Diestelmeyer (FSK-1948)

Youngest Gold Medalist, Winter, Men
19-032 Reginald Smith (ICH-1924)

Oldest Medalist/Gold Medalist, Winter, Men
38-184 Harold Simpson (ICH-1932)

Most Medals, Winter, Women
2   Nancy Greene (ASK)
1   Eleven tied with one.

Most Gold Medals, Winter, Women
1   Barbara Ann Scott (FSK)
1   Anne Heggtveit (ASK)
1   Barbara Wagner (FSK)
1   Nancy Greene (ASK)
1   Kathy Kreiner (ASK)

First Medalist, Winter, Women
06 FEB 1948 Barbara Ann Scott (FSK-Ladies)

First Gold Medalist, Winter, Women
06 FEB 1948 Barbara Ann Scott (FSK-Ladies)

Youngest Medalist, Winter, Women
17-044 Debbie Wilkes (FSK-1964)

Youngest Gold Medalist, Winter, Women
19-212 Kathy Kreiner (ASK-1976)

Oldest Medalist, Winter, Women
26-048 Francis Dafoe (FSK-1956)

Oldest Gold Medalist, Winter, Women
24-280 Nancy Greene (ASK-1968)

Most Medals, Men, Games
3   Phil Edwards (TAF-1932)
3   Alex Wilson (TAF-1932)
3   Gaeten Boucher (SSK-1984)
3   Victor Davis (SWI-1984)

Most Gold Medals, Men, Games
    2   George Hodgson (SWI-1920)
    2   Percy Williams (TAF-1928)
    2   Gaeten Boucher (SSK-1984)
    2   Alex Baumann (SWI-1984)

Most Medals, Women, Games
    3   Elaine Tanner (SWI-1968)
    3   Anne Ottenbrite (SWI-1984)

Most Gold Medals, Women, Games
    1   Fanny Rosenfeld (TAF-1928)
    1   Florence Bell (TAF-1928)
    1   Ethel Smith (TAF-1928)
    1   Myrtle Cook (TAF-1928)
    1   Ethel Catherwood (TAF-1928)
    1   Anne Ottenbrite (SWI-1984)
    1   Barbara Ann Scott (FSK-1948)
    1   Anne Heggtveit (ASK1960)
    1   Barbara Wagner (FSK-1960)
    1   Nancy Greene (ASK-1968)
    1   Kathy Kreiner (ASK-1976)

Most Medals, Winter, Men, Games
    3   Gaeten Boucher (SSK-1984)
    2   Alexander Hurd (SSK-1932)
    2   William Logan (SSK-1932)

Most Gold Medals, Winter, Men, Games
    2   Gaeten Boucher (SSK-1984)
    1   Many Canadians tied with one.

Most Medals, Winter, Women, Games
    2   Nancy Greene (ASK-1968)
    1   Many Canadians tied with one.

Most Gold Medals, Winter, Women, Games
    1   Barbara Ann Scott (FSK-1948)
    1   Anne Heggtveit (ASK1960)
    1   Barbara Wagner (FSK-1960)
    1   Nancy Greene (ASK-1968)
    1   Kathy Kreiner (ASK-1976)

CAYMAN ISLANDS (CAY)
Cayman Islands Olympic Committee - 1976

Area: 102 sq. mi.   Population (1985 est.): 18,000
Located: Three islands, south of Cuba, and northwest of Jamaica.
Language(s): English
Government: A dependency of the United Kingdom.

Olympic History: The Cayman Islands has been represented at two
    Olympic Games, those of 1976 and 1984.

CENTRAL AFRICA (CAF)
Republique Centrafricaine
Central African Republic
Comité Olympic Centrafricain - 1965

Became independent of France on 13 AUG 1960.
Area: 240,324 sq. mi. Population (1985 est.): 2,664,000
Located: In central Africa.
Language(s): French (official), local dialects
Religion(s): Roman Catholic 25%, the rest traditional tribal
Government: Republic

Olympic History: Central Africa first competed at the 1968
  Olympic Games, when Gabriel Mboa ran in the heats of the 5,000
  metres. Their next Olympic appearance occurred in 1984 when
  they were represented by two track & field athletes and three
  boxers.

CEYLON (CEY)
  See Sri Lanka.

CHAD (CHA)
République du Tchad
Republic of Chad
Comité Olympique Tchadien - 1964

Area: 495,755 sq. mi. Population (1985 est.): 5,036,000
Located: In central northern Africa
Language(s): French (official), Arabic
Religion(s): Muslims 44%, Animist 23%, Christian 33%
Government: Republic.

Olympic History: Chad first competed at the Olympic Games of
  1964. It has since appeared at the Olympic Games of 1968, 1972,
  and 1984.

CHILE (CHI)
República de Chile
Republic of Chile
Comite Olímpico de Chile - ca. 1912

Area: 292,135 sq. mi. Population (1985 est.): 12,042,000
Located: The western coast of southern South America.
Language(s): Spanish
Religion(s): Predominately Roman Catholic
Government: Republic

Olympic History: In 1896, Luis Subercaseaux ran in the 100 and
400 metres, making Chile one of the thirteen countries which was
represented at the first Olympic Games. They did not appear
again until 1912. Since that time, however, they have missed
only the Games of 1932 and 1980.
   Chile first competed at the Olympic Winter Games of 1948 and
since has competed eight times in the winter celebrations,
missing only 1972 and 1980.

Medal Count:

	Men				Women				Totals			
	GO	SI	BR	TOT	GO	SI	BR	TOT	GO	SI	BR	TOT
Summer	–	4	2	6	–	1	–	1	–	5	2	7
Winter	–	–	–	–	–	–	–	–	–	–	–	–
Totals	–	4	2	6	–	1	–	1	–	5	2	7

Most Medals, Men
   2   Oscar Cristi (EQU)
   1   Miguel Plaza Reyes (TAF)
   1   Cesar Mendoza (EQU)
   1   Ricardo Echevarria (EQU)
   1   Carlos Lucas (BOX)
   1   Ramon Tapia (BOX)
   1   Claudio Barrientos (BOX)

First Medalist, Men
   05 AUG 1928 Miguel Plaza Reyes (TAF-Marathon)

Youngest Medalist, Men
   21-335 Claudio Barrientos (BOX-1956)

Oldest Medalist, Men
   35-037 Oscar Cristi (EQU-1952)

Most Medals, Women
   1   Marlene Ahrens (TAF)

First Medalist, Women
   28 NOV 1956 Marlene Ahrens (TAF-JT)

CHINA (CHN)
Zhonghua Renmin Gonghe Guo
People's Republic of China
Chinese Olympic Committee - 1979.

Area: 3,705,390 sq. mi. Population (1985 est.): 1,037,588,000
Language(s): Mandarin Chinese (official), Shangahi, Canton,
   Fukien, Hakka dialects, Tibetan, Vigus (Turkic)
Religion(s): Officially atheist; Confucianism, Buddhism, Taoism
Government: People's Republic

Olympic History: China competed at the Olympic Games of 1932,
1936, 1948 and 1952. However, because of disputes with the
recognition of Chinese Taipei (Taiwan, aka Formosa) by the IOC,
mainland China, the People's Republic of China, did not again
take part in the Games of the Olympiad until 1984 at Los
Angeles, where they made a very successful return to action.
China had actually returned to the Olympic fold, however, in
1980 at Lake Placid. This was their first appearance in the
Olympic Winter Games.
   Although the current NOC was recognized by the IOC in 1979,
the first recognition of a Chinese Olympic Committee was in
1922. This committee furnished several members to the IOC but
withdrew from the group on 19 August 1958, in protest of the
IOC's continued recognition of Taiwan. A request to be
recognized again was submitted in 1975 and approved 25 November
1979.

Medal Count:

	Men				Women				Totals			
	GO	SI	BR	TOT	GO	SI	BR	TOT	GO	SI	BR	TOT
Summer	10	7	5	22	5	2	2	9	15	9	7	31
Winter	-	-	-	-	-	-	-	-	-	-	-	-
Totals	10	7	5	22	5	2	2	9	15	9	7	31

Most Medals, Men
   6   Ning Li (GYM)
   3   Yun Lou (GYM)

Most Gold Medals, Men
   3   Ning Li (GYM)
   2   Yun Lou (GYM)

First Medalist, Men
   29 JUL 1984   Guoqiang Zeng (WLT-52 kg.)
   29 JUL 1984   Peishun Zhou (WLT-52 kg.)
   29 JUL 1984   Haifeng Xu (SHO-Free Pistol)
   29 JUL 1984   Yifu Wang (SHO-Free Pistol)

First Gold Medalist, Men
   29 JUL 1984   Guoqiang Zeng (WLT-52 kg.)
   29 JUL 1984   Haifeng Xu (SHO-Free Pistol)

Youngest Medalist/Gold Medalist, Men
   19-011   Yuwei Li (SHO-1984)

Oldest Medalist/Gold Medalist, Men
   26-055   Weiqiang Chen (WLT-1984)

Most Medals, Women
   2   Yanhong Ma (GYM)
   2   Xiao Xuan Wu (SHO)

Most Gold Medals, Women
   1   Fifteen athletes tied with one

First Medalist, Women
  31 JUL 1984 Xiao Xuan Wu (SHO-Air Rifle)

First Gold Medalist, Women
  02 AUG 1984 Xiao Xuan Wu (SHO-Small-Bore Rifle)

Youngest Medalist, Women
  15-137 Qun Huang (GYM-1984)

Youngest Gold Medalist, Women
  19-222 Jihong Zhou (DIV-1984)

Oldest Medalist/Gold Medalist, Women
  27-119 Rongfang Zhang (VOL-1984)

Most Medals, Men, Games
  6   Ning Li (GYM)
  3   Yun Lou (GYM)

Most Gold Medals, Men, Games
  3   Ning Li (GYM)
  2   Yun Lou (GYM)

Most Medals, Women, Games
  2   Yanhong Ma (GYM)
  2   Xiao Xuan Wu (SHO)

Most Gold Medals, Women, Games
  1   Fifteen athletes tied with one

CHINESE TAIPEI (TAIWAN) (TPE)
Chung-hua Min-kuo
Republic of China
Chinese Taipei Olympic Committee - 1960

Area: 13,814 sq. mi. Population (1985 est.): 19,338,000
Located: Off the southeast coast of mainland China.
Language(s): Mandarin Chinese (official), Taiwan, Hakka dialects
Religion(s): Buddhism, Taoism, Confucianism
Government: Republic

Olympic History: Taiwan has been represented at the Olympic Games
since 1956, and has competed at six Olympic Games - those of
1956, 1960, 1964, 1968, 1972, and 1984. The country has been
embroiled in the recognition dispute with mainland China, and
has thus competed in the Olympic Games under various names -
Taiwan (1960-1972), Chinese Taipei (1984), and China (1956). It
has had two absolutely superb athletes, Chuang-Kwang "C. K."
Yang, who finished second in the 1960 decathlon; and Chi Cheng,
who finished third in the 80 metre hurdles in 1968, although
both were world record holders in those events at one time. The
third medalist was a weightlifter, Wen-Yee Tsai, who finished
third in the 60 kg. class in 1984 at Los Angeles.

Taiwan has competed at three Olympic Winter Games, those of
1972, 1976, and 1984.

The Chinese Taipei Olympic Committee was first formed in 1949
by some members of the mainland Chinese committee who had fled
to the island. Competing for several years under the banner
"China," the IOC eventually banned the country from competing
under this name. The current NOC was recognized on 26 November
1979 and on 23 March 1981 it signed an agreement with the IOC in
which the NOC agreed to change its name to the Chinese Taipei
Olympic Committee and compete under a new flag and emblem.

Medal Count:

	Men				Women				Totals			
	GO	SI	BR	TOT	GO	SI	BR	TOT	GO	SI	BR	TOT
Summer	-	1	1	2	-	-	1	1	-	1	2	3
Winter	-	-	-	-	-	-	-	-	-	-	-	-
Totals	-	1	1	2	-	-	1	1	-	1	2	3

COLOMBIA (COL)
Rupública de Colombia
Republic of Colombia
Comité Olímpico Colombiano - 1948

Area: 439,735 sq. mi. Population (1985 est.): 29,347,000
Located: At the northwest corner of South America.
Language(s): Spanish
Religion(s): Roman Catholic 97%
Government: Republic

Olympic History: Colombia first competed at the 1932 Olympic
Games, represented by marathon runner Jorgé Perry Villate. The
country has since competed at every Olympics with the exception
of 1952. They have yet to compete in the Olympic Winter Games.

Medal Count:

	Men				Women				Totals			
	GO	SI	BR	TOT	GO	SI	BR	TOT	GO	SI	BR	TOT
Summer	-	2	2	4	-	-	-	-	-	2	2	4
Winter	-	-	-	-	-	-	-	-	-	-	-	-
Totals	-	2	2	4	-	-	-	-	-	2	2	4

Most Medals, Men
    2   Helmut Bellingrodt (SHO)
    1   Clemente Rojas (BOX)
    1   Alfonso Perez (BOX)

First Medalist, Men
    01 SEP 1972   Helmut Bellingrodt (SHO-Running Deer)

Youngest Medalist, Men
    20-009   Clemente Rojas (BOX-1972)

Oldest Medalist, Men
    37-225   Helmut Bellingrodt (SHO-1984)

CONGO (CGO)
République Populaire du Congo
People's Republic of the Congo
Comité Olympique Congolais - 1964

Area: 132,046 sq. mi. Population (1985 est.):   1,798,000
Located: In western central Africa
Language(s):   French (official), Bantu dialects
Religion(s):   Roman Catholic 40%, animists 47%, Muslim 2%
Government: People's republic

Olympic History: The Congo has competed at three Olympic Games,
    starting in 1964.   They have yet to win a medal and have never
    competed at the Olympic Winter Games.

COOK ISLANDS (COK)
Cook Islands Sports and Olympic Association - 1986

Area: 93 sq. mi. Population (1983 est.):   16,900
Location: Islands in the south Pacific, 2100 miles northwest of
    New Zealand.
Language(s):   English
Religion(s):   Anglican, Protestant, Roman Catholic
Government: Self-governing dependency of New Zealand; became
    independent in 1965.

Olympic History: The Cook Islands has yet to participate in the
    Olympic Games.

COSTA RICA (CRC)
Répúblíca de Costa Rica
Republic of Costa Rica
Comité Olímpico de Costa Rica - 1954

Area: 19,575 sq. mi. Population (1985 est.): 2,644,000
Located: In central America
Language(s): Spanish (official)
Religion(s): Roman Catholic
Government: Democratic Republic

Olympic History: Costa Rica has competed at seven Olympic Games -
  1936, 1964, 1968, 1972, 1976, 1980 and 1984. They have yet to
  win a medal and have never competed at the Olympic Winter Games.

CUBA (CUB)
Rupública de Cuba
Republic of Cuba
Comité Olímpico Cubano - 1954

Area: 44,218 sq. mi. Population (1985 est.): 10,105,000
Located: Southeast of Florida
Language(s): Spanish
Religion(s): Roman Catholic 42%
Government: Communist state.

Olympic History: In 1900, the fencer Ramón Fonst competed at the
  Olympic Games, and actually won the first gold medal for the
  small Caribbean country. Fonst returned to compete in 1904 at
  St. Louis along with a few other athletes. In 1924 Cuba was
  represented by nine competitors, while in 1928, the country had
  one competitor.
  In 1948, Cuba sent a full team to the London Olympic Games and
  their participation was continuous until they elected to boycott
  the 1984 Olympic Games in Los Angeles. Cuba has had some
  success in track & field but by far their best sport has been
  boxing, in which they have probably had the top team in the
  world for the last decade. Cuban athletes have not yet competed
  in the Olympic Winter Games.

Medal Count:

	Men				Women				Totals			
	GO	SI	BR	TOT	GO	SI	BR	TOT	GO	SI	BR	TOT
Summer	20+	18	10	48+	1	1	2	4	21+	19	12	52+
Winter	-	-	-	-	-	-	-	-	-	-	-	-
Totals	20+	18	10	48+	1	1	2	4	21+	19	12	52+

Most Medals, Men
  5   Ramón Fonst (FEN)
  3   Teófilo Stevenson (BOX)

Most Gold Medals, Men
    4   Ramón Fonst (FEN)
    3   Teófilo Stevenson (BOX)

First Medalist, Men
    14 JUN 1900 Ramón Fonst (FEN-Epee)

First Gold Medalist, Men
    14 JUN 1900 Ramón Fonst (FEN-Epee)

Youngest Medalist, Men
    16-036 Carlos De Cárdenas Culmell, Jr. (YAC-1948)

Youngest Gold Medalist, Men
    16-288 Ramón Fonst (FEN-1900)

Oldest Medalist, Men
    44-223 Carlos De Cárdenas Culmell (YAC-1948)

Oldest Gold Medalist, Men
    30-154 Manuel Diaz (FEN-1904)

Most Medals, Women
    2   Silvio Chibás (TAF)
    2   Marlene Elejarde (TAF)
    2   Fulgencio Romay (TAF)

Most Gold Medals, Women
    1   Maria Colón Ruenes (TAF)

First Medalist, Women
    20 OCT 1968 Sprint Relay Team (TAF-400R)

First Gold Medalist, Women
    25 JUL 1980 Maria Colón Ruenes (TAF-JT)

Youngest Medalist, Women
    17-292 Carmen Valdés (TAF-1972)

Oldest Medalist, Women
    28-238 Fulgencio Romay (TAF-1972)

Most Medals, Men, Games
    3   Ramón Fonst (FEN-1904)
    2   Manuel Diaz (FEN-1904)
    2   Alberto Juantorena (TAF-1976)

Most Gold Medals, Men, Games
    3   Ramón Fonst (FEN-1904)
    2   Alberto Juantorena (TAF-1976)

CYPRUS (CYP)
Kypriaki Dimokratia (Greek); Kibris Cumhuriyeti (Turkish)
Republic of Cyprus
Cyprus Olympic Committee - 1978

Area: 3,572 sq. mi. Population (1985 est.): 665,000
Located: In the eastern Mediterranean, off the Turkish coast.
Language(s): Greek, Turkish (both official), English
Religion(s): Greek Orthodox 77%, Muslims 18%
Government: Republic; became independent of Britain, Greece and
    Turkey on 16 AUG 1960.

Olympic History: Cyprus has competed at the Olympic Games of 1980
    and 1984. Its first Olympic participation, however, occurred at
    the Olympic Winter Games of 1980 in Lake Placid, and they also
    appeared at Sarajevo in 1984.

CZECHOSLOVAKIA (TCH)
Ceskoslovenská Socialisticka Republika
Czechoslovak Socialist Republic
Comité Olympique Tchécoslovaque - 1920

Area: 49,365 sq. mi. Population (1985 est.): 15,502,000
Located: In eastern central Europe
Language(s): Czech, Slovak (both official)
Religion(s): Roman Catholics, Lutherans, Eastern Orthodox
Government: Communist; became a republic on 30 OCT 1918,
    combining the kingdoms of Bohemia, Moravia, and Slovakia.

Olympic History: Athletes from what is now Czechoslovakia first
    competed at the 1900 Olympics, representing Bohemia. Bohemian
    athletes also competed in 1906, 1908, and 1912. In 1920
    Czechoslovakia sent its first true Olympic team to Antwerp.
    Since that time, the only Olympic Games not attended, including
    the Olympic Winter Games, has been the 1984 Los Angeles
    Olympics.
    Czechoslovakia has excelled in many different sports at the
    Olympics. The country's most noteworthy athletes have been
    distance runner Emil Zátopek, and female gymnast Vera Cáslavská.

Medal Count:

	Men				Women				Totals			
	GO	SI	BR	TOT	GO	SI	BR	TOT	GO	SI	BR	TOT
Summer	29	36	41+	106+	13	10	5	28	42	46	46+	134+
Winter	2	6	6	14	–	1	5	6	2	7	11	20
Totals	31	42	47+	120+	13	11	10	34	44	53	57+	154+

Most Medals, Men
5   Emil Zátopek (TAF)
5   Ladislav Vacha (GYM)

Most Gold Medals, Men
    4   Emil Zátopek (TAF)
    2   Jan Brzák-Felix (CAN)
    2   Josef Holeček (CAN)

First Medalist, Men
    15 JUL 1900 František Janda-Suk (TAF-DT) (TCH/BOH)
    20 JUL 1924 Bedřich Supčik (GYM-Rope Climb)

First Gold Medalist, Men
    20 JUL 1924 Bedřich Supčik (GYM-Rope Climb)

Youngest Medalist, Men
    16-096 Ludvic Vébr (ROW-1976)

Youngest Gold Medalist, Men
    17-260 Miroslav Koranda (ROW-1952)

Oldest Medalist, Men
    40-113 Jan Brzák-Felix (CAN-1948)

Oldest Gold Medalist, Men
    36-128 Jan Brzák-Felix (CAN-1948)

Most Medals, Women
    11   Vera Cáslavská (GYM)
    4   Eva Bosáková-Vechtová (GYM)

Most Gold Medals, Women
    7   Vera Cáslavská (GYM)
    1   Twelve athletes tied with one

First Medalist, Women
    09 JUL 1900 Hedwiga Rosenbaumová (TEN-Singles/Mixed) (TCH/BOH)
    14 AUG 1948 Gymnastics Team (GYM-Team)

First Gold Medalist, Women
    14 AUG 1948 Gymnastics Team (GYM-Team)

Youngest Medalist/Gold Medalist, Women
    16-181 Milena Duchková (DIV-1968)

Oldest Medalist, Women
    37-348 Dana Zátopková (TAF-1960)

Oldest Gold Medalist, Women
    35-049 Zdenka Veřmiřovská (GYM-1948)

Most Medals, Winter, Men
    4   Jiři Holik (ICH)
    3   Teodor Cerný (ICH)
    3   Vladimir Dzurilla (ICH)
    3   Oldřich Machač (ICH)

Most Gold Medals, Winter, Men
1   Jiři Raška (NSK)
1   Ondrej Nepela (FSK)

First Medalist/Gold Medalist, Winter, Men
11 FEB 1968 Jiři Raska (NSK-70 Jump)

Youngest Medalist, Winter, Men
19-213 Jiři Holik (ICH-1964)

Youngest Gold Medalist, Winter, Men
21-020 Ondrej Nepela (FSK-1972)

Oldest Medalist, Winter, Men
35-120 Otakar Vindyš (ICH-1920)

Oldest Gold Medalist, Winter, Men
27-007 Jiři Raška (NSK-1968)

Most Medals, Winter, Women
3   Kvetoslava Jeriová (NSK)
1   Olga Charvatová (ASK)
1   Hana Mašková (FSK)
1   Helena Sikolová (NSK)
1   Gabriela Svobodová (NSK)
1   Blanka Paulu (NSK)
1   Dagmar Schvubová (NSK)

First Medalist, Winter, Women
11 FEB 1968 Hana Mašková (FSK-Ladies)

Youngest Medalist, Winter, Women
21-250 Olga Charvatová (ASK-1984)

Oldest Medalist, Winter, Women
30-353 Gabriela Svobodová (NSK-1984)

Most Medals, Men, Games
3   Robert Pražák (GYM-1924)
3   Emmanuel Löffler (GYM-1928)
3   Ladislav Vácha (GYM-1928)
3   Emil Zátopek (TAF-1952)

Most Gold Medals, Men, Games
3   Emil Zátopek (TAF-1952)
1   Many athletes tied with one

Most Medals, Women, Games
6   Vera Cáslavská (GYM-1968)
4   Vera Cáslavská (GYM-1964)

Most Gold Medals, Women, Games
   4   Vera Cáslavská (GYM-1968)
   3   Vera Cáslavská (GYM-1964)

Most Medals, Winter, Men, Games
   2   Jiri Raska (NSK-1968)
   1   Many athletes tied with one

DAHOMEY
   See Benin.

DENMARK (DEN)
Kongeriget Danmark
Kingdom of Denmark
Danmarks Olympiske Komite - 1905

Area: 16,633 sq. mi. Population (1985 est.): 5,105,000
Located: In northern Europe, separating the North and Baltic
   Seas.
Language(s): Danish
Religion(s): Predominately Lutherans
Government: Constitutional Monarchy.

Olympic History: Denmark has competed at every summer Olympic
   Games except 1904, including those of 1906. At the Olympic
   Winter Games, they have competed five times, between 1948 and
   1968, sending nine competitors - eight men and one women.

Medal Count:

	Men				Women				Totals			
	GO	SI	BR	TOT	GO	SI	BR	TOT	GO	SI	BR	TOT
Summer	25+	49	43	117+	5	8	9	22	30+	57	52	139+
Winter	-	-	-	-	-	-	-	-	-	-	-	-
Totals	25+	49	43	117+	5	8	9	22	30+	57	52	139+

Most Medals, Men
   5   Niels Larsen (SHO)
   5   Lars Madsen (SHO)

Most Gold Medals, Men
   4   Paul Elvström (YAC)
   2   Lars Madsen (SHO)
   2   Soren Jensen (WRE)
   2   Henry Hansen (CYC)
   2   Poul Jensen (YAC)
   2   Valdemar Bandolowski (YAC)
   2   Erik Hansen (YAC)

First Medalist/Gold Medalist, Men
   07 APR 1896 Viggo Jensen (WLT-Heavyweight)

Youngest Medalist/Gold Medalist, Men
  18-059 Bent Peder Rasch (CAN-1952)

Oldest Medalist/Gold Medalist, Men
  53-066 Anders Nielsen (SHO-1920)

Most Medals, Women
  3   Karen Harup (SWI)
  2   Karen Lachman (FEN)
  2   Greta Andersen (SWI)

Most Gold Medals, Women
  1   Karen Hoff (CAN)
  1   Ellen Osiier (FEN)
  1   Stefani Fryland-Clausen (DIV)
  1   Greta Andersen (SWI)
  1   Karen Harup (SWI)

First Medalist, Women
  11 MAY 1912 Thora Castenschiold (TEN-Singles)

First Gold Medalist, Women
  04 JUL 1924 Ellen Osiier (FEN-Foil Individual)

Youngest Medalist, Women
  12-024 Inge Sörensen (SWI-1936)

Youngest Gold Medalist, Women
  20-149 Stefani Fryland-Clausen (DIV-1920)

Oldest Medalist, Women
  36-058 Karen Lachmann (FEN-1952)

Oldest Gold Medalist, Women
  33-326 Ellen Osiier (FEN-1924)

Most Medals, Men, Games
  4   Viggo Jensen (WLT/SHO-1896)
  3   Anders Nielsen (SHO-1900)

Most Gold Medals, Men, Games
  2   Henry Hansen (CYC-1928)
  1   Many athletes tied with one

Most Medals, Women, Games
  3   Karen Harup (SWI-1948)
  2   Greta Andersen (SWI-1948)

DJIBOUTI (DJI)
Jumhouriyya Djibouti
Republic of Djibouti
Comité National Olympique Djiboutien - 1984

Area: 8,494 sq. mi. Population (1985 est.): 297,000
Located: On the east coast of Africa
Language(s): French (official), Somali, Saho-Afar, Arabic
Religion(s): Mostly Muslim.
Government: Republic; became independent of France, Ethiopia, and
  Somalia on 27 JUN 1977.

Olympic History: Only recently recognized by the IOC, Djibouti
  sent three track & field athletes to the 1984 Olympics, but they
  competed without distinction. The track & field world awaits,
  however, the Olympic appearance of their excellent marathon
  runners, who have been among the world's best in the past few
  years.

DOMINICAN REPUBLIC (DOM)
República Dominicana
Comité Olímpico Dominicano - 1962

Area: 18,816 sq. mi. Population (1985 est.): 6,614,000
Located: In the West Indies, sharing the island of Hispaniola
  with Haiti.
Language(s): Spanish
Religion(s): Roman Catholic 98%
Government: Representative democracy.

Olympic History: Albert Torres was the first Dominican Republic
  athlete to make an Olympic appearance, competing in the 1964 100
  metre dash. They have competed six times since, never failing
  to appear. The first medal, and only to date, won by a
  Dominican athlete occurred in 1984 at Los Angeles when Pedro
  Nolasco won a bronze medal in bantamweight boxing.

ECUADOR (ECU)
República del Ecuador
Republic of Ecuador
Comité Olímpico Ecuatoriano - 1959

Area: 109,483 sq. mi. Population (1985 est.): 9,378,000
Located: In northwest South America, on the Pacific Coast
Language(s): Spanish (official), Quechuan, Jivaroan
Religion(s): Roman Catholic
Government: Republic

Olympic History: Ecuador sent three track & field competitors to
    the 1924 Olympic Games - Alberto Jurado Gonzales, Luis Jarrin,
    and Belisario Villacis. A gap of 44 years then occurred before
    they returned to the Olympics at Mexico City and they have
    competed continuously since. They have never appeared at the
    Olympic Winter Games and have never won a medal. Their top
    performance has been a fourth-place finish in the 1972 200 metre
    butterfly swimming event by Jorgé Delgado Panchama.

EGYPT (EGY)
Jumhuriyah Misr al-Arabiya
Arab Republic of Egypt
Comité Olympique Egyptien - 1910

Area: 386,650 sq. mi. Population (1985 est.): 49,000,000
Located: Northeast corner of Africa
Language(s): Arabic, English
Religion(s): Sunni Muslim 90%
Government: Republic

Olympic History: Egypt's first Olympic appearance was at the
    Intercalated Games of 1906. Since then it has competed at all
    Olympic except those of 1908, 1932, 1956, and 1976. Egypt has
    never competed at the Olympic Winter Games. From 1960 through
    1972, Egypt competed as the United Arab Republic, joining in a
    union in 1960 with Syria.
      Egypt's greatest Olympic successes have come in the strength
    sports of weightlifting and wrestling. It has also won medals
    in the strength sports of boxing and judo, and one athlete,
    Farid Simaika, won two medals in diving in 1928.

Medal Count:

	Men				Women				Totals			
	GO	SI	BR	TOT	GO	SI	BR	TOT	GO	SI	BR	TOT
Summer	6	6	7	19	-	-	-	-	6	6	7	19
Winter	-	-	-	-	-	-	-	-	-	-	-	-
Totals	6	6	7	19	-	-	-	-	6	6	7	19

Most Medals, Men
   2   Farid Simaika (DIV)
   2   Ibrahim Shams (WLT)

Most Gold Medals, Men
   1   Mahmoud Fayad (WLT)
   1   Ibrahim Shams (WLT)
   1   Anwar Mohammed Mesbah (WLT)
   1   Khadr Sayed El-Touni (WLT)
   1   El Sayed Nosseir (WLT)
   1   Ibrahim Moustafa (WRE)

First Medalist/Gold Medalist, Men
   29 JUL 1928   El Sayed Nosseir (WLT-Light-heavyweight)

Youngest Medalist, Men
   20-039   Saleh Mohammed Soliman (WLT-1936)

Youngest Gold Medalist, Men
   21-144   Khadr Sayed El-Touni (WLT-1936)

Oldest Medalist, Men
   33-223 Attia Hamouda (WLT-1948)
   33-325   Ibrahim Shams (WLT-1948)

Oldest Gold Medalist, Men
   33-325   Ibrahim Shams (WLT-1948)

EL SALVADOR (ESA)
Republica de El Salvador
Comité Olímpico de El Salvador - 1962

Area: 8,260 sq. mi. Population (1985 est.): 4,981,000
Located: Central America
Language(s): Spanish, Nahuati (Indian language)
Religion(s): Roman Catholic
Government: Republic

Olympic History: El Salvador has competed at three Olympics -
   1968, 1972, and 1984. They have won no medals to date.

ESTONIA (EST)

Olympic History: As a separate nation, Estonia competed at the
   Olympic Games of 1920 through 1936, continuously. In 1912 at
   Stockholm, Russia was represented by 12 athletes, several of
   whom were Estonian. Since 1952, Estonia has been a republic of
   the USSR and thus has not competed as an independent nation.
   Estonia also competed at the Olympic Winter Games of 1928 and
   1936.

Medal Count:

| | Men | | | | Women | | | | Totals | | |
	GO	SI	BR	TOT	GO	SI	BR	TOT	GO	SI	BR	TOT
Summer	6	6	9	21	-	-	-	-	6	6	9	21
Winter	-	-	-	-	-	-	-	-	-	-	-	-
Totals	6	6	9	21	-	-	-	-	6	6	9	21

Most Medals, Men
   2   Kristyan Palusalu (WRE)
   2   Voldemar Väli (WRE)
   2   August Neo (WRE)
   2   Alfred Neuland (WLT)
   2   Arnold Luhaäär (WLT)

Most Gold Medals, Men
   2   Kristyan Palusalu (WRE)
   1   Alfred Neuland (WLT)
   1   Osvald Käpp (WRE)
   1   Eduard Pütsep (WRE)
   1   Voldemar Väli (WRE)

First Medalist, Men
   08 AUG 1920   Alfred Neuland (WLT-Lightweight)
   08 AUG 1920   Alfred Schmidt (WLT-Featherweight)

First Gold Medalist, Men
   08 AUG 1920   Alfred Neuland (WLT-Lightweight)

Youngest Medalist, Men
   22-120   Alfred Schmidt (WLT-1920)

Youngest Gold Medalist, Men
   23-166   Osvald Käpp (WRE-1928)

Oldest Medalist, Men
   41-079   Nikolai Wekschin (YAC-1928)

Oldest Gold Medalist, Men
   28-152   Kristyan Palusalu (WRE-1936)

ETHIOPIA (ETH)
Hebretasebawit Etyopia
Socialist Ethiopia
Comité Olympique Ethiopien - 1954

Area: 471,776 sq. mi. Population (1985 est.): 42,266,000
Located: In East Africa
Language(s): Amharic (official), Tigre (Semitic language), Galla
   (Hamitic language), Arabic
Religion(s): Christian Orthodox 40%, Muslim 40%
Government: Provisional military government

Olympic History: Ethiopia made its first Olympic appearance in
    1956. They have since missed only the 1976 Olympics, joining in
    the African boycott. The country has made no Winter Olympic
    appearances.
       Ethiopia's top athletes have been distance runners. Heading
    this list is Abebe Bikila, Olympic marathon champion in 1960 and
    1964, and generally considered the greatest marathoner of all
    time.

Medal Count:

	Men				Women				Totals			
	GO	SI	BR	TOT	GO	SI	BR	TOT	GO	SI	BR	TOT
Summer	5	1	4	10	-	-	-	-	5	1	4	10
Winter	-	-	-	-	-	-	-	-	-	-	-	-
Totals	5	1	4	10	-	-	-	-	5	1	4	10

Most Medals, Men
    3   Mamo Wolde (TAF)
    3   Miruts Yifter (TAF)

Most Gold Medals, Men
    2   Abebe Bikila (TAF)
    2   Miruts Yifter (TAF)

First Medalist/Gold Medalist, Men
    10 SEP 1960   Abebe Bikila (TAF-Marathon)

Youngest Medalist, Men
    25-313 Mohammed Kedir (TAF-1980)

Youngest Gold Medalist, Men
    28-034 Abebe Bikila (TAF-1960)

Oldest Medalist, Men
    40-090 Mamo Wolde (TAF-1972)

Oldest Gold Medalist, Men
    36-138 Miruts Yifter (TAF-1980)

FIJI (FIJ)
Dominion of Fiji
Fiji Amateur Sports Association and National Olympic Committee -
    1955

Area: 7,056 sq. mi. Population (1985 est.): 700,000
Located: In western South Pacific
Language(s): English (official), Fijian, Hindustani
Religion(s): Christian 50%, Hindu 40%
Government: Parliamentary democracy

Olympic History: Fiji has competed at all the Olympics since 1956 with the exception of the 1980 Moscow Olympics. They have never sent a very large team, as their entire Olympic contingent for all years totals sixteen men and one women. Their largest team was in 1984 at Los Angeles with six men and one women, all in track & field except for two male judoka. They have never competed in the Olympic Winter Games.

FINLAND (FIN)
Sudmen Tasavalta
Republic of Finland
Finnish Olympic Committee - 1919

Area: 130,119 sq. mi. Population (1985 est.): 4,908,000
Located: Northern Baltic region of Europe
Language(s): Finnish 94%, Swedish 6% (both official)
Religion(s): Lutheran 90%
Government: Constitutional republic

Olympic History: Finland first competed at the 1906 Intercalated Games in Athens and also appeared two years later at the 1908 London Olympics. Their first Olympic Winter appearance was in 1924 at Chamonix although they had two skaters entered in the figure skating events in 1920. Since those dates Finland's participation has been continuous, never missing an Olympic Games nor an Olympic Winter Games.

Finland's greatest successes have come in the distance running events in the summer Games. In those events, led by Hannes Kolehmainen, Paavo Nurmi, and Lasse Viren, Finland has been the preeminent nation. Prior to World War II Finland was also the dominant nation in wrestling. In the Winter Games, Finland has excelled at nordic skiing and, in the early Games, at speed skating.

Olympic Hosts:
1952 - Helsinki - The Games of the XVth Olympiad

Medal Count:

	Men				Women				Totals			
	GO	SI	BR	TOT	GO	SI	BR	TOT	GO	SI	BR	TOT
Summer	95	72	106	273	1	2	1	4	96	74	107	277
Winter	21+	31+	24	77	7+	10+	8	26	29	42	32	103
Totals	116+	103+	130	350	8+	12+	9	30	125	116	139	380

Most Medals, Men
12   Paavo Nurmi (TAF)
9   Heikki Savolainen (GYM)

Most Gold Medals, Men
9   Paavo Nurmi (TAF)
5   Ville Ritola (TAF)
5   Clas Thunberg (SSK)

First Medalist, Men
    25 APR 1906   Verner Järvinen (TAF-DT)

First Gold Medalist, Men
    01 MAY 1906   Verner Järvinen (TAF-DT Greek)
    01 MAY 1906   Verner Weckman (WRE-Middleweight)

Youngest Medalist/Gold Medalist, Men
    18-219   Tomi Poikolainen (ARC-1980)

Oldest Medalist, Men
    59-132   Ernst Westerlund (YAC-1952)

Oldest Gold Medalist, Men
    40-320   Heikki Savolainen (GYM-1948)

Most Medals, Women, Summer
    1   Sylvi Saimo (CAN)
    1   Päivi Meriluoto (ARC)
    1   Tiina Lillak (TAF)
    1   Kaisa Parviainen (TAF)

Most Gold Medals, Women, Summer
    1   Sylvi Saimo (CAN)

First Medalist/Gold Medalist, Women
    28 JUL 1952   Sylvi Saimo (CAN-Kayak Singles)

Youngest Medalist, Women, Summer
    23-114   Tiina Lillak (TAF-1984)

Oldest Medalist, Women, Summer
    37-259   Sylvi Saimo (CAN-1952)

Most Medals, Winter, Men
    7   Veikko Hakulinen (NSK)
    7   Eero Mäntyranta (NSK)
    7   Clas Thunberg (SSK)

Most Gold Medals, Winter, Men
    5   Clas Thunberg (SSK)
    3   Veikko Hakulinen (NSK)
    3   Eero Mäntyranta (NSK)

First Medalist/Gold Medalist, Winter, Men
    26 APR 1920   Walter Jakobsson (FSK-Pairs)

Youngest Medalist, Winter, Men
    19-064   Niilo Halonen (NSK-1960)

Youngest Gold Medalist, Winter, Men
    20-216   Matti Nykänen (NSK-1984)

Oldest Medalist, Winter, Men
41-359 Walter Jakobsson (FSK-1924)

Oldest Gold Medalist, Winter, Men
38-080 Walter Jakobsson (FSK-1920)

Most Medals, Winter, Women
5   Helena Takalo (NSK)
4   Marjatta Kajosmaa (NSK)
4   Kaija Mustonen (SSK)
4   Marja-Liisa Hämäläinen (NSK)

Most Gold Medals, Winter, Women
3   Marja-Liisa Hämäläinen (NSK)
1   Ludowika Jakobsson (FSK)
1   Lydia Wideman (NSK)
1   Siiri Rantanen (NSK)
1   Mirja Hietamies (NSK)
1   Sirkka Polkunen (NSK)
1   Helena Takalo (NSK)
1   Kaija Mustonen (SSK)

First Medalist/Gold Medalist, Winter, Women
26 APR 1920 Ludowika Jakobsson (FSK-Pairs)

Youngest Medalist, Winter, Women
19-012 Marjo Matikainen (NSK-1984)

Youngest Gold Medalist, Winter, Women
25-025 Mirja Hietamies (NSK-1956)

Oldest Medalist, Winter, Women
39-189 Ludowika Jakobsson (FSK-1924)

Oldest Gold Medalist, Winter, Women
35-275 Ludowika Jakobsson (FSK-1920)

Most Medals, Men, Games
6   Ville Ritola (TAF-1924)
5   Paavo Nurmi (TAF-1924)
5   Clas Thunberg (SSK-1924)
5   Veikko Huhtanen (GYM-1948)

Most Gold Medals, Men, Games
5   Paavo Nurmi (TAF-1924)
4   Ville Ritola (TAF-1924)

Most Medals, Women, Games
4   Marja-Liisa Hämäläinen (NSK-1984)
3   Marjatta Kajosmaa (NSK-1972)
3   Helena Takalo (NSK-1976)

370   *Olympic Records by Nations*

Most Gold Medals, Women, Games
  3   Marja-Liisa Hämäläinen (NSK-1984)

Most Medals, Winter, Men, Games
  5   Clas Thunberg (SSK-1924)
  3   Julius Skutnabb (SSK-1924)
  3   Birger Wasenius (SSK-1936)
  3   Veikko Hakulinen (NSK-1956)
  3   Veikko Hakulinen (NSK-1960)
  3   Eero Mäntyranta (NSK-1964)
  3   Eero Mäntyranta (NSK-1968)
  3   Juha Mieto (NSK-1980)
  3   Aki Karvonen (NSK-1984)

Most Gold Medals, Winter, Men, Games
  3   Clas Thunberg (SSK-1924)
  2   Eero Mäntyranta (NSK-1964)

Most Medals, Winter, Women, Games
  4   Marja-Liisa Hämäläinen (NSK-1984)
  3   Marjatta Kajosmaa (NSK-1972)
  3   Helena Kivioja-Takalo (NSK-1976)

Most Gold Medals, Winter, Women, Games
  3   Marja-Liisa Hämäläinen (NSK-1984)
  1   Ludowika Jakobsson (FSK-1920)
  1   Lydia Wideman (NSK-1952)
  1   Siiri Rantanen (NSK-1956)
  1   Mirja Hietamies (NSK-1956)
  1   Sirkka Polkunen (NSK-1956)
  1   Kaija Mustonen (SSK-1968)
  1   Helena Kivioja-Takalo (NSK-1976)

FRANCE (FRA)
République Française
French Republic
Comité National Olympique et Sportif Français - 1894

Area: 221,207 sq. mi. Population (1985 est.): 55,041,000
Located: Western Europe
Language(s): French; minorities speak Breton, Alsatian German,
  Flemish, Italian, Basque, and Catalan
Religion(s): Roman Catholic
Government: Republic

Olympic History: France can be said to be the home of the modern
Olympic Games, being the home of Pierre de Coubertin, their
founder. Not unexpectedly, they have competed at every
celebration of the Olympic Games and at every Olympic Winter
Games. Older sources state that they were not represented at
the 1904 Olympics in St. Louis, but finishing third in the
marathon that year was Albert Corey who ran under the colors of
the Chicago Athletic Association and for many years was listed
as representing the United States. However, Corey came to the
United States only in 1902 and was still a French citizen in
1904. In addition to appearing at all the Olympic Games, France
has hosted four Olympic Games, more than any other country save
the United States.
   France's greatest athletic successes have come in the sports
of cycling and fencing, sports at which they have often been the
dominant nation.

Olympic Hosts:
         1900 - Paris - The Games of the IInd Olympiad
         1924 - Paris - The Games of the VIIIth Olympiad
         1924 - Chamonix - The Ist Olympic Winter Games
         1968 - Grenoble - The Xth Olympic Winter Games
         1992 - Albertville - The XVIth Olympic Winter Games

Medal Count:

| | ___Men___ | | | | ___Women___ | | | | ___Totals___ | | | |
	GO	SI	BR	TOT	GO	SI	BR	TOT	GO	SI	BR	TOT
Summer	139+	153+	162+	455+	8+	6+	6+	21+	148	160	169	477
Winter	8	4	8+	20+	4	6	6+	16+	12	10	15	37
Totals	147+	157+	171	476+	12+	12+	13	37+	160	170	184	514

Most Medals, Men
    8   Philippe Cattiau (FEN)
    8   Roger Ducret (FEN)
    8   Léon Moreaux (SHO)

Most Gold Medals, Men
    4   Max Decugis (TEN)
    4   Lucien Gaudin (FEN)
    4   Christian d'Oriola (FEN)

First Medalist, Men
    06 APR 1896 Alexandre Tuffère (TAF-TJ)

First Gold Medalist, Men
    07 APR 1896 Eugène-Henri Gravelotte (FEN-Foil Individual)

Youngest Medalist, Men
    <10   Unknown coxswain (ROW-1900)
    12-233   Noël Vandernotte (ROW-1936)

Youngest Gold Medalist, Men
    <10   Unknown coxswain (ROW-1900)
    14-095   Bernard Malivoire (ROW-1952)

Oldest Medalist, Men
    58-003 André Jousseaume (EQU-1952)

Oldest Gold Medalist, Men
    54-014 André Jousseaume (EQU-1948)

Most Medals, Women
    3   Andrée Brunet-Joly (FSK)
    3   Marielle Goitschel (ASK)
    3   Suzanna Lenglen (TEN)
    3   Micheline Ostermeyer (TAF)
    3   Perrine Pelen (ASK)
    3   Brigitte Gaudin-Latrille (FEN)
    3   Pascale Trinquet-Hachin (FEN)

Most Gold Medals, Women
    3   Suzanne Lenglen (TEN)
    2   Andrée Brunet-Joly (FSK)
    2   Marielle Goitschel (ASK)
    2   Micheline Ostermeyer (TAF)
    2   Pascale Trinquet-Hachin (FEN)

First Medalist, Women
    09 JUL 1900   Helène Prevost (TEN-Singles/Mixed)

First Gold Medalist, Women
    04 JUL 1912   Marquerite Broquedis (TEN-Singles)

Youngest Medalist, Women
    18-105 Brigitte Latrille (FEN-1976)

Youngest Gold Medalist, Women
    20-020 Isabelle Bégard (FEN-1980)

Oldest Medalist, Women
    38-016 Virginie Hériot (YAC-1928)

Oldest Gold Medalist, Women
    29-079 Christine Muzio (FEN-1980)

Most Medals, Winter, Men
    3   Pierre Brunet (FSK)
    3   Jean-Claude Killy (ASK)
    3   Henri Oreiller (ASK)

Most Gold Medals, Winter, Men
    3   Jean-Claude Killy (ASK)
    2   Henri Oreiller (ASK)
    2   Pierre Brunet (FSK)

First Medalist, Winter, Men
    31 JAN 1924   Pierre Brunet (FSK-Pairs)

First Gold Medalist, Winter, Men
    19 FEB 1928 Pierre Brunet (FSK-Pairs)

Youngest Medalist, Winter, Men
    19-363 Guy Perillat (ASK-1960)

Youngest Gold Medalist, Winter, Men
    22-035 Jean Vuarnet (ASK-1960)

Oldest Medalist/Gold Medalist, Winter, Men
    29-229 Pierre Brunet (FSK-1932)

Most Medals, Winter, Women
    3   Andrée Brunet-Joly (FSK)
    3   Marielle Goitschel (ASK)
    3   Perrine Pelen (ASK)

Most Gold Medals, Winter, Women
    2   Andrée Brunet-Joly (FSK)
    2   Marielle Goitschel (ASK)

First Medalist, Winter, Women
    31 JAN 1924 Andrée Joly (FSK-Pairs)

First Gold Medalist, Winter, Women
    19 FEB 1928 Andrée Joly (FSK-Pairs)

Youngest Medalist, Winter, Women
    17-205 Danielle Debernard (ASK-1972)

Youngest Gold Medalist, Winter, Women
    18-128 Marielle Goitschel (ASK-1964)

Oldest Medalist/Gold Medalist, Winter, Women
    30-149 Andrée Brunet-Joly (FSK-1932)

Most Medals, Men, Games
    5   Léon Moreaux (SHO-1906)
    5   Julien Brulé (ARC-1920)
    5   Roger Ducret (FEN-1924)

Most Gold Medals, Men, Games
    3   Paul Masson (CYC-1896)
    3   Max Decugis (TEN-1906)
    3   Roger Ducret (FEN-1924)
    3   Robert Charpentier (CYC-1936)
    3   Jean-Claude Killy (ASK-1968)

Most Medals, Women, Games
    3   Suzanne Lenglen (TEN-1920)
    3   Micheline Ostermeyer (TAF-1948)

Most Gold Medals, Women, Games
  3   Suzanne Lenglen (TEN-1920)
  2   Micheline Ostermeyer (TAF-1948)
  2   Pascale Trinquet-Hachin (FEN-1980)

Most Medals, Winter, Men, Games
  3   Jean-Claude Killy (ASK-1968)
  3   Henri Oreiller (ASK-1948)

Most Gold Medals, Winter, Men, Games
  3   Jean-Claude Killy (ASK-1968)
  2   Henri Oreiller (ASK-1948)

Most Medals, Winter, Women, Games
  2   Christine Goitschel (ASK-1964)
  2   Marielle Goitschel (ASK-1964)
  2   Annie Famose (ASK-1968)
  2   Perrine Pelen (ASK-1984)

Most Gold Medals, Winter, Women, Games
  1   Andrée Brunet-Joly (FSK-1928)
  1   Andrée Brunet-Joly (FSK-1932)
  1   Marielle Goitschel (ASK-1964)
  1   Christine Goitschel (ASK-1964)
  1   Christine Goitschel (ASK-1968)

GABON (GAB)
République Gabonaise
Gabonese Republic
Comité Olympique Gabonais - 1968

Area: 103,346 sq. mi. Population (1985 est.): 988,000
Located: Atlantic coast of central Africa
Language(s): French (official), Bantu dialects
Religion(s): Tribal beliefs, Christian minority
Government: Republic

Olympic History: Gabon has competed at two Olympic Games, 1972
   and 1984. In 1972 they were represented by one boxer, and in
   1984 by two boxers and two women track & field athletes.

THE GAMBIA (GAM)
Republic of The Gambia
Gambia National Olympic Committee - 1976

Area: 4,361 sq. mi. Population (1985 est.): 751,000
Located: Atlantic Coast near western tip of Africa
Language(s): English (official), Mandinka, Wolof
Religion(s): Muslims 85%, Christian 14%
Government: Republic

Olympic History: Four male and three female track & field
athletes at Los Angeles in 1984 make up Gambia's entire Olympic
delegation to date.

GERMANY (GER)
See Germany, Federal Republic of; Germany, Democratic Republic
of; and The Saar

GERMANY, DEMOCRATIC REPUBLIC OF (EAST GERMANY) (GDR)
Deutsche Demokratische Republik
German Democratic Republic
Nationales Olympisches Komitee der Deutschen Demokratischen
Republik - 1955

Area: 41,768 sq. mi. Population (1985 est.): 16,686,000
Located: East central Europe
Language(s): German
Religion(s): Protestant 80%
Government: Communist

Olympic History: The GDR competed with the FRG as a combined
German team at the Olympic Games of 1956-1964. In 1968, the GDR
made its first appearance in the Olympic Games as an independent
state. In 1968, however, the GDR was forced to compete as "East
Germany," a name it does not recognize, and competing with a
common flag and anthem with the NOC of the FRG. These affronts
were corrected in 1972. Since 1972, the GDR has missed only the
1984 Los Angeles Olympics. They have become one of the three
world sporting powers, being dominant in many sports in both the
summer and winter Games. Its women, especially, are virtually
without peer in the sporting world.

Medal Count:

	Men				Women				Totals			
	GO	SI	BR	TOT	GO	SI	BR	TOT	GO	SI	BR	TOT
Summer	59	56	65	180	63	59	41	163	122	115	106	343
Winter	20	15+	21+	57	14	13+	8+	36	34	29	30	93
Totals	79	71+	86+	237	77	72+	49+	199	156	144	136	436

Most Medals, Men
    7   Roland Matthes (SWI)
    6   Rudiger Helm (CAN)

Most Gold Medals, Men
    4   Roland Matthes (SWI)
    3   Rudiger Helm (CAN)
    3   Bernard Germeshausen (BOB)
    3   Meinhard Nehmer (BOB)
    3   Siegfried Brietzke (ROW)
    3   Ulrich Wehling (NSK)

First Medalist, Men
01 DEC 1956 Wolfgang Behrendt (BOX-Bantamweight)
01 DEC 1956 Klaus Richtzenhein (TAF-1500)
15 OCT 1968 Lothar Milde (TAF-DT)

First Gold Medalist, Men
01 DEC 1956 Wolfgang Behrendt (BOX-Bantamweight)
17 OCT 1968 Christoph Hohne (TAF-50 Walk)

Youngest Medalist/Gold Medalist, Summer, Men
17-108 Jörg Woithe (SWI-1980)

Oldest Medalist/Gold Medalist, Summer, Men
38-020 Kurt Czekella (SHO-1968)

Most Medals, Women
8   Kornelia Ender (SWI)
7   Karin Janz (GYM)

Most Gold Medals, Women
4   Kornelia Ender (SWI)
4   Bärbel Wöckel-Eckert (TAF)

First Medalist, Women
26 NOV 1956 Christa Stubnick (TAF-100)
20 OCT 1968 Margitta Gummel (TAF-SP)
20 OCT 1968 Marita Lange (TAF-SP)

First Gold Medalist, Women
27 AUG 1960 Ingrid Krämer (DIV-Springboard)
20 OCT 1968 Margitta Gummel (TAF-SP)

Youngest Medalist, Women
13-308 Kornelia Ender (SWI-1972)

Youngest Gold Medalist, Women
15-072 Andrea Pollack (SWI-1976)

Oldest Medalist, Women
34-096 Karin Balzer (TAF-1972)

Oldest Gold Medalist, Women
27-279 Angelika Noack (ROW-1980)

Most Medals, Winter, Men
4   Klaus-Michael Bonsack (LUG)
4   Meinhard Nehmer (BOB)
4   Frank Ullrich (BIA)
4   Bogdan Musiol (BOB)
4   Bernhard Germeshausen (BOB)

Most Gold Medals, Winter, Men
3   Meinhard Nehmer (BOB)
3   Bernhard Germeshausen (BOB)

First Medalist, Winter, Men
 05 FEB 1956   Harry Glaß (NSK-Jump)
 18 FEB 1968   Klaus-Michael Bonsack/Thomas Köhler (LUG-Doubles)

First Gold Medalist, Winter, Men
 28 FEB 1960   Helmut Recknagel (NSK-80 Jump)
 18 FEB 1968   Klaus-Michael Bonsack/Thomas Köhler (LUG-Doubles)

Youngest Medalist, Winter, Men
 18-020   Frank Ullrich (BIA-1976)

Youngest Gold Medalist, Winter, Men
 19-206   Jens Weißflog (NSK-1984)

Oldest Medalist/Gold Medalist, Winter, Men
 39-042   Meinhard Nehmer (BOB-1980)

Most Medals, Winter, Women
 5   Karin Enke (SSK)
 3   Barbara Petzold (NSK)
 3   Andrea Schöne-Mitscherlich (SSK)

Most Gold Medals, Winter, Women
 3   Karin Enke (SSK)
 2   Barbara Petzold (NSK)

First Medalist, Winter, Women
 20 FEB 1960   Helga Haase (SSK-500)
 07 FEB 1972   Anna-Maria Müller (LUG-Singles)

First Gold Medalist, Winter, Women
 20 FEB 1960   Helga Haase (SSK-500)
 07 FEB 1972   Anna-Maria Müller (LUG-Singles)

Youngest Medalist, Winter, Women
 15-008   Manuela Groß (FSK-1972)

Youngest Gold Medalist, Winter, Women
 18-077   Katarina Witt (FSK-1984)

Oldest Medalist/Gold Medalist, Winter, Women
 24-197   Barbara Petzold (NSK-1980)

Most Medals, Men, Games
 4   Roland Bruckner (GYM-1980)
 3   Frank Wiegand (SWI-1964)
 3   Roland Matthes (SWI-1968)
 3   Roland Matthes (SWI-1972)
 3   Rudiger Helm (CAN-1976)
 3   Rudiger Helm (CAN-1980)
 3   Frank Ullrich (BIA-1980)

Most Gold Medals, Men, Games
  2   Roland Matthes (SWI-1968)
  2   Roland Matthes (SWI-1972)
  2   Rudiger Helm (CAN-1980)

Most Medals, Women, Games
  5   Karin Janz (GYM-1972)
  5   Kornelia Ender (SWI-1976)
  5   Ines Diers (SWI-1980)

Most Gold Medals, Women, Games
  4   Kornelia Ender (SWI-1976)
  3   Ulrich Richter (SWI-1976)
  3   Caren Metschuck (SWI-1980)
  3   Barbara Krause (SWI-1980)
  3   Rica Reinisch (SWI-1980)

Most Medals, Winter, Men, Games
  3   Frank Ullrich (BIA-1980)
  2   Meinhard Nehmer (BOB-1976)
  2   Bernhard Germeshausen (BOB-1976)
  2   Wolfgang Hoppe (BOB-1984)
  2   Dietmar Schauerhammer (BOB-1984)

Most Gold Medals, Winter, Men, Games
  2   Meinhard Nehmer (BOB-1976)
  2   Bernard Germeshausen (BOB-1976)
  2   Wolfgang Hoppe (BOB-1984)
  2   Dietmar Schauerhammer (BOB-1984)

Most Medals, Winter, Women, Games
  4   Karin Enke (SSK-1984)
  3   Andrea Mitscherlich-Schöne (SSK-1984)

Most Gold Medals, Winter, Women, Games
  2   Barbara Petzold (NSK-1980)
  2   Karin Enke (SSK-1984)

GERMANY, FEDERAL REPUBLIC OF (WEST GERMANY) (FRG)
Bundesrepublik Deutschland
Federal Republic of Germany
Nationales Olympisches Komitee für Deutschland - 1950

Area: 95,975 sq. mi. Population (1985 est.): 60,950,000
Located: Central Europe
Language(s): German
Religion(s): Protestant 45%, Roman Catholic 45%
Government: Federal republic

Olympic History: Germany was one of the countries which competed at the first Olympics in 1896. Germany competed with distinction through the Olympics preceding World War II, except for those of 1920 and 1924, when they were not invited because of their role in the First World War. In 1948, Germany was once again not invited to the Olympic Games. The country returned to the Olympic fold in 1952. From 1952 through 1964 Germany was represented by a combined team representing both the FRG and the GDR, although it should be noted that no GDR athletes competed in 1952. Starting in 1968 the two Germanies have competed under separate flags. Germany, later as a combined team, and later as the FRG, has competed at all Olympic Winter Games except those of 1924 and 1948, when they were not invited. In 1952 The Saar was recognized as a separate Olympic Committee by the IOC and competed at the Helsinki Olympics. The Saar was reunited with the FRG in 1956. Their athletes were absorbed by the combined German teams and The Saar OC was dissolved on 20 September 1956.

Olympic Hosts:

    1936 - Berlin - The Games of the XIth Olympiad
    1936 - Garmisch-Partenkirchen - The IVth Olympic Winter
              Games
    1972 - Munich - The Games of the XXth Olympiad

Medal Count - Germany and FRG Combined (1896-1984):

	Men				Women				Totals			
	GO	SI	BR	TOT	GO	SI	BR	TOT	GO	SI	BR	TOT
Summer	116+	140+	153+	410+	21+	32+	31+	85+	137+	173	185	495+
Winter	12+	10+	13+	36+	7+	8+	6+	22+	20	19	20	59
Totals	128+	150+	166+	446+	29+	41+	38+	108+	157+	192	205	554+

Medal Count - Germany (1896-1936, and FRG/GDR combined medals 1952-64):

	Men				Women				Totals			
	GO	SI	BR	TOT	GO	SI	BR	TOT	GO	SI	BR	TOT
Summer	65	74	70	209	6+	8	11	25+	71+	82	81	234+
Winter	2	2	3	7	2	2	-	4	4	4	3	11
Totals	67	76	73	216	8+	10	11	29+	75+	86	84	245+

Medal Count - FRG (1952-1984):

	Men				Women				Totals			
	GO	SI	BR	TOT	GO	SI	BR	TOT	GO	SI	BR	TOT
Summer	51+	66+	83+	201+	14+	24+	20+	59+	66	91	104	261
Winter	10+	8+	10+	29+	5+	6+	6+	18+	16	15	17	48
Totals	61+	74+	93+	230+	20+	31+	27+	78+	82	106	121	309

Most Medals, Men

    7   Reiner Klimke (EQU)
    7   Hans-Günter Winkler (EQU)

Most Gold Medals, Men
  5   Reiner Klimke (EQU)
  5   Hans-Günter Winkler (EQU)

First Medalist, Men
  09 APR 1896 Gymnastics Parallel Bars Team (GYM-PB Team)
  09 APR 1896 Gymnastics Horizontal Bar Team (GYM-HB Team)
  09 APR 1896 Karl Schumann (GYM-HV)
  09 APR 1896 Herman Weingartner (GYM-HB/FR/PH/HV)
  09 APR 1896 Alfred Flatow (GYM-HB)
  15 OCT 1968 Gerhard Hennige (TAF-400IH)

First Gold Medalist, Men
  09 APR 1896 Gymnastics Parallel Bars Team (GYM-PB Team)
  09 APR 1896 Gymnastics Horizontal Bar Team (GYM-HB Team)
  09 APR 1896 Karl Schumann (GYM-HV)
  09 APR 1896 Herman Weingartner (GYM-HB)
  19 OCT 1968 Eight-Oared Crew (ROW-Eights)

Youngest Medalist/Gold Medalist, Men
  14-282 Klaus Zerta (ROW-1960)

Oldest Medalist, Men
  60-094 Josef Neckermann (EQU-1972)

Oldest Gold Medalist, Men
  56-142 Josef Neckermann (EQU-1968)

Most Medals, Women
  5   Liselott Linsenhoff (EQU)
  4   Annegret Richter (TAF)

Most Gold Medals, Women
  2   Liselott Linsenhoff (EQU)
  2   Annegret Richter (TAF)
  2   Ulrike Meyfarth (TAF)
  2   Heidemarie Rosendahl (TAF)
  2   Roswitha Esser (CAN)
  2   Annemarie Zimmermann (CAN)
  2   Rosi Mittermaier (ASK)

First Medalist/Gold Medalist, Women
  05 JUL 1912 Dorothea Köring (TEN-Mixed)
  16 OCT 1968 Ingrid Becker (TAF-Pentathlon)

Youngest Medalist, Women
  14-115 Inge Schmitz (SWI-1936)
  16-113 Ulrike Meyfarth (TAF-1972)

Youngest Gold Medalist, Women
  18-038 Zita Funkenhauser (FEN-1984)

Oldest Medalist/Gold Medalist, Women
  45-012 Liselott Linsenhoff (EQU-1968)

Most Medals, Winter, Men
   4   Wolfgang Zimmerer (BOB)
   4   Peter Angerer (BIA)

Most Gold Medals, Winter, Men
   2   Andreas Ostler (BOB)
   2   Lorenz Nieberl (BOB)
   2   Erhard Keller (SSK)

First Medalist/Gold Medalist, Winter, Men
   29 OCT 1908 Heinrich Bürger (FSK-Pairs)
   11 FEB 1968 Franz Keller (NSK-Nordic Combined)

Youngest Medalist, Winter, Men
   18-022   Hans-Jürgen Baumler (FSK-1960)

Youngest Gold Medalist, Winter, Men
   20-279   Manfred Schnelldorfer (FSK-1964)

Oldest Medalist/Gold Medalist, Winter, Men
   41-103   Franz Kemser (BOB-1952)

Most Medals, Winter, Women
   3   Rosi Mittermaier (ASK)
   3   Annemarie "Mirl" Buchner (ASK)

Most Gold Medals, Winter, Women
   2   Rosi Mittermaier (ASK)
   1   Christl Cranz (ASK)
   1   Ossi Reichert (ASK)
   1   Heidi Beibl (FRG)
   1   Anna Hübler (FSK)
   1   Maxi Herber (FSK)
   1   Ria Falk (FSK)
   1   Monika Pflug (SSK)

First Medalist, Winter, Women
   29 OCT 1908 Anna Hübler (FSK-Pairs)
   29 OCT 1908 Elsa Rendschmidt (FSK-Ladies)
   11 FEB 1972 Monika Pflug (SSK-1000)

First Gold Medalist, Winter, Women
   29 OCT 1908 Anna Hübler (FSK-Pairs)
   11 FEB 1972 Monika Pflug (SSK-1000)

Youngest Medalist/Gold Medalist, Winter, Women
   15-128   Maxi Herber (FSK-1936)
   17-347   Monika Pflug (SSK-1972)

Oldest Medalist/Gold Medalist, Winter, Women
   30-033   Ossi Reichart (ASK-1956)

Most Medals, Men, Games
6   Hermann Weingartner (GYM-1896)
6   Konrad Frey (GYM-1936)

Most Gold Medals, Men, Games
4   Karl Schumann (GYM/WRE-1896)
3   Alfred Flatow (GYM-1896)
3   Konrad Frey (GYM-1936)
3   Hermann Weingartner (GYM-1936)
3   Alfred Schwarzmann (GYM-1936)

Most Medals, Women, Games
3   Annemarie "Mirl" Buchner (ASK-1952)
3   Heidemarie Rosendahl (TAF-1972)
3   Rosi Mittermaier (ASK-1976)
3   Annegret Richter (TAF-1976)
3   Karin Seick (SWI-1984)

Most Gold Medals, Women, Games
2   Heidemarie Rosendahl (TAF-1972)
2   Rosi Mittermaier (ASK-1976)

Most Medals, Winter, Men, Games
3   Peter Angerer (BIA-1984)
2   Ernst Baier (FSK-1936)
2   Andreas Ostler (BOB-1952)
2   Lorenz Nieberl (BOB-1952)
2   Wolfgang Zimmerer (BOB-1972)
2   Peter Utzschneider (BOB-1972)
2   Wolfgang Zimmerer (BOB-1976)
2   Manfred Schumann (BOB-1976)

Most Gold Medals, Winter, Men, Games
2   Andreas Ostler (BOB-1952)
2   Lorenz Nieberl (BOB-1952)

Most Medals, Winter, Women, Games
3   Annemarie "Mirl" Buchner (ASK-1952)
3   Rosi Mittermaier (ASK-1976)

Most Gold Medals, Winter, Women, Games
2   Rosi Mittermaier (ASK-1976)
1   Anna Hübler (FSK-1908)
1   Maxi Herber (FSK-1936)
1   Christl Cranz (ASK-1936)
1   Ria Falk (FSK-1952)
1   Ossi Reichert (ASK-1956)
1   Heidi Beibl (FRG-1960)
1   Monika Pflug (SSK-1972)

GHANA (GHA)
Republic of Ghana
Ghana Olympic Committee - 1952

Former Name: Gold Coast (changed and independence declared 06 MAR 1957).
Area: 92,098 sq. mi. Population (1985 est.): 13,004,000
Located: Southern coast of west Africa
Language(s): English (official), tribal languages
Religion(s): Christian 45%, tribal beliefs 45%
Government: Authoritarian

Olympic History: Ghana first appeared at the Olympics in 1952, as The Gold Coast. It did not attend the 1956 Olympics, but competed from 1960 through 1972. After boycotting the 1976 and 1980 Olympics, Ghana did attend the 1984 Olympics. Ghana has never competed at the Olympic Winter Games.

Medal Count:

	Men				Women				Totals			
	GO	SI	BR	TOT	GO	SI	BR	TOT	GO	SI	BR	TOT
Summer	-	1	2	3	-	-	-	-	-	1	2	3
Winter	-	-	-	-	-	-	-	-	-	-	-	-
Totals	-	1	2	3	-	-	-	-	-	1	2	3

Most Medals, Men
  1   Clement "Ike" Quartey (BOX)
  1   Eddie Blay (BOX)
  1   Prince Amartey (BOX)

First Medalist, Men
  05 SEP 1960 Clement "Ike" Quartey (BOX-Light-welterweight)

Youngest Medalist, Men
  22-147 Clement "Ike" Quartey (BOX-1960)

Oldest Medalist, Men
  28-076 Prince Amartey (BOX-1972)

GOLD COAST (---)
  See Ghana.

GREAT BRITAIN (GBR)
The United Kingdom of Great Britain and Northern Ireland
The British Olympic Association - 1905

Area: 94,226 sq. mi. Population (1985 est.): 56,423,000
Located: Islands off the northwest coast of Europe
Language(s): English, Welsh (southern Wales), Gaelic (N. Ireland)
Religion(s): Protestant (Anglican 19%), Roman Catholic minority
Government: Constitutional monarchy

Olympic History: Great Britain has never failed to be represented
at the Olympic Games, including all the usual exceptions. It
competed at the 1906 Intercalated Games in Athens, the 1908
figure skating events at London, the 1920 figure skating events
in Antwerp, and it competed at the 1956 Equestrian Olympics in
Stockholm. Only Switzerland can make a similar claim. Through
1920, Great Britain competed in a combined team with Ireland.

Olympic Hosts:
        1908 - London - The Games of the IVth Olympiad
        1948 - London - The Games of the XIVth Olympiad

Medal Count:

	Men				Women				Totals			
	GO	SI	BR	TOT	GO	SI	BR	TOT	GO	SI	BR	TOT
Summer	147+	169+	163+	480+	18	41+	34+	94+	165+	211+	198	575
Winter	4+	2+	6	13	2+	1+	4	8	7	4	10	21
Totals	152	172+	169+	493+	20+	43+	38+	102+	172+	215+	208	596

Most Medals, Men
   8   Henry Taylor (SWI)
   5   Jack Beresford (ROW)
   5   John Jarvis (SWI)

Most Gold Medals, Men
   4   Henry Taylor (SWI)
   3   Jack Beresford (ROW)
   3   Reginald Doherty (TEN)
   3   Richard Meade (EQU)
   3   Charles Smith (WAP)
   3   George Wilkinson (WAP)

First Medalist, Men
  07 APR 1896 Launceston Elliot (WLT-Heavyweight)
  07 APR 1896 Charles Gmelin (TAF-400)

First Gold Medalist, Men
  07 APR 1896 Launceston Elliot (WLT-Heavyweight)

Youngest Medalist, Men
  16-134 Brian Phelps (DIV-1960)

Youngest Gold Medalist, Men
  20-202 George de Relwyskow (WRE-1908)

Oldest Medalist, Men
  61-245 John Butt (SHO-1912)

Oldest Gold Medalist, Men
  56-078 Allen Whitty (SHO-1924)

Most Medals, Women
   5   Kathleen McKane (TEN)
   4   Margaret Cooper (SWI)

Most Gold Medals, Women
   2   Charlotte Cooper (TEN)
   2   Ethel Hannam (TEN)

First Medalist/Gold Medalist, Women
  09 JUL 1900 Charlotte Cooper (TEN-Singles/Mixed)

First Gold Medalist, Women
  09 JUL 1900 Charlotte Cooper (TEN-Singles/Mixed)

Youngest Medalist, Women, Summer
  15-143 Sarah Hardcastle (SWI-1984)

Youngest Gold Medalist, Women, Summer
  17-266 Bella Moore (SWI-1912)

Oldest Medalist/Gold Medalist, Women
  43-015 Winifred McNair (TEN-1920)

Most Medals, Winter, Men
   1   Many athletes tied with one

Most Gold Medals, Winter, Men
   1   Seventeen athletes tied with one

First Medalist, Winter, Men
  29 JAN 1908 James Johnson (FSK-Pairs)
  29 JAN 1908 Edgar Syers (FSK-Pairs)
  29 JAN 1908 Arthur Cumming (FSK-Special Figures)
  29 JAN 1908 George Hall-Say (FSK-Special Figures)

First Gold Medalist, Winter, Men
  16 FEB 1936 Ice Hockey Team (ICH)

Youngest Medalist/Gold Medalist, Winter, Men
  20-328 James Chappell (ICH-1936)

Oldest Medalist, Winter, Men
  45-035 John Crammond (LUG/SKE-1948)

Oldest Gold Medalist, Winter, Men
  35-046 Carl Erhardt (ICH-1936)

Most Medals, Winter, Women
   2   Jeannette Altwegg (FSK)
   2   Madge Syers (FSK)
   2   Phyllis Johnson (FSK)

Most Gold Medals, Winter, Women
    1   Madge Syers (FSK)
    1   Jeannette Altwegg (FSK)
    1   Jayne Torvill (FSK)

First Medalist, Winter, Women
    29 JAN 1908 Madge Syers (FSK-Pairs/Singles)
    29 JAN 1908 Dorothy Greenhough-Smith (FSK-Singles)
    29 JAN 1908 Phyllis Johnson (FSK-Pairs)

First Gold Medalist, Winter, Women
    29 JAN 1908 Madge Syers (FSK-Singles)

Youngest Medalist, Winter, Women
    15-076 Cecilia Colledge (FSK-1936)

Youngest Gold Medalist, Winter, Women
    21-165 Jeannette Altwegg (FSK-1952)

Oldest Medalist, Winter, Women
    35-116 Phyllis Johnson (FSK-1920)

Oldest Gold Medalist, Winter, Women
    26-303 Madge Syers (FSK-1908)

Most Medals, Men, Games
    3   Thirteen athletes tied with three

Most Gold Medals, Men, Games
    3   Henry Taylor (SWI-1908)
    2   Charles Bennett (TAF-1900)
    2   Lawrence Doherty (TEN-1900)
    2   Reginald Doherty (TEN-1900)
    2   Benjamin Jones (CYC-1908)

Most Medals, Women, Games
    3   Mary Bignal-Rand (TAF-1964)
    2   Charlotte Cooper (TEN-1900)
    2   Ethel Hannam (TEN-1912)

Most Gold Medals, Women, Games
    2   Charlotte Cooper (TEN-1900)
    2   Ethel Hannam (TEN-1912)

Most Medals, Winter, Men, Games
    1   Many athletes tied with one

Most Gold Medals, Winter, Men, Games
    1   Seventeen athletes tied with one

Most Medals, Winter, Women, Games
2	Madge Syers (FSK-1908)
1	Dorothy Greenhoulgh-Smith (FSK-1908)
1	Phyllis Johnson (FSK-1908)
1	Phyllis Johnson (FSK-1920)
1	Ethel Muckelt (FSK-1924)
1	Jeannette Altwegg (FSK-1948)
1	Jeannette Altwegg (FSK-1952)
1	Jayne Torvill (FSK-1984)

Most Gold Medals, Winter, Women, Games
1	Madge Syers (FSK-1908)
1	Jeannette Altwegg (FSK-1952)
1	Jayne Torvill (FSK-1984)

GREECE (GRE)
`Elliniki Dimokratia
Hellenic Republic
Comité Olympique Hellénique - 1894

Area: 51,146 sq. mi. Population (1985 est.): 9,921,000
Located: Southern end of Balkan peninsula in southeast Europe
Language(s): Greek
Religion(s): Greek Orthodox 97%
Government: Presidential parliamentary republic

Olympic History: Greece is the home of the Olympics, the ancient
Games having been held there from at least 776 BC through 393
AD. The Games were revived and first held in Athens in 1896.
Since that time Greek participation at the Games of the Olympiad
has been continuous. Greece has also competed at the Olympic
Winter Games, first appearing in 1936 and missing only the 1960
Squaw Valley Olympics.

Olympic Hosts:
    1896 - Athens - The Games of the Ist Olympiad
    1906 - Athens - The (Intercalated) Olympic Games of 1906

Medal Count:

	Men				Women				Totals		
	GO	SI	BR	TOT	GO	SI	BR	TOT	GO	SI	BR	TOT
Summer	21	38+	37+	97	1	1+	1+	4	22	40	39	101
Winter	-	-	-	-	-	-	-	-	-	-	-	-
Totals	21	38+	37+	97	1	1+	1+	4	22	40	39	101

Most Medals, Men
4	Nicolaos Georgantas (TAF)
4	Konstantin Tsiklitiras (TAF)

Most Gold Medals, Men
2	Jean Georgiadis (FEN)
2	Georgios Orphanidis (SHO)

First Medalist, Men
  06 APR 1896 Ioannis Persakis (TAF-TJ)

First Gold Medalist, Men
  07 APR 1896 Leon Pyrgos (FEN-Foil Professional)

Youngest Medalist, Men
  10-216 Dimitrios Loundras (GYM-1896)

Youngest Gold Medalist, Men
  16-101 Ioannis Malokinis (SWI-1896)

Oldest Medalist/Gold Medalist, Men
  36-102 Giorgios Orphanidis (SHO-1896)

Most Medals, Women
  1   Esmée Simiriotou (TEN)
  1   Sophia Marinou (TEN)
  1   Euphrosine Paspati (TEN)
  1   Aspasia Matsa (TEN)

Most Gold Medals, Women
  1   Esmée Simiriotou (TEN)

First Medalist, Women
  24 APR 1896 Esmée Simiriotou (TEN-Singles)
  24 APR 1896 Sophia Marinou (TEN-Singles)
  24 APR 1896 Euphrosine Paspati (TEN-Singles)

First Gold Medalist, Women
  24 APR 1896 Esmée Simiriotou (TEN-Singles)

Youngest Medalist, Women
  21-115 Aspasia Matsa (TEN-1906)

Youngest/Oldest Gold Medalist, Women
  22-113 Esmée Simiriotou (TEN-1906)

Oldest Medalist, Women
  25-113 Euphrosine Paspati (TEN-1906)

Most Medals, Men, Games
  3   Efstathios Choraphas (SWI-1896)
  3   Nicolaos Georgantas (TAF-1906)

Most Gold Medals, Men, Games
  2   Georgios Orphanidas (SHO-1906)
  1   Many athletes tied with one

GRENADA (GRN)
State of Grenada
Grenada Olympic Association - 1984

Area: 133 sq. mi. Population (1984 est.): 113,000
Located: Island north of Venezuela in the Caribbean Sea
Language(s): English (official), French-English patois
Religion(s): Roman Catholic 64%, Anglican 22%
Government: Independent state of United Kingdom

Olympic History: Grenada has yet to compete in the Olympic Games.

GUAM (GUM)
Guam Amateur Sports Federation - 1986

Area: 209 sq. mi. Population (1985 est.): 119,540
Located: Southwest Pacific Ocean
Language(s): English, Chamorro, Spanish
Religion(s): Protestant, Roman Catholic
Government: Self-governing unincorporated territory of the United
  States

Olympic History: Guam has yet to compete in the Olympic Games.

GUATEMALA (GUA)
República de Guatemala
Republic of Guatemala
Comité Olímpico Guatemalteco - 1947

Area: 42,042 sq. mi. Population (1985 est.): 8,346,000
Located: Central America
Language(s): Spanish, Indian dialects
Religion(s): Roman Catholic 90%, Mayan religion
Government: Military

Olympic History: Guatemala first competed in the 1952 Olympics.
  It did not appear again until 1968 but has not missed an Olympic
  Games since. It has never competed in the Olympic Winter Games.
  Its top performance has been a sixth-place finish by Edgardo
  Zachrisson in skeet shooting at Montreal.

GUINEA (GUI)
République de Guinée
Republic of Guinea
Comité Olympique Guinéen - 1965

Area: 94,964 sq. mi. Population (1985 est.): 5,597,000
Located: Atlantic coast of west Africa
Language(s): French (official), tribal languages
Religion(s): Muslim 75%, tribal 24%, Christian 1%
Government: Republic

Olympic History: Guinea has so far competed at the Olympic Games
of 1968, 1972, and 1984. They have yet to win an Olympic medal.

GUINEA, BRITISH (---)
See Guyana.

GUINEA, EQUATORIAL (GEQ)
República de Guinea Ecuatorial
Republic of Equatorial Guinea
Comité National Olympique Equato-Guinéen - 1984

Area: 10,832 sq. mi. Population (1985 est.): 350,000
Located: West Africa
Language(s): Spanish (official), Fang, English
Religion(s): Roman Catholic 83%, Protestant
Government: Unitary Republic

Olympic History: Equatorial Guinea made its first Olympic
appearance in 1984 at Los Angeles, represented by five track &
field athletes.

GUYANA (GUY)
Cooperative Republic of Guyana
Guyana Olympic Association - 1948

Former Name: British Guinea (changed and independence declared 26
MAY 1966)
Area: 83,000 sq. mi. Population (1985 est.): 768,000
Located: Northern coast of South America
Language(s): English (official), Amerindian dialects
Religion(s): Christians 57%, Hindus 34%, Muslim 9%
Government: Republic within the Commonwealth of Nations

Olympic History: Guyana has competed at nine Olympic Games since
1948, missing only 1980. They have had 47 Olympians, 42 men and
five women. In 1980 Michael Anthony won their only medal to
date, a bronze in bantamweight boxing.

HAITI (HAI)
République d'Haiti
Republic of Haiti
Comité Olympique Hatien - 1924

Area: 10,714 sq. mi. Population (1985 est.): 5,762,000
Located: West Indies - occupies western third of island of
Hispaniola
Language(s): French (official), Creole (majority)
Religion(s): Roman Catholics 80%, Protestants 10%, Voodoo widely
practised
Government: Republic

Olympic History: Haiti has an interesting Olympic history. They
sent one fencer, named Léon Thiercelin, to the 1900 Olympics in
Paris. Their next appearances were in 1924, 1928, and 1932,
followed by a long gap before their return to the Olympic fold
in 1960. Despite having appeared in five Olympics to that date,
they had only a total representation of twelve men through 1960.
They have since appeared at the 1972, 1976 and 1984 Olympics.
Haitians have won two medals. In 1928, Silvio Cator (the first
man to long jump over 26 feet) won a silver medal in the long
jump. In 1924 their free rifle shooting team (Ludovic Augustin,
Astrel Rolland, Ludovic Valborge, Destin Destine, and Eloi
Metullus) won a bronze medal.

HONDURAS (HON)
República de Honduras
Republic of Honduras
Comité Olímpico Hondureno – 1956

Area: 43,277 sq. mi. Population (1985 est.): 4,499,000
Located: Central America
Language(s): Spanish, Indian dialects
Religion(s): Roman Catholic, small Protestant minority
Government: Democratic constitutional republic

Olympic History: Honduras has competed at the Olympics Games of
1968, 1972, and 1984.

HONG KONG (HKG)
Crown Colony of Hong Kong
Amateur Sports Federation and Olympic Committee of Hong Kong –
1951

Area: 409 sq. mi. Population (1983 est.): 5,287,000
Located: At the mouth of the Canton river on the east coast of
China
Language(s): English, Mandarin Chinese (official), Cantonese
(primary)
Religion(s): Buddhism, Taoism, Confucianism, Protestants, Roman
Catholic
Government: British parliamentary state

Olympic History: Hong Kong first competed at the 1952 Olympic
Games and has since missed only the 1980 Moscow Olympics. Hong
Kong has never competed at the Olympic Winter Games.

HUNGARY (HUN)
Magyar Népköztáraság
Hungarian People's Republic
Comité Olympique Hongrois - 1895

Area: 35,919 sq. mi. Population (1985 est.): 10,644,000
Located: East central Europe
Language(s): Hungarian (Magyar)
Religion(s): Roman Catholic 67%, Protestant 25%
Government: Communist unitary state

Olympic History: Hungary was one of the countries which attended
the first Olympic Games in 1896 at Athens. Since that time the
country has missed only two Olympics, including the Winter
Games. Hungary was not invited to the 1920 Olympics in Antwerp,
having been an aggressor nation in World War I, and Hungary
chose not to attend the 1984 Los Angeles Olympics.
    Hungary has been very successful in a variety of sports, but
by far her greatest honors have come in fencing. In one fencing
discipline, the sabre, Hungary is by far the preeminent nation,
and in fact, between 1908 and 1960 won nine of eleven team
titles and ten of eleven individual titles in this event.

Medal Count:

	Men				Women				Totals		
	GO	SI	BR	TOT	GO	SI	BR	TOT	GO	SI	BR	TOT
Summer	95	88	107	290	18	18	24	60	113	106	131	350
Winter	-	1	2	3	-	1	2	3	-	2	4	6
Totals	95	89	109	293	18	19	26	63	113	108	135	356

Most Medals, Men
    10   Aládár Gerevich (FEN)
    9   Zoltán Halmay (SWI)

Most Gold Medals, Men
    7   Aládár Gerevich (FEN)
    6   Pál Kovács (FEN)
    6   Rudolf Kárpáti (FEN)

First Medalist, Men
    09 APR 1896 Nándor Dáni (TAF-800)

First Gold Medalist, Men
    11 APR 1896 Alfred Hájos (SWI-100/1200)

Youngest Medalist/Gold Medalist, Men
    17-008 Sándor Wladar (SWI-1980)

Oldest Medalist/Gold Medalist, Men
    50-179 Aládár Gerevich (FEN-1960)

Most Medals, Women
    10   Agnes Keleti (GYM)
    7   Margit Korondi (GYM)

Most Gold Medals, Women
5   Agnes Keleti (GYM)
2   Ilona Elek (FEN)
2   Margit Korondi (GYM)
2   Ildikó Saginé-Ujlakiné-Rejtö (FEN)

First Medalist, Women
03 AUG 1932 Erna Bogáthy Bogen (FEN-Foil Individual)

First Gold Medalist, Women
05 AUG 1936 Ilona Elek (FEN-Foil Individual)

Youngest Medalist, Women
14-167 Krisztina Medveczky (GYM-1972)

Youngest Gold Medalist, Women
16-346 Katalin Szöke (SWI-1952)

Oldest Medalist, Women
45-072 Ilona Elek (FEN-1952)

Oldest Gold Medalist, Women
41-078 Ilona Elek (FEN-1952)

Most Medals, Winter, Men
2   László Nagy (FSK)
2   László Szollás (FSK)

First Medalist, Winter, Men
12 FEB 1932 László Szollás (FSK-Pairs)

Youngest Medalist, Winter, Men
21-349 Ede Király (FSK-1948)

Oldest Medalist, Winter, Men
28-174 László Nagy (FSK-1956)

Most Medals, Winter, Women
2   Marianna Nagy (FSK)
2   Emilia Rotter (FSK)

First Medalist, Winter, Women
12 FEB 1932 Emilia Rotter (FSK-Pairs)

Youngest Medalist, Winter, Women
22-037 Andrea Kékessy (FSK-1948)

Oldest Medalist, Winter, Women
29-158 Emilia Rotter (FSK-1936)

Most Medals, Men, Games
    4   István Pelle (GYM-1932)
    3   Zoltán Halmay (SWI-1900)
    3   János Mogyorósi-Klencs (GYM-1948)
    3   Ferenc Pataki (GYM-1948)
    3   Tibor Berczelly (FEN-1952)
    3   Aládár Gerevich (FEN-1952)

Most Gold Medals, Men, Games
    2   Thirteen athletes tied with two

Most Medals, Women, Games
    6   Agnes Keleti (GYM-1956)
    5   Margit Korondi (GYM-1952)

Most Gold Medals, Women, Games
    4   Agnes Keleti (GYM-1956)
    2   Katalin Szöke (SWI-1952)
    2   Ildikó Saginé-Ujlakiné-Rejtö (FEN-1964)

ICELAND (ISL)
Lyoveldio Island
Republic of Iceland
Olympíunefnd Islands - 1935

Area: 39,769 sq. mi. Population (1985 est.): 241,000
Located: North end of Atlantic Ocean
Language(s): Icelandic
Religion(s): Evangelical Lutheran 97%
Government: Constitutional republic

Olympic History: Iceland sent one athlete to the 1908 Olympics,
    Johannes Josefsson, a wrestler. They also sent two athletes to
    the 1912 Olympics, but did not again appear until 1936. Since
    then they have never failed to be present at an Olympic Games.
    They have competed at all Olympic Winter Games since 1948.
    Iceland's athletes have captured two medals. In 1948,
    Vilhjalmur Einarsson won a silver medal in the triple jump
    event, while in 1984 Bjarni Fridriksson won a bronze medal in
    the 95 kg. class in judo. Also in 1984, Einarsson's son, Einar
    Vilhjalmursson finished 6th in the javelin throw.

INDIA (IND)
Bharat
Republic of India
Indian Olympic Association - 1924

Area: 1,266,595 sq. mi. Population (1985 est.): 767,681,000
Located: Occupies most of the Indian subcontinent in southern
    Asia
Language(s): Hindi (official), English (associate official)
Religion(s): Hindu 83%, Muslim 11%, Christian 3%, Sikh 2%
Government: Federal republic

Olympic History: India's first Olympic appearance can be traced
to 1900 when Norman Pritchard, an Indian citizen and later a
silent-screen star, competed in the sprints at Paris, but
represented the London Athletic Club and Great Britain.   India's
next Olympic appearance, and first real one, occurred in 1920.
In 1928, India entered its first field hockey team and won the
gold medal.   Thus was born the Indian leviathan in this sport,
as India won six consecutive gold medals and 30 consecutive
games, before losing in the 1960 finals to Pakistan.   Pritchard
won two medals in the 1900 sprints, and one Indian wrestler,
Kha-Shaba Jadav (1952 freestyle bantamweight bronze), has won a
medal but otherwise, all of India's medals in the Olympics have
been won by their field hockey team.   India sent a small
contingent of athletes to the 1964 and 1968 Olympic Winter
Games.

Medal Count:

	Men				Women				Totals			
	GO	SI	BR	TOT	GO	SI	BR	TOT	GO	SI	BR	TOT
Summer	8	3	3	14	–	–	–	–	8	3	3	14
Winter	–	–	–	–	–	–	–	–	–	–	–	–
Totals	8	3	3	14	–	–	–	–	8	3	3	14

Most Medals, Men
   4   Leslie Walter Claudius (FIH)
   4   Udham Singh (FIH)

Most Gold Medals, Men
   3   Leslie Walter Claudius (FIH)
   3   Udham Singh (FIH)
   3   Dhyan Chand (FIH)
   3   Ranganandhan Francis (FIH)
   3   Balbir Singh (FIH)
   3   Randhir Singh Gentle (FIH)

First Medalist, Men
   16 JUL 1900   Norman Pritchard (TAF-200LH) (GBR/IND)
   26 MAY 1928   Field Hockey Team (FIH)

First Gold Medalist, Men
   26 MAY 1928   Field Hockey Team (FIH)

Youngest Medalist/Gold Medalist, Men
   19-271   Chinadorai Deshmutu (FIH-1952)

Oldest Medalist/Gold Medalist, Men
   45-278   Dharam Singh (FIH-1964)

INDONESIA (INA)
Republik Indonesia
Republic of Indonesia
Komite Olympiade Indonesia - 1952

Area: 735,268 sq. mi. Population (1985 est.): 173,103,000
Located: Archipelago southeast of Asia along the equator
Language(s): Bahasa Indonesian (Malay) (official), Javanese
Religion(s): Muslims 90%
Government: Independent republic

Olympic History: Indonesia has competed at the Olympics since
   1952, missing the Games of 1964 and 1980. They have never
   competed at the Olympic Winter Games and they have never won a
   medal.

IRAN (IRN)
Jomhori-e-Islami-e-Iran
Islamic Republic of Iran
National Olympic Committee of the Islamic Republic of Iran - 1947

Area: 636,293 sq. mi. Population (1985 est.): 45,191,000
Located: Between the Middle East and southern Asia
Language(s): Farsi, Turk, Kurdish, Arabic, English
Religion(s): Shiite Muslim 93%
Government: Islamic republic

Olympic History: Iran first competed at the 1948 Olympic Games
   and their participation was continuous through 1976. They have
   not competed since. They have competed at the Olympic Winter
   Games of 1956, 1964, 1968, 1972, and 1976. All of Iran's
   success has come in the strength sports of weightlifting (9
   medals) and wrestling (20 medals).

Medal Count:

| | Men | | | | Women | | | | Totals | | | |
	GO	SI	BR	TOT	GO	SI	BR	TOT	GO	SI	BR	TOT
Summer	4	10	15	29	-	-	-	-	4	10	15	29
Winter	-	-	-	-	-	-	-	-	-	-	-	-
Totals	4	10	15	29	-	-	-	-	4	10	15	29

Most Medals, Men
   3   Mohammed Nassiri-Seresht (WLT)
   3   Gholam Reza Takhti (WRE)

Most Gold Medals, Men
   1   Mohammed Nassiri-Seresht (WLT)
   1   Emamali Habibi (WRE)
   1   Abdollah Movahed Ardabili (WRE)
   1   Gholam Reza Takhti (WRE)

First Medalist, Men
   09 AUG 1948 Jaffar Salmassi (WLT-Featherweight)

First Gold Medalist, Men
  01 DEC 1956 Emamali Habibi (WRE-Lightweight Freestyle)
  01 DEC 1956 Gholam Reza Takhti (WRE-Light-heavyweight Free.)

Youngest Medalist, Men
  16-254 Nasser Guivehtchi (WRE-1952)

Youngest Gold Medalist, Men
  23-013 Mohammed Nassiri-Seresht (WLT-1968)

Oldest Medalist, Men
  37-328 Mahmoud Namdjou (WLT-1956)

Oldest Gold Medalist, Men
  28-224 Abdollah Movahed Ardabili (WRE-1968)

IRAQ (IRQ)
al Jumhouriya al'Iraqia
Republic of Iraq
Iraqi National Olympic Committee - 1948

Area: 167,924 sq. mi. Population (1985 est.): 15,507,000
Located: Middle East, occupying most of historic Mesopotamia
Language(s): Arabic (official), Kurdish
Religion(s): Shiite Muslim 55%, Sunni Muslim 40%
Government: Ruling council

Olympic Histoy: Iraq made its first Olympic appearance in 1948 at
  London. They have since competed at six Olympics, missing 1972
  and 1980. They have yet to compete in the Olympic Winter Games.
  One Iraqi athlete has won a medal - that being Abdul Wahid Aziz
  who finished third in lightweight weightlifting in 1960 at Rome.
  Women have not yet competed in the Olympics for Iraq.

IRELAND (IRL)
Eire
Olympic Council of Ireland - 1923

Area: 27,137 sq. mi. Population (1985 est.): 3,588,000
Located: Island just west of Great Britain, off northwest
  European coast
Language(s): English, Gaelic
Religion(s): Roman Catholic 94%, Anglican 4%
Government: Parliamentary republic

Olympic History: Ireland first competed as a separate state in
  the 1924 Olympic Games at Paris. Prior to that time, however,
  many Irish athletes had competed - mostly for Great Britain. In
  addition many of the great American weight-throwers had been
  recent Irish immigrants.
    Since 1924, Ireland has competed at every Olympic Games except
  those of 1936. They have never competed in the Olympic Winter
  Games.

Medal Count:

	Men				Women				Totals			
	GO	SI	BR	TOT	GO	SI	BR	TOT	GO	SI	BR	TOT
Summer	4	5	5	14	-	-	-	-	4	5	5	14
Winter	-	-	-	-	-	-	-	-	-	-	-	-
Totals	4	5	5	14	-	-	-	-	4	5	5	14

Most Medals, Men
   2   Patrick O'Callaghan (TAF)
   1   Twelve athletes tied with one

Most Gold Medals, Men
   2   Patrick O'Callaghan (TAF)
   1   Ron Delany (TAF)
   1   Robert Tisdall (TAF)

First Medalist/Gold Medalist, Men
   11 APR 1896   John Pius Boland (TEN-Singles) (GBR/IRL)
   30 JUL 1928   Patrick O'Callaghan (TAF-HT)

Youngest Medalist, Men
   18-209   John Caldwell (BOX-1956)

Youngest Gold Medalist, Men
   21-271   Ron Delany (TAF-1956)

Oldest Medalist, Men
   30-091   David Wilkins (YAC-1980)

Oldest Gold Medalist, Men
   26-186   Patrick O'Callaghan (TAF-1932)

ISRAEL (ISR)
Medinat Israel
State of Israel
Olympic Committee of Israel - 1952

Area: 7,847 sq. mi. Population (1985 est.): 4,128,000
Located: Eastern end of Mediterranean Sea
Language(s): Hebrew, Arabic (both official), Yiddish
Religion(s): Judaism 83%, Muslim, Christian
Government: Parliamentary democracy

Olympic History: Israel competed at its first Olympics in 1952 at
   Helsinki. The country has never appeared at the Olympic Winter
   Games. Israel has missed only the 1980 Moscow Olympics since
   1952.
      The zenith of Israel participation came in 1968 when its
   football (soccer) team finished fifth. The nadir occurred four
   years later at Munich on 05 SEP 1972 when Arab terrorists
   murdered eleven Israeli athletes and officials.

ITALY (ITA)
Repubblica Italiana
Italian Republic
Comitato Olimpico Nazionale Italiano - 1915

Area: 116,303 sq. mi. Population (1985 est.): 57,116,000
Located: Southern Europe, jutting into the Mediterranean Sea
Language(s): Italian
Religion(s): Roman Catholic
Government: Republic

Olympic History: Italy has had an outstanding record of Olympic
  participation. It has never missed an Olympic Winter Games and
  has missed only the Olympic Games of 1896 and 1904. In 1896 an
  Italian runner, Carlo Airoldi, attempted to enter the marathon,
  walking from Italy to Athens, but he was denied entry because he
  could not produce amateur credentials.
    Italy has had success in many different sports. They have
  been the dominant country many times in both cycling and
  fencing.

Olympic Hosts:
        1960 - Rome - The Games of the XVIIth Olympiad

Medal Count:

| | Men | | | | Women | | | | Totals | | |
	GO	SI	BR	TOT	GO	SI	BR	TOT	GO	SI	BR	TOT
Summer	135	106+	113	354+	5	8+	7	20+	140	115	120	375
Winter	10	8	5	23	2	1	2	5	12	9	7	28
Totals	145	114+	118	377+	7	9+	9	25+	152	124	127	403

Most Medals, Men
  13   Edoardo Mangiarotti (FEN)
   9   Giulio Gaudini (FEN)

Most Gold Medals, Men
   6   Edoardo Mangiarotti (FEN)
   6   Nedo Nadi (FEN)

First Medalist, Men
  31 MAY 1900 Gian-Giorgio Trissino (EQU-Long Jump)

First Gold Medalist, Men
  02 JUN 1900 Gian-Giorgio Trissino (EQU-High Jump)

Youngest Medalist/Gold Medalist, Men
  14-012 Giorgio Cesana (ROW-1906)

Oldest Medalist/Gold Medalist, Men
  49-267 Guido Balzarini (FEN-1924)

Most Medals, Women
  3   Novella Calligaris (SWI)
  3   Antonella Lonzi-Ragno (FEN)
  3   Sara Simeoni (TAF)

Most Gold Medals, Women
  1   Irene Camber (FEN)
  1   Antonella Lonzi-Ragno (FEN)
  1   Sara Simeoni (TAF)
  1   Gabriella Dorio (TAF)
  1   Trebisonda "Ondina" Valla (TAF)

First Medalist/Gold Medalist, Women
  06 AUG 1936   Trebisonda "Ondina" Valla (TAF-80HH)

Youngest Medalist, Women
  17-247   Novella Calligaris (SWI-1972)

Youngest Gold Medalist, Women
  20-078   Trebisonda "Ondina" Valla (TAF-1936)

Oldest Medalist, Women
  40-201   Velleda Cesari (FEN-1960)

Oldest Gold Medalist, Women
  32-094   Antonella Lonzi-Ragno (FEN-1972)

Most Medals, Winter, Men
  6   Eugenio Monti (BOB)
  3   Paul Hildgartner (LUG)
  3   Gustavo Thöni (ASK)

Most Gold Medals, Winter, Men
  2   Eugenio Monti (BOB)
  2   Paul Hildgartner (LUG)
  2   Luciano De Paolis (BOB)

First Medalist/Gold Medalist, Winter, Men
  04 FEB 1948   Nino Bibbia (BOB-Skeleton)

Youngest Medalist/Gold Medalist, Winter, Men
  19-246   Paul Hildgartner (LUG-1972)

Oldest Medalist/Gold Medalist, Winter, Men
  47-217   Giacomo Conti (BOB-1956)

Most Medals, Winter, Women
  2   Giuliana Chenal-Minuzzo (ASK)
  1   Claudia Giordani (ASK)
  1   Erika Lechner (LUG)
  1   Paoletta Magoni (ASK)

Most Gold Medals, Winter, Women
    1   Erika Lechner (LUG)
    1   Paoletta Magoni (ASK)

First Medalist, Winter, Women
    17 FEB 1952 Giuliana Minuzzo (ASK-Downhill)

First Gold Medalist, Winter, Women
    15 FEB 1968 Erika Lechner (LUG-Singles)

Youngest Medalist/Gold Medalist, Winter, Women
    19-155 Paoletta Magoni (ASK-1984)

Oldest Medalist, Winter, Women
    28-089 Giuliana Chenal-Minuzzo (ASK-1960)

Oldest Gold Medalist, Winter, Women
    20-263 Erika Lechner (LUG-1968)

Most Medals, Men, Games
    5   Nedo Nadi (FEN-1920)
    4   Aldo Nadi (FEN-1920)
    4   Giulio Gaudini (FEN-1932)
    4   Edoardo Mangiarotti (FEN-1952)

Most Gold Medals, Men, Games
    5   Nedo Nadi (FEN-1920)
    3   Enrico Bruna (ROW-1906)
    3   Giorgio Cesana (ROW-1906)
    3   Emilio Fontanella (ROW-1906)
    3   Francesco Verri (CYC-1906)
    3   Aldo Nadi (FEN-1920)
    3   Romeo Neri (GYM-1932)

Most Medals, Women, Games
    3   Novella Calligaris (SWI-1972)
    1   Thirty athletes tied with one

Most Gold Medals, Women, Games
    1   Trebisonda "Ondina" Valla (TAF-1936)
    1   Irene Camber (FEN-1952)
    1   Antonella Lonzi-Ragno (FEN-1972)
    1   Sara Simeoni (TAF-1980)
    1   Gabriella Dorio (TAF-1984)

Most Medals, Winter, Men, Games
    2   Renzo Alvera (BOB-1956)
    2   Eugenio Monti (BOB-1956)
    2   Sergio Siorpaes (BOB-1964)
    2   Eugenio Monti (BOB-1964)
    2   Eugenio Monti (BOB-1968)
    2   Luciano De Paolis (BOB-1968)
    2   Gustavo Thöni (ASK-1972)

Most Gold Medals, Winter, Men, Games
  2   Eugenio Monti (BOB-1968)
  2   Luciano De Paolis (BOB-1968)

Most Medals, Winter, Women, Games
  1   Giuliana Chenal (ASK-1952)
  1   Giuliana Chenal-Minuzzo (ASK-1960)
  1   Erika Lechner (LUG-1968)
  1   Claudia Giordani (ASK-1976)
  1   Paoletta Magoni (ASK-1984)

Most Gold Medals, Winter, Women, Games
  1   Erika Lechner (LUG-1968)
  1   Paoletta Magoni (ASK-1984)

IVORY COAST (CIV)
République de la Côte d'Ivoire
Republic of Ivory Coast
Comité Olympique Ivoirien - 1963

Area: 124,503 sq. mi. Population (1985 est.): 10,090,000
Located: Southern coast of West Africa
Language(s): French (official), tribal languages
Religion(s): Muslim 15%, Christian 12%, indigenous beliefs 63%
Government: Republic

Olympic History: The Ivory Coast has competed in the Olympic
Games since 1964, missing only the 1980 Games. One athlete from
this country has won a medal, that being Gabriel Tiacoh who in
1984 at Los Angeles finished second in the men's 400 metre dash.
The country has not appeared at the Olympic Winter Games.

JAMAICA (JAM)
Jamaica Olympic Association - 1936

Area: 4,232 sq. mi. Population (1985 est.): 2,366,000
Located: West Indies in Caribbean Sea
Language(s): English, Jamaican Creole
Religion(s): Protestant 70%
Government: Constitutional monarchy

Olympic History: Jamaica has sent athletes to all the Olympic
Games since 1948. In 1960, Jamaica, Barbados and Trinidad
combined to form The Antilles team, representing the West Indies
Federation. That team won two medals, which are counted in the
list below. Of the two medals, one was won by George Kerr, a
Jamaican, in the 800 metres, while the other was a bronze in the
1600 relay. Three members of that team were Jamaican while one
(James Wedderburn) was from Barbados. Jamaica has never
competed in the Olympic Winter Games.

   Jamaica has won all its medals except one in track & field.
Their entire success has been based on the short distances, from
100 to 800 metres – both men and women. The non-track & field
medal was a bronze won in 1980 by David Weller in the 1,000
metre time trial cycling.

Medal Count:

	Men				Women				Totals			
	GO	SI	BR	TOT	GO	SI	BR	TOT	GO	SI	BR	TOT
Summer	4	8	5	17	–	–	3	3	4	8	8	20
Winter	–	–	–	–	–	–	–	–	–	–	–	–
Totals	4	8	5	17	–	–	3	3	4	8	8	20

Most Medals, Men
   4   Herb McKenley (TAF)
   4   Donald Quarrie (TAF)
   4   Arthur Wint (TAF)

Most Gold Medals, Men
   2   Arthur Wint (TAF)
   2   George Rhoden (TAF)

First Medalist, Men
   02 AUG 1948 Arthur Wint (TAF-800)

First Gold Medalist, Men
   05 AUG 1948 Arthur Wint (TAF-400)

Youngest Medalist, Men
   19-001 Gregory Meghoo (TAF-1984)

Youngest Gold Medalist, Men
   25-225 George Rhoden (TAF-1952)

Oldest Medalist, Men
   33-168 Don Quarrie (TAF-1984)

Oldest Gold Medalist, Men
   32-063 Arthur Wint (TAF-1952)

Most Medals, Women
   3   Merlene Ottey (TAF)

First Medalist, Women
   30 JUL 1980 Merlene Ottey (TAF-200)

Most Medals, Men, Games
    3   Herb McKenley (TAF-1952)
    2   Arthur Wint (TAF-1948)
    2   Arthur Wint (TAF-1952)
    2   George Rhoden (TAF-1952)
    2   George Kerr (TAF-1960)
    2   Donald Quarrie (TAF-1976)

Most Gold Medals, Men, Games
    2   George Rhoden (TAF-1952)
    1   Arthur Wint (TAF-1948)
    1   Arthur Wint (TAF-1952)
    1   Herbert McKenley (TAF-1952)
    1   Leslie Laing (TAF-1952)
    1   Donald Quarrie (TAF-1976)

Most Medals, Women, Games
    2   Merlene Ottey (TAF-1984)

JAPAN (JPN)
Nippon
The Japanese Olympic Committee - 1912

Area: 145,856 sq. mi. Population (1985 est.): 120,731,000
Located: Archipelago off east coast of Asia
Language(s): Japanese
Religion(s): Buddhism, Shintoism
Government: Parliamentary democracy

Olympic History: Japan first competed at the 1912 Olympic Games,
    its delegation and Olympic Committee led by Dr. Jigoro Kano, the
    founder of judo. Japan has since failed to compete only at the
    Games of 1948, when it was not invited, and 1980, when it chose
    to boycott the Games. At the Olympic Winter Games, Japan first
    competed in 1928 and has since missed only 1948 when it was not
    invited. The high point of their Olympic Winter history
    occurred at Sapporo, Japan, in the 1972 70-metre ski jump.
    Yukio Kasaya won the event and led a Japanese sweep of the
    medals.
        Japan has been the dominant country in men's gymnastics since
    1956. In addition, at times they have been the top country in
    swimming and one of the top in wrestling and weightlifting.

Olympic Hosts:
            1940 - Sapporo - Olympic Winter Games (not held)
            1940 - Tokyo - The Games of the XIIth Olympiad (not held)
            1964 - Tokyo - The Games of the XVIIIth Olympiad
            1972 - Sapporo - The XIth Olympic Winter Games

Medal Count:

	Men				Women				Totals			
	GO	SI	BR	TOT	GO	SI	BR	TOT	GO	SI	BR	TOT
Summer	79	68	70	217	4	4	5	13	83	72	75	230
Winter	1	4	1	6	–	–	–	–	1	4	1	6
Totals	80	72	71	223	4	4	5	13	84	76	76	236

Most Medals, Men
13   Takashi Ono (GYM)
12   Sawao Kato (GYM)

Most Gold Medals, Men
8   Sawao Kato (GYM)
6   Akinori Nakayama (GYM)

First Medalist, Men
23 AUG 1920   Ichya Kumagai (TEN-Singles/Doubles)
23 AUG 1920   Seiichiro Kashio (TEN-Doubles)

First Gold Medalist, Men
02 AUG 1928   Mikio Oda (TAF-TJ)

Youngest Medalist/Gold Medalist, Men
14-309   Kusuo Kitamura (SWI-1932)

Oldest Medalist/Gold Medalist, Men
40-344   Maseo Takemoto (GYM-1960)

Most Medals, Women
2   Miwako Motoyoshi (SWI)
2   Sumie Oinuma (VOL)
2   Toyoko Iwahara (VOL)
2   Takako Iida (VOL)
2   Mariko Okamoto (VOL)
2   Takako Shirai (VOL)

Most Gold Medals, Women
1   Twenty-six athletes tied with one

First Medalist, Women
02 AUG 1928   Kinue Hitomi (TAF-800)

First Gold Medalist, Women
11 AUG 1936   Hideko Maehata (SWI-200 breaststroke)

Youngest Medalist, Women
19-005   Sachiko Otani (VOL-1984)

Youngest Gold Medalist, Women
19-268   Yoko Shinozaki (VOL-1964)

Oldest Medalist, Women
30-345   Keiko Ikeda-Tanaka (GYM-1964)

Oldest Gold Medalist, Women
   30-178   Takako Iida (VOL-1964)

Most Medals, Winter, Men
   1   Chiharu Igaya (ASK)
   1   Yukio Kasaya (NSK)
   1   Akitsugu Konno (NSK)
   1   Seiji Aochi (NSK)
   1   Hirokazu Yagi (NSK)
   1   Yoshihiro Kitazawa (SSK)

Most Gold Medals, Winter, Men
   1   Yukio Kasaya (NSK)

First Medalist, Winter, Men
   31 JAN 1956   Chiharu Igaya (ASK-Slalom)

First Gold Medalist, Winter, Men
   06 FEB 1972   Yukio Kasaya (NSK-70 Jump)

Youngest Medalist, Winter, Men
   20-053   Hirokazu Yagi (NSK-1980)

Oldest Medalist, Winter, Men
   29-320   Seiji Aochi (NSK-1972)

Most Medals, Men, Games
   6   Takashi Ono (GYM-1960)
   6   Akinori Nakayama (GYM-1968)

Most Gold Medals, Men, Games
   4   Akinori Nakayama (GYM-1968)
   3   Takashi Ono (GYM-1960)
   3   Yukio Endo (GYM-1964)
   3   Sawao Kato (GYM-1968)
   3   Sawao Kato (GYM-1972)

Most Medals, Women, Games
   2   Miwako Motoyoshi (SWI-1984)
   1   Many athletes tied with one

Most Gold Medals, Women, Games
   1   Twenty-six athletes tied with one

JORDAN (JOR)
al Mamlaka al Urduniya al Hashemiyah
Hashemite Kingdom of Jordan
Jordan Olympic Committee - 1963

Area: 37,737 sq. mi. Population (1985 est.): 2,668,000
Located: Western Asia, near the Mediterranean coast
Language(s): Arabic (official), English
Religion(s): Sunni Muslim 93%, Christians 5%
Government: Constitutional monarchy

Olympic History: Jordan competed at the 1980 and 1984 Olympic
   Games, but has not yet appeared in the Olympic Winter Games.

KENYA (KEN)
Jamhuri ya Kenya
Republic of Kenya
Kenya Olympic Association - 1955

Area: 224,960 sq. mi. Population (1985 est.): 20,194,000
Located: Along the Indian Ocean, off the coast of East Africa
Language(s): Swahili (official), English
Religion(s): Protestant 38%, Roman Catholic 28%, Muslim 6%
Government: Republic

Olympic History: Kenya first competed at the Olympics in 1956.
   After competing in 1960, 1964, 1968, and 1972, they joined the
   boycotts of 1976 and 1980, but returned to the Olympic fold in
   1984 at Los Angeles. They have never competed in the Olympic
   Winter Games. Kenya has won five medals in boxing but all of
   the other medals it has won are due to its excellent distance
   runners, the most outstanding of these having been Kipchoge
   Keino.

Medal Count:

| | Men | | | | Women | | | | Totals | | | |
	GO	SI	BR	TOT	GO	SI	BR	TOT	GO	SI	BR	TOT
Summer	6	7	9	22	-	-	-	-	6	7	9	22
Winter	-	-	-	-	-	-	-	-	-	-	-	-
Totals	6	7	9	22	-	-	-	-	6	7	9	22

Most Medals, Men
   4   Kipchoge Keino (TAF)
   2   Wilson Kiprugut (TAF)
   2   Philip Waruinge (BOX)
   2   Julius Sang (TAF)
   2   Naftali Temu (TAF)
   2   Charles Asati (TAF)
   2   Hezakiah Nyamau (TAF)

Most Gold Medals, Men
   2   Kipchoge Keino (TAF)
   1   Charles Asati (TAF)
   1   Hezakiah Nyamau (TAF)
   1   Robert Ouko (TAF)
   1   Julius Korir (TAF)
   1   Naftali Temu (TAF)
   1   Amos Biwott (TAF)
   1   Julius Sang (TAF)

First Medalist, Men
   16 OCT 1964 Wilson Kiprugut (TAF-800)

First Gold Medalist, Men
   13 OCT 1968   Naftali Temu (TAF-10,000)

Youngest Medalist, Men
   19-022 Ibrahim Bilili (BOX-1984)

Youngest Gold Medalist, Men
   21-039 Amos Biwott (TAF-1968)

Oldest Medalist/Gold Medalist, Men
   32-237 Kipchoge Keino (TAF-1972)

KOREA (SOUTH KOREA) (KOR)
Taehan Min'guk
Republic of Korea
Korean Olympic Committee - 1947

Area: 38,025 sq. mi. Population (1985 est.): 42,643,000
Located: Northern east Asia
Language(s): Korean
Religion(s): Buddhism, Confucianism, Christian
Government: Republic

Olympic History: Korea first officially competed at the 1948
   Olympic Games in London. However, in 1936, shortly after the
   occupation of the country by the Japanese, two excellent
   marathoners were forced to wear the colors of Japan. Despite
   this affront, Kee-Chung Sohn and Seung-Yong Nam won a gold and a
   bronze medals, respectively, in that race.
     Since 1948 the Koreans have done well in combative sports,
   winning virtually all of their medals in boxing, wrestling, judo
   and weightlifting. The women have also medalled in volleyball,
   basketball, and archery.

Olympic Hosts:
   1988 - Seoul - The Games of the XXIVth Olympiad

Medal Count:

	Men				Women				Totals			
	GO	SI	BR	TOT	GO	SI	BR	TOT	GO	SI	BR	TOT
Summer	6	10	16	32	1	1	2	4	7	11	18	36
Winter	-	-	-	-	-	-	-	-	-	-	-	-
Totals	6	10	16	32	1	1	2	4	7	11	18	36

Most Medals, Men
   2   Sung-Jip Kim (WLT)
   1   Many athletes tied with one

Most Gold Medals, Men
   [1   Kee-Chung Sohn (Kitei Son) (TAF)]
   1   Yung-Mo Yang (WRE)
   1   Byeng-Keun Ahn (JUD)
   1   Hyoung-Zoo Ha (JUD)
   1   In-Tak Youh (WRE)
   1   Weon-Kee Kim (WRE)
   1   Joon-Sup Shin (BOX)

First Medalist, Men
   09 AUG 1936   Kee-Chung Sohn (Kitei Son) (KOR/JPN-TAF-Marathon)
   09 AUG 1936   Seung-Yong Nam (Shoryu Nan) (KOR/JPN-TAF-Marathon)
   10 AUG 1952   Sung-Jip Kim (WLT-Middleweight)

First Gold Medalist, Men
   09 AUG 1936   Kee-Chung Sohn (Kitei Son) (KOR/JPN-TAF-Marathon)
   31 JUL 1976   Yung-Mo Yang (WRE-Freestyle Featherweight)

Youngest Medalist, Men
   19-080   Jae-Yup Kim (JUD-1984)

Youngest Gold Medalist, Men
   22-068   Hyoung-Zoo Ha (JUD-1984)

Oldest Medalist, Men
   33-195   Sung-Jip Kim (WLT-1952)

Oldest Gold Medalist, Men
   26-214   In-Tak Youh (WRE-1984)

Most Medals, Women
   1   Many athletes tied with one.

Most Gold Medals, Women
   1   Hyang-Soon Seo (ARC)

First Medalist, Women
   30 JUL 1976   Volleyball Team

First Gold Medalist, Women
   11 AUG 1984   Hyang-Soon Seo (ARC-Women)

Youngest Medalist/Gold Medalist, Women
   17-035   Hyang-Soon Seo (ARC-1984)

Oldest Medalist, Women
   26-127   Soon-Bok Lee (VOL-1976)

KOREA, DEMOCRATIC PEOPLE'S REPUBLIC OF (NORTH KOREA) (PRK)
Chosun Minchu-chui Inmin Konghwa-guk
Democratic People's Republic of Korea
Olympic Committee of the Democratic People's Republic of Korea -
    1957

Area: 46,540 sq. mi. Population (1985 est.): 20,082,000
Located: Northern east Asia
Language(s): Korean
Religion(s): religion discouraged; traditionally Buddhism,
    Confucianism
Government: Communist state

Olympic History: The Democratic People's Republic of Korea made
    its first Olympic appearance at the Olympic Winter Games in
    Innsbruck in 1964, and again competed at the Winter Games of
    1972 and 1984. It has also competed at the Olympic Games of
    1972, 1976 and 1980, skipping the 1984 Los Angeles Olympics. It
    has had some success in various sports, winning medals in
    shooting, boxing, volleyball, wrestling, weightlifting, judo,
    and speed skating.

Olympic Hosts:
          1988 - The Games of the XXIVth Olympiad (may co-host
                 several events.)

Medal Count:

	Men				Women				Totals			
	GO	SI	BR	TOT	GO	SI	BR	TOT	GO	SI	BR	TOT
Summer	2	5	4	11	-	-	1	1	2	5	5	12
Winter	-	-	-	-	-	1	-	1	-	1	-	1
Totals	2	5	4	11	-	1	1	2	2	6	5	13

Most Medals, Men
    2   Byong-Uk Li (BOX)
    1   Nine athletes tied with one

Most Gold Medals, Men
    1   Ho-Jun Li (SHO)
    1   Yong-Jo Gu (BOX)

First Medalist/Gold Medalist, Men
    28 AUG 1972 Ho-Jun Li (SHO-Small-bore Rifle, Prone)

Youngest Medalist, Men
    20-334 Bong-Chol Ho (WLT-1980)

Youngest Gold Medalist, Men
    21-015 Yong-Jo Gu (BOX-1976)

Oldest Medalist, Men
    28-289 Ho-Pyong Li (WRE-1980)

Oldest Gold Medalist, Men
    25-271 Ho-Jun Li (SHO-1972)

Most Medals, Women
    1   Twelve athletes tied with one.

First Medalist, Women
    07SEP1972 Volleyball Team

Youngest Medalist, Women
    18-196   Myong-Suk Paek (VOL-1972)

Oldest Medalist, Women
    30-118   Su-Dae Kim (VOL-1972)

Most Medals, Women, Winter
    1   Pil-hwa Han (SSK)

First Medalist, Women, Winter
    02 FEB 1964 Pil-hwa Han (SSK-3,000)

KUWAIT (KUW)
Dowlat al-Kuwait
State of Kuwait
Kuwait Olympic Committee – 1966

Area: 6,880 sq. mi. Population (1985 est.): 1,710,000
Located: Middle East, at northern end of Persian Gulf
Language(s): Arabic
Religion(s): Islam 85%
Government: Constitutional monarchy

Olympic History: Kuwait has competed continuously at the Olympic
  Games since 1968. They have yet to win a medal and they have
  never competed at the Olympic Winter Games.

LAOS (LAO)
Sathalanalat Paxathipatai Paxaxon Lao
Lao People's Democratic Republic
Comité Olympique Lao - 1979

Area: 91,428 sq. mi. Population (1985 est.): 3,605,000
Located: Indochinese Peninsula in southeast Asia
Language(s): Lao (official), French, English
Religion(s): Buddhist 58%, tribal 34%
Government: Communist

Olympic History: Laos's sole Olympic appearance has been in 1980
    at Moscow.

LATVIA (LAT)

Olympic History: Prior to its annexation by the Soviet Union in
    1940, Latvia competed at the Olympics of 1924, 1928, 1932, and
    1936. As an independent country it won three medals. In 1932
    Janis Dalinsh finished second in the 50 kilometre walk, and in
    1936 Adalberts Bubenko finished third in the same event.
    Additionally, in 1936 Edwin Bietags won a silver medal in light-
    heavyweight Greco-Roman wrestling.

Medal Count:

	Men				Women				Totals			
	GO	SI	BR	TOT	GO	SI	BR	TOT	GO	SI	BR	TOT
Summer	-	2	1	3	-	-	-	-	-	2	1	3
Winter	-	-	-	-	-	-	-	-	-	-	-	-
Totals	-	2	1	3	-	-	-	-	-	2	1	3

LEBANON (LIB)
al-Jamhouriya al-Lubnaniya
Republic of Lebanon
Comité Olympique Libanais - 1948

Area: 4,015 sq. mi. Population (1985 est.): 2,619,000
Located: At Eastern end of Mediterranean Sea
Language(s): Arabic (official), French, Armenian
Religion(s): Muslim 60%, Christian 25% Druze 7%, Greek Orthodox
7%
Government: Parliametary republic

Olympic History: Lebanon has sent athletes to every Olympics
    since 1948 with the exception of the 1956 Olympics. Rather
    oddly, for a country from such an arid climate, they have
    participated at every Olympic Winter Games since 1948. All of
    their medals have come in the strength sports of wrestling and
    weightlifting.

Medal Count:

	Men				Women				Totals			
	GO	SI	BR	TOT	GO	SI	BR	TOT	GO	SI	BR	TOT
Summer	-	2	2	4	-	-	-	-	-	2	2	4
Winter	-	-	-	-	-	-	-	-	-	-	-	-
Totals	-	2	2	4	-	-	-	-	-	2	2	4

Most Medals, Men
```
    1       Zakaria Chihab (WRE)
    1       Khalil Taha (WRE)
    1       Mohammed Traboulsi (WLT)
    1       Hassan Bchara (WRE)
```

First Medalist, Men
```
    27 JUL 1952  Zakaria Chihab (WRE-Bantamweight Greco-Roman)
    27 JUL 1952  Khalil Taha (WRE-Welterweight Greco-Roman)
```

Youngest Medalist, Men
```
    20-052  Khalil Taha (WRE-1952)
```

Oldest Medalist, Men
```
    35-130  Hassan Bchara (WRE-1980)
```


LESOTHO (LES)
Kingdom of Lesotho
Lesotho Olympic Committee - 1972

Area: 11,716 sq. mi. Population (1985 est.): 1,512,000
Located: Southern Africa
Language(s): English, Sesotho (official)
Religion(s): Protestant 49%, Roman Catholic 43%
Government: Constitutional monarchy

Olympic History: Lesotho has competed at three Olympic Games -
  those of 1972, 1980 and 1984.

LIBERIA (LBR)
Republic of Liberia
Liberian National Olympic Committee - 1955

Area: 38,250 sq. mi. Population (1985 est.): 2,232,000
Located: Southwest coast of western Africa
Language(s): English (official), tribal dialects
Religion(s): Traditional beliefs 65%, Muslim 20%, Christian 15%
Government: Military

Olympic History: Liberia first competed at the Olympics in 1956.
  They have since missed only the Olympic Games of 1968.

LIBYA (LBA)
al-Jamahiriyah al-Arabiya al-Libya al-Shabiya al-Ishtirakiya
Socialist People's Libyan Arab Jamahiriya
National Olympic Committee Socialist People's Libyan Arab
Jamahiriya - 1963

Area: 679,359 sq. mi. Population (1985 est.): 3,752,000
Located: On Mediterranean coast of north Africa
Language(s): Arabic
Religion(s): Sunni Muslim 97%
Government: Centralized republic, under military control

Olympic History: Libya competed at the 1964, 1968, and 1972
  Olympics, sending a total of five athletes to those Games. It
  was represented at Moscow in 1980 but has boycotted the 1976 and
  1984 Olympics.

LIECHTENSTEIN (LIE)
Fürstentum Liechtenstein
Principality of Liechtenstein
Comité Olympique du Liechtenstein - 1936

Area: 62 sq. mi. Population (1985 est.): 27,000
Located: In the Alps between Switzerland and Austria
Language(s): German (official), Alemannic dialect
Religion(s): Roman Catholic 85%, Protestant 8%
Government: Hereditary constitutional monarchy

Olympic History: Liechtenstein made its first Olympic appearances
  at the Games of 1936, both Winter and Summer. Since that time
  it has failed to appear only at the 1952 Oslo Winter Olympics,
  the 1956 Melbourne Olympics, and the 1980 Moscow Olympics.
    Liechtenstein holds an unusual, but not unique, position in
  the Olympic hierarchy, being one of three countries which has
  won more medals at the Olympic Winter Games than at the Games of
  the Olympiad (Norway and Austria are the others). This is
  because of the country's outstanding alpine skiers, and
  especially the Wenzel family, Hanni and Andreas.

Medal Count:

	Men				Women				Totals			
	GO	SI	BR	TOT	GO	SI	BR	TOT	GO	SI	BR	TOT
Summer	-	-	-	-	-	-	-	-	-	-	-	-
Winter	-	1	2	3	2	1	2	5	2	2	4	8
Totals	-	1	2	3	2	1	2	5	2	2	4	8

Most Medals, Winter, Men
  2   Andreas Wenzel (ASK)
  1   Willy Frommelt (ASK)

First Medalist, Winter, Men
  14 FEB 1976 Willy Frommelt (ASK-Slalom)

Youngest Medalist, Winter, Men
  21-338 Andreas Wenzel (ASK-1980)

Oldest Medalist, Winter, Men
  25-333 Andreas Wenzel (ASK-1984)

Most Medals, Winter, Women
  4   Hanni Wenzel (ASK)
  1   Ursula Konzett (ASK)

Most Gold Medals, Winter, Women
  2   Hanni Wenzel (ASK)

First Medalist, Winter, Women
  17 FEB 1980 Hanni Wenzel (ASK-Downhill)

First Gold Medalist, Winter, Women
  21 FEB 1980 Hanni Wenzel (ASK-Giant Slalom)

Youngest Medalist, Winter, Women
  19-058 Hanni Wenzel (ASK-1976)

Youngest Gold Medalist, Winter, Women
  23-068 Hanni Wenzel (ASK-1980)

Oldest Medalist, Winter, Women
  24-094 Ursula Konzett (ASK-1984)

Oldest Gold Medalist, Winter, Women
  23-070 Hanni Wenzel (ASK-1980)

LITHUANIA (LIT)

Olympic History: Prior to its annexation by the Soviet Union in
  1940, Lithunania competed at the Olympic Games of 1924 and 1928,
  but failed to win any medals.

LUXEMBOURG (LUX)
Grand-Duché de Luxembourg
Grand Duchy of Luxembourg
Comité Olympique et Sportif Luxembourgeois - 1908

Area: 998 sq. mi. Population (1985 est.): 366,000
Located: Northwest Europe, between Belgium, Germany, and France
Language(s): French, German, Luxembourgian
Religion(s): Roman Catholic 94%
Government: Constitutional monarchy

Olympic History: Luxembourg first competed at the 1912 Olympic
   Games and has since competed at fifteen celebrations, missing
   only the 1932 Los Angeles Games. Twice they have competed at
   the Olympic Winter Games, sending bobsled teams to the Games of
   1928 and 1932. They have won one gold medal in sports, that
   being the 1,500 metre gold of 1952 win by Josef Barthel. Their
   first medal had been a silver won in 1920 by Joseph Alzin in
   heavyweight weightlifting. Jean Jacoby, an artist, also won two
   gold medals in the now defunct art competitions - in 1924 in the
   painting and graphic art category, and in 1928 in the sketches
   and water colors category.

MADAGASCAR (MAD)
Repoblika Demokratika Malagasy
Democratic Republic of Madagascar
Comité Olympique Malgache - 1964

Area: 226,657 sq. mi. Population (1985 est.):   9,941,000
Located: Indian Ocean off the southeast coast of Africa
Language(s):   Malagasy (national), French
Religion(s):   Christian 51%, animists 47%, Muslim 2%
Government: Republic

Olympic History: Madagascar has entered five Olympic Games -
   those of 1964, 1968, 1972, 1980, and 1984. Their top athlete
   has been the sprinter, Jean-Louis Ravelomanantsoa, who finished
   eighth in 1968. He was injured in 1972 and failed to make the
   final. A true announcer's nightmare occurred, however, in the
   tenth heat of the first round of the 100 metres that year:
   Ravelomanantsoa finished second in the heat, narrowly losing out
   to the top Greek sprinter, Vasili Papageorgopoulos.

MALAWI (MAW)
Republic of Malawi
Olympic and Commonwealth Games Association of Malawi - 1968

Area: 45,747 sq. mi. Population (1985 est.):   7,056,000
Located: Southeast Africa
Language(s):   English, Chichewa (both official)
Religion(s):   Christian 75%, Muslim 20%
Government: Republic

Olympic History: Malawi competed at the 1972 Olympics and then
   returned to the Olympic arena in 1984 with a four-man team.

MALAYA
   See Malaysia

MALAYSIA (MAL)
Federation of Malaysia
Olympic Council of Malaysia - 1954

Former Names: Federation of Malaya; In 1963 it joined with North
   Borneo (now Sabah) and Sarawak to form the Federation of
   Malaysia. In 1966, the Malayan States (the eleven states
   formerly comprising the Federation of Malaya, i.e., all of the
   Malay Peninsula south of Thailand) became known as West
   Malaysia, and Sabah and Sarawak together were redesignated East
   Malaysia.
Area: 127,316 sq. mi. Population (1985 est.): 15,467,000
Located: On the southeast tip of Asia and the north coast of the
   island of Borneo.
Language(s): Malay (official), English, Chinese, Indian languages
Religion(s): Muslim, Hindu, Buddhist, Taoism, Confucianism
Government: Federal parliamentary democracy with a constitutional
monarch.

Olympic History: Malaysia has competed in the Olympics since
   1956, missing only the 1980 Moscow Olympics since that time.   In
   1956 and 1960, the country competed as Malaya. In 1964,
   Singapore also competed as a part of the Malaysian team, but
   since then Singapore has competed on its own. The country has
   never competed in the Olympic Winter Games and it has never won
   a medal.

MALDIVES (MDV)
Divehi Jumhuriya
Republic Maldives
Maldives Olympic Committee - 1985

Area: 115 sq. mi. Population (1985 est.): 182,000
Located: In the Indian Ocean, southwest of India
Language(s): Divehi (Sinhalese dialect)
Religion(s): Sunni Muslim
Government: Republic

Olympic History: The Maldives has yet to compete in the Olympic
   Games.

MALI (MLI)
République de Mali
Republic of Mali
Comité Olympique Malien - 1963

Area: 478,764 sq. mi. Population (1985 est.): 7,721,000
Located: In the interior of western Africa
Language(s): French (official), Bambara
Religion(s): Muslim 90%
Government: Republic

Olympic History: Mali has competed at the Olympic Games of 1964,
    1968, 1972, 1976, and 1984. They have never won a medal and
    they have not competed at the Olympic Winter Games.

MALTA (MLT)
Repubblika Ta'Malta
Republic of Malta
Malta Olympic Committee - 1936

Area: 122 sq. mi. Population (1985 est.): 355,000
Located: Island in the center of the Mediterranean Sea
Language(s): Maltese, English (both official)
Religion(s): Roman Catholic
Government: Republic

Olympic History: Malta first competed at the Olympics in 1928.
    They have participated rather sporadically since then, appearing
    again in 1936, 1948, 1960, 1968, 1976, 1980, and 1984. They
    have never competed at the Winter Games.

MAURITANIA (MTN)
République Islamique de Mauritanie
Islamic Republic of Mauritania
Comité Olympique Mauritanien - 1979

Area: 397,954 sq. mi. Population (1985 est.): 1,656,000
Located: Western Africa
Language(s): French (official), Hassanya Arabic (national),
    Toucouleur, Fula, Sarakole, Wolof
Religion(s): Muslim
Government: Military republic

Olympic History: Mauritania has yet to compete in the Olympic
    Games.

MAURITIUS (MRI)
Mauritius Olympic Committee - 1972

Area: 790 sq. mi. Population (1985 est.): 1,024,900
Located: In the Indian Ocean, 500 miles east of Madagascar
Language(s): English (official), French, Creole
Religion(s): Hindu 51%, Christian 30%, Muslim 16%
Government: Parliamentary democracy under a constitutional
monarch

Olympic History: Mauritius made its Olympic début in 1984 at Los
    Angeles, represented by four track & field athletes - three male
    and one female.

MEXICO (MEX)
Estados Unidos Mexicanos
United Mexican State
Comité Olímpico Mexicano - 1923

Area: 761,604 sq. mi. Population (1985 est.): 79,662,000
Located: Southern North America
Language(s): Spanish
Religion(s): Roman Catholic
Government: Federal republic

Olympic History: Mexican athletes first competed at the 1900
   Olympic Games when several of their polo players played at
   Paris. They returned to the Olympic fold in 1924 and have
   competed since without fail. Mexico sent five bobsled
   competitors to the 1928 Winter Olympics but has not competed at
   the Olympic Winter Games since. In 1932 they entered another
   bobsled team but it did not compete.

Olympic Hosts:
        1968 - Mexico City - The Games of the XIXth Olympiad

Medal Count:

	Men				Women				Totals			
	GO	SI	BR	TOT	GO	SI	BR	TOT	GO	SI	BR	TOT
Summer	9	11	15	35	-	1	1	2	9	12	16	37
Winter	-	-	-	-	-	-	-	-	-	-	-	-
Totals	9	11	15	35	-	1	1	2	9	12	16	37

Most Medals, Men
   4   Joaquin Capilla Perez (DIV)
   3   Humberto Mariles Cortes (EQU)

Most Gold Medals, Men
   2   Humberto Mariles Cortes (EQU)
   1   Ernst Canto (TAF)
   1   Raul Gonzalez (TAF)
   1   Daniel Bautista (TAF)
   1   Ricardo Delgado (BOX)
   1   Antonio Roldan (BOX)
   1   Joaquin Capilla Perez (DIV)
   1   Felipe Muñoz (SWI)
   1   Rubén Uriza (EQU)
   1   Alberto Valdés (EQU)

First Medalist, Men
   13 AUG 1932 Gustavo Huet (SHO-Small-bore Rifle, Prone)
   13 AUG 1932 Francisco Cabañas (BOX-Flyweight)

First Gold Medalist, Men
   14 AUG 1948 Show Jumping Team (EQU)
   14 AUG 1948 Humberto Mariles Cortes (EQU-Jumping Individual)

Youngest Medalist, Men
  17-192   Hector Lopez (BOX-1984)

Youngest Gold Medalist, Men
  17-262   Felipe Muñoz (SWI-1968)

Oldest Medalist, Men
  44-338   Manuel Mendivil Yocupicio (EQU-1980)

Oldest Gold Medalist, Men
  34-227   Humberto Mariles Cortes (EQU-1948)

Most Medals, Women
  1   Maria Teresa Ramirez (SWI)
  1   Pilar Roldan Reyna (FEN)

First Medalist, Women
  24 OCT 1968   Maria Teresa Ramirez (SWI-800 freestyle)

Youngest Medalist, Women
  15-071   Maria Theresa Ramirez (SWI-1968)

Oldest Medalist, Women
  24-115   Pilar Roldan Reyna (FEN-1968)

Most Medals, Men, Games
  2   Humberto Mariles Cortes (EQU-1948)
  2   Rubén Uriza (EQU-1948)
  2   Joaquin Capilla Perez (DIV-1956)
  2   Joaquin Pérez de las Heras (EQU-1980)
  2   Raul Gonzalez (TAF-1984)

MONACO (MON)
Principality of Monaco
Comité Olympique Monégasque - 1953

Area: 0.73 sq. mi. Population (1984 est.): 28,000
Located: On the northwest Mediterranean coast
Language(s): French
Religion(s): Roman Catholic
Government: Constitutional monarchy

Olympic History: Monaco competed at the 1920 Olympic Games and
  has since missed only the Games of 1932, 1956, and 1980. The
  country has yet to appear at the Olympic Winter Games. No
  Monagasque athlete has won a medal in a sporting event but in
  1924 Julien Médecin won a bronze medal in the architecture
  portion of the now defunct art competitions.

MONGOLIA (MGL)
Bügd Nayramdakh Mongol Ard Uls
Mongolian People's Republic
Comité National Olympique de la République Populaire Mongolie –
1962

Area: 604,247 sq. mi. Population (1985 est.): 1,893,000
Located: East central Asia
Language(s): Khalkha Mongolian
Religion(s): Officially discouraged – Lama Buddhism prevails
Government: Communist state

Olympic History: Mongolia has competed at the Olympic Games since
1964, their only absence being the 1984 Los Angeles Olympics,
which they boycotted. Their first Olympic appearance was at the
1964 Innsbruck Olympics and they have competed continuously
since at the Olympic Winter Games. In 1964 they showed up in
Innsbruck without having entered, not realizing that was
necessary. The IOC graciously allowed them to compete despite
their late entry.

Medal Count:

| | Men | | | | Women | | | | Totals | | |
	GO	SI	BR	TOT	GO	SI	BR	TOT	GO	SI	BR	TOT
Summer	–	5	5	10	–	–	–	–	–	5	5	10
Winter	–	–	–	–	–	–	–	–	–	–	–	–
Totals	–	5	5	10	–	–	–	–	–	5	5	10

Most Medals, Men
1   Ravdan Davaadalai (JUD)
1   Tsendying Damdin (JUD)
1   Surenjav Sukhbaatar (WRE)
1   Dugarsuren Ouinbold (WRE)
1   Zeveg Oidov (WRE)
1   Sereeter Danzandarjaa (WRE)
1   Dagvasuren Purev (WRE)
1   Jamtsying Davaajav (WRE)
1   Munkbat Jigjid (WRE)
1   Khorloogyn Baianmunkh (WRE)

First Medalist, Men
20 OCT 1968   Surenjav Sukhbaatar (WRE-Flyweight Freestyle)
20 OCT 1968   Sereeter Danzandarjaa (WRE-Lightweight Freestyle)
20 OCT 1968   Dagvasuren Purev (WRE-Welterweight Freestyle)
20 OCT 1968   Munkbat Jigjid (WRE-Middleweight Freestyle)

Youngest Medalist, Men
17-154   Surenjav Sukhbaatar (WRE-1968)

Oldest Medalist, Men
28-191   Khorloogyn Baianmunkh (WRE-1972)

MOROCCO (MAR)
al-Mamlaka al-Maghrebia
Kingdom of Morocco
Comité Olympique Marocain - 1959

Area: 172,413 sq. mi. Population (1985 est.):   23,117,000
Located: Northwest coast of Africa
Language(s):   Arabic (official), Berber, French, Spanish
Religion(s):   Sunni Muslim 99%
Government: Constitutional monarchy

Olympic History: Morocco has competed at six Olympics. First
   appearing in 1960, they missed only the 1976 Games when they
   joined the African boycott. The country has won three Olympic
   medals, all by track athletes - two gold (Said Aouita [1984
   5,000] and Nawal El-Moutawakel [1984 women's 400IH]) and one
   silver (Rhadi ben Abdessalam [1960 marathon]).

Medal Count:

	Men				Women				Totals			
	GO	SI	BR	TOT	GO	SI	BR	TOT	GO	SI	BR	TOT
Summer	1	1	-	2	1	-	-	1	2	1	-	3
Winter	-	-	-	-	-	-	-	-	-	-	-	-
Totals	1	1	-	2	1	-	-	1	2	1	-	3

Most Medals, Men
   1   Said Aouita (TAF)
   1   Rhadi ben Abdesselam (TAF)

Most Gold Medals, Men
   1   Said Aouita (TAF)

First Medalist, Men
   10 SEP 1960 Rhadi ben Abdesselam (TAF-1960)

First Gold Medalist, Men
   11 AUG 1984 Said Aouita (TAF-1984)

Youngest Medalist, Men
   23-282 Said Aouita (TAF-1984)

Oldest Medalist, Men
   31-195 Rhadi ben Abdesselam (TAF-1960)

Most Gold Medals/Medals, Women
   1   Nawal El Moutawakel (TAF)

First Medalist/Gold Medalist, Women
   08 AUG 1984 Nawal El Moutawakel (TAF)

MOZAMBIQUE (MOZ)
Républica Popular de Mocambique
People's Republic of Mozambique
Comité Olímpico Nacional de Moçambique - 1979

Area: 309,494 sq. mi. Population (1985 est.): 13,638,000
Located: Southeast coast of Africa
Language(s): Portuguese (official), Bantu languages predominate
Religion(s): Traditional beliefs 50%, Christian 30%, Muslim 10%
Government: Socialist one-party state

Olympic History: Mozambique has competed in two Olympic Games,
  those of 1980 and 1984.

NEPAL (NEP)
Sri Nepala Sarkar
Kingdom of Nepal
Nepal Olympic Committee - 1963

Area: 56,136 sq. mi. Population (1985 est.): 16,966,000
Located: Astride the Himalaya Mountains in south central Asia
Language(s): Nepali (official)
Religion(s): Hindu 90%, Buddhist 7%
Government: Constitutional monarchy

Olympic History: Nepal has competed at the 1964, 1972, 1976, 1980
  and 1984 Olympic Games. This Himalayan country has still not
  competed in the Olympic Winter Games.

THE NETHERLANDS (HOL)
Konindrijk der Nederlanden
Kingdom of The Netherlands
Netherlands Olympic Committee - 1912

Area: 15,770 sq. mi. Population (1985 est.): 14,481,000
Located: Northwest Europe on the North Sea
Language(s): Dutch
Religion(s): Roman Catholic 36%, Dutch Reformed 20%
Government: Parliamentary democracy under a constitutional
      monarch

Olympic History: The Netherlands, or Holland, sent 30 athletes to
  the 1900 Paris Olympics. After skipping the 1904 St. Louis
  Olympics, Holland has never missed an Olympic Games. At the
  Winter Games, Holland appeared first in 1928, missed the 1932
  Lake Placid Games, but has appeared continuously since.
    In the summer Games, Holland has had a variety of successes in
  different sports but has never dominated any sport. In the
  Winter Olympics, however, Holland has always been one of the
  very top nations in speed skating. In 1972, Ard Schenk won
  three events and at the time was hailed as the greatest skater
  ever.

Olympic Hosts:
    1928 - Amsterdam - The Games of the IXth Olympiad

Medal Count:

	Men				Women				Totals			
	GO	SI	BR	TOT	GO	SI	BR	TOT	GO	SI	BR	TOT
Summer	25	28	45+	98+	16	17	13+	46+	41	45	59	145
Winter	5	9	6	20	5	6	4	15	10	15	10	35
Totals	30	37	51+	118+	21	23	17+	61+	51	60	69	180

Most Medals, Men
   5   Adrianus Jong (FEN)
   4   Jetze Doorman (TAF)
   4   George van Rossem (FEN)
   4   Adrianus "Ard" Schenk (SSK)
   4   Cornelis "Kees" Verkerk (SSK)

Most Gold Medals, Men
   3   Adrianus "Ard" Schenk (SSK)
   3   Adolph van der Voort van Zijp (EQU)

First Medalist, Men
  01 AUG 1900 Pistol Shooting Team (SHO-Team Pistol)

First Gold Medalist, Men
  26 AUG 1900 Pairs with Coxswain Team (ROW-Pairs with)

Youngest Medalist/Gold Medalist, Men
  14-163 Franciscus Hin (YAC-1920)

Oldest Medalist, Men
  50-119 Johannes Hoolwerff (YAC-1928)

Oldest Gold Medalist, Men
  38-100 Maurice Peeters (CYC-1920)

Most Medals, Women
   4   Francina "Fannie" Blankers-Koen (TAF)
   4   Hendrika Mastenbroek (SWI)
   3   Atje Keulen-Deelstra (SSK)
   3   Ada Kok (SWI)
   3   Marie-Louise Linssen-Vaessen (SWI)
   3   Willemijntje den Ouden (SWI)
   3   Johanna Termeulen (SWI)
   3   Anne Marie Verstappen (SWI)

Most Gold Medals, Women
   4   Francina "Fannie" Blankers-Koen (TAF)
   3   Hendrika Mastenbroek (SWI)

First Medalist, Women
  21 JUL 1924 Kornelia Bouman (TEN-Mixed)

First Gold Medalist, Women
   10 AUG 1928 Gymnastics Team (GYM)

Youngest Medalist, Women
   14-220 Willemijntje den Ouden (SWI-1932)

Youngest Gold Medalist, Women
   20-060 Martine Ohr (FIH-1984)

Oldest Medalist, Women
   35-043 Elisabeth Sevene (FIH-1984)

Oldest Gold Medalist, Women
   32-244 Ria Stalman (TAF-1984)

Most Medals, Winter, Men
   4   Adrianus "Ard" Schenk (SSK)
   4   Cornelis "Kees" Verkerk (SSK)

Most Gold Medals, Winter, Men
   3   Adrianus "Ard" Schenk (SSK)
   1   Piet Kleine (SSK)
   1   Cornelis "Kees" Verkerk (SSK)

First Medalist, Winter, Men
   17 FEB 1952 Cornelis "Kees" Broekman (SSK-5,000)

First Gold Medalist, Winter, Men
   16 FEB 1968 Cornelis "Kees' Verkerk (SSK-1,500)

Youngest Medalist, Winter, Men
   21-101 Cornelis "Kees" Verkerk (SSK-1964)

Youngest Gold Medalist, Winter, Men
   24-150 Piet Kleine (SSK-1976)

Oldest Medalist, Winter, Men
   29-102 Cornelis "Kees" Verkerk (SSK-1972)

Oldest Gold Medalist, Winter, Men
   27-144 Adrianus "Ard" Schenk (SSK-1972)

Most Medals, Winter, Women
   4   Christina Baas-Kaiser (SSK)
   3   Atje Keulen-Deelstra (SSK)

Most Gold Medals, Winter, Women
   1   Christina Baas-Kaiser (SSK)
   1   Sjoukje Dijkstra (FSK)
   1   Carolina Geijssen (SSK)
   1   Annie Borckink (SSK)
   1   Johanna Schut (SSK)

First Medalist, Winter, Women
  23 FEB 1960 Sjoukje Dijkstra (FSK-Singles)

First Gold Medalist, Winter, Women
  02 FEB 1964 Sjoukje Dijkstra (FSK-Singles)

Youngest Medalist, Winter, Women
  18-209 Ria Visser (SSK-1980)

Youngest Gold Medalist, Winter, Women
  21-031 Carolina Geijssen (SSK-1968)

Oldest Medalist/Gold Medalist, Winter, Women
  33-268 Christina Baas-Kaiser (SSK-1972)

Most Medals, Men, Games
  3   Adrianus "Ard" Schenk (SSK-1972)
  3   Hans van Helden (SSK-1976)

Most Gold Medals, Men, Games
  3   Adrianus "Ard" Schenk (SSK-1972)
  2   Wilhelm Ruska (JUD-1972)
  2   Charles Pahud de Mortanges (EQU-1928)
  2   Adolph van der Voort van Zijp (EQU-1924)

Most Medals, Women, Games
  4   Hendrika Mastenbroek (SWI-1936)
  4   Francina "Fannie" Blankers-Koen (TAF-1948)

Most Gold Medals, Women, Games
  4   Francina "Fannie" Blankers-Koen (TAF-1948)
  3   Hendrika Mastenbroek (SWI-1936)

Most Medals, Winter, Men, Games
  3   Adrianus "Ard" Schenk (SSK-1972)
  3   Hans van Helden (SSK-1976)

Most Gold Medals, Winter, Men, Games
  3   Adrianus "Ard" Schenk (SSK-1972)
  1   Cornelis "Kees" Verkerk (SSK-1968)
  1   Piet Kleine (SSK-1976)

Most Medals, Winter, Women, Games
  3   Atje-Keulen Deelstra (SSK-1972)
  2   Carolina Geijssen (SSK-1968)
  2   Christina Kaiser (SSK-1968)
  2   Christina Baas-Kaiser (SSK-1972)

Most Gold Medals, Winter, Women, Games
  1   Sjoukje Dijkstra (FSK-1964)
  1   Carolina Geijssen (SSK-1968)
  1   Johanna Schut (SSK-1968)
  1   Christina Baas-Kaiser (SSK-1972)
  1   Annie Borckink (SSK-1980)

NETHERLANDS ANTILLES (AHO)
De Nederlandse Antillen
The Netherlands Antilles
Nederlands Antilliaans Olympisch Comité - 1950

Area: 385 sq. mi. Population (1981 est.): 244,000
Located: Two groups of islands in the West Indies
Language(s): Dutch (official), English, Spanish, Papiamento
Government: Self-governing state of The Netherlands

Olympic History: The Netherlands Antilles has competed in the
  Olympics since 1952. They did not travel to Melbourne in 1956,
  and boycotted the 1980 Olympics, but otherwise have competed at
  every Olympic Games.

NEW ZEALAND (NZL)
New Zealand Olympic and Commonwealth Games Association - 1911

Area: 103,736 sq. mi. Population (1985 est.): 3,271,000
Located: Island in southwest Pacific Ocean
Language(s): English (official), Maori
Religion(s): Anglican 29%, Presbyterian 18%, Roman Catholic 15%
Government: Parliamentary

Olympic History: New Zealand was first represented at the 1908
  Olympic Games. In that year they formed a combined team with
  Australia as Australasia. One New Zealander competed, Harry
  Kerr, a walker who won a bronze in the 3,500 metre walk. In
  1912 two New Zealanders competed with Australasia. Finally in
  1920 at Antwerp, New Zealand took part in the Olympic Games as a
  separate nation. New Zealand competed at its first Olympic
  Winter Games in 1952 at Oslo. It missed the Winter Games of
  1956 and 1964, but has competed at the others since. New
  Zealand has had its greatest success in track & field with
  several of its middle-distance runners being Olympic champions.

Medal Count:

	Men				Women				Totals			
	GO	SI	BR	TOT	GO	SI	BR	TOT	GO	SI	BR	TOT
Summer	21+	4	13	38+	1	–	2	3	22+	4	15	41+
Winter	–	–	–	–	–	–	–	–	–	–	–	–
Totals	21+	4	13	38+	1	–	2	3	22+	4	15	41+

Most Medals, Men
    3   Simon Dickie (ROW)
    3   Peter Snell (TAF)
    3   Ian Ferguson (CAN)

Most Gold Medals, Men
    3   Peter Snell (TAF)
    3   Ian Ferguson (CAN)

First Medalist, Men
    14 JUL 1908   Harry Kerr (TAF-3,500 walk) (AUS/NZL)
    29 AUG 1920   Clarence Hadfield D'Arcy (ROW-Single Sculls)

First Gold Medalist, Men
    15 JUL 1912   Malcolm Champion (SWI-800 free relay) (AUS/NZL)
    11 AUG 1928   Edward "Ted" Morgan (BOX-Welterweight)

Youngest Medalist, Men
    18-079   Brett Hollister (ROW-1984)

Youngest Gold Medalist, Men
    20-001   Athol Earl (ROW-1972)

Oldest Medalist, Men
    40-042   Bruce Kendall (YAC-1984)

Oldest Gold Medalist, Men
    37-138   Christopher Timms (YAC-1984)

Most Medals, Women
    1   Yvette Williams (TAF)
    1   Ann Chamberlain (TAF)
    1   Jean Stewart (SWI)

Most Gold Medals, Women
    1   Yvette Williams (TAF)

First Medalist/Gold Medalist, Women
    23 JUL 1952 Yvette Williams (TAF-LJ)

Youngest Medalist, Women
    21-221   Jean Stewart (SWI-1952)

Oldest Medalist, Women
    28-320   Ann Chamberlain (TAF-1964)

Most Medals, Men, Games
    3   Ian Ferguson (CAN-1984)
    2   Peter Snell (TAF-1964)
    2   Paul McDonald (CAN-1984)

Most Gold Medals, Men, Games
    3   Ian Ferguson (CAN-1984)
    2   Peter Snell (TAF-1964)

Most Medals, Women, Games
    1   Yvette Williams (TAF-1952)
    1   Jean Stewart (SWI-1952)
    1   Ann Chamberlain (TAF-1964)

Most Gold Medals, Women, Games
    1   Yvette Williams (TAF-1952)

NICARAGUA (NCA)
Republica de Nicaragua
Republic of Nicaragua
Comité Olímpico Nicaragüense - 1959

Area: 50,193 sq. mi. Population (1985 est.): 2,232,000
Located: Central America
Language(s): Spanish, English
Religion(s): Roman Catholic
Government: Republic

Olympic History: Nicaragua has competed at the Olympic Games
    since 1968 and has appeared every time since then. They have
    never competed in the Olympic Winter Games and they have never
    won a medal.

NIGER (NIG)
République du Niger
Republic of Niger
Comité Olympique Nigérien - 1964

Area: 489,189 sq. mi. Population (1985 est.): 6,491,000
Located: Interior of north Africa
Language(s): French (official), Hausa, Djema
Religion(s): Muslim 85%, animists 14%
Government: Republic

Olympic History: Niger competed at the Olympics of 1964, 1968 and
    1972 but has since not competed. The country can claim one
    medal, a bronze won by Isakka Daborg in light-welterweight
    boxing in 1972.

NIGERIA (NGR)
Federal Republic of Nigeria
Nigeria Olympic Committee - 1951

Area: 356,667 sq. mi. Population (1985 est.): 102,783,000
Located: Southwest coast of Africa
Language(s): English (official), Hausa, Yoruba, Ibo
Religion(s): Muslim 47% (mostly Northern), Christian 34% (mostly
  Southern)
Government: Military

Olympic History: Nigeria first competed in the Olympics in 1952.
  They have since missed only the 1976 Games, owing to the African
  boycott.

Medal Count:

		Men				Women				Totals		
	GO	SI	BR	TOT	GO	SI	BR	TOT	GO	SI	BR	TOT
Summer	–	1	3	4	–	–	–	–	–	1	3	4
Winter	–	–	–	–	–	–	–	–	–	–	–	–
Totals	–	1	3	4	–	–	–	–	–	1	3	4

Most Medals, Men
  1   Nojim Maiyegun (BOX)
  1   Isaac Ikhouria (BOX)
  1   Peter Konyegwachie (BOX)
  1   Sunday Uti (TAF)
  1   Moses Ugbusien (TAF)
  1   Rotimi Peters (TAF)
  1   Innocent Egbunike (TAF)

First Medalist, Men
  23 OCT 1964 Nojim Maiyegun (BOX-Light-middleweight)

Youngest Medalist, Men
  18-259 Peter Konyegwachie (BOX-1984)

Oldest Medalist, Men
  28-237 Rotimi Peters (TAF-1984)

NORTH BORNEO
  See Malaysia

NORTHERN RHODESIA (---)
  See Zambia.

NORWAY (NOR)
Kongeriket Norge
Kingdom of Norway
Norwegian Olympic Committee - 1900

Area: 125,081 sq. mi. Population (1985 est.): 4,152,000
Located: Western portion of the Scandanavian peninsula
Language(s): Norwegian (official), Lapp
Religion(s): Lutheran 97%
Government: Hereditary constitutional monarchy

Olympic History: Norway competed at the Olympics of 1900 and has
 missed only the 1904 Olympic Games since. Norway has competed
 at every Olympic Winter Games.
  Until 1984, Norway could claim to be the top nation at the
 Olympic Winter Games in terms of medals and gold medals won. In
 that year, however, the Soviet Union surpassed Norway in both
 categories. Norway shares with Liechtenstein and Austria the
 unusual distinction of having won more medals in the Winter
 Games than in the Summer Olympics.

Olympic Hosts:
      1952 - Oslo - The VIth Olympic Winter Games

Medal Count:

	Men				Women				Totals			
	GO	SI	BR	TOT	GO	SI	BR	TOT	GO	SI	BR	TOT
Summer	39	29+	33	101+	–	1+	1	2+	39	31	34	104
Winter	48	54+	45	147+	6	2+	7	15+	54	57	52	163
Totals	87	84+	78	249+	6	3+	8	17+	93	88	86	267

Most Medals, Men
   8   Otto Olsen (SHO)
   7   Ivar Ballangrud (SSK)
   7   Albert Helgerud (SHO)
   7   Einar Liberg (SHO)
   7   Gudbrand Skatteboe (SHO)

Most Gold Medals, Men
   5   Ole Lilloe-Olsen (SHO)
   4   Otto Olsen (SHO)
   4   Ivar Ballangrud (SSK)
   4   Einar Liberg (SHO)
   4   Gudbrand Skatteboe (SHO)

First Medalist, Men
   15 JUL 1900 Carl Albert Andersen (TAF-PV)

First Gold Medalist, Men
   11 JUL 1908 Free Rifle Shooting Team (SHO-Free Rifle Team)

Youngest Medalist/Gold Medalist, Men
   17-292 Harald Eriksen (GYM-1906)

Oldest Medalist/Gold Medalist, Men
57-045 Johan Anker (YAC-1928)

Most Medals, Women, Summer
1   Molla Bjurstedt (TEN)
1   Vibeke Lunde (YAC)
1   Grete Waitz (TAF)

First Medalist, Women, Summer
04 JUL 1912 Molla Bjurstedt (TEN-Ladies' Singles)

Youngest Medalist, Women
28-120 Molla Bjurstedt (TEN-1912)

Oldest Medalist, Women
31-130 Vibeke Lunde (YAC-1952)

Most Medals, Winter, Men
7   Ivar Ballangrud (SSK)
6   Roald Larsen (SSK)
6   Johan Gröttumsbråten (NSK)

Most Gold Medals, Winter, Men
4   Ivar Ballangrud (SSK)
3   Johan Gröttumsbråten (NSK)
3   Thorleif Haug (NSK)
3   Hjalmar Andersen (SSK)

First Medalist, Winter, Men
26 APR 1920 Yngvar Bryn (FSK-Pairs)

First Gold Medalist, Winter, Men
30 JAN 1924 Thorleif Haug (NSK-50 km)

Youngest Medalist, Winter, Men
18-137 Alv Gjestvang (SSK-1956)

Youngest Gold Medalist, Winter, Men
20-173 Birger Ruud (NSK-1932)

Oldest Medalist, Winter, Men
44-078 Martin Stixrud (FSK-1920)

Oldest Gold Medalist, Winter, Men
35-005 Magnar Solberg (BIA-1972)

Most Medals, Winter, Women
3   Inger Aufles (NSK)
3   Sonja Henie (FSK)
3   Berit Mördre-Lammedal (NSK)
3   Berit Aunli (NSK)
3   Brit Pettersen (NSK)

Most Gold Medals, Winter, Women
```
3       Sonja Henie (FSK)
1       Björg Eva Jensen (SSK)
1       Inger Nybraaten (NSK)
1       Anne Jahren (NSK)
1       Berit Aunli (NSK)
1       Brit Pettersen (NSK)
1       Inger Aufles (NSK)
1       Babben Enger-Damon (NSK)
1       Berit Mördre (NSK)
```

First Medalist, Winter, Women
```
26 APR 1920  Alexis Bryn (FSK-Pairs)
```

First Gold Medalist, Winter, Women
```
18 FEB 1928  Sonja Henie (FSK-Singles)
```

Youngest Medalist/Gold Medalist, Winter, Women
```
15-315  Sonja Henie (FSK-1928)
```

Oldest Medalist, Winter, Women
```
31-301  Berit Lammedal-Mördre (NSK-1972)
```

Oldest Gold Medalist, Winter, Women
```
27-250  Berit Aunli (NSK-1984)
```

Most Medals, Men, Games
```
5       Otto Olsen (SHO-1920)
5       Roald Larsen (SSK-1924)
```

Most Gold Medals, Men, Games
```
3       Gudbrand Skatteboe (SHO-1906)
3       Otto Olsen (SHO-1920)
3       Ole Lilloe-Olsen (SHO-1920)
3       Thorleif Haug (NSK-1924)
3       Ivar Ballangrud (SSK-1936)
3       Hjalmar Andersen (SSK-1952)
```

Most Medals, Winter, Men, Games
```
5       Roald Larsen (SSK-1924)
4       Thorleif Haug (NSK-1924)
4       Ivar Ballangrud (SSK-1936)
```

Most Gold Medals, Winter, Men, Games
```
3       Thorleif Haug (NSK-1924)
3       Ivar Ballangrud (SSK-1936)
3       Hjalmar Andersen (SSK-1952)
```

Most Medals, Winter, Women, Games
```
2       Berit Mördre (NSK-1968)
2       Inger Aufles (NSK-1968)
2       Berit Aunli (NOR-1984)
2       Brit Pettersen (NSK-1984)
2       Anne Jahren (NSK-1984)
```

Most Gold Medals, Winter, Women, Games
    1   Sonja Henie (FSK-1928)
    1   Sonja Henie (FSK-1932)
    1   Sonja Henie (FSK-1936)
    1   Inger Aufles (NSK-1968)
    1   Babben Enger-Damon (NSK-1968)
    1   Berit Mördre (NSK-1968)
    1   Björg Eva Jensen (SSK-1980)
    1   Inger Nybraaten (NSK-1984)
    1   Anne Jahren (NSK-1984)
    1   Berit Aunli (NSK-1984)
    1   Brit Pettersen (NSK-1984)

OMAN (OMA)
Saltanat 'Uman
Sultanate of Oman
National Olympic Committee of Oman - 1982

Area: 82,030 sq. mi. Population (1985 est.): 1,228,000
Located: Southeast coast of the Arabian peninsula
Language(s): Arabic (official), English, Urdu
Religion(s): Ibadhi Muslim 75%, Sunni Muslim
Government: Absolute monarchy

Olympic History: Oman made its Olympic début in 1984 at Los
    Angeles, represented by nine shooters and seven track & field
    athletes.

PAKISTAN (PAK)
Islamic Republic of Pakistan
Pakistan Olympic Association - 1948

Area: 310,403 sq. mi. Population (1985 est.): 99,199,000
Located: Western part of southern Asia
Language(s): Urdu, English (both official)
Religion(s): Muslim 97%
Government: Martial law régime

Olympic History: Pakistan first competed at the Olympic Games in
    1948. They did not attend the 1980 Moscow Olympics but
    otherwise have attended all Games since. They have never
    competed at the Olympic Winter Games. Pakistan owes almost its
    entire Olympic success to one sport - field hockey. They have
    won a medal in this sport at every celebration since 1956, and
    finished fourth in 1948 and 1952. In 1960 they won the gold
    medal, defeating India in the final and ending its 32-year
    Olympic winning streak. The only non-hockey medal won was a
    1960 bronze by Mohammad Bashir in freestyle welterweight
    wrestling.

Medal Count:

	Men				Women				Totals			
	GO	SI	BR	TOT	GO	SI	BR	TOT	GO	SI	BR	TOT
Summer	3	3	2	8	-	-	-	-	3	3	2	8
Winter	-	-	-	-	-	-	-	-	-	-	-	-
Totals	3	3	2	8	-	-	-	-	3	3	2	8

Most Medals, Men
4	Abdul Rashid (FIH)
3	Saeed Anwar (FIH)
3	Manzur Hussain Atif (FIH)
3	Munir Ahmad Dar (FIH)
3	Abdul Hamid (FIH)
3	Anwar Ahmad Khan (FIH)
3	Mohammed Asad Malik (FIH)
3	Mutih Ullah (FIH)

Most Gold Medals, Men
2	Abdul Rashid (FIH)
1	Many athletes tied with one

First Medalist, Men
06 DEC 1956 Field Hockey Team (FIH)

First Gold Medalist, Men
09 SEP 1960 Field Hockey Team (FIH)

Youngest Medalist, Men
17-025 Haneef Khan (FIH-1976)

Youngest Gold Medalist, Men
19-228 Shahid Ali Khan (FIH-1984)

Oldest Medalist/Gold Medalist, Men
38-101 Abdul Rashid (FIH-1960)

PANAMA (PAN)
República de Panama
Republic of Panama
Comité Olímpico de Panama - 1947

Area: 29,208 sq. mi. Population (1985 est.): 2,180,000
Located: Central America
Language(s): Spanish (official), English
Religion(s): Roman Catholic 93%, Protestant
Government: Constitutional monarchy with a centralized republic

Olympic History: Panama was represented at the Olympics in 1928,
   1948, and 1952 by a single athlete. They have sent larger
   contingents since 1960, although they did not attend the 1980
   Moscow Olympics. They have never competed in the Olympic Winter
   Games. Their lone competitor in 1948 did quite well, as Lloyd
   LaBeach won Panama's only two Olympic medals to date, finishing
   third in both the 100 and 200 metre dashes.

PAPUA-NEW GUINEA (NGU)
Papua New Guinea Olympic Committee and Commonwealth Games
Association - 1974

Area: 178,259 sq. mi.   Population (1985 est.):   3,326,000
Located: Eastern half of island of New Guinea
Language(s):   English (official), Melanesian Pidgin, Police Motu
Religion(s):   Protestant 63%, Roman Catholic 31%
Government: Parliamentary democracy

Olympic History: Papua-New Guinea has competed at the Olympic
   Games of 1976 and 1984.

PARAGUAY (PAR)
Répública del Paraguay
Republic of Paraguay
Comité Olímpico Paraguayo - 1968

Area: 157,047 sq. mi.   Population (1985 est.):   3,989,000
Located: Landlocked in the center of South America
Language(s):   Spanish (official), Guarani (used by 90%)
Religion(s):   Roman Catholic (official) 97%
Government: Constitutional republic with a powerful executive
   branch

Olympic History: Paraguay has competed at the Olympic Games of
   1968, 1972, 1976, and 1984.   They have never won a medal and
   they have never competed at the Olympic Winter Games.

PERU (PER)
Répública del Peru
Republic of Peru
Comité Olímpico Peruano - 1936

Area: 496,222 sq. mi.   Population (1985 est.):   19,698,000
Located: Pacific coast of South America
Language(s):   Spanish, Quechua (both official), Aymara
Religion(s):   Roman Catholic 90+%
Government: Constitutional republic

Olympic History: Peru first competed at the 1936 Olympic Games.
   They have since missed only the 1952 Games in Helsinki.   Peru
   has won two medals in Olympic competition, both in shooting.   In
   1948 Edwin Vasquez Cam won a gold medal in free pistol shooting
   and in 1984 Francisco Boza won a silver medal in trap shooting.
   The country has not competed at the Olympic Winter Games.

THE PHILIPPINES (PHI)
Republic of the Philippines
Philippine Olympic Committee - 1929

Area: 115,831 sq. mi. Population (1985 est.): 56,808,000
Located: Archipelago off the southeast corner of Asia
Language(s): Filipino (based on Tagalog), English (both official)
Religion(s): Roman Catholic 83%, Protestant 9%, Muslim 5%
Government: Republic

Olympic History: The Philippines first competed at the Olympics
   in 1924, and has since missed only the 1980 Moscow Olympics.
   They have yet to competed at the Olympic Winter Games. Their
   six medals have been evenly divided among boxing, swimming, and
   track & field.

Medal Count:

	Men				Women				Totals			
	GO	SI	BR	TOT	GO	SI	BR	TOT	GO	SI	BR	TOT
Summer	–	1	5	6	–	–	–	–	–	1	5	6
Winter	–	–	–	–	–	–	–	–	–	–	–	–
Totals	–	1	5	6	–	–	–	–	–	1	5	6

Most Medals, Men
   2   Teofilo Yldefonzo (SWI)
   1   José Villanueva (BOX)
   1   Anthony Villanueva (BOX)
   1   Miguel White (TAF)
   1   Simeon Toribio (TAF)

First Medalist, Men
   08 AUG 1928 Teofilo Yldefonzo (SWI-200 breaststroke)

Youngest Medalist, Men
   19-220 Anthony Villanueva (BOX-1964)

Oldest Medalist, Men
   29-186 Teofilo Yldefonzo (SWI-1932)

POLAND (POL)
Polska Rzeczpospolita Ludowa
Polish People's Republic
Comité Olympique Polonais - 1919

Area: 120,727 sq. mi. Population (1985 est.): 37,160,000
Located: On Baltic Sea in eastern Europe
Language(s): Polish
Religion(s): Officially discouraged - Roman Catholic 95%
Government: Communist

Olympic History: Poland competed continuously at the Olympic
Games from 1924 through 1980. Prior to that several Poles
probably competed for other countries. In 1908, Jerzy Gajdzyk,
his name Americanized to George Gaidzik, won a diving bronze
medal for the United States. The 1912 Russian Olympic team
included eight Poles. Poland has also competed at all the
Olympic Winter Games.

Medal Count:

	Men				Women				Totals			
	GO	SI	BR	TOT	GO	SI	BR	TOT	GO	SI	BR	TOT
Summer	32	41	73	146	6	10	13	29	38	51	86	175
Winter	1	–	1	2	–	1	1	2	1	1	2	4
Totals	33	41	74	148	6	11	14	31	39	52	88	179

Most Medals, Men
  5   Jerzy Pawłowski (FEN)
  4   Witold Woyda (FEN)

Most Gold Medals, Men
  2   Witold Woyda (FEN)
  2   Waldemar Baszanowski (WLT)
  2   Jerzy Kulej (BOX)
  2   Józef Szmidt (TAF)
  2   Józef Zapedzki (SHO)

First Medalist, Men
  27 JUL 1924 Cycling Pursuit Team (CYC-4000 TP)
  27 JUL 1924 Adam Królikiewicz (EQU-Jumping Individual)

First Gold Medalist, Men
  31 JUL 1932 Janusz Kusociński (TAF-10,000)

Youngest Medalist, Men
  18-146 Benedykt Kocot (CYC-1972)

Youngest Gold Medalist, Men
  20-058 Lech Łasko (VOL-1976)

Oldest Medalist, Men
  38-296 Marian Zieliński (WLT-1968)

Oldest Gold Medalist, Men
  33-048 Edward Skorek (VOL-1976)

Most Medals, Women
  7   Irena Szewińska-Kirszenstein (TAF)
  3   Teresa Ciepły-Wieczorkowna (TAF)

Most Gold Medals, Women
```
3       Irena Szewińska-Kirszenstein (TAF)
1       Teresa Ciepły-Wieczorkowna (TAF)
1       Elzbieta Krzesińska (TAF)
1       Halina Górecka-Richterówna (TAF)
1       Halina Konopacka (TAF)
1       *Stanisława Walasiewiczówna [Stella Walsh] (TAF)
1       *Ewa Kłobukowska (TAF)
```

First Medalist/Gold Medalist, Women
```
31 JUL 1928   Halina Konopacka (TAF-DT)
```

Youngest Medalist/Gold Medalist, Women
```
18-021 *Ewa Kłobukowska (TAF-1964)
```

Oldest Medalist, Women
```
44-226 Irena Szydłowska (ARC-1972)
```

Oldest Gold Medalist, Women
```
30-067 Irena Szewińska-Kirszenstein (TAF-1976)
```

Most Medals, Winter, Men
```
1       Franciszek Gasienica Groń (NSK)
1       Wojciech Fortuna (NSK)
```

Most Gold Medals, Winter, Men
```
1       Wojciech Fortuna (NSK)
```

First Medalist, Winter, Men
```
31 JAN 1956   Franciszek Gasienica Groń (NSK-Nordic Combined)
```

First Gold Medalist, Winter, Men
```
11 FEB 1972   Wojciech Fortuna (NSK-90 Jump)
```

Youngest Medalist, Winter, Men
```
19-188 Wojciech Fortuna (NSK-1972)
```

Oldest Medalist, Winter, Men
```
24-185 Franciszek Gasienica Groń (NSK-1956)
```

Most Medals, Winter, Women
```
1       Elwira Seroczyńska (SSK)
1       Helena Pilejczykówna (SSK)
```

First Medalist, Winter, Women
```
21 FEB 1960   Elwira Seroczyńska (SSK-1,500)
21 FEB 1960   Helena Pilejczykówna (SSK-1,500)
```

Youngest Medalist, Winter, Women
```
28-296 Elvira Seroczyńska (SSK-1960)
```

Oldest Medalist, Winter, Women
```
28-326 Helena Pilejczykówna (SSK-1960)
```

Most Medals, Men, Games
    2   MichaŁ Antoniewicz (EQU-1928)
    2   Jerzy Braun (ROW-1932)
    2   Jerzy Skolimowski (ROW-1932)
    2   Janusz Slazak (ROW-1932)
    2   Jerzy PawŁowski (FEN-1956)
    2   Egon Franke (FEN-1964)
    2   MieczysŁaw Nowicki (CYC-1976)

Most Gold Medals, Men, Games
    1   Many athletes tied with one

Most Medals, Women, Games
    3   Irena Szewińska-Kirszenstein (TAF-1964)
    2   Teresa CiepŁy-Wieczorkówna (TAF-1964)
    2   *Ewa KŁobukowska (TAF-1964)

Most Gold Medals, Women, Games
    1   Halina Konopacka (TAF-1928)
    1   Elzbieta Krzesińska (TAF-1956)
    1   Halina Górecka-Richterówna (TAF-1964)
    1   Teresa Ciepóy-Wieczorkówna (TAF-1964)
    1   Irena Kirszenstein (TAF-1964)
    1   Irena Kirszenstein (TAF-1968)
    1   Irena Szewińska-Kirszenstein (TAF-1976)
    1   *StanisŁawa Walasiewiczówna [Stella Walsh] (TAF-1932)
    1   *Ewa KŁobukowska (TAF-1964)

*Though listed as females, KŁobukowska failed a sex test in 1966
    and Walasiewiczówna (Americanized to Walsh after her emigration
    to the United States) was found at autopsy in 1981 to possess
    both male and female sexual organs.

PORTUGAL (POR)
Répúblíca Portuguesa
Republic of Portugal
Comité Olímpico Português - 1909

Area: 35,553 sq. mi. Population (1985 est.): 10,046,000
Located: At southwest extreme of Europe, on the western half of
    the Iberian Peninsula
Language(s): Portuguese
Religion(s): Roman Catholic 97%
Government: Parliamentary democracy

Olympic History: Portugal has competed at the Olympic Games
    continuously since 1912. In the Olympic Winter Games they have
    appeared once with only one competitor. That was Duarte
    Espirito Santo Silva who competed in alpine skiing events in
    1952 at Oslo.

Medal Count:

	Men				Women				Totals			
	GO	SI	BR	TOT	GO	SI	BR	TOT	GO	SI	BR	TOT
Summer	1	4	6	11	–	–	1	1	1	4	7	12
Winter	–	–	–	–	–	–	–	–	–	–	–	–
Totals	1	4	6	11	–	–	1	1	1	4	7	12

Most Medals, Men
    2   Carlos Lopes (TAF)
    2   Luiz Mena e Silva (EQU)

Most Gold Medals, Men
    1   Carlos Lopes (TAF)

First Medalist, Men
    27 JUL 1924 Show Jumping Team (EQU-Jumping Team)

First Gold Medalist, Men
    12 AUG 1984 Carlos Lopes (TAF-Marathon)

Youngest Medalist, Men
    18-0945 Antonio Borges de Almeida (EQU-1924)

Oldest Medalist, Men
    46-198 Luiz Mena e Silva (EQU-1948)

Oldest Gold Medalist, Men
    37-176 Carlos Lopes (TAF-1984)

Most Medals, Women
    1   Rosa Mota (TAF)

First Medalist, Women
    05 AUG 1984 Rosa Mota (TAF-Marathon)

PUERTO RICO (PUR)
Estado Libre Asociado de Puerto Rico
Commonwealth of Puerto Rico
Comité Olímpico de Puerto Rico – 1948

Area: 3,435 sq. mi. Population (1985 est.): 3,279,231
Located: Easternmost island in the West Indies
Language(s): English, Spanish
Religion(s): Roman Catholic
Government: Independently governed part of the United States

Olympic History: Puerto Rico first competed at the 1948 Olympics
    in London and has not failed to compete at the Olympic Games
    since then. They have also sent one athlete to the Olympic
    Winter Games. In 1984, George Tucker, born in Puerto Rico but a
    native of New York, competed in the men's singles luge event and
    finished last. All of Puerto Rico's medals have been won in
    boxing.

Medal Count:

	Men				Women				Totals			
	GO	SI	BR	TOT	GO	SI	BR	TOT	GO	SI	BR	TOT
Summer	-	1	3	4	-	-	-	-	-	1	3	4
Winter	-	-	-	-	-	-	-	-	-	-	-	-
Totals	-	1	3	4	-	-	-	-	-	1	3	4

Most Medals, Men
    1   Juan Evangelista Venegas (BOX)
    1   Orlando Maldonado (BOX)
    1   Luiz Ortiz (BOX)
    1   Aristides Gonzales (BOX)

First Medalist, Men
    13 AUG 1948 Juan Evangelista Venegas (BOX-Bantamweight)

Youngest Medalist, Men
    17-071 Orlando Maldonado (BOX-1976)

Oldest Medalist, Men
    23-181 Aristides Gonzales (BOX-1984)

QATAR (QAT)
Dawlet al-Qatar
State of Qatar
Qatar National Olympic Committee - 1980

Area: 4,247 sq. mi. Population (1985 est.): 301,000
Located: Occupies peninsula on the west coast of the Persian Gulf
Language(s): Arabic (official), English
Religion(s): Muslim 95%
Government: Traditional emirate

Olympic History: Qatar made its initial Olympic appearance in Los
    Angeles in 1984 with a team of eight track & field athletes, a
    football (soccer) team, and four shooters.

RHODESIA (RHO)
    See Zimbabwe.

ROMANIA (ROM)
Republica Socialista România
Socialist Republic of Romania
Comité Olympique Roumain - 1914

Area: 91,699 sq. mi. Population (1985 est.): 22,734,000
Located: Southeast Europe on the Black Sea
Language(s): Romanian, Hungarian, German
Religion(s): Eastern Orthodox 80%, Roman Catholic 6%
Government: Communist

Olympic History: Romania first competed at the 1924 Olympic
Games, and has missed only the 1932 Olympics since. They defied
pressure from their neighbors and valiantly were the only
Eastern European country to compete at the 1984 Olympics in Los
Angeles. Romania has also competed at every Olympic Winter
Games since their inception in 1924. They are best known now
for their outstanding women gymnasts, notably Nadia Comăneci,
Ecaterina Szabo, Teodora Ungereanu, and Simona Pauca. They also
produce excellent canoeists. Romania's lone Winter Olympic
medal came in the 1968 two-man bobsled event.

Medal Count:

	Men				Women				Totals			
	GO	SI	BR	TOT	GO	SI	BR	TOT	GO	SI	BR	TOT
Summer	23	35	50+	108+	25	18	25+	68+	48	53	76	177
Winter	–	–	1	1	–	–	–	–	–	–	1	1
Totals	23	35	51+	109+	25	18	25+	68+	48	53	77	178

Most Medals, Men
5   Ivan Patzaichin (CAN)
4   Vasile Diba (CAN)

Most Gold Medals, Men
4   Ivan Patzaichin (CAN)
2   Toma Simionov (CAN)
2   Leon Rotman (CAN)

First Medalist, Men
18 MAY 1924 Rugby Team (RUG)

First Gold Medalist, Men
29 JUL 1952 Iosif Sirbu (SHO-Small-bore Rifle, prone)

Youngest Medalist, Men
17-018 Dumitru Raducanu (ROW-1984)

Youngest Gold Medalist, Men
18-334 Ivan Patzaichin (CAN-1968)

Oldest Medalist, Men
57-283 Petre Rosca (EQU-1980)

Oldest Gold Medalist, Men
35-046 Ion Dumitrescu (SHO-1960)

Most Medals, Women
9   Nadia Comăneci (GYM)
5   Ecaterina Szabo (GYM)

Most Gold Medals, Women
5   Nadia Comăneci (GYM)
4   Ecaterina Szabo (GYM)

First Medalist, Women
   29 NOV 1956   Olga Orban (FEN-Foil Individual)

First Gold Medalist, Women
   08 SEP 1960   Iolanda Balas (TAF-HJ)

Youngest Medalist, Women
   14-163   Christina Grigoras (GYM-1980)

Youngest Gold Medalist, Women
   14-250   Nadia Comăneci (GYM-1976)

Oldest Medalist/Gold Medalist, Women
   36-176   Lia Manoliu (TAF-1968)

Most Medals, Winter, Men
   1   Ion Panturu (BOB)
   1   Nicolae Neagoe (BOB)

First Medalist, Winter, Men
   06 FEB 1968   Ion Panturu/Nicolae Neagoe (BOB-Two-man)

Youngest Medalist, Winter, Men
   26-188   Nicolae Neagoe (BOB-1968)

Oldest Medalist, Winter, Men
   33-148   Ion Panturu (BOB-1968)

Most Medals, Men, Games
   2   Leon Rotman (CAN-1956)
   2   Leon Patzaichin (CAN-1984)
   2   Toma Simionov (CAN-1984)

Most Gold Medals, Men, Games
   2   Leon Rotman (CAN-1956)
   1   Many tied with one

Most Medals, Women, Games
   5   Nadia Comăneci (GYM-1976)
   5   Ecaterina Szabo (GYM-1984)

Most Gold Medals, Women, Games
   4   Ecaterina Szabo (GYM-1984)
   3   Nadia Comăneci (GYM-1976)

RUSSIA (---)

Olympic History: Prior to the Communist Revolution, Russia
   competed at the Olympics of 1900, 1906, 1908, and 1912.
   Although at the first three celebrations their representation
   was only three, six, and five athletes, respectively, in 1912
   they sent a large team of 169 athletes.   At those Olympics,
   Russia won one gold medal, four silver medals, and three bronze
   medals.   Their first medal was won by Aleksandr Petrov in 1908
   in heavyweight Greco-Roman wrestling.   Their first gold medal,
   and first winter medal of any type, was won by Nikolai Panin (né
   Nikolai Kolomenkin) who in 1908 won the special figures figure
   skating event.   See also USSR.

RWANDA (RWA)
Republika y'u Rwanda
Republic of Rwanda
Comité National Olympique du Rwanda - 1984

Area: 10,169 sq. mi.   Population (1985 est.):   6,115,000
Located: East central Africa
Language(s):   French, Kinyarwandu (both official), Swahili
Religion(s):   Christian 68%, traditional 23%
Government: Republic

Olympic History: Rwanda has not yet competed in the Olympic
   Games.

SAAR (---)

Olympic History: In 1952 The Saar was recognized as a separate
   Olympic Committee by the IOC and competed at the Helsinki
   Olympics, represented by 31 athletes but winning no medals.   The
   Saar was reunited with the FRG in 1956.   Their athletes were
   absorbed by the combined German teams and The Saar OC was
   dissolved on 20 September 1956.

SAINT VINCENT AND THE GRENADINES (VIN)
Saint Vincent and the Grenadines
St. Vincent and the Grenadines Olympic Association - 1987

Area: 150 sq. mi.   Population (1985 est.):   102,000
Located: Eastern Caribbean
Language(s):   English
Religion(s):   Methodist, Anglican, Roman Catholic
Government: Independent state of the British Commonwealth

Olympic History: St. Vincent and the Grenadines has never
   competed in the Olympic Games.

SAMOA, AMERICAN (SAO)
American Samoa
American Samoa National Olympic Committee - 1987

Area: 77 sq. mi. Population (1984 est.): 33,800
Located: Six small islands 2,600 miles southwest of Honolulu
Language(s):   English, local dialects
Religion(s):   Protestant, Roman Catholic, native beliefs
Government: Independent part of the United States

Olympic History: American Samoa has never competed in the Olympic
   Games.

SAMOA, WESTERN (SAM)
Malotuto'atasi o Samoa i Sisifo
Independent State of Western Samoa
Western Samoa Amateur Sports Federation - 1983

Area: 1,133 sq. mi. Population (1985 est.):   160,000
Located: South Pacific Ocean
Language(s):   Samoan, English (both official)
Religion(s):   Protestant, Roman Catholic
Government: Parliamentary democracy

Olympic History: Western Samoa's first Olympic appearance came in
   1984 at Los Angeles.

SAN MARINO (SMR)
Serenissima Repubbica di San Marino
Most Serene Republic of San Marino
Comitato Olimpico Nazionale Sammarinese - 1959

Area: 24 sq. mi. Population (1985 est.):   22,300
Located: North central Italy near Adriatic coast
Language(s):   Italian
Religion(s):   Roman Catholic
Government: Independent republic

Olympic History: San Marino has competed at six summer Olympics -
   those of 1960, 1968, 1972, 1976, 1980, and 1984. It has twice
   been represented at the Olympic Winter Games - those of 1976 and
   1984. No San Marinan athlete has yet won a medal.

SAUDI ARABIA (SAU)
al-Mamlaka al-'Arabiya as-Sa'udiya
Kingdom of Saudi Arabia
Saudi Arabia Olympic Committee - 1965

Area: 839,996 sq. mi. Population (1985 est.): 11,152,000
Located: Occupies most of Arabian peninsula in Middle East
Language(s): Arabic
Religion(s): Muslim 99%
Government: Monarchy with council of ministers

Olympic History: Saudi Arabia has competed at the Olympics of
    1972, 1976, and 1984. They have never competed in the Olympic
    Winter Games.

SENEGAL (SEN)
République di Sénégal
Republic of Senegal
Comité Olympique Sénégalais - 1963

Area: 75,750 sq. mi. Population (1985 est.): 6,755,000
Located: Western extreme of Africa
Language(s): French (official), tribal languages
Religion(s): Muslim 75%, Christians 5%
Government: Republic

Olympic History: Senegal first competed at the 1964 Olympic Games
    and has competed at every Olympics since. They have never
    competed at the Olympic Winter Games nor have they yet to win a
    medal. Their top finish was in 1968 when Amadou Gakou finished
    fourth in the 400 metre dash in track & field.

SEYCHELLES (SEY)
Republic of Seychelles
Seychelles Olympic Committee - 1979

Area: 171 sq. mi. Population (1985 est.): 66,000
Located: In Indian Ocean, 700 miles northeast of Madagascar
Language(s): English, French (both official), Creole
Religion(s): Roman Catholic 96%
Government: Single party republic

Olympic History: The Seychelles has competed at two Olympic
    Games, those of 1980 and 1984. They have won no medals.

SIERRA LEONE (SLE)
Republic of Sierra Leone
Sierra Leone Olympic and Overseas Games Committee - 1964

Area: 27,699 sq. mi. Population (1985 est.): 3,883,000
Located: West coast of Africa
Language(s): English (official), tribal languages
Religion(s): Muslim 60%, animist 30%
Government: Republic

Olympic History: Sierra Leone has competed at two Olympic Games,
    those of 1968 and 1980.

SINGAPORE (SIN)
Republic of Singapore
Singapore National Olympic Council - 1948

Area: 224 sq. mi. Population (1985 est.): 2,556,000
Located: Off tip of Malayan peninsula in southeast Asia
Language(s): Chinese, Malay, Tamil, English (all official)
Religion(s): Buddhism, Taoism, Islam, Hinduism, Christianity
Government: Parliamentary democracy

Olympic History: Singapore has competed at eight Olympic Games -
    those of 1948, 1952, 1956, 1960, 1968, 1972, 1976, and 1984. In
    1964 Singaporean athletes competed under the banner of Malaysia
    in a combined team with Malaysia and North Borneo. Singapore
    has not competed at the Olympic Winter Games. In 1960 at Rome,
    Howe-Liang Tan won a silver medal in lightweight weightlifting,
    the only medal won to date by a Singapore athlete.

SOLOMON ISLANDS (SOL)
Solomon Islands National Olympic Committee - 1983

Area: 10,640 sq. mi. Population (1985 est.): 267,000
Located: Melanesian archipelago in the western south Pacific
Language(s): English (official), Pidgin
Religion(s): Anglican 34%, Evangelical 24%, Roman Catholic 19%
Government: Parliamentary democracy within the Commonwealth of
    Nations

Olympic History: The Solomon Islands' first Olympic appearance
    came in 1984 at the Los Angeles Olympics. They were represented
    by one weightlifter and one track & field athlete.

SOMALIA (SOM)
Jamhuriyadda Dimugradiga Somaliya
Somali Democratic Republic
Somali National Olympic Committee - 1972

Area: 246,300 sq. mi. Population (1985 est.): 7,595,000
Located: Occupies the eastern horn of Africa
Language(s): Somali, Arabic (both official)
Religion(s): Sunni Muslim 99%
Government: Independent republic

Olympic History: Somalia has competed at only two Olympic Games -
those of 1972 and 1984. They have yet to win a medal.

SOUTH AFRICA (SAF)
Republiek van Suid-Afrika
Republic of South Africa

Area: 472,359 sq. mi. Population (1985 est.): 32,465,000
Located: Southern tip of Africa
Language(s): Afrikaans, English (both official), Bantu languages
predominate
Religion(s): Christian
Government: Tricameral parliamentary, with one chamber each for
Caucasians, blacks, and Asians.

Olympic History: With the exception of the Intercalated Games of
1906, South Africa's participation was continuous from 1904
through 1960. Since that time, however, they have not been
allowed to compete at the Olympics. This has been due to the
country's policy of apartheid and, in particular, its use of the
policy in choosing its athletic teams, which is forbidden by IOC
policy. In 1968 the IOC almost allowed a mixed South African
team to compete, but withdrew the invitation under threat of
mass boycotts. Eventually the South African Olympic Committee
was also ejected from the IOC. In 1976, the South African
question again became prominent when several African nations
boycotted in protest of a New Zealand rugby team having played
several games on tour in South Africa. Ironically rugby has not
been an Olympic sport since 1924 and the New Zealand rugby team
was named the All-Blacks. It is also ironic that the first
South African Olympians were two Kaffir tribesmen who ran in the
1904 marathon; named Lentauw and Yamasini, they were both black
men. South African participation in future Olympics is not
imminent.

Medal Count:

	Men				Women				Totals			
	GO	SI	BR	TOT	GO	SI	BR	TOT	GO	SI	BR	TOT
Summer	14	14	16	44	2	1	4	7	16	15	20	51
Winter	-	-	-	-	-	-	-	-	-	-	-	-
Totals	14	14	16	44	2	1	4	7	16	15	20	51

Most Medals, Men
    3   Bevil Rudd (TAF)
    3   Charles Winslow (TEN)

Most Gold Medals, Men
    2   Charles Winslow (TEN)
    1   Thirteen athletes tied with one

First Medalist, Men
    01 MAY 1906 Vincent de Villiers Duncker (TAF-110HH)

First Gold Medalist, Men
    22 JUL 1908 Reginald Walker (TAF-100)

Youngest Medalist, Men
    17-045 William Meyers (BOX-1960)

Youngest Gold Medalist, Men
    18-326 Gerald Dreyer (BOX-1948)

Oldest Medalist, Men
    42-202 George Harvey (SHO-1920)

Oldest Gold Medalist, Men
    38-018 Harold Kitson (TEN-1912)

Most Medals, Women
    1   Thirteen athletes tied with one

Most Gold Medals, Women
    1   Joan Harrison (SWI)
    1   Esther Brand (SWI)

First Medalist, Women
    09 AUG 1928 Freestyle Relay Team (SWI-400R)

First Gold Medalist, Women
    27 JUL 1952 Esther Brand (TAF-HJ)

Youngest Medalist, Women
    16-081 Jeanette Myburgh (SWI-1956)

Youngest Gold Medalist, Women
    16-245 Joan Harrison (SWI-1952)

Oldest Medalist/Gold Medalist, Women
    27-301 Esther Brand (TAF-1952)

Most Medals, Men, Games
    2   Charles Winslow (TEN-1920)
    2   Harold Kitson (TEN-1920)

Most Gold Medals, Men, Games
```
   2        Charles Winslow (TEN-1920)
   1        Thirteen athletes tied with one
```

SPAIN (ESP)
España
Spanish State
Comité Olímpico Español - 1924

Area: 194,896 sq. mi. Population (1985 est.): 38,829,000
Located: Southwest Europe, occupying most of the Iberian
  peninsula
Language(s): Spanish (official), Catalan, Galician, Basque
Religion(s): Roman Catholic
Government: Constitutional monarchy

Olympic History: In 1900 Spain was represented by five rowers at
  the Paris Olympics. Spain next appeared on the Olympic stage in
  1920, and has since missed only the 1936 Berlin Olympics.
  Spain's first winter appearance was in 1936 at Garmisch-
  Partenkirchen and they have never failed to compete in the
  Olympic Winter Games since.

Olympic Hosts:
        1992 - Barcelona - The Games of the XXVth Olympiad
                    (scheduled)

Medal Count:

	Men				Women				Totals			
	GO	SI	BR	TOT	GO	SI	BR	TOT	GO	SI	BR	TOT
Summer	3	11	7	21	-	-	-	-	3	11	7	21
Winter	1	-	-	1	-	-	-	-	1	-	-	1
Totals	4	11	7	22	-	-	-	-	4	11	7	22

Most Medals, Men
```
   3        Herminio Menéndez (CAN)
   2        José Navarro Morenés (EQU)
   2        Luis Ramos Missione (CAN)
```

Most Gold Medals, Men
```
   1        José Navarro Morenés (EQU)
   1        José Alvaro de los Trujillos (EQU)
   1        Julio Garcia Fernandez (EQU)
   1        Alejandro Abascal (YAC)
   1        Miguel Noguer (YAC)
   1        Luis Doreste (YAC)
   1        Roberto Molina (YAC)
```

First Medalist, Men
  29 JUN 1920 Polo Team (POL)

First Gold Medalist, Men
  12 AUG 1928 Show Jumping Team (EQU-Jumping Team)

Youngest Medalist, Men
    20-296 Enrique Rodriquez-Cal (BOX-1972)

Youngest Gold Medalist, Men
    22-110 Antonio Gorostequi (YAC-1976)

Oldest Medalist, Men
    50-250 José Navarro Morenés (EQU-1948)

Oldest Gold Medalist, Men
    33-225 Julio Garcia Fernandez (EQU-1928)

Most Medals/Gold Medals, Winter, Men
    1   Francisco Fernandez Ochoa (ASK)

First Medalist/Gold Medalist, Winter, Men
    13 FEB 1972 Francisco Fernandez Ochoa (ASK-Slalom)

Most Medals, Men, Games
    2   Herminio Menéndez (CAN-1980)
    1   Many athletes tied with one

Most Gold Medals, Men, Games
    1   José Navarro Morenés (EQU-1928)
    1   José Alvaro de los Trujillos (EQU-1928)
    1   Julio Garcia Fernandez (EQU-1928)
    1   Alejandro Abascal (YAC-1980)
    1   Miguel Noguer (YAC-1980)
    1   Luis Doreste (YAC-1984)
    1   Roberto Molina (YAC-1984)

SRI LANKA (SRI)
Sri Lanka Prajathanthrika Samajavadi Janarajaya
Democratic Socialist Republic of Sri Lanka
National Olympic Committee of Sri Lanka - 1937

Former Name: Ceylon (changed 22 MAY 1972)
Area: 25,332 sq. mi. Population (1985 est.): 16,344,000
Located: Indian Ocean off the coast of India
Language(s): Sinhala (official), Tamil, English
Religion(s): Buddhist 69%, Hindu 15%, Christian 7%, Muslim 7%
Government: Republic

Olympic History: Sri Lanka, as Ceylon, competed at the Olympics
    from 1948 through 1968. After its changed its name to Sri
    Lanka, it has competed at the Olympics of 1972, 1976, 1980 and
    1984, making its participation continuous since its début in
    1948. Sri Lanka has yet to compete in the Olympic Winter Games.
    One medal has been won by a Sri Lankan athlete. In 1948, Duncan
    White, then representing Ceylon, finished second in the 400
    metre hurdles.

THE SUDAN (SUD)
Jamhuryat as-Sudan
Democratic Republic of the Sudan
Sudanese Olympic Committee - 1959

Area: 966,757 sq. mi. Population (1985 est.): 22,972,000
Located: At the eastern end of the Sahara Desert in north Africa
Language(s): Arabic (official), tribal languages
Religion(s): Muslim 73%, animist 18%, Christian 9%
Government: Republic

Olympic History: The Sudan has competed at three Olympic Games,
  those of 1960, 1968, and 1972. It has never competed at the
  Olympic Winter Games.

SURINAME (SUR)
Republic of Suriname
Surinaams Olympisch Comité - 1959

Area: 63,037 sq. mi. Population (1985 est.): 395,000
Located: Northern coast of South America
Language(s): Dutch (official), Sranan (Creole), English
Religion(s): Muslim, Hindu, Christian
Government: Military-civilian executive

Olympic History: Surinam has competed at four Olympic Games since
  its début in 1968. It has missed only the 1980 Moscow Olympics.
  Its Olympic delegation to date totals ten men - seven in track &
  field and three judoka.

SWAZILAND (SWZ)
Kingdom of Swaziland
Swaziland Olympic and Commonwealth Games Association - 1972

Area: 6,704 sq. mi. Population (1985 est.): 636,000
Located: Southern Africa, near the Indian Ocean coast
Language(s): Siswati, English (both official)
Religion(s): Christian 77%, animist 23%
Government: Monarchy

Olympic History: Swaziland has competed at two Olympic Games -
  those of 1972 and 1984.

SWEDEN (SWE)
Konungariket Sverige
Kingdom of Sweden
The Swedish Olympic Committee - 1913

Area: 173,731 sq. mi. Population (1985 est.): 8,348,000
Located: On Scandanavian Peninsula in northern Europe
Language(s): Swedish, Finnish
Religion(s): Lutheran (official) 95%, other Protestant 5%
Government: Constitutional monarchy

Olympic History: With the exception of the 1904 St. Louis
    Olympics, Sweden has competed at every Olympic Games and every
    Olympic Winter Games. In addition to having been one of the two
    or three top countries in the Winter Games, they have also been
    outstanding in equestrian sport and canoeing at the summer
    Olympics.

Olympic Hosts:
        1912 - Stockholm - The Games of the Vth Olympiad
        1956 - Stockholm - The Equestrian Games of the XVIth
                    Olympiad

Medal Count:

	Men				Women				Totals			
	GO	SI	BR	TOT	GO	SI	BR	TOT	GO	SI	BR	TOT
Summer	124+	130+	148+	403+	5	7+	12+	25+	129+	138	161	428+
Winter	28	22	26	76	4	3	3	10	32	25	29	86
Totals	152+	152+	174+	479+	9	10+	15+	35+	161+	163	190	514+

Most Medals, Men
    9   Sixten Jernberg (NSK)
    8   Vilhelm Carlberg (SHO)
    8   Gert Fredriksson (CAN)

Most Gold Medals, Men
    6   Gert Fredriksson (CAN)
    4   Sixten Jernberg (NSK)
    4   Eric Lemming (TAF)
    4   Henri St. Cyr (EQU)

First Medalist, Men
    16 JUL 1900   Tug-of-War Team (Half of team) (SWE/DAN)
    19 JUL 1900   Ernst Fast (TAF-Marathon)

First Gold Medalist, Men
    16 JUL 1900   Tug-of-War Team (Half of team) (SWE/DAN)
    27 APR 1906   Eric Lemming (TAF-JT)

Youngest Medalist, Men
    14-011 Nils Skoglund (DIV-1920)

Youngest Gold Medalist, Men
    15-226 Per Daniel Bertilsson (GYM-1908)

Oldest Medalist, Men
  72-280 Oscar Swahn (SHO-1920)

Oldest Gold Medalist, Men
  64-258 Oscar Swahn (SHO-1912)

Most Medals, Women
  4   Toini Gustafsson (NSK)
  3   Ulrike Knape (SWI)
  3   Britt Strandberg (NSK)
  3   Agneta Andersson (CAN)
  3   Ann-Sofi Colling-Petterson (GYM)

Most Gold Medals, Women
  2   Agneta Andersson (CAN)
  2   Toini Gustafsson (NSK)

First Medalist, Women
  13 JUL 1912 Greta Johanson (DIV-Platform)
  13 JUL 1912 Lisa Regnell (DIV-Platform)

First Gold Medalist, Women
  13 JUL 1912 Greta Johanson (DIV-Platform)

Youngest Medalist, Women
  16-228 Eva Ollivier (DIV-1920)

Youngest Gold Medalist, Women
  17-130 Ulrika Knape (DIV-1972)

Oldest Medalist, Women
  46-274 Ulla Håkanson (EQU-1984)

Oldest Gold Medalist, Women
  27-261 Ingrid Sandahl (GYM-1952)

Most Medals, Winter, Men
  9   Sixten Jernberg (NSK)
  4   Gillis Grafström (FSK)
  4   Gunde Anders Swan (NSK)

Most Gold Medals, Winter, Men
  4   Sixten Jernberg (NSK)
  3   Gillis Grafström (FSK)

First Medalist, Winter, Men
  29 OCT 1908 Ulrich Salchow (FSK-Singles)
  29 OCT 1908 Richard Johansson (FSK-Singles)
  29 OCT 1908 Per Thorén (FSK-Singles)

First Gold Medalist, Winter, Men
  29 OCT 1908 Ulrich Salchow (FSK-Singles)

Youngest Medalist/Gold Medalist, Winter, Men
    20-363   Jonny Nilsson (SSK-1964)

Oldest Medalist, Winter, Men
    38-247   Gillis Grafström (FSK-1932)

Oldest Gold Medalist, Winter, Men
    35-002   Sixten Jernberg (NSK-1964)

Most Medals, Winter, Women
    4   Toini Gustafsson (NSK)
    3   Britt Strandberg (NSK)

Most Gold Medals, Winter, Women
    2   Toini Gustafsson (NSK)
    1   Magda Julin-Mauroy (NSK)
    1   Sonja Ruthström-Edström (NSK)
    1   Britt Strandberg (NSK)
    1   Irma Johansson (NSK)

First Medalist, Winter, Women
    25 APR 1920   Magda Julin-Mauroy (FSK-Singles)
    25 APR 1920   Svea Norén (FSK-Singles)

First Gold Medalist, Winter, Women
    25 APR 1920   Magda Julin (FSK-Singles)

Youngest Medalist, Winter, Women
    24-203   Svea Noren (FSK-1920)

Youngest Gold Medalist, Winter, Women
    25-276   Magda Julin-Mauroy (FSK-1920)

Oldest Medalist, Winter, Women
    33-322   Britt Strandberg (NSK-1968)

Oldest Gold Medalist, Winter, Women
    29-100   Sonja Ruthström-Edström (NSK-1960)

Most Medals, Men, Games
    5   Vilhelm Carlberg (SHO-1912)
    4   Eric Lemming (TAF-1906)
    4   Eric Carlberg (SHO-1912)
    4   Johann Holst (SHO-1912)
    4   Erik Backman (TAF-1920)
    4   Sixten Jernberg (NSK-1956)
    4   Gunde Anders Swan (NSK-1984)

Most Gold Medals, Men, Games
    3   Vilhelm Carlberg (SHO-1912)
    2   Many athletes tied with two

Most Medals, Women, Games
    3   Toini Gustafsson (NSK-1968)
    3   Agneta Andersson (CAN-1984)

Most Gold Medals, Women, Games
    2   Toini Gustafsson (NSK-1968)
    2   Agneta Andersson (CAN-1984)

Most Medals, Winter, Men, Games
    4   Sixten Jernberg (NSK-1956)
    4   Gunde Anders Swan (NSK-1984)

Most Gold Medals, Winter, Men, Games
    2   Sixten Jernberg (NSK-1964)
    2   Ingemar Stenmark (ASK-1980)
    2   Gunde Anders Swan (NSK-1984)
    2   Thomas Wassberg (NSK-1984)
    2   Martin Lundström (NSK-1984)

Most Medals, Winter, Women, Games
    3   Toini Gustafsson (NSK-1968)
    2   Sonja Edstrom (NSK-1956)

Most Gold Medals, Winter, Women, Games
    2   Toini Gustafsson (NSK-1968)
    1   Magda Julin-Mauroy (NSK-1920)
    1   Sonja Ruthström-Edstrom (NSK-1960)
    1   Britt Strandberg (NSK-1960)
    1   Irma Johansson (NSK-1960)

SWITZERLAND (SUI)
Swiss Confederation
Comité Olympique Suisse - 1912

Area: 15,941 sq. mi. Population (1985 est.): 6,457,000
Located: Central Europe
Language(s): German 65%, French 18%, Italian 12%, Romansh 1% (all official)
Religion(s): Roman Catholic 49%, Protestant 48%
Government: Federal state

Olympic History: Switzerland first competed at the 1896 Olympic Games when it was represented by Louis Zutter, a gymnast from Neuchâtel. Switzerland also competed at the first Olympic Winter Games in 1924, and was represented before that in 1920 at Antwerp in both the figure skating and ice hockey events. They have been represented at every Olympic Games and every Olympic Winter Games, one of only two countries to make this claim (Great Britain is the other).

Switzerland has really never been the dominant country in any sport. In the early Games they had top-notch gymnasts. Until the GDR became dominant they were the top nation in bobsledding in the Winter Games.

Olympic Hosts:
        1928 - Saint Moritz - The IInd Olympic Winter Games
        1948 - Saint Moritz - The Vth Olympic Winter Games

Medal Count:

	Men				Women				Totals			
	GO	SI	BR	TOT	GO	SI	BR	TOT	GO	SI	BR	TOT
Summer	40	61+	56+	158	1	1+	1+	4	41	63	58	162
Winter	11	17	17	45	7	3	3	13	18	20	20	58
Totals	51	78+	73+	203	8	4+	4+	17	59	83	78	220

Most Medals, Men
    8   Eugen Mack (GYM)
    8   Georges Miez (GYM)
    8   Konrad Stäheli (SHO)

Most Gold Medals, Men
    5   Konrad Stäheli (SHO)
    5   Louis Richardet (SHO)

First Medalist/Gold Medalist, Men
    09 APR 1896 Louis Zutter (GYM-PH)

Youngest Medalist/Gold Medalist, Men
    14-222 Hans Bourquin (ROW-1928)

Oldest Medalist, Men
    66-155 Louis Noverraz (YAC-1968)

Oldest Gold Medalist, Men
    53-055 Herman de Pourtales (YAC-1900)

Most Medals, Summer, Women
    3   Christine Stückelberger (EQU)
    2   Marianne Gossweiler (EQU)

Most Gold Medals, Women
    2   Marie-Theres Nadig (ASK)
    1   Yvonne Rüegg (ASK)
    1   Renée Colliard (ASK)
    1   Hedy Schlunegger (ASK)
    1   Michela Figini (ASK)
    1   Madeleine Berthod (ASK)
    1   Christine Stückelberger (EQU)

Youngest Medalist, Women
    21-162 Marianne Gossweiler (EQU-1964)

Oldest Medalist, Women
    40-193 Amy Catherine de Bary (EQU-1984)

Youngest/Oldest Gold Medalist, Women
    29-069 Christine Stückelberger (EQU-1976)

Most Medals, Winter, Men
5   Fritz Feierabend (BOB)
4   Erich Schärer (BOB)

Most Gold Medals, Winter, Men
1   Twenty-five athletes tied with one

First Medalist/Gold Medalist, Winter, Men
03 FEB 1924 Five-Man Bobsled Team (BOB-Five-Man)

Youngest Medalist, Winter, Men
16-141 Richard "Bibi" Torriani (ICH-1928)

Youngest Gold Medalist, Winter, Men
18-279 Heinrich Schläppi (BOB-1924)

Oldest Medalist, Winter, Men
46-342 Albert Madörin (BOB-1952)

Oldest Gold Medalist, Winter, Men
40-172 Heinrich Angst (BOB-1956)

Most Medals, Winter, Women
3   Marie-Theres Nadig (ASK)
1   Ten athletes tied with one

Most Gold Medals, Winter, Women
2   Marie-Theres Nadig (ASK)
1   Yvonne Rüegg (ASK)
1   Renée Colliard (ASK)
1   Hedy Schlunegger (ASK)
1   Michela Figini (ASK)
1   Madeleine Berthod (ASK)

First Medalist/Gold Medalist, Winter, Women
02 FEB 1948 Hedy Schlunegger (ASK-Downhill)

Youngest Medalist/Gold Medalist, Winter, Women
17-315 Michela Figini (ASK-1984)

Oldest Medalist, Winter, Women
27-230 Antoinette Meyer (ASK-1948)

Oldest Gold Medalist, Winter, Women
25-000 Madeleine Berthod (ASK-1956)

Most Medals, Men, Games
    5   Eugen Mack (GYM-1936)
    4   Konrad Stäheli (SHO-1900)
    4   Konrad Stäheli (SHO-1906)
    4   Jean Reich (SHO-1906)
    4   Louis Richardet (SHO-1906)
    4   Fritz Kucher (SHO-1920)
    4   Hermann Hanggi (GYM-1928)
    4   Georges Miez (GYM-1928)
    4   Josef Stalder (GYM-1952)

Most Gold Medals, Men, Games
    3   Louis Richardet (SHO-1906)
    3   Konrad Stäheli (SHO-1906)
    3   Georges Miez (GYM-1928)

Most Medals, Winter, Women, Games
    2   Marie-Theres Nadig (ASK-1972)
    1   Ten athletes tied with one

Most Gold Medals, Winter, Women, Games
    2   Marie-Theres Nadig (ASK-1972)
    1   Hedy Schlunegger (ASK-1948)
    1   Renée Colliard (ASK-1956)
    1   Madeleine Berthod (ASK-1956)
    1   Yvonne Rüegg (ASK-1960)
    1   Michela Figini (ASK-1984)

SYRIA (SYR)
al-jamhouriya al-Arabia as-Souriya
Syrian Arab Republic
Comité Olympique Syrien - 1948

Former Name: United Arab Republic (with Egypt; FEB 1958 to 20 SEP
    1961)
Area: 71,498 sq. mi. Population (1985 est.): 10,535,000
Located: At eastern end of Mediterranean Sea
Language(s): Arabic (official), Kurdish, Armenian, French,
    English
Religion(s): Sunni Muslim 70%, Christian 13%
Government: Socialist

Olympic History: Syria sent one athlete to the 1948 Olympic
    Games. In 1960, the United Arab Republic (Egypt and Syria)
    competed at Rome with 74 athletes. Syria was a member of the
    UAR at that time but it is unknown how many, if any, of the 74
    athletes were Syrian. Syria returned to the Olympic fold in
    1968 and their participation has been continuous since. They
    have yet to compete in an Olympic Winter Games. In 1984, Joseph
    Atiyeh won Syria's first medal, a silver in the 100 kg. class in
    freestyle wrestling.

TAIWAN (---)
  See Chinese Taipei.

TANGANYIKA (---)
  See Tanzania.

TANZANIA (TAN)
Jamhuri ya Mwungano wa Tanzania
United Republic of Tanzania
Tanzanie Olympic Committee - 1968

Former Names: Tanganyika and Zanzibar (merged 26 APR 1964)
Area: 364,886 sq. mi. Population (1985 est.): 21,701,000
Located: Coast of East Africa - Zanzibar is an island off the
  coast
Language(s): Swahili, English (both official)
Religion(s): Muslim 35%, Christian 35%, traditional beliefs 30%
Government: Republic

Olympic History: As Tanganyika, Tanzania had three athletes at
  the 1964 Olympic Games. As Tanzania they have competed at the
  1968, 1972, 1980, and 1984 Olympics. They have never competed
  at the Olympic Winter Games. In 1980 at Moscow, two Tanzanian
  distance runners won silver medals - Suleiman Nyambui on the
  5,000 metres and Filbert Bayi in the steeplechase. In 1976,
  Bayi had been a co-favorite with New Zealand's John Walker in
  the 1,500 metres and the battle between them was anticipated to
  be one of the great races in track history. It never occurred
  as Tanzania joined the 1976 African boycott in protest of a New
  Zealand rugby team playing in South Africa.

THAILAND (THA)
Muang Thai or Prathet Thai
Kingdom of Thailand
Olympic Committee of Thailand - 1950

Former Name: Siam (changed 1949)
Area: 198,456 sq. mi. Population (1985 est.): 51,546,000
Located: On Indochinese and Malayan Peninsulas in southeast Asia
Language(s): Thai, Chinese
Religion(s): Buddhist 95%, Muslim 4%
Government: Constitutional monarchy

Olympic History: Competing in the Olympics since 1952, Thailand
  has missed only the 1980 Moscow Olympics. They have never
  competed in the Olympic Winter Games. They have won two medals.
  In 1976 Payao Pooltarat won a bronze in light flyweight boxing.
  In 1984 Dhawee Umponmaha won a silver medal in light-
  welterweight boxing.

TOGO (TOG)
République Togolaise
Republic of Togo
Comité National Olympique Togolais - 1965

Area: 21,622 sq. mi. Population (1985 est.): 3,023,000
Located: Southern coast of west Africa
Language(s): French (official)
Religion(s): Traditional 60%, Christian 20%, Muslim 20%
Government: Republic

Olympic History: Togo has competed at two Olympic Games - those
   of 1972 and 1984.

TONGA (TGA)
Pule'anga Tonga
Kingdom of Tonga

Area: 270 sq. mi. Population (1985 est.): 103,000
Located: Western south Pacific Ocean
Language(s): Tongan, English
Religion(s): Free Wesleyan 47%, Roman Catholic 14%, Free Church
   of Tonga 14%, Mormons 9%, Church of Tonga 9%
Government: Constitutional monarchy

Olympic History: Tonga has not yet competed at the Olympic Games.

TRINIDAD AND TOBAGO (TRI)
Republic of Trinidad and Tobago
Trinidad and Tobago Olympic Association - 1962

Area: 1,970 sq. mi. Population (1985 est.): 1,186,000
Located: Off eastern coast of Venezuela
Language(s): English (official), Hindi, French, Spanish
Religion(s): Roman Catholic 33%, Hindu 24%, Protestant 14%,
   Muslim 6%
Government: Parliamentary democracy

Olympic History: Trinidad and Tobago has competed continuously at
   the Olympics since their début in 1948, competing only as
   Trinidad through 1964. In 1960 they had one cyclist and one
   track & field athlete competing in a combined team with Jamaica
   under the name The Antilles, and representing the West Indies
   Federation. Trinidad and Tobago has not yet competed in the
   Olympic Winter Games. The country has won medals in
   weightlifting and track & field.

Medal Count:

	Men				Women				Totals			
	GO	SI	BR	TOT	GO	SI	BR	TOT	GO	SI	BR	TOT
Summer	1	2	4	7	–	–	–	–	1	2	4	7
Winter	–	–	–	–	–	–	–	–	–	–	–	–
Totals	1	2	4	7	–	–	–	–	1	2	4	7

Most Medals, Men
    2   Rodney Wilkes (WLT)
    2   Edwin Roberts (TAF)
    2   Wendell Mottley (TAF)

Most Gold Medals, Men
    1   Hasely Crawford (TAF)

First Medalist, Men
    09 AUG 1948   Rodney Wilkes (WLT-Featherweight)

First Gold Medalist, Men
    24 JUL 1976   Hasely Crawford (TAF-100)

Youngest Medalist, Men
    22-148   Kent Bernard (TAF-1964)

Youngest/Oldest Gold Medalist, Men
    25-343   Hasely Crawford (TAF-1976)

Oldest Medalist, Men
    27-137   Rodney Wilkes (WLT-1952)

Most Medals, Men, Games
    2   Edwin Roberts (TAF-1964)
    2   Wendell Mottley (TAF-1964)

TUNISIA (TUN)
al Jumhuriyah at-Tunisiyah
Republic of Tunisia
Comité Olympique Tunisien - 1957

Area: 63,170 sq. mi. Population (1985 est.): 7,259,000
Located: Northern coast of Africa
Language(s): Arabic (official), French
Religion(s): Mainly Muslim with Christian and Jewish minorities
Government: Republic

Olympic History: Tunisia has competed at the Olympic Games since
   1960, missing only the Games of 1976 at Montreal. They have
   never competed at the Olympic Winter Games. Their top athlete
   has been Mohamed Gammoudi, a distance runner.

Medal Count:

	Men				Women				Totals			
	GO	SI	BR	TOT	GO	SI	BR	TOT	GO	SI	BR	TOT
Summer	1	2	2	5	–	–	–	–	1	2	2	5
Winter	–	–	–	–	–	–	–	–	–	–	–	–
Totals	1	2	2	5	–	–	–	–	1	2	2	5

Most Medals, Men
   4   Mohamed Gammoudi (TAF)
   1   Habib Galhia (BOX)

Most Gold Medals, Men
   1   Mohamed Gammoudi (TAF)

First Medalist, Men
   14 OCT 1964 Mohamed Gammoudi (TAF-10,000)

First Gold Medalist, Men
   17 OCT 1968 Mohamed Gammoudi (TAF-5,000)

Youngest Medalist, Men
   23-163 Habib Galhia (BOX-1964)

Oldest Medalist, Men
   34-212 Mohamed Gammoudi (TAF-1972)

Youngest/Oldest Gold Medalist
   30-249 Mohamed Gammoudi (TAF-1968)

TURKEY (TUR)
Turkiye Cumhuriyeti
Republic of Turkey
Turkish Olympic Committee - 1911

Area: 301,381 sq. mi. Population (1985 est.): 50,661,000
Located: Asia Minor, between the Black and Mediterranean Seas
Language(s): Turkish (official), Kurdish, Arabic
Religion(s): Muslim 98%, Christian, Jews
Government: Republic

Olympic History: In 1907, Pierre de Coubertin visited Turkey and
  had as his guide, Aleko Mulas, a young gymnast who was studying
  at the Galatasaray Lycée. Coubertin invited Mulas to attend the
  Olympic Games and in 1908, Mulas became Turkey's first Olympic
  athlete when he competed in the gymnastic events. In 1912,
  Turkey had two athletes at Stockholm, but they did not enter a
  real team until 1924 at Paris. Since then they have missed only
  the Games of 1932 and 1980. Turkey first competed at the
  Olympic Winter Games in 1936 and has since missed the Winter
  Games of 1952, 1972, and 1980.
    As noted below, Turkey has won 44 Olympic medals. Probably no
  other country can "pin" its Olympic success so much to one
  sport, as Turkey has won all but three of these medals in
  wrestling (41), the others coming in boxing (2) and track &
  field (1).

Medal Count:

	Men				Women				Totals			
	GO	SI	BR	TOT	GO	SI	BR	TOT	GO	SI	BR	TOT
Summer	23	12	9	44	-	-	-	-	23	12	9	44
Winter	-	-	-	-	-	-	-	-	-	-	-	-
Totals	23	12	9	44	-	-	-	-	23	12	9	44

Most Medals, Men
  3   Hamit Kaplan (WRE)
  2   Hüseyin Akbas (WRE)
  2   Ahmet Ayik (WRE)
  2   Mithat Bayrak (WRE)
  2   Mustafa Dagistanli (WRE)
  2   Hasan Güngör (WRE)
  2   Ahmet Kireççi (WRE)
  2   Ismail Ogan (WRE)

Most Gold Medals, Men
  2   Mithat Bayrak (WRE)
  2   Mustafa Dagistanli (WRE)

First Medalist, Men
  04 AUG 1936 Ahmet Kireççi (WRE-Middleweight FS)

First Gold Medalist, Men
  09 AUG 1936 Yasar Erkan (WRE-Featherweight GR)

Youngest Medalist, Men
  20-008 Eyup Can (BOX-1984)

Youngest Gold Medalist, Men
  21-282 Ahmet Kireççi (WRE-1936)

Oldest Gold Medalist/Medalist, Men
  34-205 Mahmut Atalay (WRE-1968)

UGANDA (UGA)
Republic of Uganda
Uganda Olympic Committee - 1956

Area: 93,354 sq. mi. Population (1985 est.): 14,689,000
Located: East central Africa
Language(s): English (official), Luganda, Swahili
Religion(s): Christian 63%, Muslim 6%, traditional beliefs
Government: Military

Olympic History: Uganda competed at the Olympics for the first
  time in 1956. Their participation was continuous through 1972 -
  the highlight that year being John Akii-Bua winning their first
  gold medal with his world record performance in the 400 metre
  intermediate hurdles. In 1976, after the overthrow of Idi Amin,
  and joining in the 1976 African protest, Uganda did not
  participate at Montreal. They have competed, however, in both
  1980 and 1984. Uganda has never competed at the Olympic Winter
  Games.

Medal Count:

	Men				Women				Totals			
	GO	SI	BR	TOT	GO	SI	BR	TOT	GO	SI	BR	TOT
Summer	1	3	1	5	-	-	-	-	1	3	1	5
Winter	-	-	-	-	-	-	-	-	-	-	-	-
Totals	1	3	1	5	-	-	-	-	1	3	1	5

Most Medals, Men
  2   Leo Rwabwogo (BOX)
  1   John Akii-Bua (TAF)
  1   Eridari Mukwanga (BOX)
  1   John Mugabi (BOX)

Most Gold Medals, Men
  1   John Akii-Bua (TAF)

First Medalist, Men
  26 OCT 1968 Leo Rwabwogo (BOX-Flyweight)
  26 OCT 1968 Eridari Mukwanga (BOX-Bantamweight)

First Gold Medalist, Men
  02 SEP 1972 John Akii-Bua (TAF-400IH)

Youngest Medalist, Men
19-146 Leo Rwabwogo (BOX-1968)

Oldest Medalist, Men
25-107 Eridari Mukwanga (BOX-1968)

Youngest/Oldest Gold Medalist, Men
22-274 John Akii-Bua (TAF-1972)

UNION OF SOVIET SOCIALIST REPUBLICS/SOVIET UNION/U.S.S.R. (URS)
Soyuz Sovetskykh Sotsialisticheskikh Respublic
    (SSSR - CCCP in Cyrillic)
Comité Olympique d'U.R.S.S. - 1951

Area: 8,649,496 sq. mi. Population (1985 est.): 277,504,000
Located: From east Europe across north Asia to the Pacific Ocean
Language(s): Russian, Ukrainian, Byelorussian, Polish, Turkish
Religion(s): Officially discouraged - Russian Orthodox 18%,
    Muslim 9%, other Orthodox, Protestant, Jewish and Buddhist
    groups
Government: Federal Union

Olympic History: The Soviet Union has had two distinct periods of
Olympic participation. From 1900 through 1912 they competed
without fail at the Olympics as Russia. However, after the
Communist Revolution they withdrew from international sport
until the late 40's. After World War II they competed in the
European Championships in track & field but they did not return
to the Olympic fold until 1952 at Helsinki. They made their
inaugural Winter Olympic appearance in 1956 at Cortina. They
have competed at every Olympics since with the exception of the
1984 Los Angeles Olympics. Since returning to the Olympics the
Soviet Union has been a dominant force in almost all Olympic
sports.

Olympic Hosts:
        1980 - Moscow - Games of the XXIInd Olympiad.

Medal Count:

| | Men | | | | Women | | | | Totals | | | |
	GO	SI	BR	TOT	GO	SI	BR	TOT	GO	SI	BR	TOT
Summer	257+	223+	178	659	82+	68+	74	225	340	292	252	884
Winter	40	27+	27+	95	28	20+	21+	70	68	48	49	165
Totals	297+	251+	205+	754	110+	88+	95+	295	408	340	301	1049

Most Medals, Men
    15   Nikolai Andrianov (GYM)
    13   Boris Shakhlin (GYM)

Most Gold Medals, Men
    7   Nikolai Andrianov (GYM)
    7   Boris Shakhlin (GYM)
    7   Viktor Chukarin (GYM)

First Medalist, Men
  24 JUL 1908 Aleksandr Petrov (RUS/URS-WRE-Greco Heavyweight)
  20 JUL 1952 Aleksandr Anufriev (TAF-10K)

First Gold Medalist, Men
  21 JUL 1952 Men's Gymnastic Team
  21 JUL 1952 Viktor Chukarin (GYM-All-Around, Horse Vault,
                 Pommeled Horse)
  21 JUL 1952 Grant Shaginyan (GYM-Rings)

Youngest Medalist, Men
  16-319 Vladimir Aleinik (DIV-1976)

Youngest Gold Medalist, Men
  18-310 Aleksandr Portnov (DIV-1980)

Oldest Medalist, Men
  45-235 Yuriy Lorentsson (ROW-1976)

Oldest Gold Medalist, Men
  41-345 Valentin Mankin (YAC-1980)

Most Medals, Women
  18   Larisa Latynina (GYM)
  10   Polina Astakhova (GYM)

Most Gold Medals, Women
  9   Larisa Latynina (GYM)
  6   Lidiya Skoblikova (SSK)
  5   Polina Astakhova (GYM)
  5   Nelli Kim (GYM)

First Medalist, Women
  20 JUL 1952 Nina Romashkova (TAF-DT)
  20 JUL 1952 Elisaveta Bagryantseva (TAF-DT)
  20 JUL 1952 Nina Dumbadze (TAF-DT)

First Gold Medalist, Women
  20 JUL 1952 Nina Romashkova (TAF-DT)

Youngest Medalist, Women
  14-052 Sirvard Emirzian

Youngest Gold Medalist, Women
  15-000 Maria Filatova (GYM-1976)

Oldest Medalist, Women
  37-307 Antonina Seredina (CAN-1968)

Oldest Gold Medalist, Women
  36-239 Lyudmila Pinaeeva-Khvedosyuk (CAN-1972)

Most Medals, Winter, Men
```
5        Evgeniy Grishin (SSK)
5        Nikolai Zimyatov (NSK)
5        Aleksandr Tikhonov (BIA)
```

Most Gold Medals, Winter, Men
```
4        Evgeniy Grishin (SSK)
4        Nikolai Zimyatov (NSK)
4        Aleksandr Tikhonov (BIA)
```

First Medalist, Winter, Men
```
29 OCT 1908  Nikolai Panin (Kolomenkin) (FSK-Special Figures)
27 JAN 1956  Pavel Kolchin (NSK-30K)
```

First Gold Medalist, Winter, Men
```
29 OCT 1908  Nikolai Panin (Kolomenkin) (FSK-Special Figures)
28 JAN 1956  Evgeniy Grishin (SSK-500)
```

Youngest Medalist/Gold Medalist, Winter, Men
```
19-009  Igor Malkov (SSK-1984)
```

Oldest Medalist/Gold Medalist, Winter, Men
```
35-222  Oleg Protopopov (FSK-1968)
```

Most Medals, Winter, Women
```
8        Galina Kulakova (NSK)
7        Raisa Smetanina (NSK)
6        Lidiya Skoblikova (SSK)
```

Most Gold Medals, Winter, Women
```
6        Lidiya Skoblikova (SSK)
4        Galina Kulakova (NSK)
```

First Medalist, Winter, Women
```
28 JAN 1956  Lyubov Kozyreva (NSK-10K)
28 JAN 1956  Radya Eroshina (NSK-10K)
```

First Gold Medalist, Winter, Women
```
28 JAN 1956  Lyubov Kozyreva (NSK-10K)
```

Youngest Medalist, Winter, Women
```
15-091  Marina Cherkasova (FSK-1980)
```

Youngest Gold Medalist, Winter, Women
```
20-350  Lidiya Skoblikova (SSK-1960)
```

Oldest Medalist, Winter, Women
```
38-005  Alevtina Kolchina (NSK-1968)
```

Oldest Gold Medalist, Winter, Women
```
33-362  Alevtina Kolchina (NSK-1968)
```

Most Medals, Men, Games
```
8         Aleksandr Dityatin (GYM-1980)
7         Boris Shakhlin (GYM-1960)
7         Mikhail Voronin (GYM-1968)
7         Nikolai Andrianov (GYM-1976)
```

Most Gold Medals, Men, Games
```
4         Viktor Chukarin (GYM-1952)
4         Boris Shakhlin (GYM-1960)
4         Nikolai Andrianov (GYM-1976)
```

Most Medals, Women, Games
```
7         Mariya Gorokhovskaya (GYM-1952)
6         Larisa Latynina (GYM-1956)
6         Larisa Latynina (GYM-1960)
6         Larisa Latynina (GYM-1964)
```

Most Gold Medals, Women, Games
```
4         Lidiya Skoblikova (SSK-1964)
3         Larisa Latynina (GYM-1960)
3         Klaudiya Boyarskikh (NSK-1964)
3         Olga Korbut (GYM-1972)
3         Galina Kulakova (NSK-1972)
3         Nelli Kim (GYM-1976)
```

Most Medals, Winter, Men, Games
```
3         Pavel Kolchin (NSK-1956)
3         Anatoli Aliabiev (BIA-1980)
3         Nikolai Zimyatov (NSK-1980)
```

Most Gold Medals, Winter, Men, Games
```
3         Nikolai Zimyatov (NSK-1980)
2         Evgeniy Grishin (SSK-1956)
2         Evgeniy Grishin (SSK-1960)
2         Vyacheslav Vedenin (NSK-1972)
```

Most Medals, Winter, Women, Games
```
4         Lidiya Skoblikova (URS-1964)
4         Tatyana Averina (URS-1976)
```

Most Gold Medals, Winter, Women, Games
```
4         Lidiya Skoblikova (SSK-1964)
3         Klaudiya Boyarskikh (NSK-1964)
3         Galina Kulakova (NSK-1972)
```


UNITED ARAB EMIRATES (UAE)
Ittihad al-Imarat al-Arabiyah
United Arab Emirates Olympic Committee - 1980

Area: 32,000 sq. mi. Population (1985 est.): 1,283,000
Located: Southern shore of the Persian Gulf
Language(s): Arabic (official), Farsi, English, Hindi, Urdu
Religion(s): Muslim 90%, Christian, Hindu
Government: Federation of Emirates

Olympic History: The United Arab Emirates first competed at the
1984 Olympics in Los Angeles where they were represented by
eight male track & field athletes.

UNITED ARAB REPUBLIC (UAR)
  See Egypt and Syria.

UNITED STATES (USA)
United States of America
United States Olympic Committee - 1895

Area: 3,618,770 sq. mi. Population (1985 est.): 238,631,000
Located: Central North America
Language: English
Religion(s): Protestant, Roman Catholic, Judaism
Government: Democratic republic

Olympic History: The United States has competed at every Olympic
  Games with the exception of the 1980 Moscow Games, and has never
  failed to be repesented at the Olympic Winter Games. In
  addition, they had skaters present in both 1908 and 1920 when
  those events were held with the summer celebration. They have
  been the dominant country in terms of medals won since the
  inception of the Games. However, in the past three decades, the
  Soviet Union has won slightly more medals, and the German
  Democratic Republic now also threatens this dominance. The
  United States has also been host to the Olympic Games more than
  any other country.

Olympic Hosts:
          1904 - St. Louis - The Games of the IIIrd Olympiad
          1932 - Lake Placid - The IIIrd Olympic Winter Games
          1932 - Los Angeles - The Games of the Xth Olympiad
          1960 - Squaw Valley - The VIIIth Olympic Winter Games
          1980 - Lake Placid - The XIIIth Olympic Winter Games
          1984 - Los Angeles - The Games of the XXIIIrd Olympiad

Medal Count:

	Men				Women				Totals			
	GO	SI	BR	TOT	GO	SI	BR	TOT	GO	SI	BR	TOT
Sum.	594+	442+	386	1423+	122+	93+	75+	292	717+	536+	461+	1715+
Win.	28	25+	16+	70	12	19+	15+	47	40	45	32	117
Tot.	622+	468+	402+	1493+	134+	113+	91	339	757+	581+	493+	1832+

Most Medals, Men
  11   Carl Osburn (SHO)
  11   Mark Spitz (SWI)

Most Gold Medals, Men
  10/8   Ray Ewry (TAF)
  9   Mark Spitz (SWI)

First Medalist, Men
  06 APR 1896   James Connolly (TAF-TJ)

First Gold Medalist, Men
  06 APR 1896   James Connolly (TAF-TJ)

Youngest Medalist, Men
  15-041   Donald Douglas (YAC-1932)

Youngest Gold Medalist, Men
  16-162   Jackie Fields (BOX-1924)

Oldest Medalist, Men
  68-194   Samuel Duvall (ARC-1904)

Oldest Gold Medalist, Men
  64-002   Galen Spencer (ARC-1904)

Most Medals, Women
  8   Shirley Babashoff (SWI)
  5   Mary Lou Retton (GYM)

Most Gold Medals, Women
  4   Pat McCormick (DIV)
  3   Fourteen athletes tied

First Medalist, Women
  09 JUL 1900   Marion Jones (TEN-Singles/Mixed)

First Gold Medalist, Women
  04 OCT 1900   Margaret Abbott (GOL-Ladies)

Youngest Medalist, Women
  13-024   Dorothy Poynton (DIV-1936)

Youngest Gold Medalist, Women
  13-268   Marjorie Gestring (DIV-1936)

Oldest Medalist/Gold Medalist, Women
  45-025   Lida Howell (ARC-1904)

Most Medals, Winter, Men
  5   Eric Heiden (SSK)
  3   John Heaton (BOB/SKE)
  3   Pat Martin (BOB)

Most Gold Medals, Winter, Men
  5   Eric Heiden (SSK)
  2   Dick Button (FSK)
  2   Jack Shea (SSK)
  2   Irving Jaffee (SSK)
  2   Billy Fiske (BOB)
  2   Clifford Gray (BOB)

First Medalist, Winter, Men
  <u>30 APR 1920 Ice Hockey Team</u>
  26 JAN 1924 Charles Jewtraw (SSK-500)

First Gold Medalist, Winter, Men
  26 JAN 1924 Charles Jewtraw (SSK-500)

Youngest Medalist, Winter, Men
  14-363 Scott Allen (FSK-1964)

Youngest Gold Medalist, Winter, Men
  16-260 Billy Fiske (BOB-1928)

Oldest Medalist/Gold Medalist, Winter, Men
  43-057 Francis Tyler (BOB-1948)

Most Medals, Winter, Women
  4   Dianne Holum (SSK)
  3   Beatrix Loughran (FSK)
  3   Leah Poulos-Mueller (SSK)
  3   Sheila Young (SSK)

Most Gold Medals, Winter, Women
  2   Andrea Mead-Lawrence (ASK)
  1   Ten athletes tied

First Medalist, Winter, Women
  <u>25 APR 1920 Theresa Weld (FSK-Ladies)</u>
  29 JAN 1924 Beatrix Loughran (FSK-Ladies)

First Gold Medalist, Winter, Women
  05 FEB 1948 Gretchen Fraser (ASK-Slalom)

Youngest Medalist, Winter, Women
  16-013 Carol Heiss (FSK-1956)

Youngest Gold Medalist, Winter, Women
  16-157 Anne Henning (SSK-1972)

Oldest Medalist, Winter, Women
  31-226 Beatrix Loughran (FSK-1932)

Oldest Gold Medalist, Winter, Women
  28-359 Gretchen Fraser (ASK-1948)

Most Medals, Men, Games
  7   Willis Lee (SHO-1920)
  7   Lloyd Spooner (SHO-1920)
  7   Mark Spitz (SWI-1972)

Most Gold Medals, Men, Games
     7   Mark Spitz (SWI-1972)
     5   Anton Heida (GYM-1904)
     5   Willis Lee (SHO-1920)
     5   Eric Heiden (SSK-1980)

Most Medals, Women, Games
     5   Shirley Babashoff (SWI-1976)
     5   Mary Lou Retton (GYM-1984)

Most Gold Medals, Women, Games
     3   Ethelda Bleibtrey (SWI-1920)
     3   Helene Madison (SWI-1932)
     3   Wilma Rudolph (TAF-1960)
     3   Chris Von Saltza (SWI-1960)
     3   Sharon Stouder (SWI-1964)
     3   Debbie Meyer (SWI-1968)
     3   Melissa Belote (SWI-1972)
     3   Sandra Neilson (SWI-1972)
     3   Valerie Brisco-Hooks (TAF-1984)
     3   Mary T. Meagher (SWI-1984)
     3   Nancy Hogshead (SWI-1984)
     3   Tracy Caulkins (SWI-1984)

Most Medals, Winter, Men, Games
     5   Eric Heiden (SSK-1980)
     2   Jack Shea (SSK-1932)
     2   Irving Jaffee (SSK-1932)
     2   Stanley Benham (BOB-1952)
     2   Pat Martin (BOB-1952)

Most Gold Medals, Winter, Men, Games
     5   Eric Heiden (SSK-1980)
     2   Jack Shea (SSK-1932)
     2   Irving Jaffee (SSK-1932)

Most Medals, Winter, Women, Games
     3   Sheila Young (SSK-1976)
     2   Gretchen Fraser (ASK-1948)
     2   Andrea Mead-Lawrence (ASK-1952)
     2   Penny Pitou (ASK-1960)
     2   Jean Saubert (ASK-1964)
     2   Anne Henning (SSK-1972)
     2   Dianne Holum (SSK-1972)
     2   Dianne Holum (SSK-1976)

Most Gold Medals, Winter, Women, Games
     2   Andrea Mead Lawrence (ASK-1952)
     1   Ten athletes tied

UPPER VOLTA (VOL)
  See Burkina-Faso

URUGUAY (URU)
República Oriental del Uruguay
Oriental Republic of Uruguay
Comité Olímpico Uruguayo - 1923

Area: 68,037 sq. mi. Population (1985 est.): 2,936,000
Located: In southern South America, on the Atlantic
Language: Spanish
Religion(s): Roman Catholic
Government: Republic

Olympic History: Uruguay first competed at the 1924 Olympics in
  Paris and has competed at every Games since, with the exception
  of the 1980 Games in Moscow. They had only one competitor in
  1932 but he did quite well; Douglas Guillermo won a silver
  medal in the single sculls rowing.
    Uruguay has won two gold medals. In 1924 and 1928 their
  football (soccer) team won the Olympics title, and several
  members of these teams later helped Uruguay win the inaugural
  World Cup title in that sport. In another team sport,
  basketball, Uruguay has also done well, winning bronze medals in
  1952 and 1956 and placing as high as sixth in 1984.
    No Uruguayan woman has won an Olympic medal and they have had
  only a few women compete. Uruguay has never competed at the
  Olympic Winter Games.

Medal Count:

	Men				Women				Totals			
	GO	SI	BR	TOT	GO	SI	BR	TOT	GO	SI	BR	TOT
Summer	2	1	6	9	–	–	–	–	2	1	6	9
Winter	–	–	–	–	–	–	–	–	–	–	–	–
Totals	2	1	6	9	–	–	–	–	2	1	6	9

Most Medals, Men
    2   Andrés Mazali (SOC)
    2   José Nasazzi (SOC)
    2   Pedro Arispe (SOC)
    2   José Andrade (SOC)
    2   Santos Urdinaran (SOC)
    2   Hector Scarone (SOC)
    2   Pedro Petrone (SOC)
    2   Pedro Cea (SOC)
    2   Juan Rodriguez (ROW)
    2   Héctor Costa (BAS)
    2   Nelson Demarco (BAS)
    2   Héctor Garcia Otero (BAS)
    2   Sergio Matto (BAS)

Most Gold Medals, Men
   2   Andrés Mazali (SOC)
   2   José Nasazzi (SOC)
   2   Pedro Arispe (SOC)
   2   José Andrade (SOC)
   2   Santos Urdinaran (SOC)
   2   Hector Scarone (SOC)
   2   Pedro Petrone (SOC)
   2   Pedro Cea (SOC)

First Medalist, Men
   09 JUN 1924 Football Team (SOC)

First Gold Medalist, Men
   09 JUN 1924 Football Team (SOC)

Youngest Medalist/Gold Medalist, Men
   18-364 Pedro Petrone (SOC-1924)

Oldest Medalist, Men
   30-336 Oscar Moglia (BAS-1956)
   30-336 Nelson Demarco (BAS-1956)

Oldest Gold Medalist, Men
   29-161 Alfredo Ghierra (SOC-1924)
   29-161 Angel Romano (SOC-1924)

VANUATU (VAN)
Ripablik Blong Vanuatu
Republic of Vanuatu
Vanuatu Olympic Committee - 1987

Area: 5,700 sq. mi. Population (1985 est.): 140,000
Located: Southwest Pacific, 1,200 miles north of Australia
Language(s): Bislama (national), French, English (both official)
Religion(s): Protestant 55%, Roman Catholic 16%, animists 15%
Government: Republic

Olympic History: Vanuatu has never competed in the Olympic Games.

VENEZUELA (VEN)
República de Venezuela
Republic of Venezuela
Comité Olímpico Venezolano - 1935

Area: 352,143 sq. mi. Population (1985 est.): 17,317,000
Located: On the Caribbean coast of South America
Language: Spanish
Religion(s): Roman Catholic
Government: Federal Republic

Olympic History: The Venezuelans have been represented at the
   Summer Olympics without fail since 1948, one of the few
   countries to claim this. They have competed in athletics,
   boxing, cycling, equestrian, fencing, soccer, judo,
   weightlifting, wrestling, swimming, and shooting. Boxing has
   been their best sport, as they have won five medals, two of them
   in 1984, which was the first time they have won more than one
   medal at any Games. They have never competed in the Olympic
   Winter Games.

Medal Count:

	Men				Women				Totals		
	GO	SI	BR	TOT	GO	SI	BR	TOT	GO	SI	BR	TOT
Summer	1	2	5	8	-	-	-	-	1	2	5	8
Winter	-	-	-	-	-	-	-	-	-	-	-	-
Totals	1	2	5	8	-	-	-	-	1	2	5	8

Most Medals, Men
   1   Francisco Rodriguez (BOX)
   1   José Marcellino Bolivar (BOX)
   1   Omar Catari Paraza (BOX)
   1   Bernardo Pinango (BOX)
   1   Pedro Gamaro (BOX)
   1   Enrico Forcella Pelliccioni (SHO)
   1   Rafael Vidal Castro (SWI)
   1   Arnaldo Devonish (TAF)

Most Gold Medals, Men
   1   Francisco Rodriguez (BOX)

First Medalist, Men
   23 JUL 1948 Arnaldo Devonish (TAF-TJ)

First Gold Medalist, Men
   26 OCT 1968 Francisco Rodriguez (BOX-Light-flyweight)

Youngest Medalist, Men
   20-027 José Marcellino Bolivar (BOX-1984)

Youngest/Oldest Gold Medalist, Men
   23-036 Francisco Rodriguez (BOX-1968)

Oldest Medalist, Men
   52-328 Enrico Forcella Pelliccioni (SHO-1960)

VIETNAM (VIE)
Cong Hoa Xa Hoi Chu Nghia Viet Nam
Socialist Republic of Vietnam
Comité Olympique du Vietnam - 1979

Area: 128,401 sq. mi. Population (1985 est.): 60,492,000
Located: On the east coast of the Indochinese peninsula in
   southeast Asia.
Language(s): Vietnamese (official), French, English
Religion(s): Buddhism, Confucianism, Taoism
Government: Communist republic

Olympic History: The original NOC for Vietnam was founded on 25
   November 1951 and was recognized by the IOC in 1952. After the
   Vietnam War the committee was restructured on 20 December 1976
   and waited four years for IOC recognition. Vietnam appeared at
   every Summer Olympics from 1952 through 1968 and again competed
   in 1980. They have yet to win a medal and they have never
   competed at the Olympic Winter Games.

VIRGIN ISLANDS, BRITISH (IVB)
British Virgin Islands
British Virgin Islands Olympic Committee - 1982

Area: 24 sq. mi. Population (1985 est.): 9,000
Located: In the Caribbean, 75 miles east of Puerto Rico
Language: English
Religion(s): Protestant, Roman Catholic
Government: Self-governing possession of the United Kingdom

Olympic History: The British Virgin Islands has been represented
   at only two Olympic Games and, strangely enough, one was the
   1984 Olympic Winter Games. At Sarajevo they were represented by
   Erroll Fraser, a speed skater born in the British Virgin Islands
   but who grew up in New York city. At Los Angeles, they had a
   team of four athletes and six yachtsmen. They have won no
   medals.

VIRGIN ISLANDS, U.S. (ISV)
United States' Virgin Islands
Virgin Islands Olympic Committee - 1967

Area: 133 sq. mi. Population (1985 est.): 101,500
Located: In the Caribbean, 70 miles east of Puerto Rico
Language: English
Religion(s): Roman Catholic
Government: Self-governing possession of the United States

Olympic History: The U.S. Virgin Islands has been represented at
   four Olympic Games, those of 1968, 1972, 1976, and 1984. They
   have yet to win a medal. They have not competed at the Olympic
   Winter Games.

YEMEN ARAB REPUBLIC (NORTH YEMEN) (YAR)
al-Jumhuriyat al-Arabiyah al-Yamaniyah
Yemen Arab Republic
The Yemen Arab Republic Committee - 1981

Area: 75,290 sq. mi. Population (1985 est.): 6,159,000
Located: On the southern Red Sea Coast of the Arabian Peninsula
Language: Arabic
Religion(s): Sunni Muslim 50%, Shiite Muslim 50%
Government: Republic

Olympic History: Although recognized by the IOC in 1981, the
Yemen Arab Republic has yet to be represented at the Olympic
Games.

YEMEN DEMOCRATIC REPUBLIC (SOUTH YEMEN) (YMD)
Jumhuriyat al-Yaman ad-Dimuqratiyah ash-Sha'biyan
People's Democratic Republic of Yemen
Yemen Olympic Committee - 1981

Area: 128,559 sq. mi. Population (1985 est.): 2,209,000
Located: On the southern coast of the Arabian peninsula
Language: Arabic
Religion(s): Sunni Muslim 91%, Christian 4%, Hindis 4%
Government: Republic

Olympic History: Although recognized by the IOC in 1981, the
Yemen Democratic Republic has yet to be represented at the
Olympic Games.

YUGOSLAVIA (YUG)
Socijalistička Federativna Republika Jugoslavija
Socialist Federal Republic of Yugoslavia
Comité Olympique Yougoslave - 1920

Area: 98,766 sq. mi. Population (1985 est.): 23,124,000
Located: On the Adriatic coast of the Balkan peninsula in
southeast Europe
Language(s): Serbo-Croatian, Macedonian, Slovenian (all
official), Albanian
Religion(s): Eastern Orthodox 50%, Roman Catholic 30%, Muslim 10%
Government: Federal Republic

Olympic History: Yugoslavia was first represented at the 1912
Olympics in Stockholm. Since then, they have appeared at every
summer Olympic celebration, although in 1932 they were
represented by a lone track & field athlete. They first
appeared at the Olympic Winter Games at their inception in 1924
and have returned every four years with the exception of 1932
and 1960.

Olympic Hosts:
          1984 - Sarajevo - The XIVth Olympic Winter Games

Medal Count:

	Men				Women				Totals			
	GO	SI	BR	TOT	GO	SI	BR	TOT	GO	SI	BR	TOT
Summer	21	23	22	66	2	2	1	5	23	25	23	71
Winter	-	1	-	1	-	-	-	-	-	1	-	1
Totals	21	24	22	67	2	2	1	5	23	26	23	72

Most Medals, Men
    6   Leon Stukelj (GYM)
    3   Krešimir Cošić (BAS)
    3   Dražen Dalipagić (BAS)
    3   Andro Knego (BAS)
    3   Rajko Žižić (BAS)
    3   Matijya Ljubek (CAN)
    3   Miroslav Cerar (GYM)

Most Gold Medals, Men
    3   Leon Stukelj (GYM)
    2   Miroslav Cerar (GYM)
    2   Matija Ljubek (CAN)

First Medalist, Men
    20 JUL 1924   Leon Stukelj (GYM-All-Around, Horizontal Bar)

First Gold Medalist, Men
    20 JUL 1924   Leon Stukelj (GYM-All-Around, Horizontal Bar)

Youngest Medalist, Men
    14-362   Josip Reić (ROW-1980)

Youngest Gold Medalist, Men
    17-264   Perica Bukić (WAP-1984)

Oldest Medalist/Gold Medalist, Men
    32-246   Krešimir Cošić (BAS-1980)

Most Medals, Women
    2   Djurdjica Bjedov (SWI)
    2   Mirjana Ognjenović (THA)
    2   Svetlana Anastasovski (THA)
    2   Svetlana Dasić-Kitić (THA)
    2   Mirjana Djurica (THA)
    2   Biserka Višnjić (THA)
    2   Jasna Kolar-Merdan (THA)

Most Gold Medals, Women
    1   Thirteen athletes tied with one.

First Medalist, Women
    19 OCT 1968   Djurdica Bjedov (SWI-100 breaststroke)

First Gold Medalist, Women
  19 OCT 1968   Djurdica Bjedov (SWI-100 breaststroke)

Youngest Medalist, Women
  19-042   Rada Savić (THA-1980)

Youngest Gold Medalist, Women
  19-269   Svetlana Mugosa (THA-1984)

Oldest Medalist, Women
  30-336   Vera Djurašković (BAS-1980)

Oldest Gold Medalist, Women
  30-327   Mirjana Ognjenović (THA-1984)

Most Medals, Winter, Men
  1   Jure Franko (ASK)

First Medalist, Winter, Men
  14 FEB 1984   Jure Franko (ASK-Giant Slalom)

Most Medals, Men, Games
  3   Leon Stukelj (GYM-1928)
  2   Miroslav Cerar (GYM-1964)
  2   Matija Ljubek (CAN-1976)

Most Gold Medals, Men, Games
  2   Leon Stukelj (GYM-1924)
  1   Many athletes tied with one.

Most Medals, Women, Games
  2   Djurdjica Bjedov (SWI-1968)
  1   Many athletes tied with one.

ZAIRE (ZAI)
République du Zaiere
Republic of Zaire
Comité National Olympique Zarois - 1968

Former name: Belgian Congo; changed 27 OCT 1971
Area: 905,563 sq. mi. Population (1985 est.): 30,505,000
Located: In Central Africa
Language(s): French (official), Bantu dialects
Religion(s): Christian 70%, Muslim 10%
Government: Republic with strong Presidential authority

Olympic History: Zaire was represented by five cyclists at the
  Mexico City Olympics in 1968. Their second Olympic appearance
  came sixteen years later at Los Angeles where they were
  represented by three track & field athletes - two men and woman.
  They have yet to win an Olympic medal.

ZAMBIA (ZAM)
Republic of Zambia
National Olympic Committee of Zambia - 1963

Former name: Northern Rhodesia; changed 24 OCT 1964
Area: 290,586 sq. mi. Population (1985 est.): 6,832,000
Located: In southern central Africa
Language(s): English (official), Bantu dialects
Religion(s): Predominately animists, Roman Catholic 21%
Government: Republic

Olympic History: Zambia first competed at the 1964 Olympic Games
    and has since taken part at five celebrations, missing only
    1968. They have never competed at the Olympic Winter Games. In
    1984 Keith Mwila won their first medals when he finished third
    in light-flyweight boxing.

ZANZIBAR
    (see Tanzania)

ZIMBABWE (ZIM)
National Olympic Committee of Zimbabwe - 1980

Former Name: Rhodesia; changed 18 APR 1980
Area: 150,803 sq. mi. Population (1985 est.): 8,678,000
Located: In southern Africa
Language(s): English (official), Shona, Sindebele
Religion(s): Mostly tribal beliefs, Christian minority
Government: Parliamentary democracy

Olympic History: As Rhodesia, Zimbabwe competed at three Olympic
    Games - those of 1928, 1960, and 1964. They competed again
    under their new name at Moscow in 1980 and the highlight of
    their appearance was the gold medal performance of their women's
    field hockey team. This is the only medal they have won. They
    have not competed in the Winter Games.

Youngest Medalist/Gold Medalist, Women
    22-194 Brenda Joan Philips (FIH-1980)

Oldest Medalist/Gold Medalist, Women
    35-253 Anthea Doreen Stewart (FIH-1980)

THE GAMES OF THE OLYMPIADS

Following are summaries of all the previous Olympic Games, including those not held. The summaries include number of nations and competitors, torch bearers, the name of the person officially opening the Games, and a list of the top medal-winning nations. Following that is a list of the top individual performers at each Olympic Games, including every athlete who won either two gold medals or four medals at a single Olympic Games. Finally a one-deep list of the age records for each Olympic Games is given.

THE GAMES OF THE 1ST OLYMPIAD

Dates: 06-15 April 1896
Site: Athens, Greece
Official Opening By: King George I
Number of Countries Competing: 13
Number of Athletes Competing: 311

Medals Won by Countries

	G	S	B	Tot
Greece	10	19	18	47
United States	11	7	1	19
Germany	6½	5	3	14½
France	5	4	2	11
Great Britain	2½	3	2	7½
Denmark	1	2	4	7

Top Individual Performances

	G	S	B	Tot
Karl Schumann (GER-GYM/WRE)	4	–	–	4
Herman Weingärtner (GER-GYM)	3	2	1	6
Alfred Flatow (GER-GYM)	3	1	–	4
Paul Masson (FRA-CYC)	3	–	–	3
Fritz Hofmann (GER-TAF/GYM)	2	1	2	5
Robert Garrett (USA-TAF)	2	1	1	4
Viggo Jensen (DEN-WLT/SHO)	1	2	1	4

Youngest Medalist, Men
10-216   Dimitrios Loundras (GRE-GYM)*
16-101   Ioannis Malokinis (GRE-SWI)
*Date of birth as given in Kamper but this is felt to be doubtful, even by Kamper himself.

Youngest Gold Medalist, Men
    10-216   Dimitrios Loundras (GRE-GYM)*
    18-070   Alfred Hajos (HUN-SWI)
    *Date of birth as given in Kamper but this is felt to be
    doubtful, even by Kamper himself.

Oldest Medalist/Gold Medalist, Men
    36-102   Giorgios Orphanidas (GRE-SHO)

THE GAMES OF THE 2ND OLYMPIAD

Dates: 20 May - 28 October, 1900
Site: Paris, France
Official Opening By: none
Number of Countries Competing: 22
Number of Athletes Competing: 1330

Medals Won by Countries

	G	S	B	Tot
France	28	34	32	94
United States	19	14	12	45
Great Britain	12	7	7	26
Belgium	5	5	4	14
Switzerland	6	1	1	8

Top Individual Performances

	G	S	B	Tot
Alvin Kraenzlein (USA-TAF)	4	-	-	4
Konrad Stäheli (SUI-SHO)	3	-	1	4
Ray Ewry (USA-TAF)	3	-	-	3
Irving Baxter (USA-TAF)	2	3	-	5
Walter Tewksbury (USA-TAF)	2	2	1	5
Emil Kellenberger (SUI-SHO)	2	1	-	3
Charles Bennett (GBR-TAF)	2	1	-	3
Hubert van Innis (BEL-ARC)	2	1	-	3
Hugh Doherty (GBR-TEN)	2	-	1	3
Laurie Doherty (GBR-TEN)	2	-	1	3
Achille Paroche (FRA-SHO)	1	2	1	4
Stanley Rowley (AUS/GBR-TAF)	1	-	3	4
Ole Östmo (NOR-SHO)	-	2	2	4

Youngest Medalist, Men
    <10   unknown French boy (ROW)
    15-306   Paul Vasseur (FRA-WAP)

Youngest Medalist, Women
    20-250   Marion Jones (USA-TEN)

Youngest Gold Medalist, Men
    <10   unknown French boy (ROW)
    16-288   Ramon Fonst (CUB-FEN)

Youngest Gold Medalist, Women
   22-112   Margaret Abbott (USA-GOL)

Oldest Medalist/Gold Medalist, Men
   53-055   Herman de Pourtales (SUI-YAC)

Oldest Medalist, Women
   38-278   Daria Pratt (USA-GOL)

Oldest Gold Medalist, Women
   29-291   Charlotte Cooper (GBR-TEN)

THE GAMES OF THE 3RD OLYMPIAD

Dates: 01 July - 23 November 1904
Site: St. Louis, Missouri, United States
Candidate Cities: Chicago, Illinois, USA (Chicago was originally
  selected but the site was later moved to St. Louis)
Official Opening By: Mr. David Francis, President of the
  Louisiana Purchase Exposition (The 1904 World's Fair)
Number of Countries Competing: 13
Number of Athletes Competing: 625

Medals Won by Countries

	G	S	B	Tot
United States	81+	88	83	242+
Germany	4	4	5	15
Canada	4	1	-	5
Hungary	2	1	1	4
Cuba	3+	-	-	3+

Top Individual Performances

	G	S	B	Tot
Anton Heida (USA-GYM)	5	1	-	6
Marcus Hurley (USA-CYC)	4	-	-	4
George Eyser (USA-GYM)	3	2	-	5
James Lightbody (USA-TAF)	3	1	-	4
Charles Daniels (USA-SWI)	3	1	-	4
Archie Hahn (USA-TAF)	3	-	-	3
Harry Hillman (USA-TAF)	3	-	-	3
Ray Ewry (USA-TAF)	3	-	-	3
Ramon Fonst (CUB-FEN)	3	-	-	3
Lida Howell (USA-ARC)	3	-	-	3
Burton Downing (USA-CYC)	2	3	1	6
William Merz (USA-GYM)	-	1	4	5
Francis Gailey (USA-SWI)	-	3	1	4
Frank Kungler (USA-TOW/WRE/WLT)	-	3	1	4
Teddy Billington (USA-CYC)	-	1	3	4

Youngest Medalist, Men
   15-126   Henry Richardson (USA-ARC)

Youngest Gold Medalist, Men
    19-168   Ralph Rose (USA-TAF)

Oldest Medalist, Men
    68-194   Samuel Duvall (USA-ARC)

Oldest Medalist/Gold Medalist, Women
    45-025   Lida Howell (USA-ARC)

Oldest Gold Medalist, Men
    64-002   Galen Spencer (USA-ARC)

THE INTERCALATED OLYMPIC GAMES OF 1906

Dates: 22 April - 02 May 1906
Site: Athens, Greece
Official Opening By: King George I
Number of Countries Competing: 20
Number of Athletes Competing: 884

Medals Won by Countries

	G	S	B	Tot
France	15	9	16	40
Greece	8	13	13	34
Great Britain	8	11	5	24
United States	12	6	6	24
Italy	7	6	3	16

Top Individual Performances

	G	S	B	Tot
Louis Richardet (SUI-SHO)	3	3	-	6
Gudbrand Skatteboe (NOR-SHO)	3	1	-	4
Francesco Verri (ITA-CYC)	3	-	-	3
Giorgio Cesana (ITA-ROW)	3	-	-	3
Enrico Bruna (ITA-ROW)	3	-	-	3
Emilio Fontanella (ITA-ROW)	3	-	-	3
Max Decugis (FRA-TEN)	3	-	-	3
Martin Sheridan (USA-TAF)	2	3	-	5
Konrad Stäheli (SUI-SHO)	2	2	1	5
Léon Moreaux (FRA-SHO)	2	1	2	5
Geo. Dillon-Kavanagh (FRA-FEN)	2	1	-	3
Geo. de la Falaise (FRA-FEN)	2	-	-	2
Paul Pilgrim (USA-TAF)	2	-	-	2
Ray Ewry (USA-TAF)	2	-	-	2
Gustav Casmir (GER-FEN)	2	2	-	4
Jean Reich (SUI-SHO)	1	1	3	5
Eric Lemming (SWE-TAF)	1	-	3	4

Youngest Medalist/Gold Medalist, Men
    14-012   Giorgio Cesana (ITA-ROW)

Youngest Medalist, Women
   21-115   Aspasia Matsa (GRE-TEN)

Youngest Gold Medalist, Women
   21-261   Marie Decugis (FRA-TEN)

Oldest Medalist, Men
   52-196   Charles Newton-Robinson (GBR-FEN)

Oldest Medalist, Women
   25-113   Euphrosine Paspati (GRE-TEN)

Oldest Gold Medalist, Men
   52-031   Maurice Lecoq (FRA-SHO)

Oldest Gold Medalist, Women
   22-113   Esmée Simiriotou (GRE-TEN)

THE GAMES OF THE 4TH OLYMPIAD

Dates: 27 April - 31 October 1908
Site: London, England
Candidate Cities: Berlin, Germany; Milan, Italy; Rome, Italy
  (Rome was originally selected but the site was later moved to
  London)
Official Opening By: King Edward VII
Number of Countries Competing: 22
Number of Athletes Competing: 2056

Medals Won by Countries

	G	S	B	Tot
Great Britain	55	50	39	144
United States	23	12	12	47
Sweden	8	6	11	25
France	5	5	9	19
Canada	3	3	10	16

Top Individual Performances

	G	S	B	Tot
Mel Sheppard (USA-TAF)	3	-	-	3
Henry Taylor (GBR-SWI)	3	-	-	3
Benjamin Jones (GBR-CYC)	2	1	-	3
Martin Sheridan (USA-TAF)	2	-	1	3
Oscar Swahn (SWE-SHO)	2	-	1	3

Youngest Medalist/Gold Medalist, Men
   15-226   Per Daniel Bertilsson (SWE-GYM)

Youngest Medalist/Gold Medalist, Women
   24-274   Gwendoline Eastlake-Smith (GBR-TEN)

Oldest Medalist/Gold Medalist, Men
    60-265   Oscar Swahn (SWE-SHO)

Oldest Medalist, Women
    39-332   Märtha Adlerstråhle (SWE-TEN)

Oldest Gold Medalist, Women
    29-316   Dorothea Chambers (GBR-TEN)

THE GAMES OF THE 5TH OLYMPIAD

Dates: 05 May - 22 July 1912
Site: Stockholm, Sweden
Official Opening By: King Gustav V
Number of Countries Competing: 28
Number of Athletes Competing: 2546

Medals Won by Countries
	G	S	B	Tot
Sweden	24	24	17	65
United States	25	18	20	63
Great Britain	10	15	16	41
Finland	9	8	9	26
Germany	5	13	7	25

*The above medals reflect the actual results of the decathlon and
pentathlon in track & field athletics, i.e., Decathlon - 1)
Thorpe (USA), 2) Weislander (SWE), 3) Lomberg (SWE); Pentathlon
- 1) Thorpe (USA), 2) Bie (NOR), 3) Donahue (USA).

Top Individual Performances
	G	S	B	Tot
Hannes Kolehmainen (FIN-TAF)	3	1	-	4
Vilhelm Carlberg (SWE-SHO)	3	1	-	4
Alfred Lane (USA-SHO)	3	-	-	3
Johan von Holst (SWE-SHO)	2	1	1	4
Eric Carlberg (SWE-SHO)	2	1	-	3
Ake Lundberg (SWE-SHO)	2	1	-	3
Fred Hird (USA-SHO)	1	-	3	4
Carl Osburn (USA-SHO)	1	2	1	4

Youngest Medalist, Men
    17-229   Ture Persson (SWE-TAF)

Youngest Medalist/Gold Medalist, Women
    17-186   Greta Johanson (SWE-DIV)

Youngest Gold Medalist, Men
    18-030   Nedo Nadi (FEN-ITA)

Oldest Medalist/Gold Medalist, Men
64-258   Oscar Swahn (SWE-SHO)

Oldest Medalist/Gold Medalist, Women
38-132   Edith Hannam (GBR-TEN)

THE GAMES OF THE 6TH OLYMPIAD

Dates: not held due to World War I
Scheduled Site: Berlin, Germany
Candidate Cities: Alexandria, Egypt; Budapest, Hungary;
  Cleveland, Ohio, USA

THE GAMES OF THE 7TH OLYMPIAD

Dates: 20 April - 12 September 1920
Site: Antwerp, Belgium
Candidate Cities: Budapest, Hungary; Lyon, France
Speaker of the Athlete's Oath: Victor Boin (Water Polo/Fencing)
Official Opening By: King Albert
Number of Countries Competing: 29
Number of Athletes Competing: 2692

Medals Won by Countries

	G	S	B	Tot
United States	41	27	28	96
Sweden	19	20	26	65
Great Britain	15	15	13	43
Belgium	14	11	10	36
Finland	15	10	9	34

Top Individual Performances

	G	S	B	Tot
Willis Lee (USA-SHO)	5	1	1	7
Nedo Nadi (ITA-FEN)	5	-	-	5
Hubert van Innis (BEL-ARC)	4	2	-	6
Lloyd Spooner (USA-SHO)	4	1	2	7
Carl Osburn (USA-SHO)	4	1	1	6
Otto Olsen (NOR-SHO)	3	2	-	5
Paavo Nurmi (FIN-TAF)	3	1	-	4
Dennis Fenton (USA-SHO)	3	-	1	4
Julien Brulé (FRA-ARC)	1	3	1	5
Östen Ostensen (NOR-SHO)	-	2	2	4
Erik Backman (SWE-TAF)	-	1	3	4
Fritz Kucher (SUI-SHO)	-	-	4	4

Youngest Medalist, Men
14-011   Nils Skoglund (SWE-DIV)

Youngest Medalist/Gold Medalist, Women
14-120   Aileen Riggin (USA-DIV)

Youngest Gold Medalist, Men
14-163   Franciscus Hin (HOL-YAC)

Oldest Medalist, Men
72-280   Oscar Swahn (SWE-SHO)

Oldest Medalist/Gold Medalist, Women
43-015   Winifred McNair (GBR-TEN)

Oldest Gold Medalist, Men
54-187   Hubert van Innis (BEL-ARC)

THE GAMES OF THE 8TH OLYMPIAD

Dates: 04 May - 27 July 1924
Site: Paris, France
Candidate Cities: Amsterdam, The Netherlands; Barcelona, Spain;
  Los Angeles, California, USA; Prague, Czechoslovakia; Rome,
  Italy
Speaker of the Athlete's Oath: Georges André (Athletics)
Official Opening By: President Gaston Doumergue
Number of Countries Competing: 44
Number of Athletes Competing: 3092

Medals Won by Countries

	G	S	B	Tot
United States	45	27	27	99
France	13	15	10	38
Finland	14	13	10	37
Great Britain	9	13	12	34
Sweden	4	13	12	29

Top Individual Performances

	G	S	B	Tot
Paavo Nurmi (FIN-TAF)	5	-	-	5
Ville Ritola (FIN-TAF)	4	2	-	6
Roger Ducret (FRA-FEN)	3	1	-	4
Johnny Weissmuller (USA-SWI/WAP)	3	-	1	4
Vincent Richards (USA-TEN)	2	1	-	3
Ole Lilloe-Olsen (NOR-SHO)	2	1	-	3

Youngest Medalist, Men
14-307   Marcel Lepan (FRA-ROW)

Youngest Medalist/Gold Medalist, Women
16-177   Martha Norelius (USA-SWI)

Youngest Gold Medalist, Men
16-162   Jackie Fields (USA-BOX)

Oldest Medalist, Men
    56-091   Ernst Linder (SWE-EQU)

Oldest Gold Medalist, Men
    56-078   Allen Whitty (GBR-SHO)

Oldest Medalist/Gold Medalist, Women
    37-213   Hazel Wightman (USA-TEN)

THE GAMES OF THE 9TH OLYMPIAD

Dates: 17 May - 12 August 1928
Site: Amsterdam, The Netherlands
Speaker of the Athlete's Oath: Harry Denis (Football)
Official Opening By: HRH Prince Hendrik
Number of Countries Competing: 46
Number of Athletes Competing: 3014

Medals Won by Countries
	G	S	B	Tot
United States	22	18	16	56
Germany	10	7	14	31
Finland	8	8	9	25
Sweden	7	6	12	25
France	6	10	5	21

Top Individual Performances
	G	S	B	Tot
Georges Miez (SUI-GYM)	3	1	-	4
Lucien Gaudin (FRA-FEN)	2	2	-	4
Hermann Hänggi (SUI-GYM)	2	1	1	4
Eugen Mack (SUI-GYM)	2	-	1	3

Youngest Medalist/Gold Medalist, Men
    14-222   Hans Bourquin (SUI-ROW)

Youngest Medalist, Women
    13-024   Dorothy Poynton (USA-DIV)

Youngest Gold Medalist, Women
    16-343   Betty Robinson (USA-TAF)

Oldest Medalist/Gold Medalist, Men
    57-045   Johan Anker (NOR-YAC)

Oldest Medalist, Women
    41-073   Olga Oelkers (GER-FEN)

Oldest Gold Medalist, Women
    38-016   Virginie Hériot (FRA-YAC)

THE GAMES OF THE 10TH OLYMPIAD

Dates: 30 July - 14 August 1932
Site: Los Angeles, California, United States
Speaker of the Athlete's Oath: George Calnan (Fencing)
Official Opening By: Vice President Charles Curtis
Number of Countries Competing: 37
Number of Athletes Competing: 1408

Medals Won by Countries

	G	S	B	Tot
United States	42	32	31	105
Italy	12	12	12	36
Finland	5	8	12	25
Sweden	9	5	9	23
Germany	4	12	5	21

Top Individual Performances

	G	S	B	Tot
Helene Madison (USA-SWI)	3	-	-	3
Romeo Neri (ITA-GYM)	3	-	-	3
Istvan Pelle (HUN-GYM)	2	2	-	4
Babe Didrikson (USA-TAF)	2	1	-	3
Giulio Gaudini (ITA-FEN)	-	3	1	4
Heikki Savolainen (FIN-GYM)	-	1	3	4

Youngest Medalist/Gold Medalist, Men
    14-309   Kusuo Kitamura (JPN-SWI)

Youngest Medalist, Women
    14-058   Katherine Rawls (USA-SWI)

Youngest Gold Medalist, Women
    16-117   Claire Dennis (AUS-SWI)

Oldest Medalist/Gold Medalist, Men
    46-290   Xavier Lesage (FRA-EQU)

Oldest Medalist/Gold Medalist, Women
    27-312   Lillian Copeland (USA-TAF)

THE GAMES OF THE 11TH OLYMPIAD

Dates: 01 - 16 August 1936
Site: Berlin, Germany
Candidate Cities: Alexandria, Egypt; Barcelona, Spain; Budapest,
  Hungary; Buenos Aires, Argentina; Cologne, Germany; Dublin,
  Ireland; Frankfurt/Main, Germany; Helsinki, Finland; Nuremburg,
  Germany; Rome, Italy
Torch Bearer: Fritz Schilgen (first torch run)
Speaker of the Athlete's Oath: Rudolf Ismayr (Weightlifting)
Official Opening By: Chancellor Adolf Hitler
Number of Countries Competing: 49
Number of Athletes Competing: 4066

Medals Won by Countries

	G	S	B	Tot
Germany	33	26	30	89
United States	24	20	12	56
Italy	8	9	5	22
Sweden	6	5	9	20
Finland	7	6	6	19

Top Individual Performances

	G	S	B	Tot
Jesse Owens (USA-TAF)	4	-	-	4
Konrad Frey (GER-GYM)	3	1	2	6
Hendrika Mastenbroek (HOL-SWI)	3	1	-	4
Alfred Schwarzmann (GER-GYM)	3	-	2	5
Robert Charpentier (FRA-CYC)	3	-	-	3
Guy Lapébie (FRA-CYC)	2	1	-	3
Eugen Mack (SUI-GYM)	-	4	1	5

Youngest Medalist, Men
    12-233   Noël Vandernotte (FRA-ROW)

Youngest Medalist, Women
    12-024   Inge Sörensen (DEN-SWI)

Youngest Gold Medalist, Men
    17-124   Edoardo Mangiarotti (ITA-FEN)

Youngest Gold Medalist, Women
    13-268   Marjorie Gestring (USA-DIV)

Oldest Medalist/Gold Medalist, Men
    52-020   Friedrich Gerhard (GER-EQU)

Oldest Medalist/Gold Medalist, Women
    29-078   Ilona Elek (HUN-FEN)

THE GAMES OF THE 12TH OLYMPIAD

Dates: not held due to World War II
Scheduled Site: originally to have been Tokyo, Japan; Helsinki,
    Finland awarded the Games on 16 July 1938
Candidate Cities: Alexandria, Egypt; Athens, Greece; Barcelona,
    Spain; Budapest, Hungary; Buenos Aires, Argentina; Dublin,
    Ireland; Lausanne, Switzerland; London, England; Montreal,
    Quebec, Canada; Rio de Janeiro, Brazil; Rome, Italy; Toronto,
    Ontario, Canada

THE GAMES OF THE 13TH OLYMPIAD

Dates: not held due to World War II
Scheduled Site: London, England
Candidate Cities: Athens, Greece; Budapest, Hungary; Detroit,
    Michigan, USA; Lausanne, Switzerland

THE GAMES OF THE 14TH OLYMPIAD

Dates: 29 July - 14 August 1948
Site: London, England
Candidate Cities: Baltimore, Maryland, USA; Lausanne,
    Switzerland; Los Angeles, California, USA; Minneapolis,
    Minnesota, USA; Philadelphia, Pennsylvania, USA
Torch Bearer: John Mark
Speaker of the Athlete's Oath: Donald Finlay (Athletics)
Official Opening By: King George VI
Number of Countries Competing: 59
Number of Athletes Competing: 4099

Medals Won by Countries

	G	S	B	Tot
United States	38	27	19	84
Sweden	16	11	17	44
France	10	6	13	29
Italy	8	12	9	29
Hungary	10	5	12	27

Top Individual Performances

	G	S	B	Tot
Fanny Blankers-Koen (HOL-TAF)	4	-	-	4
Veikko Huhtanen (FIN-GYM)	3	1	1	5
Paavo Aaltonen (FIN-GYM)	3	-	1	4
James McLane (USA-SWI)	2	1	-	3
Ann Curtis (USA-SWI)	2	1	-	3
Humb. Mariles Cortés (MEX-EQU)	2	-	1	3
Mal Whitfield (USA-TAF)	2	-	1	3

Youngest Medalist, Men
16-036   Carlos De Cárdenas Culmell, Jr. (CUB-YAC)

Youngest Medalist/Gold Medalist, Women
17-136   Thelma Kalama (USA-SWI)

Youngest Gold Medalist, Men
17-263   Bob Mathias (USA-TAF)

Oldest Medalist/Gold Medalist, Men
56-212   Paul Smart (USA-YAC)

Oldest Medalist/Gold Medalist, Women
41-078   Ilona Elek (HUN-FEN)

THE GAMES OF THE 15TH OLYMPIAD

Dates: 19 July - 03 August 1952
Site: Helsinki, Finland
Candidate Cities: Amsterdam, The Netherlands; Athens, Greece;
    Chicago, Illinois, USA; Detroit, Michigan, USA; Lausanne,
    Switzerland; Minneapolis, Minnesota, USA; Philadelphia,
    Pennsylvania, USA; Stockholm, Sweden
Torch Bearers: Paavo Nurmi and Hannes Kolehmainen
Speaker of the Athlete's Oath: Heikki Savolainen (Gymnastics)
Official Opening By: President Juho Paasikivi
Number of Countries Competing: 69
Number of Athletes Competing: 4925

Medals Won by Countries

	G	S	B	Tot
United States	40	19	17	76
USSR	22	30	19	71
Hungary	16	10	16	42
Sweden	12	13	10	35
FRG	-	7	17	24

Top Individual Performances

	G	S	B	Tot
Viktor Chukarin (URS-GYM)	4	2	-	6
Emil Zátopek (TCH-TAF)	3	-	-	3
Mariya Gorokhovskaya (URS-GYM)	2	5	-	7
Edoardo Mangiarotti (ITA-FEN)	2	2	-	4
Grant Schaginyan (URS-GYM)	2	2	-	4
Nina Bokharova (URS-GYM)	2	2	-	4
Margit Korondi (HUN-GYM)	1	1	3	5
Agnes Keleti (HUN-GYM)	1	1	2	4
Josef Stalder (SUI-GYM)	-	2	2	4

Youngest Medalist/Gold Medalist, Men
14-095   Bernard Malivoire (FRA-ROW)

Youngest Medalist/Gold Medalist, Women
   15-124   Pearl Jones (USA-TAF)

Oldest Medalist, Men
   59-132   Ernst Westerlund (FIN-YAC)

Oldest Medalist, Women
   45-072   Ilona Elek (HUN-FEN)

Oldest Gold Medalist, Men
   59-113   Everard Endt (USA-YAC)

Oldest Gold Medalist, Women
   37-259   Sylvi Saimo (FIN-CAN)

THE GAMES OF THE 16TH OLYMPIAD

Dates: 22 November - 08 December 1956; 10 - 17 June 1956
   (Equestrian Games)
Site: Melbourne, Australia; Stockholm, Sweden (Equestrian Games)
Candidate Cities: Buenos Aires, Argentina; Chicago, Illinois,
   USA; Detroit, Michigan, USA; Los Angeles, California, USA;
   Mexico City, Mexico; Minneapolis, Minnesota, USA; Montreal,
   Quebec, Canada; Philadelphia, Pennsylvania, USA; San Francisco,
   California, USA
Candidate Cities for the Equestrian Games: Berlin, Germany;
   Buenos Aires, Argentina; Los Angeles, California, USA; Paris,
   France; Rio de Janeiro, Brazil
Torch Bearer: Ron Clarke
Speaker of the Athlete's Oath: John Landy (Athletics)
Official Opening By: His Royal Highness The Duke of Edinburgh
Number of Countries Competing: 67
Number of Athletes Competing: 3184

Medals Won by Countries
	G	S	B	Tot
USSR	37	29	32	98
United States	32	25	17	74
Australia	13	8	14	35
Hungary	9	10	7	26
Italy	8	8	9	25

Top Individual Performances

	G	S	B	Tot
Agnes Keleti (HUN-GYM)	4	2	-	6
Larisa Latynina (URS-GYM)	4	1	1	6
Viktor Chukarin (URS-GYM)	3	1	1	5
Valentin Muratov (URS-GYM)	3	1	-	4
Murray Rose (AUS-SWI)	3	-	-	3
Bobby Joe Morrow (USA-TAF)	3	-	-	3
Betty Cuthbert (AUS-TAF)	3	-	-	3
Dawn Fraser (AUS-SWI)	2	1	-	3
Lorraine Crapp (AUS-SWI)	2	1	-	3
Edoardo Mangiarotti (ITA-FEN)	2	-	1	3
Takashi Ono (JPN-GYM)	1	3	1	5
Sofiya Muratova (URS-GYM)	1	-	3	4
Masao Takemoto (JPN-GYM)	-	1	3	4
Yuriy Titov (URS-GYM)	-	1	3	4

Youngest Medalist/Gold Medalist, Men
17-331   Murray Rose (AUS-SWI)

Youngest Medalist, Women
14-156   Sylvia Ruuska (USA-SWI)

Youngest Gold Medalist, Women
14-184   Sandra Morgan (AUS-SWI)

Oldest Medalist/Gold Medalist, Men
54-094   Henri St. Cyr (SWE-EQU)

Oldest Medalist/Gold Medalist, Women
35-182   Agnes Keleti (HUN-GYM)

THE GAMES OF THE 17TH OLYMPIAD

Dates: 25 August - 11 September 1960
Site: Rome, Italy
Candidate Cities: Athens, Greece; Brussels, Belgium; Budapest,
    Hungary; Buenos Aires, Argentina; Chicago, Illinois, USA;
    Detroit, Michigan, USA; Lausanne, Switzerland; Los Angeles,
    California, USA; Mexico City, Mexico; Minneapolis, Minnesota,
    USA; New York, New York, USA; Philadelphia, Pennsylvania, USA;
    Rio de Janeiro, Brazil; San Francisco, California, USA; Tokyo,
    Japan
Torch Bearer: Giancarlo Peris
Speaker of the Athlete's Oath: Adolfo Consolini (Athletics)
Official Opening By: President Giovanni Gronchi
Number of Countries Competing: 83
Number of Athletes Competing: 5346

Medals Won by Countries
```
                   G   S   B   Tot
USSR              43  29  31  103
United States     34  21  16   71
Italy             13  10  13   36
FRG/GDR          10* 10   6*  26*
Australia          8   8   6   22
```

*In 1960, the FRG competed as a combined team with the GDR. The following medals were shared between combined teams: Men's Canoeing - Kayak Relay (gold); and Women's Swimming - 400 metre freestyle relay, and 400 metre medley relay (both bronze).

Top Individual Performances
```
                              G   S   B  Tot
Boris Shakhlin (URS-GYM)      4   2   1    7
Larisa Latynina (URS-GYM)     3   2   1    6
Takashi Ono (JPN-GYM)         3   1   2    6
Chris von Saltza (USA-SWI)    3   1   -    4
Wilma Rudolph (USA-TAF)       3   -   -    3
Polina Astakhova (URS-GYM)    2   1   1    4
Sofiya Muratova (URS-GYM)     1   2   1    4
```

Youngest Medalist, Men
    16-134   Brian Phelps (GBR-DIV)

Youngest Medalist/Gold Medalist, Women
    14-260   Carolyn Wood (USA-SWI)

Youngest Gold Medalist, Men
    16-073   Michael Obst (FRG-ROW)

Oldest Medalist, Men
    55-104   Manfred Metzger (SUI-YAC)

Oldest Medalist, Women
    40-201   Velleda Cesari (ITA-FEN)

Oldest Gold Medalist, Men
    50-179   Aládár Gerevich (HUN-FEN)

Oldest Gold Medalist, Women
    31-132   Nina Ponomareva-Romashkova (URS-TAF)

THE GAMES OF THE 18TH OLYMPIAD

Dates: 10 - 24 October 1964
Site: Tokyo, Japan
Candidate Cities: Brussels, Belgium; Detroit, Michigan, USA;
    Vienna, Austria
Torch Bearer: Yoshinori Sakai
Speaker of the Athlete's Oath: Takashi Ono (Gymnastics)
Official Opening By: Emperor Hirohito
Number of Countries Competing: 93
Number of Athletes Competing: 5140

Medals Won by Countries

	G	S	B	Tot
USSR	30	31	35	96
United States	36	26	28	90
FRG/GDR	7	14*	15*	36*
Japan	16	5	8	29
Italy	10	10	7	27

*In 1964, the FRG competed as a combined team with the GDR. The
following medals were shared between combined teams: Men's
Swimming - 400 metre freestyle relay, 800 metre freestyle relay,
and 400 metre medley relay (all silver); Men's Gymnastics - Team
Combined Competition (bronze); and Equestrian - Three-Day Event,
Team Competition (bronze).

Top Individual Performances

	G	S	B	Tot
Don Schollander (USA-SWI)	4	–	–	4
Vera Cáslavská (TCH-GYM)	3	1	–	4
Yukio Endo (JPN-GYM)	3	1	–	4
Sharon Stouder (USA-SWI)	3	1	–	4
Steve Clark (USA-SWI)	3	–	–	3
Larisa Latynina (URS-GYM)	2	2	2	6
Polina Astakhova (URS-GYM)	2	1	1	4
Kathy Ellis (USA-SWI)	2	–	2	4
Hans-Joachim Klein (FRG-SWI)	–	3	1	4
Viktor Lisitskiy (URS-GYM)	–	4	–	4
Shuji Tsurumi (JPN-GYM)	1	3	–	4
Boris Shakhlin (URS-GYM)	1	2	1	4

Youngest Medalist, Men
    17-013   Klaus Dibiasi (ITA-DIV)

Youngest Medalist/Gold Medalist, Women
    14-097   Debra "Pokey" Watson (USA-SWI)

Youngest Gold Medalist, Men
    17-019   Dick Roth (USA-SWI)

Oldest Medalist, Men
    60-025   Lars Thörn (SWE-YAC)

Oldest Medalist, Women
35-216   Glorianne Perrier (USA-CAN)

Oldest Gold Medalist, Men
59-024   William Northman (AUS-YAC)

Oldest Gold Medalist, Women
31-327   Katalin Juhász-Nagy (HUN-FEN)

THE GAMES OF THE 19TH OLYMPIAD

Dates: 12 - 27 October 1968
Site: Mexico City, Mexico
Candidate Cities: Buenos Aires, Argentina; Detroit, Michigan,
USA; Lyon, France
Torch Bearer: Norma Enriqueta Basilio de Sotela
Speaker of the Athlete's Oath: Pablo Garrido (Athletics)
Official Opening By: President Gustavo Diaz Ordaz
Number of Countries Competing: 112
Number of Athletes Competing: 5530

Medals Won by Countries
	G	S	B	Tot
United States	45	28	34	107
USSR	29	32	30	91
Hungary	10	10	12	32
FRG	5	11	10	26
Japan	11	7	7	25

Top Individual Performances
	G	S	B	Tot
Vera Cáslavská (TCH-GYM)	4	2	-	6
Akinori Nakayama (JPN-GYM)	4	1	1	6
Charles Hickcox (USA-SWI)	3	1	-	4
Sawao Kato (JPN-GYM)	3	-	1	4
Debbie Meyer (USA-SWI)	3	-	-	3
Mikhail Voronin (URS-GYM)	2	4	1	7
Susie Pederson (USA-SWI)	2	2	-	4
Michael Wenden (AUS-SWI)	2	1	1	4
Mark Spitz (USA-SWI)	2	1	1	4
Jan Henne (USA-SWI)	2	1	1	4
Roland Matthes (GDR-SWI)	2	1	-	3
Ken Walsh (USA-SWI)	2	1	-	3
Natalia Kukhinskaya (URS-GYM)	2	-	2	4
Zinaida Voronina (URS-GYM)	1	1	2	4

Youngest Medalist/Gold Medalist, Men
14-175   Günther Tiersch (FRG-ROW)

Youngest Medalist, Women
14-289   Karen Moras (AUS-SWI)

Youngest Gold Medalist, Women
   15-002   Susie Pedersen (USA-SWI)

- Oldest Medalist, Men
   66-155   Louis Noverraz (SUI-YAC)

Oldest Medalist/Gold Medalist, Women
   41-060   Liselott Linsenhoff (FRG-EQU)

Oldest Gold Medalist, Men
   56-142   Josef Neckermann (FRG-EQU)

THE GAMES OF THE 20TH OLYMPIAD

Dates: 26 August - 10 September 1972
Site: Munich, Federal Republic of Germany (FRG)
Candidate Cities: Detroit, Michigan, USA; Madrid, Spain;
   Montreal, Quebec, Canada
Torch Bearer: Günter Zahn
Speaker of the Athlete's Oath: Heidi Schüller (Athletics)
Official Opening By: President Gustave Heinemann
Number of Countries Competing: 122
Number of Athletes Competing: 7156

Medals Won by Countries

	G	S	B	Tot
USSR	50	27	22	99
United States	33	31	30	94
GDR	20	23	23	69
FRG	13	11	16	40
Hungary	6	13	16	35

Top Individual Performances

	G	S	B	Tot
Mark Spitz (USA-SWI)	7	-	-	7
Sawao Kato (JPN-GYM)	3	2	-	5
Shane Gould (AUS-SWI)	3	1	1	5
Olga Korbut (URS-GYM)	3	1	-	4
Melissa Belote (USA-SWI)	3	-	-	3
Sandra Neilson (USA-SWI)	3	-	-	3
Karin Janz (GDR-GYM)	2	2	1	5
Jerry Heidenreich (USA-SWI)	2	1	1	4
Roland Matthes (GDR-SWI)	2	1	1	4
Akinori Nakayama (JPN-GYM)	2	1	1	4
Lyudmila Turishcheva (URS-GYM)	2	1	1	4
Shigeru Kasamatsu (JPN-GYM)	1	1	2	4
Tamara Lazakovich (URS-GYM)	1	1	2	4

Youngest Medalist/Gold Medalist, Men
   16-276   Uwe Benter (FRG-ROW)

Youngest Medalist, Women
13-308   Kornelia Ender (GDR-SWI)

Youngest Gold Medalist, Women
15-115   Deena Deardurff (USA-SWI)

Oldest Medalist, Men
60-094   Josef Neckermann (FRG-EQU)

Oldest Medalist, Women
46-258   Maud von Rosen (SWE-EQU)

Oldest Gold Medalist, Men
46-050   Hans-Günter Winkler (FRG-EQU)

Oldest Gold Medalist, Women
45-012   Liselott Linsenhoff (FRG-EQU)

THE GAMES OF THE 21ST OLYMPIAD

Dates: 17 July - 01 August 1976
Site: Montreal, Quebec, Canada
Candidate Cities: Los Angeles, California, USA; Moscow, USSR
Torch Bearer: Stéphane Prefontaine and Sandra Henderson
Speaker of the Athlete's Oath: Pierre St. Jean (Weightlifting)
Official Opening By: Queen Elizabeth II
Number of Countries Competing: 92
Number of Athletes Competing: 6085

Medals Won by Countries

	G	S	B	Tot
USSR	49	41	35	125
GDR	40	25	25	90
United States	34	35	25	94
FRG	10	12	17	39
Romania	4	9	14	27

Top Individual Performances

	G	S	B	Tot
Nikolai Andrianov (URS-GYM)	4	2	1	7
Kornelia Ender (GDR-SWI)	4	1	-	5
John Naber (USA-SWI)	4	1	-	5
Nadia Comăneci (ROM-GYM)	3	1	1	5
Nelli Kim (URS-GYM)	3	1	-	4
James Montgomery (USA-SWI)	3	-	1	4
Ulrike Richter (GDR-SWI)	3	-	-	3
Andrea Pollack (GDR-SWI)	2	2	-	4
Mitsuo Tsukahara (JPN-GYM)	2	1	2	5
John Hencken (USA-SWI)	2	1	-	3
Shirley Babashoff (USA-SWI)	1	4	-	5
Lyudmila Turishcheva (URS-GYM)	1	2	1	4

Youngest Medalist, Men
16-096   Ludvic Vébr (TCH-ROW)

Youngest Medalist, Women
13-341   Robin Corsiglia (CAN-SWI)

Youngest Gold Medalist, Men
17-110   Brian Goodell (USA-SWI)

Youngest Gold Medalist, Women
14-250   Nadia Comăneci (ROM-GYM)

Oldest Medalist/Gold Medalist, Men
46-158   Harry Boldt (FRG-EQU)

Oldest Medalist, Women
43-339   Edith Master (USA-EQU)

Oldest Gold Medalist, Women
34-254   Ivanka Christova (BUL-TAF)

THE GAMES OF THE 22ND OLYMPIAD

Dates: 19 July - 03 August 1980
Site: Moscow, Union of Soviet Socialist Republics
Candidate City: Los Angeles, California, USA
Torch Bearer: Sergei Belov
Speaker of the Athlete's Oath: Nikolai Andrianov (Gymnastics)
Official Opening By: President Leonid Brezhnev
Number of Countries Competing: 81
Number of Athletes Competing: 5326

Medals Won by Countries

	G	S	B	Tot
USSR	80	69	46	195
GDR	47	37	42	126
Bulgaria	8	16	17	41
Hungary	7	10	15	32
Poland	3	14	15	32

Top Individual Performances

	G	S	B	Tot
Aleksandr Dityatin (URS-GYM)	3	4	1	8
Caren Metschuck (GDR-SWI)	3	1	-	4
Nikolai Andrianov (URS-GYM)	3	-	-	3
Barbara Krause (GDR-SWI)	3	-	-	3
Rica Reinisch (GDR-SWI)	3	-	-	3
Vladimir Salnikov (URS-SWI)	3	-	-	3
Vladimir Parfenovich (URS-CAN)	3	-	-	3
Ines Diers (GDR-SWI)	2	2	1	5
Nadia Comăneci (ROM-GYM)	2	2	-	4
Elena Davydova (URS-GYM)	2	1	-	3
Sergei Kopliakov (URS-SWI)	2	1	-	3
Aleksandr Tkachev (URS-GYM)	2	1	-	3
Natalya Shaposhnikova (URS-GYM)	2	-	2	4
Rüdiger Helm (GDR-CAN)	2	-	1	3
Roland Brückner (GDR-GYM)	1	1	2	4
Maxi Gnauck (GDR-GYM)	1	1	2	4

Youngest Medalist, Men
14-362   Josip Reić (YUG-ROW)

Youngest Medalist, Women
14-052   Sirvard Emirzyan (URS-DIV)

Youngest Gold Medalist, Men
17-005   Sándor Wladár (HUN-SWI)

Youngest Gold Medalist, Women
15-106   Rica Reinisch (GDR-SWI)

Oldest Medalist, Men
57-283   Petre Rosca (ROM-EQU)

Oldest Medalist/Gold Medalist, Women
35-353   Anthea Stewart (ZIM-FIH)

Oldest Gold Medalist, Men
41-345   Valentin Mankin (URS-YAC)

THE GAMES OF THE 23RD OLYMPIAD

Dates: 28 July - 12 August 1984
Site: Los Angeles, California, United States
Torch Bearer: Rafer Johnson
Speaker of the Athlete's Oath: Edwin Moses (Athletics)
Official Opening By: President Ronald Reagan
Number of Countries Competing: 140
Number of Athletes Competing: 7344

Medals Won by Countries

	G	S	B	Tot
United States	83	61	30	174
FRG	17	19	23	59
Romania	20	16	17	53
Canada	10	18	16	44
Great Britain	5	10	22	37

Top Individual Performances

	G	S	B	Tot
Ecaterina Szabo (ROM-GYM)	4	1	-	5
Carl Lewis (USA-TAF)	4	-	-	4
Ning Li (CHN-GYM)	3	2	1	6
Nancy Hogshead (USA-SWI)	3	1	-	4
Rick Carey (USA-SWI)	3	-	-	3
Tracy Caulkins (USA-SWI)	3	-	-	3
Ian Ferguson (NZL-CAN)	3	-	-	3
Mary T. Meagher (USA-SWI)	3	-	-	3
Lars-Erik Moberg (SWE-CAN)	3	-	-	3
Michael Groß (FRG-SWI)	2	2	-	4
Agneta Andersson (SWE-CAN)	2	1	-	3
Chandra Cheeseborough (USA-TAF)	2	1	-	3
Mike Heath (USA-SWI)	2	1	-	3
Peter Vidmar (USA-GYM)	2	1	-	3
Simona Pauca (ROM-GYM)	2	-	1	3
Mary Lou Retton (USA-GYM)	1	2	2	5
Mitchell Gaylord (USA-GYM)	1	1	2	4

Youngest Medalist, Men
17-018   Dumitri Raducanu (ROM-ROW)

Youngest Medalist/Gold Medalist, Women
14-317   Simona Pauca (ROM-GYM)

Youngest Gold Medalist, Men
17-264   Perica Bukić (YUG-WAP)

Oldest Medalist/Gold Medalist, Men
49-092   William E. Buchan (USA-YAC)

Oldest Medalist, Women
52-143   Patricia Dench (AUS-SHO)

Oldest Gold Medalist, Women
40-212   Linda Thom (CAN-SHO)

THE GAMES OF THE 24TH OLYMPIAD

Dates: 17 September - 05 October 1988
Scheduled Site: Seoul, Republic of Korea (some events may be held
   in the Democratic People's Republic of Korea)
Candidate Cities: Athens, Greece; Melbourne, Australia; Nagoya,
   Japan

THE GAMES OF THE 25TH OLYMPIAD

Dates: to be announced
Scheduled Site: Barcelona, Spain
Candidate Cities: Amsterdam, The Netherlands; Belgrade,
  Yugoslavia; Birmingham, England; Brisbane, Australia; Paris,
  France

THE OLYMPIC WINTER GAMES

THE 1ST OLYMPIC WINTER GAMES

Dates: 25 January - 04 February 1924
Site: Chamonix, France
Speaker of the Athlete's Oath: Camille Mandrillon (Skiing)
Official Opening By: Under-Secretary for Physical Education
Gaston Vidal
Number of Countries Competing: 16
Number of Athletes Competing: 294

Medals Won by Countries

	G	S	B	Tot
Norway	4	7	6	17
Finland	4	3	3	10
United States	1	2	1	4
Austria	2	1	-	3
Great Britain	-	1	2	3

Top Individual Performances

	G	S	B	Tot
Clas Thunberg (FIN-SSK)	3	1	1	5
Thorleif Haug (NOR-NSK)	3	-	-	3
Julius Skutnabb (FIN-SSK)	1	1	1	3
Roald Larsen (NOR-SSK)	-	2	3	5
Johan Gröttumsbråten (NOR-NSK)	-	1	2	3

Youngest Medalist/Gold Medalist, Men
18-279   Heinrich Schläppi (SUI-BOB)

Youngest Medalist/Gold Medalist, Women
21-341   Herma Planck-Szabo (AUT-FSK)

Oldest Medalist, Men
42-194   Irving Small (USA-ICH)
42-034   René Mortiaux (BEL-BOB)

Oldest Medalist, Women
39-189   Ludowika Jakobsson (FIN-FSK)

Oldest Gold Medalist, Men
34-229   Julius Skutnabb (FIN-SSK)

Oldest Gold Medalist, Women
25-356   Helen Engellman (AUT-FSK)

THE 2ND OLYMPIC WINTER GAMES

Dates: 11 - 19 February 1928
Site: St. Moritz, Switzerland
Candidate Cities: Davos, Switzerland; Engelberg, Switzerland
Speaker of the Athlete's Oath: Hans Eidenbenz (Skiing)
Official Opening By: President Edmund Schulthess
Number of Countries Competing: 25
Number of Athletes Competing: 495

Medals Won by Countries

	G	S	B	Tot
Norway	6	4	5	15
United States	2	2	2	6
Sweden	2	2	1	5
Finland	2	1	1	4
Austria	-	3	1	4

Top Individual Performances

	G	S	B	Tot
Johan Gröttumsbråten (NOR-NSK)	2	-	-	2
Clas Thunberg (FIN-SSK)	2	-	-	2
Bernt Evensen (NOR-SSK)	1	1	1	3
Ivar Ballangrud (NOR-SSK)	1	-	1	2

Youngest Medalist, Men
    15-129   Thomas Doe (USA-BOB)

Youngest Medalist/Gold Medalist, Women
    15-315   Sonja Henie (NOR-FSK)

Youngest Gold Medalist, Men
    16-260   Billy Fiske (USA-BOB)

Oldest Medalist, Men
    44-362   Jay O'Brien (USA-BOB)

Oldest Medalist, Women
    27-232   Beatrix Loughran (USA-FSK)

Oldest Gold Medalist, Men
    42-182   Nion Tucker (USA-BOB)

Oldest Gold Medalist, Women
    26-156   Andrée Brunet-Joly (FRA-FSK)

THE 3RD OLYMPIC WINTER GAMES

Dates: 04 - 15 Feburary 1932
Site: Lake Placid, New York, United States
Candidate Cities: Bear Mountain, New York, USA; Denver, Colorado,
  USA; Duluth, Minnesota, USA; Minneapolis, Minnesota, USA;
  Montreal, Quebec, Canada; Yosemite Valley, California, USA (two
  separate applications)
Speaker of the Athlete's Oath: Jack Shea (Speed Skating)
Official Opening By: New York Governor Franklin D. Roosevelt
Number of Countries Competing: 17
Number of Athletes Competing: 306

Medals Won by Countries

	G	S	B	Tot
United States	6	4	2	12
Norway	3	4	3	10
Canada	1	1	5	7
Sweden	1	2	-	3
Finland	1	1	1	3

Top Individual Performances

	G	S	B	Tot
Jack Shea (USA-SSK)	2	-	-	2
Irving Jaffee (USA-SSK)	2	-	-	2
Veli Saarinen (FIN-NSK)	1	-	1	2

Youngest Medalist, Men
    19-342   Reto Capadrutt (ITA-BOB)

Youngest Medalist/Gold Medalist, Women
    19-306   Sonja Henie (NOR-FSK)

Youngest Gold Medalist, Men
    20-173   Birger Ruud (NOR-NSK)

Oldest Medalist/Gold Medalist, Men
    48-358   Jay O'Brien (USA-BOB)

Oldest Medalist, Women
    31-226   Beatrix Loughran (USA-FSK)

Oldest Gold Medalist, Women
    30-149   Andrée Brunet-Joly (FRA-FSK)

THE 4TH OLYMPIC WINTER GAMES

Dates: 06 - 16 Feburary 1936
Site: Garmisch-Partenkirchen, Germany
Candidate Cities: Montreal, Quebec, Canada; St. Moritz,
  Switzerland
Speaker of the Athlete's Oath: Wilhelm Bogner (Skiing)
Official Opening By: Chancellor Adolf Hitler
Number of Countries Competing: 28
Number of Athletes Competing: 755

Medals Won by Countries

	G	S	B	Tot
Norway	7	5	3	15
Sweden	2	2	3	7
Germany	3	3	-	6
Finland	1	2	3	6
United States	1	-	3	4

Top Individual Performances

	G	S	B	Tot
Ivar Ballangrud (NOR-SSK)	3	1	-	4
Oddbjörn Hagen (NOR-NSK)	1	2	-	3
Ernest Baier (GER-FSK)	1	1	-	2
Erik-August Larsson (SWE-NSK)	1	-	1	2
Birger Wasenius (FIN-SSK)	-	2	1	3

Youngest Medalist, Men
  15-300   Erik Pausin (AUT-FSK)

Youngest Medalist, Women
  15-076   Cecilia Colledge (GBR-FSK)

Youngest Gold Medalist, Men
  20-328   James Chappell (GBR-ICH)

Youngest Gold Medalist, Women
  15-127   Maxi Herber (GER-FSK)

Oldest Medalist/Gold Medalist, Men
  36-126   Alan Washbond (USA-BOB)

Oldest Medalist, Women
  29-158   Emilia Rotter (HUN-FSK)

Oldest Gold Medalist, Women
  23-312   Sonja Henie (NOR-FSK)

THE 5TH OLYMPIC WINTER GAMES

Dates: 30 January - 08 February 1948
Site: St. Moritz, Switzerland
Candidate Cities for the Games of 1940: Garmisch-Partenkirchen,
Germany; Oslo, Norway; Sapporo, Japan; St. Moritz, Switzerland
(Sapporo was originally selected but withdrew. The Games were
awarded to St. Moritz. St. Moritz withdrew on 09 June 1938 and
the Games were awarded to Garmisch-Partenkirchen. The Games
were not held due to World War II.)
Candidate Cities for the Games of 1944: Cortina d'Ampezzo, Italy;
Montreal, Quebec, Canada; Oslo, Norway; St. Moritz, Switzerland
(Cortina d'Ampezzo was originally selected. The Games were not
held due to World War II.)
Candidate Cities for the Games of 1948: Lake Placid, New York,
USA
Speaker of the Athlete's Oath: Richard "Bibi" Torriani (Ice
Hockey)
Official Opening By: President Enrico Celio
Number of Countries Competing: 28
Number of Athletes Competing: 713

Medals Won by Countries

	G	S	B	Tot
Sweden	4	3	3	10
Norway	4	3	3	10
Switzerland	3	4	3	10
United States	3	4	2	9
Austria	1	3	4	8

Top Individual Performances

	G	S	B	Tot
Henri Oreiller (FRA-ASK)	2	-	1	3
Martin Lundström (SWE-NSK)	2	-	-	2
Nils Östensson (SWE-NSK)	1	1	-	2
Trude Beiser (AUT-ASK)	1	1	-	2
Gretchen Fraser (USA-ASK)	1	1	-	2
Ake Seyffarth (SWE-SSK)	1	1	-	2

Youngest Medalist, Men
    18-037   Wallace Diestelmeyer (CAN-FSK)

Youngest Medalist, Women
    17-151   Jeannette Altwegg (GBR-FSK)

Youngest Gold Medalist, Men
    18-202   Dick Button (USA-FSK)

Youngest Gold Medalist, Women
    19-272   Barbara Ann Scott (CAN-FSK)

Oldest Medalist, Men
    49-038   Max Houben (USA-BOB)

Oldest Medalist/Gold Medalist, Women
    28-359   Gretchen Fraser (USA-ASK)

Oldest Gold Medalist, Men
    43-057   Francis Tyler (USA-BOB)

THE 6TH OLYMPIC WINTER GAMES

Dates: 14 - 25 February 1952
Site: Oslo, Norway
Candidate Cities: Cortina d'Ampezzo, Italy; Lake Placid, New
    York, USA
Torch Bearer: Eigil Nansen
Speaker of the Athlete's Oath: Torbjörn Falkanger (Ski Jumping)
Official Opening By: Her Royal Highness Princess Ragnhild
Number of Countries Competing: 22
Number of Athletes Competing: 732

Medals Won by Countries

	G	S	B	Tot
Norway	7	3	6	16
United States	4	6	1	11
Finland	3	4	2	9
Austria	2	4	2	8
FRG	3	2	2	7

Top Individual Performances

	G	S	B	Tot
Hjalmar Andersen (NOR-SSK)	3	-	-	3
Andrea Mead-Lawrence (USA-ASK)	2	-	-	2
Andreas Ostler (FRG-BOB)	2	-	-	2
Lorenz Noeberl (FRG-BOB)	2	-	-	2
Stein Eriksen (NOR-ASK)	1	1	-	2
Hallgeir Brenden (NOR-NSK)	1	1	-	2
Heikki Hasu (FIN-NSK)	1	1	-	2
Tapio Mäkelä (FIN-NSK)	1	1	-	2
Othmar Schneider (AUT-ASK)	1	1	-	2

Youngest Medalist/Gold Medalist, Men
    20-308   Robert Dickson (CAN-ICH)

Youngest Medalist, Women
    16-297   Tenley Albright (USA-FSK)

Youngest Gold Medalist, Women
    19-300   Andrea Mead-Lawrence (USA-ASK)

Oldest Medalist, Men
    46-342   Albert Mädorin (SUI-BOB)

Oldest Medalist/Gold Medalist, Women
    31-281   Lydia Wideman (FIN-NSK)

Oldest Gold Medalist, Men
    41-103   Franz Kemser (FRG-BOB)

THE 7TH OLYMPIC WINTER GAMES

Dates: 26 January - 05 February 1956
Site: Cortina d'Ampezzo, Italy
Candidate Cities: Colorado, USA (city not specified); Lake
    Placid, New York, USA; Oslo, Norway
Torch Bearer: Guido Caroli (Speed Skating)
Speaker of the Athlete's Oath: Guiliana Chenal-Minuzzo (Skiing)
Official Opening By: President Giovanni Gronchi
Number of Countries Competing: 32
Number of Athletes Competing: 819

Medals Won by Countries

	G	S	B	Tot
USSR	7	3	6	16
Austria	4	3	4	11
Sweden	2	4	4	10
Finland	3	3	1	7
United States	2	3	2	7

Top Individual Performances

	G	S	B	Tot
Anton "Toni" Sailer (AUT-ASK)	3	-	-	3
Evgeniy Grishin (URS-SSK)	2	-	-	2
Sixten Jernberg (SWE-NSK)	1	2	1	4
Veikko Hakulinen (FIN-NSK)	1	2	-	3
Lyubov Kozyreva (URS-NSK)	1	1	-	2
Sigvard Ericsson (SWE-SSK)	1	1	-	2
Pavel Kolchin (URS-NSK)	1	-	2	3

Youngest Medalist, Men
    18-054   John McKenzie (CAN-ICH)

Youngest Gold Medalist, Men
    20-073   Anton "Toni" Sailer (AUT-ASK)

Youngest Medalist, Women
    15-260   Ingrid Wendl (AUT-FSK)

Youngest Gold Medalist, Women
    19-259   Elisabeth Schwarz (AUT-FSK)

Oldest Medalist/Gold Medalist, Men
    47-217   Giacomo Conti (ITA-BOB)

Oldest Medalist/Gold Medalist, Women
  31-048   Siiri Rantanen (FIN-NSK)

THE 8TH OLYMPIC WINTER GAMES

Dates: 18 - 28 February 1960
Site: Squaw Valley, California, United States
Candidate Cities: Garmisch-Partenkirchen, Federal Republic of
  Germany; Innsbruck, Austria; Karachi, USSR; St. Moritz,
  Switzerland
Torch Bearer: Ken Henry
Speaker of the Athlete's Oath: Carol Heiss (Figure Skating)
Official Opening By: Vice-President Richard Nixon
Number of Countries Competing: 30
Number of Athletes Competing: 665

Medals Won by Countries

	G	S	B	Tot
USSR	7	5	9	21
United States	3	4	3	10
Finland	2	3	3	8
Sweden	3	2	2	7
Norway	3	3	-	6
Austria	1	2	3	6

Top Individual Performances

	G	S	B	Tot
Lidiya Skoblikova (URS-SSK)	2	-	-	2
Evgeniy Grishin (URS-SSK)	2	-	-	2
Veikko Hakulinen (FIN-NSK)	1	1	1	3
Mariya Gusakova (URS-NSK)	1	1	-	2
Sixten Jernberg (SWE-NSK)	1	1	-	2
Helga Haase (GDR-SSK)	1	1	-	2
Viktor Kosichkin (URS-SSK)	1	1	-	2
Knut Johannesen (NOR-SSK)	1	1	-	2
Ernst Hinterseer (AUT-ASK)	1	-	1	2

Youngest Medalist, Men
  18-022   Hans-Jürgen Bäumler (FRG-FSK)

Youngest Medalist, Women
  16-145   Traudl Hecher (AUT-FSK)

Youngest Gold Medalist, Men
  19-316   Tom Williams (USA-ICH)

Youngest Gold Medalist, Women
  19-003   Heidi Biebl (FRG-ASK)

Oldest Medalist/Gold Medalist, Men
  35-052   Veikko Hakulinen (FIN-NSK)

Oldest Medalist, Women
37-184   Eevi Huttunen (FIN-SSK)

Oldest Gold Medalist, Women
29-100   Sonja Ruthström (SWE-NSK)

THE 9TH OLYMPIC WINTER GAMES

Dates: 29 January - 09 February 1964
Site: Innsbruck, Austria
Candidate Cities: Calgary, Alberta, Canada; Lahti, Sweden
Torch Bearer: Joseph Rieder
Speaker of the Athlete's Oath: Paul Aste (Bobsledding)
Official Opening By: President Dr. Adolf Schärf
Number of Countries Competing: 36
Number of Athletes Competing: 1093

Medals Won by Countries

	G	S	B	Tot
USSR	11	8	6	25
Norway	3	6	6	15
Austria	4	5	3	12
Finland	3	4	3	10
France	3	4	-	7
Sweden	3	3	1	7

Top Individual Performances

	G	S	B	Tot
Lidiya Skoblikova (URS-SSK)	4	-	-	4
Klaudiya Boyarskikh (URS-NSK)	3	-	-	3
Eero Mäntyranta (FIN-NSK)	2	1	-	3
Sixten Jernberg (SWE-NSK)	2	-	1	3
Evdokiya Mekshilo (URS-NSK)	1	1	-	2
Asser Rönnlund (SWE-NSK)	1	1	-	2
Christine Goitschel (FRA-ASK)	1	1	-	2
Marielle Goitschel (FRA-ASK)	1	1	-	2
Veikko Kankkonen (FIN-NSK)	1	1	-	2
Toralf Engan (NOR-NSK)	1	1	-	2
Josef "Pepi" Stiegler (AUT-ASK)	1	-	1	2

Youngest Medalist, Men
14-363   Scott Ethan Allen (USA-FSK)

Youngest Medalist/Gold Medalist, Women
18-128   Marielle Goitschel (FRA-ASK)

Youngest Gold Medalist, Men
17-306   Manfred Stengl (AUT-LUG)

Oldest Medalist, Men
36-015   Eugenio Monti (ITA-BOB)

Oldest Medalist/Gold Medalist, Women
33-362   Alevtina Kolchina (URS-NSK)

Oldest Gold Medalist, Men
35-002   Sixten Jernberg (SWE-NSK)

THE 10TH OLYMPIC WINTER GAMES

Dates: 06 - 18 February 1968
Site: Grenoble, France
Candidate Cities: Calgary, Alberta, Canada; Lahti, Sweden; Lake
    Placid, New York, USA; Oslo, Norway; Sapporo, Japan
Torch Bearer: Alain Calmat
Speaker of the Athlete's Oath: Leo Lacroix (Skiing)
Official Opening By: President Charles de Gaulle
Number of Countries Competing: 37
Number of Athletes Competing: 1293

Medals Won by Countries

	G	S	B	Tot
Norway	6	6	2	14
USSR	5	5	3	13
Austria	3	4	4	11
France	4	3	2	9
Netherlands	3	3	3	9

Top Individual Performances

	G	S	B	Tot
Jean-Claude Killy (FRA-ASK)	3	-	-	3
Toini Gustafsson (SWE-NSK)	2	1	-	3
Harald Grönningen (NOR-NSK)	2	-	-	2
Ole Ellefsaeter (NOR-NSK)	2	-	-	2
Eugenio Monti (ITA-BOB)	2	-	-	2
Luciano de Paolis (ITA-BOB)	2	-	-	2
Eero Mäntyranta (FIN-NSK)	-	1	2	3

Youngest Medalist, Men
19-281   Alfred Matt (AUT-ASK)

Youngest Medalist, Women
16-266   Dianne Holum (USA-SSK)

Youngest Gold Medalist, Men
20-155   Wolfgang Schwarz (AUT-FSK)

Youngest Gold Medalist, Women
19-198   Peggy Fleming (USA-FSK)

Oldest Medalist/Gold Medalist, Men
40-023   Eugenio Monti (ITA-BOB)

Oldest Medalist, Women
38-005   Alevtina Kolchina (URS-NSK)

Oldest Gold Medalist, Women
32-084   Lyudmila Belousova (URS-FSK)

THE 11TH OLYMPIC WINTER GAMES

Dates: 03 - 13 February 1972
Site: Sapporo, Japan
Candidate Cities: Banff, Alberta, Canada; Lahti, Sweden; Salt
  Lake City, Utah, USA
Torch Bearer: Hideki Takada
Speaker of the Athlete's Oath: Keichi Suzuki (Speed Skating)
Official Opening By: Emperor Hirohito
Number of Countries Competing: 35
Number of Athletes Competing: 1232

Medals Won by Countries

	G	S	B	Tot
USSR	8	5	3	16
GDR	4	3	7	14
Norway	2	5	5	12
Switzerland	4	3	3	10
Netherlands	4	3	2	9

Top Individual Performances

	G	S	B	Tot
Galina Kulakova (URS-NSK)	3	-	-	3
Ard Schenk (HOL-SSK)	3	-	-	3
Vyacheslav Vedenin (URS-NSK)	2	-	1	3
Marie-Theres Nadig (SUI-ASK)	2	-	-	2
Pål Tyldum (NOR-NSK)	1	2	-	3
Gustavo Thöni (ITA-ASK)	1	1	-	2
Fedor Simashev (URS-URS)	1	1	-	2
Dianne Holum (USA-SSK)	1	1	-	2
Christina Baas-Kaiser (HOL-SSK)	1	1	-	2
Alevtina Olyunina (URS-NSK)	1	1	-	2
Marjatta Kajosmaa (FIN-NSK)	-	2	1	3
Atje Keulen-Deelstra (HOL-SSK)	-	1	2	3

Youngest Medalist, Men
16-261   Mark Howe (USA-ICH)

Youngest Medalist, Women
15-008   Manuela Groß (GDR-FSK)

Youngest Gold Medalist, Men
19-188   Wojciech Fortuna (POL-NSK)

Youngest Gold Medalist, Women
    16-157   Anne Henning (USA-SSK)

Oldest Medalist/Gold Medalist, Men
    38-238   Jean Wicki (SUI-BOB)

Oldest Medalist, Women
    34-009   Marjatta Kajosmaa (FIN-NSK)

Oldest Gold Medalist, Women
    33-268   Christina Baas-Kaiser (HOL-SSK)

THE 12TH OLYMPIC WINTER GAMES

Dates: 04 - 15 February 1976
Site: Innsbruck, Austria
Candidate Cities: Lahti, Sweden; Grenada, France; Vancouver,
    British Columbia, Canada; Denver, Colorado, USA (Denver was
    originally selected but withdrew. The Games were awarded to
    Innsbruck which had not originally made application for them.)
Torch Bearer: Christl Haas and Josef Feistmantl
Speaker of the Athlete's Oath: Werner Delle-Karth (Bobsledding)
Official Opening By: President Dr. Rudolf Kirchschläger
Number of Countries Competing: 37
Number of Athletes Competing: 1128

Medals Won by Countries

	G	S	B	Tot
USSR	13	6	8	27
GDR	7	5	7	19
United States	3	3	4	10
FRG	2	5	3	10
Norway	3	3	1	7
Finland	2	4	1	7

Top Individual Performances

	G	S	B	Tot
Raisa Smetanina (URS-NSK)	2	1	-	3
Rosi Mittermaier (FRG-ASK)	2	1	-	3
Tatyana Averina (URS-SSK)	2	-	2	4
Nikolai Kruglov (URS-BIA)	2	-	-	2
Meinhard Nehmer (GDR-BOB)	2	-	-	2
Bernhard Germeshausen (GDR-BOB)	2	-	-	2
Helena Takalo (FIN-NSK)	1	2	-	3
Sheila Young (USA-SSK)	1	1	1	3
Hans van Helden (HOL-SSK)	-	-	3	3

Youngest Medalist, Men
    17-320   Anton Innauer (AUT-NSK)

Youngest Medalist/Gold Medalist, Women
    19-212   Kathy Kreiner (CAN-ASK)

Youngest Gold Medalist, Men
   20-218   Sergei Babinov (URS-ICH)

Oldest Medalist, Men
   37-244   Esko Saira (FIN-BIA)

Oldest Medalist, Women
   38-009   Marjatta Kajosmaa (FIN-NSK)

Oldest Gold Medalist, Men
   35-032   Meinhard Nehmer (GDR-BOB)

Oldest Gold Medalist, Women
   33-289   Galina Kulakova (URS-NSK)

THE 13TH OLYMPIC WINTER GAMES

Dates: 13 - 24 February 1980
Site: Lake Placid, New York, United States
Torch Bearer: Dr. Charles Morgan Kerr
Speaker of the Athlete's Oath: Eric Heiden (Speed Skating)
Official Opening By: Vice-President Walter Mondale
Number of Countries Competing: 37
Number of Athletes Competing: 1067

Medals Won by Countries

	G	S	B	Tot
GDR	9	7	7	23
USSR	10	6	6	22
United States	6	4	2	12
Norway	1	3	6	10
Finland	1	5	3	9

Top Individual Performances

	G	S	B	Tot
Eric Heiden (USA-SSK)	5	-	-	5
Nikolai Zimyatov (URS-NSK)	3	-	-	3
Henni Wenzel (LIE-ASK)	2	1	-	3
Anatoli Alyabiev (URS-BIA)	2	-	1	3
Barbara Petzold (GDR-NSK)	2	-	-	2
Ingemar Stenmark (SWE-ASK)	2	-	-	2
Frank Ullrich (GDR-BIA)	1	2	-	3
Juha Mieto (FIN-NSK)	-	2	1	3

Youngest Medalist, Men
   18-323   Manfred Deckert (GDR-NSK)

Youngest Medalist, Women
   15-091   Marina Cherkasova (URS-FSK)

Youngest Gold Medalist, Men
   19-082   Mike Ramsey (USA-ICH)

Youngest Gold Medalist, Women
   18-240   Karin Enke (GDR-SSK)

Oldest Medalist/Gold Medalist, Men
   39-042   Meinhard Nehmer (GDR-BOB)

Oldest Medalist, Women
   37-298   Galina Kulakova (URS-NSK)

Oldest Gold Medalist, Women
   30-158   Irina Rodnina (URS-FSK)

THE 14TH OLYMPIC WINTER GAMES

Dates: 08 - 19 February 1984
Site: Sarajevo, Yugoslavia
Candidate Cities: Göteburg, Sweden; Sapporo, Japan
Torch Bearer: Sandra Dubravcic
Speaker of the Athlete's Oath: Bojan Krizaj (Skiing)
Official Opening By: President Mika Spiljak
Number of Countries Competing: 49
Number of Athletes Competing: 1437

Medals Won by Countries

	G	S	B	Tot
USSR	6	10	9	25
GDR	9	9	6	24
Finland	4	3	6	13
Norway	3	2	4	9
United States	4	4	-	8
Sweden	4	2	2	8

Top Individual Performances

	G	S	B	Tot
Marja-Liisa Hämäläinen (FIN-NSK)	3	-	1	4
Karin Enke (GDR-SSK)	2	2	-	4
Gunde Anders Swan (SWE-NSK)	2	1	1	4
Gaeten Boucher (CAN-SSK)	2	-	1	3
Wolfgang Hoppe (GDR-BOB)	2	-	-	2
Dietmar Schauerhammer (GDR-BOB)	2	-	-	2
Thomas Wassberg (SWE-NSK)	2	-	-	2
Andrea Schöne (GDR-SSK)	1	2	-	3
Peter Angerer (FRG-BIA)	1	1	1	3
Eirik Kvalfoss (NOR-BIA)	1	1	1	3
Igor Malkov (URS-SSK)	1	1	-	2
Tomas Gustafsson (SWE-SSK)	1	1	-	2
Berit Aunli (NOR-NSK)	1	1	-	2
Matti Nykänen (FIN-NSK)	1	1	-	2
Jens Weißflog (GDR-NSK)	1	1	-	2
Nikolai Zimyatov (URS-NSK)	1	1	-	2
Brit Pettersen (NOR-NSK)	1	-	1	2
Anne Jahren (NOR-NSK)	1	-	1	2
Aki Karvonen (FIN-NSK)	-	1	2	3

Youngest Medalist/Gold Medalist, Men
    19-009   Igor Malkov (URS-SSK)

Youngest Medalist/Gold Medalist, Women
    18-077   Katarina Witt (GDR-FSK)

Oldest Medalist, Men
    35-098   Bernhard Lehmann (GDR-BOB)

Oldest Medalist, Women
    31-354   Raisa Smetanina (URS-NSK)

Oldest Gold Medalist, Men
    32-248   Paul Hildgartner (ITA-LUG)

Oldest Gold Medalist, Women
    28-161   Marja-Liisa Hämäläinen (FIN-NSK)

THE 15TH OLYMPIC WINTER GAMES

Dates: 23 February - 06 March 1988
Scheduled Site: Calgary, Alberta, Canada
Candidate Cities: Cortina d'Ampezzo, Italy; Falun, Sweden

THE 16TH OLYMPIC WINTER GAMES

Dates: to be announced
Scheduled Site: Albertville, France
Candidate Cities: Anchorage, Alaska, USA; Berchtesgaden, FRG;
  Cortina d'Ampezzo, Italy; Falun, Sweden; Lillehammer, Norway;
  Sofia, Bulgaria